THE NEW ENCYCLOPEDIA OF
GOLF

THE NEW ENCYCLOPEDIA OF
GOLF

MALCOLM CAMPBELL

A DORLING KINDERSLEY BOOK

LONDON, NEW YORK,
MUNICH, MELBOURNE, DELHI

A Penguin Company

Produced for Dorling Kindersley by
KINSEY & Harrison

DORLING KINDERSLEY
Senior Editor Edward Bunting
Senior Art Editor Kevin Ryan
Managing Editor Sharon Lucas
Senior Managing Art Editor Derek Coombes
DTP Designer Sonia Charbonnier
Production Controller Mel Alsopp

This completely revised edition first published in
Great Britain in 2001 by Dorling Kindersley Ltd.
80 Strand, London WC2R ORL
First published in 1991, revised 1994
2 4 6 8 10 9 7 5 3 1

ISBN 0-7513-2790-5

Publisher's note Golf course and hole lengths in
this book are given in either yards or metres,
according to the style adopted by the management
of the courses themselves. The † symbol used
throughout this book denotes amateur status.

Colour reproduction by Colourscan, Singapore

Printed and bound in the Slovak Republic by TBB

Half-title (page 1) *Bronze statuette of J.H. Taylor*
Title (pages 2–3) *Tiger Woods at Blue Canyon Golf Course,
Thailand; and Sergio Garcia, after driving*

See our complete catalogue at
WWW.DK.COM

CONTENTS

*A Willie Park Snr putter of 1875 and feathery ball contrast
with their modern counterparts of a century later (top)*

Sunrise over the 16th hole at Oakland Hills, Michigan, USA

Image of a golfer from a whisky advertisement of about 1905

5
RECORDS AND
REFERENCE 360

Official souvenir programme from the Ryder Cup of 1933, hosted at Southport and Ainsdale – the fourth match played between the United States and Great Britain and Ireland

FOREWORD

By the 41st President of the United States of America

It has been argued since the days of antiquity – convincingly, I maintain – that the gods should not count the hours spent fishing against one's time on Earth. To this, I might offer but one amendment: time spent on the golf course.

There is something about golf, this greatest of games as Bobby Jones rightly dubbed it, which brings out the best in all of us. Granted, it does not always bring out our best as golfers, but it inevitably brings out our best as people – as men and women of honor and integrity, who play according to time-honored rules (and who hopefully play briskly at that!).

Happily, as much as golf has changed through the years, it remains inescapably beholden to certain traditions dating back to its origins. Every young player – regardless of race, creed, or nationality – who picks up a club today is bound through the ages not only to the members of the Society of St Andrews Golfers (later the Royal & Ancient) who founded the first "Thirteen Rules of Golf" nearly 250 years ago, but also to all who have abided the letter and spirit of fair play since. We all become part of a continuum that transcends any one player or even the "Auld Grey Toon" itself.

In this light, *The New Encyclopedia of Golf* offers golfers of all ages and handicaps a valuable resource through which they might trace golf's history – its timeless heroes, its hallowed courses, its touchstone moments. Only by respecting golf's storied past might we preserve it intact for future generations – so that they, too, might come to know the indescribable pleasure, and pain, of this greatest of games. Enjoy!

George Bush, Houston, Texas, March 2001

INTRODUCTION

"Golf is a wonderful game. It is more than a game to me: it is a life's work, a career, a profession. Whether it is a science or an art I do not know – it is probably half and half – but it is a noble occupation all the same."

Three-time Open Champion Sir Henry Cotton

Noble occupation
The author (left) hands Henry Cotton a club at the 1982 Open.

When I was six, maybe seven-years-old, my mother bought me a set of golf clubs from a Boy Scout jumble sale. She paid only a few pennies for a modest collection of old hickory-shafted clubs with rusty iron heads, all gathered together in an old and battered canvas bag. Her motive I have no doubt was to give her son something to occupy an active body and mind to keep him from under her feet during the long weeks of the summer school break. Looking back on that childhood more than half a century ago, it is clear to me now that of all the material things that I was given as a child, none has had such a telling effect on the outcome of my life than that collection of battered old cleeks.

That bag of clubs was my introduction to a game and a lifestyle that would take me in time to the far corners of the world; it was an introduction to a game that has taken me into contact with some of the greatest names not only in golf but in many other sports as well. It has brought me into contact with royalty and captains of business and industry as well as into the locker rooms of the most modest of clubs where the spirit of the game was equally shared, the welcome just as grand. That old bag of clubs has been responsible for me being privileged to visit and to play – with but a few exceptions – most of the great golf courses of the world, as well as scores with little or no fame attached to them.

Dressing the part (1)
Golf and fashion have always gone together, but manners and sportsmanship define the true golfer.

Dressing the part (2) (left) *Bobby Jones learned to play golf by mimicking the rhythmical swing of his local professional. Jones not only dressed the part but played the part, respecting the special ethic and great traditions of golf.*

Old clubs and new belts (right) *A hundred years might separate this Scottish, lancewood-shafted, steel-headed wood (top) from the space-age materials of a modern graphite-shafted American metal wood (right). But the essential design of a driver has changed little. The clubface buckle, however, might be a different matter!*

THE GREATEST GAME

But more important than all of that this "greatest game", as the legendary Bobby Jones called it so simply and eloquently, has been the key that has opened doors to countless friendships in every corner of the world where the game of golf is played. I consider myself to have been fortunate indeed.

But golf is much more than a game. Bobby Jones knew that as well as anyone in the 600 years or so of golf's history, and no one appreciated it more than the modest lawyer from Atlanta, Georgia, the greatest amateur in the history of sport.

Around the world there are now countless millions who understand what Bobby Jones meant. Golf brings people of all races and rank together in a way that the United Nations could not dream of in a thousand years. It is the game that crosses the social divide in a way that politicians have singularly failed to do with mountains of legislation.

Golf is the game for everyone, and its great traditions and values stand out as a blueprint for life as relevant as any religion.

Golf offers a lead; the open door to a dignified and honest lifestyle for those who choose to walk through it, where the essence of good manners, humour and good taste lie at the heart of its great traditions. More than any other game, it is the true test of character in the individual. In golf there is no hiding place for the mean of spirit or for those who choose not to embrace its simple creed of honesty and self-discipline.

GOLF – THE GREAT LEVELLER

While it is inconceivable that a once-a-week tennis player could ever enjoy a competitive match on the Centre Court at Wimbledon with Pete Sampras, it is perfectly feasible for a novice to stand on the first tee of the Old Course at St Andrews and embark on an enjoyable and competitive game with Tiger Woods. The ability to close the skill gap, and make that competitiveness possible, comes courtesy of golf's sometimes abused but largely equitable handicap system that is unique to the game.

For the professional, a combination of ability and endless hours of practice, provides the means to a living which, in the case of Tiger

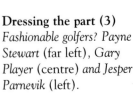

Dressing the part (3) *Fashionable golfers? Payne Stewart (far left), Gary Player (centre) and Jesper Parnevik (left).*

Time-honoured traditions (right) *Standing majestically at the edge of one of the world's oldest courses, the Royal & Ancient clubhouse at St Andrews embodies the spirit and traditions of the noble game.*

as a one time bastion of old Corinthian values. At the start of the twenty-first century soccer and rugby stand hostage to the forces of exploitation in which the values of honest sport and competition appear ever more to have been sacrificed on the alter of commercial expediency. Where once there were heroes there now remain only stars.

Woods, for instance, amounts to wealth beyond the wildest dreams. For the rest of us, blessed with altogether less golfing dexterity, golf is a game of immense pleasure in which the companionship and the surroundings are as important as the result and the activity itself.

THE CIVILIZED GAME

It was the Scots who took the game from their famous links courses to the far corners of the earth. Yet it matters not whether golfers gather around the long table at the Prestwick Golf Club in Ayrshire, Scotland, or at golf clubs in the United States or the Far East. Wherever they meet in the name of the game they share a rich experience and are part of the great traditions and spirit of golf's origins.

Golf may now be the last civilized game in a world where so many sports have become tainted at the edges by scandal and commercial exploitation. Arguments over money have ended in strikes among baseball players in the United States; even cricket, that paragon of English public school virtue and stiff upper lip, has been rocked by match fixing; a stream of athletes have been sent home in drugs disgrace from the Olympic Games now discredited

THE CONTROVERSIAL GAME

Golf, of course, is not entirely without flaw, the happenings at Brookline, Massachusetts, in the 1999 Ryder Cup remain vivid in most people's memory, but they were an embarrassment rather than a symptom of an underlying malaise. However, they remain a clear warning of the dangers of hijacking the professional game to force it into an amphitheatre of national confrontation for huge outside commercial gain, which some believe the Ryder Cup has now become.

Certainly it is no longer the gathering together of professional golfers in the name of friendship and honest competition which was how Samuel Ryder envisioned it when he underwrote the expenses of the Great Britain and Ireland side and put up the famous gold trophy for first time competition – ironically as it happens in Massachusetts – back in 1927.

There have been other occasions when the golfing escutcheon has been stained. Old Tom Morris, two down with six to play to Willie Park in the last battle they ever fought, famously left the course at Musselburgh and retired to Mrs Forman's public house with Robert Chambers the referee, as a protest against the Park supporters taking judicious kicks at the golf balls in their efforts to help the Willie Park cause. The year was 1882. In 1925 the expatriate Scot, Macdonald Smith, left

Happy players, sad scene (right) *The over-enthusiasm of United States spectators and team players sadly marred the 1999 Ryder Cup matches at Brookline, Massachusetts, doing considerable damage to the image of the event. Here the American players swamp the green in celebration of their narrow victory.*

The Golf Research Group reported that by the year 2000 there were just over three million golfers in Britain and that figure had remained almost static through the decade of the 1990s. In the UK one of the key growth sectors going into the twenty-first century was women golfers. Again, according to the Golf Research Group, only seven percent of golfers in England were women, the lowest percentage in any European country. In the United States the figure was put at 23 percent, although there were some indications that US numbers were beginning to fall.

In Japan, the world's second biggest golf market worth some $3 billion, efforts to take the game to a wider audience were set back by the collapse of the Japanese economy in the late 1990s. In a country where the game is prohibitively expensive for the vast majority of ordinary Japanese golfers, a new policy of lower green fees had succeeded in making the game more accessible.

the old course at Prestwick a sad and embittered man with a final round score of 82 in the British Open Championship he had all but won before he was trampled into defeat by a well-meaning but over-enthusiastic crowd which invaded the course. It was the last time Prestwick ever hosted the Championship. But such incidents thankfully remain isolated. Golf remains in essence true to the legacy of the underlying values developed from its historic past. And long may it continue.

THE GLOBAL GAME

There have been two major periods of growth in the game in the past 120 years. The first was in the last two decades of the nineteeth century when golf moved across the Atlantic and took hold in the United States. The second came in the last two decades of the twentieth century when the demand for golf, fuelled by exposure to television, brought a massive influx of new players into a game that struggled for some time to provide facilities for them. Two million golfers in America in the 1920s doubled to four million by 1950. In 1960 it was estimated that five million were playing and that figure had expanded to 11 million by 1970. By the beginning of the new millennium there were close to 27 million golfers.

Four corners of the globe (above) *Vijay Singh from Fiji was catapulted in the 2000 Masters at Augusta to superstar status, having once been a humble pro in Borneo.*

Versatile view (below) *Large crowds make viewing of the action difficult at times, but fold-away platforms and periscopes have now become essential golf viewing accessories.*

The biggest draw (left) *The arrival of Tiger Woods on the world stage of golf in the late 1990s has had a major impact on the game. In the words of Tom Watson, Woods has raised the bar in competition at the highest level of the game but he still has a long way to go to equal the championship winning record of Jack Nicklaus.*

Star attractions (above and below) *Pro-Am games involving the likes of Se Ri Pak (above), Tiger Woods or Michael Douglas (below) draw a whole new raft of celebrity followers.*

But at the beginning of the twenty-first century the majority of Japanese golfers still seemed destined to play their golf on driving ranges. Around 13 million golfers were estimated to actually play golf in Japan, but many were restricted in the number of rounds they could afford to play.

Perhaps the start of the twenty-first century will mark a gradual slowing down of development as happened at the start of the twentieth century.

TIGERMANIA

The arrival of Tiger Woods on the stage of world sport at the very end of the last millennium provided the potential for yet another major boost. A whole new raft of interest was created, particularly in the United States among young African-Americans, who had previously been exposed to a diet of baseball and American football. Woods quickly became the most famous sportsman in the world and is well on the way to becoming the wealthiest. He enjoys the standing that was once the preserve of Hollywood stars. He is the brightest among a galaxy of stars now playing for vast sums of money around the world's golf circuits.

Whether he is yet a hero in the sense that Jack Nicklaus has been a hero to golfers for four decades, the golfing world has still to find out.

Presidential seal of approval (above) *Former US President Bill Clinton, like many of his predecessors, was a keen golfer during his time at the White House. Even when he travelled abroad he took his clubs with him – as at Ireland's famous Ballybunion course.*

Sporting hero (below) *In the 2000 Olympic Games in Sydney the Great White Shark, Greg Norman, who has won two majors and a host of other international championships in a distinguished career, took a leading part in the ceremonies.*

Multi-tiered driving range (below) *For many enthusiastic Japanese golfers the driving range is as close as they ever get to a golf course. Multi-tier versions meet the huge demand for space.*

MORE THAN JUST A GAME

Equipment and golf courses have changed out of all recognition, but the game itself still stands much as it has done since the first players put club to ball on an open, windswept stretch of linksland on the east coast of Scotland all those centuries ago.

The preservation of the value and traditions that developed from those earlier times, and remain at the heart of the game, are a responsibility for all of us who call ourselves golfers to protect. It is a responsibility that we must hand on to future generations and by so doing retain that which the great champion Sir Henry Cotton described as something "*more important than just a game*".

In *The New Encyclopedia of Golf* I have tried to give a flavour of what this game of golf is about, its history, its statistics, the people who have influenced its development, and the great courses upon which it is played. If I have succeeded in even a small way to do any justice to such a wonderful subject, I will be be very thankful for that bag of cleeks all those years ago.

Malcolm Campbell
Lower Largo, Scotland

THE EARLY GAME

There is no dispute that golf, or a pastime similar to the game we know today, has been played for centuries, but exactly how and when this game of club-and-ball first arrived to test and frustrate the human soul remains a matter of speculation. Some trace golf's origins back to the game of paganica, played in the time of the Roman Empire, while others see it as evolving from the French jeu de mail or the Dutch game of kolven.

Whatever the truth of these speculations, the pioneers of golf were undoubtedly the Scots. It was the Scots who developed the game on their seaside links and transported it with them all over the world.

A 1920s Doulton jug showing a Jacobean golfer

Inspired by their passion for the game, they taught other nations to play. But just as importantly, they provided the first implements for golf and the courses to play on, and they laid down the standards and basic rules that still, to a large degree, prevail today.

Kolven in Holland,1668 (left)
A painting by Adriaen van de Velde shows this early club-and-ball game being played on ice near Haarlem.

Early "golfer" from a 1384 Flemish manuscript

MISTY ORIGINS

Set the ball rolling
Although the first golf ball was probably made of beechwood, there was no lack of design experimentation. This early relative of the golf ball is made of animal hair and thread in a linen pouch.

Hours of pleasure
A Flemish Book of Hours from 1530, illustrated under the supervision of the famous miniaturist Simon Bennink, displays perhaps the first true image of golf.

L IKE SO MANY *other forms of human activity, golf has no clear recorded origins. With little solid evidence available, accounts of the early history of the game often depend heavily on the writer's imagination. Accepting that, as Voltaire sagely observed, the ancient histories are but fables that have been agreed upon, there are many mythological starting points from which to embark upon an account of the game.*

The danger of fable is that it is too readily confused with fact. Quite simply, there is no documentary evidence of golf, as we know it today, prior to the middle of the fifteenth century, and there is no hard evidence to disprove the most obvious and well-documented theory that the game began on the east coast of Scotland. But the quest to find earlier evidence of the game in its present form has taxed the minds of eminent men over many decades.

QUEST FOR ORIGINS

Most research has centred on establishing the relationship between golf and other pastimes in Europe, and seeking support for the theory that one or other of them was the forerunner of golf. There have been so many different types of club-and-ball games throughout the course of history that speculation knows almost no limit. Although the lack of solid facts frustrates attempts to reach a

substantial conclusion, however, it is both illuminating and fascinating to compare other club-and-ball games with golf, consider any areas of overlap between them, and judge their possible influence on the game's development.

ROMAN COUNTRY SPORT

Some historians have gone back as far as Ancient Rome and forged a link between golf and paganica, a game that was popular with country folk in the early days of the Roman Empire. Little is known about the rules of the game, but legend has it that paganica was played with a bent stick and a ball made from leather filled with feathers. The interesting connection here is that early golf balls were also made with feathers stuffed into leather covers (see page 30), although the paganica ball is believed to have been about 4–7in (10–18cm) in diameter, so its resemblance to a golf "feathery" is not that close.

The expansion of the Roman Empire north and west from the Mediterranean could well have carried paganica across Europe. The legions who supported the Roman governors were recruited from the country districts, and it would have been natural for the occupying forces to have indulged their rural pastimes in foreign lands as they did at home.

This theory suggests that paganica was at the root of the later development of various other club-and-ball games in northern Europe, particularly in France and the Low Countries, which have also been proposed as the forerunners of golf. The principal

candidates among them are cambuca, jeu de mail, chole, crosse, kolven and pell mell. Cambuca (or cambuta) was played in England in the mid-fourteenth century during the reign of Edward III. There are close similarities with paganica: cambuca players used a curved club and a ball made from feathers which, it is thought, was propelled towards a mark set in the ground. In 1363 a royal proclamation was issued banning able-bodied men from all games on feast days. The list ranged from cock-fighting to football and "other vain games",

Mail shot
Lauthier's Nouveaux Règles pour le Jeu de Mail *of 1717 shows the wooden mallet swung by a player of the game.*

but also included cambuca and club ball, which was a form of hockey. Instead, the men were urged, on penalty of imprisonment, to practise shooting with bow and arrow. Less than 100 years later, a Scottish Act of Parliament was to ban golf for the same reasons and threaten the same penalty of imprisonment for those caught playing it.

In the Great East Window of Gloucester Cathedral in the west of England, also dating from the mid-fourteenth century, a headless figure in stained glass is depicted swinging a curved club. The object of his attention is a yellow ball on a green background. Although the figure is known as the "golf player", it is more likely the game in question was cambuca, as the window is contemporary with the game and the ban that went with it.

THE GAMES OF FRANCE

Another game that appears to have owed much in its origins to the Roman game of paganica was the southern French sport of jeu de mail. The game was played with a *mail* (wooden mallet) and a wooden ball. The mallet was quite flexible and the ball could be struck substantial distances.

The object of the game was to play the ball along a designated course about a half a mile long to a fixed point. Jeu de mail seems to have resembled golf in being an individual game, with each player retaining the use of his own ball throughout the game. The

The swing of it
A small roundel in Gloucester Cathedral's Great East Window appears to portray a person performing a golf swing, yet the sport is generally thought to be cambuca.

Players at pell mell
An engraving from the Stuart period depicts pell mell being played in St James's Park, London. Golf evolved either from or alongside the other club-and-ball games of Europe.

Art and craft
In his painting, dated 1624, Flemish painter Paul Bril provides a fascinating visual record of the cross-country game of jeu de mail. In the lower right corner of the oil painting, a clubmaker, surrounded by his products, can be seen crafting a wooden ball.

Choleurs in action
Unlike golfers, chole players shared a single ball, as seen in the Duchess of Burgundy's 1450 Book of Hours. Opponents hit the ball in different directions.

winner of jeu de mail was the player who required the least number of strokes to reach the designated mark, which is obviously not unlike the basic concept of scoring in golf. A game in most respects similar to the ancient form of jeu de mail was still being played at Montpellier in the south of France around the start of the twentieth century. In his Historical Gossip about Golf and Golfers, published in 1863, A. Robb offers an interesting account of jeu de mail, describing it as strikingly similar to the game of golf. "The club is made in the shape of a hammer," Robb writes. "The handle is rather longer than that of a golf club, of the same size and thickness, and having a good deal of spring in it." The *mail* club was even designed to cope with a bad lie: "One end of the club is nearly flat, like the flat end of a hammer, with which the ball is usually hit, while the other is more sloped, so as to give a facility for striking the ball when it gets into a position of difficulty. Both ends are strongly bound with iron, which is necessary to give weight to the club as well as prevent the wood from breaking." The ball was also not unlike a golf ball, being "solid and round, made of the root of the box tree, about two inches [5cm] in diameter."

CHOLE AND CROSSE

A later version of jeu de mail was chole, which dates back to the mid-fourteenth century in Belgium and France. Chole was played cross-country, using clubs with long wooden shafts and balls that were made of either beechwood or leather, stuffed with whatever material was readily available. The ball was teed up for the first stroke and spare clubs and balls were probably carried around for the players.

The game itself was played in open fields with the object of reaching a fixed point, often some considerable distance away, and touching it with the ball in a specified number of strokes. However, unlike golf, there was only one ball, which all players, including opponents, played. Three members of the striking side each played strokes to advance the ball towards their objective. Then a member of the opposing team was allowed to strike the ball back from where it had come, or towards any hazard that would impair the progress of the striking team. This backward stroke was called a decholade, after which the striking team was allowed another three strokes. Crosse seems to have been simply another version of chole. The name for the game is derived from the French word for a hooked stick. It is known that the heads of the clubs were made of iron, similar to golf clubs, but like chole, the game seems actually to have had more resemblance to hockey than to golf.

KOLVEN AND THE CASE FOR HOLLAND

Those who believe that the origins of golf are to be found in Holland present kolven (or kolf) as the basis of their case. Quite a lot is known about the game (in fact, it is still played in Friesland and north Holland), but its similarity to golf is limited.

Although occasionally played outside on ice, kolven is essentially an indoor game played on a wooden floor, or in kolf courts specifically built for the purpose. In *The Statistical Account of Scotland in 1795*, there is a graphic account of the Dutch game that reinforces the view that kolf and golf are separated by more than their initial letter.

In this account by the Rev. Walker, one of the ministers at the Canongate Church in Edinburgh, there is confirmation that kolven was played in a confined area of about 20 by 60ft (6 by 18m) and indoors. The reverend

From pillar to post
The sport that appears on this early Delft tile is certainly the Dutch game of kolven, in which the players took their aim at fixed marks, such as posts. It was sometimes played indoors, and at other times in open country or even on ice.

Dutch winter scene
In winter, a version of kolven was played outside on Holland's frozen rivers and canals.

gentleman's recollection of the game comes from a period when he was resident in Holland and can therefore be assumed to be close to the mark. He writes: "The floor, which is composed of sand, clay and pitch, is made as level as a billiard table, and the inclosing walls are, for 2ft [60cm] above the floor, faced either with polished stone or sheet lead, that they may cause the ball to rebound with accuracy. At about 8 to 10ft [2.5 to 5.5m] from each end wall, a circular post of about 5in [13cm] diameter is placed precisely in the middle of the area with regard to breadth, consequently opposite the one to the other, at the distance of 40ft [12m] or thereby."

Neither the balls nor the clubs were close to their golf equivalents in design: "The balls used in the game are about the size of cricket balls [or baseballs], made perfectly round and elastic, covered with soft leather and sewed with fine

Kolf in Amsterdam
The limited dimensions of an outdoor kolf court are clearly shown in N.M. Aartman's engraving of kolven players behind the Stadlander Inn in the Amsterdam of 1755.

wire. The clubs are from 3 to 4ft [1 to 1.2m] long, with stiff shafts. The heads are of brass, and the face, with which the ball is struck, is perfectly smooth, having no inclination, such as might have a tendency to raise the ball from the ground." The target in kolven was two posts: "The game may be played by any number, either in parties against each other, or each person for himself; and the contest is, who shall hit the two posts in the fewest strokes and make his ball retreat from the last one with such an accurate length as that it shall lie nearest to the opposite wall of the area."

It seems kolven bears only a limited resemblance to golf. It is more likely to have influenced hockey and, by its transfer on to frozen canals in winter, ice hockey.

Pell mell was another ball-and-mallet game played in a restricted area with palisades, but nonetheless similar in concept to jeu de mail. In the sixteenth century, the game was introduced to Scotland from France, and Mary Queen of Scots is recorded as having played pell mell. But since it is separately recorded that the Scottish queen also played golf, the two games can hardly have been confused in anybody's mind.

MAGIC OF THE HOLE

There is a single, simple element missing from these various club-and-ball pastimes that separates them from the game of golf as we know it today: the hole. All use targets of one sort or another, but all of them above ground. Golf is unique in that the object of the exercise is to propel a ball across a course, which is liberally littered with obstacles designed to prevent that accomplishment, from a point where it is balanced in mid-air to another point where it finishes underneath the ground.

It may be a fiendish game, the aim of which is, as Sir Winston Churchill allegedly remarked, "to hit a very small ball into an even smaller hole, with weapons singularly ill designed for the purpose", but the hole is the vital factor. It is the existence of the hole that locates the game's origins firmly in Scotland. In effect, the history of golf is contained

The kolf club
Kolven was played with sturdy, heavy wooden clubs with brass plates to reinforce the head. Sixteenth-century examples of the fearsome-looking weapons used in this particular Dutch pastime are rare, but a few survive.

Hole change (right)
It is the hole, the unique feature of golf, that has taxed the skill and patience of countless generations of golfers. A light-hearted look at Jacobean golfers on this 1920s Doulton Seriesware Trophy shows a caddie directing the ball in the direction of the ever-tricky hole with a helpful puff of breath.

Prohibition
In the middle of the fifteenth century, James II decreed that "golfe be utterly cryed downe, and not to be used", in order to return the priority to archery, jousting and allied martial activities crucial to the defence of the Scottish realm.

within the record of Scottish golf. Golf has been a Scottish national pastime since long before the Scots' ignominious defeat at the hands of the English in 1513, when they lost their king and the flower of their noble families at the Battle of Flodden Field.

THE BANNING OF "GOLFE"

It is not too difficult to make the case that golf was at least one contributing factor in that merciless defeat. The Scots were no match for the English archers in the first assault and were eventually routed. It was only a matter of 50 years earlier that King James II of Scotland had been so concerned that golf was interfering with the practice of archery that he banned the game in the Scottish Act of Parliament of 1457 – the first documented reference to today's game. There is every evidence that the people of Scotland took little notice of the Act.

Subsequent bans were introduced only to be as widely ignored; it can be fairly assumed that the nation's collective ability to put a club to a ball grew in equal proportion to the decline in their prowess with bow and arrow. Indeed, so determined were the Scots to pursue the "golfe" that the Act banning it was repealed just over 40 years later.

Even in Scotland, golf's origins remain obscure. However, it is thought that it was being played there as much as a century before James II ordered that "golfe be utterly cryed downe". It was, indeed, probably already a Scottish pastime as early as 1319,

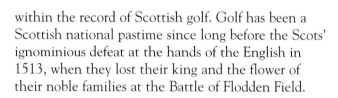

when the French authorities banned all ball games for the same reasons that had been given by the Scottish monarch – to encourage martial skills.

How golf actually originated will remain a mystery. One theory is that fishermen on the east coast of Scotland invented the game to amuse themselves as they returned home from their boats. What would be more natural than for a young fisherman, making his way across the rolling stretches of fine turf among the sand dunes, to pick up a stick of driftwood and aim a blow at a pebble? If he knocked the pebble forward, the competitive instinct inborn in man would demand that he hit it again to see if he could send it even farther.

INVENTING THE BUNKER

If the pebble rolled into a hollow, where sheep had huddled for shelter and their hooves had broken through to the sand just below, then the first obstacle to forward progress of the pebble had been found: the player would then have experienced the frustration that guarantees further attempts. It does not require a great leap of the imagination to develop that scene into a game between competing fishermen played across the links from boat to village, finishing at the same point each time, perhaps close to the local hostelry. If the pebble fell into a rabbit hole then the

game of golf had almost been "invented". There are copious links at St Andrews, and at the Old Course there is probably the most ancient stretch of land in the world in continuous use for the pursuit of golf. It is the classic links formed by nature, with the hand of man having played little part in its development over the centuries.

As to where the game was first played in Scotland, there can only be conjecture. King James II would not have banned golf in 1457, had it not been widely popular by then and probably much earlier. There is good evidence that it was played at Leith at this time and possibly earlier.

Those who claim that Leith predated St Andrews as a golf links point to what was then called the German Ocean to uphold the claim, maintaining that St Andrews could not have been used because the links was then covered by the sea at high tide. However, the links at St Andrews was almost certainly further inland than it is now because the sea has receded. There is no doubt that golf was played at St Andrews early in the sixteenth century. The citizens of the town were given the rights to use the links for "golf, futball,

Holemarker
Golf's connections with fisherfolk are retained in an early holemarker, comprising a wicker lobster pot on top of a bamboo pole. Such devices were deemed to be more challenging than flags because they did not give the players any indication of the direction of the wind.

St Andrews (left)
The east coast of Scotland was the birth-place of golf, and St Andrews was probably the first course there. This detail from an anonymous oil painting shows golfers on the Old Course, in front of the distinctive St Andrews skyline. The painting dates from around 1720 and is thought to be the earliest image of golf in Scotland.

shuteing at all times with all other manner of pastimes" by a charter dated 15 January 1552. And it is almost certain that golf was played there a century before that. Much of the other evidence about early golf is found in Kirk Session (church court) records in the sixteenth and seventeenth centuries. In many parts of the east coast of Scotland, parishioners were being punished for playing golf "at the time of the preaching of the Sermon". At St Andrews in 1599, miscreants were fined small sums for the first two offences, before the more ominous use of "the repentance pillar". After that, the culprits were "deprived of office" – excommunicated! Had there been as keen an appreciation of art in Britain as there was in the Low Countries at that time, more pictorial evidence might have survived of the early courses. But, as golf historian Robert Browning states: "The fact that the Flemish pictures of chole and the Dutch picture of kolven have no parallel of similarly early date in English or Scottish pictures of golf, is evidence of nothing except the superior artistic sense of the Continent, for it is a remarkable fact that up to the middle of the seventeenth century the art of painting made no appeal to the English taste."

ROYAL PATRONAGE

During the sixteenth century, the game became firmly established on the east coast of Scotland and began to spread farther afield. By this time, golf had gained respectability among the highest levels of society and was certainly played by James VI of Scotland before he acceded to the English throne, as James I, in 1603. His mother, Mary Queen of Scots, was also a notable player. We know that she played golf with one of her attendants, Mary Seton, because the queen lost a match against her and presented her conqueror with a still famous necklace. She also fell foul of the Church for playing golf only a few days after the

murder of her husband, Lord Darnley, in 1567. But royal interest in the game in Scotland went back further than this. We know that golf was played as far north as Montrose and had moved inland to Perth by the beginning of the sixteenth century, probably taken there by King James IV. Grandson of the Scottish king who had first tried to ban the game, James IV had in his turn tried to stop the Scots from playing golf, but eventually he was converted to the

Golf royalty (right)
Mary Queen of Scots was one of the first known devotees of golf.

King of clubs (left)
James VI of Scotland is said to have taken his clubs with him when he acceded to the English throne as James I in 1603. Its court connections gave golf a firm foothold in its progress.

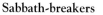

Sabbath-breakers
Two children suffer the wrath of the Church for indulging in golf on the Sabbath. Habitual offenders who "passis to play at the goufe" on Sundays faced a series of fines – and eventual excommunication – for their passion for the burgeoning game.

game himself. By 1502, the king's treasurer had paid 14 shillings to a bowmaker in Perth to supply clubs. From then onwards there was a series of bills paid from the royal coffers for golf balls, and even for lost bets incurred at the game. There is one account of the royal treasurer having to pay the Earl of Bothwell 14 shillings that the king had lost in a wager on a golfing combat somewhere out on the links.

GOLF SPREADS ACROSS SCOTLAND

It was this royal interest in golf that contributed greatly to its spread throughout Scotland and, ultimately, to its export farther afield. The earliest centres of golf all had associations with royalty or, in the case of St Andrews, with two other influential pillars of Scots society – education and the Church. St Andrews is Scotland's oldest seat of learning and it was also a powerful Church stronghold.

Scotland's capital, Edinburgh, was the head-quarters of the court, and golf blossomed around the city, aided by royal patronage. The same was true in other towns, such as Dunfermline and Perth, where there were royal palaces. The Bishop of Galloway became a player, possibly through court connections, and was probably responsible for the spread of the game to the south-west of the country. The Marquis

of Montrose was another keen player, which may well account for that town having a link with early golf. By the start of the seventeenth century, golf was actively pursued from the south-east of the country to as far north as the remote and windswept Orkney Islands, where it is believed to have been taken by two men, David Monteith and James Dickson.

Despite golf's popularity, it would be another 150 years before efforts were made to bring an organized structure to the game. But there was no lack of space for the enthusiasts to play. From as far north as Wick

Golf in Edinburgh
One of the first English watercolourists, Paul Sandby, painted soldiers' golf on the links at Bruntsfield in the mid-eighteenth century. Edinburgh Castle, once home to the Scottish court which did so much to spread golf, dominates the scene.

Matching pairs
The Scottish painter Charles Lees completed his Summer Evening at Musselburgh in 1859. As Edinburgh expanded, the seaside links at Musselburgh superseded Bruntsfield and Leith as the chief local course for the city's golfers, becoming the leading centre of golf until eclipsed by St Andrews in the 1890s.

Sand tees (right)
On the earliest courses, there were no separate teeing-grounds. A handful of sand was excavated from the previous hole and moulded into a cone, on which to set the ball.

Classic ground
The gently undulating terrain of east Scotland is covered in beautifully springy turf and coarse, hazardous gorse and heather. Allied to a fickle climate – prone to rapid changes of wind direction – this land remains the classic environment for golf.

in Caithness to well south of Edinburgh, the east coast of Scotland is blessed with mile upon mile of linksland, quite unsuitable for the growing of crops, but perfect terrain for the leisurely pursuit of golf.

The links evolved from great tracts of unsheltered sand, left by the sea as it receded over the centuries; in confirmation of the fact that they were once covered by the ocean, many courses around Britain are still peppered with seashells. Rivers running through this sandy wasteland to the sea deposited silt and seeds. Off-shore breezes blew the sand into great dunes that constantly moved until wild grasses took root and made them stable, permanent features. Fertilizer was supplied by the birds and water by the Scottish climate to encourage the grasses further. The links was land just waiting for golf to be invented.

GOLF'S NATURAL LANDSCAPE

The humps and hollows left by the shifting sand and sea and the tight turf cropped short by rabbits and grazing sheep were perfect for the game. The championship courses of Great Britain and Ireland stand testimony to this truth. All the courses

currently on the Open Championship rota in Britain, from St Andrews (currently the farthest north) to Royal St George's in south-east England, have evolved from linksland. And there are dozens of other links courses in the British Isles – from Royal Dornoch in the far north-east of Scotland to the marvellous links of Ireland, such as Portmarnock, Royal Portrush and Ballybunion. There are also examples of this terrain in courses in France, Belgium and the Netherlands, as well as a particularly fine example at Falsterbo in southern Sweden.

However, the early courses were not like those of today. There were no putting greens or tees as such; the courses were rough and were afforded little or no attention. The hole was a crude affair and served not only as the ultimate resting-place for the ball but also as a continuous supply of sand for the building of a tee from which to play the next drive.

PINCH OF SAND

The player took a handful of damp sand from the hole when he removed his ball and pinched it together to form a small mound, on which to place his ball. The tee was right beside the hole, which became deeper as more sand was removed. Finally it was dug so deep that a player could scarcely retrieve his ball, at which point a new hole was started.

The areas between the sandhills developed into smooth stretches of turf, probably as a result of continual tracking over the decades by animals such as rabbits and foxes, and by the men who hunted them. These tracks developed into the fairways and the areas around the holes, worn out by continual play, were expanded to form greens that were allocated exclusively for the delicate task of putting. This meant that eventually a separate, fresh area had to be set aside for teeing. Rabbits grazed the turf and kept it short; there was no machinery to do the job. Many of Britain's seaside links courses, such as

Saunton Sands in north Devon, relied exclusively on rabbits to keep their fairways tightly cropped until well into the second half of the twentieth century. Only recently, when the amount of play created damage to the turf faster than nature's ability to repair it, did science take a hand in golf's evolution with artificial fertilizer and irrigation.

TRADITION OF THE SILVER CLUBS

During the eighteenth century, golf experienced the first stirrings of a desire for organization of the game when clubs devoted exclusively to golf and the development of an accepted set of rules were formed.

The earliest club for which there is concrete proof is the Gentlemen Golfers of Leith (later to become, as they now are, the Honourable Company of Edinburgh Golfers), instituted in 1744. Royal Black-heath and Royal Burgess both declare they are older, but so far no evidence has been found to substantiate their claims. Blackheath has been entered in *The Golfer's Handbook* as "instituted traditionally in 1608", but the earliest evidence for the existence of the club dates from 1766, when the first ball was

attached to their silver club. It was common among eighteenth-century clubs to have a competition, the winner of which was declared captain for the ensuing year. A silver ball was attached to a silver club with the date and the captain's name inscribed on it.

The Society of St Andrews Golfers (later awarded the title of "Royal and Ancient" by King William IV in 1834) purchased their silver club in 1754. It was stated in their minutes book that it was open for competition to all clubs in Great Britain and Ireland. But when looking around for more senior clubs with whom to play they could only find the Gentlemen Golfers. It seems strange that if the Royal Burgess Golfing Society was formed in 1735, as they claim, they did not make contact.

The early clubs were as much a place to eat and drink vast quantities of claret as they were for the more healthy pursuit of

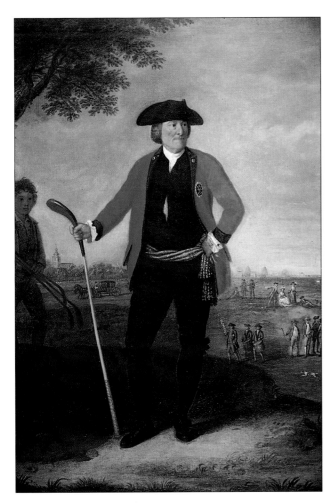

Captain of the Golf (left)
An oil painting by David Allan portrays William Inglis, captain of the Honourable Company of Edinburgh Golfers from 1782–4. Behind him, on Leith links, two drummers announce the procession of the annually contested silver club, for which the first set of formal rules was established.

golf. It is no coincidence that the trophy for the Open Championship is a claret jug. It would be hard to find an exception to the rule that the majority of golf clubs were formed by small groups of like-minded souls brought together in drinking and eating establishments of one sort or another. Once the clubs were formed, members could more easily combine their appetites for all three activities. Some may feel little has substantially changed in the last 250 years.

As golf became more popular, it inevitably spread out from its beginnings on the east coast of Scotland. The Scots had strong trading links with the Low Countries and a diplomatic "Auld Alliance" with the French. In the same way that the Romans brought paganica to southern Europe, so the Scots took golf to the south and east and, ultimately, to virtually every country on the map of the world.

Fact and figures
This 1908 pair of Staffordshire figurines, representing William Innes and his caddie, was modelled on the subjects of a 1790 painting by Lemuel Francis Abbott. Innes wears the captain's coat of the Blackheath club, which officially dates back to 1766 but claims a heritage from 1608.

THE PLAYCLUB ERA

A WEALTH OF *equipment has survived from the early years of golf in Scotland, and the collecting of antique golf clubs is now a special interest that fascinates many golfing enthusiasts. From the start of the eighteenth century to well beyond the middle of the nineteenth, a golfer would head out to do battle on the links armed with some eight to twelve clubs, the essential implements typically comprising a couple of playclubs, a grassed driver, three or more spoons, a baffing spoon, a wooden niblick and a wooden putter.*

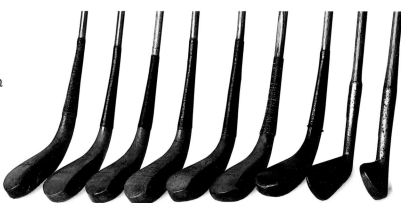

It is assumed that the first clubs used in Scotland, during the fifteenth century, were fashioned from wood, comprising a sturdy shaft, a weighted head and a padded handle, bound with hide from sheep, pig, horse or cow, or chamois. Later, from around 1700, metal-headed clubs joined the player's set, initially as additional implements for specialist tasks, but eventually taking the place of certain of the long-nosed wooden clubs.

SUPPLE DRIVERS

It was the elegant playclubs that above all characterized this whole era of golf in the eighteenth and nineteenth centuries. They were long-nosed, long-shafted, supple driving clubs that gave distance from the tee. Straight in the face, they made the ball run on when swept off the tee with a flat swing. Playclubs could easily split and golfers usually carried two of them in case one broke.

Shorter than the playclub was the grassed driver. This club was used to lift the ball off good fairway lies or to give the ball height when hit down wind. It had some loft on the clubface. Spoons (otherwise known as scrapers) came in long, middle and short sizes for dealing with various fairway lies. The clubs differed in the length of the shaft and the degree of loft of the clubface. The baffing spoon was a sturdy implement for taking turf with the ball to create maximum lift and minimum run. The wooden niblick was short and well-lofted and used to remove the ball from bunkers and difficult situations.

Finally came the wooden putter. It was broader- and shorter-headed, and shorter-shafted, than the other woods. Upright in lie, the club was straight-faced and surprisingly heavy in the head. One might expect all of

Set of 1850 clubs
Left to right: a playclub for tee-shots; spoons *for fairway strokes; a putter; and two irons for escaping trouble.*

SPLICED WOODS

Early woods were constructed from a strong, straight-grained shaft, tapering to a long, flat wedge, which was joined to a taper on the socket of the clubhead. After being glued, the joint was bound with twine whipping to hold it in place and to prevent damage.

Shaft

Tapering splice

Spliced joint

Clubhead

Whipping

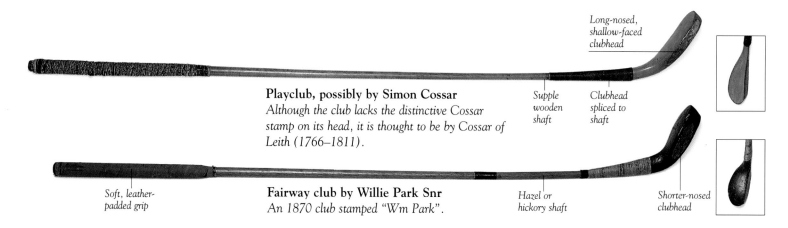

Long-nosed, shallow-faced clubhead

Playclub, possibly by Simon Cossar
Although the club lacks the distinctive Cossar stamp on its head, it is thought to be by Cossar of Leith (1766–1811).

Supple wooden shaft

Clubhead spliced to shaft

Soft, leather-padded grip

Fairway club by Willie Park Snr
An 1870 club stamped "Wm Park".

Hazel or hickory shaft

Shorter-nosed clubhead

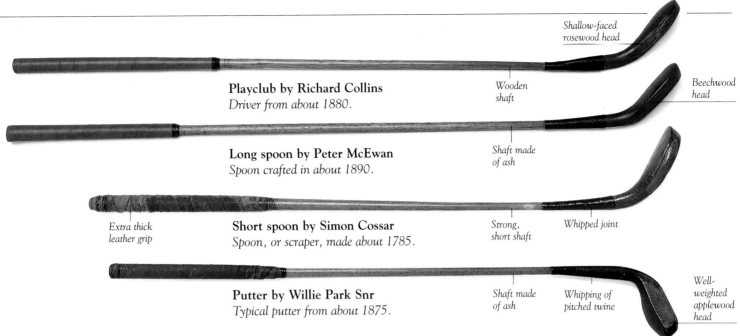

Playclub by Richard Collins
Driver from about 1880.

Shallow-faced rosewood head

Wooden shaft

Beechwood head

Long spoon by Peter McEwan
Spoon crafted in about 1890.

Shaft made of ash

Short spoon by Simon Cossar
Spoon, or scraper, made about 1785.

Extra thick leather grip

Strong, short shaft

Whipped joint

Putter by Willie Park Snr
Typical putter from about 1875.

Shaft made of ash

Whipping of pitched twine

Well-weighted applewood head

these early clubs to be unwieldy but this was not so. Heads, though differing in width, were elegantly shaped, nicely balanced and attractively coloured in ochre or dark "keel" stain.

CHOICE OF WOOD

The timber chosen to fashion the wooden clubs varied greatly. Most of the fruit-woods, including apple, pear, plum and cherry, were used for heads, along with hornbeam, dogwood, thornwood, beech and eventually, and most effectively, persimmon – a dense, straight-grained wood that was imported to Scotland from North America. The shafts, attached to the underside of the neck of the clubhead by a simple splice, were slender and finely tapered to ensure the "spring" or "kick" was in the correct position. The integrity of the splice was maintained by whipping, a tight binding of pitched twine or cord that was wrapped around the joint.

Shafts were made from ash, hazel, green-heart, lemonwood or lancewood, until hickory was found to be ahead of others in strength and straightness of grain.

Hard on the heels of the wooden-headed clubs came the irons. The first irons looked like weapons of war. With square-toed blades, thick sockets, sturdy shafts and well-padded grips, they were made for hard-hitting golfers.

Modifications to the heavy irons came along in the mid-nineteenth century. The first was the track iron, a small, round-headed, well-weighted tool for removing the ball from cart tracks, hoof marks and rabbit scrapes. Next came the cleek, a long-shafted, parallel-bladed iron with the loft of a middle spoon, for playing out of tight lies or light sand. The lofter, which vied with the baffing spoon, also became popular during this time.

Club comparison
Club design varied little for over 100 years, with playclubs and spoons having long, slim heads.

HAND-FORGED IRONS

Early iron heads were hand-forged with a socket, the opening of which was nicked with a cold chisel to grip the wooden shaft. The shaft of the club was filed to a slight taper to rest snugly in the socket before being driven into the clubhead to ensure a firm, secure fit.

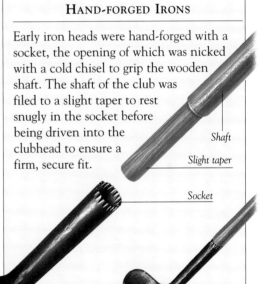

Shaft

Slight taper

Socket

Iron head

Thickly padded cloth grip

Square-toed iron
Sturdy iron from about 1750.

Strong wooden shaft

Thick hosel

Large, heavy head with concave face

Square toe

Driving iron by Robert Forgan
Crafted in the 1850s, the club may have belonged to Allan Robertson.

Strong wooden shaft

Slim hosel

Oval head

Track iron
Replacing the niblick, this iron lifted balls from cart tracks and hoof prints.

Strong, short-shafted upright club

Thick hosel

Small, heavy round clubhead

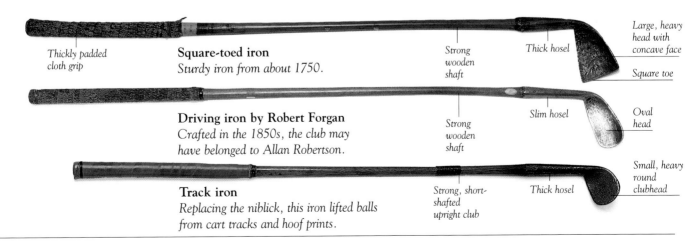

THE CLUBMAKER PROFESSIONAL

T HE CRAFTSMEN WHO *made golf clubs during the eighteenth and nineteenth centuries were a fascinating group of individuals who played a vital part in the history of the game. The earliest clubs were fashioned by bow-makers, wood-turners and carpenters, and their clubmaking skills were passed from father to son. Their family businesses were often associated with individual clubs such as Musselburgh, St Andrews or Leith. Many of the clubmakers were also among the leading golfers of their day – men such as Willie Park Snr, winner of the first Open Championship in 1860, Willie Dunn Jnr, winner of the first unofficial US Open, and the legendary Old Tom Morris.*

The clubs these men produced were the long-nosed woods that predominated in golf until the 1880s. Before the arrival of machine tools, all the parts of a wooden club were made by hand. To make a playclub, for instance, the clubmaker had to form a rough block of wood into a shaped head with a curved socket that tapered into a splice to fit the shaft. He used a special vice fitted to his bench and supported by a rod fixed to the floor to give complete rigidity while he worked.

Many of his tools were typical of any carpenter – saws, hammers, screwdrivers, files, planes and drills. A bunsen burner

Hammer

Screw-driver

Chisel (left) for cutting grooves in the back of the clubhead for lead inserts

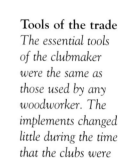

Weights (right) for weighing lead

Ladle (right) for pouring lead

Tools of the trade
The essential tools of the clubmaker were the same as those used by any woodworker. The implements changed little during the time that the clubs were made by hand.

Varnish or shellac pot and brush

Glue pot

Wood block with template for measuring the correct angle of the clubhead's lie

Protective ram's horn inserts for the leading edge of the clubhead

Old Tom Morris
A famous clubmaker, Old Tom Morris for many years served as the professional to the R & A, where his duties included repairing members' clubs.

Plane for shaft

Spliced clubheads

Oil can

Gouge

Bradawl

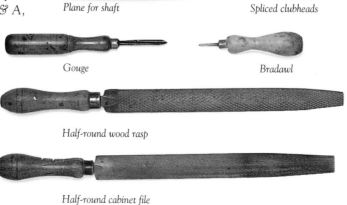

Half-round wood rasp

Half-round cabinet file

Stain pot and brush

was employed to melt lead, which was then ladled into a groove in the back of the club to give the head more balance, power and "feel". Ram's horn was used as an insert in the sole and face of the clubhead to minimize damage from rocks and stones. The clubmakers also used name-stamps to identify their output, which conveniently allows them to be identified today. Among the famous names from between the late eighteenth and late nineteenth centuries were the Dickson family of Leith; Simon Cossar, also of Leith; Hugh Philp of St Andrews, the first clubmaker to concentrate on balancing and streamlining wooden clubs;

Andrew Strath, also a noted player, winning the 1865 Open Championship; and the Patrick family from Leven in Fife.

While some of these craftsmen were solely clubmakers, others were employed at the links as a "ranger" or "keeper of the green", a jack-of-all-trades who could play golf, supervise the upkeep of the course, give tuition, collect fees, organize caddies, regulate play, and repair anything from a scythe to a sand-iron. This role evolved into that of the modern club professional. Irons were much less common than woods until the late nineteenth century. As golf gained in popularity, however, the range

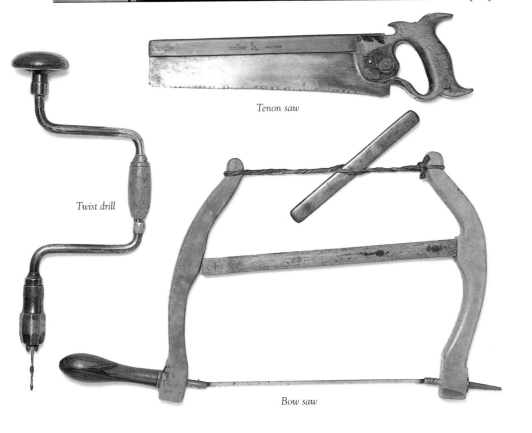

Workplace (left)
This room, as set out for use by a club professional in 1904, shows the round-topped, flat-faced vice fixed to the workbench.

Hand-forging (right)
There were few early makers of irons due to a lack of forges, anvils and tools. Here a blacksmith hand-forges heads for irons at the Premier Golf Company in 1909.

and variety of irons increased. Makers who hand-forged heads included Robert Brodie, James Anderson of Anstruther, the Carrick family, John Gray, Robert White and Robert Wilson. Some early blade-and-socket irons were made from two pieces of metal, a process followed by drop-forging and cast-moulding. The names of the "cleekmakers" appearing on such early clubs include those of Craigie, Brand, Nicholson and Stewart.

Tenon saw

Twist drill

Bow saw

Wooden shaft-former

Full-length shafts

THE GOLF REVOLUTION

SCOTTISH GOLF CLUBS *numbered about 30 in 1864; in the same year there were just three English clubs – Royal Blackheath, Old Manchester and Westward Ho! But by 1900 there were over two thousand clubs in Britain, and most of them were south of the border.*

Golf coaches
A publicity photograph that appeared in the coaches of the London and North Eastern Railway around 1900 shows golfers on the Holy Island links. The coming of the railway was a major factor in the rapid spread of golf around Britain.

This revolutionary growth of golf occurred as the industrial and imperial expansion of the Victorian era brought new prosperity to the English middle-class. With increasing money and leisure time, many of these affluent Victorians imitated the royal family in their habit of holidaying in Scotland. There they discovered the delights of golf and became infused with a love of the game, which they then took back to England with them.

The golf boom was made possible by two major developments: the advent of the "guttie" ball and the expansion of the railways. Balls made from gutta percha (see page 31) were introduced around the mid-nineteenth century and were about a quarter of

the price of the short-lived feathery balls they replaced, bringing golf within the financial reach of the Scottish working man. As gutties could also be produced in greater quantity, there was a ready supply of balls to meet the exploding demand.

The great improvement in transport provided by the expanding railway system (the railway reached St Andrews in 1850) gave enthusiasts access to the existing courses and to the newly developed seaside resorts of England and Scotland. Towards the latter part of the century, seaside towns built courses as an attraction for their new visitors. Many links courses of Britain have had, or still have, railway lines running along one of their boundaries. Inland courses were built within train distance of the cities to satisfy the craze for this newly popular sport.

BOOM IN BRITAIN

The number of clubs in Britain was thought to be about 60 in 1880; 387 in 1890; and 2,330 in 1900. There were less courses than clubs, as several clubs shared each course. But clearly the rise in the number of clubs points to a dramatic increase in both the popularity of golf and the number of courses.

The people who knew most about golf were the Scottish professionals. They were a hardy group of individuals who originally earnt money making clubs and balls and acting as caddies for their more wealthy employers. They played in some of the earliest matches for money and they counted among their number such great names as

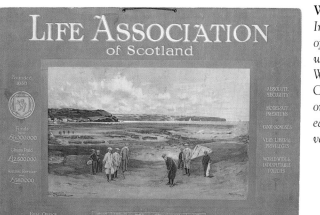

Wind skill (right)
In the shadow of its famous windmill, Wimbledon Common was one of London's earliest golfing venues.

The golfing life
A calendar of the year 1913, advertising the Life Association insurance company, incorporates a water-colour by J. Michael Brown depicting Horace Hutchinson's approach to the 4th hole at Royal North Devon, one of England's first clubs.

THE DEVELOPMENT OF THE RULES OF GOLF

The first written rules of golf were formulated by the Gentlemen Golfers of Leith in 1744. The presentation of a valuable silver club by the City of Edinburgh as a prize necessitated a common agreement on the way the game should be played, so Leith drew up 13 "Articles & Laws in Playing at Golf". New clubs continued to draw up their own rules, but looked to Leith for guidance until the Society of St Andrews Golfers became more influential from the mid-nineteenth century. In 1897 the Royal & Ancient Golf Club of St Andrews (as it had then become) was invited by the leading clubs of the day to compile a uniform code of rules.

During the first half of the 20th century the Royal & Ancient and the USGA, the governing body of American golf, both applied the same basic rules, but they made separate interpretations of decisions. These differences were largely resolved at a special conference in 1951, which was also attended by representatives from Canada and Australia.

The only stumbling-block was ball size, and some minor points on play. Importantly, the Royal & Ancient and the USGA agreed that they would meet every four years to review the rules and they set up a Joint Decisions Committee to establish uniformity.

A book of Decisions on the Rules is now jointly published by the two organizations and revised annually. It first appeared in 1984, marking a breakthrough in cooperation.

National Inter-club Championship, 1857
Competitors in an early R & A championship, congregating from numerous different clubs, highlighted the need for a uniform set of rules.

Duncan Forbes (left)
Lord President of the Court of Session, and an influential member of the Gentlemen Golfers of Leith, Duncan Forbes was instrumental in drawing up the first rules in 1744. Until then, golf had survived without a written set of rules for some 300 years.

Allan Robertson (see page 324) and Old Tom Morris (see page 298). Scottish professionals were imported south of the border to lay out courses and were much in demand to teach golf to the wealthy English at the new clubs that were being set up all over the country.

FIRST ENGLISH LINKS
The oldest existing seaside links in England, at Westward Ho! in north Devon, was created in 1864 when Old Tom Morris came down from Scotland to lay out the holes. Much of the early golfing history of England came out of the course at Westward Ho! and its Royal North Devon Club, along with top players, including J.H. Taylor, the first Englishman to break the Scottish dominance of golf when he won the Open Championship in 1894.

As the game spread gradually throughout England more clubs were founded. All around the south-east coast of England, prospective golfers explored links-land for its suitability for the game. Nearer the capital, the London Scottish Club was formed in 1865 when members of the London Scottish regiment were granted permission to play over Wimbledon Common. The civilian members were not happy with the way the military ran the club, and broke away to form what is now the Royal Wimbledon Club, playing on a heath by the Common. Among other early clubs, the Royal Liverpool Club at Hoylake, founded in 1869, played a major role in the development of English golf, hosting the first Amateur Championship in 1885.

Whereas in Scotland golf was played by all levels of society, in England the game attracted the majority of its devotees from the middle- and upper-classes, and clubs tended to evolve traditions of exclusivity. Although Scots were largely responsible for spreading the game to the rest of the world, this English identification of the game as the preserve of the gentleman was to become a firm component of golf's image when it arrived in the United States.

Beer and bunkers
A 1910 poster for a Glasgow beer harnesses a significant image of Scottish culture. The Scots exported golf to England, marketing their professional expertise in the game.

FEATHERIES AND GUTTIES

N O SINGLE ELEMENT *has had greater influence on golf's development than the ball. The nature and effectiveness of the various types of ball have shaped the way that the game has evolved and greatly influenced club design. In the early seventeenth century, the "feathery" superseded the wooden missile, probably made of beech, that was the earliest known ball. Expensive and easily damaged, these feather-filled balls held sway until the momentous advent of the gutta percha ball in 1848.*

Featheries (below)
Hard to make and easy to damage, featheries were expensive. They responded badly to poor weather, and if the leather or stitching was cut by a club, the ball was rendered useless. The antique featheries shown here are from the Royal & Ancient Club at St Andrews.

As well as being arduous, the task of crafting a feathery was detrimental to the maker's health. His lungs filled with feather dust, and his chest was weakened by the constant pressure of filling the ball, which was cupped in a wooden mould strapped against his body. Even the most experienced maker could only complete four balls a day; this accounted for their price of three to four shillings, often more than the price of a club. Despite its drawbacks, the feathery did noble service for

THE FEATHERY BALL

The feathery cover was made from three specially shaped lobes of dampened horse- or bull-hide (below), which were sewn together with thin twine,

leaving a small aperture, and then turned outside in. Wetted feathers were crammed into the hole with a special crutch-handled stuffing rod before it was stitched. On drying, the feathers expanded as the hide shrank, forming a hard ball. Its roundness depended on the skill of the cutting and stitching.

Shaped hide for feathery cover

Large strip was oblong to "hourglass" in shape

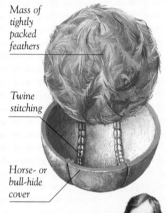

Mass of tightly packed feathers

Twine stitching

Horse- or bull-hide cover

Feathery ball used by Allan Robertson in 1842 when playing the Old Course at St Andrews in 87 strokes

Allan Robertson feathery ball of 1843

Red feather ball for use in snow

Last feathery made by Robertson, in 1852

Feathery made by John Gourlay of Musselburgh around 1840

Feathery by Old Tom Morris, formerly Robertson's employee

Feathery made by William Gourlay of Bruntsfield

Allan Robertson (right)
Perhaps the finest golfer of his era, Robertson was the most famous of a family of feathery-makers. He unsuccessfully resisted the arrival of the new gutta percha ball.

Rare feathery owned by J.H. Taylor

Top-hat rule (left)
Tradition has it that as many poultry feathers as it took to fill an entire top hat to the brim were needed to stuff a single feathery.

Old feathery, dated 1820 on the ball, by an unknown maker

Rare feather ball by Tom Alexander "famed on the Burntisland links"

Feather ball stamped "William" in Gothic script, date unknown

Undated ball with sprung seam that shows feather inside

over 200 years until the middle of the nineteenth century. Of the early makers of featheries, the Gourlay and Robertson families are the best known.

In 1848, a dramatic change came with the arrival of gutta percha, a rubber-like substance from the tropical percha tree. It was found to be malleable when boiled in water, and was easily pressed into the shape of a ball, which hardened when cooled. Moreover, when misshapen or broken, the parts could be reshaped after reboiling. The new gutta percha ball (or "guttie") heralded the demise of the expensive feathery and brought the game within the reach of the less well-off. It made standardization easier, and detailed attention was given to ball size and weight. Makers stamped the weight, between 26 and 31 pennyweights, on each ball, along with their name. With golf's new popularity, more ballmakers set up in business; most tyre and rubber companies were making balls before the end of the century. The reign of the guttie lasted until the introduction of the rubber-core Haskell ball at the start of the twentieth century.

THE GUTTIE BALL

The first gutta percha balls, shaped by gloved hand or by rolling the hot material between two flat boards, were smooth. Players discovered that the guttie flew better after it had been indented by mishit strokes, leading to the idea of marking the complete ball with a cold chisel or the claw end of a hammer. This hand-marking method was used until the introduction of the engraved iron or brass mould. Gutties made in a mould were more precisely round and had the flight-assisting marks built in.

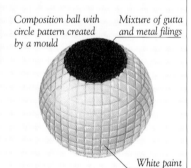

Moulds were either smooth or patterned to indent the ball. These are two smooth types: one with interlocking teeth; one with a lip.

Hand-rolled guttie with indents made by a chisel

Pure black gutta percha

White paint

Composition ball with circle pattern created by a mould

Mixture of gutta and metal filings

White paint

Collecting gutta
Gutta percha was tapped from the base of tropical trees, such as the Malaysian Palaquium gutta. Before tapping was introduced, the trees used to be cut down to extract their resin, each tree yielding 13lb (6kg) of gutta percha.

Well-used, black gutta percha ball

Badly marked, white-painted guttie

Gutta percha balls
The black gutta percha was painted white to make the ball more visible. "Composition" gutties had admixtures of other materials, such as cork or metal filings.

Smooth ball made by Robertson in 1852

Hand-hammered Robertson guttie from the 1850s

Red, hand-hammered guttie for use in snow

Composition guttie with smooth finish

Paterson's original "New Composite" guttie ball

Guttie with which Robertson played the St Andrews Old Course in a record 79

Guttie ball stamped with a distinctive circle marking

Black ball of about 1852 with mould-stamped marking

Gutta percha (right)
Once collected, the hardened sap of the gutta percha tree is wound in strips. It becomes malleable when it is boiled.

BULGERS, BRASSIES AND BAFFIES

T HE ARRIVAL OF *the guttie ball dramatically altered club design. The harder and heavier new ball was difficult to control with the slender, long-nosed woods and easily damaged them. Consequently, from 1880, wooden heads became shorter, broader and deeper, leading to the introduction of the "bulger", a driver with a convex face, which was designed to minimize a sliced or hooked stroke.*

Also towards the end of the nineteenth century, the spoons gradually disappeared from the set, being replaced by a baffy and a brassie, the heads of which were fitted with a brass striking-plate on the sole. At the same time, the number of iron clubs increased, primarily because they were cheaper to manufacture and could not harm the guttie, as they had the feathery. Around 1900, the irons, each with a different degree of loft, comprised the driving cleek, iron cleek, lofter, mashie, sand iron, niblick and putting cleek.

HEADS AND JOINTS

The new shape of wooden heads allowed clubmakers to alter the way the shaft was attached to the head. The bulkier, wider head could accommodate a hole drilled to take a round, tapered shaft, typically of hickory, which was less "whippy". This method was superseded by the

The bulger driver
The new clubhead shape focused the club weight in a small area.

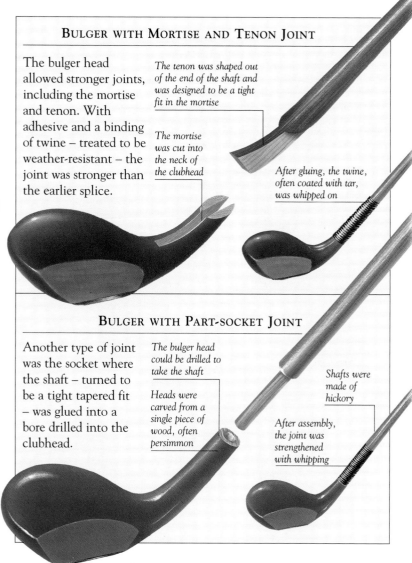

BULGER WITH MORTISE AND TENON JOINT

The bulger head allowed stronger joints, including the mortise and tenon. With adhesive and a binding of twine – treated to be weather-resistant – the joint was stronger than the earlier splice.

The tenon was shaped out of the end of the shaft and was designed to be a tight fit in the mortise

The mortise was cut into the neck of the clubhead

After gluing, the twine, often coated with tar, was whipped on

BULGER WITH PART-SOCKET JOINT

Another type of joint was the socket where the shaft – turned to be a tight tapered fit – was glued into a bore drilled into the clubhead.

The bulger head could be drilled to take the shaft

Heads were carved from a single piece of wood, often persimmon

Shafts were made of hickory

After assembly, the joint was strengthened with whipping

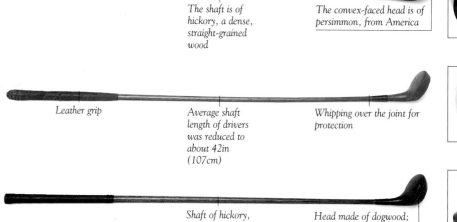

The shaft is of hickory, a dense, straight-grained wood

The convex-faced head is of persimmon, from America

Leather grip

Average shaft length of drivers was reduced to about 42in (107cm)

Whipping over the joint for protection

Shaft of hickory, replacing hazel or ash of playclubs

Head made of dogwood; leather insert in face

Socket-headed bulger driver
This club, made in 1903, is stamped "Jack White", Open Champion in 1904. The convex face gave a small striking area for accurate players.

Mortise and tenon joint driver
This driver was made around 1900 by A.H. Scott of Elie, Fife. This joint was used locally before being displaced by the through socket.

Old Tom Morris baffy
The baffy replaced the longer-headed baffing spoon. This club was made in Tom Morris's shop in about 1905, three years before his death.

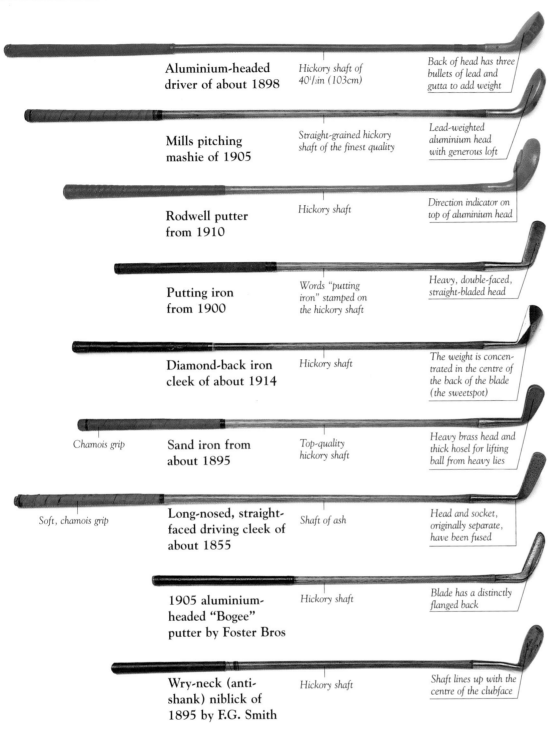

Aluminium-headed driver of about 1898 — Hickory shaft of 40¹/₂in (103cm) — Back of head has three bullets of lead and gutta to add weight

Mills pitching mashie of 1905 — Straight-grained hickory shaft of the finest quality — Lead-weighted aluminium head with generous loft

Rodwell putter from 1910 — Hickory shaft — Direction indicator on top of aluminium head

Putting iron from 1900 — Words "putting iron" stamped on the hickory shaft — Heavy, double-faced, straight-bladed head

Diamond-back iron cleek of about 1914 — Hickory shaft — The weight is concentrated in the centre of the back of the blade (the sweetspot)

Chamois grip — **Sand iron from about 1895** — Top-quality hickory shaft — Heavy brass head and thick hosel for lifting ball from heavy lies

Soft, chamois grip — **Long-nosed, straight-faced driving cleek of about 1855** — Shaft of ash — Head and socket, originally separate, have been fused

1905 aluminium-headed "Bogee" putter by Foster Bros — Hickory shaft — Blade has a distinctly flanged back

Wry-neck (anti-shank) niblick of 1895 by F.G. Smith — Hickory shaft — Shaft lines up with the centre of the clubface

THE ODD, THE BANNED AND THE UGLY

Around the turn of the twentieth century there was an explosion of experimentation in club design. Alongside their mass-produced clubs, many leading manufacturers invested time and money in prototypes designed to aid convenience, improve performance or keep abreast of changes in playing technique. From 1893 to 1906, the Urquhart family worked to perfect an iron with an adjustable blade (left) that enabled the loft to be varied as desired. J. Brown's rake mashie, "The Major" (centre left), was useful when playing out of rye grass or fine sand bunkers. The small, mallet-headed dual-purpose club (centre right) had varying lofts on each side. And in their spring-faced cleek (right), Spalding sandwiched a strip of gutta behind a scored steel face, which was riveted to an iron head. Many patented clubs were short-lived, either proving impractical or being banned.

"through socket", where the shaft fitted in a hole drilled through to the sole of the head. Other techniques were the mortise and tenon, twin-splice and V-insert.

Many curious variants found their way to the clubmaker's shop, including the "one-piece" club. It was made of ash, thornwood or dogwood, usually fashioned from the root or thicker low branches of a mature shrub or small tree. The bulbous root formed the head, and the shaft was shaped from the slimmed-down branch.

Other oddities included the vast range of inserts used on driving and fairway clubs to protect the face from the impact with the tougher ball. These ranged from glass, rubber and slate to ivory and rhinoceros and elephant skins. Also tried were small rollers fitted into driver soles. On the face of the club, a coil spring with a strip of metal, or with a ball-bearing, was tested to speed the ball. Lead weights were placed in the heel and toe of the head to aid the player who was unable to flight his

ball as intended. Most of these ambitious inventions failed to conquer the market, although face inserts are still fitted today.

Clubs with aluminium heads also appeared on the scene. First came putters, with heads shaped in the style of a short wooden-headed putter. These proved popular, and by 1895 the demand was sufficient for manufacturers to make a full range of clubs from this light metal, including drivers, cleeks and mashies.

Up to about 1900 the clubface was left unmarked, reducing the amount of "stop" or backspin that could be put on the ball. But it proved popular when manufacturers took to marking the centre of the club-face, by indenting or grooving the metal.

TEES

G OLF HISTORIANS BELIEVE *that the practice of using the green as a teeing-ground to the next hole was phased out during the eighteenth century. Instead, after holing out, players moved a short distance from the green and teed-up on a specially formed patch of turf. This meant that the green was spared the ravages of divot-lifting playclubs and boot-stud scratches. More importantly, the game speeded up as players moved promptly off the green.*

Along with the evolution of the teeing-ground came the iron sand box. This contained dense sand, which enabled the caddie or player to form a cone or mound of sand for the ball to sit on. The box also marked the driving-off area.

Over the years the sand box became more sophisticated. First it was fitted with runners to enable the greenkeepers to pull the heavy container to a new position on the teeing-ground. Later, legs were added to bring the box up to waist height.

Even after the arrival of celluloid tees at the beginning of the 1900s, followed by others made from cardboard, wood and rubber (for use on hard, frozen ground), a variety of moulds and gadgets were patented to help form a sand tee. These "tee stamps" were usually made of brass in the shape of a miniature inverted bell.

Eventually, as the use of cheap ready-made tees became almost universal, sand boxes were used instead as receptacles for broken tees and other litter.

Paper tees (below)
A popular alternative to sand was the disposable tee cup, a ring of cardboard that lifted the ball off the turf. They were even sold in perforated booklets; the golfer had to tear off one of these along the perforation and shape it by rolling it between the fingers.

This sand mould has two heights: one for teeing up with a driver, the shorter one for use with an iron

On the teeing-ground
Golfers teed up their balls on small mounds of sand (above); a mould (left) was used to form sand cones.

Colonel Bogey's brand from Illinois was designed to "eliminate bothersome sand tees"

Booklet of cardboard tees, "Novel-tees", from Chicago

Tees advertising shops and services

Circular wooden tee-holder

Rubber ball support

"Perfect Golf Tee", for use on hard ground

Experimental tees (above)
Many innovative devices were marketed, including the circular tee-holder. The "Perfect Golf Tee" of 1927 had a nail to anchor the ball support, so that it would not fly off.

Rubber tees (below)
Rubber tees were introduced for use on hard ground or in snow. The tees are of different heights: the low one was employed with irons and the taller one with drivers.

Low tee for use with irons

Tall tee for shots with drivers

Cord to tie tees to bag or clothing

Canvas bag of 100 wooden tees for one shilling

"Rite-Hite" tee box from 1925

Collar to ensure uniform height

Wooden tees
The advantage of wooden tees was that they did not damage clubheads.

Canadian celluloid tees from 1932

Bright finish to tees made them easier to find in the grass

Pack of tees with a book of matches

Plastic tees advertising Dewar's whisky in Scotland

Celluloid and plastic tees
In addition to being cheap to produce, plastic tees did not break easily.

CARRYING THE CLUBS

T HE MODIFICATIONS AND *improvements made to clubs and balls during the latter half of the nineteenth century were accompanied by advances in ancillary equipment not directly related to play. One major leap forward was the introduction of the club-carrier or golf bag. Previously clubs had been carried about loose under the arm of the golfer or his caddie and the bag was a welcome addition to their comfort.*

Golf bags first appeared on the market between 1885 and 1895 in the style of a slender, tubular wicker basket, or of a wooden tripod supporting a canvas pocket, which could be carried by a single handle. The tripod was constructed so that the legs opened automatically when the base of the bag was placed on the ground. By the end of the century the golf bag had become an essential part of the golfer's equipment,

Wooden dowel wrapped in American green cloth

Aluminium rod to separate straps

Noosed leather straps for holding clubs

Rare club-carrier
To transport the clubs around the course, they were suspended between the two straps of this nineteenth-century club-carrier.

Leather pouch for carrying balls

enabling many accessories to be carried including a tee mould for sand tees, a pouch-shaped ball cleaner, finger tape for treating blisters and multi-purpose tape for carrying out running repairs.

CADDIES FOR PENNIES

The word "caddie" derives from the French cadet, a title given to a youth serving in the armed forces or at court. Cadets were looked upon as page-boys, porters and bearers, and in local parlance caddie was applied to those who carried the golfers' clubs. Mainly young boys, they were expected to select the correct clubs, tee-up the ball and attend to the flag-stick on the green. They were also required to remain as silent as possible.

As golf has changed, so too has the fortune of caddies. For a long time they were treated as mere club-carriers, given a few pennies for two-and-a-half hours at the player's beck and call. Today, however, caddying has become a serious profession, with the best caddies highly prized and paid, travelling the world in the employ of professional golfers, many of whom started as caddies.

Carrying handles

The Bussey (right)
This club-carrier had a club-retainer that could be adjusted according to the varying length of the clubs. The twin legs swung out on hinges every time the carrier was put on the ground.

Adjustable leather club-retainer

Canvas ball pouch at top

Before the bag (above)
Caddies used to carry the bundle of clubs under their arm before the introduction of golf bags. Caddying is almost as old as the game itself.

Canvas ball pocket

Bipod supporting legs

Leather handles

Canvas club-retainer

Mahogany board

The Osmond (right)
The Osmond had a canvas club-retainer and ball pocket. The carrying handles were made of leather. This particular model, "The Automaton", was patented in 1893.

Supporting legs

Golfer and bag
The bag made it easier for golfers to manage their equipment on the course. Clubs could be kept dry and sundry accessories could be carried.

TAKING GOLF TO THE WORLD

THE SPREAD OF *golf across the world since the late nineteenth century has been rapid but uneven. The game boomed in the United States long before its current explosion in Japan and the Far East. The early apostles of golf were almost invariably Scots, who set up golf courses wherever they travelled, so they could indulge in their favourite sporting pastime. They were largely responsible for establishing the game in the United States.*

The pioneers (left)
The first photo of golf in the United States, dated 1888, shows play at the St Andrew's cow-pasture course.

John Reid (right)
US golf's founder was president of the first club: St Andrew's, Yonkers, New York.

The men credited with much of the early pioneering effort in the United States were John Reid and Robert Lockhart, two expatriate Scottish schoolfriends from Dunfermline in Fife, a town famous for its linen and not far from St Andrews itself. Reid, a resident of Yonkers, New York, and manager of an iron works, is now generally regarded as the "father of American golf", but Lockhart, a New York linen merchant, had an extremely significant part to play

Farewell dinner
To celebrate leaving their course in the orchard on the Weston estate at the end of 1893, the members of the St Andrew's club held a dinner. The "Apple Tree Gang" and their guests signed the menu for H.O. Tallmadge, later the first USGA secretary. Their new quarters were at Grey Oaks.

as well. Lockhart was in the habit of bringing unusual gifts back from Scotland, which he visited in pursuit of his linen business. On one trip he brought back tennis racquets and balls, but failed to create much interest in that game amongst his acquaintances.

FATEFUL TRIP
In the summer of 1887, Lockhart visited Old Tom Morris's shop in St Andrews and ordered six golf clubs and two dozen gutta percha golf balls, presumably with the intention of taking them back with him over the Atlantic. However, it seems that the order for the clubs was not completed in time for his departure and his implements had to be despatched by sea, reaching him some time later.

The clubs were ordered on behalf of John Reid, but before he passed them on, Lockhart, who had played as a youth on Musselburgh links and at least knew the rudiments and basic rules of the game, decided to put the clubs to the test himself. There are several accounts of what happened that day in late autumn 1887, including one which claims that Lockhart had to be bailed out by Reid after being arrested for playing golf in a public place. The most accurate description of the event is probably that given by Robert Lockhart's son, Sydney. He recalled accompanying his father and his brother Leslie one Sunday morning to "a place on the river which is now Riverside Drive". There his father selected a teeing-ground, watched by a mounted policeman.

"Father teed up the first little white ball," Sydney Lockhart writes, "and, selecting one of the long wooden clubs, dispatched it far down the meadow. He tried all the clubs and then we boys were permitted to drive some balls too." Their efforts attracted the policeman's attention and he asked if he could join in. "The officer got down off his horse and went through the motions of teeing up, aping father in waggling and squaring off to the ball and other preliminaries. Then he let go and hit a beauty straight down the field which went fully as far as any that father had hit. Being greatly encouraged and proud of his natural ability at a game that involved a ball and stick, he tried again. This time he missed the ball completely and then in rapid succession he missed the little globe three more times; so with a look of disgust on his face he mounted his horse and rode away."

THE GIFT OF GOLF

Thus initiated, the products of the craft of Old Tom Morris, three woods and three irons acquired for around $2 each, were presented to Lockhart's friend, John Reid, who then embarked – although one suspects he did not know it at the time – on a mission that was to change the sporting future of his country for ever. It was in mid-winter, on 22 February 1888, Washington's birthday, that Reid and five of his friends – John B. Upham, Henry O. Tallmadge, Harry Holbrook, Kingman H. Putman and Alexander P.W. Kinnan – took themselves into a cow pasture opposite Reid's home in Lake Avenue, Yonkers, to lay out their course. They found it difficult to make six clubs serve the needs of so many players, but they played the first "round". That they

Champion of American golf
Charles Blair Macdonald was an important figure in the early years of golf in the United States, as player, administrator and architect. His Chicago course design, the first US 18-holer, influenced many subsequent courses.

were able to do so was only by the good fortune of a sudden thaw, however. Their pioneering efforts on their three-hole course lasted less than three weeks, for a blizzard left it under 3ft (90cm) of snow and the American golf revolution came to a temporary halt.

GOLFING TIES

Once the snow had cleared, however, Reid and his friends were back on the course, and they were soon looking for another place to build a bigger one. They moved round the corner to a 30-acre (12ha) site owned by a German butcher by the name of John C. Shotts. Reid and his friends had neither asked nor been given permission to use the land for their new course, but since they were among Mr Shotts's best customers he felt it prudent not to make any complaint. So the game had begun and the pioneering players persevered in their pastime.

Through the summer they played on, incurring in turn the ridicule of other local residents and the wrath of the clergy for playing on the Sabbath. But since the Scots had been ignoring clerical edicts on the subject for centuries they were little concerned on that front. Indeed, criticism rather strengthened their resolve to bring a more structured form to their activities. To this end Reid invited his golfing friends to his home after their round on 14 November 1888. There they formed the St Andrew's Golf Club, named after the famous links course on the east coast of Scotland known throughout the world as the home of golf. The club was distinguished from its name-sake in Scotland by the use of the apostrophe (St Andrew's, not St Andrews), but the same principles and traditions of the game were to apply to both. It was hoped that the name would help inspire and generate the same enthusiasm for the game in the United States as existed in Scotland. It turned out to be a propitious choice, as the subsequent history of golf in North America was to prove.

Home golf
There was such enthusiasm for golf in the United States in the early years of the twentieth century that many board games, such as this one made in 1910 in New York, were sold. They enabled would-be golfers to practise tactics away from crowded courses.

Following the example of their predecessors in St Andrews, Scotland, more than a hundred years before, the founders adjourned to dinner to celebrate their new club and to toast the future of golf in their country. Reid was elected as president, with Upham as secretary and treasurer, and the game of golf had officially arrived in the United States.

APPLE TREE GANG

In 1892 the club moved to another site, set in an apple orchard on the Weston estate, with views over the Hudson River and Palisades in New Jersey. It took only a day to design the new layout, which was threaded between the apple trees, and when it was finished the St Andrew's Club at Yonkers could boast six holes measuring a total of 1,500 yards. Reid and his colleagues became known as the "Apple Tree Gang", after the apple tree under which they sat for shade while taking suitable refreshment after a round of golf.

By that time a handful of other clubs had joined the St Andrew's pioneers. Among them were Shinnecock Hills and Meadow Brook on Long Island, White Plains in Westchester, Richmond on Staten Island, Greenwich in Connecticut, and across the river in New Jersey, Lakewood, New Brunswick, Montclair, Paterson and Baltusrol. From that trickle there started a flood, and by the turn of the century the United States had more than 1,000 golf clubs. The Apple Tree Gang could have had no idea, when they took their first tentative golf steps little over a decade before, of what they were unleashing on the United States.

Great as the influence of the St Andrew's founders was, however, it should be noted that they were not the first people actually to play golf in America; neither was their club the first in the country. It

Golf cup
A drinking stein, made in the United States by O'Hara around 1899, carries a Harvard University crest on its lid. Many of the golf clubs that burgeoned in the States at the turn of the century were created by groups of drinking companions.

President Havermeyer
The first president of the USGA, the ruling body of American golf, was Theodore Augustus Havermeyer, builder of the course at Newport, Rhode Island. The USGA was formed in 1894 by six golf clubs in the north-east United States.

is known that Scottish officers who fought during the American War of Independence, which began in 1775, brought golf with them across the Atlantic. Four years later an advertisement appeared in *Rivington's Royal Gazette*, New York, which, under a heading "To the Golf Players", pronounced: "The season for this pleasant and healthy exercise now advancing Gentlemen may be furnished with excellent CLUBS and the veritable CALEDONIAN BALLS by enquiring at the Printer's." Charleston in South Carolina was the site of the formation of the South Carolina Golf Club in 1786 and the Savannah Golf Club was operating in Georgia in 1796. But although it is clear that there was a certain interest in the game over a century before John Reid and his friends first played in their cow pasture, it did not endure. Thus it was not until the Apple Tree Gang introduced the game to the north-east United States that the American passion for golf began to take hold, and they are justly credited as the founding fathers of the American game.

FOUNDING THE USGA

Among the other early American golf pioneers was Theodore Havermeyer who, despite some lack of enthusiasm among his contemporaries, built a course at Newport, Rhode Island, a resort for the wealthy. In 1894 Havermeyer was elected the first president of the United States Golf Association (USGA) when it was formed at a meeting of five of the newly established clubs: St Andrew's, the Country Club of Brookline, Newport, Shinnecock Hills and Chicago. Newport was selected as the venue for the first official US Open and US Amateur Championships that were held the following year.

Other important figures in the game at that time were Henry O. Tallmadge, the first secretary of the association, and Charles Blair Macdonald, who became a golf addict while studying at St Andrews, Scotland. Influenced by the Scottish links,

Macdonald built the Chicago Golf Club, which is credited with having the first 18-hole course in the United States. Macdonald's work affected much of the early thinking on courses in the United States, and this explains why the first layouts on the eastern seaboard bear such a resemblance to Scottish courses.

TAKING ROOT AROUND THE WORLD

Canada had already been bitten by the golf bug as it spread from Scotland. The country's first club at Montreal, later to become Royal Montreal, was founded in 1873, 15 years before the Apple Tree Gang first put club to ball. The Royal Quebec Club was formed in 1875, and these two clubs played the first inter-club match in Canada, at Cove Fields, in 1876.

Postcard from Pinehurst (right)
Pictures of famous holes made excellent greetings, as in this image of the 16th at Pinehurst's Number 2.

Gone golfing (below)
Golf was the great escape from everyday cares. Bunking off to battle with bunkers had more appeal than tiresome toil on the treadmill.

Beginning **The Peddler** – By Henry C. Rowland

That year another club was formed in Toronto, but golf did not subsequently spread as quickly in Canada as in the United States. This was perhaps partly due to the smaller population north of the border, and partly to the colder climate, which made the golf season much shorter. Yet the influence of Canada on golf on the North American continent has been considerable, and today there are more than 1,600 courses across the country.

It was not only to the other side of the Atlantic that the Scots took their game; they played a part in its introduction to most of the countries in the expanding British Empire. In fact, the Royal Calcutta Club in India, formed in 1829, is among the oldest of all clubs; Royal Bombay dates back to 1842. Both clubs were founded by Scottish golfing enthusiasts engaged in trade with India. The Royal Calcutta Club inaugurated the Amateur Championship of India and the Far East in 1892, by which time there were clubs not only in India but in Ceylon (now Sri Lanka), Singapore and Burma. The first Amateur Championship was played over 54 holes of the nine-hole layout and until 1948 British players still dominated the event. As the standard of the home players' game improved, the British influence faded. There are now some 150 golf courses in India.

FARTHER AFIELD

There is some confusion over precisely when the game spread to Australia. It is thought that golf was played in some form as early as 1870 in Adelaide, although the Royal Adelaide Club officially dates back only to 1892. The Royal Melbourne Club had been founded a year earlier, in 1891, and the Royal Sydney Club came along shortly afterwards in 1893. Across the Tasman Sea, the Royal Christchurch Club in New Zealand dates back even earlier to 1867 and the Otago Club to 1871.

South Africa had pioneering clubs too, of which Royal Cape, founded in 1885, is generally accepted as the oldest. Even the island of Mauritius took to golf in 1844 when the Mauritius Naval and Military Gymkhana Club is believed to have been formed. The Royal Hong Kong Golf Club was founded in 1889, but since the colony was handed back to the Chinese in 1997, the "Royal" title, granted by Queen Victoria in 1897, has been dropped.

Fowl stroke
A memento of the earlier days of golf in the United States: a ceramic figure of Walt Disney's Donald Duck has a swing at a golf ball. He has learned the first lesson of keeping his eye on the ball.

Golf at Pau

The first golf club on the continent of Europe was at Pau in France, close to the border with Spain and in the gentle foothills of the Pyrenees. The club was founded in 1856 in the fashionable British holiday colony there. Golf had originally been played in the area by Scottish officers of the Duke of Wellington's army towards the end of the Napoleonic Wars.

In continental Europe, the Golf Club de Pau in south-west France is generally accepted as the oldest club, having been founded by British visitors in 1856, while the Royal Antwerp Club in Belgium was founded in 1888, the same year that the Apple Tree Gang were finding a new use for their cow pasture. Strangely, despite all the speculation over the origins of the game and its possible connections with the Low Countries (see page 17), the first golf club in the Netherlands did not appear until almost the end of the nineteenth century. This honour belongs to the Rosendaelsche Club in Arnhem, which was founded by Dutch golfing enthusiasts in 1896.

The twentieth century has seen golf develop all over the world on a major scale. The great boost to the game given by the United States at the turn of that century, when hundreds of clubs were formed, followed over the years by the development of resort golf courses to cater for holiday golf, has made the Americans by far the biggest golfing nation in the world. But there have been major golf booms as significant in their own way elsewhere in the world, especially since the Second World War.

There was also increasing awareness of golf in continental Europe and since the early 1970s there has been a rapid expansion of the game, particularly in France and Germany, where interest was stimulated by the emergence of international stars such as Catherine Lacoste and Bernhard Langer. In Spain and Portugal, the construction of golf courses has been largely to provide facilities for visiting players from further north in Europe escaping the winter weather, rather than to cater for local demand. But the existence of these courses has encouraged the development of local talent, especially in Spain, which has produced brilliantly gifted players such as Seve Ballesteros, José-Maria Olazábal, and Sergio Garcia.

PLAYING THE GREEN CARD

Sweden has been a major golfing nation for many years and has the largest number of active golfers in Europe outside the British Isles. The Swedes have made a significant impact on the game through their "green card" system, which requires newcomers to the game to pass a written and practical examination before they are licensed to play on a full-length course. The golfing authorities have an aggressive youth policy and the country has been producing players capable of winning on the European Tour. Joakim Haeggman became the first Swedish player to win Ryder Cup honours when he was included in the European Team at The Belfry in 1993. Since then several Swedish players have won Ryder Cup honours, including Jesper Parnevik and Per Ulrik Johansson.

Golf was played in most of the countries of central and eastern Europe before the Second World War, including Hungary, Poland, Yugoslavia, Romania and Czechoslovakia. Africa too has been affected by the expansion of golf. In addition to the many fine courses

Come to Italy

An Italian state tourist department brochure of 1932 tempts British players to head south for golfing holidays. After the First World War, golf spread quite rapidly over the European continent.

in South Africa, of which Royal Cape and Royal Johannesburg are probably the most impressive, there are more than 70 courses in Zimbabwe with the Bulawayo Club, founded in 1896, the oldest.

The expansion in the popularity of the game since the Second World War has been especially intense in the Far East. By 1987 Taiwan could boast 23 courses and 200,000 players. In Lu Liang Huan the island produced a player capable of taking second place in the Open Championship in 1971 and helping win the World Cup for Taiwan the following year.

It is the Japanese, however, who have taken to the game with an enthusiasm unmatched by any other recent converts. Golf was first played in Japan almost as early as the end of the nineteenth century, when a Scot named Arthur Groome built a few holes on top of Mount Rokko, near Kobe, for a group of English and Scottish expatriates. The Kobe Club soon had 18 holes and other clubs followed at Yokohama and around Tokyo, but most of the early members were foreigners. Today the Japanese themselves flock to play golf. There were fewer than 30 clubs in Japan at the end of the Second World War. Today there are many hundreds, despite the fact that the country has a severe shortage of suitable land on which to build courses.

THE JAPANESE GOLF BOOM
It is estimated that there are more than 13 million Japanese golfers, but high green fees mean they spend more time on the driving ranges than on the golf course. Before the economic crisis in Japan in the late 1990s, golf club memberships in Japan were often

viewed as major investment opportunities and have been traded for figures in excess of $1 million. With space at home at such a premium, many affluent Japanese companies also took the opportunity to invest in golf course developments and golf resorts in other parts of the world. The Riviera Club in the United States and the Old Course Hotel Golf Resort and Spa in St Andrews, Scotland, are examples. Meanwhile, the average Japanese golfer plays his or her golf on one of the 4,000 and more driving ranges – often a multi-storey construction and always a high-tech operation.

There is no sign of an end to the expansion of golf as a world game. China and Taiwan have an aggressive golf course building programme, central European countries such as Poland and Slovenia are expanding into golf and post-Cold-War Russia is fast opening up to the game. The sport is now played by an estimated 30 million golfers in 80 countries world-wide.

Iberian golf
The dramatic setting for golf at Vale do Lobo, in the Portuguese Algarve, provides a stern challenge to tourists, who make use of one of the most popular resort courses built to cater for the needs of golfing holidaymakers.

Tobacco jar (left)
The famous ceramic works of Noritake in Japan made this golf-motif tobacco jar in the 1930s, showing that golf had some followers in Asia before the Second World War.

Precious few courses (right) *The enormous Shiba Park in Tokyo is a three-storey range where hundreds of golfers can practise at any one time, shooting balls out 280yd (256m) to a sloping rubber mat.*

②

THE MODERN GAME

 The great golf-course building explosion of the late nineteenth century – in the United States alone 1,000 golf courses were built in the 1890s – coupled with the invention of the superior-quality rubber-core ball, which made golf altogether easier to play, set the game well on the way to becoming today's mass-particiption sport. The large number of clubs around the world celebrating centenaries at the end of the twentieth century was a testament to the scale of the golf revolution at that time.

With the new courses came players keen to learn and the professional golfer came of age. New technology brought rapid advances in golfing equipment.

Golf continues to boom around the world, encouraged by the televised exploits of

French ceramic golfing figure from the 1950s

the new generation of superstar players – not least by the phenomenon that is Tiger Woods.

Popular spectator sport (left)
The 1988 US Open is watched by a huge gallery of avid golf enthusiasts.

Modern, wide-bodied carbon graphite woods with boron-reinforced shafts

COMPETING FOR GLORY

GOLF HAS COME *a long way since its tentative beginnings five or six centuries ago on the east coast of Scotland. The pastime of the Scots has become the passion of millions of people, as well as being, for a celebrated few, a passport to untold riches. At around the end of the nineteenth century, as the game expanded and became better organized, the professional golfer first rose to the status of a popular hero.*

Model player (above)
Enthusiasm for golf permeated other leisure areas. This lead toy is part of a board game from the beginning of the century.

Top trio
Clement Flower's 1913 portrait of the Triumvirate shows, left to right, Taylor, Braid, Vardon (driving) at the 2nd tee on the Old Course at St Andrews.

Until then, golf had been very much an amateur pursuit. Early in the development of the game, the job of the golf professional was to make clubs and balls and to carry the clubs, and later the bags, of the amateur players. Even in the late Victorian period, golf professionals were much less highly regarded than they are now.

GOLF PROFESSIONAL OR PROFESSIONAL GOLFER

Essentially, the professional was there to provide a service for club players, although he played in occasional money matches and, increasingly, in organized tournaments. Today, of course, golf professionals still aid their club members in much the same way. But no equivalent to the modern tournament players – professional golfers who play golf for a living on the various tours around the world – existed until the emergence of three masters of the game in the 1890s heralded a new era.

The British players Harry Vardon (see page 344), James Braid (see page 240) and J.H. Taylor (see page 339) dominated the game for two decades and were known as the Great Triumvirate. The trio, who between them won 16 Open Championships from 1894 to 1914, became the first golfing superstars. Spectators flocked to see them, and they were in demand to open new courses and clubhouses. The combined impact of these

three champions on the growth of golf cannot be overstated. Harry Vardon brought a new artistry to the game, while Braid made an outstanding contribution to course architecture. And Taylor, despite his fabulous record of five Open Championship wins, is famed as much for improving the lot of the professional golfer as for his prowess as a player. It was largely due to him that the first Professional Golfers' Association was formed in 1901.

CHALLENGE FROM THE AMERICANS

In the days of the Great Triumvirate, British players dominated the game of golf. But the Americans, by building 1,000 courses between 1890 and 1900 and importing hundreds of Scottish professionals to teach the game, soon started to catch up. In 1911 Johnny McDermott became the first home-bred American to

Cigarette-card hero (right)
Gene Sarazen dominated the game during the 1920s and 1930s, winning international fame.

On the way up (below)
Walter Hagen was instrumental in raising the status of professional golfers, winning them the right to use the clubhouse.

Magazine cover (left)
As the popularity of the game grew, the volume of golf-related literature swelled, particularly in the United States. A plethora of books and magazines with golfing themes was made available to an increasingly golf-mad general public.

win the US Open Championship, but the real breakthrough followed two years later with the memorable victory of Francis Ouimet (see page 312), a 20-year-old amateur from Brookline. Taking time off work to play in the Open, which was being held that year on his local course, Ouimet defeated the experienced visiting British professionals, Harry Vardon and Ted Ray (see page 322), to take the title. It was an immensely popular triumph and golf in the United States never looked back.

It was not until 1922 that an American defeated the British on their home ground, when the flamboyant Walter Hagen (see page 266) won the Open Championship. Following his victory, his fellow Americans Bobby Jones (see page 274), Gene Sarazen (see page 327) and Densmore Shute held sway over the event for more than a decade. Henry Cotton (see page 246) restored British ascendancy at home by winning the Open in 1934 at St George's, but the balance of power in the world of golf had shifted radically in the direction of the United States.

TOURNAMENT PLAY

The first three decades of the twentieth century witnessed the transition from a professional game dominated by challenge matches between individual players or teams of two, to modern tournament golf. The great days of the man-to-man encounter were before the First World War. Although these matches went on into the 1920s and, to some extent, even later, tournament play then held the primacy.

Until the 1930s the amateur game still produced formidable players who were a match for the professionals. The four championships generally regarded as the Major events were the US and British Opens and the US and British Amateur Championships – the four titles won by Bobby Jones

in his "Grand Slam" of 1930. But with the advent of the Masters Tournament in 1934, all four of the championships now regarded as the Majors – the British and US Open Championships, the Masters and the USPGA Championship – were in place, and the professional game was establishing its predominance.

BIG-MONEY GOLF

After the Second World War the game blossomed in the United States. Between 1945 and 1970, the number of courses in the country more than doubled and the prize money available to the top US professionals increased dramatically. Ben Hogan (see page 268) was the first dominant American in the post-war game. In 1953 he came closer than any other player to winning the four professional Majors in one year. All he missed was the USPGA

Great year
America saluted Ben Hogan with a victory parade in New York after he won the British Open in 1953. With victories in the US Open and Masters that year, Hogan became the player closest to winning the four professional Majors in a single season.

Top trophies
These glittering prizes are the trophies for the four Majors, the apex of achievement for professional golfers today: from left to right, the Open Championship, the USPGA Championship, the US Masters and the US Open.

TV golf

The arrival of television had a remarkable effect on golf. It brought millions of dollars into the professional game in the United States through advertising and sponsorship, and its influence quickly spread to Europe.

The last of the Majors to abandon matchplay was the USPGA Championship in 1958. Four rounds of strokeplay on separate days became the standard formula, players pitting their skills against the course rather than against individual opponents. Rare exceptions include the World Matchplay Championship, the hybrid Dunhill Cup, and the WGC Andersen Consulting Match Play. The amateur game, however, retained its allegiance to matchplay, and the majority of ordinary players still compete in their club matches on a matchplay basis today.

REVIVING THE OPEN

Ben Hogan's decision to cross the Atlantic to play in the British Open in 1953 was not typical of its time. So great were the incentives to play in the United States that the leading American players ignored the British Open during much of the 1950s. Despite the absence of the Americans, however, the British professionals rarely won the championship after the Second World War. The end of hostilities heralded the emergence of new centres of golfing excellence, including most notably the British Dominions. Of the 12 Open Championships between 1949 and 1960, South African and Australian players won ten, including four each for Bobby Locke (see page 284) and Peter Thomson (see page 340). Thomson was to win a fifth in 1965.

Championship, which he could not contest because it clashed with the British Open. Later in the 1950s Arnold Palmer (see page 316) seized centre stage. Thanks to his manager, Mark McCormack, and to the emerging medium of television, Palmer became a legend first in the United States and then across the world. He was a hero whose exploits were viewed by millions on television and he started a new international boom in the popularity of the game both as a spectator and a participant sport. Television changed the nature of professional golf in many ways. It was a major factor in the virtual disappearance of matchplay – which sets individual players against one another – from professional tournament play.

The world's greatest championship was languishing through lack of the money that would bring the new breed of financially motivated professional players to Britain. The Royal & Ancient Golf Club, which runs the Open, saw that investment was needed to attract the top players. For the Centenary Open in 1960, the prize money was increased as well as the amenities at St Andrews.

The great Palmer

An exciting player, Arnold Palmer breathed new life into the British Open, helping to restore it to its rightful place as the most prestigious of all golf events. He also promoted a new boom in golf's overall popularity.

Major money (right)
The administration of major golf championships is big business. This tented village, housing a network of sponsors, retailers and exhibitors, was set up at Turnberry for the 1986 Open Championship.

Golf in art (left)
American LeRoy Neiman's vivid golf paintings are famous. The Eighteenth at Pebble Beach shows the 1983 Bing Crosby Pro-Am. The players are: ex-President Gerald Ford, Jack Nicklaus (putting), Tom Watson and actor Clint Eastwood.

Taylor half a century before. Their only British challenge came from Tony Jacklin, who won the British Open in 1969 and the US Open the following year.

The USA dominated the golf scene during the 1960s and 1970s with the reign of Palmer followed by that of Nicklaus. However, a sustained European revival was signalled in 1979 when Severiano Ballesteros (see page 234) won the Open Championship at Royal Lytham and St Annes. Ballesteros won the Open at St Andrews in 1984 and again at Lytham in 1988. Sandy Lyle (see page 290) was the first home-based Scot to win the championship since 1920 when he won at Royal St George's, Sandwich, in 1985.

The emergence of Germany's Bernhard Langer (see page 279) – who won the US Masters in 1985 and again in 1993 – and of promising young professionals from Sweden and Spain, reflected the gathering strength of European golf. This revival culminated in the victory of the European team in the Ryder Cup. This biennial event, instituted in 1927, between professionals of

Despite this, few top Americans came. But one who did was Arnold Palmer. The appearance of Palmer revivified the championship, and he returned to win it in 1961 and 1962. His example was followed by Jack Nicklaus (see page 304), Lee Trevino (see page 342) and Tom Watson (see page 348). The Americans had returned to Britain with a vengeance.

In the 1960s Arnold Palmer, Jack Nicklaus and the South African Gary Player (see page 318) featured prominently in exhibition matches, usually staged for television. They became, in effect, a "Modern Triumvirate" and took golf into a new era in much the same way as had Vardon, Braid and

Out of this world
Golf is the only sport to have been played away from Earth. On 6 February 1971, Apollo 14 astronaut Alan B. Shepard Jnr used a 6-iron head attached to a soil-sampler to hit a ball about 200 yards.

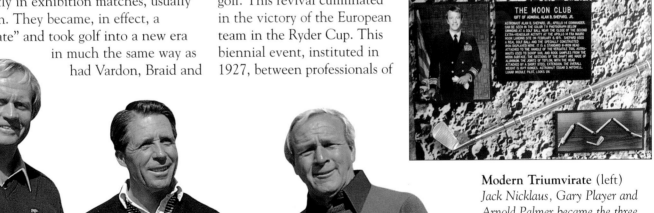

Modern Triumvirate (left)
Jack Nicklaus, Gary Player and Arnold Palmer became the three most popular and successful champions of the 1960s. In that decade alone, they won a total of 18 Majors between them.

Masters record
Jack Nicklaus became the oldest winner of the Masters when he took the title in 1986 for a record sixth time – his twentieth win in a Major. Here, before an enthralled crowd at Augusta's 15th green, Nicklaus sinks a crucial 12-foot (3.4m) putt for an eagle-3, on a final round of 65. The unsurpassed record-holder in the Majors, Nicklaus has also distinguished himself as a top course designer.

Britain and the United States, had become such a one-sided affair by the 1970s that its continued existence was in danger. In 1979, in order to make the matches more competitive, Europeans became eligible to play against the United States.

THE EUROPEAN INVASION

Although the European team just failed to win in 1983 in the US, they triumphed in 1985, and retained the trophy with a win in 1987 and a tie in 1989. In the 1990s honours were even with two wins apiece, although the US victory at Brookline in 1999 was marred by bad crowd behaviour and unpleasant scenes among the players.

In addition to participating in the expanding European Tour, which has been systematically built up since 1975, the best of the European players had an ever-increasing impact in the United States. Englishman Nick Faldo (see page 258) not only won the British Open Championship three times, in 1987, 1990 and 1993, but also captured the coveted Masters Tournament in two consecutive years, 1989

and 1990. Welshman Ian Woosnam (see page 356) won at Augusta in 1991, with Spaniard José-Maria Olazábal (see page 308) coming second, confirming the resurgence of European players. Olazábal went on to win the Masters in 1994 and again in 1999.

By the end of the twentieth century a wave of European players were making their presence felt on the United States PGA Tour. Colin Montgomerie of Scotland (see page 296), Lee Westwood from England (see page 352), Darren Clark of Ireland, Jesper Parnevik of Sweden (see page 315), Thomas

Jug logo (above)
The logo on this distinctive caddie's bib shows the Open Championship trophy, the famous claret jug. The first Open drew eight entrants; by 1990 there were 1,707.

Ryder Cup triumph
Tony Jacklin lifts the Ryder Cup after the European win at The Belfry in 1985. He had led his team to the first victory over the United States in 28 years. When the Europeans beat the Americans for the first time on their home soil in 1987, the balance of power in world golf had decisively shifted.

MANAGING THE GAME

Back in the 1920s, Walter Hagen had been assisted by Bob Harlow who, along with another American, Fred Corcoran, were the first managers. Today the management role is filled by companies like Mark McCormack's International Management Group, which runs the affairs of leading players and organizes tournaments around the world.

With financial rewards so great, the amateur game has become little more than a breeding-ground for would-be professionals. Fewer players of real ability decide to retain their amateur status – although there have been notable exceptions, such as Jay Sigel, Michael Bonallack (see page 239) and Charlie Green. However, even Sigel eventually gave in to the lure of professional golf when he turned 50 and became eligible to play on the lucrative Seniors Tour in the United States. He set aside his lifelong commitment to amateur golf, qualified at the Senior Tour School and joined the paid ranks.

In the 1990s the demand for golf continued to grow, particularly in the latter part of the decade when the exploits of Tiger Woods (see page 354) fuelled a huge surge of interest, particularly among young black Americans. The strong US economy of the Bill Clinton years saw a steady rise in "high end" golf developments and public access courses. In 1989 the Royal & Ancient Golf Club published a research document entitled *The Demand for Golf*, forecasting that Britain would require 700 new golf courses in the 1990s to keep pace with demand. But by the end of the 1990s only just over half that figure had been built.

Ballesteros's ball
The amateur game supports a worldwide industry manufacturing clothing and equipment. Today's bewildering choice includes several ranges endorsed by golf's top professionals.

Bjorn of Denmark and the young Spaniard, Sergio Garcia (see page 262), were leading examples. From further afield, Ernie Els of South Africa (see page 256), Nick Price from Zimbabwe (see page 320) and Vijay Singh from Fiji (see page 328) had not only won on the US Tour but all three had won major championships by 2000.

Professional golf now has lucrative tours, not only in America and Europe, but also in Australia, the Far East, and Japan, and this has encouraged a new generation of top professionals from these countries. Although the Japanese are extremely successful in Japan, where they regularly beat many of the world's leading players, so far victory in the Majors has eluded them.

Separate divisions of the British PGA and the USPGA – the PGA European Tour in Britain and the PGA Tour in America – represent the tournament players on their various tours and organize and administer the many events in which they play. In addition, golf management has become a major business in the financially-oriented environment of the modern professional game, where the top stars can command considerable sums in "appearance money".

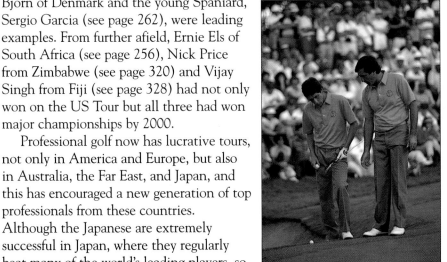

Spanish stars (above)
In Ryder Cup partnership, Seve Ballesteros (right) advises fellow Spaniard José-Maria Olazábal. Spain is now providing the game with some of its finest players.

Facing the future
One of the leading players of recent years, Nick Faldo, assisted by caddie Fanny Sunneson, has earnt a large fortune from his golfing triumphs.

TEACHING THE GAME

Early lessons
(below) *J.H. Taylor was among the first golf professionals to see the possibilities of teaching golf for a living.*

RUNNING LIKE AN *endless stream through the history of the modern game has been the search for "the secret" of how to play golf more proficiently. The quest to find the special move or key to unlock the door to golfing success has been at the core of a whole industry devoted to teaching and coaching both the physical and mental game – from exercise manuals to the inner game.*

Arnold's musical interlude (below)
Long before the days of video analysis, Arnold Palmer rode on the back of his immense popularity at the start of the 1960s with an attempt to transfer his genius on to vinyl in the shape of this double long-playing record.

Few sports encourage a passion for learning in the way that golf has done in the past 150 years and still continues to do. However, it was not really until the arrival of the gutta percha ball around 1848 that golfers first began to seek out teachers and instructional material.
The stream of new players coming into the game, made possible by the arrival of the "affordable" golf ball, quickly fostered the interest in instruction.

Swing gizmo
(below) *With the invention of swing simulators anyone could emulate the perfect swing in theory and in practice.*

THE FIRST MANUALS

Initially it was slow to develop but by the early years of the twentieth century a steady stream of golf instruction books was rolling off the presses. The first book solely devoted to golf and how to play it, *The Golfers' Manual*, was published in 1857

and written by a Scottish golfer by the name of Henry B. Fernie, who took as his pen name "A Keen Hand". The early writers were the gentlemen players of the day – literate, articulate gentlemen of some means and in marked contrast to their professional golfer counterparts of the same period.

The arrival of the Great Triumvirate of Harry Vardon, James Braid and J.H. Taylor changed all that. They were the first of the great professionals and sporting icons of their day, and they were not slow to appreciate the financial benefits that could accrue from exploiting their success on the fairways. All three supplied a steady stream of instructional material in the early part of the nineteenth century.

Countless hundreds of golf instruction books have been published since, often it seems inspired by a desire to capitalize on a "name" rather than to make a useful contribution to golf tuition.

Cigarette cards
(above) *Like so many sports of the time, golf proved a popular subject for cigarette cards, with a whole series devoted to the golf stars' instructional hints and tips.*

Texan guru (left) *Harvey Penick (centre) advised some of the world's top players, notably Tom Kite (on his right) and Ben Crenshaw (on his left). Crenshaw was a pall bearer at Penick's funeral just days before winning the 1995 US Masters.*

Magazines (right) *Golfing magazine were not slow to see the lure of offering ways of improving their readers' golfing techniques.*

There have been notable exceptions. Tommy Armour's guide *How to Play Your Best Golf All the Time*, first published in 1954, was still being reprinted going into the new millennium and Ben Hogan's *The Modern Fundamentals of Golf*, another classic that has stood the test of time, was one of the first books to use top quality illustrations rather than photography, a format repeated countless times since.

The legendary Bobby Jones (see page 274) was also a great writer. He took to the writer's pen from the very point when he stopped playing competitively, supplying syndicated columns and magazine articles throughout the United States.

PENICK'S LITTLE RED BOOK

In more recent times *Harvey Penick's Little Red Book* (1992) stands out as one of golf's most famous and best-selling works, reflecting on more than half a century of top-class golf tuition and advice. Ben Crenshaw and Tom Kite were two of the world's top players who benefited from the advice of Harvey Penick.

John Jacobs (right) *One of the first players to bring golf driving ranges and instruction to the UK masses, John Jacobs also passed on his expertise to top players.*

GADGETS AND GIZMOS

Along with instruction books there developed a whole industry devoted to the creation of special apparatus and gadgets claiming to help golfers become better players. As early as the 1930s there was complicated machinery designed to simulate the perfect golf swing to provide a benchmark from which the pupil could learn and develop. Circular tube structures to guide the club through the perfect arc are still available today.

Undoubtedly the major development in instruction came with the development of high-speed film and later video. The ability to provide slow-motion analysis of the swings of the world's great players brought an entirely new dimension to golf instruction. For the first time it was possible to see what actually happened during the swing rather than what was thought to happen. Film and video exposed the limitations of still photography where different types of camera shutters produced seemingly conflicting data for analysis, especially on what was happening to the shaft of the club during the swing.

THE SWING COMES OUT ON VIDEO

If high-speed film brought a new dimension, then video created a revolution in golf instruction. The video camera is the spy in the golf instructor's armoury and allows him or her (the number of women professional instructors had increased markedly by the end of the twentieth century) to monitor pupils' progress, and the pupil has a reference to take away and work on.

There are very few professional instructors today who do not utilize video analysis in their teaching schedules. Invariably that video imagery is used in conjunction with fast developing computer technology to pinpoint swing flaws and monitor attempts at correction.

Until well into the twentieth century in Britain, and particularly in Scotland, the cultural capital of the game, golfers did not practise. It was considered not the sporting thing to do and almost tantamount to cheating in some circles. The result was a lack of adequate practice facilities at many golf clubs in Britain, while in others there was none at all. This was not the case in the rest of Europe or in the United States, where tuition and regular practice have always been very much more part of the game.

The golf boom of the last two decades of the twentieth century witnessed a significant shift in attitudes in Britain to teaching and practice. Driving ranges became more popular, particularly among newcomers to the game who found it difficult or impossible to join clubs.

GOLF ACADEMIES

Universally, this period also saw major developments in the concept of the golf academy, where the provision of first class practice facilities is coupled to the very latest in teaching technology, with an instructional staff trained to make the very best use of both.

The golf academy has become the natural successor to the long-established golf school concept pioneered by eminent teachers such as former GB & I Ryder Cup captain John Jacobs, working extensively in Europe and the United States. There has been further specialization in the academy concept with the Colin Montgomerie Links Golf Academy at the Turnberry Hotel in Scotland. The academy specializes in teaching the peculiarities of traditional links golf through a programme developed by the Ryder Cup star.

GURUS

At the very top of the golf teaching food chain are the gurus of golf, the teachers, mentors, soul-searchers, fixers and in some cases the friends without whom, it seems, many of the top players would be unable to compete successfully.

Some gurus have been great players in their own right, such as Americans Bob Toski and Byron Nelson who have contributed to the success of Tom Watson, while Jack Grout was the only teacher Jack Nicklaus entrusted with his swing mechanics.

However, it is Zimbabwean expert David Leadbetter, perhaps more than anyone else, who created the aura and image of the modern golf guru, along with the modern academy.

Golf Academy
(above)
Colin Montgomerie's Golf Academy at the Turnberry Hotel, Scotland, teaches the subtleties of links golf.

Leadbetter and Faldo
(left) *In the 1980s Leadbetter helped Faldo modify his game to become the world's best. But it all fell apart in the 1990s.*

Hole in One (right)
Exhibition games, Pro-Am tournaments, and hole-in-one challenges (often with a car for the prize) are all part of the modern game attracting huge crowds, larger TV audiences and plenty of advertising revenue.

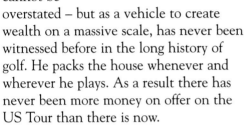

Money, Money (right) *Women golfers, such as Annika Sorenstam, can now earn good prize money on the Tour.*

the "Tiger Woods" factor. His influence on the game not just as a player – and that cannot be overstated – but as a vehicle to create wealth on a massive scale, has never been witnessed before in the long history of golf. He packs the house whenever and wherever he plays. As a result there has never been more money on offer on the US Tour than there is now.

Some sceptics have suggested that if Woods is not competing in an event it becomes a second-class tournament, making it inevitably damaging to the long-term future of the Tour. This seems unlikely. Nicklaus at the height of his powers averaged around 18 while Tiger Woods in 2000, when he won three of the four majors, only played 17 events. The absence of Nicklaus in many events did not diminish the viability of the Tour, and this should hold true for the Tiger.

Tiger in London (above) *A par-3 hole was specially created in London's Hyde Park for an exhibition by Tiger Woods – seen here driving and watched by English soccer star Gary Lineker.*

THE LEADBETTER PHENOMENON

David Leadbetter's work with Nick Faldo, which resulted in the Englishman rising to the top of the world rankings and winning five major titles, turned Leadbetter into the most eminent golf teacher of the time. Sadly, this successful partnership was to end rather less amicably than it began when Faldo went into a slump from which he seemed destined never to escape.

Leadbetter straddled the whole field of golf instruction. Academies on both sides of the Atlantic, a line of swing and putting aids, best-selling books and videos all bear the Leadbetter name. His reputation as the greatest of the gurus came under challenge in the 1990s with the arrival on the scene of Tiger Woods and his friend and guru, Butch Harmon.

Harmon was another successful player in his own right and enjoyed a reputation as a top teacher, but after he became attached to the Tiger Woods machine he was

catapulted to guru stardom. Like Leadbetter with Nick Faldo, Harmon was not slow to capitalize on the success of his star pupil and there are now academies and instructional material with his name.

THE FUTURE FOR GOLF

At the start of the new millennium there is no apparent reason why golf should not continue its multi-billion-dollar world-wide commercial boom, fuelled now by

Harmon and his pupil (left) *have superseded the Leadbetter–Faldo partnership.*

WOMEN IN GOLF

Fashion victims
Conforming to the styles of the 1890s, women golfers were severely restricted by long, billowing skirts and corsets designed to shape a narrow waist at the expense of free bodily movement.

Required reading
Genevieve Hecker, twice US Women's Amateur Champion, published this useful book for women golfers in 1904.

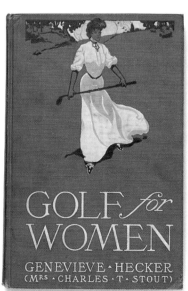

WOMEN'S GOLF HAS *changed dramatically since the Second World War, when the few women's professional tournaments barely paid enough to cover expenses. Today's top money-earners like Laura Davies and Karrie Webb (see pages 250, 347) can expect rewards on a scale to rival all but the greatest male players.*

The first women's golf clubs came into existence in the second half of the nineteenth century, when golf was played by genteel ladies of leisure, but only as a glorified form of pitch-and-putt. It was considered indelicate to raise the club above shoulder height, and restrictive clothing severely limited movement. Voluminous full-length skirts were secured just above the ankle with elastic belts.

But such decorous and inhibiting behaviour and attire were not to last long after the formation of the Ladies' Golf Union in 1893. The major influence behind this new group of golfing women was its secretary, Issette Pearson, runner-up to Lady Margaret Scott in the first British Ladies' Amateur Championship in that same year.

WOMEN TAKE THE LEAD
Also in 1893, across the Atlantic, American women were taking the initiative. Members of the newly formed Shinnecock Hills Club, New York, were persuaded by their wives to build them a separate nine-hole course. Where men refused to share or build a course, women created their own. By 1894, a group of female golfers had founded their own club and created a seven-hole course in Morristown, New Jersey. It would take only a few years for American women to match the level of British female golfing activity.

The first superstar of British women's golf was Charlotte Cecilia Pitcairn Leitch, who reached the semi-finals of the British Ladies' Amateur in 1908 at the age of 17. She shortened her name to Cecil Leitch from 1914 and went on to win 12 titles in Britain,

Ladies' star (above)
Cecil Leitch was the preeminent player in Britain between about 1914 and 1926.

Lady Scott (above)
Margaret Scott (second left) won the 1895 British Ladies' at Portrush, where the women's game was especially encouraged.

France and Canada. With her strong, flat swing, she dominated the game until finally overcome by Joyce Wethered (see page 351), who played a strongly contrasting, stylish and elegant game.
Wethered was so effective that she captured eight titles in four years before retiring from competitive play in 1925. She made a comeback to win the British Ladies' Amateur for the fourth and last time at St Andrews four years later.

TRANSATLANTIC RIVALRY
Wethered's opponent in the final on that occasion was Glenna Collett (see page 347), who held an equal supremacy over golf in the United States and was to win the Women's Amateur Championship there six times. Women's international golf had begun when an American team travelled to Britain in 1905 to play in the British Ladies' Amateur. The first international women's trophy, the Curtis Cup, was

Americans abroad (left)
The American women golfers who visited Britain in 1930 included Glenna Collett (standing, second from right) who that year lost in the final of the British Ladies' Amateur.

Freer styles
This 1930s bronze statuette shows how comfort and elegance started to combine in women's attire to make golf easier to play.

True professional
Women golfers, such as Canada's Sandra Post, are now able to earn good prize money on the Tour.

donated by two American sisters, Harriot and Margaret Curtis, who had taken part in the original 1905 event. The Americans won the first Curtis Cup match in 1932, and were not beaten until 20 years later. The British amateurs won in 1952 and 1956, but the Americans proved their domination with 13 successive victories up to 1986. In that year, the British women recorded an historic victory at Prairie Dunes, and they won again in 1988. The Americans reasserted themselves at Somerset Hills in 1990.

POST-WAR GROWTH

Unlike the men's game, women's golf remained predominantly amateur until well after the Second World War. In 1949 a fledgling Ladies' Professional Golf Association (LPGA) was created in the United States, led by Patty Berg and Babe Zaharias (see pages 238, 358), but for some years tournaments remained sparse, and prize money far below the levels available to male players.

Zaharias was the most successful female player of the immediate post-war period, winning 17 tournaments in 1946 alone. She dominated the early days of the LPGA Tour with her talent and enthusiasm. Her leading role was later taken over by Mickey Wright (see page 352), who emerged in the 1950s, and then by Kathy Whitworth (see page 353) and Nancy Lopez (see page 286). Only one European player of that period challenged American superiority – Catherine Lacoste of France. In 1967, at the age of 22, she

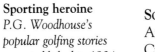

Sporting heroine
P.G. Woodhouse's popular golfing stories were published in 1904.

became the youngest winner of the US Women's Open, as well as being the first amateur and the first overseas player to take the title.

By the time the charismatic Lopez achieved superstar status in the late 1970s, women's professional golf in the United States had truly come of age, with extensive television coverage and annual prize money counted in millions of dollars. In Britain, by contrast, the professional game did not begin until 1979 and it struggled for years without arousing a great deal of public interest or attracting much financial sponsorship.

Yet with the emergence of a growing number of European competitors and a rise in playing standards, a regular Tour in Britain and Europe was eventually established. One star of the Tour is Laura Davies (see page 250), who became the first British woman to win the US Women's Open in 1987. Other proven women players are Alison Nicholas, Liselotte Neumann, Helen Alfredsson, Janice Moodie and Annika Sorenstam (see page 330). Meanwhile, Australian Karrie Webb and South Korean Se Ri Pak (see page 315) have made women's golf truly international.

SOLHEIM CUP

After 70 years of the Ryder Cup, women professionals at last established their own equivalent in 1990, the Solheim Cup, a mixture of foursomes, fourballs and singles. The first match was won by the American team, by the large margin of $11\frac{1}{2}$ to $4\frac{1}{2}$. In 1992, however, at Dalmahoy, Scotland, the European women confirmed the emerging strength of their Tour by defeating the USA $11\frac{1}{2}$ to $6\frac{1}{2}$. They repeated the victory at Loch Lomond in 2000 after a run of US wins.

THE RISE OF THE RUBBER-CORE BALL

T HE INVENTION OF *the wound rubber-core Haskell ball at the turn of the century was a momentous event in golf history, ushering in the modern age of the game. Created by winding lengths of rubber around a solid core, the Haskell's added "spring" offered golfers greater distance, as the new ball flew and bounced farther than its guttie predecessor and performed better, even when mis-hit.*

Mesh-marked balls
This collection of a dozen named rubber-core balls, with a variety of recessed mesh or lattice patterns, dates from around the early 1930s.

THE RUBBER-CORE BALL

The rubber-core ball, developed by Coburn Haskell in 1898 and first made commercially in 1901, could be hit farther and faster than previous designs. It was made by winding great lengths of rubber yarn, stretched under tension, around a rubber core. A livelier core enabled golfers to exercise more control over the ball's spin and flight. Early models had a gutta percha covering, on to which was moulded a flight-assisting pattern.

Rubber thread

Gutta percha cover

The rubber-core ball was invented by a wealthy American amateur golfer Coburn Haskell in collaboration with Bertram Work, an engineer with the Goodrich Rubber Company at Akron, Ohio. The earliest prototypes were not successful, because the hand-wound balls tended to duck and curve. However, the creation of an automatic winding machine coupled with the use of a bramble cover facilitated greater control, and Work's company began mass manufacturing.

Walter J. Travis won the US Amateur Championship with a Haskell in the autumn of 1901, and the following year, on the other side of the Atlantic, Sandy Herd won the Open Championship using a Haskell. The adoption of the new ball, with its much livelier feel and greater distance, led to

a surge in the popularity of the game. To find a missile that would outdo the Haskell, rival manufacturers tried many different materials for the cores, such as cork, lead, mercury and ball bearings. Research went into the role of ball covers, and in the 1910s and 1920s players were able to select from at least 200 different named balls. They were finished with covers of varying thicknesses and with multiform markings, from bramble (raised, round bumps) to recessed crescent moons, triangles and squares (or "mesh"), each of which was claimed to outfly the others.

Box of Scottish rubber-core balls dating from around 1910

Box of repainted, recycled balls from the early 1930s of practice quality for beginners

Cheap balls, numbered for identification, made by Dunlop Rubber in London around 1938

American rubber-core balls from about 1925, "guaranteed for 54 holes"

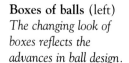

Non-floating dimpled balls; the first dimples appeared on balls in 1908

The 1940s Dunlop Warwick brand of ball, with recessed dimple marks

Boxes of balls (left)
The changing look of boxes reflects the advances in ball design.

High flyer (right)
The makers of the core-wound "Kite", with distinctive bramble markings, were sued by Haskell for breach of patent, but in vain.

The study of golf-ball aerodynamics and the laws governing a ball's trajectory has come a long way since then. Today, the patterns have been replaced by dimples, which accentuate the effects of lift and minimize the amount of drag on the ball.

In 1921 the USGA and the R & A decided that the uniform diameter for a golf ball should be 1.62in (41mm). Ten years later the USGA increased the ball size to 1.68in (43mm) and it was not until 1987 that the R & A agreed that the American standard should become mandatory worldwide.

Multi-layer Golf Ball

Until the end of the twentieth century there were three basic types of golf ball construction (*see panel, right*). At the start of the new millennium another type of golf ball featuring a multi-layer construction was beginning to capture a significant share of the market. The multi-layer ball commonly consists of a solid inner core around which is moulded an inner layer or mantle encased in an outer layer usually of a soft cover material such as "urethane elastomer".

The introduction of the multi-layer ball, and the rapid acceptance of it by top name professionals keen to exploit its claimed advantages of more length with maximum control, effectively sounded the death knell for the traditional three-piece, wound construction ball. When Tiger Woods switched to the multi-layer ball, the three-piece went into free fall.

1940s American balls, sold as adding "distance and accuracy"

English balls, with dimple markings, of the late 1950s

Bromford balls manufactured in Great Britain in the 1960s

Have a ball
This 1920s hand-painted, plaster-of-Paris statuette, 16in (40cm) tall, was distributed to Pro shops to encourage sales of Dunlop balls.

THREE-PIECE (SURLYN COVER)

This version of the three-piece wound ball has a solid rubber core over which rubber yarn is wound for good control. The cover is made from Surlyn, a thermoplastic resin that is harder than balata and is thus considerably more durable; it is virtually uncuttable.

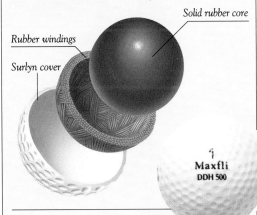

Rubber windings

Solid rubber core

Surlyn cover

Maxfli
DDH 500

TWO-PIECE

A high-energy acrylate or resin core with a tough cut-proof blended cover gives the two-piece more length than any other ball. It is also virtually indestructible which, with its top roll distance, makes it by far the most popular ball among ordinary golfers. However, because it has a lower spin rate, it is less easy to control.

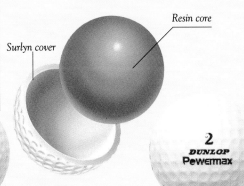

Resin core

Surlyn cover

2
DUNLOP
Pewermax

ONE-PIECE

Seldom used as a playing ball, the one-piece, made from a solid piece of Surlyn with dimples moulded in, is most usually found on practice grounds and driving ranges. It is the least expensive golf ball and extremely durable, but it gives less distance because of its lower compression. The one-piece has a distinctly soft feel on impact with the clubface.

Solid Surlyn

THREE-PIECE (BALATA COVER)

Until the arrival of the multi-layer ball, the balata-covered, liquid-centred, three-piece ball was the most advanced of golf balls. The wound construction over a liquid centre, combined with a soft, synthetic balata cover, produced the highest spin rate.

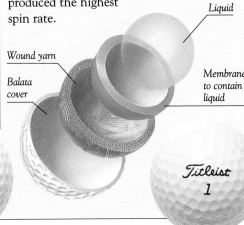

Liquid

Wound yarn

Balata cover

Membrane to contain liquid

Titleist
1

MODERN CLUB DESIGN

N EW MATERIALS AND *advancing technology have always been the major influences in the development of golf clubs. Just as hickory shafts, introduced by club-maker Forgan, were a radical innovation, so modern designers have revolutionized the clubmaker's craft. The most significant advance in the first years of the twentieth century was the introduction of the steel shaft. Experiments with steel shafts began as early as the 1890s by blacksmith Thomas Horsburgh and by professional Willie Dunn Jnr. Horsburgh patented the idea but let the patent lapse. The first seamless, steel shafts were made in Britain by 1912.*

1890 aluminium-headed driver with hickory shaft

1990 steel-headed driver with steel shaft

Head to head
Metal-headed woods, increasingly popular, are not new, however. Aluminium-headed clubs have been available since the late nineteenth century. The construction, materials and details, such as the slim hosel, may have altered, but the modern club differs little in basic design.

Types of driver construction
Virtually all of today's woods are made of metal, rather than wood, hence the unusual term "metal woods". The steel-headed and the titanium-headed drivers are more forgiving to mis-hits.

Persimmon driver *Steel-headed driver* *Titanium-headed driver*

A wide variety of grips in various textures to suit all weather conditions is now available for woods and irons

Graphite is now the most popular material for the shaft of the modern driver

---

Range of modern iron clubs
Irons are either traditionally hand-forged blades – preferred by better players and perceived to have more feel at impact – or peripherally-weighted cast-iron clubs that give a larger sweet spot. Rescue clubs are a cross between an iron and a fairway wood.

Hand-forged 5-iron *Peripherally weighted 5-iron* *Kasco K2K44 rescue club*

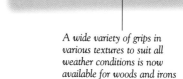

Irons are supplied with either steel or graphite shafts available in a range of shaft flexes; a typical length is about 37¹/₂in (95cm)

Wedges and special-purpose irons
Wedges are used to loft the ball high over short distances. The sand wedge is used for escaping from bunkers, and the pitching wedge (or 10-iron) to play the ball on to the green and make it stop quickly. The utility wedge serves both functions.

Sand wedge *Utility wedge* *Pitching wedge*

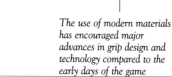

The use of modern materials has encouraged major advances in grip design and technology compared to the early days of the game

Wedges are rarely used when a full swing is required so the amount of flexibility of the shaft is less important; the average length is 35¹/₂in (90cm)

"Toe-and-heel" putters
Putters come in a larger variety of shapes than any other club. Many are peripherally weighted to maximize the size of the sweet spot. "Toe-and-heel" putters concentrate the weight at both ends of the head to reduce torque.

Straight-set toe-and-heel *Toe-and-heel with large head* *Offset toe-and-heel*

Shaped "pistol grip" with flat side at right angles to the clubface for aligning the putter and ensuring accurate aim

Stainless steel shaft; putters are generally between 32–35in (81–90cm) in length

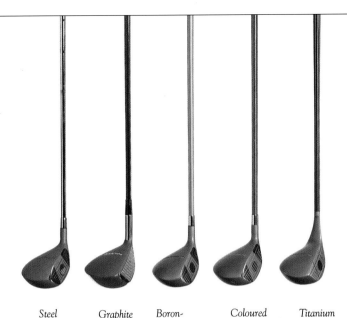

Shaft types

Major advances have been made in shaft construction since the days of hickory. Steel shafts revolutionized the game in the late 1920s, and steel is still the most common material for the modern golf club. But graphite, which is light but extremely strong, is gradually replacing it.

Steel shaft

Graphite shaft

Boron-reinforced shaft

Coloured graphite shaft

Titanium shaft

By the late 1920s steel was being used freely in the United States. But it was not until 1929 that the Royal & Ancient Club legalized steel shafts when the Prince of Wales (the future King Edward VIII) played with a set of steel-shafted clubs on the Old Course at St Andrews. It is said the Royal & Ancient had either to legalize them or disqualify the Prince.

MASS PRODUCTION

Mass-produced clubs followed and with them came matched sets with numbered, instead of named, clubs (*see page 60*). Steel is still the main shaft material for the irons, but carbon fibre (or graphite) in a range of flexes and colours, is gradually taking over.

When persimmon, used to make wooden heads, became scarce, steel heads shaped like traditional wooden heads replaced it. Steel and titanium are now the most popular materials.

The majority of golf manufacturers' production is now geared to "game improvement clubs" such as peripherally weighted irons. With new casting techniques the mass of a clubhead can be redistributed around the outside edges of metal woods and irons. This minimizes the effects of poor shots. Customized clubs tailored to fit individuals in terms of shaft length and flexibility, lie (angle between head and shaft) and swingweight (weight distribution) are now widely available.

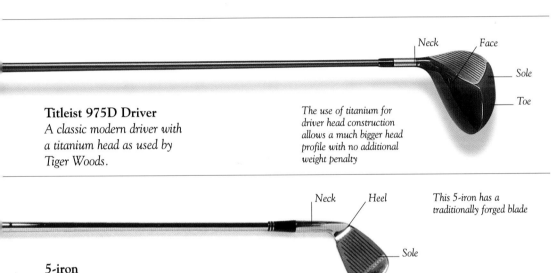

Neck

Face

Sole

Toe

Titleist 975D Driver
A classic modern driver with a titanium head as used by Tiger Woods.

The use of titanium for driver head construction allows a much bigger head profile with no additional weight penalty

Neck

Heel

This 5-iron has a traditionally forged blade

Sole

Toe

5-iron
The 5-iron is a useful mid-iron for combining reasonable distance with accuracy.

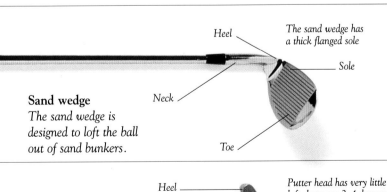

Heel

The sand wedge has a thick flanged sole

Sole

Neck

Toe

Sand wedge
The sand wedge is designed to loft the ball out of sand bunkers.

Shape of soles and bounce
The sand wedge has a thick, rounded "bounce" on the sole to prevent it digging into the sand. The medium bounce of the utility wedge suits its dual purpose. The pitching wedge has less bounce, which is better for approach shots to the green.

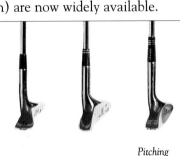

Sand wedge

Utility wedge

Pitching wedge

Heel

Putter head has very little loft, between 2–4 degrees

Neck

Face

Toe

Putter
Designed for precision play on the greens, the putter rolls the ball.

Wide variety of putter heads
The traditional, centre-shafted putter still has many adherents. The offset mallet-head putter continues to grow in popularity, while the centre-shafted onset-headed putter is an example of the many alternative styles available.

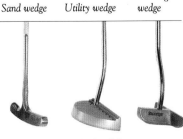

Centre-shafted putter

Mallet-headed putter

Onset-headed putter

THE FULL SET OF CLUBS

WITH THE ADOPTION *of steel shafts in the 1930s came the possibility of matched sets of clubs, produced to precise specifications regarding size, flex and weight. Manufacturers devised special clubs for every conceivable eventuality, and some golfers carried as many as 20 or more clubs of various kinds. The USGA imposed a 14-club limit on 1 January 1938, and the Royal & Ancient followed suit the following year. The decision to limit the number was taken "to restore the making of individual shots, and increase the skill of the player."*

Within this limit, however, there is scope to choose the clubs needed to deal with virtually all circumstances. The driver and fairway woods are designed for striking the ball the farthest distances from tee or fairway. The iron clubs are divided into long, medium and short, relative to the distance they send the ball. Long irons send the ball farther than short irons, which are designed for accuracy or getting out of trouble. The putter is used

Whole in one (above)
An adjustable iron had all the range of a set by means of its variable loft.

Matched set
A contemporary set comprises a driver and two fairway woods with irons normally numbered from 3 to 9, a pitching wedge, and a sand iron. A putter makes up the set.

| Driver | 3-wood | 5-wood | 3-iron | 4-iron | 5-iron | 6-iron | 7-iron | 8-iron |

WOODEN CLUB CONSTRUCTION

Production of the traditional wooden head owes more to craftsmanship than to the pure engineering of stainless steel and graphite, but very few wooden heads are still made today. The construction of wooden-headed clubs has changed little over the decades.

The shape of the head was marked out on a piece of close-grained wood, such as persimmon. The basic shape of the head was then cut out and worked to its final form. A hole was bored into the neck or hosel to receive the shaft.

Graphite clubs (right)
Despite retaining their traditional names, woods and irons are today often made from carbon fibre.

Space-age profile
Carbon fibres bonded together in layers produce a strong and lightweight clubhead.

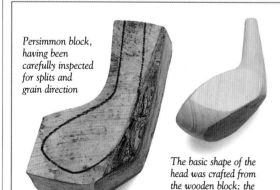

Persimmon block, having been carefully inspected for splits and grain direction

The basic shape of the head was crafted from the wooden block; the streamlined back of the head was all-important

Slots were cut for a plastic insert in the face and a metal plate on the bottom of the club to protect it from damage

Weight could be added by pouring molten lead into a hole under the sole-plate, or by adding lead to the back of the head

After fine sanding, staining added to the visual appeal, and varnishing sealed the wood from the elements

almost exclusively on the green or on the closely cut fringes surrounding the green. Woods are usually numbered from 1 (the driver) to 5. A set of irons normally ranges from 3 to 9 or 10. The loft on the face of the club (the angle the clubface makes with vertical) increases with the number, while the shaft length of the club decreases. Irons number 1 and 2 are also produced, although they are usually only available on special order from manufacturers. These two long irons are specialist clubs for the better players and are not recommended for average golfers, who often find it easier to use a wood.

9-iron

10-iron
(Pitching
wedge)

Sand iron
(Sand
wedge)

Strong fibre (left)
Carbon fibre woven into a cloth strip and then coupled with bonding materials makes for an incredibly strong, useful material.

MODERN MATERIALS

The most successful new material is carbon fibre (or graphite), although other composite materials are gaining converts. The material is used for clubheads but is most commonly found in the production of a wide range of lightweight variable flex shafts. Early problems in poor resistance to twisting were soon overcome by improved production techniques. The saving of weight in shafts allows mass to be concentrated in the head with no penalty in increased overall weight.

DRIVER TECHNOLOGY

Ultra-lightweight titanium construction in metal-headed drivers has allowed the production of large-headed drivers with claims of more distance from these clubs. However, the new technology has created problems for golf's rule makers.

The Rules of Golf says that the face of the club must not have "the effect at impact of a spring". The USGA introduced a test protocol in November 1998, to test for "spring-effect" while the R & A considered if a test was necessary.

DRIVERS AND RULES

When Callaway's ERC driver was introduced it was declared non-conforming under the USGA test protocol because of "spring-effect" and therefore illegal for competition in the United States and Mexico (where USGA rules apply). With no test in the rest of the world under the R & A rules the club was quite legal. In September 2000 the R & A decided that a conformance test for "spring-like" effect in golf clubs was "not necessary at present" leaving the two ruling bodies split on the issue.

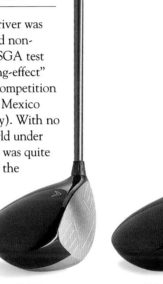

ERC II
does not conform to USGA protocol

Titleist 975D
conforms to USGA protocol

Ping ISI
conforms to USGA protocol

SPECIALIST WEDGES

The modern range of pitching clubs or wedges has made getting the ball close to the hole from 80 to 100 yards much easier and as a result scoring much lower. Wedges are most commonly available with lofts of between 53 degrees and 60 degrees but others with even steeper lofts are made. These clubs provide a high degree of control close to the green, from deep rough or the steepest bunkers.

Cleveland
Gunmetal 53

Cleveland "Trusty
Rusty" 56

Cleveland
BeCu

Cleveland Reg
485 "Chrome" 60

COURSE ARCHITECTS

Neat cutter
One of the basic tools of the greenkeeper, and one of the first to be invented, is the hole cutter. It is used to remove a plug of turf and soil to create a neat hole of uniform size in the green.

N ATURE WAS THE *first golf architect, shaping the links of eastern Scotland out of the undulating dunes along the shoreline. But as golf developed, leading professionals were called in to lay out courses, and the construction of tests for the player's skills became ever more elaborate.*

Initially the methods of the architects were simple in the extreme. They would pace the available ground, dotting the landscape with coloured stakes to indicate tees and greens. The job would usually be completed in under a day and when a mower had been run over the areas designated as greens, the course was deemed ready for play.

In 1894, Old Tom Morris, one of the leading course architects of his era, charged £1 per day, plus travelling expenses, to design a course. A hundred years later Jack Nicklaus could command $1million for the same task, but it would entail a great deal more than banging stakes in the ground.

Course architecture took a leap forward when the possibility of using inland sites was realized. The pioneer was golf professional Willie Park Jnr, who is largely held responsible for taking golf away from its seaside origins. He discovered the potential of a sand-based heath to the west of London, where he laid out Sunningdale in the 1890s. Park was followed by five-time Open Champion James Braid, a prolific architect in the early years of the twentieth century. Braid designed the Gleneagles courses, and many other famous layouts.

ST. GEORGE'S HILL GOLF COURSE. *Blowing up roots during construction.*

Blasting out
Architects are not prepared to let a few tree roots stand in their way during the construction or improvement of a course. Explosives have long been used to clear the way, as at the St George's Hill course, Surrey, England, before the First World War.

INTERNATIONAL DESIGN
Sunningdale was later modified by its secretary, H.S. Colt, who then designed the more exposed New course at the club. He became one of Britain's finest designers in an era that produced courses such as Wentworth and The Berkshire, and talented architects including Tom Simpson, Charles Alison and Herbert Fowler, who also worked in the United States.

The Chicago golf-course architect Charles Blair Macdonald began researching British golf courses in 1902 to help him create the first course of real quality

in the United States, The National Golf Links. He also inspired George Crump, A.W. Tillinghast and Hugh Wilson to produce courses at Pine Valley, Baltusrol and Merion. Two Scots, Alister MacKenzie and Donald Ross, left a legacy of fine courses in the United States and around the world. Pinehurst Number 2 is the best of the Ross collection, while MacKenzie partnered Bobby Jones in creating Augusta National. Their creation, with its emphasis on strategic rather than penal design, revolutionized course design in the United States.

The renowned Robert Trent Jones (see page 65) first attracted attention and controversy when he

---

THE CUTTING EDGE OF GREENKEEPING

Before grass-cutting machines, greenkeepers relied on hungry sheep and rabbits to graze on the fairways and keep them close-cropped. The development of the mower meant that conditions for play improved dramatically and greenkeepers were not dependent on natural grass cutters.

Early model (above)
This motor mower, used on the Old Course at St Andrews in 1913, replaced the work done by sheep.

Later designs (left)
Mowers have moved on to greatly reduce the time spent cutting the green and leave a finely cut finish.

adapted the Oakland Hills course in Birmingham, Michigan, for the 1951 US Open, with dramatic results. He became by far the most prominent golf course architect in the United States during the 1960s and 1970s, leaving his trademarks of lakes and massive bunkers on an extraordinary number of courses across the breadth of the continent.

THE MODERN LAYOUT

Course design has continued to evolve, and many would say that it entered its modern phase in the late 1960s, when Pete Dye teamed up with Jack Nicklaus on the Harbour Town Golf Links in South Carolina. They combined different-textured grasses to demarcate areas of the course and used railway-sleeper bulkheads as boundaries. Nicklaus and Dye went on to dominate the course-design business in the late 1970s and the 1980s.

Meanwhile in Europe, Dave Thomas and Peter Alliss came into golf-course architecture from the professional tour, to join men of vast experience such as C.K. Cotton, Charles Lawrie, Henry Cotton, Frank Pennink, John Harris and Fred Hawtree.

By the 1980s, leading professionals had again begun to dominate the business, as they had done almost a century earlier. Australian Peter Thomson, Arnold Palmer from America, Seve Ballesteros from Spain, Bernhard Langer from Germany, Britain's Tony Jacklin, Neil Coles and Brian Huggett, and dozens more have all been caught up with the worldwide demand for courses.

The power and scope of modern machinery and the development of irrigation techniques and new

grass strains, have enabled spectacular feats of course design and construction. For instance, in Florida, Georgia and South Carolina, massive drainage and earth-filling operations have allowed courses to emerge out of swampland, leaving only an occasional alligator to remind golfers of what existed before. And such is the shortage of land in Japan that courses are constructed out of seemingly impossible hilly terrain. Some Japanese courses have installed escalators to transport golfers from one secluded valley hole up a steep incline to the next tee, ready to swoop down into an adjoining valley.

Where golfers in desert terrain were once content to play through scrubland to greens made from a stodgy mixture of sand and oil, at a golf course like Jack Nicklaus's Desert Highlands they now play on manicured grass fairways and perfect greens, kept alive by millions of gallons of water pumped out each night by computer-controlled irrigation systems.

But despite modern technology, the best courses are still those that fit easily and naturally into their surroundings. This is why the features of legendary links courses such as St Andrews continue to be an inspiration to architects the world over.

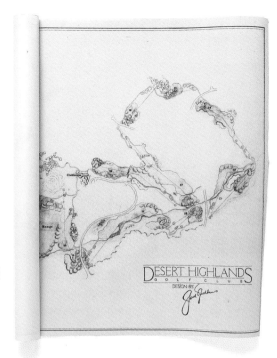

Blueprint for success
The value of a layout depends on the course architect's ability to create challenges for players of every skill level and fit the holes into the existing landscape. Jack Nicklaus succeeded brilliantly at Desert Highlands in Arizona.

Designer flair (left)
Gary Player (far left) teamed up with architect Pete Dye (left) at Sawgrass, Florida. The course has the Dye trademark, an island green.

Dual career (right)
Great golfer Jack Nicklaus is also one of the most prolific course designers. He created the popular Huis Ten Bosch course for Japanese clients in Nagasaki.

MODERN COURSE DESIGN

Pete Dye (above) *This leading American golf course architect likes to utilize railway sleepers in his designs, as at Harbour Town in South Carolina.*

Tom Weiskopf (below) *Open Champion (1973) and now a successful course designer with Loch Lomond under his belt – to name just one of his courses.*

T HE INCREASE IN *demand for golf world-wide in the last two decades of the twentieth century brought with it a rapid increase in the number of new golf course architects and designers along with a stronger realization of the value of good design and construction.*

The period since 1980 has seen significant improvements in turf grass management. New strains of grass have been introduced that make it possible to maintain courses to a high standard throughout the year regardless of climate. New grass strains have not only affected play; they have transformed the management of the course. This was necessary, for the demand was not only for more courses but for better courses. The exposure of the professional game on television, with often very expensively prepared courses, fuelled the demand from ordinary golf club members for similar playing conditions. Modern methods in agronomy and course maintenance can now meet that demand – but at a price.

SO-CALLED CHAMPIONSHIP COURSES

There has been a trend to create so-called "championship" golf courses, a trend largely inspired by commercial golf course developers as part of their marketing strategies to sell property built around golf courses. "Championship" became the golf course design buzzword during this period although the vast majority of golf courses carrying the label would never host championship golf in the proper sense.

At the other end of the scale is the "set aside" scheme for agricultural land in Europe. Under this scheme the European Union offers grants to farmers who take land out of agricultural use, often into leisure use. This has led to the creation of many golf courses. The scheme has encouraged many French farmers for instance to build golf courses,

and this has sometimes been with dubious results. In Britain the rush to build courses was influenced to some degree at least by a Royal & Ancient Golf Club Report published in 1989 entitled *The Demand for Golf*, which forecast that 700 new golf courses would be required in Great Britain alone to meet demand by the year 2000.

In fact little more than half that number were actually constructed, and a significant percentage of that number failed commercially soon after construction was completed. Extravagant designs, over-ambitious facilities and an over-optimistic assessment of the market, have been the most common reasons behind these failures.

By the start of the new millennium a more rational mood was abroad with the type of courses being built more reflective of the genuine

Greg Norman (right) *supervises the construction of his designs at Doonbeg (below) in Ireland. Norman is typical of the modern breed of player- businessman-designer.*

demand. One excellent example is the Kingsbarns Links (see page 104) built by Kyle Phillips just outside St Andrews in Scotland. Phillips, one of the new breed of course designers, transformed a two-tiered flat agricultural site into a spectacular traditional Scottish links course, which now stands as a tribute to modern construction allied to sympathetic design.

NOT AN ALL-MALE ARCHITECTS' CLUB

For most of the last century the world of the golf course architects was predominantly male orientated. There were, however, one or two notable exceptions, the most famous being Alice Dye, wife of Pete Dye, who became the first woman member of the American Society of Golf Course Architects (ASGCA) in 1982. In 1969 she was probably the only woman designer in the United States when she worked with her husband on the design of many significant courses including the famous Harbour Town Links in South Carolina.

The second woman to become a full member of the ASGCA was Jan Beljan, who studied landscape architecture at the University of West Virginia and eventually became chief designer with Tom Fazio. Like the other women golf course architects now making a mark in modern golf course design in the United States, including Sandy Bigler and Victoria Martz who worked with Arnold Palmer's Design company, Jan Beljan does not see that gender and age matter much in golf course design. She believes the main obstacle for women is the limited number of opportunities available to them to show what they can create.

The increase in women golfers has brought about a slow realization that their needs have not always been met in golf course design. Forward tees for women would have often been an afterthought or pushed to the side of the fairway away from the natural line of the hole. A new sensitivity to the needs of women players is emerging and with it opportunities for more women golf course designers. This is reflected in the interest of professionals such as Amy Alcott, Hollis Stacy and Jan Stephenson in lending their names and experience on tour to the design of new courses.

Father and son
Robert Trent Jones Snr (above left), *the father of modern golf course architecture, was born in England in 1904 and died just before the US Open in June 2000. He designed nearly 500 new golf courses in 43 American States and 34 countries around the world (and almost as many redesigns) in a career that spanned seven decades. His son Robert Trent Jones Jnr* (above) *continues in his father's footsteps.*

In the family (left)
The design talents of Rees Jones, younger son of Robert Trent Jones Snr, make him the first-choice designer for clubs planning to host a major championship.

③

CHAMPIONSHIP COURSES OF THE WORLD

Any selection of 100 of the world's greatest championship courses has to be a subjective exercise. The choice that follows is not intended as a simple ranking of courses in terms of difficulty or quality. It is rather a worldwide voyage of discovery across a landscape of the game's outstanding venues. The courses featured include fabled old links of stunning beauty with wild, remote fairways,

and cunningly crafted modern layouts created by the most influential of course architects, such as Robert Trent Jones, Pete Dye and Jack Nicklaus. Alongside world-famous

The centuries-old natural links of St Andrews

championship venues, some lesser-known courses are profiled here, as well as many golf clubs that have a special story to relate. In addition, there are those courses built in the most unlikely and hostile of environments utilizing all the latest technology, fine examples of human ingenuity without which a comprehensive review of the world's golf courses would be sadly incomplete.

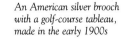

An American silver brooch with a golf-course tableau, made in the early 1900s

Widening horizons (left)
An aerial view of Shinnecock Hills shows its splendid Long Island setting.

AUGUSTA NATIONAL

AUGUSTA NATIONAL GOLF CLUB, AUGUSTA, GEORGIA, USA

O NE OF THE *few courses almost every golfer harbours dreams of playing is at Augusta National Golf Club, birthplace and home of the US Masters tournament. The course's beauty and cunning design have played a great part in making the Masters – the first of the year's Majors – an attractive and testing event. But the course was originally made for one man's pleasure.*

Course creator
Bobby Jones said of the course: "There isn't a single hole out there that can't be birdied if you just think. But there isn't one that can't be double-bogeyed if you ever stop thinking."

Master guide (below)
President in Perpetuity of Augusta National, Bobby Jones's spectators' guide is reproduced annually.

Soon after Bobby Jones's victories in the Open and Amateur Championships of Britain and the United States in the single triumphant year of 1930, he decided to retire, aged just 28, and build his own golf course. It was to be a private place where he could play with friends, away from the attentions of the thousands of golf fans who followed him everywhere he went.

Jones set out to build his dream course in collaboration with a close friend, the New York financier Clifford Roberts.

Ben Hogan Bridge
The crossing over Rae's Creek by the 12th celebrates Hogan's then record score of 274 in 1953.

They chose Augusta because it was a favourite venue for Jones to play in the winter months. Lying in a valley near the South Carolina border, at its low point only 137ft (42m) above sea level, it was much milder than his home town of Atlanta in western Georgia, which sits at an elevation of more than 1,000ft (300m). Roberts had also wintered there.

The site Jones and Roberts acquired for the new course was a 365-acre (148ha) property called Fruitlands Nursery, and recommended by a mutual friend, Thomas Barrett Jnr of Augusta. The land was already beautiful as many trees and shrubs had been left behind after the nursery closed, including a splendid avenue of magnolia trees, leading to the old colonial building that today forms the central part of the Augusta National clubhouse complex.

PARTNERS IN DESIGN

To this magnificent setting Bobby Jones brought Dr Alister MacKenzie, a Scotsman who had given up medicine and turned to the design of golf courses. Fruitlands Nursery provided MacKenzie with a piece of mildly rolling ground ideal for the style of course he had in mind – an inland version of his native Scottish links. Sadly he died in 1934, just before the course opened for play, but in the knowledge that Augusta was his greatest creation.

Almost as soon as the course was finished, Jones invited a band of amateur and professional players to a tournament, and the US Masters was born. Today the course is still exclusive, being set aside for a select group of Augusta National members; but it is shared by millions of viewers watching the Masters on television each April, as they did in 1997 when Tiger Woods won by 12 shots – the biggest winning margin

Augusta flag
The flag outside the clubhouse sports Augusta's distinctive map logo.

Winner's jacket
The presentation of the Green Jacket to the Masters Champion by the previous year's winner is now the climax of the event. Here Sandy Lyle hands the jacket to Nick Faldo in 1989.

Masters trophy
The permanent trophy (above), modelled on the colonial clubhouse was introduced in 1961.

Downhill all the way
The view from the 10th green (right), looking back towards the fairway which rises some 100ft (30m) back towards the tee.

ever. Woods not only became the youngest Masters winner, but his score of 270 over 72 holes set yet another new record.

There have been many developments but few major changes to the Augusta layout in the last 60 years. The nines were reversed after the first Masters Tournament and over the years the greens have been made considerably faster with bent grass on the greens replacing the original Bermuda grass. For the 2000 Masters, rough appeared on the course for the first time, and alterations were made to the 15th to make the drive slightly more demanding for the longer hitters.

NATURAL BEAUTY AND HAZARDS

The attractive flowering trees and shrubs and the carefully tended margins of the course are matched by the painstakingly manicured fairways and greens. Jones's basic idea was to create a course that made the most of the natural advantages of the site and that did not rely on man-made hazards or deep rough to make the test interesting. The fairways are inviting, the greens large and fast, and the bunkers sparingly distributed.

This is a prime example of strategic design, where the golfer is challenged to think through each shot carefully. There are several ways to play each hole and players have to choose the route according to their ability. At the foot of the hill on which the clubhouse stands,

through the pine trees in the bottom corner of the course, lurks a group of three holes, the 11th, 12th and 13th, called Amen Corner. This is where the Masters has often been won and lost.

At the 11th, a par 4 of 455 yards with a pond to the front and left rear of the green, Nick Faldo won play-offs for the Masters in consecutive years, 1989 and 1990. There are some players, the great Jack Nicklaus among them, who believe that the 12th, a par 3 of 155 yards, is the most demanding of the holes, needing extreme care from the tee to avoid running into trouble.

The dogleg 13th, which is a par 5 of 485 yards, is almost as challenging. Many a player has been tempted to go for the green from too far out, only to land in the stream that crosses in front of the hole. There is a similar problem at the par-5 15th. A player has to decide whether to try for the green and risk dropping short into the water. It was here that Gene Sarazen played one of the most famous shots in Masters history for an albatross-2 in 1935. The 18th hole ends the course in classic style, although it was originally the 9th, until Jones reversed the front and back nines in 1935.

THE NAMES OF AUGUSTA

1ST TEA OLIVE	10TH CAMELLIA
2ND PINK DOGWOOD	11TH WHITE DOGWOOD
3RD FLOWERING PEACH	12TH GOLDEN BELL
4TH FLOWERING CRAB APPLE	13TH AZALEA
5TH MAGNOLIA	14TH CHINESE FIR
6TH JUNIPER	15TH FIRETHORN
7TH PAMPAS	16TH REDBUD
8TH YELLOW JASMINE	17TH NANDINA
9TH CAROLINA CHERRY	18TH HOLLY

Each hole is named after one of the many shrubs, trees or flowers on the course. The 5th is named after the 21 magnolia trees that bloom in May alongside its fairway and green.

On in two
Before players hit the notorious Amen Corner they play the 10th, a deceptive 485-yard par 4. The 10th starts the second leg with a downhill drive from the tee near the clubhouse. There are few modern players who cannot reach the green in two.

AUGUSTA NATIONAL CHAMPIONSHIP COURSE

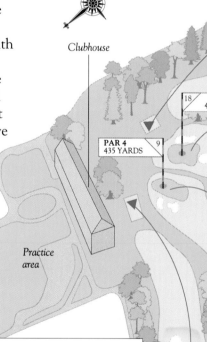

Clubhouse

Practice area

PAR 4 405 YARDS	18
PAR 4 435 YARDS	9
PAR 5 535 YARDS	8
PAR 4 400 YARDS	1

CHAMPIONSHIP LENGTHS

OUT	3,500 YARDS	PAR 36
IN	3,485 YARDS	PAR 36
TOTAL	6,985 YARDS	PAR 72

COURSE RECORD

63 NICK PRICE, US MASTERS 1986; GREG NORMAN US MASTERS 1996

US MASTERS CHAMPIONS

SEE PAGE 366

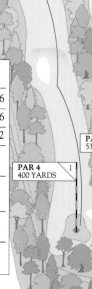

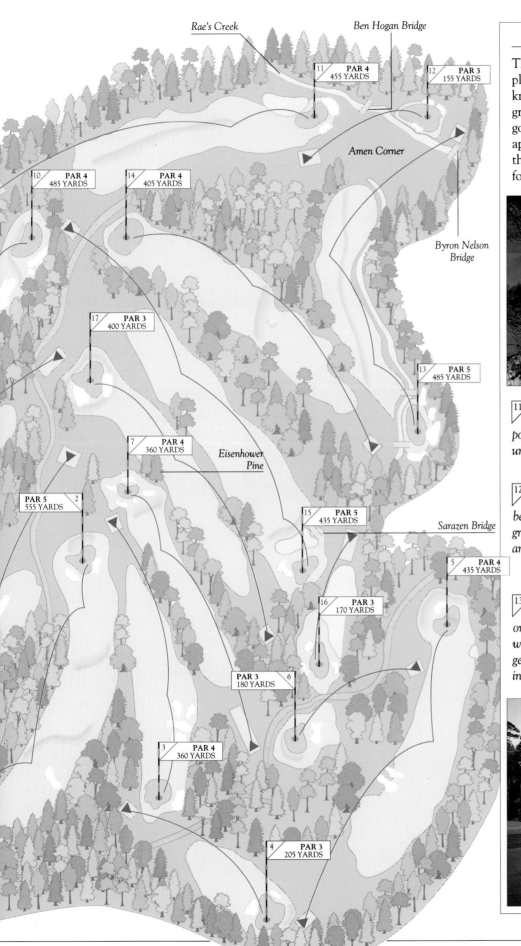

Rae's Creek

Ben Hogan Bridge

| 11 | PAR 4 455 YARDS |

| 12 | PAR 3 155 YARDS |

Amen Corner

Byron Nelson Bridge

| 10 | PAR 4 485 YARDS |

| 14 | PAR 4 405 YARDS |

| 17 | PAR 3 400 YARDS |

| 13 | PAR 5 485 YARDS |

| 7 | PAR 4 360 YARDS |

Eisenhower Pine

| PAR 5 555 YARDS | 2 |

| 15 | PAR 5 435 YARDS |

Sarazen Bridge

| 5 | PAR 4 435 YARDS |

| 16 | PAR 3 170 YARDS |

| PAR 3 180 YARDS | 6 |

| 3 | PAR 4 360 YARDS |

| 4 | PAR 3 205 YARDS |

AMEN CORNER

The 11th, 12th and 13th holes are the vital key to playing the back nine at Augusta. They have become known as Amen Corner, first christened such by the great American golf writer, Herb Warren Wind, who got the name from a jazz song. The difficulty of the approach shots combined with the extreme speed of the greens, which is typical of Augusta, make them a formidable test of golfing skills.

11 Sand trap
A bunker and a pond ensnare the unwary at the 11th.

12 Tee-shot
Rae's Creek before the 12th green, bunkered front and back, demands a perfect tee-shot.

13 Hit long
Long hitters, or those who gamble with the stream, might get on the 13th green in two.

BALLYBUNION

BALLYBUNION GOLF CLUB, BALLYBUNION, COUNTY KERRY, REPUBLIC OF IRELAND

T UCKED AWAY DEEP *in the south-west of Ireland, in the county of Kerry, lies one of the truly great links golf courses of the world. It takes not a little effort and determination to reach Ballybunion, but the rewards for persistence are great indeed. The course threads its way among huge dunes of sand, scattered at random along a shoreline of outstanding beauty and splendour. The natural features of the links have been exploited so effectively in the creation of the course that some respected critics have dubbed Ballybunion "the best golf course in the world".*

The club had a chequered early history. It was originally founded in March 1893 but five years later suffered a severe financial crisis. The first minutes book records its final entry in August 1898. It was only the fortuitous appearance of a retired Indian Army officer, Colonel Bartholomew, that led to a revival of Ballybunion's fortunes.

Together with a small group of his associates, the Colonel formed the club as it exists today in 1906. He brought in Lionel Hewson, the former editor of *Irish Golf*, to lay out nine holes. It was another 21 years before the course was extended to 18, but by 1937 Ballybunion had gained

15 **Testing target** (above)
The 15th is the toughest of the course's par 3s, particularly when the wind blows off the Atlantic. The green presents a tiny target below the tee with a huge sandhill on the left and punitive bunkering on the right.

18 **Emerald Isle desert** (left)
A wasteland of rough sand, known as the Sahara, has to be crossed at the 18th. The second shot is blind to the green, adding to the challenge of a fine finishing hole.

16 **In from the sea**
The drive must hit the fairway which slopes up from the ocean. The second shot is threatened by a bunker on the left and the green is guarded by two bunkers on the right.

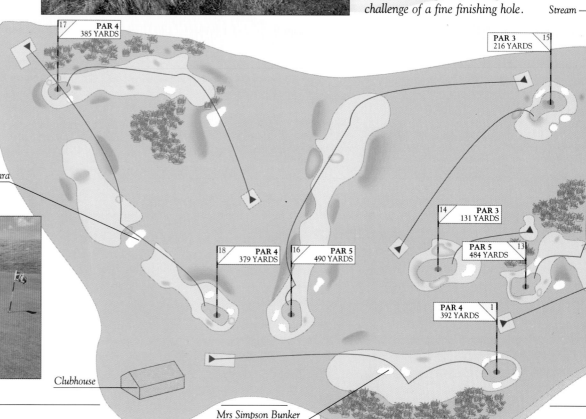

Atlantic Oc

Stream —

17 **PAR 4** 385 YARDS

PAR 3 216 YARDS **15**

Sahara

14 **PAR 3** 131 YARDS

18 **PAR 4** 379 YARDS

16 **PAR 5** 490 YARDS

PAR 5 484 YARDS **13**

PAR 4 392 YARDS **1**

Clubhouse

Mrs Simpson Bunker

sufficient reputation to be chosen to host the Irish Men's Close Championship. English golf-course architect Tom Simpson was brought in before the 1937 Championship to suggest alterations to the course, but he found little that needed attention. He confined his labours to the resiting of three greens and the addition of a controversial fairway bunker at the 14th hole. The order of the holes changed in 1971, when a new clubhouse was built, and the course now begins at the original 14th. But the bunker is still known as Mrs

Simpson – after the architect's wife, but appropriate for a feature that caused as much argument as the American divorcée who led Edward VIII to abdicate in 1936.

SAVING BALLYBUNION

In the late 1970s a campaign had to be launched to save the course from erosion on the cliff face. "Friends of Ballybunion" raised more than £100,000 under the leadership of Jackie Hourigan and the erosion was checked. But the sea also gives the course its character; the links

is virtually treeless and there are many sharp contours to the land. Despite the long grass that covers the rolling sandhills, the course is not unfair. Even on the blind shots there is usually at least some indication of the line of play.

But it is the contours that really create the challenge. The course is crammed with uphill, downhill and sidehill lies. The greens, too, are heavily contoured. As a whole, the course is demanding enough to provide a serious test of the skill and patience of any golfer.

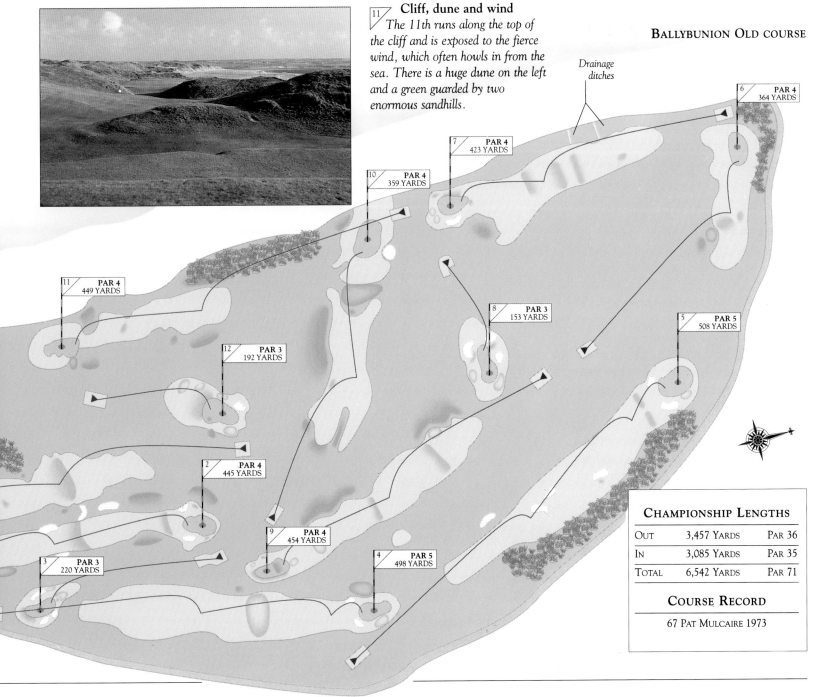

Cliff, dune and wind
The 11th runs along the top of the cliff and is exposed to the fierce wind, which often howls in from the sea. There is a huge dune on the left and a green guarded by two enormous sandhills.

BALLYBUNION OLD COURSE

Drainage ditches

6   PAR 4   364 YARDS

7   PAR 4   423 YARDS

10   PAR 4   359 YARDS

11   PAR 4   449 YARDS

8   PAR 3   153 YARDS

5   PAR 5   508 YARDS

12   PAR 3   192 YARDS

2   PAR 4   445 YARDS

9   PAR 4   454 YARDS

3   PAR 3   220 YARDS

4   PAR 5   498 YARDS

CHAMPIONSHIP LENGTHS		
OUT	3,457 YARDS	PAR 36
IN	3,085 YARDS	PAR 35
TOTAL	6,542 YARDS	PAR 71

COURSE RECORD
67 PAT MULCAIRE 1973

BALTUSROL

BALTUSROL GOLF CLUB, SPRINGFIELD, NEW JERSEY, USA

BALTUSROL GOLF CLUB *has a special place in American golf history. Not only has it hosted a record seven US Opens, but it is one of the oldest clubs in the country: golf was first played there in 1895. Unlike most country clubs, Baltusrol remains dedicated to golf alone and does not have the usual fringe activities. In fact, the original constitution of the club states that: "The object of this Club shall be the playing, cultivation, and advancement of the royal and ancient game of golf."*

The course was laid out by Louis Keller, owner and publisher of the *New York Social Register*, on land he owned at the foot of Baltusrol Mountain about 17 miles (27km) from New York City. He wrote inviting some of his friends to join, explaining that nine holes had been laid out "upon sandy hills, naturally adapted for the purpose, and now ready for use".

OPEN WINNER
In 1903 the USGA took the US Open to Baltusrol for the first time where it was won, appropriately, by Willie Anderson, whom Keller had appointed as the club's first professional. Little is known about Anderson, a shy and retiring man originally from North Berwick, Scotland. However, during his brief life – he died in his early 30s in 1910 – he won no fewer than four US Opens, a record since matched only by Bobby Jones, Ben Hogan and Jack Nicklaus. Anderson won his four titles within a space of five years and he remains the only player in the history of the US Open to win three in a row.

Baltusrol hosted its second US Open in 1915 when the amateur Jerome Travers won with a score of 297. Shortly afterwards the members decided that a tougher Baltusrol was needed and they brought in A.W. Tillinghast to supervise the construction of two completely new 18-hole layouts. Additional land was acquired for the purpose and work began

High green
This is the longest hole in the US Open. Even if the second shot avoids the "Sahara Desert", the hole still needs a long third to the elevated green.

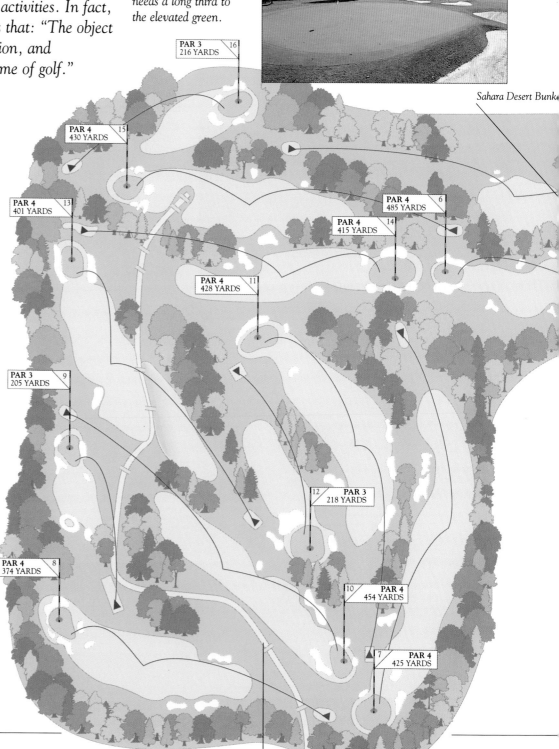

Sahara Desert Bunker

Drainage ditch

in 1920. The following year the Upper and Lower courses were opened for play. Although changes have been made to both courses over the years, notably by Robert Trent Jones on the Lower course before the 1954 US Open, the layouts are essentially as Tillinghast created them.

The Lower course has been the scene of four US Opens – 1954, 1967, 1980 and 1993 – while the Upper course hosted the 1936 Championship. Baltusrol therefore has the unique distinction in the history of the US Open of having played host to seven of the Championships on three different courses at the same club.

Tricky second shot
18 *Although it is more than 540 yards long, the finishing par 5 plays shorter, because the tee-shot is sharply downhill. This puts the green within reach of most professionals in two, but the second shot is extremely demanding. The hole doglegs left, with water crossing the fairway. A gaggle of bunkers protects the green; a long carry is needed to clear them and reach the green in two.*

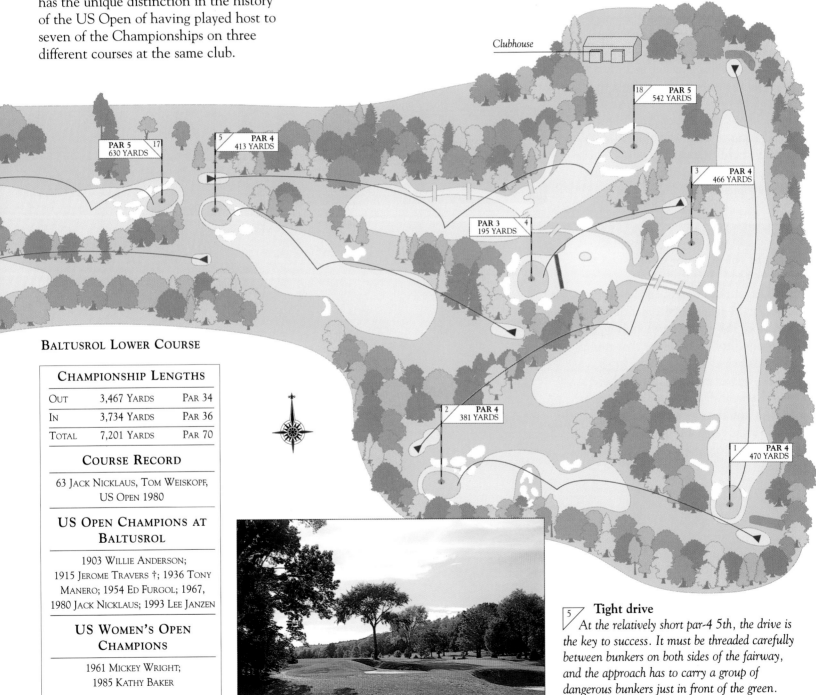

BALTUSROL LOWER COURSE

CHAMPIONSHIP LENGTHS		
OUT	3,467 YARDS	PAR 34
IN	3,734 YARDS	PAR 36
TOTAL	7,201 YARDS	PAR 70

COURSE RECORD

63 JACK NICKLAUS, TOM WEISKOPF, US OPEN 1980

US OPEN CHAMPIONS AT BALTUSROL

1903 WILLIE ANDERSON;
1915 JEROME TRAVERS †; 1936 TONY MANERO; 1954 ED FURGOL; 1967, 1980 JACK NICKLAUS; 1993 LEE JANZEN

US WOMEN'S OPEN CHAMPIONS

1961 MICKEY WRIGHT;
1985 KATHY BAKER

Clubhouse

| PAR 5 | 17 | 630 YARDS |

| 5 | PAR 4 | 413 YARDS |

| 18 | PAR 5 | 542 YARDS |

| 3 | PAR 4 | 466 YARDS |

| PAR 3 | 4 | 195 YARDS |

| 2 | PAR 4 | 381 YARDS |

| 1 | PAR 4 | 470 YARDS |

Tight drive
5 *At the relatively short par-4 5th, the drive is the key to success. It must be threaded carefully between bunkers on both sides of the fairway, and the approach has to carry a group of dangerous bunkers just in front of the green.*

BLUE CANYON

BLUE CANYON COUNTRY CLUB, MAI KHAO, PHUKET, THAILAND

SINCE IT OPENED *in 1991 the Blue Canyon Country Club has emerged as one of the finest and most picturesque among Thailand's wonderful array of golf courses. The course came to the world's attention when Tiger Woods beat Ernie Els in a dramatic play-off here at the 1998 Johnnie Walker Classic for a hugely popular win in his mother's homeland.*

18th/clubhouse
Water threatens on the right along the entire length of this very demanding par-4. Blue Canyon is not a resort, although it does welcome guests. It is a private club with 48 guestrooms, appointed with sufficient but not overbearing lavishness.

Blue Canyon had already hosted the Johnnie Walker Classic in 1994, when Greg Norman was the victor, and in 1998 it became the only course to host the tournament twice in its eleven-year history. Two years earlier Australia's Steve Elkington had won the $300,000 Honda City Invitational on the Canyon Course to further enhance the country club's reputation.

TRANQUILLITY BASE

This is quite simply a stunning place. It is not just the delicate perfume and the colour of the bougainvillea, or the splendour of the orchids, or the mirror images in the lakes, or the richness of the vegetation, it is the overwhelming peace and tranquillity of the place that leaves such an impression.

There is wonderful creativity here; a sympathetic understanding by Japanese architect and developer Yoshikazu Kato of what turns an outstanding piece of land into a very special golf course.

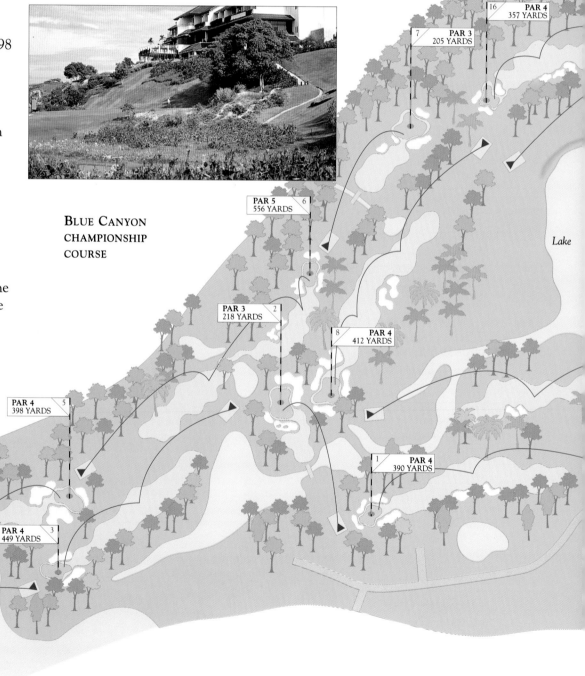

BLUE CANYON
CHAMPIONSHIP
COURSE

Tiger and the Elephants
(right) *Tiger Woods standing on the 9th green holds the Johnnie Walker Classic trophy. Woods had come from nine strokes behind going into the final round to earn a play-off with Ernie Els. He went on to win with a birdie at the second extra hole.*

The Blue Canyon Country Club has been built on what was once a tin mine and rubber plantation. The result is a sometimes daunting natural challenge with acres of water, although not all of it by any means in play, towering rubber trees, and simply breathtaking surroundings.

There are four sets of tees and there would need to be, for there are serious challenges to be found here for even the world's top professionals. From the very back tees it measures more than 7,100 yards depending on how it is set up. Low handicap amateur players find it difficult enough from the blue tees at just over 6,600 yards, and most visitors are rewarded when they play it from much farther forward than that.

There are great holes lurking here: for example the dogleg 13th over a deep canyon is spectacular and needs a carry of 180 yards to reach the fairway even at the shortest crossing point.

PAR 5 586 YARDS — 15

PAR 3 221 YARDS — 17

PAR 5 600 YARDS — 11

PAR 4 440 YARDS — 12

PAR 3 194 YARDS — 14

PAR 4 403 YARDS — 18

PAR 4 390 YARDS — 13

PAR 4 392 YARDS — 10

Clubhouse

Stunning backdrop
Tiger Woods at the 18th on his way to eventual victory in the 1998 Johnnie Walker Classic.

CHAMPIONSHIP LENGTHS		
OUT	3,598 YARDS	PAR 36
IN	3,583 YARDS	PAR 36
TOTAL	7,181 YARDS	PAR 72

COURSE RECORD
64 GREG NORMAN 1994 JOHNNIE WALKER CLASSIC

CARNOUSTIE

CARNOUSTIE GOLF LINKS, CARNOUSTIE, ANGUS, TAYSIDE, SCOTLAND

THE CARNOUSTIE CHAMPIONSHIP *course lies like a discarded string of pearls on links retreating from the ravages of the Tay estuary on the east coast of Scotland. Its 18 holes present one of the greatest challenges for any player at the top level of the game. In a world where the word "championship" has been devalued, Carnoustie remains a true test for those who would be real champions.*

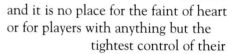

Crow crest
This region was once cursed with a plague of crows, and thus named Craw's Nestie, later changed to Carnoustie.

Carnoustie players
Carnoustie has given many great players to the game, and none better than the three Smith brothers, Alex, Willie and Macdonald. Alex Smith twice won the US Open.

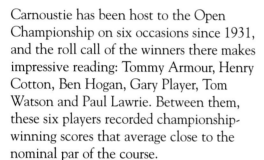

Carnoustie has been host to the Open Championship on six occasions since 1931, and the roll call of the winners there makes impressive reading: Tommy Armour, Henry Cotton, Ben Hogan, Gary Player, Tom Watson and Paul Lawrie. Between them, these six players recorded championship-winning scores that average close to the nominal par of the course. At Carnoustie this is a standard that only the great players have any hope of matching over four hard rounds of tournament play.

WIND POWER

As with all the highest quality British links courses, part of the challenge of Carnoustie lies in the whim of the weather. The battle is always with the elements as much as with the course itself. It is the wind that really makes the difference; when it blows at Carnoustie, the course is not only unrelenting and unforgiving, but it can be virtually unplayable. The course is laid out in such a way that there are never more than two consecutive holes played in the same direction, and so presents a constantly changing challenge to the players, who have to cope with the wind from all quarters.

There is no such thing as a simple hole at Carnoustie and the difficult ones are among the fiercest to be found anywhere.

East coast championship
The 1968 Open was the fourth hosted by Carnoustie.

THE OPEN CHAMPIONSHIP

CARNOUSTIE 1968

The course has no chinks in its armour and it is no place for the faint of heart or for players with anything but the tightest control of their game. Fast-running streams are a notable hazard. Jockie's Burn comes into play on four of the first six holes and the infamous Barry Burn, where so many players have come to grief in Carnoustie history – either playing into it or trying and failing to jump over it – gives this majestic course its famous finish.

As with most of the courses that developed on the east coast of Scotland, Carnoustie has little in the way of recorded history relating to its origins. It is known that golf was played on the Barry links next to Carnoustie as early as the sixteenth century. Sir Robert Maule, whom history records as being one of the first players, is known to have enjoyed the "gouff" on the Barry links, and parish records confirm the existence of the game there in 1560.

Allan Robertson, the first of the great early professionals, laid out ten holes at Carnoustie around the time of the formation of the Carnoustie Club, which

Birdie Route (above)
The 6th is where Ben Hogan birdied twice on the last day of the 1953 Open. The route he took is now known as Hogan's Alley.

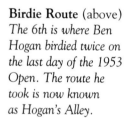

Hogan hero (above)
Ben Hogan's victory in the 1953 British Open was a masterful display; he finished four shots ahead of his rivals.

Barry Burn (right)
Frenchman Jean Van de Velde fights for a play-off at the 18th hole after landing in the tidal water of Barry Burn. The grandstands and hotel form the backdrop to the high drama.

10 Avoid the Burn

A short distance before the green at the par-4 10th, the Barry Burn offers a watery threat, while farther down by the green and to the left, a pair of bunkers waits for shots played too short. To the right of the green lurks another bunker, not far from the site of the new 11th tee. The 10th is 452 yards long and the drive requires a solid hit. The shot is threatened by a number of bunkers both to the right and left sides of the fairway.

THE NAMES OF CARNOUSTIE

1ST CUP	10TH SOUTH AMERICA
2ND GULLEY	11TH DYKE
3RD JOCKIE'S BURN	12TH SOUTHWARD HO!
4TH HILLOCKS	13TH WHINS
5TH BRAE	14TH SPECTACLES
6TH LONG	15TH LUCKYSLAP
7TH PLANTATION	16TH BARRY BURN
8TH SHORT	17TH ISLAND
9TH RAILWAY	18TH HOME

The 10th recalls the story of a young caddie, "Hairy" Nicol, who, the worse for drink, set off to seek his fortune in South America one night, only to wake up the next morning by the 10th hole.

CARNOUSTIE CHAMPIONSHIP COURSE

9 PAR 4 474 YARDS

11 PAR 4 358 YARDS

10 PAR 4 452 YARDS

Jack Nicklaus's Bunker

Drainage ditch

Barry Burn

14 Long carry

The par-5 14th is very tough for its relatively modest length. The second shot must carry the famous Spectacles, a pair of bunkers cut out of a slope about 75 yards from the centre of the double green, which is shared with the 4th.

Spectacle Bunkers

is accepted as occurring between 1839 and 1842. The course was extended to 18 holes by Old Tom Morris in 1857 and he had the satisfaction of seeing his son, "Young Tom", win a tournament there the same year, when the lad was only 16.

James Braid was brought in to revamp the course in 1926 and five years later Tommy Armour, a Scot from Edinburgh who had emigrated to America, won the first Open Championship played at Carnoustie.

In 1937 Henry Cotton took on a field which included the entire United States Ryder Cup team and beat them all, ending with a round of 71 in appalling weather. But the most memorable Open victory at Carnoustie was unquestionably Ben Hogan's matchless triumph in 1953.

8 PAR 3 183 YARDS

12 PAR 5 475 YARDS

13 PAR 3 168 YARDS

6 PAR 5 575 YARDS

7 PAR 4 397 YARDS

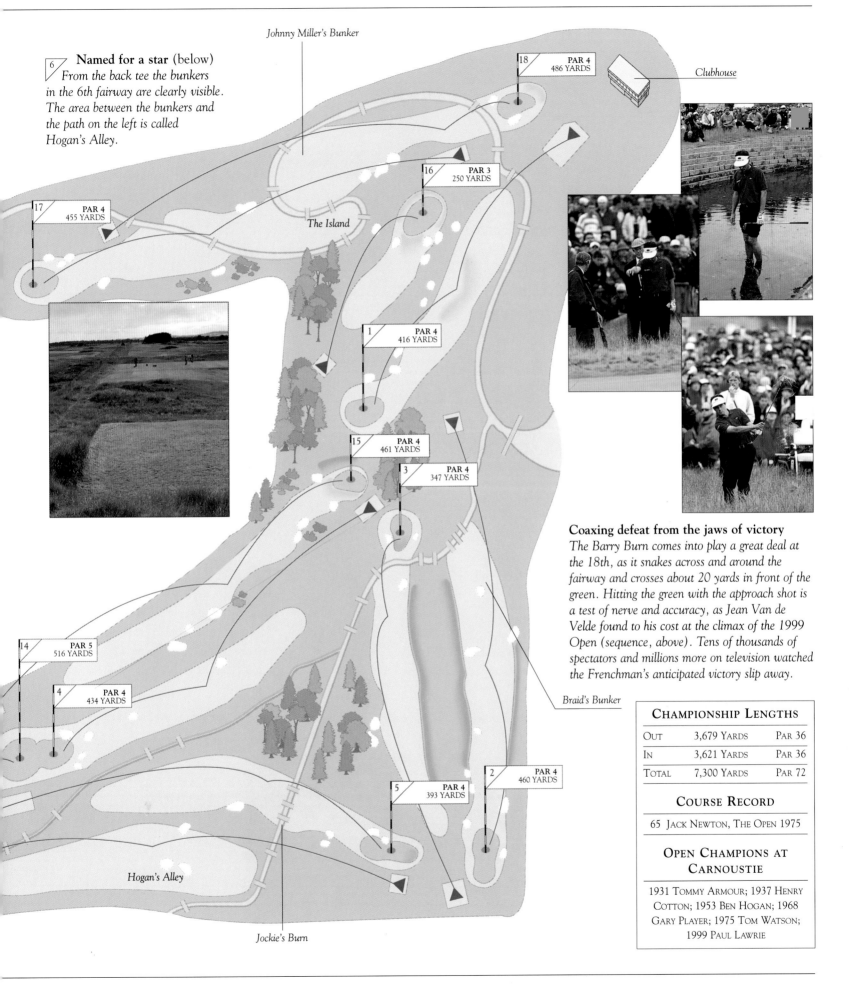

Johnny Miller's Bunker

6 Named for a star (below)
From the back tee the bunkers in the 6th fairway are clearly visible. The area between the bunkers and the path on the left is called Hogan's Alley.

| 18 | PAR 4 486 YARDS |

Clubhouse

| 16 | PAR 3 250 YARDS |

| 17 | PAR 4 455 YARDS |

The Island

| 1 | PAR 4 416 YARDS |

| 15 | PAR 4 461 YARDS |

| 3 | PAR 4 347 YARDS |

Coaxing defeat from the jaws of victory
The Barry Burn comes into play a great deal at the 18th, as it snakes across and around the fairway and crosses about 20 yards in front of the green. Hitting the green with the approach shot is a test of nerve and accuracy, as Jean Van de Velde found to his cost at the climax of the 1999 Open (sequence, above). Tens of thousands of spectators and millions more on television watched the Frenchman's anticipated victory slip away.

| 14 | PAR 5 516 YARDS |

| 4 | PAR 4 434 YARDS |

Braid's Bunker

| 2 | PAR 4 460 YARDS |

| 5 | PAR 4 393 YARDS |

Hogan's Alley

Jockie's Burn

CHAMPIONSHIP LENGTHS		
OUT	3,679 YARDS	PAR 36
IN	3,621 YARDS	PAR 36
TOTAL	7,300 YARDS	PAR 72

COURSE RECORD

65 JACK NEWTON, THE OPEN 1975

OPEN CHAMPIONS AT CARNOUSTIE

1931 TOMMY ARMOUR; 1937 HENRY COTTON; 1953 BEN HOGAN; 1968 GARY PLAYER; 1975 TOM WATSON; 1999 PAUL LAWRIE

CHANTILLY

GOLF DE CHANTILLY, VINEUIL-SAINT-FIRMIN, CHANTILLY, FRANCE

CHANTILLY IS WIDELY *regarded as the finest course in France and is one of the oldest in the country. It dates back to 1908 and has hosted the French Open Championship many times. There are shades of some of the great heathland courses, such as Sunningdale and The Berkshire, in this beautiful setting only 25 miles (40km) north of Paris. Much of the course is relatively open, despite the surrounding woodland, and Chantilly's 6,597 metres are among the most testing in Europe.*

13 Hollow shot
The 13th is one of the toughest of the course's long par 4s. A good drive is needed to open up the green on this sharp dogleg left, to leave a demanding second shot over a deep grassy hollow to a green surrounded by trees.

15 Testing trio
The 15th is the third of a group of three holes, starting at the 13th, that present a stern test and are crucial to any round at Chantilly. The drive must be long and straight to open up a green well protected by deep bunkers.

In the early part of the 1920s, Tom Simpson was commissioned to redesign the holes that make up today's course; one of his acts was to remove many of the bunkers. His work was badly damaged in the Second World War, but the championship course retains much of his original design. It contains three uncompromising par 5s and four tough par 3s, three of them more than 190m long, to make up the overall par of 71. Of the par 4s, eight exceed 380m. Much of the bunkering is penal and, particularly on the short holes, there is a premium on length combined with precision.

This peaceful course is set in beautiful woodland and there is plenty of space to enjoy; the solemn calm of the surrounding forest shuts out the world, and the mind can focus on golf alone.

The list of French Open Champions is an indication of the quality of the test. George Duncan won the first French

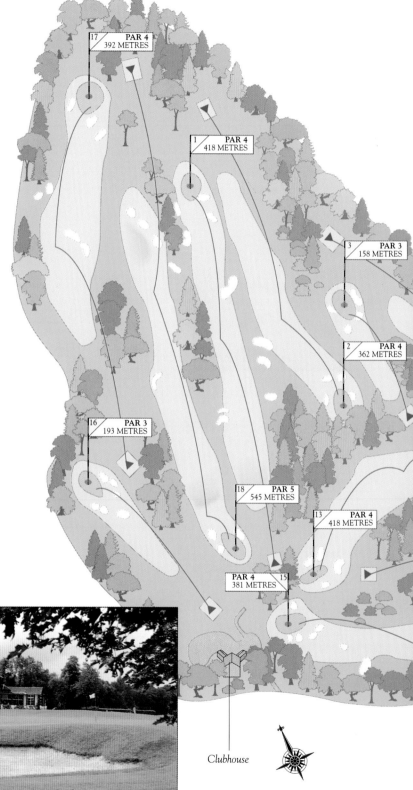

17 / PAR 4 / 392 METRES

1 / PAR 4 / 418 METRES

3 / PAR 3 / 158 METRES

2 / PAR 4 / 362 METRES

16 / PAR 3 / 193 METRES

18 / PAR 5 / 545 METRES

13 / PAR 4 / 418 METRES

PAR 4 / 381 METRES / 15

Clubhouse

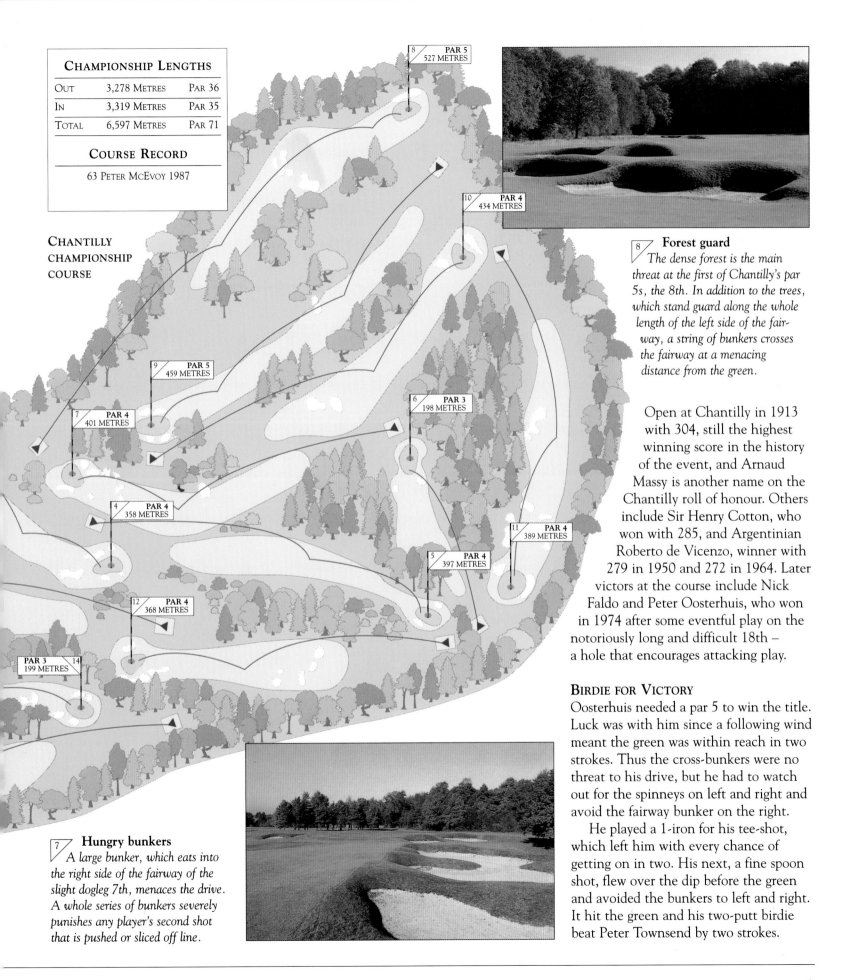

CHAMPIONSHIP LENGTHS

Out	3,278 Metres	Par 36
In	3,319 Metres	Par 35
Total	6,597 Metres	Par 71

COURSE RECORD

63 Peter McEvoy 1987

**CHANTILLY
CHAMPIONSHIP
COURSE**

8 **Forest guard**
The dense forest is the main threat at the first of Chantilly's par 5s, the 8th. In addition to the trees, which stand guard along the whole length of the left side of the fairway, a string of bunkers crosses the fairway at a menacing distance from the green.

Open at Chantilly in 1913 with 304, still the highest winning score in the history of the event, and Arnaud Massy is another name on the Chantilly roll of honour. Others include Sir Henry Cotton, who won with 285, and Argentinian Roberto de Vicenzo, winner with 279 in 1950 and 272 in 1964. Later victors at the course include Nick Faldo and Peter Oosterhuis, who won in 1974 after some eventful play on the notoriously long and difficult 18th – a hole that encourages attacking play.

BIRDIE FOR VICTORY
Oosterhuis needed a par 5 to win the title. Luck was with him since a following wind meant the green was within reach in two strokes. Thus the cross-bunkers were no threat to his drive, but he had to watch out for the spinneys on left and right and avoid the fairway bunker on the right.
He played a 1-iron for his tee-shot, which left him with every chance of getting on in two. His next, a fine spoon shot, flew over the dip before the green and avoided the bunkers to left and right. It hit the green and his two-putt birdie beat Peter Townsend by two strokes.

7 **Hungry bunkers**
A large bunker, which eats into the right side of the fairway of the slight dogleg 7th, menaces the drive. A whole series of bunkers severely punishes any player's second shot that is pushed or sliced off line.

CLUB ZUR VAHR

CLUB ZUR VAHR, COURSE GARLSTEDT, BREMEN, GERMANY

L ONG AND ACCURATE HITTING *are the keys to playing the magnificent Garlstedter Heide course, which is part of the Club zur Vahr sports club, near Bremen. The layout is heavily forested and makes the best possible use of abundant natural hazards. This fine 18-hole layout, which is rated among the finest championship courses in Europe, is only one part of a club complex also featuring a nine-hole course and other sports and leisure facilities.*

Although there was a nine-hole course at Bremen from as early as 1895, the present layout dates back only to 1970. It was the brainchild of August Weyhausen, a former German Junior Champion. He chose a 220-acre (90ha) site in undulating countryside 12 miles (20km) from Bremen. Weyhausen brought in course architect Dr Bernhard von Limburger, a former German Amateur Champion.

Von Limburger created a course that could be enjoyed by the ordinary club members and that would also be worthy of championship golf. When it is stretched to its full championship potential of 7,147 yards, it is a fearsome test for even the world's finest players. Trees dominate the course and many of the holes are doglegged, demanding long and accurate driving to open up the green for the

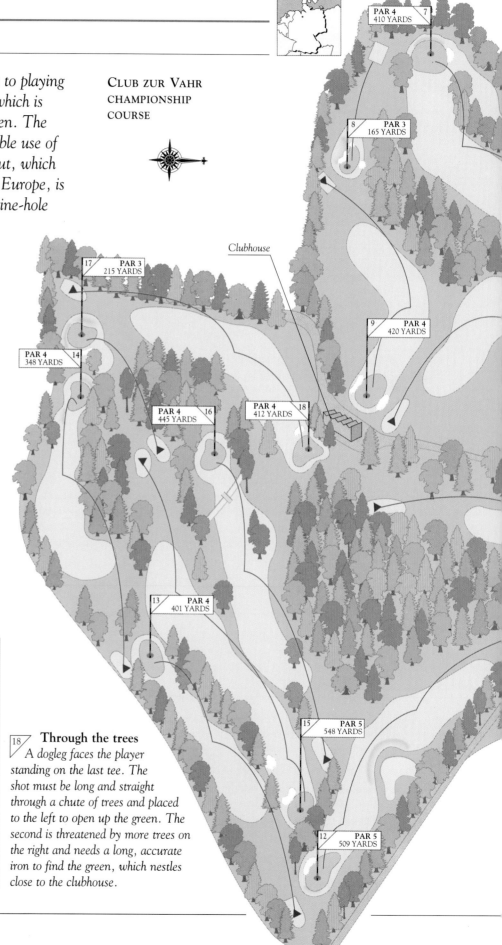

CLUB ZUR VAHR
CHAMPIONSHIP
COURSE

Clubhouse

18 **Through the trees**
A dogleg faces the player standing on the last tee. The shot must be long and straight through a chute of trees and placed to the left to open up the green. The second is threatened by more trees on the right and needs a long, accurate iron to find the green, which nestles close to the clubhouse.

Solid iron
3

As with most of the Club zur Vahr course, trees provide the main problems at the first of the short holes – the par-3 206-yard 3rd. A solid blow with a long iron is needed to reach the sanctuary of the green. Trees are a threat on both sides of a green that is also well protected by two strategically placed bunkers. Among the trees, which are predominantly silver birch and pines, there is extremely thick undergrowth in which it is only too easy to lose a stroke – or a ball.

second shot. This is a course that demands careful tactical planning. Wayward shots are punished harshly, often running into the thick undergrowth between the pine trees bordering the fairways. Because of the trees, few artificial hazards, such as fairway bunkers, have been added to the terrain. There are fewer than 30 bunkers, with all but one sited near the greens.

HOSTING THE GERMAN OPEN

A year after it was officially opened, Club zur Vahr hosted the German Open with an outstanding field from more than 20 countries. A crowd of well over 6,000 people – a record for a German golf event – turned out to watch England's Neil Coles win with a remarkable score of 279, 17 below par. Coles rated the Bremen course as one of the best championship courses in Europe, and few would disagree.

The German Open has been played at Club zur Vahr on two subsequent occasions, in 1975 and 1985. Bernhard Langer won the 1985 event which was hit by rain, forcing the organizers to reduce the championship to 54 holes.

Stream

1	PAR 4 366 YARDS
6	PAR 5 555 YARDS
3	PAR 3 206 YARDS
2	PAR 5 529 YARDS
5	PAR 4 320 YARDS
11	PAR 3 183 YARDS
10	PAR 5 568 YARDS
4	PAR 5 547 YARDS

ving range

Tight down the left
2

Only a perfect drive tight down the left side – but avoiding the trees – gives any hope of reaching the green of this long par 5 in two strokes. A stream crosses the fairway around 300 yards from the tee, with a pond just beyond. A couple of trees stand sentinel in the centre of the fairway.

CHAMPIONSHIP LENGTHS		
OUT	3,518 YARDS	PAR 37
IN	3,629 YARDS	PAR 37
TOTAL	7,147 YARDS	PAR 74

COURSE RECORD

68 NEIL COLES, PETER THOMSON, GERMAN OPEN 1971

COLONIAL

COLONIAL COUNTRY CLUB, FORT WORTH, TEXAS, USA

AT OVER 7,000 *yards and with a par of only 70, the course where Ben Hogan learned his golf puts an absolute premium on accurate driving. The Trinity River and the mass of trees through which the course is cut are supplemented by craftily strategic bunkering that makes tee-shots extremely tight. This, in turn, creates demanding second shots on a course where only three of the 12 par-4 holes are less than 400 yards long.*

There is a strong body of opinion that believes that much of Ben Hogan's success was due to the fact that he played his early golf on this tough layout in Fort Worth, Texas. Every other course in the world, so the argument goes, is simple by comparison. Hogan was for many years the dominant player at the Colonial course, winning the Colonial National Invitation Tournament (NIT) five times.

Colonial was founded in 1935 by Marvin Leonard, a local golfing enthusiast. The original course was designed by John Bredemus, and Perry Maxwell was brought in to strengthen the 3rd, 4th and 5th holes in preparation for the 1941 US Open. This was the only time that Colonial staged the men's Open; it was won by Craig Wood,

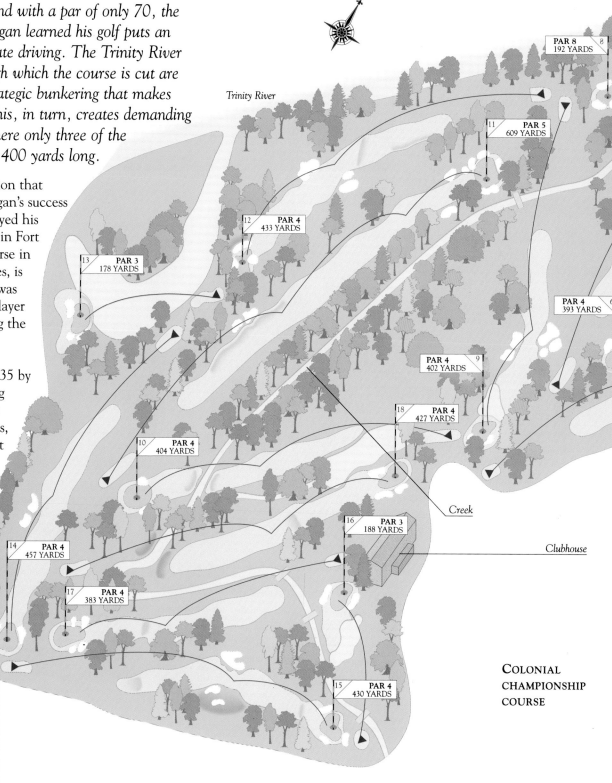

Trinity River

Creek

Clubhouse

**COLONIAL
CHAMPIONSHIP
COURSE**

CHAMPIONSHIP LENGTHS		
OUT	3,571 YARDS	PAR 35
IN	3,509 YARDS	PAR 35
TOTAL	7,080 YARDS	PAR 70

COURSE RECORD

61 KEITH CLEARWATER AND
LEE JANZEN 1993, GREG CRAFT 1999

US OPEN CHAMPIONS

1941 CRAIG WOOD

Precision is the key
Only an accurate drive down the centre of the fairway avoids trouble at the 5th. The river on the player's right, and rough and a ditch on his left, menace the tee-shot.

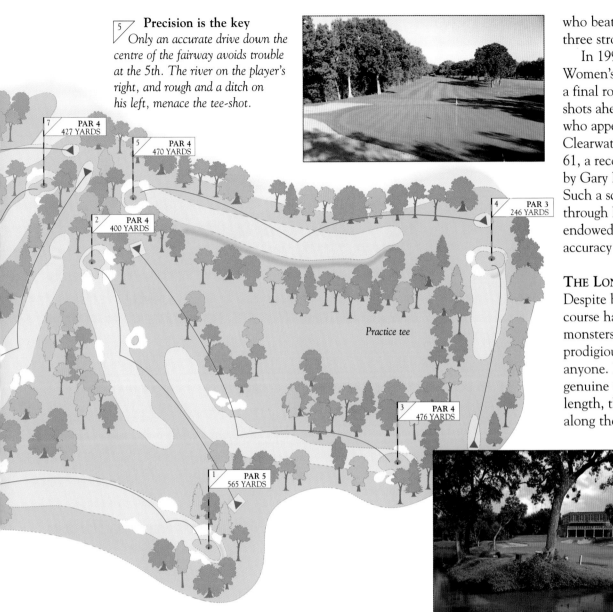

PAR 4
427 YARDS

PAR 4
470 YARDS

PAR 4
400 YARDS

PAR 3
246 YARDS

Practice tee

PAR 4
476 YARDS

PAR 5
565 YARDS

who beat his rival, Densmore Shute, by three strokes.

In 1991 the Colonial hosted the US Women's Open won by Meg Mallon with a final round of 67 for a total of 283, two shots ahead of Pat Bradley. Another player who appeared to tame Colonial was Keith Clearwater. In 1993 he shot an incredible 61, a record equalled by Lee Janzen, and by Gary Kraft in the Masterclass Colonial. Such a score could only be achieved through long and straight hitting; players endowed with strength but without accuracy will not succeed at Colonial.

THE LONG AND THE SHORT

Despite being more than 7,000 yards, the course has only two par 5s, but both are monsters. The 1st, at 565 yards, is a prodigious enough start to a course for anyone. But the 11th, at 609 yards, is a genuine three-shotter, and apart from its length, there is the added hazard of trees along the fairway on the right.

Ending up
There is no let-up at Colonial, right up to the finishing hole. The 18th is a tough par 4, which demands a long and accurate tee-shot. Water to the left of the green and menacing greenside bunkers add to the challenge of the final approach shot.

Stage fright
The last of the par-3 holes, the 16th is not unduly long at 188 yards, but it demands an accurate tee-shot over water to reach the green. Mistakes can be most embarrassing as the green, guarded by some extremely intrusive bunkers, is next to the clubhouse.

The four short holes are modest in length, with only the 4th stretching to more than 200 yards, but all demand precision. Supreme accuracy from the tee is certainly needed for the long par-4 5th. The hole doglegs to the right and those players favouring the bold shot from the tee, with a fade to cut off part of the corner, must be careful as the Trinity River lurks dangerously behind the trees. On the left, thick trees and rough combine to threaten the tee-shot struck too far through the dogleg. There is no option but to strike a perfect drive to the centre of the fairway to avoid trouble.

THE COUNTRY CLUB, BROOKLINE

THE COUNTRY CLUB, BROOKLINE, MASSACHUSETTS, USA

G ARY PLAYER ONCE *commented that The Country Club at Brookline was "more English than most English golf courses", and indeed the setting is straight out of Berkshire rather than nearby Boston. The oldest Country Club in the USA, golf tradition and golfing incident – not least the infamous 1999 Ryder Cup – ooze from the pores of this history-drenched course.*

Ryder Cup (above) *Payne Stewart in typical flamboyant attire helping the US team beat the Europeans in 1999.*

Crowd control (below) *Davis Love III backed by supporters at the controversial 33rd Ryder Cup held at Brookline.*

There is no pretentiousness in the name given to this venerable club. It is The Country Club simply because it was the only country club in the United States after a group of 34 influential Bostonians gathered together in 1882 to form a social club in the country, principally to play tennis, listen to music in the afternoons and most importantly to hold horse race meetings on which the members could enjoy a little flutter. Golf was not high on the agenda at that time, in fact it was not on the agenda at all.

It took the arrival of Miss Florence Boit, an American lady living in France, to introduce the royal and ancient game to the genteel Bostonians. Visiting the city in 1892 she brought with her a set of golf clubs, and left behind a mashie as a gift to her host, her uncle Arthur Hunnewell (a member at The Country Club). He took the old mashie and a new-found enthusiasm for the game to his club, and with the help of fellow members Laurence

Curtis and Robert Bacon, convinced the club that golf should be added to the list of the club's activities.

OUIMET'S CHALLENGE
In 1913 the course became the setting for a watershed in the history of American golf when it played host to the US Open Championship and to a 20-year-old amateur and former caddie by the name of Francis Ouimet, who beat two of Great Britain's finest players, Harry Vardon (then five times winner of the British Open), and Ted Ray. Ouimet inflicted a heavy defeat on the Britons and the effect of his victory had much more significance than the initial indication that the British were about to lose their domination of the game.

Ouimet's victory was an inspiration to Americans, and his victory created a massive surge in interest in golf. At that time fewer than 400,000 Americans were playing golf but within ten years of Ouimet's historic victory, more than two million were playing.

The present championship course is a composite layout using holes from two courses. Fifteen holes are retained from the regular course and four holes from the

Ladies a-fluttering (above) *Edwardian Bostonians gather at the clubhouse to take a flutter on the horses. They could also pursue genteel sports such as croquet and tennis.*

Clubhouse (above) *Today the clubhouse is adorned in a bright primrose yellow and is a bastion of American golf tradition.*

Downhill all the way (right) *Sergio Garcia faces a daunting prospect during the tense 1999 Ryder Cup at Brookline.*

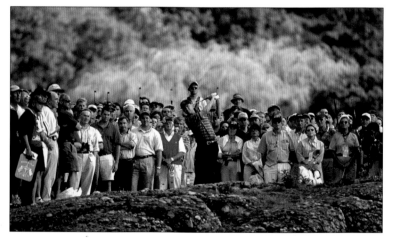

Primrose nine – a layout added in 1927 "for ladies, children and beginners" – two of them combined to form the 11th.

TESTING HOLES

Of the many testing holes, the par-4 4th is a good example, with a ring of six bunkers surrounding the green, waiting to trap long hitters who attempt to reach the green from the tee on this short dogleg. Stands of strategically placed pine trees also focus the mind to find the fairway.

Discretion is usually the better part of valour at the short par 4, 6th. A mere 310 yards in length, the temptation for the longer hitters to attempt to drive the green, particularly when the wind is up and helping, is hard to resist. The penalties for miscalculation, however, are severe, and potentially very damaging in the early stages of the round.

US Captain, Ben Crenshaw, ordered a new pot bunker to be added to the hole's defences for the infamous Ryder Cup match of 1999 when the United States won a torrid encounter amid unfortunate scenes and much recrimination.

A measure of the 6th's danger is the fact that most players in the 1988 US Open laid up to the bottom of the hill, refusing to be lured into trying for the green from the tee. Curtis Strange went on to defeat Britain's Nick Faldo in a

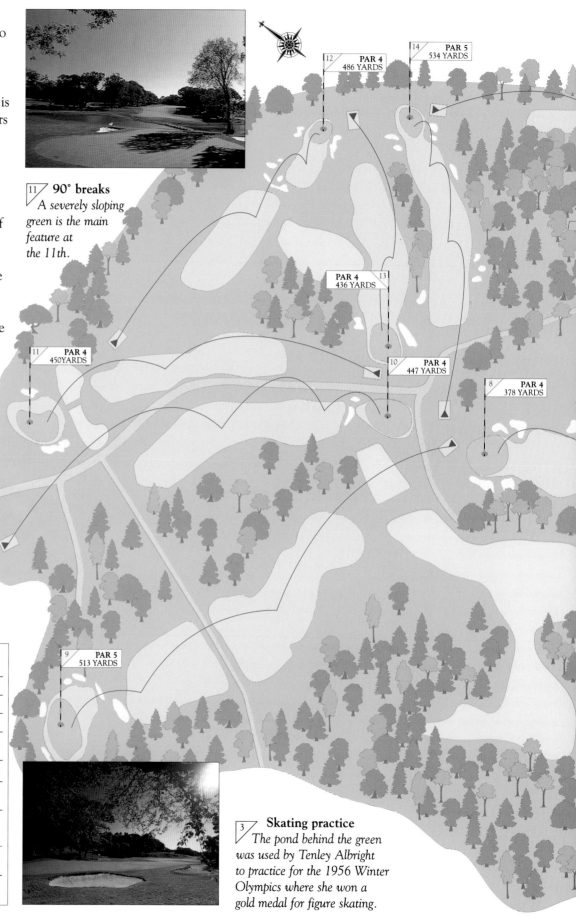

11 **90° breaks**
A severely sloping green is the main feature at the 11th.

3 Skating practice
The pond behind the green was used by Tenley Albright to practice for the 1956 Winter Olympics where she won a gold medal for figure skating.

CHAMPIONSHIP LENGTHS		
OUT	3,256 YARDS	PAR 35
IN	3,777 YARDS	PAR 36
TOTAL	7,033 YARDS	PAR 71

COURSE RECORD

64 PETER JACOBSEN, US OPEN 1988

US OPEN CHAMPIONS AT BROOKLINE

1913 FRANCIS OUIMET †; 1963 JULIUS BOROS;
1998 CURTIS STRANGE

RYDER CUP WINNERS

1999 USA

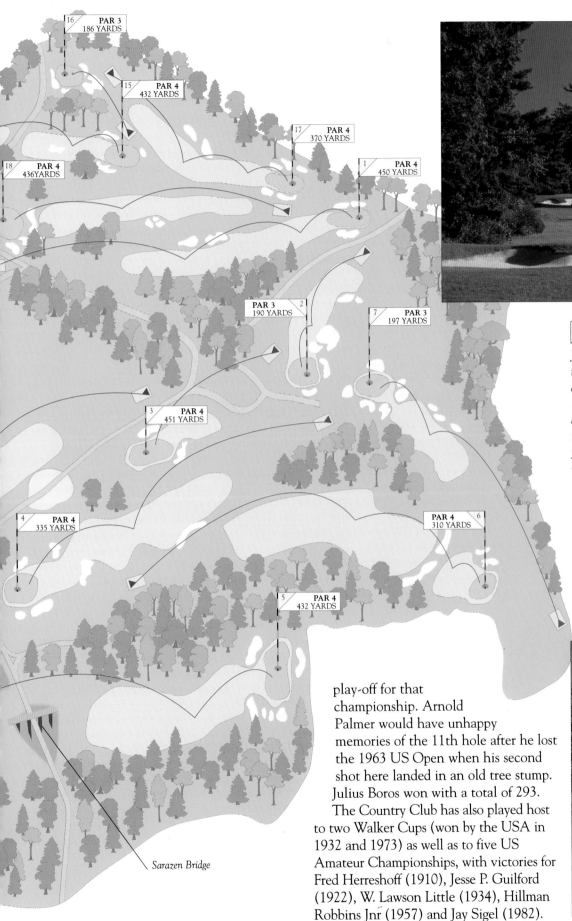

16 PAR 3
186 YARDS

15 PAR 4
432 YARDS

17 PAR 4
370 YARDS

18 PAR 4
436 YARDS

1 PAR 4
450 YARDS

PAR 3
190 YARDS 2

7 PAR 3
197 YARDS

3 PAR 4
451 YARDS

4 PAR 4
335 YARDS

PAR 4
310 YARDS 6

5 PAR 4
432 YARDS

Sarazen Bridge

Double-tiered green

17 *A double-tiered green, as redesigned by Rees Jones, is a frightening prospect, particularly when the hole is cut on the upper level. The hole was crucial in Ouimet's victory over Vardon in the 1913 US Open: he birdied it in the fourth round and again in the play-off. Julius Boros also birdied the hole 50 years later in the 1963 US Open to force his way into a play-off which he eventually won against Jacky Cupit and Arnold Palmer.*

Well-protected

4 *Although it can be driven by the longest players, the 4th green is well-protected and there are severe penalties just off the fairway for those who take a chance and fail. The hole is known as "Hospital" after the Brookline Hospital for Infectious Diseases, which is situated behind the green.*

play-off for that championship. Arnold Palmer would have unhappy memories of the 11th hole after he lost the 1963 US Open when his second shot here landed in an old tree stump. Julius Boros won with a total of 293.

The Country Club has also played host to two Walker Cups (won by the USA in 1932 and 1973) as well as to five US Amateur Championships, with victories for Fred Herreshoff (1910), Jesse P. Guilford (1922), W. Lawson Little (1934), Hillman Robbins Jnr (1957) and Jay Sigel (1982).

CYPRESS POINT

CYPRESS POINT GOLF CLUB, PEBBLE BEACH, CALIFORNIA, USA

T**HE SOUTHERN TIP** of the Monterey Peninsula in California is home to Cypress Point, generally rated as one of the most spectacular courses in the world. The 1921 US Women's Amateur Champion, Marion Hollins, fell in love with California after a visit to the state and bought the 175-acre (71ha) clifftop site with the support of local businesspeople for $175,000. Here, high above the crashing waves of the Pacific Ocean, the great course architect Dr Alister MacKenzie created a masterpiece.

13 Barred by sand
The drive at the par-4 13th must carry a sandbar in the centre of the narrowing fairway. The two-tiered green is defended by a necklace of bunkers.

The first course architect engaged to look at this stunning natural location was Seth Raynor, but he died unexpectedly and MacKenzie was appointed to continue the work. The Cypress Point Golf Club eventually opened in 1928.

The natural setting of the course, in the foothills of the Santa Lucia Mountains, is superb. Huge Monterey cypress trees brood quietly by the fairways and greens, and deer wander the course in the early morning and in the dusk.

The MacKenzie layout makes the best use of the landscape for golf. He resisted the temptation to create holes just to take advantage of the majestic views, and put the need for challenge by the course before everything else.

PAR 4
362 YARDS — 13

PAR 4
418 YARDS — 1

14 — PAR 4
383 YARDS

15 — PAR 3
139 YARDS

Clubhouse

18 — PAR 4
342 YARDS

16 Over the Pacific
The par-3 16th demands a carry of 233 yards from the back tee across the ocean and into the prevailing wind to a green thronged by bunkers.

16 — PAR 3
233 YARDS

Pacific Ocean

17 — PAR 4
376 YARDS

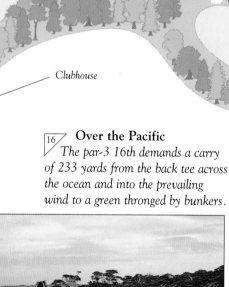

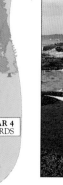

Cypress Point is highly unusual among the world's greatest courses in having both consecutive par 5s and consecutive par 3s. All its par 5s are in the first ten holes and two of the par 3s in the last four.

MacKenzie was careful to build plenty of contour and slope into the greens, in order to compensate for the course's modest length of 6,506 yards. The first green has a sharp slope, for instance, and the 5th has a two-tier green on a plateau at the end of a fairway that winds its way uphill through the pine forest. MacKenzie also emphasized the approach to the greens. At the 3rd, the challenge is to avoid bunkers of glittering sand on a short par 3. The green at the 6th is protected by five bunkers and a group of pines.

CLIFFTOP CHALLENGE

The high spots of the course come at the 15th, 16th and 17th, a great trio of holes along the clifftop beside the Pacific. Some of the most exciting golf in the world takes place here, where breathtaking views and challenging play combine.

Cypress Point was once described by the fine American player Jimmy Demaret as "the best 17-hole golf course in the world". Demaret considered that the 18th hole, a modest 342-yard dogleg, lacked sufficient strength for a finishing hole on a major course, and many other players have agreed with him since.

Today, Cypress Point is one of the world's most exclusive clubs, with only 250 members, who come from all over the United States and abroad. Exclusivity takes its toll, however, and Cypress Point is a somewhat anonymous place, where members avoid publicity and guard their prerogatives jealously.

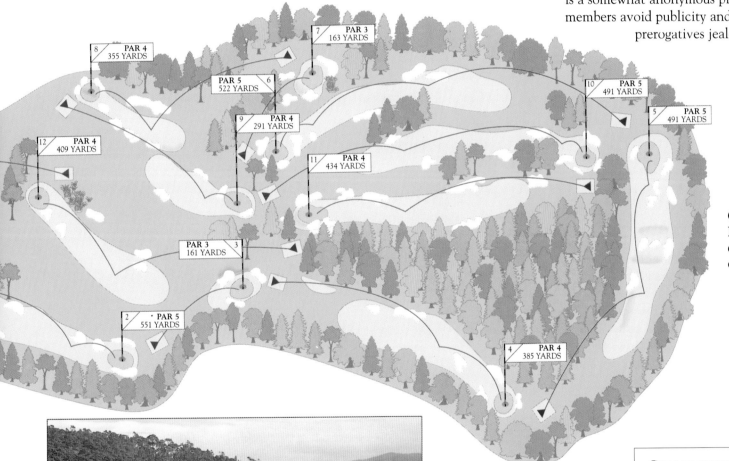

CYPRESS
POINT
CHAMPIONSHIP
COURSE

17 Tree trouble
The fairway at the 17th is wide along the clifftop but the shot from the tee, high on a cliff, must carry a stretch of ocean and be placed left to give a clear shot to the green. Too far right brings a pine tree on the front right of the green into play. There are massive bunkers to the left and back of the green, and a knot of cypress trees has to be avoided.

CHAMPIONSHIP LENGTHS		
OUT	3,337 YARDS	PAR 37
IN	3,169 YARDS	PAR 35
TOTAL	6,506 YARDS	PAR 72

COURSE RECORD

64 CRAIG STADLER, AT & T
NATIONAL PRO-AM 1982

WALKER CUP WINNERS

1981 USA

DESERT HIGHLANDS

DESERT HIGHLANDS GOLF CLUB, SCOTTSDALE, ARIZONA, USA

A SMALL PART *of the old and fabled land of the Arizona Desert, where once the native American Indians lived, has been transformed into a new-style reservation for wealthy, upwardly mobile Americans. At the heart of the Desert Highlands community is a quite remarkable Jack Nicklaus golf course, like a series of green footprints in the desert. It is a supreme example of what technology and careful planning can do to balance the aspirations of man with sensitivity to the environment.*

The days are long past when the desert was regarded as a hostile wasteland, inimical to golf as to most other human activities. Today, golf architects realize that the warmth of the desert offers a near-perfect climate for spectacular courses, provided enough water can be supplied.

PROTECT AND CONSERVE

It took Nicklaus two years of study and 20 visits to the site in the early 1980s to achieve what he was after at Desert Highlands. At the heart of all the design thinking was the need to protect the desert environment, its plants and wildlife. The conservation of water had the highest priority: only 80 acres (32ha) of the course need irrigation and recycling ensures that every drop counts.

18 Jack's view
Only the brave try to get home in two at the 18th. Most players will play short of the narrow green, which is protected by a mound. It was from Clubhouse Rock, close to the 18th, that Nicklaus first surveyed the desert and planned his course.

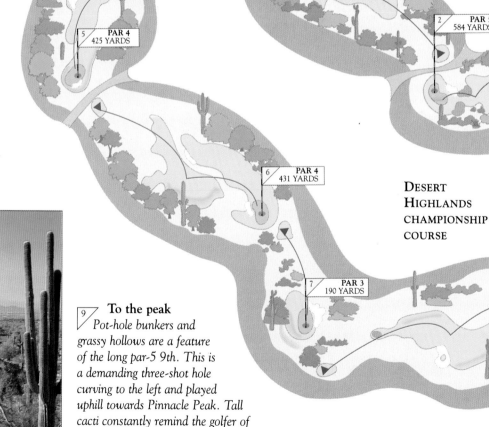

DESERT HIGHLANDS CHAMPIONSHIP COURSE

4 | PAR 3 / 211 YARDS
3 | PAR 4 / 452 YARDS
2 | PAR 5 / 584 YARDS
5 | PAR 4 / 425 YARDS
6 | PAR 4 / 431 YARDS
7 | PAR 3 / 190 YARDS
8 | 438 Y.

9 To the peak
Pot-hole bunkers and grassy hollows are a feature of the long par-5 9th. This is a demanding three-shot hole curving to the left and played uphill towards Pinnacle Peak. Tall cacti constantly remind the golfer of the arid desert setting for the finely maintained greens and fairways.

Nicklaus has achieved a harmony between the course and the boulder-strewn desert terrain with its distinctive vegetation. The fairways are, in essence, landing areas. They have an edge of semi-rough that runs into what Nicklaus calls "transitional bunkers", meaning that they border the cultivated area on one side and merge into the desert itself on the other.

The course lies 2,400ft (730m) above sea level and is 7,099 yards at champion-ship length. Nicklaus has used craggy mounds for the teeing areas, with the first hole a classic example; the drive is played out into space towards a green 120ft (37m) below. There are bent grass greens, typical of Nicklaus with their undulating contours, and fiendish pot bunkers.

A unique feature of the Desert Highlands complex is the remarkable par-41 18-hole putting course, designed by architect Gary Panks. It is so hard that Jack Nicklaus only managed 45 on it.

16 Long and low
The long par-3 16th has a three-tiered green. It is best played with a long, low shot that can run up on to the green. A bunker on the left threatens wayward drives, and a series of the hostile humps and hollows that are characteristic of the course waits for short, off-line shots.

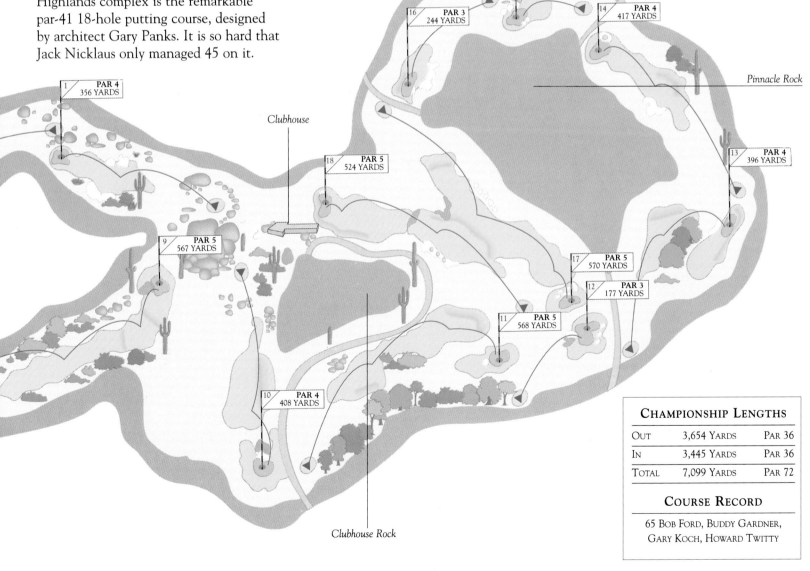

CHAMPIONSHIP LENGTHS

OUT	3,654 YARDS	PAR 36
IN	3,445 YARDS	PAR 36
TOTAL	7,099 YARDS	PAR 72

COURSE RECORD

65 BOB FORD, BUDDY GARDNER, GARY KOCH, HOWARD TWITTY

FALSTERBO

FALSTERBO GOLFKLUBB, FYRVAGEN, FALSTERBO, SWEDEN

D OWN AT THE *southernmost tip of Sweden, on a peninsula where the Baltic Sea and the waters of the Öresund meet, lies one of Europe's most dramatic courses, Falsterbo. It is a classic links course, one of the few fine examples of this type of golf to be found in continental Europe. Challenging to play, it is also a home to wildlife.*

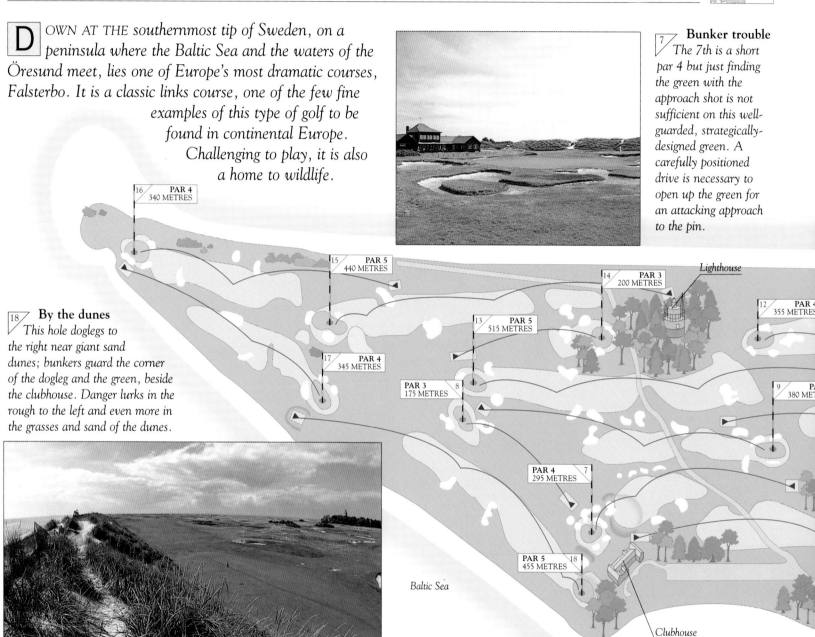

Bunker trouble
The 7th is a short par 4 but just finding the green with the approach shot is not sufficient on this well-guarded, strategically-designed green. A carefully positioned drive is necessary to open up the green for an attacking approach to the pin.

By the dunes
This hole doglegs to the right near giant sand dunes; bunkers guard the corner of the dogleg and the green, beside the clubhouse. Danger lurks in the rough to the left and even more in the grasses and sand of the dunes.

16 | PAR 4 340 METRES
15 | PAR 5 440 METRES
14 | PAR 3 200 METRES
Lighthouse
12 | PAR 4 355 METRES
13 | PAR 5 515 METRES
17 | PAR 4 345 METRES
PAR 3 175 METRES | 8
9 | PA 380 MET
PAR 4 295 METRES | 7
PAR 5 455 METRES | 18
Baltic Sea
Clubhouse

Though Falsterbo dates back to 1909, it is not the oldest club in Sweden. That distinction belongs to Hovas, near Gothenburg. But Falsterbo is the only true links course in the country, even though there are some that are partly links, such as Falsterbo's neighbour, Flommen.

Robert Turnbull, the professional at Copenhagen Golf Club, laid out the original nine holes of Falsterbo. The course was expanded to 18 holes in 1930 by Gunnar Bauer. In 1995 a project "FGK 2009" was started to update the course and the greens. Architects Peter Chamberlain and Peter Nordwall were given the task of totally reconstructing all 18 greens.

A lighthouse stands in the middle of a course which has fine turf and magnificent natural surroundings. The course is also an important nature reserve: the marshes at the northern end are a haven for bird life, as well as a challenging set of golfing hazards. But no player can afford to let his concentration wander for too long over the natural surroundings. Frequent changes in wind direction also add to the demands for the most careful attention. The toughness of the course manifests itself right from the beginning.

The tee-shot at the 1st must avoid the out-of-bounds down the right side and the trees on the other side of the fairway, which swings slightly to the right. A par at this 400m hole is not a bad start. A shortish par 3 and a relatively benign par 5 follow, but when the player turns back alongside the marsh the going gets tougher.

DOWN BY THE MARSH

The uncompromising 360m par-4 4th is the first hole beside the marsh and is usually played into the prevailing wind. The water hazard is clearly defined by tall reeds down the right side of the fairway; the green is tucked into a corner of the

marsh. The second shot often requires a wood and must cross the corner of the marsh which defends the green.

Internal water hazards – natural here, but unusual on a links course – present a dangerous prospect on the next two holes. Further on, the holes around the central lighthouse are delightful, but from the 15th the golf is played alongside the great sand dunes that are the mark of this fine course. The 16th, a beautiful 340m par 4, gently doglegs its way into the corner of the peninsula. On one side the views to Denmark, with the newly constructed bridge from Sweden, are spectacular, on the other lies the open Baltic Sea.

THE NAMES OF FALSTERBO

1ST VÄGEN	10TH KÅLHAGEN
2ND DICKENS	11TH VATTENHÅLET
3RD TÅNGVALLEN	12TH STRANDSKATAN
4TH FLOMMEN	13TH TIPPERARY
5TH CHICAGO	14TH FYRHÅLET
6TH VANNINGEN	15TH ÖRESUND
7TH 1911	16TH GUNNAR BAUER
8TH SAHARA	17TH NABBEN
9TH SYDVÄSTEN	18TH KLITTERNA

The holes at Falsterbo are named in a mixture of Swedish and English. The 5th hole is called Chicago after the gangster days of the 1920s, because it holds dangers lurking at every turn. The name of the 15th refers to a geographical feature, the sound alongside Falsterbo, while the 16th celebrates the architect of the 18-hole course.

Öresund

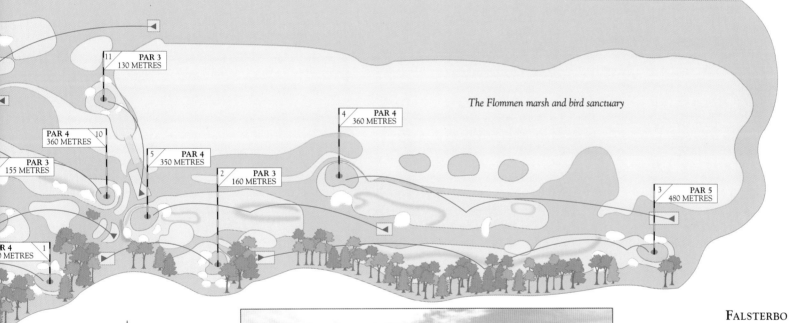

The Flommen marsh and bird sanctuary

CHAMPIONSHIP LENGTHS		
OUT	2,860 METRES	PAR 34
IN	3,205 METRES	PAR 37
TOTAL	6,065 METRES	PAR 71

COURSE RECORD

64 PETER SENIOR, PLM OPEN 1986

FALSTERBO
CHAMPIONSHIP
COURSE

11 Bridge over water trouble
The fourth of Falsterbo's five par 3s is the most spectacular. The hole is a modest 130m long, but it is surrounded on three sides by water. It is death or glory here, particularly if, as so often, a brisk breeze is blowing from left to right across the hole. Access to the green is over a long footbridge that has been built across the middle of the inlet.

GANTON

GANTON GOLF CLUB, GANTON, SCARBOROUGH, NORTH YORKSHIRE, ENGLAND

P URE HEATHLAND GOLF *is the closest substitute for the classic links of the seaside, where the game was born and nurtured. There are numerous similarities, for in many cases the "inland" heath was at one stage covered by the sea and appeared to the light of day only as the ocean receded. This is almost certainly true of Ganton, which lies only a few miles from the sea and is a course of charm, challenge and outstanding quality.*

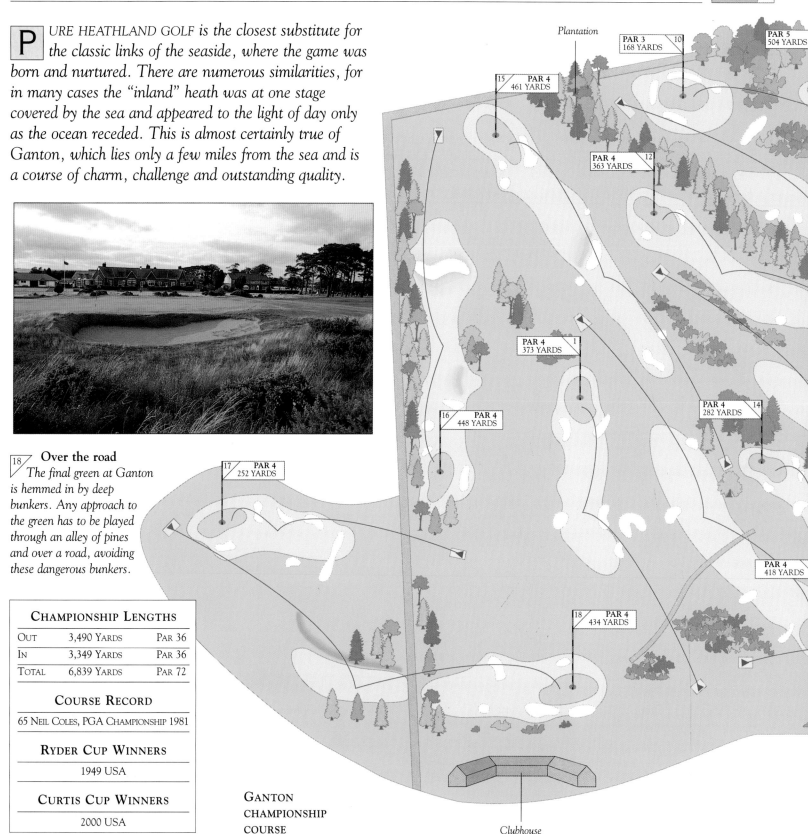

Over the road
The final green at Ganton is hemmed in by deep bunkers. Any approach to the green has to be played through an alley of pines and over a road, avoiding these dangerous bunkers.

Plantation

PAR 3
168 YARDS — 10

PAR 5
504 YARDS

15 — PAR 4
461 YARDS

PAR 4
363 YARDS — 12

PAR 4
373 YARDS — 1

PAR 4
282 YARDS — 14

16 — PAR 4
448 YARDS

17 — PAR 4
252 YARDS

PAR 4
418 YARDS — 2

18 — PAR 4
434 YARDS

CHAMPIONSHIP LENGTHS		
OUT	3,490 YARDS	PAR 36
IN	3,349 YARDS	PAR 36
TOTAL	6,839 YARDS	PAR 72

COURSE RECORD

65 NEIL COLES, PGA CHAMPIONSHIP 1981

RYDER CUP WINNERS

1949 USA

CURTIS CUP WINNERS

2000 USA

GANTON
CHAMPIONSHIP
COURSE

Clubhouse

Demanding length

The 6th is the longest par 4 on the front nine and requires two long and accurately played shots to reach it in regulation. Dangerous bunkers and thick gorse leave little room for error.

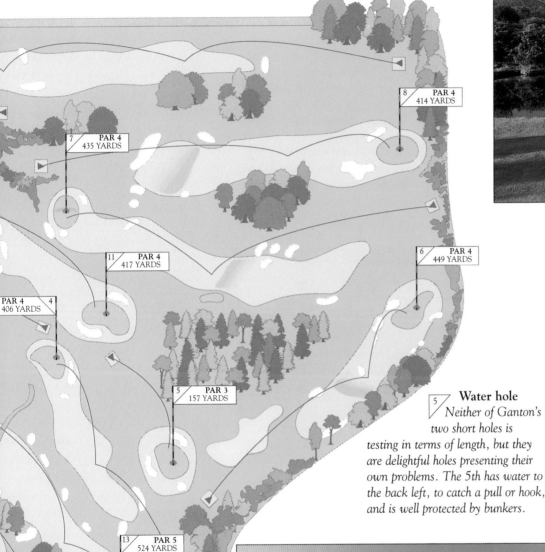

PAR 4
414 YARDS

7 PAR 4
435 YARDS

8

11 PAR 4
417 YARDS

6 PAR 4
449 YARDS

PAR 4
406 YARDS 4

5 PAR 3
157 YARDS

13 PAR 5
524 YARDS

3 PAR 4
334 YARDS

Water hole

Neither of Ganton's two short holes is testing in terms of length, but they are delightful holes presenting their own problems. The 5th has water to the back left, to catch a pull or hook, and is well protected by bunkers.

While on many courses of its period trees were introduced to define fairways and as a consequence the natural openness of the heath was destroyed, Ganton did not follow suit. Although some Scots and Corsican pines have now been planted, Ganton remains a rare example of a genuine open heathland course.

Harry S. Colt was one of the many eminent architects and players who have left their mark on the course since it came into being in 1891. Among the others were the great amateur Harold Hilton, Tom Dunn, Horace Hutchinson and Frank Pennink, as well as all three members of the Great Triumvirate. Harry Vardon was also the club professional from 1896 until 1903. In the 1920s, Dr Alister MacKenzie introduced the tiered greens that were his trademark. The best examples of his work are at the 3rd, 7th and 9th holes. The course was further strengthened by Ken Cotton in preparation for the Ryder Cup match that was held at Ganton in 1949.

Ganton has always been regarded as one of the world's finest inland courses. It hosted the very successful Curtis Cup in June 2000, won by the United States, and was awarded the Walker Cup for 2003.

GLEN ABBEY

GLEN ABBEY GOLF CLUB, OAKVILLE, ONTARIO, CANADA

GLEN ABBEY WAS *one of the first courses designed specifically to meet the demands of modern professional tournament golf. In the mid-1970s, Jack Nicklaus was brought in to create a permanent home for the Canadian Open on this spectacular site, with its wooded ravine carved over the centuries by Sixteen Mile Creek on its way towards Lake Ontario. Nicklaus made the most imaginative use of the magnificent natural terrain to create a fine championship course. Today the Golf House, once used by the Jesuit Fathers as a retreat, houses the Royal Canadian Golf Association.*

15 Out of the valley
The last of Glen Abbey's par 3s, the 15th, is one of the most demanding holes, despite being only 141 yards from the back tee. The shot is to a greatly elevated green, shaped like the continent of Africa. The green, sloping sharply from back to front, has bunkers to its front and rear. Choice of club is critical. An extra club might be felt necessary to make sure of reaching the green, but putts from above the hole are difficult to stop down the slope.

The concept to which Nicklaus worked was that of a truly championship-standard course, designed for tournament play with spectators very much in mind. It became the forerunner of the current crop of so-called "stadium" courses, aimed at providing maximum viewing areas.

To assist spectators, the ground has been elevated behind the tees and gentle, grassy slopes curve behind and to the sides of the greens. The course layout means that six of the greens and five of the tees are within 100 yards of the clubhouse. This allows the spectators to see plenty of golf without moving too far.

EASY VIEWING

Wide spaces have purposely been left between the fairways to accommodate the enormous crowds attracted by the Open, and the 18th green is set in an amphitheatre that provides comfortable viewing for thousands on the last day of this prestigious USPGA event.

Nicklaus did not start from scratch in designing Glen Abbey; there had been a golf course on the site since the time it was sold by the Jesuit Order in the early 1960s. But Nicklaus completely rebuilt it, remodelling all 18 holes. He added fresh bunkers, trees and lakes to produce a challenging new layout, while exploiting to the full the natural test presented by

the Sixteen Mile Creek ravine. The 11th to the 15th, set in the ravine and known as the "Valley" holes, are among the toughest on the whole Glen Abbey course.

The course was opened in June 1976 – an occasion when Nicklaus played an 18-hole exhibition match with Tom Weiskopf, who had won the 1975 Canadian Open. In 1977 Glen Abbey hosted the Open for the first time, Lee Trevino taking the title. The event has been played there every year since, with the exception of 1980 when it returned to Royal Montreal to fulfil an earlier commitment. Winners at Glen Abbey include Greg Norman and Curtis Strange.

Despite its severity for the tournament players, the course still presents an enjoyable test from the forward tees for those mortals possessed of more modest golfing ability.

Practice green

GLEN
ABBEY
CHAMPIONSHIP
COURSE

Sixteen Mile Creek

The Abbey car park

| 11 | PAR 4 452 YARDS |

| 12 | PAR 3 187 YARDS |

| 13 | PAR 5 529 YARDS |

| 16 | PAR 5 516 YARDS |

| 10 | PAR 4 443 YARDS |

| 2 | PAR 4 414 YARDS |

| 18 | PAR 5 508 YARDS |

Clubhouse

| 3 | PAR 3 156 YARDS |

| 1 | PAR 5 435 YARDS |

| 9 | PAR 4 458 YARDS |

| 4 | PAR 4 417 YARDS |

| 7 | PAR 3 197 YARDS |

| 6 | PAR 4 437 YARDS |

| 5 | PAR 5 527 YARDS |

Dorval Drive

CHAMPIONSHIP LENGTHS		
OUT	3,474 YARDS	PAR 36
IN	3,638 YARDS	PAR 37
TOTAL	7,112 YARDS	PAR 73

COURSE RECORD

62 GREG NORMAN, CANADIAN
OPEN 1987

12 Watch the length

The first short hole on the back nine, the 12th is deceptive in length. It is 187 yards from the back tee, but tends to play longer. The player needs to take an extra club and favour the right. The undulating green requires careful putting.

14 Crossing the creek

The tee-shot at the 14th carries Sixteen Mile Creek. The aim line of the ideal shot is between the two fairway bunkers, but a choice has to be made on how much of the dogleg is to be cut off.

HARBOUR TOWN

HARBOUR TOWN GOLF LINKS, HILTON HEAD ISLAND, SOUTH CAROLINA, USA

A T A TIME *when the trend in the United States was towards longer and longer courses, Pete Dye, with Jack Nicklaus as his consultant, swam against the tide in designing the famous Harbour Town links. The course is only of moderate length, and Dye made the greens small, keeping the number of bunkers to a minimum. There are only 56 bunkers on the course and a dozen of these are hardly ever visited. The rest are relatively flat – a buried lie in the sand is almost unheard of at Harbour Town.*

HARBOUR
TOWN
CHAMPIONSHIP
COURSE

18 | **Carry over the marsh**
The farthest back tee at the last hole is called the "Nicklaus tee" by the members. So difficult and long is the flight across the marsh, along the shore of Calibogue Sound, that it is seldom used, even by the USPGA for the MCI Heritage Classic event.

The Harbour Town golf links is only 6,912 yards long when stretched to its limit and virtually flat, with fairways often more than 40 yards wide. The fall between the highest and lowest points on the course is no greater than the height of the average man; consequently there are no uphill or downhill lies for those who live in fear of such features. The three par-5 holes are modest in length, and although there are some long par 4s, there are just as many on the course that are short.

So why is it such a highly regarded course in world golf? The answer lies in the subtlety of the design. Dye and Nicklaus hacked their way through sub-tropical trees and vegetation, leaving just enough trees in their wake to make the layout a classic test of nerve and patience.

Many of the trees were carefully left in strategic positions to confound the golfer. Wonderful live oaks festooned with Spanish moss, enormous pines and magnificent magnolias abound in this most spectacular of settings, in the holiday playground of Hilton Head Island.

ACCURACY WINS OUT
Wayward shots from the tee are often punished severely by water or trees. The care required over second shots, and the variety of them needed, is phenomenal. Dye's design demands unusual accuracy, and long hitters who cannot place the ball with pin-point precision will lose any advantage that they may usually have over those of more modest length. The greens offer few putts of any testing length.

Coastal splendour (below)
The lush beauty of sub-tropical land at the edge of the sea gives Harbour Town Golf Links an exotic backdrop. It is enhanced by the lighthouse, which is a distinctive landmark as well known as the course itself. The trees are a constant hazard.

Heritage Road

1 PAR 4
414 YARDS

2 PAR 5
505 YARDS

6 PAR 4
419 YARDS

5 PAR 5
535 YARDS

8 PAR 4
462 YARDS

7 PAR 3
180 YARDS

3 PAR 4
411 YARDS

4 PAR 3
198 YARDS

PAR 4 10
436 YARDS

11 PAR 4
438 YARDS

PAR 5 15
575 YARDS

12 PAR 4
413 YARDS

Baynard
Cove Road

Plantation Drive

14 PAR 3
165 YARDS

13 PAR 4
378 YARDS

CHAMPIONSHIP LENGTHS

OUT	3,461 YARDS	PAR 36
IN	3,451 YARDS	PAR 35
TOTAL	6,912 YARDS	PAR 71

COURSE RECORD

63 J. NICKLAUS 1975; D. WATSON
1979; J. HALLETT 1988; W. LEVI 1989;
R. FLOYD 1992

Dye believed that long putting had no place in the game and once quipped "Something that makes a golfer chip with finesse is a lot more interesting to him than a 95ft putt."

Harbour Town is now home to the South Carolina Golf Club, which has claims to be the oldest golf club in the United States. There is evidence the club originated in Charleston as far back as 1786, more than a hundred years before the formation of the St Andrew's Club in Yonkers, New York (more widely accepted as America's oldest club). In recognition of its age, the club holds the annual MCI Heritage Classic, traditionally in the week after the Masters. Arnold Palmer, Jack Nicklaus, Bernhard Langer and Nick Faldo are past winners of the Heritage event.

17 Flying over trouble
The tee-shot at Harbour Town's par-3 17th hole is one of the most daunting anywhere. It must carry water for two-thirds of its flight to a green propped up by railway sleepers, the trademark of architect Pete Dye. As an added hazard, a long ribbon of a bunker runs down the left side and around the back of a green which is narrow at the front but widens towards the rear.

KINGSBARNS LINKS

KINGSBARNS LINKS GOLF CLUB, KINGSBARNS, NEAR ST ANDREWS, FIFE, SCOTLAND

*N*O LESS A *luminary than Sir Michael Bonallack, former Secretary and a past Captain of the Royal & Ancient Golf Club of St Andrews, has said that Kingsbarns Links may be the last true seaside links site capable of development in Scotland. Whatever the final outcome, it is certainly now the standard against which any new links golf course yet to be built anywhere, is likely to be judged.*

When the course was opened in 2000 it was hailed as a masterpiece of modern design and immediately leapt high into the listings, not only of the world's new courses, but more significantly into many overall world rankings as well.

Kyle Phillips designed the course with American developers Mark Parsinen and Art Dunkley on a site where golf is believed to have been played from as far back as 1793.

Situated in the ancient Kingdom of Fife only four miles from St Andrews itself, Kingsbarns is a small village fringing the North Sea and looking north almost directly across the estuary to the mighty links of Carnoustie.

2nd hole par
The contour of the large green tends to throw approach shots to the right towards a deep gathering bunker on the front right, while a deep hollow protects the left side.

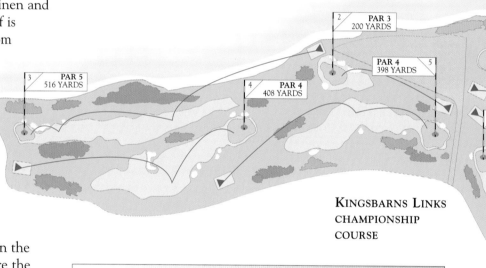

KINGSBARNS LINKS
CHAMPIONSHIP
COURSE

MILITARY MANOEUVRES

The new course has been built on the site of the nine-hole course where the Kingsbarns Golf Club was officially founded in 1815. The original course was lost to the game in 1939 when the Royal Air Force commandeered the site for military manoeuvres and despite many efforts after the Second World War to resurrect the old links it was not until the first year of the new millennium that Kingsbarns was finally back on the golfing map.

The land with which Kyle Phillips and the Kingsbarns developers had to work was essentially a two-tiered stretch of sandy agricultural land hard against the Fife shoreline. The challenge was to turn this relatively featureless tract of land into

Tricky approach
An unusually shaped and steep downward sloping green from front to back makes the 6th a tricky hole that requires the utmost care. This is part of the course that dates back to 1793.

a test of golf that could genuinely stand comparison with the great natural seaside links courses that are strung out all along the east coast of Scotland.

THE ESSENCE OF LINKS GOLF

Unlike early course construction in Scotland, where the designer had to work with the contours he was given (for there was no mechanical way to move massive amounts of land), Kyle Phillips and Mark Parsinen "created" the dunes and land movement with the earthscraper and bulldozer. The result is spectacular and significant because the land looks as if it has stood in this form for a thousand years. Kyle Phillips and the developers have proved beyond

doubt that it is possible to blend the classic early days of golf course architecture with the technology of the modern day.

On every hole there is a view of sea and more often than not in the frame of play. The short 15th is the classic example. A spectacular short hole played across the rocks and sea to a long, angled green set on a lick of land jutting out into the estuary.

But the 15th is only one of many great holes on a golf course that has set a benchmark for new golf courses in the new millennium.

CHAMPIONSHIP LENGTHS		
OUT	3,469 YARDS	PAR 36
IN	3,657 YARDS	PAR 36
TOTAL	7,126 YARDS	PAR 72

COURSE RECORD
NO SIGNIFICANT TOUR EVENT PLAYED

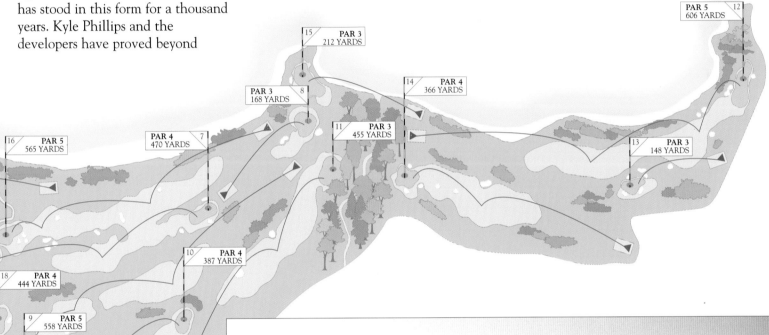

Clubhouse

16 Bunker threat

There are a multiplicity of problems to be solved on the long par-5 16th. A total of ten bunkers create a minefield of opportunity for disasters, particularly the fairway bunker down the right, which threatens the tee shot. A burn behind the green is another dangerous and unseen hazard.

LINDRICK

LINDRICK GOLF CLUB, WORKSOP, NOTTINGHAMSHIRE, ENGLAND

T HE FAMOUS COURSE *architect Dr Alister MacKenzie, designer of Augusta National, declared that Lindrick "has the best terrain of any inland course in Britain". Such an emphatic declaration by someone with such impeccable credentials is high praise indeed. But it is no more than this fine example of heathland golf, on the border between Nottinghamshire and South Yorkshire, deserves.*

Over the hill
A bunker guards the left of the fairway on the 4th, a short par 5 of 480 *yards. The second shot is played blind over a hill, towards a green that lies in front of a river.*

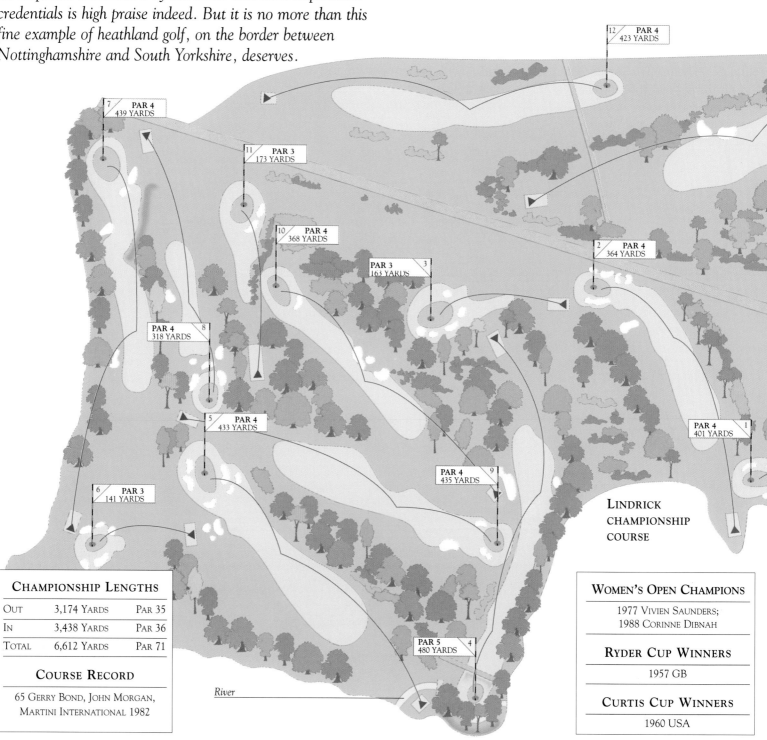

LINDRICK CHAMPIONSHIP COURSE

CHAMPIONSHIP LENGTHS		
OUT	3,174 YARDS	PAR 35
IN	3,438 YARDS	PAR 36
TOTAL	6,612 YARDS	PAR 71

COURSE RECORD

65 GERRY BOND, JOHN MORGAN, MARTINI INTERNATIONAL 1982

WOMEN'S OPEN CHAMPIONS
1977 VIVIEN SAUNDERS; 1988 CORINNE DIBNAH

RYDER CUP WINNERS
1957 GB

CURTIS CUP WINNERS
1960 USA

River

The Lindrick club was formed in 1891 as the Sheffield and District Golf Club. Laid out on heathland overlying limestone, the course has not changed greatly over the years. Only the 2nd and 18th holes have been subject to major alterations.

Gorse is the predominant shrub at Lindrick, but birch trees have invaded the area over the years and it is no longer as open a heath as it originally was.

The club has been in the vanguard of the movement to preserve traditional British golfing turf, a movement led by the late Eddie Park and his son Nicholas. They have practised what they preach at Lindrick. Top priority is accorded to sustaining the bent and fescue grasses that provide such marvellous turf for fairways and greens. Lindrick has, in fact, some of the best putting surfaces found anywhere

in the world. A great deal of care is taken to keep the course in the finest playing condition all through the year.

Lindrick has a justifiably famous place in golfing history as the course on which Great Britain and Ireland last won the Ryder Cup against the Americans, without recourse to reinforcements from Europe. It was in 1957 that

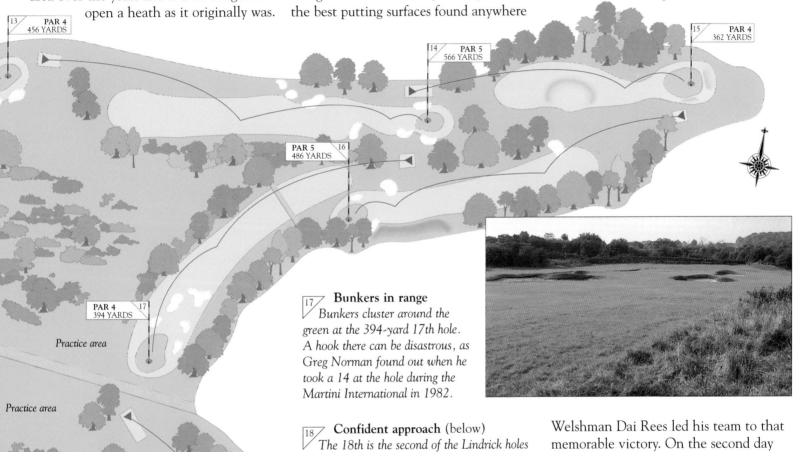

13 PAR 4 456 YARDS

14 PAR 5 566 YARDS

15 PAR 4 362 YARDS

16 PAR 5 486 YARDS

17 PAR 4 394 YARDS

Practice area

Practice area

18 PAR 3 210 YARDS

Clubhouse

17 Bunkers in range
Bunkers cluster around the green at the 394-yard 17th hole. A hook there can be disastrous, as Greg Norman found out when he took a 14 at the hole during the Martini International in 1982.

18 Confident approach (below)
The 18th is the second of the Lindrick holes to have undergone a change from the original layout. It is a testing 210-yard short hole that demands a solid shot to carry across bunkers to a well guarded green. All the greens at Lindrick are very fine putting surfaces.

Welshman Dai Rees led his team to that memorable victory. On the second day the British trailed by three matches to one, but they then won six of the eight singles to take the trophy. Even in defeat the US captain, Jackie Burke, recognized the true worth of Lindrick. "The course is a golfing paradise," Burke said. "The turf is perfect and the greens flawless."

The most famous hole at Lindrick is the 4th. This challenging hole also has a colourful history. At one time, before the county boundaries were changed, the hole straddled the borders of Nottinghamshire, Derbyshire and Yorkshire. It was a popular spot for illegal activities such as cock-fighting. To evade the police from any one county, the participants had only to step over the border and continue.

MEDINAH

MEDINAH COUNTRY CLUB, MEDINAH, CHICAGO, ILLINOIS, USA

THE GOLF CLUB at Medinah, in the suburbs of Chicago, is an unusual place by any standards. Built in the 1920s as a private club for the Ancient Arabic Order of Nobles of the Mystic Shrine – popularly known as the Shriners – its clubhouse is a mock-Moorish, temple-like building with a huge dome. But if the clubhouse lacks a traditional golfing atmosphere, the Number 3 course more than compensates. The course has hosted three US Opens since 1949, the most recent in 1990, and many players place it at the top of the "difficulty" list for the country's foremost professional championship.

MEDINAH NUMBER 3 COURSE

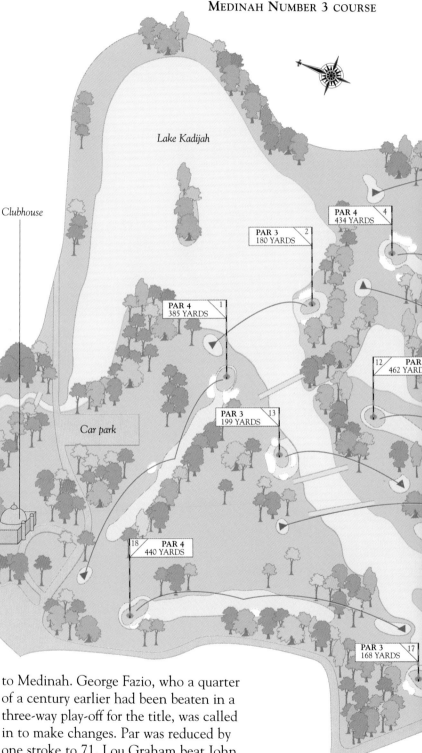

17 Over the lake
Like the 12th at Augusta, the par-3 17th at Medinah is a critical factor in victory or defeat. At a length of 168 yards, it is played from a raised tee down to a narrow green, mostly over water. Whereas Rae's Creek guards the 12th green at Augusta, Medinah's 17th has to carry Lake Kadijah, named after the Prophet Mohammed's wife.

Medinah's Number 3 course was originally designed by Tom Bendelow, an expatriate Scotsman. He intended it for women's golf, but it was considered too difficult and was soon handed over to the men. Bendelow had a dubious reputation as a golf-course designer and many changes have since been made to his course to bring it up to standard.

After Harry Cooper shot 63 on his way to winning the 1930 Medinah Open, five new holes were laid out, and the course was again much altered before the US Open was first played there in 1949. Cary Middlecoff won with a score of 286. It was not until 1975 that the US Open returned to Medinah. George Fazio, who a quarter of a century earlier had been beaten in a three-way play-off for the title, was called in to make changes. Par was reduced by one stroke to 71. Lou Graham beat John Mahaffey in the play-off.

For the 1990 Open, the USGA, in collaboration with the Medinah Club,

16 **The sharpest dogleg**

Originally the 13th hole, before the USGA made various changes to the back nine prior to the 1990 US Open, Medinah's 16th is a notorious dogleg left. Heavy trees on both sides of the fairway add to the other hazards, which include a very small, elevated green. Two bunkers lie in wait short of the green to the sides, with another behind.

CHAMPIONSHIP LENGTHS		
OUT	3,582 YARDS	PAR 36
IN	3,613 YARDS	PAR 36
TOTAL	7,195 YARDS	PAR 72

COURSE RECORD

66 S. SIMPSON, T. SIMPSON, J. SLUMAN, US OPEN 1990; R. PRICE 1990

US OPEN CHAMPIONS

1949 CARY MIDDLECOFF; 1975 LOU GRAHAM; 1990 HALE IRWIN

US PGA CHAMPIONS

1999 TIGER WOODS

US SENIOR OPEN CHAMPIONS

1988 GARY PLAYER

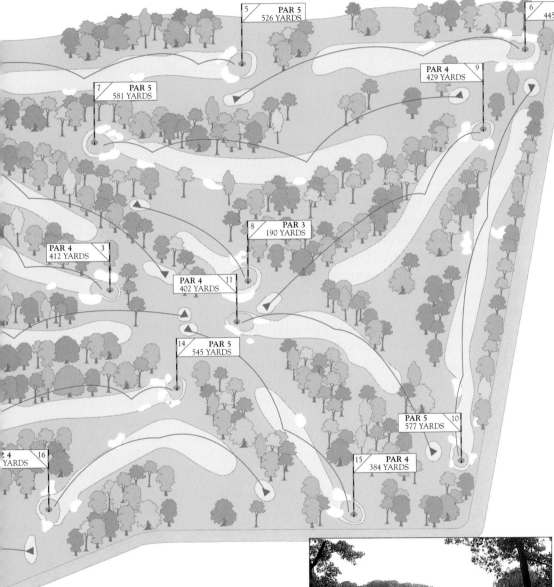

contrived to make the course even tougher. Two new holes were added to the course, another hole was lengthened, and the back nine holes were extensively re-routed. Fazio's par of 71 was raised to 72 again, and the redesigned course measured a formidable 7,195 yards, the longest ever test set for the US Open.

MEMORABLE OPEN

Before the 1990 championship began, the greens were honed until they were wickedly fast, like polished marble. But nobody could control the weather, and the greens became drenched by a thunderstorm that took much of the sting out of them. Hale Irwin carried off the title with a leading score of 280 after a thrilling contest. Irwin holed a massive 45ft (13.5m) putt on the last green – the ball ran for seven seconds before falling into the cup – to enter a play-off with Mike Donald. The following day, he sank a 6ft (1.8m) birdie putt at the 16th to tie again with Donald, and then holed an 8ft (2.4m) putt for a birdie on the first sudden-death hole to win. At 45, Irwin became the oldest winner in US Open history, and he was the first champion to have gone 91 holes for victory.

13 **Lovely but deadly**

The famous par-3 13th is another hole that crosses the long inlet from Lake Kadijah. The beauty of the landscape should not lure golfers into a false sense of security: the green is hard to hold and great accuracy is needed to negotiate the water and avoid the encircling bunkers.

MERION

MERION GOLF CLUB, ARDMORE, PHILADELPHIA, PENNSYLVANIA, USA

THE EAST COURSE at Merion was designed by Hugh Wilson, an expatriate Scot, despite the fact that he had never previously laid out a golf course. Wilson received his commission after revealing an unexpected grasp of the principles behind course design while acting as a member of his club committee researching championship courses.

Novel markers
The wicker baskets that are used to cap the pins at Merion are a unique feature of the course.

Bobby's success
A plaque at Merion's 11th tee commemorates Bobby Jones's victories in both the Amateur and Open Championships on both sides of the Atlantic in one year – known as the "Impregnable Quadrilateral". He then retired from competition golf.

Golf at Merion was originally run by the Merion Cricket Club, which had been founded in 1865, just after the end of the American Civil War. When golf took a hold in the United States in the late nineteenth century, the club members adopted the game with relish. They leased a nearby 100-acre (40ha) plot at Haverford, and here a nine-hole course was opened for play in 1896. In 1900 this was expanded to 18 holes on adjacent land loaned by Clement A. Griscomb.

The club hosted the US Women's Amateur Championship on the Haverford course in 1904, and again in 1909. But it was then decided that the course was too short to satisfy the growing demands of championship golf. The club acquired new land in Ardmore, a fashionable Philadelphia suburb, while Hugh Wilson and his committee set out to study classic courses. They visited The National Golf Links of America several times, and Wilson spent six months in Britain. When he returned from his fact-finding mission, he brought with him several unusual ideas for the new course at Merion. Among them was the use of wicker baskets instead of flags on the pins, which is now one of Merion's hallmarks. The baskets are supposed to have the advantage that, unlike flags, they do not reveal the wind direction.

The ground that the club had acquired for Wilson's new layout was hardly ideal. It was covered in trees and shrubs, and there was an old stone quarry, which

had been redundant for many years. But Wilson clearly had a natural gift and feel for golf-course architecture – no doubt a product of his Scottish background. He transformed the unlikely property into a magnificent course: a masterpiece of parkland golf that is now recognized as

one of America's finest courses. The East course was opened for play in 1912, and since then it has hosted no fewer than 13 USGA championships – more than any other course in the United States and a glowing tribute to its quality. Sadly, Wilson died at the age of 46, not long after completing the course.

UNUSUALLY SHORT

The restricted confines of the East course – a mere 110 acres (44ha) – are reflected in Wilson's design, which features tight greens, a total of 120 bunkers, and a par-70 length of 6,482 yards. This makes it one of the shortest courses on the USGA's championship rota. Set up at that length for the 1971 US Open, it was in fact the second-shortest course used for the event since the First World War.

But although the East course is of modest length, it does have two par 5s. These two holes, which alone account for a good percentage of the total course length, are in the first four holes.

White faces (right)
The bunkers at Merion were dubbed "the white faces" by Chick Evans – US Amateur Champion there in 1916. Jack Nicklaus is dwarfed by one on the 10th.

Water course (above)
The narrow streams that weave their way around Merion prove an unforgiving grave for any errant shot.

Hogan iron (below)
The USGA museum displays the 1-iron Ben Hogan used for his long second shot at the 18th during the 1950 Open at Merion.

The 2nd is a 536-yard hole, played uphill alongside Ardmore Avenue, which runs through the course and has to be crossed twice. The second par 5 is the 4th, which stretches a massive but somewhat unspectacular 600 yards. A stream relieves the otherwise plain aspect of the hole. It runs in front of the green and makes it almost impossible to reach in two strokes.

The bunkers and the small fast greens are the key to the Merion defences, and Wilson did a masterful job with both. Typical is the 8th hole which, although only 360 yards, is one of the toughest par 4s to be found anywhere. A large bunker down the right-hand side threatens the short hitter, while the longer hitter has to watch out for a dangerous bunker that eats into the fairway on the left.

HOGAN'S COMEBACK

Merion's East course was where Ben Hogan made the most incredible comeback in golfing history. He won the 1950 US Open just over a year after the terrible car crash that all but took his life. Hogan was still in great pain, and both his legs were bandaged throughout. As he started the final nine holes, he was gripped by terrible cramp in his left leg and almost had to retire. When he reached the 13th, close to the clubhouse, the pain was almost more than he could bear. Despite this he valiantly played on and fought his way into the play-off with Lloyd Mangrum and George Fazio. His second shot with a 1-iron at the last hole of the last round is still remembered, and the club is displayed in the USGA museum at Far Hills, New Jersey. Hogan won comfortably in the play-off the following day.

Another legendary player, Bobby Jones, led the field after the first round of his first US Amateur Championship at Merion in 1916, at the tender age of 14. But when Jones reached the short par-3 6th hole on the West course in the second round, he was faced with a 30ft (10m) downhill putt from behind the pin. He putted right off the green and into the stream in front of it. Shattered, he ended the round with a score of 89.

CHAMPIONSHIP LENGTHS		
OUT	3,420 YARDS	PAR 36
IN	3,062 YARDS	PAR 34
TOTAL	6,482 YARDS	PAR 70

COURSE RECORD
64 LEE MACKEY, US OPEN 1950

US OPEN CHAMPIONS AT MERION
1934 OLIN DUTRA; 1950 BEN HOGAN; 1971 LEE TREVINO; 1981 DAVID GRAHAM

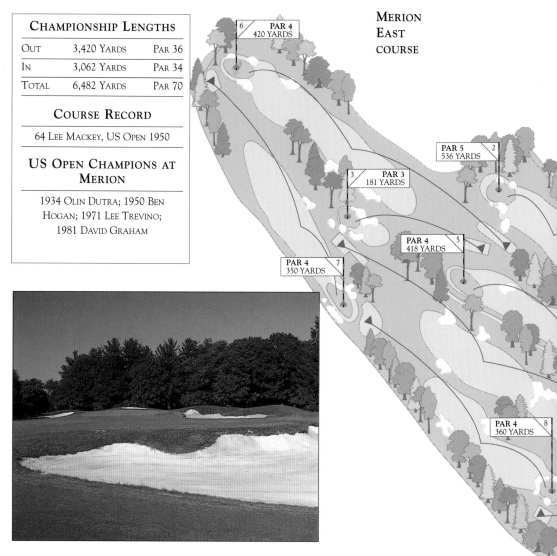

MERION
EAST
COURSE

Challenging opening (above)
The 362-yard 1st has a dogleg to the right and severe bunkering, which makes it one of the toughest holes on the course. The second shot, although short, must be extremely accurate to a green that has a wide option of pin placements.

Frustration point (right)
In the 1934 US Open, the unfortunate Bobby Cruickshank threw his niblick into the air after a poor shot had landed in the stream at the 11th. The club fell and struck him on the head, knocking him to the ground. Fortunately he was not seriously hurt.

Jones went back to Merion, however, to win the first of his five Amateur titles in 1924, and six years later, returning yet again, he won an historic victory over Eugene Homans by eight and seven in the final of the 1930 Amateur to complete his memorable Grand Slam.

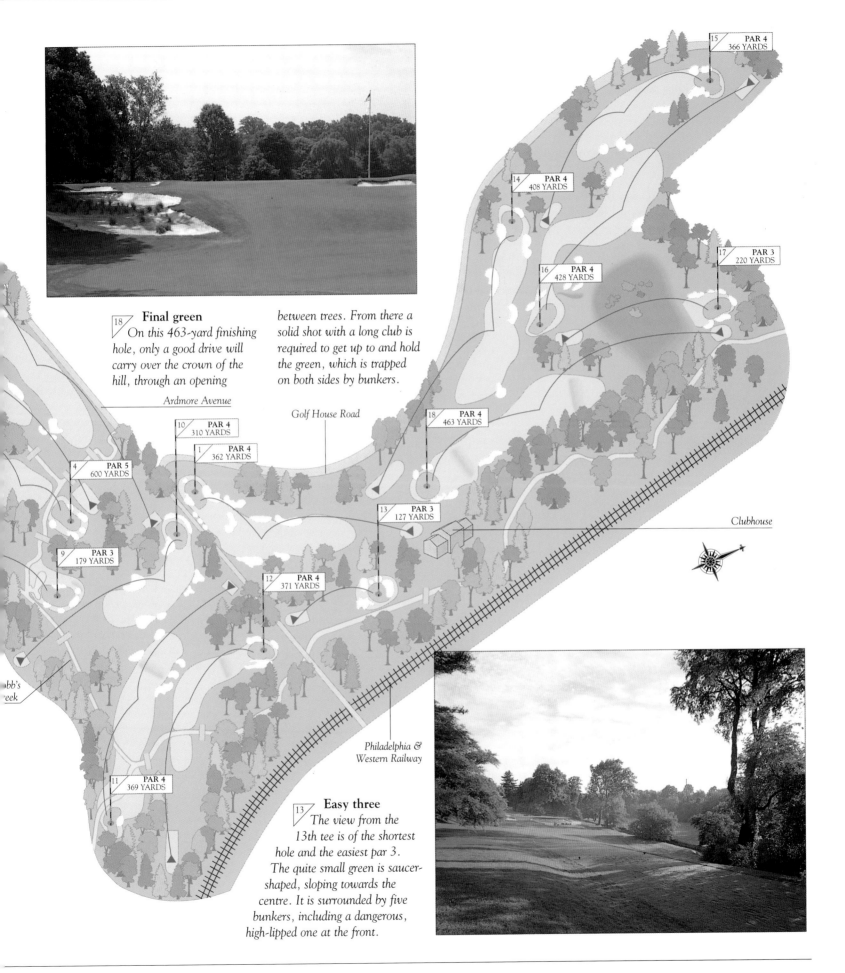

PAR 4
366 YARDS
15

PAR 4
408 YARDS
14

PAR 3
220 YARDS
17

PAR 4
428 YARDS
16

Final green
18
On this 463-yard finishing hole, only a good drive will carry over the crown of the hill, through an opening between trees. From there a solid shot with a long club is required to get up to and hold the green, which is trapped on both sides by bunkers.

Ardmore Avenue

Golf House Road

PAR 4
310 YARDS
10

PAR 4
362 YARDS
1

PAR 5
600 YARDS
4

PAR 4
463 YARDS
18

PAR 3
127 YARDS
13

Clubhouse

PAR 3
179 YARDS
9

PAR 4
371 YARDS
12

bb's eek

Philadelphia & Western Railway

PAR 4
369 YARDS
11

Easy three
13
The view from the 13th tee is of the shortest hole and the easiest par 3. The quite small green is saucer-shaped, sloping towards the centre. It is surrounded by five bunkers, including a dangerous, high-lipped one at the front.

MUIRFIELD

THE HONOURABLE COMPANY OF EDINBURGH GOLFERS, MUIRFIELD, GULLANE, EAST LOTHIAN, SCOTLAND

THERE ARE MANY *who believe that Muirfield is the fairest examination of golf among all Scotland's great championship courses. There are no hidden bunkers or subtle humps, no blind shots, few trees and no water hazards. Muirfield is a scrupulously honest but demanding test where the dangers are in open view for all to see.*

Pioneering golfer
To emphasize its long golfing traditions, the Honourable Company of Edinburgh Golfers depicted its 1771 club captain, William St Clair of Roslin, on the programme for the 1966 Open Championship at Muirfield.

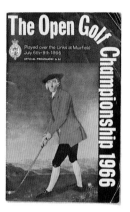

Golfing elite
This subscription receipt for the Honourable Company dates from 1895. Membership has always been exclusive.

The mighty Jack Nicklaus paid Muirfield the ultimate compliment by giving the name of Muirfield Village to his own course in Dublin, Ohio, out of respect for the course where he won his first Open Championship in 1966. He is not alone among the great players who consider Muirfield so exceptional.

The course was built in 1891, which is relatively recent by comparison with the antiquity of the club itself. The Honourable Company was formed in 1744 when "several Gentlemen of Honour skilful in the ancient and healthful exercise of Golf" petitioned the Edinburgh City Council to donate a silver club for their annual competition on Leith links.

EARLIEST RULES

There were then only five holes and the members had to share the ground with the local citizens and occasionally the military. The Company established the first rules of the game in the year of their formation – ten years before the Royal & Ancient Golf Club of St Andrews was founded.

In 1836, when the Leith links became too populated for the Company to continue to play there happily, it moved to Musselburgh, 6 miles (10km) eastwards along the coast, to share the course there with the Musselburgh Golf Club.

With the passage of time, Musselburgh in turn became too crowded, so the Honourable Company made another move east – this time to Gullane, where

Drum call
In early years, drummers announced the annual competition for the Silver Club, given by the City of Edinburgh to the Honourable Company of Edinburgh Golfers when it was founded in 1744. The first winner, John Rattray, was declared Captain of the Golf.

the present course, laid out by Old Tom Morris, was opened for play in 1891. The following year, on the new course, the Open Championship was played over 72 holes for the first time. It was won by the English amateur Harold Hilton.

There was some resentment that the Honourable Company had taken the Open Championship with it when moving from Musselburgh to Gullane, and the course was also criticized by some players as being too short and too easy.

Since those days, however, Muirfield has evolved into one of the world's outstanding courses. The present layout owes much to the changes made by Harry Colt, designer of the New course at Sunningdale, and Tom Simpson in the mid-1920s.

Unlike the great links of St Andrews and Carnoustie, Muirfield is in no way a public course. The home of the Honourable Company is a private place indeed, where the members play on uncrowded

Fired-up Faldo (right)
Nick Faldo celebrates his third Open Championship in 1992, and the second one clinched on Muirfield's fine natural setting. Back in the 1890s, however, Andrew Kirkaldy described the then new course as "an auld watermeadie".

Tricky traps (below)
Muirfield has more than 160 bunkers, many of them with walls of turf sod.

CHAMPIONSHIP LENGTHS

OUT	3,518 YARDS	PAR 36
IN	3,452 YARDS	PAR 35
TOTAL	6,970 YARDS	PAR 71

COURSE RECORD

64 RODGER DAVIS, THE OPEN 1987;
NICK FALDO, THE OPEN 1992;
STEVE PATE, THE OPEN 1992

OPEN CHAMPIONS AT MUIRFIELD

1892 HAROLD HILTON †; 1896 HARRY
VARDON; 1901 JAMES BRAID; 1906
JAMES BRAID; 1912 TED RAY; 1929
WALTER HAGEN; 1935 ALF PERRY;
1948 HENRY COTTON; 1959 GARY
PLAYER; 1966 JACK NICKLAUS;
1972 LEE TREVINO; 1980 TOM
WATSON; 1987, 1992 NICK FALDO

fairways and where the great traditions of the game are jealously guarded.

·Of many memorable Muirfield Opens, the 1972 confrontation between Lee Trevino and Tony Jacklin was most dramatic. The two men were level when Trevino's fourth shot at the par-5 17th ran through the green and into the short rough. With Jacklin well placed for a par or birdie, Trevino thought he had lost. But when he rather hurriedly chipped back on to the putting surface, the ball landed softly and ran into the hole. Clearly shaken, Jacklin three-putted and Trevino went on to take the title. American teams have been victors here too in the Ryder Cup (1973) and Walker Cup (1959, 1979).

17 Fearsome bunkers
The 550-yard 17th at Muirfield is one of three magnificent long holes. Guarded by a string of deep bunkers down the left side, it demands a precise drive. After the dogleg there is rough ground with four more bunkers. The green is surrounded by harsh rough.

MUIRFIELD
CHAMPIONSHIP
COURSE

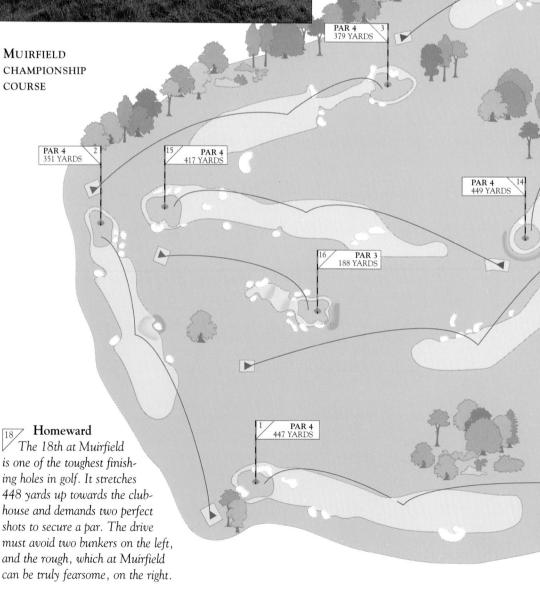

PAR 3 | 4
180 YARDS

PAR 4 | 3
379 YARDS

PAR 4 | 2
351 YARDS

15 | PAR 4
417 YARDS

PAR 4 | 14
449 YARDS

16 | PAR 3
188 YARDS

1 | PAR 4
447 YARDS

18 Homeward
The 18th at Muirfield is one of the toughest finishing holes in golf. It stretches 448 yards up towards the clubhouse and demands two perfect shots to secure a par. The drive must avoid two bunkers on the left, and the rough, which at Muirfield can be truly fearsome, on the right.

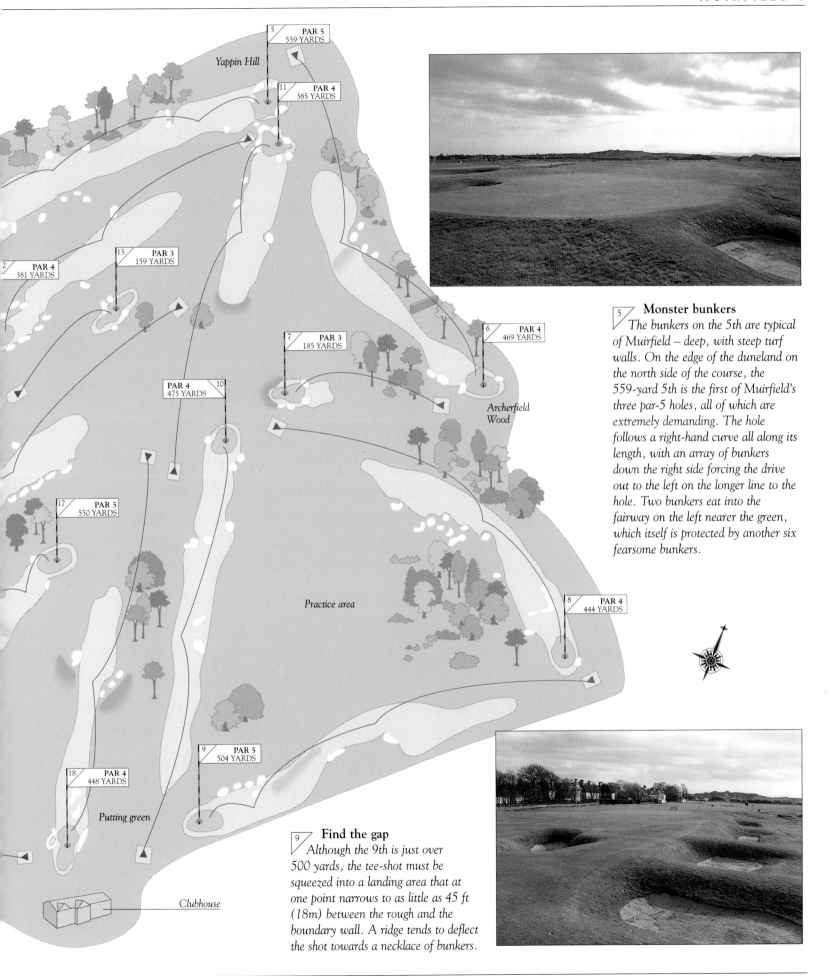

PAR 5
559 YARDS
5

Yappin Hill

PAR 4
385 YARDS
11

PAR 3
159 YARDS
13

PAR 4
381 YARDS
2

PAR 3
185 YARDS
7

PAR 4
475 YARDS
10

PAR 4
469 YARDS
6

Archerfield
Wood

PAR 5
550 YARDS
17

Practice area

PAR 4
444 YARDS
8

PAR 4
448 YARDS
18

PAR 5
504 YARDS
9

Putting green

Clubhouse

5 Monster bunkers

The bunkers on the 5th are typical of Muirfield – deep, with steep turf walls. On the edge of the duneland on the north side of the course, the 559-yard 5th is the first of Muirfield's three par-5 holes, all of which are extremely demanding. The hole follows a right-hand curve all along its length, with an array of bunkers down the right side forcing the drive out to the left on the longer line to the hole. Two bunkers eat into the fairway on the left nearer the green, which itself is protected by another six fearsome bunkers.

9 Find the gap

Although the 9th is just over 500 yards, the tee-shot must be squeezed into a landing area that at one point narrows to as little as 45 ft (18m) between the rough and the boundary wall. A ridge tends to deflect the shot towards a necklace of bunkers.

MUIRFIELD VILLAGE

MUIRFIELD VILLAGE GOLF CLUB, DUBLIN, COLUMBUS, OHIO, USA

W HEN JACK NICKLAUS, *the greatest player in the modern game, decided he wanted to build a course of his own, he called it Muirfield Village out of nostalgia for the Scottish links where he had won the first of his three Open Championships. But the seed for the idea was sown at that other shrine where he had stamped his mark in the course of his fabulous career – Augusta National.*

Trophy emblem
The crest of Muirfield Village encompasses a silhouette of the claret jug that serves as the British Open trophy.

It was at Augusta in 1966, while sitting on the verandah chatting to a friend, that Nicklaus first suggested the idea of building a course in his native town of Columbus, Ohio, to the same standard as the home of the US Masters. Nicklaus won the Masters that year and went on to triumph in the Open Championship at Muirfield three months later. The idea that he had first mooted on the verandah in Georgia was then given its name.

NO RESEMBLANCE
In fact, lest anyone should be under any misapprehension, the course that Jack Nicklaus built at Muirfield Village bears no resemblance whatsoever to the home of the Honourable Company of Edinburgh Golfers at Muirfield in Scotland. Nicklaus chose for his dream course a piece of richly rolling ground into which he built

The Tiger and the Bear (above)
The Memorial Tournament was so named because Jack Nicklaus wanted to honour an outstanding player each year for his contribution to the game. Nicklaus does just that with Tiger Woods in 2000.

a vast array of water hazards, in keeping with contemporary thinking in golf architecture. It could not be more different from the old links of Muirfield, where what water there is runs in the burns and even the Firth of Forth is mostly hidden from view by dunes.

Many people, including his former manager Mark McCormack, thought Nicklaus was foolish to take his concept to Columbus. McCormack said it would be like "standing on the street corner and burning $100 bills" and urged him to rethink the whole affair. But Jack knew exactly what he wanted. He ignored the warnings and eventually overcame the many difficulties that confronted him, including obtaining the finance.

When Nicklaus had raised the capital to go ahead, he brought in Desmond Muirhead to assist with the routing and infrastructure, and set about building a course that would test the best players in the world, and yet be "playable" for lesser mortals. It is often believed that Pete Dye had a major hand in the design but in fact his contribution was confined to some friendly and informal discussions with Nicklaus.

Another important consideration was to provide an element that previously had

Greenkeeper's pride
From the 16th tee, the course looks typically verdant and well kept.

Jack of all trades (left)
Putter in hand, Nicklaus ponders the borrow on a green. Muirfield Village greens are famous for their speed and their superb condition.

Siege mentality (right)
A pre-sartorial Payne Stewart chips onto the heavily guarded 12th green during the 1987 Ryder Cup. If the water that dissects the hole doesn't entrap the unwary player, the massive bunkers may.

played little part in the thinking of course designers – vantage points for spectators. Muirfield Village was to be in the vanguard of the so-called "stadium" style of golf course, which is designed almost as much for viewing the game as for playing it.

Nicklaus has gone to immense lengths to produce a truly outstanding course. Over the years Muirfield Village has undergone more than 100 changes, some major and some a matter of detail. Money has been no object for "The Course that Jack Built".

The prestigious Memorial Tournament, Muirfield Village's annual US Tour event, was first played there in 1976, when it was won by Roger Maltbie in a play-off. For that opening event the course measured 7,027 yards and it was lengthened to 7,101 for the next three years. Since then it has been consistently over 7,100 yards, making it one of the toughest tests on the Tour.

DOWNHILL DRIVE

It was the late Sir Henry Cotton who once said that there was no more satisfying thing in golf than to stand on an elevated tee with a driver, surveying the fairway stretching below and into the distance. Nicklaus is clearly also a subscriber to this view. On the first five holes of the Muirfield Village course the drive is from an elevated

Splashing out
When Nicklaus played the long par-5 11th in its original design, it had a lake in front of the green. Jack did not like the fact that the lake was invisible from the drive landing area so he ordered a small stream to be sited in its place. Among the more expensive changes to the course, this improvement alone cost close to $250,000.

MUIRFIELD
VILLAGE
GOLF CLUB
MEMORIAL COURSE

| 12 | PAR 3 156 YARDS |
| 11 | PAR 5 538 YARDS |
| Stream |
13	PAR 4 442 YARDS
10	PAR 4 441 YARDS
14	PAR 4 363 YARDS
15	PAR 5 490 YARDS
16	PAR 3 204 YARDS
17	PAR 4 430 YARDS
9	PAR 4 410 YARDS
18	PAR 4 437 YARDS

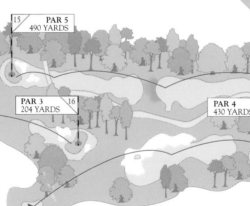

Water hole
There are shades of that most magnificent of Augusta holes, the 16th, in Nicklaus's 12th hole at Muirfield Village. There is water to be carried all the way to a green that has been built into a beautiful setting in the side of a hill and is guarded both front and back by bunkers.

CHAMPIONSHIP LENGTHS		
OUT	3,603 YARDS	PAR 36
IN	3,501 YARDS	PAR 36
TOTAL	7,104 YARDS	PAR 72

COURSE RECORD
63 KENNY PERRY

RYDER CUP WINNERS
1987 EUROPE

SOLHEIM CUP WINNERS
1998 USA

Clubhouse

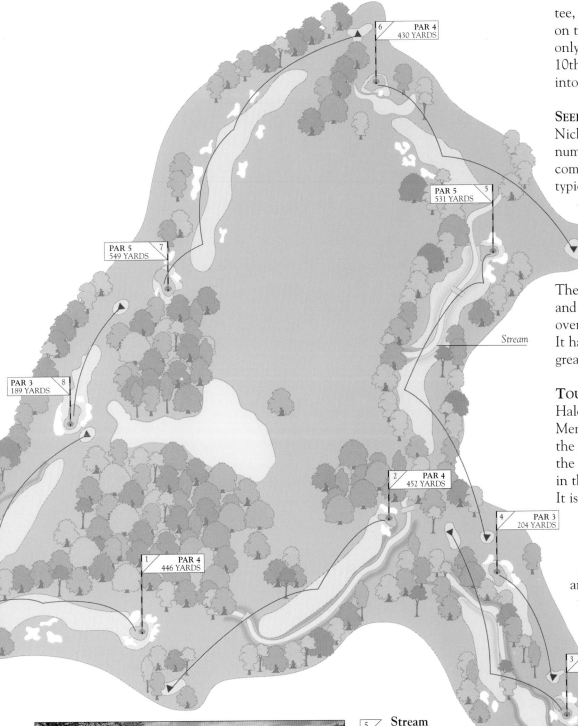

tee, and there are several more examples on the way round the course. There are only two tee-shots played uphill, at the 10th and at the 15th where the drive is into the summit of a hill.

SEEKING DRY LAND

Nicklaus has confined himself to a modest number of bunkers – 70 in all – but water comes into play on 11 of the holes. A typical example is at the 3rd, where the drive is over a stream that crosses the fairway. The stream then runs down the entire left side of the fairway to open out into a lake immediately in front of the green. The hole is just short of 400 yards long and the second shot to a two-tier green over the water is extremely demanding. It has caused many problems both to the great players and to more humble golfers.

TOUGH GREENS

Hale Irwin, a two-time winner of the Memorial Tournament, once described the greens at Muirfield Village as "some of the most beautiful and well-conditioned in the world – and some of the toughest." It is hardly surprising that Nicklaus, renowned as one of the game's greatest putters, should excel at green design. Much thought has gone into the siting of the teeing areas, in line with Nicklaus's intention to create a course suitable for those of modest ability as well as for pros. There are at least three separate tees at each hole, some of them as much as 50 yards apart. This has almost the effect of creating three separate courses, with different problems set in each one. Few golfers will have the confidence to tackle the course from the back tees, as it is certainly not a circuit for the faint of heart. Yet from the members' tees there is charm and challenge for the most modest players. With an apparently limitless budget lavished on maintenance, there are few courses in the world better to look at for spectators and players alike.

5 Stream in the centre

The 5th hole is the first of four par 5s. It is a dogleg to the right with water very much in play on the second half of the hole. A stream runs up the centre of the fairway threatening the second shot, before running away close to the front left of the green. Two bunkers menace the right of the green, as does one at the back.

THE NATIONAL

THE NATIONAL GOLF CLUB, WOODBRIDGE, ONTARIO, CANADA

G IL BLECHMAN'S DISILLUSIONMENT *with the atmosphere of country club life in the suburbs of Toronto drove this soft-spoken American car-parts manufacturer, living in Canada, to form what he described as "a real golf club" in 1972. Tom Fazio was employed to realize the Blechman dream in Ontario, and today The National Golf Club is the top-rated course in Canada.*

Leaf logo
The crest of The National is a simple contemporary design showing the leaf of the red maple, a tree that has been an emblem of Canada since the nineteenth century.

Blechman's concept of the new course was clear and stunningly ambitious: "What I wanted was a course you could play the US Open on at a week's notice without gimmicking it up," he said.

When Blechman called designer Tom Fazio to give him the contract, his instructions were simple. He told the designer he wanted the best golf course in the world, the project was to start immediately, and money was no object. Fazio's first reaction was to dismiss it as a crank call. But in the space of a few months the Blechman dream was well on its way to becoming a reality.

THE RIGHT PLACE
The site chosen for The National was a previously existing course called Pine Valley. It bore little resemblance to its splendid namesake in New Jersey, where Fazio's uncle George, a former Canadian Open winner, had played for many years. In fact, The National might never have

been built there, had Fazio not discovered some additional ground bordering the course. He argued that the existing course was not worth spending a lot of money on, but that with the additional ground the site offered real possibilities. This extra land now forms a five-hole section of the course beginning at the 11th, which is acknowledged as the most difficult, and yet scenically spectacular, stretch of golf course in the country.

Blechman's golf course was built in 1973, the year after Blechman had formed The National Golf Club. It was officially opened for play by its founder and owner in 1975. The actual construction of the course was completed in little over three months, however. The building schedule

Fall glory (above)
In autumn, the many deciduous trees colour the course a flaming red and gold. Winters can be tough in Canada and the course is closed for five months each year.

Wild water (right)
The view across the lake to the 18th green is typical of The National in its scenic splendour. The course abounds with wildlife; the water hazards are home to swans and geese.

New land, new holes
Five of the holes on the course, including the 11th shown here, were built on extra land acquired by Blechman alongside the original Pine Valley golf course. Designer Tom Fazio considered this area essential to his plans for constructing the finest course in Canada.

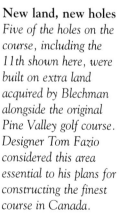

Talented family
Tom Fazio (left), the architect of the course, is the nephew of the talented George Fazio (right), a winner of the Canadian Open. George, a prolific course designer, was a valued source of advice to his nephew during the building of The National.

coincided with an early spring and 80 consecutive days of sunshine, a rare occurrence in such northern latitudes. The National very much reflects the Blechman idea of a golf club. His antipathy to the stereotypic atmosphere of suburban country club golf is easily felt; the emphasis is firmly on the game of golf rather than other diversions.

PLAYING THE NATIONAL

There are 72 bunkers on the course and water is a hazard on nine of the holes. Some of the holes can be fearsomely difficult and even Fazio admits that the course is not meant to be played from the back tees on every hole.

The front nine is long and severely guarded by bunkers. Water comes into play on four of the holes and because this half of the course is situated on the high ground, play is liable to be affected by the wind. There is great variety in these nine holes, with many changes in direction. The back nine is in a river valley more than 100ft (30m) below the front nine. The holes are shorter and tighter, winding through a mass of pines.

Viewing areas for an estimated 50,000 spectators have been provided in the design, using the natural hillsides. After the official opening of The National, its quality was immediately recognized. The club's first director of golf, Al Balding, undertook an interesting exercise when an informal tournament for Toronto's top

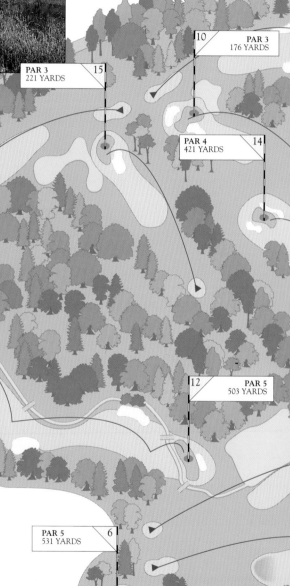

Dodge the bunkers
16 *Large bunkers distract the eye at the par-4 16th, but long hitters have a decided advantage from the tee. The second shot has to hold the green or it will finish in the back bunkers.*

THE NATIONAL
CHAMPIONSHIP
COURSE

PAR 3
176 YARDS
10

PAR 3
221 YARDS
15

PAR 4
421 YARDS
14

PAR 4
406 YARDS
11

Dead Man's Creek

PAR 5
503 YARDS
12

PAR 5
531 YARDS
6

Testing time
12 *Although not a long par 5, the 12th can be tricky. It is a narrow, snaking dogleg left, with drives hit too close to the left threatened by the stream. Drives right are menaced by a bunker. The second shot has to avoid a large bunker on the left and the approach should clear the stream that comes round in front of the green.*

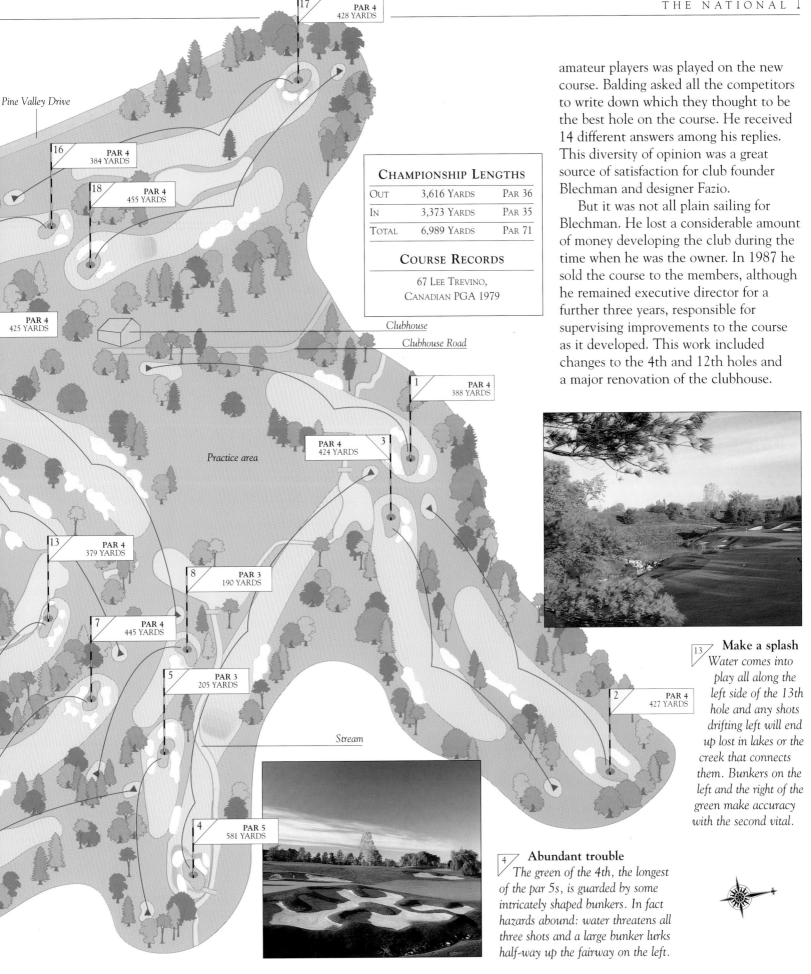

Pine Valley Drive

17 PAR 4 428 YARDS

16 PAR 4 384 YARDS

18 PAR 4 455 YARDS

PAR 4 425 YARDS

Clubhouse

Clubhouse Road

Practice area

1 PAR 4 388 YARDS

3 PAR 4 424 YARDS

13 PAR 4 379 YARDS

8 PAR 3 190 YARDS

7 PAR 4 445 YARDS

5 PAR 3 205 YARDS

2 PAR 4 427 YARDS

Stream

4 PAR 5 581 YARDS

CHAMPIONSHIP LENGTHS

OUT	3,616 YARDS	PAR 36
IN	3,373 YARDS	PAR 35
TOTAL	6,989 YARDS	PAR 71

COURSE RECORDS

67 LEE TREVINO,
CANADIAN PGA 1979

amateur players was played on the new course. Balding asked all the competitors to write down which they thought to be the best hole on the course. He received 14 different answers among his replies. This diversity of opinion was a great source of satisfaction for club founder Blechman and designer Fazio.

But it was not all plain sailing for Blechman. He lost a considerable amount of money developing the club during the time when he was the owner. In 1987 he sold the course to the members, although he remained executive director for a further three years, responsible for supervising improvements to the course as it developed. This work included changes to the 4th and 12th holes and a major renovation of the clubhouse.

13 Make a splash
Water comes into play all along the left side of the 13th hole and any shots drifting left will end up lost in lakes or the creek that connects them. Bunkers on the left and the right of the green make accuracy with the second vital.

4 Abundant trouble
The green of the 4th, the longest of the par 5s, is guarded by some intricately shaped bunkers. In fact hazards abound: water threatens all three shots and a large bunker lurks half-way up the fairway on the left.

OAKLAND HILLS

OAKLAND HILLS COUNTRY CLUB, BIRMINGHAM, MICHIGAN, USA

FOR THE 1951 US Open, the USGA called in the eminent American golf-course architect Robert Trent Jones to make changes to the Oakland Hills course outside Detroit. This famous course had hosted the championship twice before – in 1924 and 1937 – but it was felt that some modernization was needed to bring it into line with the developing game. Even the greatest players of the day were hardly prepared for Trent Jones's "alterations".

Oakland Hills was already a very fine course before Trent Jones started work on it. No less a personage than Donald Ross, the great pioneering course architect, had laid out the original course in 1917 on a perfect site which, he claimed, "the Lord had intended" for a golf course.

TEST FOR THE BEST
When Trent Jones presented the course for the 1951 US Open, eyebrows were raised. The fairways were narrower, the rough was punishing, and there were well in excess of 100 bunkers, most of them deep and dangerous, to threaten fairway landing areas and greens alike.

The Jones strategy was to force the players to hit clearly defined but well-defended landing areas from the tee.

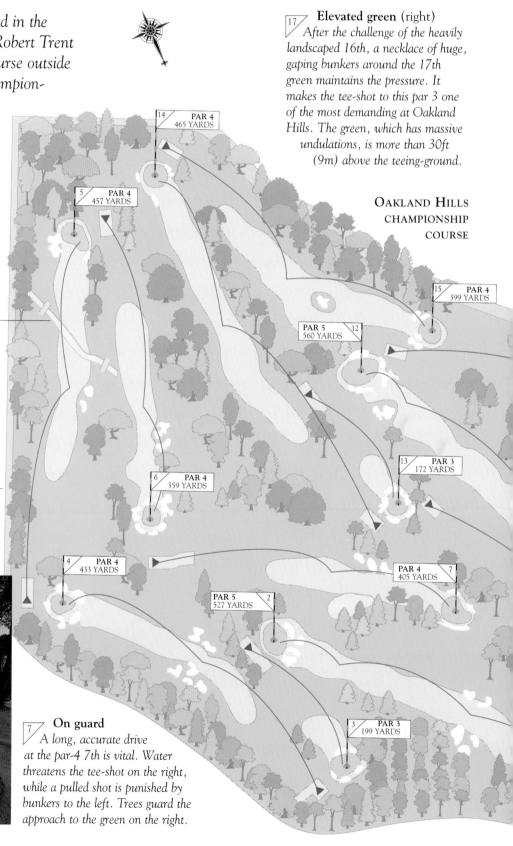

17 **Elevated green** (right)
After the challenge of the heavily landscaped 16th, a necklace of huge, gaping bunkers around the 17th green maintains the pressure. It makes the tee-shot to this par 3 one of the most demanding at Oakland Hills. The green, which has massive undulations, is more than 30ft (9m) above the teeing-ground.

OAKLAND HILLS CHAMPIONSHIP COURSE

14 **PAR 4** 465 YARDS

5 **PAR 4** 457 YARDS

15 **PAR 4** 399 YARDS

Stream

PAR 5 560 YARDS **12**

Lahser Road

6 **PAR 4** 359 YARDS

13 **PAR 3** 172 YARDS

4 **PAR 4** 433 YARDS

PAR 5 527 YARDS **2**

PAR 4 405 YARDS **7**

3 **PAR 3** 199 YARDS

7 **On guard**
A long, accurate drive at the par-4 7th is vital. Water threatens the tee-shot on the right, while a pulled shot is punished by bunkers to the left. Trees guard the approach to the green on the right.

CHAMPIONSHIP LENGTHS

OUT	3,472 YARDS	PAR 35
IN	3,524 YARDS	PAR 35
TOTAL	6,996 YARDS	PAR 70

COURSE RECORD

65 GEORGE ARCHER 1964; ALAN TAPIE, DAVID GRAHAM 1979; T. CHEN, A. NORTH, D. WATSON 1985; JACK NICKLAUS 1991

US OPEN CHAMPIONS AT OAKLAND HILLS

1924 CYRIL WALKER; 1937 RALPH GULDAHL; 1951 BEN HOGAN; 1961 GENE LITTLER; 1985 ANDY NORTH; 1996 STEVE JONES

USPGA CHAMPIONS

1972 GARY PLAYER; 1979 DAVID GRAHAM

US SENIOR OPEN CHAMPIONS

1981 ARNOLD PALMER; 1991 JACK NICKLAUS

Disaster awaited any loose approach shots to the green, in the form of deep bunkers with overhanging faces.

Ben Hogan was the defending Open Champion at Oakland Hills in 1951, and his opening round of 76 proved the severity of the test set by Trent Jones and the USGA. A second round of 73 took him to within five strokes of the leader, Bobby Locke, and he went into the final round only two strokes behind Locke and Jimmy Demaret, who were joint-leaders.

SLAYING THE MONSTER

It was then that Ben Hogan produced one of the greatest rounds in the history of championship golf. Playing conservatively from the tee to avoid trouble, Hogan put together a magnificent round of 67 to win comfortably from Clayton Heafner. The expression "monster" was first applied to a golf course by Hogan after that victory, when he said: "I am glad that I brought this course, this monster, to its knees."

Miracle stroke *Trees add to the menace of the pond on the right at the 16th. In the 1972 USPGA, Gary Player cut his drive behind them, but made an impossible shot over trees and lake to the green for a birdie.*

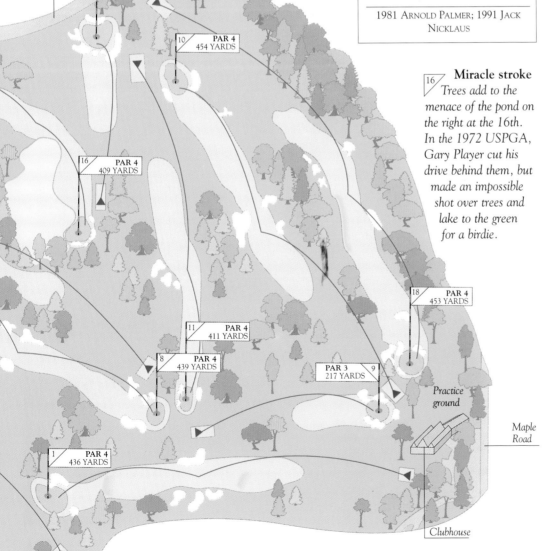

Oakland Hills has mellowed since that memorable Open, but it remains a tough challenge. The last five holes are the peak of the test. From the 14th, the longest par-4 on the course, through to the dogleg 18th with its fiendish, narrow approach to a hump-backed green, there is unrelenting pressure on the player's nerve and skill. Trent Jones said of his own course: "The player with the best shots, swing and nerve control has the best chance to win."

Since 1951, Oakland Hills has staged the US Open three times, the USPGA Championship twice, and two US Senior Opens, in 1981 and in 1991.

OAKMONT

OAKMONT COUNTRY CLUB, OAKMONT, PENNSYLVANIA, USA

T HE MEMORABLE ROUND *that gave Johnny Miller victory in the US Open at Oakmont in 1973 is one of the leading candidates for the coveted title of "best round ever played". Miller's record-breaking final 63, on rain-soaked greens, would have been remarkable anywhere. But it almost defies belief that he should have achieved it at Oakmont, on a course that has humiliated some of the greatest players. Oakmont is widely considered one of the most difficult rounds of 18 holes ever designed.*

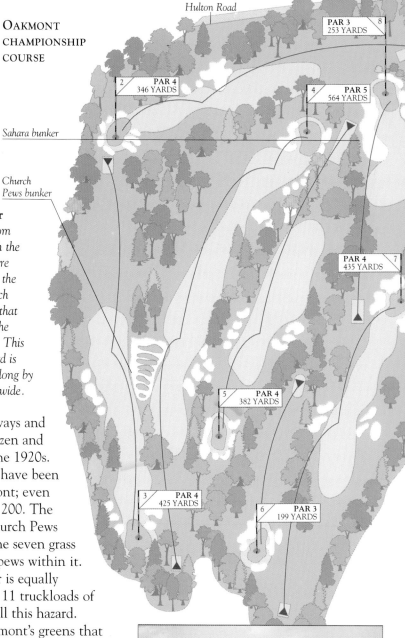

OAKMONT CHAMPIONSHIP COURSE

Hulton Road

Sahara bunker

Church Pews bunker

PAR 3 253 YARDS — 8

2 — PAR 4 346 YARDS

4 — PAR 5 564 YARDS

PAR 4 435 YARDS — 7

5 — PAR 4 382 YARDS

3 — PAR 4 425 YARDS

6 — PAR 3 199 YARDS

Railu

Not a prayer
The drives from the tee at both the 3rd and 4th are dominated by the famous Church Pews bunker that lies between the two fairways. This massive hazard is 180ft (55m) long by 120ft (36m) wide.

The Oakmont Country Club layout was the brainchild of the club's first president, the industrialist Henry C. Fownes, who designed and built the course in 1903–04. The Fownes philosophy of golf-course design was brutally simple: he wanted the toughest golf course it was possible to have. And he went ahead and built it.

BUILDING OAKMONT

In the autumn of 1903, using 150 men and 25 mule teams, Fownes had the first 12 holes completed in six weeks. They stopped work for the winter, but when spring returned so did Fownes's assault force, and the remaining six holes were ready for play by the following autumn.

Oakmont was constructed just as the rubber-core ball was replacing the old gutta ball, but the course was able to make the transition virtually intact because it was so long and difficult. Par has been reduced to compensate for improvements in technology, but golfers today still play

on the same tees, fairways and greens that Gene Sarazen and Bobby Jones used in the 1920s.

Initially there may have been 350 bunkers at Oakmont; even today there are nearly 200. The most famous is the Church Pews bunker, named after the seven grass ridges set like church pews within it. But the Sahara bunker is equally intimidating. It is said 11 truckloads of sand were needed to fill this hazard.

However, it is Oakmont's greens that do most to make this magnificent course such a great challenge. They are said to be the fastest and most difficult in the United States. Jimmy Thomson claimed that, during the 1935 US Open, he marked his ball with a dime at the 5th, but the green was so fast that when he went back to putt, "the dime had slid off!"

In 1987 Oakmont was designated a National Historic Landmark, the only US golf course to have this distinction.

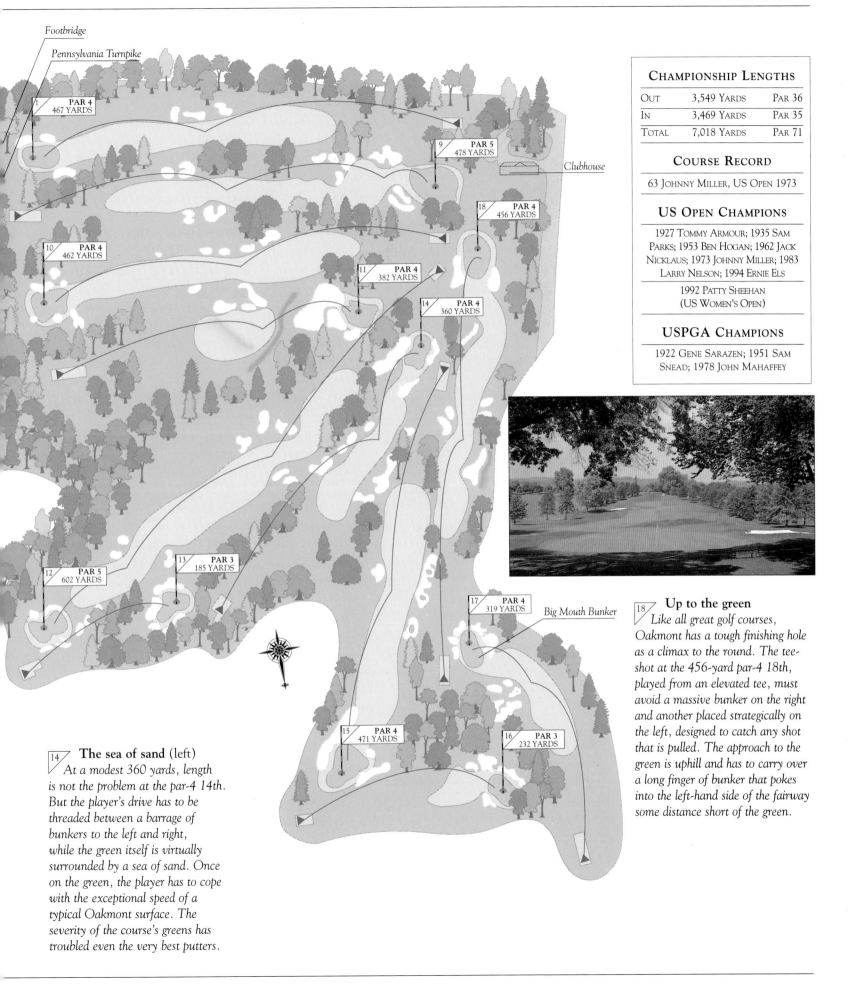

Footbridge

Pennsylvania Turnpike

Clubhouse

Big Mouth Bunker

1 PAR 4 467 YARDS

9 PAR 5 478 YARDS

18 PAR 4 456 YARDS

10 PAR 4 462 YARDS

11 PAR 4 382 YARDS

14 PAR 4 360 YARDS

12 PAR 5 602 YARDS

13 PAR 3 185 YARDS

17 PAR 4 319 YARDS

15 PAR 4 471 YARDS

16 PAR 3 232 YARDS

CHAMPIONSHIP LENGTHS

OUT	3,549 YARDS	PAR 36
IN	3,469 YARDS	PAR 35
TOTAL	7,018 YARDS	PAR 71

COURSE RECORD

63 JOHNNY MILLER, US OPEN 1973

US OPEN CHAMPIONS

1927 TOMMY ARMOUR; 1935 SAM PARKS; 1953 BEN HOGAN; 1962 JACK NICKLAUS; 1973 JOHNNY MILLER; 1983 LARRY NELSON; 1994 ERNIE ELS

1992 PATTY SHEEHAN (US WOMEN'S OPEN)

USPGA CHAMPIONS

1922 GENE SARAZEN; 1951 SAM SNEAD; 1978 JOHN MAHAFFEY

14 The sea of sand (left)
At a modest 360 yards, length is not the problem at the par-4 14th. But the player's drive has to be threaded between a barrage of bunkers to the left and right, while the green itself is virtually surrounded by a sea of sand. Once on the green, the player has to cope with the exceptional speed of a typical Oakmont surface. The severity of the course's greens has troubled even the very best putters.

18 Up to the green
Like all great golf courses, Oakmont has a tough finishing hole as a climax to the round. The tee-shot at the 456-yard par-4 18th, played from an elevated tee, must avoid a massive bunker on the right and another placed strategically on the left, designed to catch any shot that is pulled. The approach to the green is uphill and has to carry over a long finger of bunker that pokes into the left-hand side of the fairway some distance short of the green.

OARAI

OARAI GOLF CLUB, OARAI CITY, IBARAGI, JAPAN

IN A COUNTRY *with such a scarcity of land on which to build golf courses the opportunity to construct a seaside links golf course, dotted among the sand dunes on the Pacific Coast some 75 miles (120 kilometres) from Tokyo, was a dream come true for Japanese designer Seiichi Inoue. Oarai was Inoue's eighth golf course and it opened in 1953. It still remains Japan's most outstanding and demanding seaside golf course.*

OARAI
CHAMPIONSHIP
COURSE

Seiichi Inoue built the course amid an abundant forest of black pines as the natural shield against the winds that howl in from the ocean in this exposed part of the country's coastline. He avoided moving land or creating man-made obstacles to detract from the natural flow of the landscape. He wanted to emulate as far as possible the natural characteristics of the traditional links of Scotland.

EMULATING SCOTTISH LINKS
He accomplished this by retaining deep rough just off the fairways and by creating a layout where the lies are sandy and unpredictable on delicately undulating fairways. There is no shortage of space on this links, and only 30 bunkers in total, including three cross bunkers which reflect the designer's desire to keep the layout as simple as possible and to avoid that which is artificial. Pine roots protrude here and there through the sandy surface to add a little more spice and an unusual hazard to a layout that calls for considerable power when played as a tournament course.

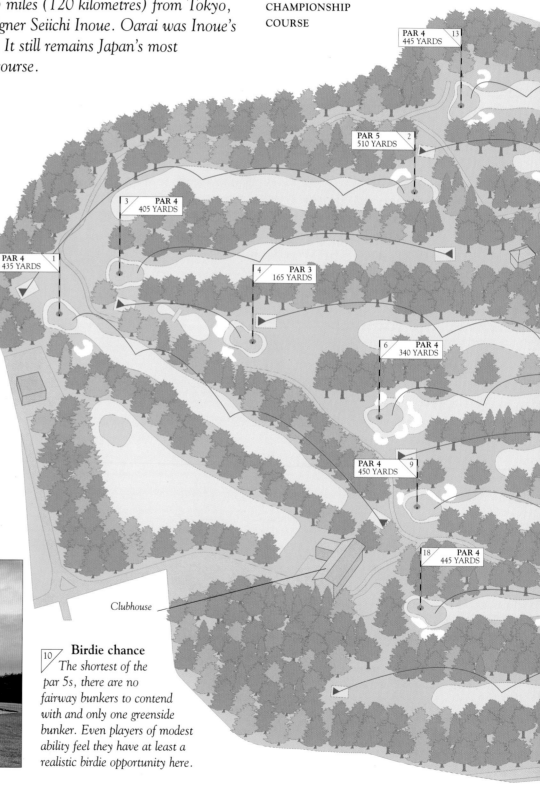

PAR 4
445 YARDS — 13

PAR 5
510 YARDS — 2

3 — PAR 4
405 YARDS

PAR 4
435 YARDS — 1

4 — PAR 3
165 YARDS

6 — PAR 4
340 YARDS

PAR 4
450 YARDS — 9

18 — PAR 4
445 YARDS

Clubhouse

10 **Birdie chance**
The shortest of the par 5s, there are no fairway bunkers to contend with and only one greenside bunker. Even players of modest ability feel they have at least a realistic birdie opportunity here.

4 **Searching test**
At 165 yards, the par-3 4th at Oarai might be the shortest hole on the course, but it presents a searching challenge. Accuracy rather than power is the key on a hole which features two severe bunkers guarding a long, rather narrow green.

PAR 3
ARDS

PAR 4
385 YARDS | 12

5 | PAR 4
460 YARDS

PAR 5
545 YARDS | 15

11 | PAR 4
405 YARDS

PAR 5
590 YARDS | 7

PAR 3
215 YARDS | 8

16 | PAR 3
245 YARDS

17 | PAR 4
460 YARDS

PAR 5
500 YARDS | 10

Oarai has been host to many major events on the Japanese golf calendar including the Japan Open in 1998, the Japan Amateur Championship twice and no fewer than five Mitsubishi tournaments.

TOUGH JAPANESE LINKS
Delicacy and precision have to be carefully added to power and distance and very few low-scoring rounds are returned here. Of its total of ten par 4 holes, only two are shorter than 400 yards from the back tees and the course rating of 74.4 marks it out as one of the toughest golf courses in the country. Of the four par 5 holes the 7th is certainly the most formidable although it is rated only third in the handicap ranking. From the back tees this monster stretches only a few yards short of 600. The last three holes are among the toughest on the course.

CHAMPIONSHIP LENGTHS		
OUT	3,570 YARDS	PAR 36
IN	3,620 YARDS	PAR 36
TOTAL	7,190 YARDS	PAR 72

COURSE RECORD		
66 TAKAHIRO NAKAGAWA 1985		

13 **Narrow approach**
The dogleg 13th is a demanding par 4 where the drive must reach the corner of the dogleg to leave a realistic chance of then reaching the green. Two dangerous bunkers guard the narrow approach to the green.

PEBBLE BEACH

PEBBLE BEACH GOLF LINKS, PEBBLE BEACH, CALIFORNIA, USA

I T WAS AT *Pebble Beach Golf Links in June 2000 that Tiger Woods rewrote US Open history books* with an astonishing 15-stroke victory, setting scoring records that few could even believe. The Woods victory did much to further enhance the reputation of this spectacular course with its cliff-top setting on the Monterey Peninsula.

CHAMPIONSHIP LENGTHS		
OUT	3,277 YARDS	PAR 36
IN	3,551 YARDS	PAR 36
TOTAL	6,828 YARDS	PAR 72

COURSE RECORD

62 TOM KITE 1983

US OPEN CHAMPIONS

1972 JACK NICKLAUS;
1982 TOM WATSON; 1992 TOM KITE;
2000 TIGER WOODS

USPGA CHAMPIONS

1977 LANNY WADKINS

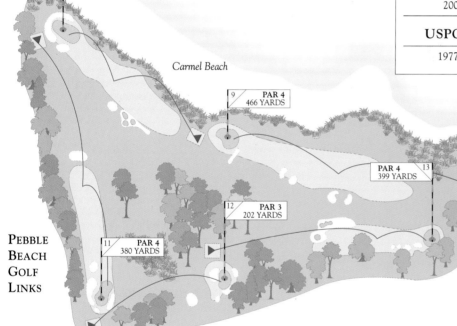

Carmel Beach

PEBBLE
BEACH
GOLF
LINKS

Pebble Beach is the only public golf course in the United States to have hosted multiple US Opens. Tiger Woods was the fourth champion to be crowned there. Prior to that it was the scene of a great climax to the 1982 US Open, when Jack Nicklaus was looking for his fifth US Open title and Tom Watson was seeking his elusive first. The course has also hosted one other of the game's "majors", the 1977 USPGA Championship, won by Lanny Wadkins.

In all of championship golf, there are few prospects more daunting than needing to make par on the last two holes at

Uphill work
The 6th hole, the second of Pebble Beach's par 5s, starts out in a copse of trees and finishes in spectacular style on the cliffs above Stillwater Cove. The second shot, threatened by the ocean, has to be played uphill towards the green.

Pebble Beach – which is what Watson needed for a play-off – let alone playing them under par to win. But Watson memorably birdied both holes to beat Nicklaus by two strokes.

This was only the second time the US Open had been played at Pebble Beach, widely regarded as the finest "ocean" course on the American continent. The USGA had been reluctant to take the US Open to Pebble Beach mainly because it seemed far from a major city – it lies some 120 miles (190km) south of San Francisco. However, the course was selected to host the 1992 US Open, as

well as the 100th playing of the US Open in 2000, which confirmed its prestige.

Opened for play in 1919, Pebble Beach was brought into being through the vision of Samuel F.B. Morse, grand-nephew of the inventor of Morse code, who bought the area from the Pacific Improvement Company. To build the course, Morse recruited Jack Neville, a man who was not a golf-course architect but a real-estate salesman. What emerged was a spectacular layout, that also annually hosts the National Pro-Am, sponsored by AT & T, but better known as "The Crosby" which is televised to a huge audience.

Monterey Bay

18	PAR 5 / 543 YARDS
17	PAR 3 / 208 YARDS
3	PAR 4 / 390 YARDS
	PAR 4 / 331 YARDS
16	PAR 4 / 403 YARDS
1	PAR 4 / 381 YARDS
2	PAR 5 / 484 YARDS
15	PAR 4 / 397 YARDS

llwater Cove

Pier

The Lodge

Palmero Road

18 **Test of nerves**
The final hole at Pebble Beach is one of the great finishing holes in golf. It curves left all the way, following the line of the cliffs. The tee-shot is played across the corner of the cliffs – how much of the dogleg is cut depends on the player's bravery.

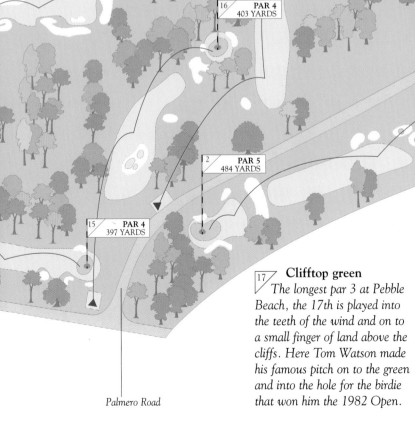

17 **Clifftop green**
The longest par 3 at Pebble Beach, the 17th is played into the teeth of the wind and on to a small finger of land above the cliffs. Here Tom Watson made his famous pitch on to the green and into the hole for the birdie that won him the 1982 Open.

PEVERO

PEVERO GOLF CLUB, PORTO CERVO, COSTA SMERALDA, SARDINIA, ITALY

R OBERT TRENT JONES, *a man not known for a feeble sense of the dramatic, was commissioned by the Aga Khan to build a golf course in that marvellous playground of the well-heeled, the Costa Smeralda in north-eastern Sardinia. What Trent Jones produced in this natural, craggy paradise, with its temperate climate, was one of the most beautiful and spectacular courses in Europe. It is almost infinitely challenging and, from the back tees, well-nigh impossible for all but the finest players.*

Careful aim
The drive from the 4th tee down into the valley is memorable; the view across Pevero Bay and the challenge of the hole are both superb. Bunkers guard the approach and accuracy is of prime importance.

Whatever the standard of the golfer, and no matter which tees are played from, there is great, pleasurable golf on the Pevero course, with its panoramic views and stunning, untamed beauty.

The course rises and plunges in great waves of scrub through alleys of jagged rock, some of which had to be blasted away to let Trent Jones realize his design. Despite this, the course is not artificial in any sense. Trent Jones admitted openly to great affection for Pevero, rating it among the best work he had ever done.

LOST IN THE ROUGH

It is just as well that the design built generous width into the fairways, for the rough is punishing to play from even if the ball can be found. A firm rein on ambition and a little restraint are the qualities best suited to this marvellous layout.

The course nestles in a valley between two spectacular bays: Pevero Bay is on one side and the glorious sandy beach of Cala di Volpe (Bay of Foxes) on the other. The course rises through hills resplendent with dwarf pine, broom and gorse, where, in spring, wild flowers and shrubs splash riotous colour across the landscape.

Lush fairways run into large and, for the most part, elevated greens, but it is hard to concentrate upon them, so strong is the influence of the panoramic views. Complementing the beauty of the natural surroundings, the clubhouse and other

associated facilities are equipped in suitable Mediterranean fashion, with a terrace looking out over the view and a pool for those wishing to cool down after a round in the heat of the day.

From the 3rd tee the course tracks a dangerous golfing path uphill to a green

which, when reached, reveals an expansive vista of the Mediterranean fading away towards Italy. A change of direction to the 4th tee produces one of the most stunning views in European golf. Beyond the green far below and over the azure waters of Pevero Bay can be seen the snow-capped mountains of Corsica.

The first of two lakes, which Trent Jones built into the design, dominates the 6th and 7th holes, two of the best on the course. Played from a tee set back in a spectacular rockery garden of flowers and

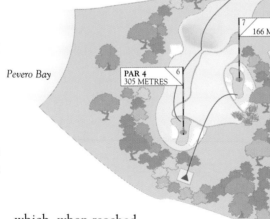

Pevero Bay

| PAR 4 | 4 |
| 351 METRES | |

| 5 | PAR 3 |
| | 175 METRES |

| 7 | PAR 3 |
| | 166 METRES |

| PAR 4 | 6 |
| 305 METRES | |

| PAR 4 | 1 |
| 376 METRES | |

| PAR 4 | 8 |
| 339 METRES | |

CHAMPIONSHIP LENGTHS		
OUT	2,991 METRES	PAR 36
IN	2,848 METRES	PAR 36
TOTAL	5,839 METRES	PAR 72

COURSE RECORD

67 DALE HAYES, ITALIAN OPEN 1978

shrubs, the 6th is a short par 4 to a narrow fairway. The lake eats into the fairway on the left and only the most accurate of tee-shots will survive. Even when the sanctuary of the fairway is reached, the player's troubles are not over. The short pitch has to carry the lake to the green. A cool nerve and steady hand are needed since the green slopes viciously towards the water. The lake also dominates the 7th, a long par 3 of 166 metres. It requires a very solid blow with a long iron from the elevated tee to make the carry over the lake and reach the safety of a narrow green. The second lake influences play at the 16th and 17th, with the tee-shot at the penultimate hole requiring a long carry over the water to a generous but deceptively sloping target.

This is golf in the most rarefied of sporting atmospheres, where there is no room for doubt that the hand of man has, for once, complemented the already magnificent work of Mother Nature.

15 **Green with a view**
The second shot at the 15th is over a hill to a green well guarded by bunkers. The greenside view is stunning.

16 **Tricky second**
One of the toughest strokes anywhere is the second shot at the 16th. A lake guards the right of the long, narrow hole and a selection of three bunkers guards the left. Mistakes are punished severely.

PEVERO CHAMPIONSHIP COURSE

3 / PAR 5 / 474 METRES

2 / PAR 4 / 350 METRES

12 / PAR 4 / 351 METRES

14 / PAR 3 / 170 METRES

13 / PAR 4 / 354 METRES

PAR 5 / 485 METRES / 11

9 / PAR 5 / 454 METRES

18 / PAR 5 / 489 METRES

10 / PAR 3 / 169 METRES

17 / PAR 3 / 132 METRES

15 / PAR 5 / 436 METRES

16 / PAR 4 / 262 METRES

Clubhouse

PINE VALLEY

PINE VALLEY GOLF CLUB, CLEMENTON, NEW JERSEY, USA

GEORGE CRUMP, WEALTHY *Philadelphia businessman and avid golfer, spent many years and the best part of his fortune in pursuit of his dream of building the best and most demanding golf course in the world. At Pine Valley, he certainly succeeded in creating one of the world's toughest inland courses. Crump picked 184 acres (74ha) of forest and marshland on the highest piece of ground in southern New Jersey – land he spotted from his railway carriage while travelling from Philadelphia to Atlantic City.*

Devil's work
The 10th green is surrounded by many sand traps, but this deep conical one, nicknamed the Devil's Arse, is particularly vicious. The only way out is to play away from the green because the lip is too steep.

The records of the Pine Valley Club give no insight into the reasons that might have led Crump to think this stretch of unpromising land, once the home of the Delaware Indians, suitable for fashioning into a great inland links. But he had no doubts and in 1912, after persuading 18 friends to put up $1,000 each, he bought the ground. Sadly, Crump did not live to see the completion of his golfing dream; he died in 1918, when only 14 of the 18 holes were finished. The Pine Valley course eventually opened a year later.

What Crump created was a series of green islands in a sea of dense under-growth, trees, water and sand. This has given Pine Valley the reputation of being the biggest bunker in the world. There are

no fairways as such. The landing areas are precisely defined and generous enough in their own way; but the penalty for missing any of them is severe, and the damage to one's score will be terminal. Many of them are encircled by steep-sided potholes.

PSYCHOLOGICAL PRESSURE

Pine Valley therefore presents as much a psychological challenge as a physical test. Most people who play the course for the first time are awe-struck by its terrifying reputation. Pine Valley members are so confident of their course's capacity that they offer a standing bet that nobody can break 80 on his first game over the course. One of the very few players to prove that this feat could be achieved was Arnold

Trapped
The 17th is a shortish par 4, but it makes up for its lack of length by being uphill all the way. By the standards of the rest of the course the green is smallish, and in line with Pine Valley's vicious penal design, it is comprehensively guarded by sand traps that begin 50 yards in front of the green.

PAR 4
344 YARDS 12

PAR 4
13 448 YARDS

PAR 3
14 184 YARDS

PAR 4
433 YARDS 16

Railway

Palmer, who went to Pine Valley for the first time in 1954 as the reigning US Amateur Champion and shot a marvellous round of 68. Palmer took all the bets he could before the round because, as he recalled later: "I was getting married and I was desperate for money at the time."

In addition to being famous for the severity and toughness of the challenge it presents, beautiful Pine Valley is notable for its undiluted devotion to the game. Unlike many modern clubs, it remains, as it always has been, strictly a golf club, with no pretensions to being anything else. This is reflected in the very traditional feel of a well lived-in clubhouse.

CHAMPIONSHIP LENGTHS		
OUT	3,352 YARDS	PAR 35
IN	3,304 YARDS	PAR 35
TOTAL	6,656 YARDS	PAR 70

COURSE RECORD

64 ROBERT LEWIS JNR, LAWRENCE BATLEY INTERNATIONAL 1981

WALKER CUP WINNERS

1936 USA; 1985 USA;

18 Dangerous waters

The 18th is played from a high tee, which makes the 185-yard carry over sand and scrub to the fairway landing area easier to achieve. The second shot has to cross water in front of the green from a downhill lie, with attendant dangers. The large green runs uphill from the front, and there is always a risk of three-putting.

PINE VALLEY CHAMPIONSHIP COURSE

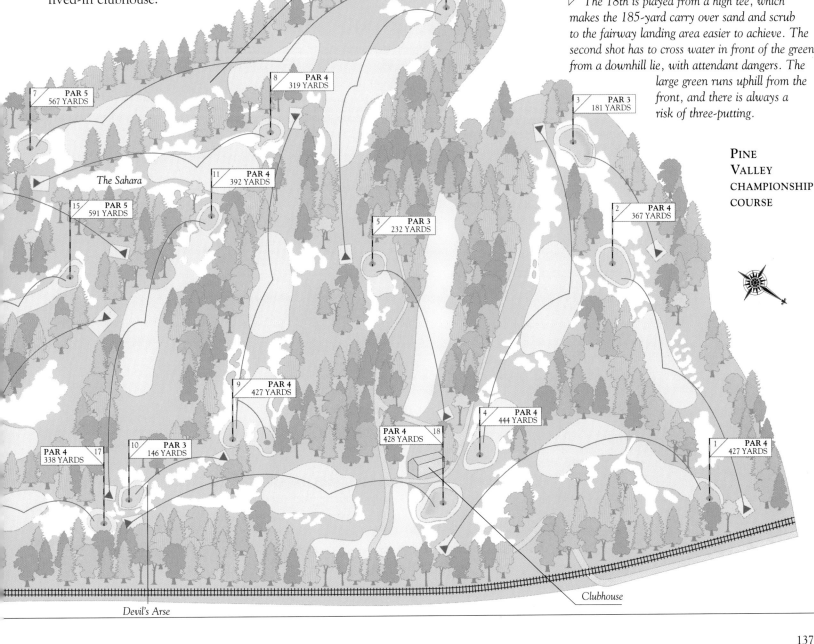

Hell's half-acre

6 PAR 4 388 YARDS

7 PAR 5 567 YARDS

8 PAR 4 319 YARDS

3 PAR 3 181 YARDS

The Sahara

11 PAR 4 392 YARDS

15 PAR 5 591 YARDS

5 PAR 3 232 YARDS

2 PAR 4 367 YARDS

9 PAR 4 427 YARDS

4 PAR 4 444 YARDS

PAR 4 428 YARDS 18

1 PAR 4 427 YARDS

PAR 4 338 YARDS 17

10 PAR 3 146 YARDS

Clubhouse

Devil's Arse

PINEHURST

PINEHURST RESORT & COUNTRY CLUB, PINEHURST, NORTH CAROLINA, USA

THERE IS NO *golf resort in the United States with a better claim to the title of "Golf Capital of America" than Pinehurst in North Carolina, which boasts no fewer than eight golf courses. This small community of only a few thousand people has a deep understanding of, and respect for, golf, matched only by that of enthusiasts in Scotland, the cradle of the game. This shared feeling for golf probably reflects the community's early connections with Scotland. The main influence on Pinehurst was Donald J. Ross, a Scottish professional from Dornoch.*

Telling emblem
The Pinehurst logo incorporates the Putter Boy, after the design of a sundial once found on the club's practice putting green.

Seal of office
US President Gerald Ford, an avid golfer, has strong links with Pinehurst. He opened the World Golf Hall of Fame there after taking office in 1974. Since then it has moved to Jacksonville, Florida.

Donald Ross settled in Pinehurst, a small community situated between Raleigh and Charlotte, after emigrating from Scotland to the United States in 1898. Previously he had been an apprentice to Old Tom Morris in St Andrews. At about the same time as Ross was making his way to a new life in America, a Boston pharmacist by the name of James W. Tufts suddenly became captivated by the new game of golf that was then growing in popularity on the east coast. He had already bought a 5,000-acre (2,000ha) site in Pinehurst, at a mere $1 an acre, with the grand scheme of developing a resort where New Englanders like himself could escape the ravages of the northern winter.

Tufts built a golf course at Pinehurst, primitive by present-day standards. But after Harry Vardon played four rounds there in 1900, golf took off. Tufts brought in Donald Ross as resident professional and the man from Dornoch set about building Pinehurst Number 2, now recognized as one of the world's greatest golf courses.

The Carolina sandhills on which Ross laid out his course were perfect for the purpose. The land, barren and of little use for anything else, was similar in many ways to the

seaside links of his native country. Ross made the most of it, refining it over the years into a true masterpiece. He went on to become involved in the design of many more courses, including Oakland Hills, Seminole, Oak Hill and Scioto.

Although Pinehurst Number 2 can be stretched to more than 7,000 yards when necessary, it is not designed to be punitively long. Ross's vision was of a

challenge that requires accuracy and planning, rather than strength. It puts the emphasis on a tight, short game around the slightly raised greens, as well as a fine touch with the putter on the subtle slopes of the putting surfaces.

There is a wonderful feeling of tranquillity, almost of solitude, when playing this marvellous course. The growth of the trees over the years has resulted in each hole becoming virtually

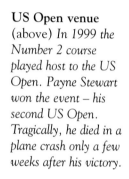

US Open venue
(above) *In 1999 the Number 2 course played host to the US Open. Payne Stewart won the event – his second US Open. Tragically, he died in a plane crash only a few weeks after his victory.*

Capital house (left)
The large clubhouse complex serves five of the eight courses at the Pinehurst resort, which is widely regarded as being the "Golf Capital of America".

Shady pines (right)
Turf and woodland typically blend in around the Pinehurst Number 2 course, as seen here with Tiger Woods competing for the 1999 US Open.

a course on its own. The sandhills and the mild climate are the perfect combination for developing the crisp Pinehurst turf. This is a course for the game's "thinkers", and it will not surrender to a frontal assault. Sam Snead once warned, "You've got to hit every shot on old Number 2". For those who do not, humiliation lies in wait around every corner.

CHAMPIONSHIP VENUE

Had it been blessed with a more accessible location, there is no doubt that Donald Ross's masterpiece would have hosted many more championships than it has. Important events staged at Pinehurst over the years have, however, included the USPGA Championship in 1936, the

Ryder Cup in 1951 (won by the USA) and the US Amateur Championship in 1962. Since 1901, the North and South Championship, an amateur event that ranks second only to the Amateur Championship itself, has been played regularly at Pinehurst. For the first eight years the event was played over the original Number 1 course, which was then a little short. From 1909, play was moved to the Number 2 course, where it has remained.

Pinehurst also hosted the World Open, the inaugural event being played there in 1973; Miller Barber took the $100,000 winner's prize. The Colgate Hall of Fame Classic was staged there in 1977, as was the 1991 US Tour Championship and the 1994 US Senior Open. Five years later it

was the venue for the memorable US Open won amid such great drama by Payne Stewart.

The long association between Pinehurst and the Tufts family continued over the decades. Richard S. Tufts, grandson of the community's founding father, made a major contribution not only to Pinehurst but to the development of the game in the US. He was a leading figure in the USGA and played a major part in the standardization of the Rules of Golf between the USGA and the Royal & Ancient Golf Club in 1951. He was also the prime mover in inaugurating the World Amateur Team Championship, known as the Eisenhower Trophy, which the USA team won here in 1980.

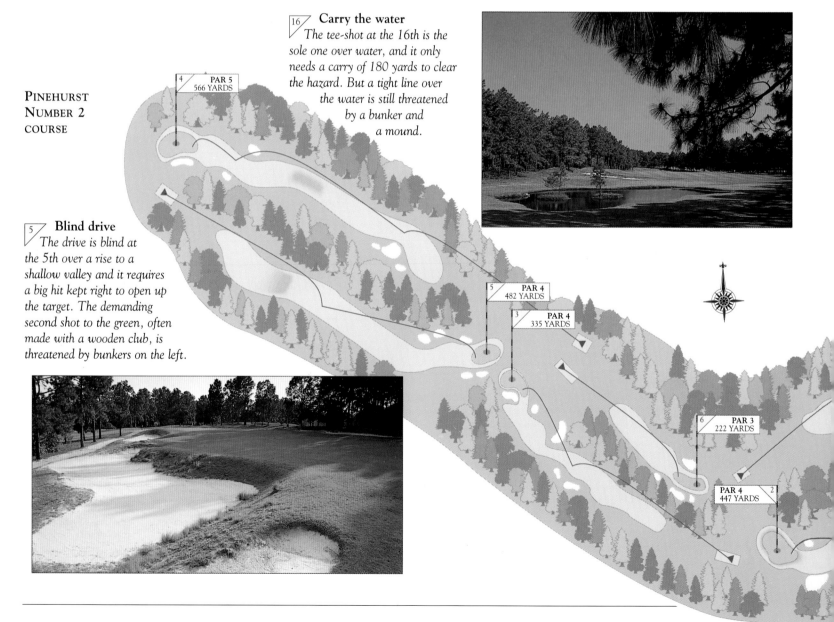

PINEHURST NUMBER 2 COURSE

4 PAR 5 566 YARDS

16 Carry the water
The tee-shot at the 16th is the sole one over water, and it only needs a carry of 180 yards to clear the hazard. But a tight line over the water is still threatened by a bunker and a mound.

5 Blind drive
The drive is blind at the 5th over a rise to a shallow valley and it requires a big hit kept right to open up the target. The demanding second shot to the green, often made with a wooden club, is threatened by bunkers on the left.

5 PAR 4 482 YARDS

3 PAR 4 335 YARDS

6 PAR 3 222 YARDS

PAR 4 447 YARDS 2

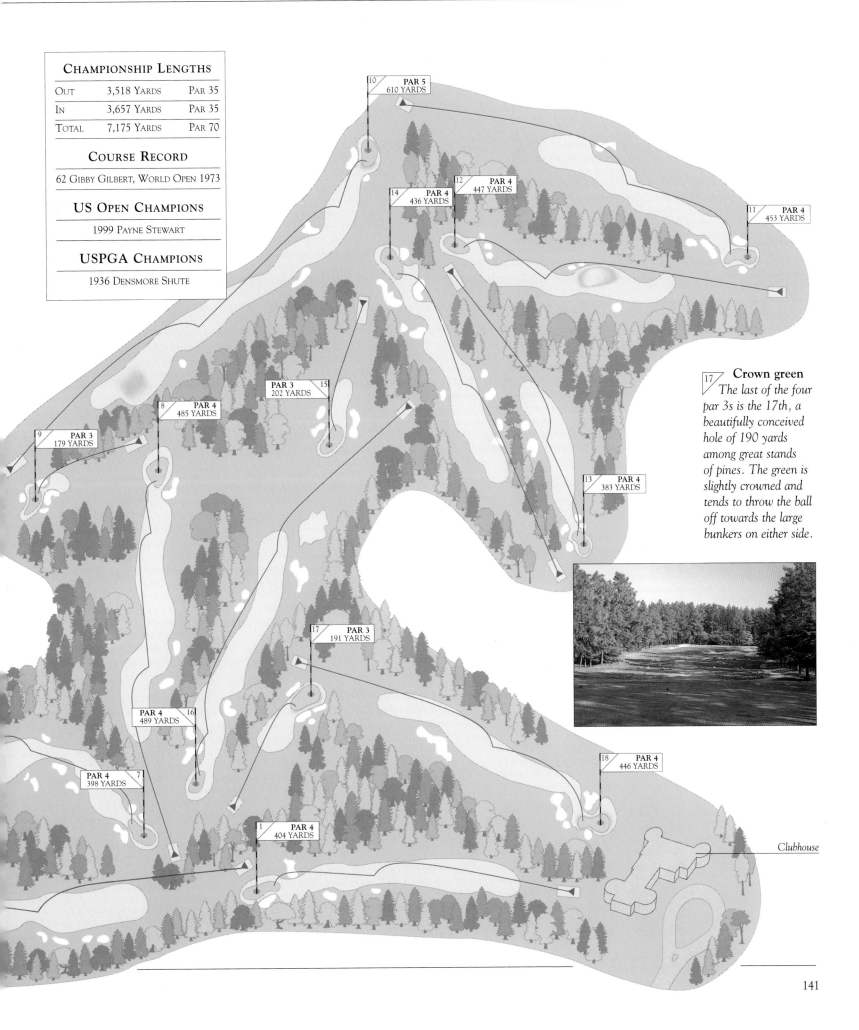

CHAMPIONSHIP LENGTHS

Out	3,518 Yards	Par 35
In	3,657 Yards	Par 35
Total	7,175 Yards	Par 70

COURSE RECORD

62 Gibby Gilbert, World Open 1973

US Open Champions

1999 Payne Stewart

USPGA Champions

1936 Densmore Shute

10 PAR 5 610 YARDS

12 PAR 4 447 YARDS

14 PAR 4 436 YARDS

11 PAR 4 453 YARDS

PAR 3 202 YARDS 15

8 PAR 4 485 YARDS

9 PAR 3 179 YARDS

13 PAR 4 383 YARDS

17 PAR 3 191 YARDS

PAR 4 489 YARDS 16

PAR 4 398 YARDS 7

1 PAR 4 404 YARDS

18 PAR 4 446 YARDS

Crown green
The last of the four par 3s is the 17th, a beautifully conceived hole of 190 yards among great stands of pines. The green is slightly crowned and tends to throw the ball off towards the large bunkers on either side.

Clubhouse

141

PORTMARNOCK

PORTMARNOCK GOLF CLUB, COUNTY DUBLIN, REPUBLIC OF IRELAND

T HE GREAT FOUR-TIME *winner of the British Open, Bobby Locke, rated the magnificent links of Portmarnock in County Dublin, Ireland, among the very finest anywhere in Europe. There are few who would argue with that judgement, for Portmarnock has all the qualities of the truly great seaside championship courses. It also offers the additional challenge of an unpredictable and capricious climate, changing swiftly from sunlight to storm.*

Local birdie
In the club's coat of arms there is a Grey Plover, a species found on the links. The shield is capped by a bishop's mitre with crossed golf clubs behind.

Unlike many other courses of its calibre, Portmarnock's origins are quite well documented. It was set up by two men called W.C. Pickeman and George Ross, who rowed across the estuary from Sutton in 1894. Although only ten miles (16km) north-east of Dublin, it was a remote spot, but the two men felt it was the ideal place for a golf course. In fact, there had already been a course of sorts on the peninsula, owned by the Irish whiskey family, Jameson. Pickeman and Mungo Park designed the first nine holes of the new course and, four years later, it was extended to 18 holes by Pickeman alone. A shed was provided as basic accommodation, but it burnt down early in the twentieth century. Today, the clubhouse is a much more elegant affair, shining clean and white in the Irish sunshine. Fred W. Hawtree laid out a third nine holes in the 1970s.

Like all the great links courses, however, Portmarnock ultimately owes far more to nature than it does to the hand of man.

Nowadays Portmarnock is, of course, accessible by road. Originally, however, it could only be reached by the ferry used by Pickeman and Ross on their original voyage of discovery. There are many strange stories attached to the passage across the estuary. None is stranger, nor perhaps more apocryphal, than that concerning the club ferryman who had a disagreement with a clergyman on the crossing. The ferryman was not renowned for his tolerance and it is said that the unfortunate cleric, apparently not of the same faith as his captain, did not make it across the water to Portmarnock.

Those who are privileged to play on this marvellous stretch of classic links will undergo an examination of the most testing nature. Like many of its contemporaries among great courses, Portmarnock is a place of moods governed by wind and weather. On a sunny and calm day looking across

Warm hosts (above)
The present clubhouse at Portmarnock dates from 1906, after the first, a mere shack, burnt down. The club is renowned for the warmth of its welcome.

Over the water (left)
When W.C. Pickeman and George Ross rowed across the estuary in 1894 to the peninsula on which Portmarnock now lies, they found a wilderness of sand dune and bracken, inhabited only by farmers and fishing folk.

Irish links (right)
Home of the Irish Open for many years, Portmarnock's gently rolling course provides ideal spectator views. It is set on an exposed peninsula and playing conditions there are greatly affected by capricious changes in the wind and weather.

Not easy
The undulating, humped surface of a links course shows up at the 7th hole. Links courses can often appear deceptively straightforward.

the estuary back to the mainland there is a magical tranquillity about the place, and yet it can transform itself rapidly, putting on a fierce and forbidding face.

There are no hidden problems on the Portmarnock course. It is a truly honest test; its inherent difficulty and the terrain are quite sufficient to provide a wonderful challenge without having recourse to modern design trickeries.

Portmarnock has hosted many fine tournaments over the years, including the Dunlop Masters, the Canada Cup (now the World Cup), the Walker Cup in 1991 and, of course, the Irish Open. In 1949 Portmarnock hosted the only Amateur Championship to be played outside the United Kingdom. While it played host to the Carroll's Irish Open, Portmarnock was voted by the players themselves as the best PGA European Tour tournament venue.

LENGTH OF THE COURSE

When the course was originally extended to 18 holes it measured just over 5,350m. In response to improvements in equipment, and particularly in the golf ball, that length has since been extended to 6,520m for the top professional events. Of the par 4s, four are in excess of 380m in length, and one of the three par 5s measures up at 550m.

Two holes are critical to any score at Portmarnock and they run consecutively: the 14th and 15th. The 14th is 350m long but it is one of the best holes on the course. The great Henry Cotton once took seven here to lose an Irish Open. Playing the short par-3 15th in the 1960 Canada Cup, Arnold Palmer shot through the stiff sea breeze to within a yard of the stick with a 3-iron.

Despite the length and challenge of this great links, when the wind does not blow its worst and the course has been softened by some rain, Portmarnock can offer little defence against the skill of the greatest players. When Bernhard Langer won his second Carroll's Irish Open in 1987, his worst round was 68 and his winning total of 269 was no fewer than 19 strokes under the course card.

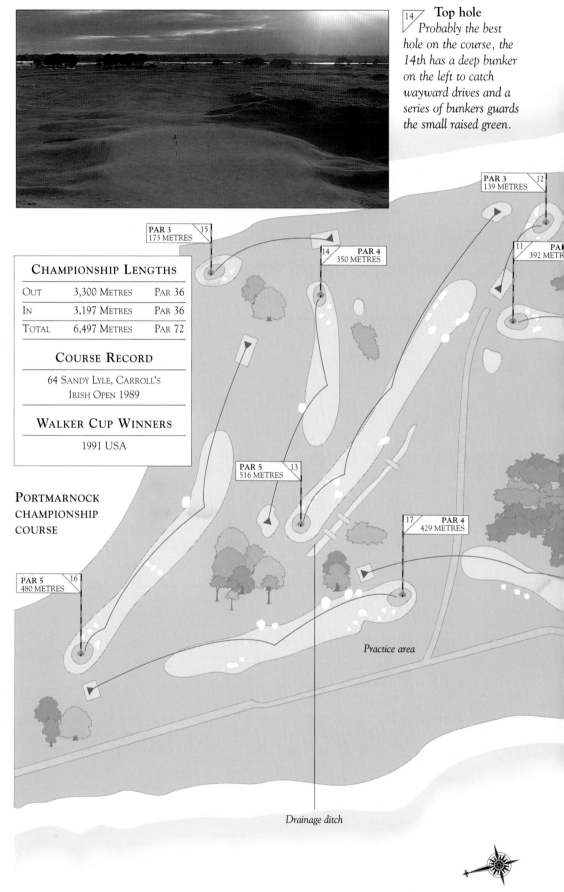

Top hole

Probably the best hole on the course, the 14th has a deep bunker on the left to catch wayward drives and a series of bunkers guards the small raised green.

CHAMPIONSHIP LENGTHS		
OUT	3,300 METRES	PAR 36
IN	3,197 METRES	PAR 36
TOTAL	6,497 METRES	PAR 72

COURSE RECORD

64 SANDY LYLE, CARROLL'S
IRISH OPEN 1989

WALKER CUP WINNERS

1991 USA

PORTMARNOCK
CHAMPIONSHIP
COURSE

PAR 3
173 METRES 15

PAR 3
139 METRES 12

PAR 4
350 METRES 14

11 PAR
392 METR

PAR 5
516 METRES 13

PAR 4
429 METRES 17

PAR 5
480 METRES 16

Practice area

Drainage ditch

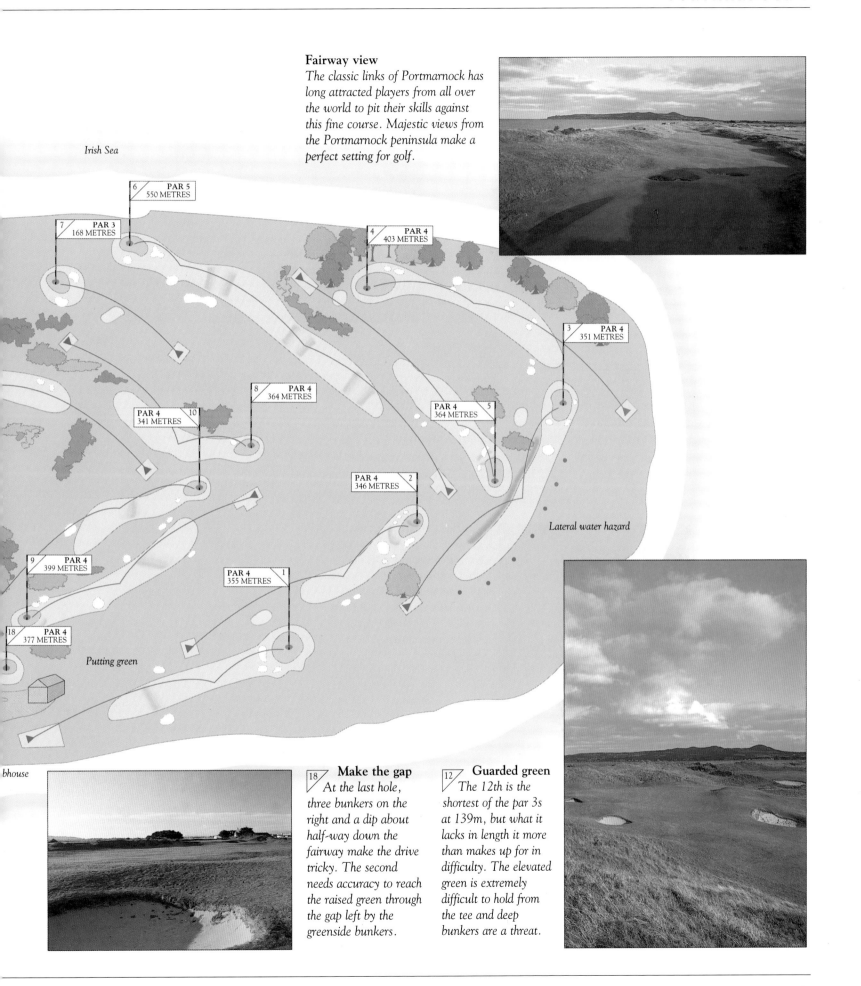

Fairway view
The classic links of Portmarnock has long attracted players from all over the world to pit their skills against this fine course. Majestic views from the Portmarnock peninsula make a perfect setting for golf.

Irish Sea

6 / PAR 5
550 METRES

7 / PAR 3
168 METRES

4 / PAR 4
403 METRES

3 / PAR 4
351 METRES

8 / PAR 4
364 METRES

PAR 4
364 METRES / 5

PAR 4 / 10
341 METRES

PAR 4 / 2
346 METRES

9 / PAR 4
399 METRES

PAR 4 / 1
355 METRES

18 / PAR 4
377 METRES

Lateral water hazard

Putting green

bhouse

18 **Make the gap**
At the last hole, three bunkers on the right and a dip about half-way down the fairway make the drive tricky. The second needs accuracy to reach the raised green through the gap left by the greenside bunkers.

12 **Guarded green**
The 12th is the shortest of the par 3s at 139m, but what it lacks in length it more than makes up for in difficulty. The elevated green is extremely difficult to hold from the tee and deep bunkers are a threat.

RIVIERA

RIVIERA COUNTRY CLUB, PACIFIC PALISADES, CALIFORNIA, USA

G EORGE THOMAS *laid out the uncompromising course of the Riviera Country Club at Pacific Palisades near Los Angeles in 1927. Golfer-architect Ben Crenshaw followed the integrity and character of the Thomas design when he restored all 18 greens and greenside bunkers in 1993. Riviera enjoys a deserved reputation worldwide as a challenging course that demands the use of all the shots in a golfer's repertoire. Its qualities are said by some to be as solid and enduring as the quiet mountains overlooking it.*

Set in the rich landscape of southern California, the Riviera course has been graphically described as "an agitated green wave rolling down historic canyons of the ancient Boca de Santa Monica ranchos." It is the golfing playground of the show-business fraternity and for many years has been the most regular home of the Los Angeles Open. Great names who have

comeback at Riviera after a car crash had almost taken his life. He entered the Los Angeles Open to test whether his mind and body could tackle an important tournament. He not only survived the four rounds but tied for first with Sam Snead (though he lost the play-off).

Riviera is a course that leaves no hiding place for a player's weaknesses. In

won this event at Riviera include Byron Nelson, Tom Watson, Sam Snead and Ben Hogan. The USPGA has been played there twice, and the US Senior Open was won there in 1998 by Hale Irwin.

It was at Riviera in 1948 that Ben Hogan won his first US Open, so far the only one to be played there, with a score of 276 that stood as a course record for 19 years. Two years later, Hogan made his

18 Looking for trouble
Many players have come unstuck while being watched by thousands of spectators from the 18th green's natural amphitheatre. The approach needs a firm blow with a long iron or wood.

6 Bunker in the green
A small bunker almost in the centre of the green is only one of the problems at the short 6th. Another bunker lies in the centre of the fairway immediately in front of the green, while another lurks at the back to penalize overclubbing.

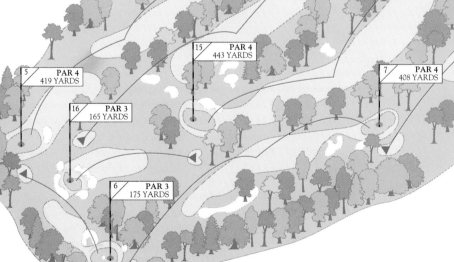

PAR 4 / 3
434 YARDS

PAR 5 / 17
576 YARDS

PAR 3 / 14
176 YARDS

PAR 4 / 4
236 YARDS

15 / PAR 4
443 YARDS

5 / PAR 4
419 YARDS

7 / PAR 4
408 YARDS

16 / PAR 3
165 YARDS

6 / PAR 3
175 YARDS

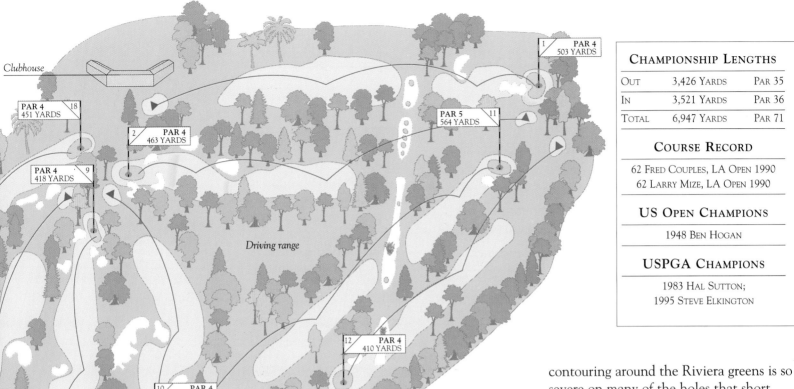

Clubhouse

PAR 4	18
451 YARDS	

2	PAR 4
	463 YARDS

1	PAR 4
	503 YARDS

PAR 5	11
564 YARDS	

PAR 4	9
418 YARDS	

Driving range

12	PAR 4
	410 YARDS

10	PAR 4
	315 YARDS

13	PAR 4
	421 YARDS

8	PAR 4
	370 YARDS

RIVIERA
CHAMPIONSHIP
COURSE

CHAMPIONSHIP LENGTHS		
OUT	3,426 YARDS	PAR 35
IN	3,521 YARDS	PAR 36
TOTAL	6,947 YARDS	PAR 71

COURSE RECORD

62 FRED COUPLES, LA OPEN 1990
62 LARRY MIZE, LA OPEN 1990

US OPEN CHAMPIONS

1948 BEN HOGAN

USPGA CHAMPIONS

1983 HAL SUTTON;
1995 STEVE ELKINGTON

his design, George Thomas managed to combine a demand for long and accurate shots from the tee with the need for precision approach play with the iron clubs. He built big greens for the long holes, desperately small greens for the short holes, and for the remainder allowed a happy medium. He defended all of them tenaciously with clever bunkering. The contouring around the Riviera greens is so severe on many of the holes that short chip shots are rarely straightforward. At just under 7,000 yards, the course is not overlong by present-day championship standards, but with lush fairways it plays every one of those yards. The lushness leads to rather soft and spongy turf, which means the ball does not roll: the par 5s especially require great power, noticeably the enormously long 17th.

AMERICAN BEAUTY

But sheer strength is certainly not all that is needed at Riviera. The bunkering is a constant danger and the ravine that winds around the edge of the course threatens the careless player. The eucalyptus, redwood, sycamore and pine trees that line the fairways not only add to the beauty of the scene, but also constitute a hazard. The course demands precision, accuracy and ball control and remains one of the world's great examinations of golf.

The Riviera course was extensively reconstructed in the mid-1970s. The work reclaimed 17 acres (7ha) of land and restored the course to its former glory. The clubhouse, on a rise overlooking the fairways, perfectly matches the luxuriant beauty of the course. Further restoration work was carried out on all 18 greens and greenside bunkers in 1993.

10 Jack's rating
Jack Nicklaus rates the 10th as one of the "great holes" in golf. The landing area at this par-4 hole is extremely tight, with two looping bunkers on the right. Some players gamble and go for the green from the tee.

ROYAL BIRKDALE

THE ROYAL BIRKDALE GOLF CLUB, SOUTHPORT, LANCASHIRE, ENGLAND

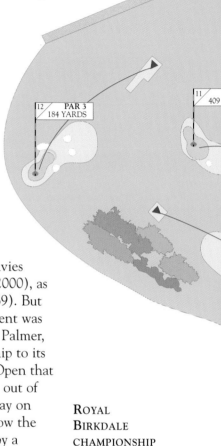

Drainage ditch

Irish Sea

T HIS SUPERB SEASIDE *course has been by far the most important venue for tournaments in England since the Second World War, hosting over thirty championships and international matches. One of a group of fine courses set among the large sand dunes that dominate the landscape along much of the Lancashire coast, it was once summed up by the great Australian player Peter Thomson as "man-sized but not a monster".*

₁₆ **Palmer's hole**
The par-4 16th is extremely demanding. It was here that the 1961 Open winner Arnold Palmer drove into rough under a bush 150 yards

from the green and looked set to drop a shot. But in an astonishing display of strength he thrashed the ball with a 6-iron and forced it over cross-bunkers and on to the green.

formidable is the rough and scrub that grows wildly on the great dunes. There is an abundance of willow scrub, which in many ways presents a more punitive threat than heather and is just as unyielding as gorse.

There have been many memorable tournaments at Birkdale, including the 100th Open Championship in 1971, when Lee Trevino triumphed over Lu Liang Huan of Taiwan. It has also hosted three Women's British Opens, won by amateur Marta Figueras-Dotti (1982), Laura Davies (1986) and Sophie Gustafson (2000), as well two Ryder Cups (1965, 1969). But perhaps the most memorable event was the 1961 Open, won by Arnold Palmer, which restored the Championship to its full prestige. It was during this Open that Palmer played his famous stroke out of the heavy rough along the fairway on what was then the 15th hole, now the 16th, which is commemorated by a plaque on the course.

ROYAL
BIRKDALE
CHAMPIONSHIP
COURSE

Birkdale is a club with a long history; it celebrated its centenary in 1989. But the club does not play on its original course. The first layout of nine holes was about a mile away from the present 18. It survived for only eight years before George Low, from the neighbouring course of Royal Lytham and St Annes, was brought in to supervise the layout of the new Birkdale course.

BETWEEN THE DUNES
Low threaded the fairways through the valleys between the giant sandhills rather than over the top of them, with the result that Birkdale has in many ways more of the character of an inland course than a true links. What makes it particularly

Arnold Palmer plaque

Scylla and Charybdis Dunes

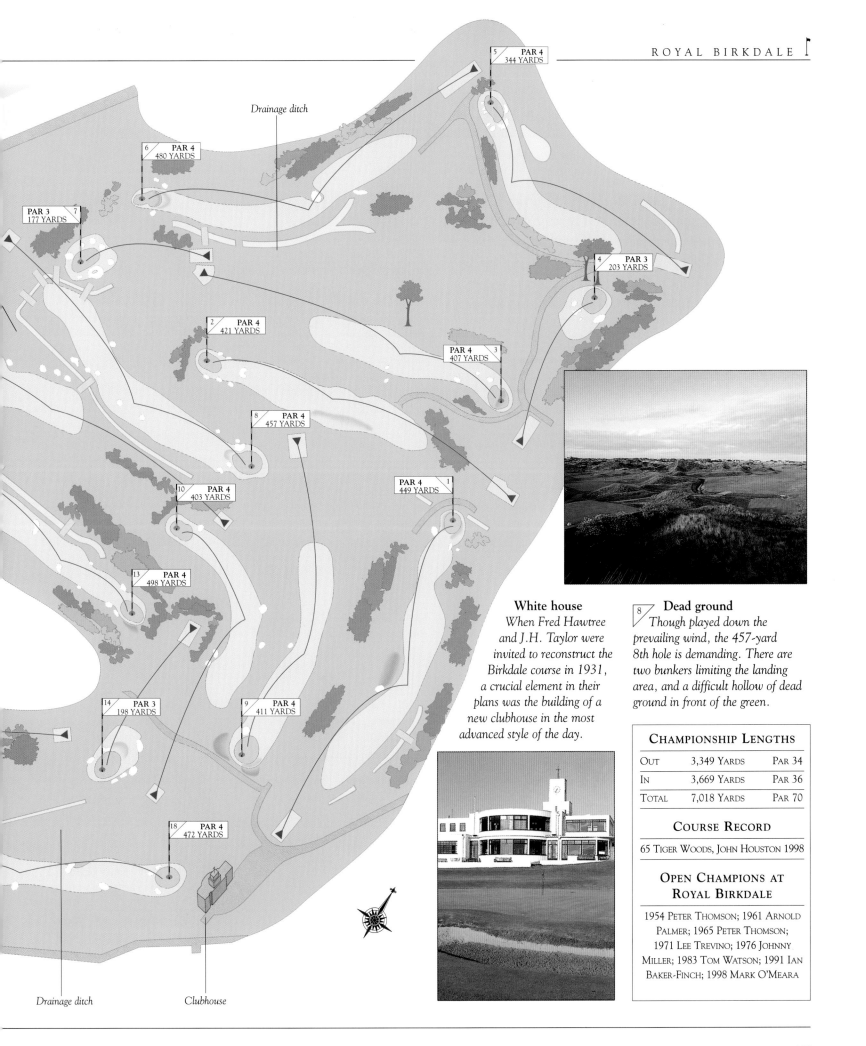

Drainage ditch

5 PAR 4
344 YARDS

6 PAR 4
480 YARDS

PAR 3 7
177 YARDS

4 PAR 3
203 YARDS

2 PAR 4
421 YARDS

PAR 4 3
407 YARDS

8 PAR 4
457 YARDS

10 PAR 4
403 YARDS

PAR 4 1
449 YARDS

13 PAR 4
498 YARDS

14 PAR 3
198 YARDS

9 PAR 4
411 YARDS

18 PAR 4
472 YARDS

Drainage ditch   *Clubhouse*

White house
When Fred Hawtree
and J.H. Taylor were
invited to reconstruct the
Birkdale course in 1931,
a crucial element in their
plans was the building of a
new clubhouse in the most
advanced style of the day.

Dead ground
8   Though played down the
prevailing wind, the 457-yard
8th hole is demanding. There are
two bunkers limiting the landing
area, and a difficult hollow of dead
ground in front of the green.

CHAMPIONSHIP LENGTHS		
OUT	3,349 YARDS	PAR 34
IN	3,669 YARDS	PAR 36
TOTAL	7,018 YARDS	PAR 70

COURSE RECORD

65 TIGER WOODS, JOHN HOUSTON 1998

OPEN CHAMPIONS AT ROYAL BIRKDALE

1954 PETER THOMSON; 1961 ARNOLD
PALMER; 1965 PETER THOMSON;
1971 LEE TREVINO; 1976 JOHNNY
MILLER; 1983 TOM WATSON; 1991 IAN
BAKER-FINCH; 1998 MARK O'MEARA

ROYAL CAPE

ROYAL CAPE GOLF CLUB, WYNBERG, CAPE TOWN, SOUTH AFRICA

L IEUTENANT-GENERAL SIR *Henry D'Oyley Torrens, a soldier of some distinction when the British Empire was at its zenith, is the man credited with introducing golf to South Africa and also with founding what is now the Royal Cape Golf Club. Early records show the General was a fanatical enthusiast for the royal and ancient game.*

Tight option
The 9th is one of the most difficult par-4 holes at Royal Cape. Lined with trees and doglegged to the left, the hole has a ditch along the right side. The farther the tee-shot is hit to the left, the tighter the hole becomes because of the trees and a bunker.

Within nine days of his arrival in South Africa, General Torrens had convened a meeting, on 14 November 1885, "for the purpose of introducing the game of golf and starting a club for same in South Africa". All those present at the meeting, with the exception of one, were military men and most of them Scots into the bargain. With the help of an officer of the Royal Engineers, a nine-hole course was eventually laid out on Waterloo Green, immediately in front of the Wynberg barracks. Each stage of its design had to receive the General's approval.

Since then the club has moved its location twice, in 1891 and 1905, and there have been many changes to the

Railway

Keep right
The long par-4 opening hole at Royal Cape is usually played into the prevailing south-east wind. It demands a long straight drive favouring the right of the fairway.

ROYAL CAPE
CHAMPIONSHIP
COURSE

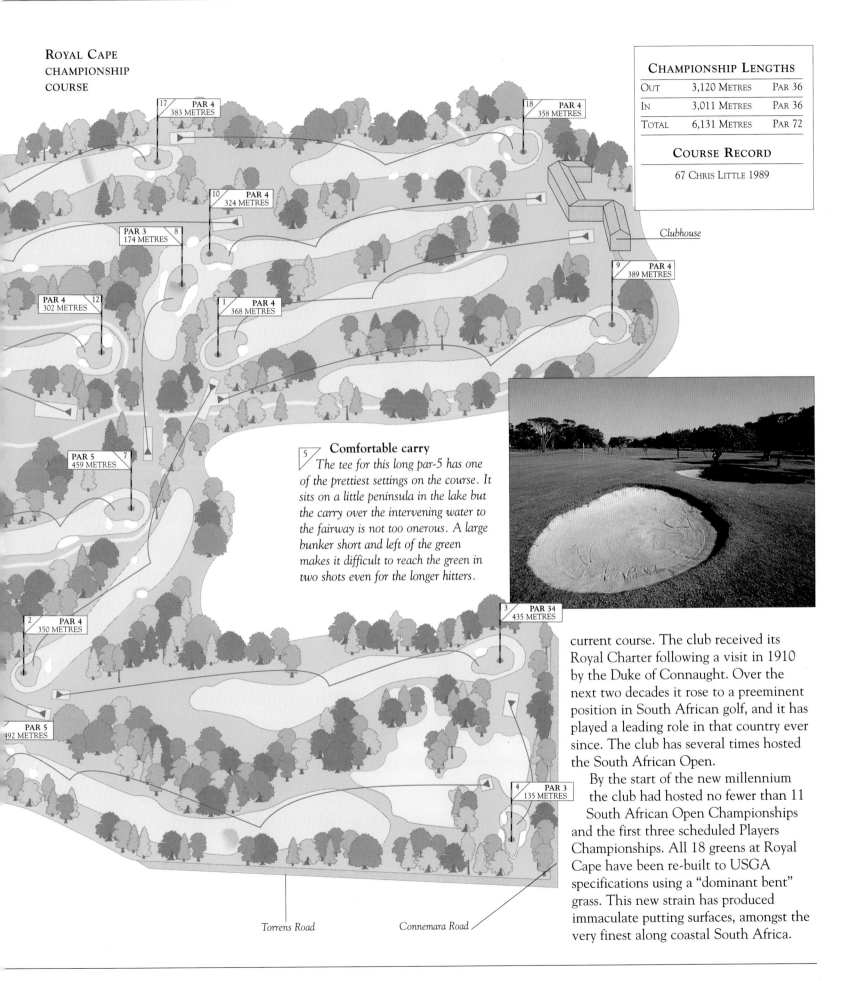

CHAMPIONSHIP LENGTHS		
OUT	3,120 METRES	PAR 36
IN	3,011 METRES	PAR 36
TOTAL	6,131 METRES	PAR 72
COURSE RECORD		
67 CHRIS LITTLE 1989		

17 / PAR 4
383 METRES

18 / PAR 4
358 METRES

10 / PAR 4
324 METRES

PAR 3 / 8
174 METRES

Clubhouse

9 / PAR 4
389 METRES

PAR 4 / 12
302 METRES

1 / PAR 4
368 METRES

PAR 5 / 7
459 METRES

5 / **Comfortable carry**
*The tee for this long par-5 has one
of the prettiest settings on the course. It
sits on a little peninsula in the lake but
the carry over the intervening water to
the fairway is not too onerous. A large
bunker short and left of the green
makes it difficult to reach the green in
two shots even for the longer hitters.*

2 / PAR 4
350 METRES

3 / PAR 34
435 METRES

PAR 5
192 METRES

4 / PAR 3
135 METRES

current course. The club received its
Royal Charter following a visit in 1910
by the Duke of Connaught. Over the
next two decades it rose to a preeminent
position in South African golf, and it has
played a leading role in that country ever
since. The club has several times hosted
the South African Open.

By the start of the new millennium
the club had hosted no fewer than 11
South African Open Championships
and the first three scheduled Players
Championships. All 18 greens at Royal
Cape have been re-built to USGA
specifications using a "dominant bent"
grass. This new strain has produced
immaculate putting surfaces, amongst the
very finest along coastal South Africa.

Torrens Road

Connemara Road

ROYAL COUNTY DOWN

ROYAL COUNTY DOWN GOLF CLUB, NEWCASTLE, COUNTY DOWN, NORTHERN IRELAND

S OME SAY THAT *next to Pine Valley in the United States, Royal County Down is the world's most difficult golf course. Such an assessment depends very much on personal opinion, but Welshman Dai Rees, captain of the last successful British Ryder Cup team before assistance arrived from the Continent, certainly supported such a view. Royal County Down is also one of the most beautiful courses, lying around the curve of Dundrum Bay within the shadow of the Mountains of Mourne.*

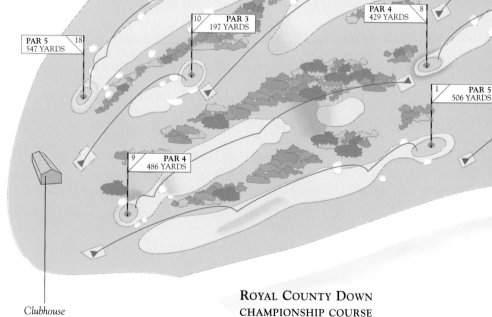

5 Blind challenge (above)
A dogleg to the right from the 5th tee invites the player to cut off as much as he dares with a blind drive across heather. A long second shot to the green is menaced by a defensive phalanx of bunkers and sand dunes.

1 Distracting scene
Looking down to the first green, the scenery is fine enough to challenge the concentration of the most dedicated player, yet the first tee-shot requires the closest attention. The drive to a narrow fairway in a valley, with sandhills on either side, demands a long and straight shot.

On a clear day the view from Royal County Down embraces both the peak of Slieve Donard and, 40 miles (64km) away to the east, the Isle of Man. On the other side, the hills of Ballynahinch complete a picture of breathtaking splendour.

Old Tom Morris laid out the original course for £4 in 1889, according to the minutes of the club, which was formed in March of that year. The course soon gained a reputation as being one of the finest in all Ireland. George Combe, the club captain in 1895–96, was largely responsible

PAR 4
427 YARDS   17

PAR 4
438 YARDS   11

PAR 4
429 YARDS   8

PAR 3
197 YARDS   10

PAR 5
547 YARDS   18

PAR 5
506 YARDS   1

PAR 4
486 YARDS   9

Clubhouse

ROYAL COUNTY DOWN
CHAMPIONSHIP COURSE

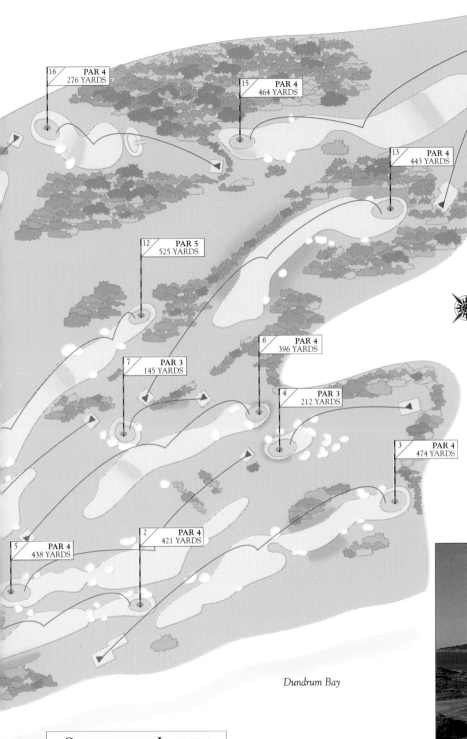

14	PAR 3 213 YARDS
16	PAR 4 276 YARDS
15	PAR 4 464 YARDS
13	PAR 4 443 YARDS
12	PAR 5 525 YARDS
6	PAR 4 396 YARDS
7	PAR 3 145 YARDS
4	PAR 3 212 YARDS
3	PAR 4 474 YARDS
2	PAR 4 421 YARDS
5	PAR 4 438 YARDS

Dundrum Bay

for its layout then being changed to two loops of nine holes returning to the clubhouse – a revolutionary concept at the time. Improvements to the course continued, influenced by club professional Seymour Dunn in 1904, Harry Vardon in 1908, and Harry Colt in 1926. Since then the course has changed little aside from the odd bunker and some yardage amendments.

TESTING AND UNCOMPROMISING

This is a marvellous links, with splendid individual holes running through narrow valleys of rich, crisp turf, flanked by great swathes of gorse, wild roses and uncompromising sand dunes. The championship course offers the most severe of challenges for the best of the world's players. In 2000 Christy O'Connor Jnr secured the Senior British Open here.

Five holes – the 2nd, 5th, 6th, 9th and 15th – call for blind tee-shots and others impose blind shots to the green. Three of the par-3 holes are 200 yards or more and very demanding, severely punishing any mistake from the tee with threatening bunkers, gorse and heavy rough. Only the 9th among the par-5 holes is under 500 yards, while the 18th is 545 yards.

CHAMPIONSHIP LENGTHS		
OUT	3,507 YARDS	PAR 35
IN	3,530 YARDS	PAR 36
TOTAL	7,037 YARDS	PAR 71

COURSE RECORD

66 JAMES BRUEN, IRISH OPEN 1939

CURTIS CUP WINNERS

1968 USA

4 **Green in the gorse**
Spectacular scenery and a testing challenge are the hallmarks of Royal County Down. Gorse and wild flowers abound in the duneland around the curve of Dundrum Bay. All the par-3 holes on the course are magnificent, and the 4th, although not the toughest, is no exception.

ROYAL DORNOCH

ROYAL DORNOCH GOLF CLUB, DORNOCH, SUTHERLAND, SCOTLAND

I N THE FAR *north-east corner of Scotland lies a golf course that is unsurpassed in its wild beauty. Royal Dornoch, an historic links where records show golf has been played since 1616, has a unique atmosphere born of its remoteness as well as the undoubted quality of its layout. It is a course for the traditionalist and the purist.*

Local folk legend
On the Dornoch crest, a Sutherland wild mountain cat holds a horseshoe torn from the rear leg of an invading Norseman's mount.

To reach Royal Dornoch requires a journey through some of the finest of Scotland's landscapes. And what a joy is in store for the intrepid traveller who reaches the historic old town, with its air of peace and remoteness and the open friendliness of its population.

Only St Andrews and Leith can claim greater antiquity than Dornoch. In 1630 Sir Robert Gordon wrote in his *History of Sutherland*: "About this toun there are the fairest and largest links of any pairt of Scotland, fit for Archery, Golfing, Ryding, and all other exercises; they doe surpasse the fields of Montrose and St Andrews." Thus, some form of the royal

Postcard home
Among the game's wealthy and famous who journeyed to Dornoch were Joyce and Roger Wethered, who were regular summer visitors and helped to spread Dornoch's fame.

Railway town
The coming of the railway in 1903 put Dornoch on the golfing map, and the small Scottish town soon became a popular holiday resort.

and ancient game has probably been played at Dornoch for more than 370 years. Organized modern golf came to Dornoch in the autumn of 1876 when the local chief constable, Alex McHardy, who originated from Fife, and Dr Hugh Gunn, a graduate of St Andrews University, arranged a meeting to establish the

Dornoch Golf Club. The club was formed the following spring, originally with a nine-hole course. Some ten years later Old Tom Morris from St Andrews was called in to add a further nine holes. The man who most influenced the development of Dornoch, however, was John

Arctic winds (above)
The homeward nine is played alongside the Dornoch Firth, fully exposed to the wild moods of the weather.

Sutherland, in his time one of the most revered names in Scottish golf. An estate agent and factor in the town of Dornoch, he was appointed secretary of the club in 1883, a position he was to hold for more than 50 years. He made several revisions to the course layout in collaboration with J.H. Taylor, who became a regular visitor.

John Sutherland was one of the early pioneers of greenkeeping and course maintenance. The construction of greens was his speciality, but he was also an architect in his own right and planned several northern courses. He was a fine player and unrivalled administrator.

The present course at Dornoch has four par 3s and only two par 5s. It follows a natural soft S-shape along the line of the shore, a classic "out-and-back" configuration. As in all classic links, the wind is the key factor. When it is from the prevailing west, the first eight holes may lull the player into a false sense of wellbeing, although if the course is fast and dry the ability to judge approaches will have been well tested by then.

Bumpy ride (right)
Some 45 miles (72km) north of Inverness, Royal Dornoch nestles by the sea. Gorse, bunkers and bumps await any wayward shot.

Influential Scot
Donald Ross based the design of many US courses on Dornoch.

From the 9th tee the battle for home is on and there is no let-up. Only the 17th reverses the direction of the homeward journey, but it allows little respite, because the drive into a hidden valley is fraught with danger from the bunkers and the gorse on the left side. The pitch to the green will seldom be of much length, but it requires a deft touch over a gaggle of awkward bunkers to a plateau green, which is difficult to hold.

The home hole requires two solid blows to make the open green, even in normal circumstances. When the weather boils up, as it so quickly can in this isolated corner of Sutherland in the far north of Scotland, it often requires three strokes from even the strongest player, and all must be substantially struck.

5 High tee
Dornoch's 357-yard par-4 5th hole is without doubt one of the most beautiful on the course. The tee is set high on the ridge of sand dunes and lost in a sea of whin which, when in bloom, creates one of golf's most spectacular sights.

4 High ridge
The 4th hole is a medium-length par 4 running in the shadow of the high ridge that dominates the outward holes. There is an elevated tee and the approach is played over a nest of bunkers.

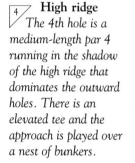

Clubhouse

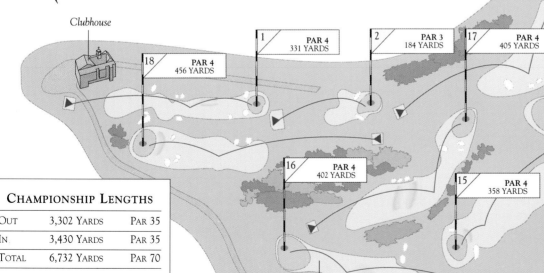

Old quarry

PAR 4		
4	PAR 4	427 YARDS
12	PAR 5	557 YARDS
3	PAR 4	414 YARDS
13	PAR 3	180 YARDS
1	PAR 4	331 YARDS
2	PAR 3	184 YARDS
17	PAR 4	405 YARDS
18	PAR 4	456 YARDS
14	PAR 4	445 YARDS
16	PAR 4	402 YARDS
15	PAR 4	358 YARDS

CHAMPIONSHIP LENGTHS

OUT	3,302 YARDS	PAR 35
IN	3,430 YARDS	PAR 35
TOTAL	6,732 YARDS	PAR 70

COURSE RECORD

66 CP CHRISTY,
CARNEGIE SHIELD 1994

14 Foxy (right)
The 14th, known as Foxy, does not possess a single bunker, and this reflects the quality of what is widely accepted as the best and most subtle of holes on this great links.

ROYAL
DORNOCH
CHAMPIONSHIP
COURSE

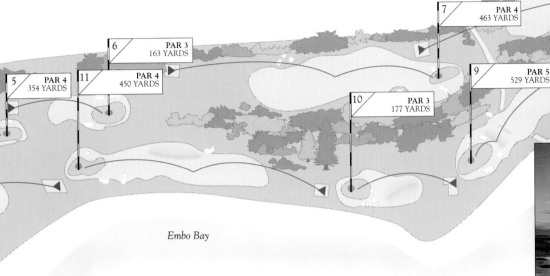

| 8 | PAR 4 437 YARDS |

Old quarry

| 7 | PAR 4 463 YARDS |

| 6 | PAR 3 163 YARDS |

| 5 | PAR 4 354 YARDS |

| 11 | PAR 4 450 YARDS |

| 9 | PAR 5 529 YARDS |

| 10 | PAR 3 177 YARDS |

Embo Bay

Dornoch's very remoteness has mitigated against its hosting as many major events as it might otherwise have done. The Scottish Ladies' Amateur Championship was played there in 1971 and again in 1984. The next year the Amateur Championship went to Dornoch, Garth McGimpsey emerging victorious, and the club hosted the Ladies Home Internationals in 1999. The first Scottish Amateur of the New Millennium was played at Dornoch, reflecting a growing acceptance, perhaps, that with new road connections Dornoch is not now so remote. There is no doubting its pedigree and Tom Watson, five-times Open Champion and an honorary member of the club, rates Dornoch as one of the truly great courses. "I have played none finer," he has said. "It is a natural masterpiece."

The influence of Dornoch has been enormous, through the club's former professional and head greenkeeper, Donald Ross. Ross went to the United States in the 1900s and designed some of the game's greatest golf courses, notably Pinehurst.

8 Out to sea
The 8th hole, known as Dunrobin, is a 437-yard par 4. It is played north-east towards the sea across an old quarry, the drive sailing downhill into a hidden hollow. The green is, as usual, well defended by bunkers. The course then turns back along the shore for the remaining ten holes.

THE NAMES OF ROYAL DORNOCH

1ST FIRST	10TH FUARAN
2ND ORD	11TH A'CHLACH
3RD EARL'S CROSS	12TH SUTHERLAND
4TH ACHINCHANTER	13TH BENTS
5TH HILTON	14TH FOXY
6TH WHINNY BRAE	15TH STULAIG
7TH PIER	16TH HIGH HOLE
8TH DUNROBIN	17TH VALLEY
9TH CRAIGLAITH	18TH HOME

The 5th hole is named for the great Hoylake amateur, Harold Hilton. Other names, such as Ord (for the Ord of Caithness) and Sutherland, relate to geographical features of the area. The 14th is called Foxy because it is considered exceptionally tricky to play.

ROYAL LIVERPOOL

ROYAL LIVERPOOL GOLF CLUB, HOYLAKE, THE WIRRAL, MERSEYSIDE, ENGLAND

D ESPITE ITS SOMEWHAT *austere first appearance, the links of the Royal Liverpool Golf Club at Hoylake lies at the very heart of the history of the royal and ancient game in England, and golf owes a large debt of gratitude to the club for its pioneering spirit. The Hoylake course is without question among the toughest and most demanding of the great seaside championship courses.*

Seaside memento
The Royal Liverpool Golf Club crest depicts a mythical bird holding a piece of seaweed, or "liver", in its beak.

Open landscape
Hoylake's enduring quality is evident in this 1957 oil painting by Arthur Weaver, probably golf's leading contemporary artist.

Built in 1869 on the Warren, a racecourse owned by the Royal Liverpool Hunt Club, Hoylake is the oldest of English seaside courses, save only for Westward Ho! in Devon. Robert Chambers and George Morris built the original course, which was enlarged to 18 holes in 1871.

For its first seven years, the course doubled as a racetrack, and Hoylake's racing origins are still remembered in the name of the 18th hole, known as the Stand, and in the ringing of the original saddling bell to summon members to dine.

Until 1895, Royal Liverpool's clubhouse was at the Royal Hotel, which was owned by the father of one of Hoylake's most famous players, the amateur John Ball. Hoylake was also the home of Ball's arch-rival Harold Hilton, another great amateur of the same era.

For many decades Hoylake was recognized as the most important course in England, and it is steeped in golfing

history. The Amateur Championship – the oldest event of its kind in the world – had its origins there in 1885 and the first international match between Scotland and England was played at Hoylake in 1902. The first competition between an amateur men's team from the United States and one from Great Britain was also held there, in 1921; this match was the precursor of the Walker Cup.

The Royal Liverpool Golf Club was also one of the earliest arbiters of amateur and professional status. When the club staged the first Amateur Championship, an entry was received from a Scotsman by the name of Douglas Rolland who, the previous year, had finished second in the Open Championship. His application was rejected, but this still left the club with a problem to resolve: how precisely was an "amateur" to be defined?

SOVEREIGN ISSUE

John Ball was a crucial case in point. He wished to enter for the Amateur event, but in 1878 he had taken money from the game. Still only 15 years old, he had finished tied for fourth place in the Open Championship. He lost the play-off, but there was a money prize due to him.

There is some doubt as to whether the sum involved was a sovereign or a half sovereign, but the young John Ball put the money in his pocket. This incident was brought up against Ball when he wanted to enter the Amateur Championship. However, a diplomatic solution was found to the problem. The age limit for receiving cash prizes was fixed at 16 and so John Ball, only 15 when he had taken the money, did not forfeit his amateur status. He went on to win the Amateur Championship eight times.

The Hoylake course is a classic links course exposed to the vagaries of wind and weather. There is little in the way of great scenic splendour here, although the

Home player (above)
John Ball was born at Hoylake in 1862 and was always considered unbeatable on his home ground, where he had honed his golfing skills.

Treasury (right)
The magnificent old clubhouse of the Royal Liverpool Golf Club, with its traditional smoke room on the first floor, is an Aladdin's cave of fascinating historic golfing artifacts.

hills of North Wales come into view towards the middle of the round and Hilbre Island rises out of the vast expanse of sandbanks in majestic solitude.

The course is unique among Open Championship venues because a player can hit the ball out-of-bounds even within the course boundaries. It has one of the most fearsome opening shots in championship golf. The practice ground runs along the entire right side of the hole, turning sharply right in the landing area for the drive and continuing all the way to the green. It is the most unnerving start whether with or against the wind.

All the great players of the past, including Bobby Jones and Walter Hagen, have faced this particular challenge and the many other ones that follow. The short, controversial 7th hole, known as Dowie, is a splendid example of Hoylake's need for accurate play. The hole is well protected by bunkers and swales. The drive has to carry 200 yards to reach the green and there is absolutely no margin for error.

The five holes to the finish are extremely long, totalling 2,401 yards, and as difficult as will be found anywhere. The 17th, a 420-yard par 4, is generally regarded as the toughest among them. The second shot here requires precision and good judgement to avoid bunkers on the left and the road to the right. If there is an adverse wind, the problems multiply.

ROYAL
LIVERPOOL
CHAMPIONSHIP
COURSE

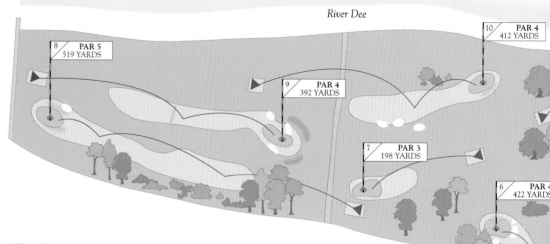

River Dee

The Open Championship has been played at Hoylake ten times. Bobby Jones took the second of his four Grand Slam wins in 1930 on this course, despite taking a seven at the 8th hole in the last round. The last occasion Royal Liverpool hosted the Open was in 1967, when popular Argentinian Roberto de Vicenzo was the winner.

Hoylake has not been on the Open rota since de Vicenzo's win, primarily because the trappings and infrastructure grew enormously. But there has never been any doubt that the course is of the required standard, and hopes for an early return of the Open were much improved after an R & A announcement in 2001 that Hoylake was again being considered.

Aim

11 Alpine remoteness (above)
In among the dunes at the far end of the course from the clubhouse, the 11th – known as the Alps is a superb one-shot hole. It demands a prodigious blow to reach the remote oblong green. Some players tackle it with a wooden club.

THE NAMES OF ROYAL LIVERPOOL	
1ST COURSE	10TH DEE
2ND ROAD	11TH ALPS
3RD LONG	12TH HILBRE
4TH NEW	13TH RUSHES
5TH TELEGRAPH	14TH FIELD
6TH BRIARS	15TH LAKE
7TH DOWIE	16TH DUN
8TH FAR	17TH ROYAL
9TH PUNCH BOWL	18TH STAND

The 11th hole is named the Alps for its extremely high sandhills, which demand a long carry from the tee.

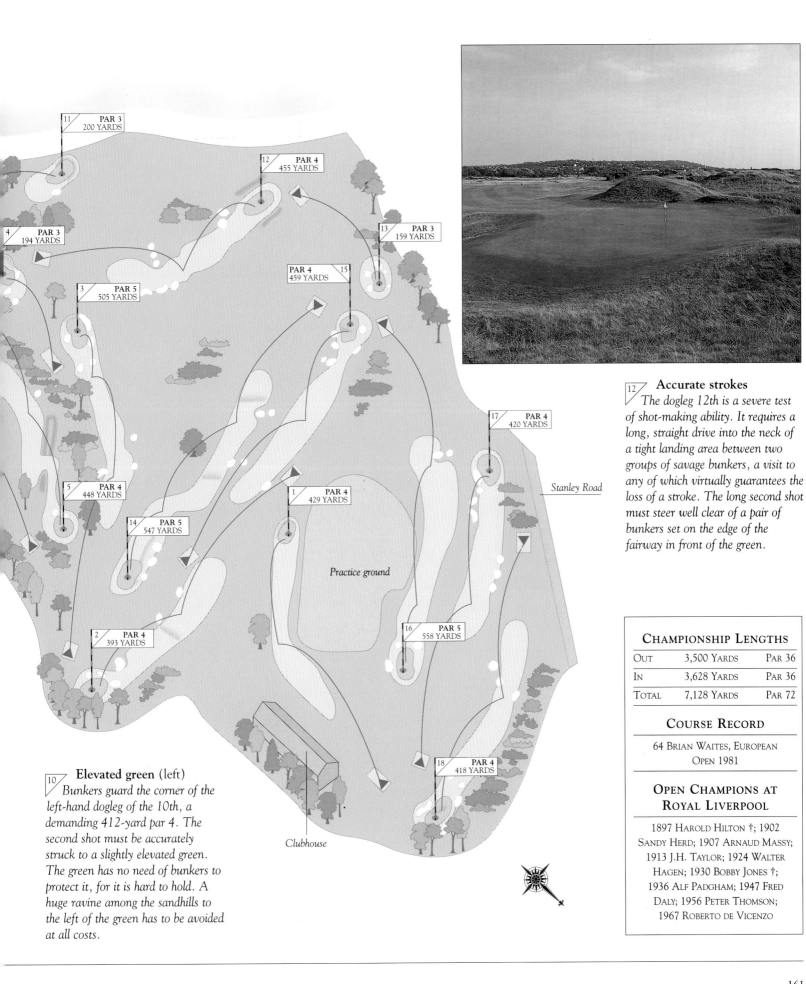

11 / PAR 3
200 YARDS

12 / PAR 4
455 YARDS

13 / PAR 3
159 YARDS

4 / PAR 3
194 YARDS

PAR 4 / 15
459 YARDS

3 / PAR 5
505 YARDS

17 / PAR 4
420 YARDS

Stanley Road

5 / PAR 4
448 YARDS

1 / PAR 4
429 YARDS

14 / PAR 5
547 YARDS

Practice ground

2 / PAR 4
393 YARDS

16 / PAR 5
558 YARDS

18 / PAR 4
418 YARDS

Clubhouse

12 / Accurate strokes

The dogleg 12th is a severe test of shot-making ability. It requires a long, straight drive into the neck of a tight landing area between two groups of savage bunkers, a visit to any of which virtually guarantees the loss of a stroke. The long second shot must steer well clear of a pair of bunkers set on the edge of the fairway in front of the green.

10 / Elevated green (left)

Bunkers guard the corner of the left-hand dogleg of the 10th, a demanding 412-yard par 4. The second shot must be accurately struck to a slightly elevated green. The green has no need of bunkers to protect it, for it is hard to hold. A huge ravine among the sandhills to the left of the green has to be avoided at all costs.

CHAMPIONSHIP LENGTHS		
OUT	3,500 YARDS	PAR 36
IN	3,628 YARDS	PAR 36
TOTAL	7,128 YARDS	PAR 72

COURSE RECORD

64 BRIAN WAITES, EUROPEAN
OPEN 1981

OPEN CHAMPIONS AT ROYAL LIVERPOOL

1897 HAROLD HILTON †; 1902
SANDY HERD; 1907 ARNAUD MASSY;
1913 J.H. TAYLOR; 1924 WALTER
HAGEN; 1930 BOBBY JONES †;
1936 ALF PADGHAM; 1947 FRED
DALY; 1956 PETER THOMSON;
1967 ROBERTO DE VICENZO

ROYAL LYTHAM AND ST ANNES

ROYAL LYTHAM AND ST ANNES GOLF CLUB, LYTHAM ST ANNES, LANCASHIRE, ENGLAND

L AST OF THE *great line of golf courses along the edge of the Irish Sea, which begins at Hoylake and is strung out northwards along the Lancashire coast, Royal Lytham and St Annes is one of England's most difficult championship courses. Since the first 18 holes were laid out here in 1897, it has changed in character from a pure seaside links to a rather softer, lusher course. But the roll call of Open Champions at Lytham includes many of the game's finest players and is a tribute to the quality of the challenge that the course continues to present.*

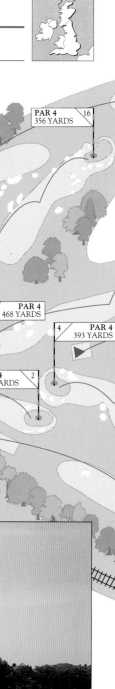

Clubhouse

18 PAR 4 386 YARDS
PAR 4 356 YARDS 16
1 PAR 3 206 YARDS
PAR 4 413 YARDS 17
15 PAR 4 468 YARDS
4 PAR 4 393 YARDS
PAR 4 420 YARDS 2

Changing outlook
Over the years, the Lytham course has become more hemmed in and it now has a distinctly urban setting: three sides are overlooked by houses *and the fourth runs alongside a railway. Although it is now some way from the sea and is greener than it once was, the course still retains many of the qualities of a true links.*

CHAMPIONSHIP LENGTHS		
OUT	3,270 YARDS	PAR 35
IN	3,415 YARDS	PAR 36
TOTAL	6,685 YARDS	PAR 71

COURSE RECORD

65 CHRISTY O'CONNOR SNR, THE OPEN 1969; BRIAN HUGGETT, DUNLOP MASTERS 1970; BILL LONGMUIR, SEVE BALLESTEROS, THE OPEN 1979

OPEN CHAMPIONS AT ROYAL LYTHAM AND ST ANNES

1926 BOBBY JONES †; 1952 BOBBY LOCKE; 1958 PETER THOMSON; 1963 BOB CHARLES; 1969 TONY JACKLIN; 1974 GARY PLAYER; 1979, 1988 SEVE BALLESTEROS; 1996 TOM LEHMAN

1998 SHERRI STEINHAUER (BRITISH WOMEN'S OPEN)

Alexander Doleman, a schoolteacher from Musselburgh in Scotland, was the driving force behind the formation of the Lytham and St Annes Golf Club in 1886. Grounds were leased from the St-Annes-on-Sea Land and Building Company and an 18-hole course was built, with an additional nine holes for ladies.

The club had negotiated only a short lease, however, and the leasing company was not keen to extend it. So, in 1897, the club moved to its present location. By 1903 the club had 751 members, and

nine years later the membership was able to raise £8,500 for the building of a magnificent new clubhouse, which still stands today. This sum must have seemed a king's ransom in those days.

George Lowe is credited with the design of the original course on the present site, but such notable architects as Harry Colt, Herbert Fowler and G.K. Cotton have also left their mark at Royal Lytham and St Annes over the years. Their course has withstood the onslaught of the modern game extremely well.

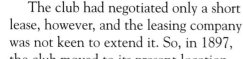

Recalling his first visit to Lytham in the 1920s, Henry Cotton likened the greens, burned by the hot summer, to "putting on ice". Anyone who has ever played on traditional British golfing turf during a drought, when no water is available to temper the speed, will know what Cotton meant. Modern watering systems have ended the days of ice-like greens at Lytham, but the greens can still be quick in dry conditions, and they have retained the fine links grasses that many great courses have lost in recent times through overuse of the sprinkler.

The Open Championship was first played at Lytham in 1926, when Bobby Jones scored the first of his three Open victories. Bobby Locke, Peter Thomson and left-hander Bob Charles all survived dramas to win Opens there in later years.

TIGHT FINISHES

In 1974 Gary Player made his final shot to the last green left-handed, using the back of his putter, after he had run through the green with his approach and the ball had lodged against the wall of the clubhouse. That hole was also the scene of great emotion in 1969, when Tony Jacklin became the first Briton for 18 years to win the Championship. A decade later the crowds were cheering the first Open win by Severiano Ballesteros, a victory that he was to repeat when the Championship returned to Lytham again in 1988. Curiously, the Open Championship has not yet been won at Lytham by an American professional – it is the only course on the regular Championship rota where this has not occurred.

Although Peter Thomson played the front nine in 29 strokes in the 1963 Open – amazing Henry Cotton, who said it was a "puzzle to anyone" to know just how Thomson had done it – low scores are not common at Royal Lytham, unless the weather is particularly benign. There is too much trouble abounding for the course to fail to extract a penalty over four rounds of championship golf.

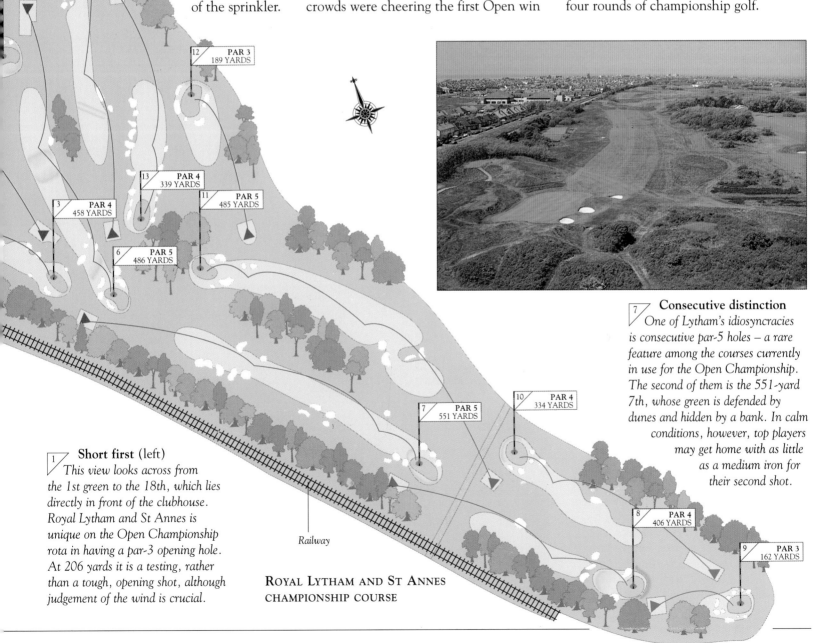

ROYAL LYTHAM AND ST ANNES
CHAMPIONSHIP COURSE

Railway

Short first (left)
This view looks across from the 1st green to the 18th, which lies directly in front of the clubhouse. Royal Lytham and St Annes is unique on the Open Championship rota in having a par-3 opening hole. At 206 yards it is a testing, rather than a tough, opening shot, although judgement of the wind is crucial.

Consecutive distinction
One of Lytham's idiosyncracies is consecutive par-5 holes – a rare feature among the courses currently in use for the Open Championship. The second of them is the 551-yard 7th, whose green is defended by dunes and hidden by a bank. In calm conditions, however, top players may get home with as little as a medium iron for their second shot.

ROYAL MELBOURNE

ROYAL MELBOURNE GOLF CLUB, BLACK ROCK, VICTORIA, AUSTRALIA

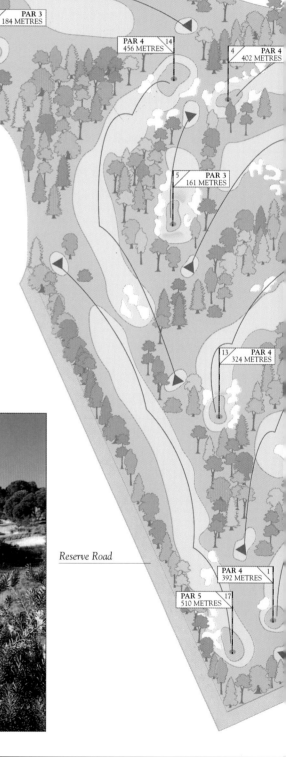

T HE CHAMPIONSHIP COURSE *at Royal Melbourne is an amalgamation of some of the finest work of two great golf-course designers: Alex Russell, the 1924 Australian Open Champion, who was responsible for the East course, and Dr Alister MacKenzie, architect of Augusta National, who laid out the West course. The two courses were blended at the end of the 1950s to form the finest course in Australia, and one of the world's greatest.*

The enthusiastic immigrants who founded the Royal Melbourne Club in 1891 were strongly influenced by the traditions of St Andrews, many of them having arrived in Australia from the "auld grey toon". When the club's members were seeking a new site for their course in 1924, it was natural they should be attracted by a stretch of duneland covered in heather and bracken, reminiscent of a Scottish links, and that MacKenzie, a Scotsman, should be imported as a designer.

COMBINING THE BEST
The current championship course was devised so as to avoid the busy roads that crossed the existing East and West courses and was first used for the Canada (now World) Cup in 1959 and again in 1972 and 1988. It comprises two holes from Russell's designs and 16 from MacKenzie's.

Amalgamation produced a composite course of outstanding quality. The short 304m par-4 3rd and the formidable 395m par-4 18th – a quite stupendous finishing hole – are among the most challenging anywhere in the world. But it is the Royal Melbourne greens that mark the calibre of

this course. They are a joy to putt on, and there are none faster or truer anywhere the game is played. The credit for these masterpieces, which are preserved in the finest traditions of links golf, belongs to Claude Crockford, head greenkeeper at the club for many years.

The rough-hewn bunkers, dug out by horse and scoop in the same manner as the rest of the course, are another remarkable feature of this outstanding layout. There is nothing of the sterile prissiness so evident in modern bunker design. In 1998, Royal Melbourne played host to the third Presidents Cup, the USA losing to the International team.

Reserve Road

5 Slippery slope
A steep slope in front of the 5th green ensures that any shot left short will trickle down the hill, leaving an extremely difficult

chip back. The green itself slopes steeply from the back to the front, and the player requires a deft stroke with the putter to avoid three-putting.

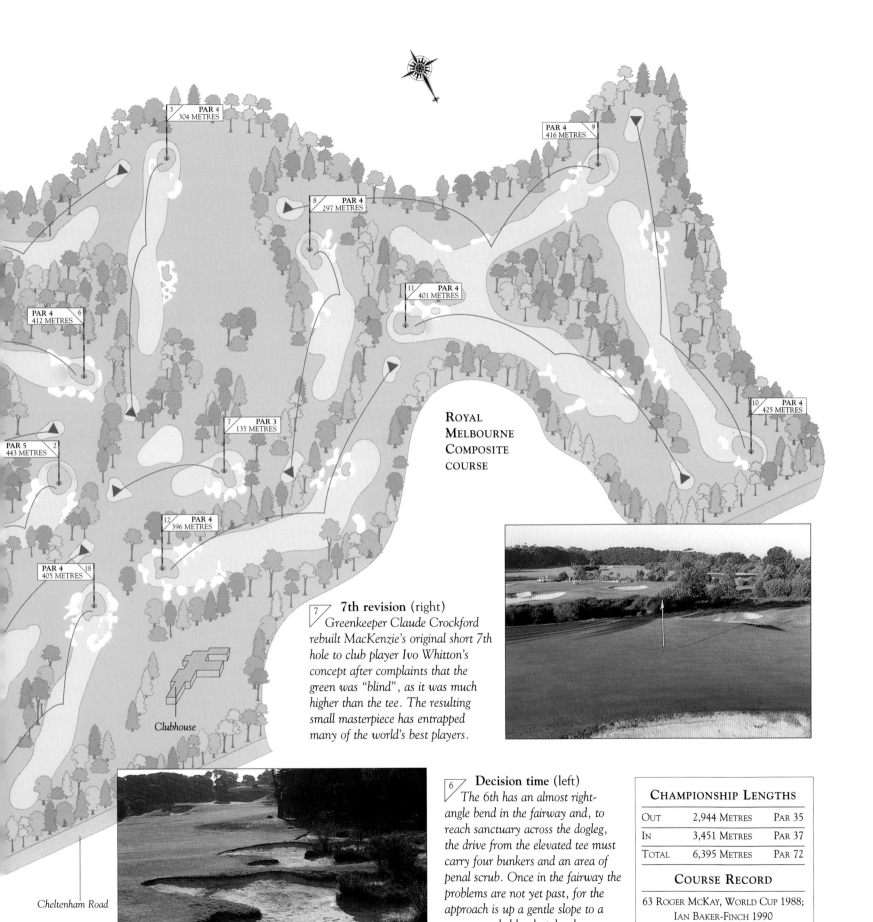

3 | PAR 4 | 304 METRES

PAR 4 | 416 METRES | 9

8 | PAR 4 | 297 METRES

11 | PAR 4 | 401 METRES

PAR 4 | 412 METRES | 6

ROYAL
MELBOURNE
COMPOSITE
COURSE

10 | PAR 4 | 425 METRES

7 | PAR 3 | 135 METRES

PAR 5 | 443 METRES | 2

12 | PAR 4 | 396 METRES

PAR 4 | 405 METRES | 18

Clubhouse

Cheltenham Road

7 **7th revision** (right)
Greenkeeper Claude Crockford rebuilt MacKenzie's original short 7th hole to club player Ivo Whitton's concept after complaints that the green was "blind", as it was much higher than the tee. The resulting small masterpiece has entrapped many of the world's best players.

6 **Decision time** (left)
The 6th has an almost right-angle bend in the fairway and, to reach sanctuary across the dogleg, the drive from the elevated tee must carry four bunkers and an area of penal scrub. Once in the fairway the problems are not yet past, for the approach is up a gentle slope to a green guarded by deep bunkers.

CHAMPIONSHIP LENGTHS

OUT	2,944 METRES	PAR 35
IN	3,451 METRES	PAR 37
TOTAL	6,395 METRES	PAR 72

COURSE RECORD

63 ROGER MCKAY, WORLD CUP 1988;
IAN BAKER-FINCH 1990

ROYAL NORTH DEVON

ROYAL NORTH DEVON GOLF CLUB, WESTWARD HO!, BIDEFORD, DEVON, ENGLAND

T HE LINKS COURSE *of the Royal North Devon Club at Westward Ho! is the oldest in England and a supreme example of natural seaside golf. The layout is nearly the same as it was over 80 years ago and, while some people might call it a museum piece, it is no less a challenge now than it was then. It requires dedication to make the journey to Westward Ho!, as it is a remote place, but the trip is well worth while. Were it not so difficult to reach, the course would surely have hosted many more championships than it has in its long history.*

Royal plumes
The club's crest is dominated by the plumes of the Prince of Wales, later Edward VII, who awarded the North Devon Club its Charter in 1865.

Golf has been played at Westward Ho! since the early 1850s, and Old Tom Morris travelled all the way from Scotland to have a look at the first primitive layout in 1860. But it was not until 1864 that the club itself was founded. It was then called the North Devon and West of England Club and the Rev. I.H. Gossett, vicar of the nearby village of Northam, whose family had been instrumental in developing the game there, was elected to be the first captain of the club.

Old Tom Morris again made the long journey from Scotland that year and laid out two courses, one of 17 holes and the other of 22. There were several alterations before the turn of the century, but the layout today is much as Herbert Fowler left it after he reconstructed it in 1908. The course has always been on common land, known as the Burrows, and the commoners have

Novel name
Charles Kingsley's famous adventure novel Westward Ho!, *written in 1855, gave the course its name.*

rights to graze animals there. They still exercise those rights to the present day, and sheep and horses may be encountered by the golfer, sometimes in large numbers.

Westward Ho!, named after the famous novel of that name by Charles Kingsley, is characterized by several other striking features, not least of them the sea rushes that threaten not only a player's score but his physical wellbeing into the bargain. On the inland holes these rushes form the rough and are often 6ft (1.8m) tall. They are tipped with steel-hard spikes that have been known to impale a golf ball and would do the same to its owner were he fool enough to do battle with them.

The course is famous, too, for the numerous top players who have emanated from it. J.H. Taylor, one of the members of the Great Triumvirate, learned to play at Westward Ho!. He became interested in the game when he caddied for the teenage Horace Hutchinson, who was later to win the Amateur Championship twice and become an eminent writer on golf. Taylor was then a houseboy in the Hutchinson household, but within a few years he

Grazed turf (above)
The difference between the totally untended linksland and that of the course at Westward Ho! shows up clearly. The course is relatively smooth – it is grazed by livestock as well as being cared for by greenkeepers – and has become a little more mellow with the passage of time.

Taylor's links with the past (left)
Royal North Devon's most famous son, J.H. Taylor, owed his Open Championship triumphs to the lessons he learned on its fine Devon linksland.

Threatening traps
(right) *The colossal sleepered Cape bunker awaits the poorly driven tee-shot from the 4th. Other obstacles on the course include threatening hillocks and animals that graze the common land. The course abounds with white-painted marker stones.*

became the first English professional to beat the Scots at their own game, winning the Open Championship five times between 1894 and 1913. In 1957 he was made president at North Devon, the club where he had been a caddie as a boy.

HOSTING THE AMATEUR

The course has hosted the Amateur Championship three times in its history. In 1912 John Ball from Hoylake won the last of his eight titles, beating Abe Mitchell at the 38th hole. The Amateur returned there in 1925, Robert Harris

taking the honours, and Eric Martin Smith was something of a surprise winner when the Amateur Championship was last played there back in 1931.

This historic links has never been easy to score on, even for the finest players. In the first 100 years of the history of Royal North Devon, there were only four rounds under 70 recorded in any of the club's regular medal competitions.

In more recent years, as with so many other great links courses, the greens have become far more meadow-like in character and

much of the fire has gone from them. In fact, there are many who feel Westward Ho! would be the finest links course in all of England were it to be returned to its original, more natural, condition.

The clubhouse and concomitant facilities are comfortable and welcoming, and the atmosphere within reeks of the tradition behind this most ancient of

ROYAL NORTH DEVON CHAMPIONSHIP COURSE

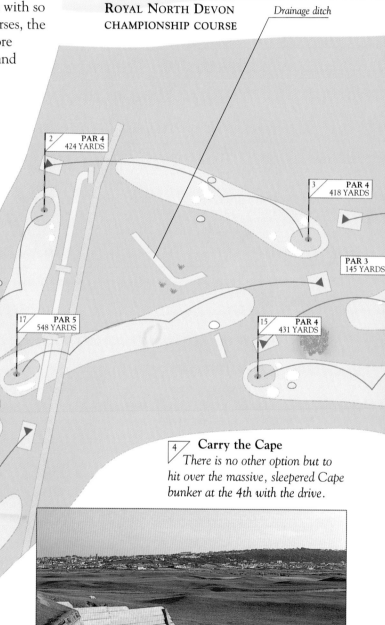

Drainage ditch

2 PAR 4 424 YARDS

3 PAR 4 418 YARDS

PAR 3 145 YARDS

17 PAR 5 548 YARDS

15 PAR 4 431 YARDS

PAR 5 485 YARDS 1

18 PAR 4 416 YARDS

Clubhouse

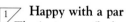

1 Happy with a par

The 1st is a par 5 of a modest 485 yards, but the player who goes to the second without having conceded a stroke to the course will be well pleased. The outlook from the tee may appear flat and featureless but the course is actually full of natural hazards, including grazing livestock.

CHAMPIONSHIP LENGTHS		
OUT	3,309 YARDS	PAR 36
IN	3,353 YARDS	PAR 35
TOTAL	6,662 YARDS	PAR 71

COURSE RECORD
66 KEL NAGLE, MARTINI INTERNATIONAL 1975

4 Carry the Cape

There is no other option but to hit over the massive, sleepered Cape bunker at the 4th with the drive.

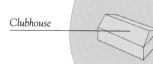

English golf courses. The wide open skies of a virtually treeless links give the course an almost limitless sense of freedom. In golfing terms, however, it is a freedom that allows a player to score well or else to get into deep trouble, and the course demands constant concentration. Westward Ho! will continue to delight golf connoisseurs for many years to come.

Over humps
The 6th runs through the humps and hollows towards the River Torridge estuary. It has an open plateau green and demands a very solid second shot.

Bristol Channel

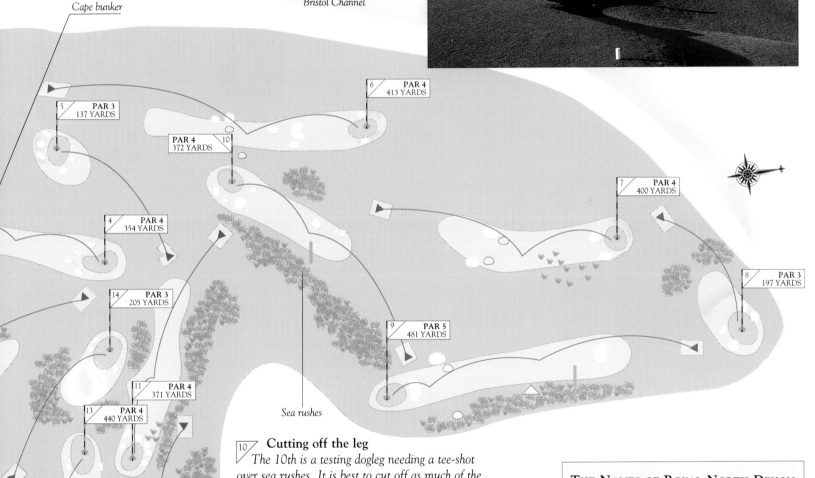

Cape bunker

5 PAR 3 137 YARDS
6 PAR 4 413 YARDS
PAR 4 372 YARDS 10
4 PAR 4 354 YARDS
7 PAR 4 400 YARDS
8 PAR 3 197 YARDS
14 PAR 3 205 YARDS
9 PAR 5 481 YARDS
11 PAR 4 371 YARDS
13 PAR 4 440 YARDS
Sea rushes
12 PAR 4 425 YARDS

Cutting off the leg
The 10th is a testing dogleg needing a tee-shot over sea rushes. It is best to cut off as much of the dogleg as possible on the way to the small green.

THE NAMES OF ROYAL NORTH DEVON

1ST BURN	10TH RUSH
2ND BAGGY	11TH APPLEDORE
3RD SANDYMERE	12TH HINDE
4TH CAPE	13TH LUNDY
5TH TABLE	14TH IRON HUT
6TH CREST	15TH CHURCH
7TH BAR	16TH PUNCH BOWL
8TH ESTUARY	17TH ROAD
9TH WESTWARD HO!	18TH HOME

The 14th hole at Westward Ho! is named Iron Hut after a strange building that served as a substitute for a clubhouse in the early days of the Royal North Devon Club. It did yeoman service for the members for many years, despite its primitive amenities.

169

ROYAL PORTRUSH

ROYAL PORTRUSH GOLF CLUB, PORTRUSH, COUNTY ANTRIM, NORTHERN IRELAND

T HE CHAMPIONSHIP COURSE *at Portrush in Northern Ireland is one of the finest and most historic links anywhere in the British Isles. The Royal Portrush Golf Club, founded in 1888, actually has three courses set amid its 480 acres (190ha) of duneland. Of these, the world-famous Dunluce course is as stern a test of golf as any of the great links, and has the distinction of being the only Irish course to have been selected to host the Open Championship (in 1951). From 1995 to 1999 it was also the venue for the Senior Open Championships.*

13 Bunker danger
Three bunkers guard the outer corner of the sharp dogleg 13th. An accurate tee-shot is needed to pass them. Once on the fairway, the approach is simple, except for a fiendish bunker short of the green to the left.

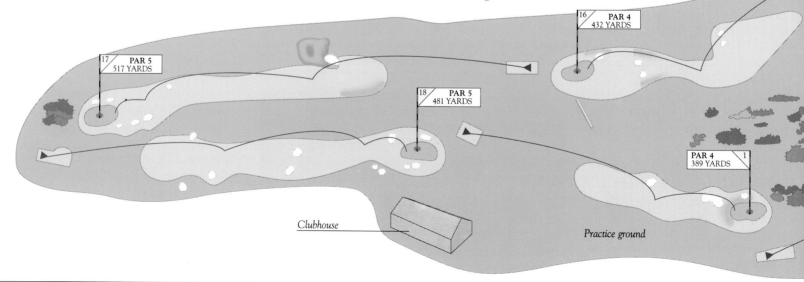

14 Calamity corner
The 213-yard 14th on Dunluce is one of the most famous holes in Ireland. Depending on the wind, the tee-shot demands anything from a medium iron to a solid blow with the driver. A chasm to the green's right leaves no margin for error and the hole is aptly named Calamity.

Royal Portrush was originally founded in May 1888 as the County Club, with Colonel J.M. McCalmont, MP, and J.S. Alexander (known as the "Admiral of Portglenone") as the founding fathers. Portraits of these pioneers still hang in the clubhouse. In 1892 the club was granted royal patronage by the Duke of York. Three years later, it became the Royal Portrush Golf Club, with the Prince of Wales, later King Edward VII, as patron.

The original layout at Portrush in 1888 was nine holes, but within a year another nine had been added. At that time eight holes were on the landward side of the coast road that runs out to the famous rock formations of the Giant's Causeway, but over the years substantial changes have resulted in the course moving further out into the dunes. The towering

sandhills provide a vast panorama. To the west are the Donegal hills, and north over the sea lie Islay and the Hebrides. The Causeway and the Skerries are to the east.

NARROW FAIRWAYS
The Dunluce fairways are narrow and all, except the 1st and the 18th, dogleg one way or the other, demanding accuracy as well as length from the tee. Max Faulkner won the Open Championship here in 1951 thanks to a fiercely curved second shot to the green at the last hole.

In 1995 his son-in-law Brian Barnes won the Senior Open Championship on the Dunluce course, followed, also on Portrush's links turf by Gary Player (1997), Brian Huggett (1998) and Christy O'Connor Jnr in 1999.

16 **PAR 4** 432 YARDS

17 **PAR 5** 517 YARDS

18 **PAR 5** 481 YARDS

PAR 4 389 YARDS 1

Clubhouse

Practice ground

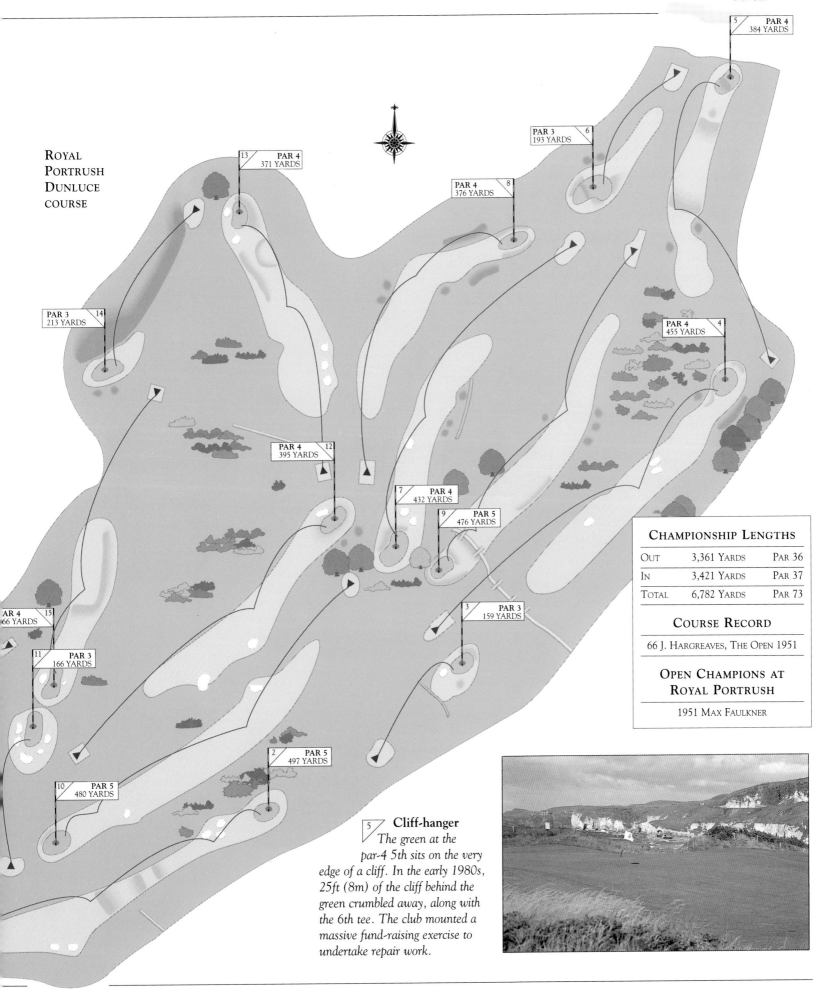

Irish Sea

ROYAL
PORTRUSH
DUNLUCE
COURSE

| 5 | PAR 4 384 YARDS |

| PAR 3 193 YARDS | 6 |

| 13 | PAR 4 371 YARDS |

| PAR 4 376 YARDS | 8 |

| PAR 3 213 YARDS | 14 |

| PAR 4 455 YARDS | 4 |

| PAR 4 395 YARDS | 12 |

| 7 | PAR 4 432 YARDS |

| 9 | PAR 5 476 YARDS |

| 3 | PAR 3 159 YARDS |

| AR 4 66 YARDS | 15 |

| 11 | PAR 3 166 YARDS |

| 2 | PAR 5 497 YARDS |

| 10 | PAR 5 480 YARDS |

CHAMPIONSHIP LENGTHS

OUT	3,361 YARDS	PAR 36
IN	3,421 YARDS	PAR 37
TOTAL	6,782 YARDS	PAR 73

COURSE RECORD

66 J. HARGREAVES, THE OPEN 1951

OPEN CHAMPIONS AT ROYAL PORTRUSH

1951 MAX FAULKNER

5 Cliff-hanger
The green at the par-4 5th sits on the very edge of a cliff. In the early 1980s, 25ft (8m) of the cliff behind the green crumbled away, along with the 6th tee. The club mounted a massive fund-raising exercise to undertake repair work.

171

ROYAL ST GEORGE'S

ROYAL ST GEORGE'S GOLF CLUB, SANDWICH, KENT, ENGLAND

T HIS FINE LINKS, *with its towering sandhills and rumpled fairways, has a long and distinguished history in English golf dating back to the mid-1880s. It began when Dr Laidlaw Purves, a Scot who had come down from Edinburgh and who was a member at Royal Wimbledon, set out in search of a suitable seaside site for a course to serve the needs of London golfers. At that time inland courses were not highly thought of and Dr Purves wanted to create a links course inspired, no doubt, by the fine examples he had left behind in his native country.*

It is said the good doctor surveyed the links of Sandwich from the tower of St Clement's church and declared it perfect. In 1887 he formed the Sandwich Golfing Association and plans were drawn up. Since then there have been changes, the most recent of which have been to the 14th where the green has been moved to the right and is now tucked against the boundary fence.

Sloping lies on the fairways are a common factor on the undulating ground and have prompted several famous players to criticize the Kent links as "unfair". But this is a harsh judgement as St George's is certainly a classic seaside links.

The great Henry Cotton, who won the first of his three Open titles at Sandwich, was a firm admirer of this famous links.

ROYAL ST GEORGE'S CHAMPIONSHIP COURSE

Suez Canal

13 PAR 4 443 YARDS

PAR 4 365 YARDS 12

PAR 4 478 YARDS 15

14 PAR 5 551 YARDS

PAR 3 163 YARDS 16

Practice area

PAR 4 468 YARDS 18

Duncan's Hollow

Clubhouse

Putting green

1 **Stay out of the Kitchen**
A thatched starter's hut stands alongside the 1st tee. A short drive at this opening hole means that the second shot will have to be played from a hollow known as the Kitchen.

6 **Against the breeze**
The par-3 6th needs a tricky shot into the prevailing wind to the green, which is guarded by four bunkers. The one to the left of the green is particularly dangerous.

wich Flats

5 Bottled out

In the celebrated 1949 Open Championship, the Irish player Harry Bradshaw was leading the field in the final round when he found his ball lying inside a broken beer bottle behind the 5th green. He elected to play the ball as it lay and smashed it out. But he ran up a 6 and was eventually beaten by Bobby Locke in a play-off. It is argued that his famous "bottle shot" cost him the Open, as he was entitled to a free lift and drop. If he had taken it he would probably have had a putt for a 4.

Cotton once remarked: "The turf at Sandwich gives lies one dreams about. The ball is always 'lying a treat', so with larks singing and the sun shining on the waters of Pegwell, it is a golfer's heaven."

COURSE OF CHAMPIONS

In 1894 it was decided that the Open Championship should be moved to England for the first time and Royal St George's was chosen as the venue. The Championship was won for the first time by an English professional, the legendary J.H. Taylor, marking the start of the domination of the event by the Great Triumvirate of Vardon, Braid and Taylor. The course has thus long been associated with the Open and hosted it nine times up to Bobby Locke's win there in 1949. It fell out of favour after that because the Open had become too big an event for the little town of Sandwich to handle comfortably. Eventually the Royal & Ancient decided to take the Open back to St George's in 1981, and in 1985, when Sandy Lyle won the first British victory in 16 years, and again in 1993 when Greg Norman won his second Open Championship title. The course is firmly back on the Open rota.

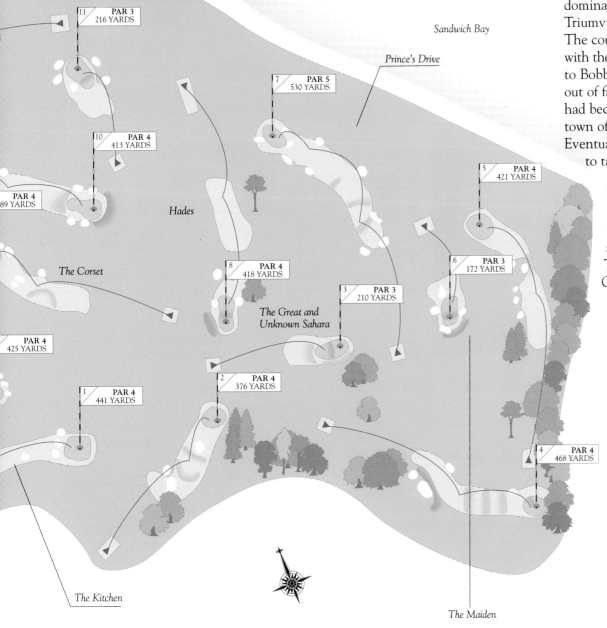

Sandwich Bay

Prince's Drive

11 PAR 3 216 YARDS

7 PAR 5 530 YARDS

10 PAR 4 413 YARDS

5 PAR 4 421 YARDS

PAR 4 89 YARDS

Hades

The Corset

8 PAR 4 418 YARDS

6 PAR 3 172 YARDS

3 PAR 3 210 YARDS

The Great and Unknown Sahara

PAR 4 425 YARDS

2 PAR 4 376 YARDS

1 PAR 4 441 YARDS

4 PAR 4 468 YARDS

The Kitchen

The Maiden

CHAMPIONSHIP LENGTHS		
OUT	3,425 YARDS	PAR 35
IN	3,522 YARDS	PAR 35
TOTAL	6,947 YARDS	PAR 70

COURSE RECORD

63 PAYNE STEWART, THE OPEN 1993;
NICK FALDO, THE OPEN 1993

OPEN CHAMPIONS AT ROYAL ST GEORGE'S

1894 J.H. TAYLOR; 1899 HARRY VARDON; 1904 JACK WHITE; 1911 HARRY VARDON; 1922 WALTER HAGEN; 1928 WALTER HAGEN; 1934 HENRY COTTON; 1938 REG WHITCOMBE; 1949 BOBBY LOCKE; 1981 BILL ROGERS; 1985 SANDY LYLE; 1993 GREG NORMAN

ROYAL SYDNEY

THE ROYAL SYDNEY GOLF CLUB, ROSE BAY, NEW SOUTH WALES, AUSTRALIA

UNDULATING GREENS, NARROW *fairways and fearsome rough combine to give Royal Sydney its reputation as one of the finest courses in Australia. When the Royal Sydney Golf Club was founded in 1893, the members played on a nine-hole layout. Three years later, under the direction of the club's new professional, James Scott, the course was extended to 18 holes. These holes were built on the inside of the original nine on sandy soil, a terrain that gives Royal Sydney something of the flavour of links golf. S.J. Robbie is generally credited with the original design, but Dr Alister MacKenzie, famous for his work at Augusta National and Royal Melbourne, stamped his unmistakable mark on the course in the 1920s.*

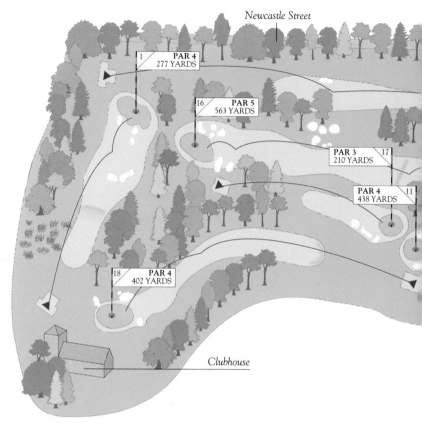

Drawing round the bend
The 18th is one of the best finishing holes in Australia. A stiff dogleg left of 402 yards, it needs a drive long enough to pass the elbow of the bend to leave a clear approach to the green. Shots less than 230 yards from the tee may be blocked out by trees but the big hitters, who can draw the ball round the corner, have a significant advantage. The green is large, but care must be taken to avoid bunkers that threaten any shots dragged short and to the right.

MacKenzie concentrated on alterations to the bunkers, making them bigger and deeper as well as adding to the number. The sand is dazzling white and soft – it is quite common to find the ball in a plugged lie in a Royal Sydney bunker.

Further alterations were made to the course during the 1980s, in preparation for Royal Sydney to host the Australian Open in 1988. In particular, the greens were enlarged significantly.

As with all courses close to the sea, the wind is a constant factor. It can change from being off the sea in the morning to off the land in the afternoon, as the land heats up relative to the sea. Generally, the weather is good, as would be expected from a course sited on this clement part of the Australian continent, although the occurrence of violent thunderstorms can be a hazard for golfers in October.

SUCCESS STORY

In 1897, four years after the club was founded, it was granted royal patronage. It quickly became established as one of the best courses in Australia, and has now developed into a vast golf, tennis and social club with almost 6,000 members.

Royal Sydney lies only ten minutes away from the centre of Sydney and is surrounded by the fashionable houses of the city suburbs. The course has a high proportion of elevated tees looking down to open fairways below, with greens stretching out into the distance. This attractive feature was made possible by the natural site. The ground forms a saucer shape, allowing the tees to be cut into the higher ground around the slopes.

The variable wind is the course's main defence. On those occasions when it does not blow too strongly, Royal Sydney is vulnerable to the skills of the world's top professionals. Mark Calcavecchia proved this conclusively in the 1988 Australian Open. The American's winning score was 19 under the course's par.

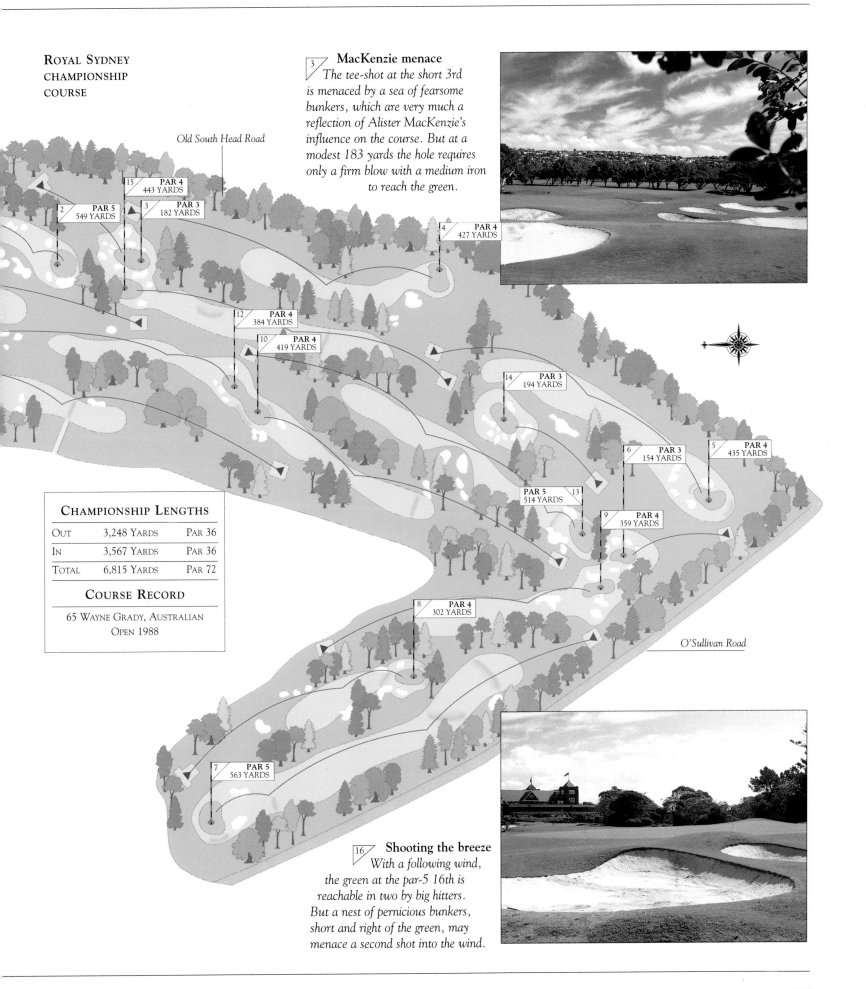

ROYAL SYDNEY
CHAMPIONSHIP
COURSE

Old South Head Road

15 **PAR 4** 443 YARDS

2 **PAR 5** 549 YARDS

3 **PAR 3** 182 YARDS

4 **PAR 4** 427 YARDS

12 **PAR 4** 384 YARDS

10 **PAR 4** 419 YARDS

14 **PAR 3** 194 YARDS

6 **PAR 3** 154 YARDS

5 **PAR 4** 435 YARDS

PAR 5 514 YARDS 13

9 **PAR 4** 359 YARDS

8 **PAR 4** 302 YARDS

7 **PAR 5** 563 YARDS

O'Sullivan Road

3 **MacKenzie menace**
The tee-shot at the short 3rd is menaced by a sea of fearsome bunkers, which are very much a reflection of Alister MacKenzie's influence on the course. But at a modest 183 yards the hole requires only a firm blow with a medium iron to reach the green.

CHAMPIONSHIP LENGTHS

OUT	3,248 YARDS	PAR 36
IN	3,567 YARDS	PAR 36
TOTAL	6,815 YARDS	PAR 72

COURSE RECORD

65 WAYNE GRADY, AUSTRALIAN
OPEN 1988

16 **Shooting the breeze**
With a following wind, the green at the par-5 16th is reachable in two by big hitters. But a nest of pernicious bunkers, short and right of the green, may menace a second shot into the wind.

ROYAL TROON

ROYAL TROON GOLF CLUB, TROON, AYRSHIRE, SCOTLAND

T HE MARVELLOUS COURSE *at Royal Troon lies at the southern end of a long run of duneland stretching from Irvine to Prestwick, that is host to most of the best links courses on the west side of Scotland. Troon is an exceptionally demanding course, recognized as one of the sternest tests on the Open Championship rota. The club was awarded its royal charter in 1978, its centenary year.*

Troon emblem
The serpent circling the clubs is the symbol of medicine – a reference to Dr Highet, instigator of the club, and its first honorary secretary and treasurer. The motto means "as much by skill as by strength".

In at the finish
Members can watch the action at the last green from the comfort of the clubhouse smoke room, out of the wind.

There are many stories of golf being played on the links at Troon long before there was a recognized golf course on this beautiful stretch of Ayrshire coastline. There is evidence in Ian Mackintosh's excellent history of the club that a "course" of four or five holes existed as early as 1870. The holes on this course were cut with a knife and "were neither round nor square, but were large enough!"

PLANNING TROON

The club itself, however, did not come into existence until March 1878. The prospective members met for the first time to lay their plans in a local hostelry, the Portland Arms Hotel, at the instigation of Dr John Highet. Another of the founding fathers was James Dickie from Paisley, a town on the outskirts of

Glasgow. Although he did not live in Troon, Dickie was no stranger to the area, where he had a summer house. It was Dickie who approached the 6th Duke of Portland, the owner of the Estate of Fullarton upon which he wanted to build the course.

He was granted permission for a golf club to play on the land between Craigend and the Pow Burn. Part of this ground turned out to be unsuitable and the founding fathers of Troon Golf Club had to make do with the ground from Craigend to Gyaws Burn. Today the Craigend Burn is piped under the road in front of the clubhouse, while the Gyaws Burn is still a part of the course.

The original design of the Old course at Troon is credited to George Strath, and the 1883 Open Champion Willie Fernie who was also the club professional. Over the years changes have been made to lengthen the course and refine the bunkering, with contributions from James Braid, Dr Alister MacKenzie and Frank Pennink.

James Braid
In the mid 1920s James Braid was asked by the club for advice on bunkering.

Arthur Havers won the first Open played at Troon in 1923 and many illustrious names have joined him in Troon's list of Open Champions since. It was 27 years after Havers's victory before the Open was back there again, when the great South African, Bobby Locke, won with a score of 279, the first time 280 had been broken in the Championship.

In 1962 Arnold Palmer came to defend his Open title at Troon and won with a new record score of 276. Tom Weiskopf was a popular winner in 1973, equalling Palmer's score, and Tom Watson won the fourth of his five Open

Holiday golf (above)
This postcard shows the clubhouse before the First World War. The combination of a railway and a golf course meant that golfers flocked on holiday to Troon, to sample the delights of this west-coast links and the hospitality of the clubhouse.

Golf doctor (above)
Local doctor John Highet called the original small group of members together in the Portland Arms Hotel to start the club in March 1878.

Rough escape (right)
Tiger Woods plays his second shot from the rough to the 18th green in the 1997 Open. Despite Tiger's record round of 64, the title went to Justin Leonard.

THE NAMES OF ROYAL TROON

1st	Seal	10th	Sandhills
2nd	Black Rock	11th	The Railway
3rd	Gyaws	12th	The Fox
4th	Dunure	13th	Burmah
5th	Greenan	14th	Alton
6th	Turnberry	15th	Crosbie
7th	Tel-El-Kebir	16th	Well
8th	Postage Stamp	17th	Rabbit
9th	The Monk	18th	Craigend

The 12th is named the Fox not because it is tricky, but because there was once a copse alongside the present tee that sheltered foxes. Tel-el-Kebir, the name of the 7th, recalls a battle fought in Egypt in 1882.

Wind and sand
The 17th is one of the toughest par 3s in championship golf. It is 223 yards long to a plateau green that is difficult to hold. Five bunkers guard the green, with the three on the right dangerous in the prevailing wind, which blows over the player's left shoulder. The green slopes away on all sides, so missing it leaves a difficult pitch back to salvage a par.

titles there in 1982. In 1989 the Open went to a four-hole play-off for the first time, with Mark Calcavecchia pitted against Greg Norman and Wayne Grady. Norman lost his chance when he took three from the back of the green at the notorious 17th, and Calcavecchia birdied on the 18th to win. The 1997 Open Championship at Troon saw Justin Leonard catch up on Jesper Parnevik's six-shot lead on the final day to clinch victory.

THE LONG AND THE SHORT
There are several famous holes at Royal Troon, including the long and fearsome 6th, known as Turnberry. It has a long carry into the wind off the tee to reach a narrow strip of fairway guarded by a

triangle of bunkers, two to the left and one to the right. The drive is best placed just to the right of the left-hand bunkers, while the second shot must avoid a bunker on the left side of the fairway 50 yards short of the green and a cavernously deep bunker, situated on the right-hand side 20 yards farther on.

A long line of high dunes covered in impenetrable rough runs along the right side of the fairway and the green itself sits in the lee of a massive dune. It is guarded by a wickedly deep bunker that eats into the front left of the green.

Even when conditions are favourable there are few who can reach the green in two strokes – or who are brave enough even to try – and when the wind is

blowing against the player, usually with a hint of right quarter to it, the green is simply out of anyone's reach in two.

POSTAGE STAMP
The shortest hole in Open Championship golf is Troon's 8th, known as the Postage Stamp. This is where, in the 1973 Open, American Gene Sarazen, a winner in his time of all the game's Major

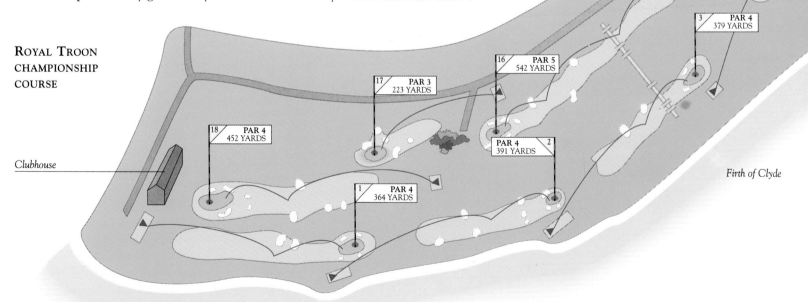

ROYAL TROON CHAMPIONSHIP COURSE

Clubhouse

Firth of Clyde

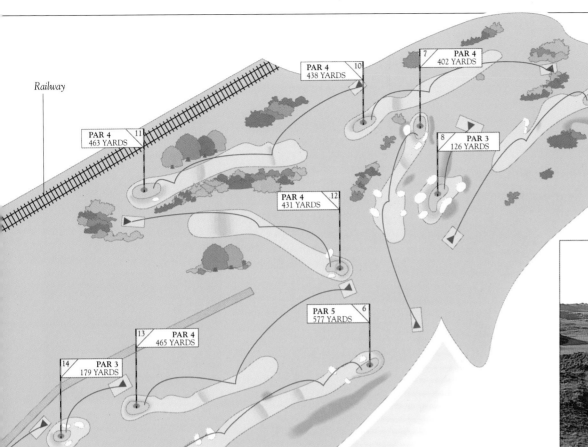

Railway

PAR 4
11 463 YARDS

PAR 4
10 438 YARDS

7 PAR 4
402 YARDS

9 PAR 4
423 YARDS

PAR 4
12 431 YARDS

8 PAR 3
126 YARDS

PAR 5
577 YARDS 6

13 PAR 4
465 YARDS

14 PAR 3
179 YARDS

5 PAR 3
210 YARDS

4 PAR 5
557 YARDS

8 Short but deadly
*The 8th at Royal Troon,
famous throughout the world
as the Postage Stamp, is the
shortest hole in British Open
golf. It is a modest 126 yards
long but it is, as Henry Leach
once wrote, "as full of
wickedness as it is of beauty."*

11 Off the rails
*The long par-4 11th is fraught with
danger. Hitting out-of-bounds over
the railway is a real risk approaching
the green. There is so much gorse that
only one bunker is needed as an
extra hazard.*

CHAMPIONSHIP LENGTHS		
OUT	3,429 YARDS	PAR 36
IN	3,650 YARDS	PAR 35
TOTAL	7,079 YARDS	PAR 71

COURSE RECORD

64 GREG NORMAN, THE OPEN 1989;
TIGER WOODS, THE OPEN 1997

OPEN CHAMPIONS AT ROYAL TROON

1923 ARTHUR HAVERS; 1950 BOBBY
LOCKE; 1962 ARNOLD PALMER;
1973 TOM WEISKOPF; 1982 TOM
WATSON; 1989 MARK CALCAVECCHIA;
1997 JUSTIN LEONARD

championships, paid a sentimental visit to
play honorary rounds with two former
champions, Fred Daly and Max Faulkner.
Sarazen needed only a total of three
strokes to play the 8th hole twice –
without using his putter at all.

In the first round he punched a 5-iron
at the Postage Stamp. The ball pitched
short of the hole and rolled in. It was an
astounding stroke witnessed by millions
on television. Sarazen observed: "When
the clubhead came in contact with the
ball, I had the same feeling I'd had when
I hit my second shot at the Masters in
Augusta in 1935 for the double eagle."

The following day Sarazen played the
same club at the same hole and found one
of the five deep bunkers that surround the
green. His recovery shot from the sand
went straight into the hole for an even
more remarkable two. Sarazen presented
his 5-iron to the Royal & Ancient Golf
Club at St Andrews, where it now remains.

RYE

RYE GOLF CLUB, CAMBER, RYE, EAST SUSSEX, ENGLAND

*T**HE ANCIENT WALLED** town of Rye on the south coast of England is a place of history and tradition, and so too is the great course that bears its name. This is not the world of brash, modern commercial golf. It is a place where there is still respect for the older and, some might say, better values of the game.*

New clubhouse
The Rye course suffered badly during the Second World War and the old clubhouse was badly damaged by a flying bomb that exploded on the 15th fairway in 1944. The clubhouse was not rebuilt until 1949.

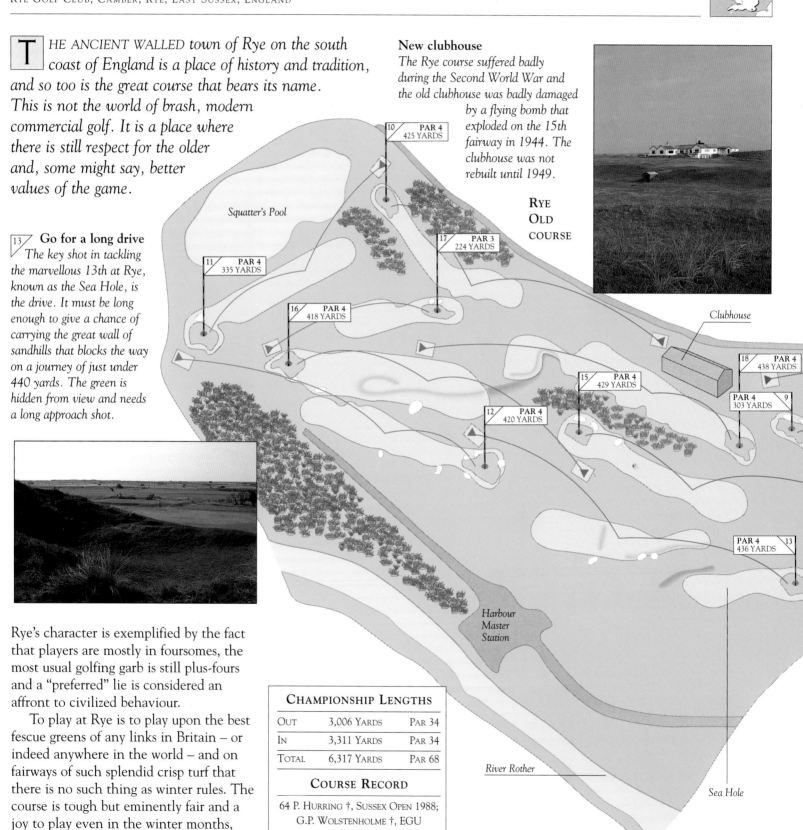

Go for a long drive
The key shot in tackling the marvellous 13th at Rye, known as the Sea Hole, is the drive. It must be long enough to give a chance of carrying the great wall of sandhills that blocks the way on a journey of just under 440 yards. The green is hidden from view and needs a long approach shot.

RYE OLD COURSE

Rye's character is exemplified by the fact that players are mostly in foursomes, the most usual golfing garb is still plus-fours and a "preferred" lie is considered an affront to civilized behaviour.

To play at Rye is to play upon the best fescue greens of any links in Britain – or indeed anywhere in the world – and on fairways of such splendid crisp turf that there is no such thing as winter rules. The course is tough but eminently fair and a joy to play even in the winter months, when the fairways are always dry, and the

CHAMPIONSHIP LENGTHS		
OUT	3,006 YARDS	PAR 34
IN	3,311 YARDS	PAR 34
TOTAL	6,317 YARDS	PAR 68

COURSE RECORD

64 P. HURRING †, SUSSEX OPEN 1988;
G.P. WOLSTENHOLME †, EGU
CHAMPIONS 1994

greens fast and true. It is a salutary reminder of the need to preserve traditional British golfing turf. No artificial fertilizers have been used on this land and Rye is all the better for it.

Rye is an excellent links course and many of the holes are quite deceptively difficult. The wind is a key factor when it blows, and at Rye it is usually blowing. A typical Rye hole is the par-4 16th. It needs a good drive to have any chance of a par. At 418 yards the 16th is not unduly long, but the tee-shot must carry over a ridge running diagonally across the fairway. Even with the drive well placed, there is still much work to be done. The second demands a substantial blow with a long iron, or even a wood, to reach the green.

There have been many changes at Rye since the first course was built in 1894. Most of them have been brought about by the increase in traffic along the road that runs along the northern boundary. There was considerable upheaval to the course just before the start of the First World War and more changes were made after hostilities ceased. New holes have also been built since the Second World War, with the result that the first half of the course has changed completely and retains only the 5th from earlier times.

CONSERVING TRADITION

But if the layout has changed, little else has at Rye. It is a conservative place where the old corrugated pavilion might well still be there, were it not for the German bomb that destroyed it in 1944. The new one is a comfortable replacement which presents the prospect of an excellent lunch and good company.

As home of the Oxford and Cambridge Golfing Society, Rye is also the venue for the Society's annual tournament for the President's Putter,

4 **Tough going**
The 4th ranks among golf's greatest holes. The drive on to the narrow fairway is always hard enough, but when the wind blows, as it often does at Rye, it is a searching test of nerve and technique. There are rough sandhills on the left and a drop down to the plain on the other side. The 4th is not nearly the longest of the two-shot holes, but there is none harder.

Rye–Camber Road

always held in the month of January. The heavy snow of the winter of 1979 forced cancellation that year, but that is the only time since the first Putter was played for in 1920 that the weather prevented play. On one occasion play had to be transferred to Littlestone because of frost in the opening rounds, but otherwise the Putter goes on regardless.

The putter for which contestants play was originally owned by the 1891 Open Champion, Hugh Kirkaldy. The club was used by the Society's first president, John L. Low, when he was narrowly beaten by Harold Hilton in the final of the Amateur Championship at St Andrews in 1901. Today it hangs on the clubhouse wall. Attached to it is a row of balls that commemorate the winners of the Putter.

5 **Green in the hills**
The attractive 5th is a par 3 across a wide gully. The green sits high up in the sandhills and is slightly saucer-shaped. A medium iron is all that is called for under reasonable conditions for a hole of just over 160 yards, but the stroke must be truly and carefully struck if the ball is to hold the green and not run over.

ST ANDREWS

ST ANDREWS LINKS MANAGEMENT COMMITTEE, ST ANDREWS, FIFE, SCOTLAND

P ERHAPS THE MOST *thrilling sight in golf is that of the ancient buildings and dramatic spires of the town of St Andrews standing sentinel over the most famous stretch of golf links in the world. Here lies the cradle of the game, its historical and cultural home, the Mecca to which every golfer who ever put club to ball wants to make a pilgrimage at least once during his golfing life.*

It is here that great deeds have been done and rules and standards set. And it is here that the golfing world still looks today for example and guidance.

Golf has been played on the Old Course itself for more than 400 years, and on the links of the town for longer still. The course is unique in that it owes little to the hand of man in its design or layout. It has evolved over the centuries at the whim of time and tide, a masterpiece that stands as a lasting tribute to the shaping power of nature itself.

All the great names in the history of the game (with the exception of Ben Hogan) have walked across the famous little stone bridge over the Swilcan Burn on to the final fairway with, before them, the most famous view in golf.

The Royal & Ancient clubhouse stands guard over the vast expanse of the fairway shared by the first and last holes. Crossing that antique bridge and looking towards the clubhouse, the wide stretch of the West Sands lies to the left, sweeping away towards the Eden Estuary.

To the right is the ancient town itself, which is the home not only of the game of golf but also of Scotland's most ancient and respected seat of higher academic learning, the University of St Andrews. The Old Course is the classic seaside links, although the sea is seldom in view, except on the first and last holes where the view of St Andrews Bay is dramatic.

There are none of the great dunes found at, for example, Royal Birkdale, only undulating fairways with little elevation, crossed at intervals by the huge double greens. There are only four single greens on the Old course – the 1st, the 9th, the famous 17th and the 18th.

The 1st tee is directly in front of the big window of the Royal & Ancient clubhouse. Before the player stretches the most inviting fairway in the game. Shared with the 18th, it is more than 100 yards wide. But despite this tempting expanse, the stroke from the 1st tee on the Old Course at St Andrews remains the most nerve-racking for openers anywhere in the world.

Once across the Swilcan Burn that guards the 1st green, and where the shot is always one more club than you think, the course turns right and follows the sweep of St Andrews Bay, sharing fairways and greens along the way,

Crossed clubs
The St Andrews Links crest has an image of the saint with crossed clubs in place of the normal cross of the St Andrews flag.

R & A trophy room
The R & A clubhouse exhibits in its trophy room the silver clubs, to which each captain adds a silver or gold ball after taking office.

Golfing party
On the 1st fairway golfers and their caddies contemplate the shot. Clubs used to be carried loose; the bag is a comparatively recent invention.

Early putters (above)
This engraving purports to show a group of players holing out on the 1st green in 1798. However, the clubhouse, visible in the top left of the picture, was not built until 1854.

Stone bridge (right)
The stone span of Swilcan Bridge, once the route into the ancient city from the west, has been crossed by almost all the great names in the history of the game. It shows the way to the magnificent old clubhouse that dominates the view over the links.

until it turns right again at the start of what is known as the Loop. It is here, starting at the 7th and finishing at the 11th, where the fairways of these two holes cross, that game-winning scores have to be made.

Within this run of five holes, the Old Course's only two short holes are found – the 8th and the wickedly difficult 11th, known as the High Hole (in). From there the course starts for home back along the path already trodden, often sharing the fairways of the journey out and playing to the other side of the huge double greens. White flags mark the pins on the outward journey, whereas red distinguishes the

Rainy day (left)
This painting by J. Michael Brown (1880–1916), titled A Rainy Day at St Andrews, is probably of the 13th hole. It records the match between Harold Hilton and Robert Harris in the 1913 Amateur Championship. Hilton won by 6-and-5.

THE ROYAL & ANCIENT GOLF CLUB

The Royal & Ancient Golf Club came into existence in 1754 when the first members gathered for copious eating and drinking, either at Baillie Glass's or the Black Bull Tavern. The club was known as the Society of St Andrews Golfers, until King William IV became the Society's patron in 1834 and the title of the Royal & Ancient Golf Club of St Andrews was conferred.

Ten years after the Society was formed, it decreed that the number of holes on the Old Course should be reduced from 22 to 18, the standard that has prevailed to this day. Contrary to widespread belief, the Royal & Ancient Golf Club does not own the Old Course. The course is held in trust by the local authority under an Act of Parliament. This ensures that the world's most famous course remains, as it has always been, a municipal links that is open to anyone to play upon payment of a green fee.

The Royal & Ancient is the governing body of golf throughout the world, with the exception of the United States and Mexico. It sets and reviews the rules and standards of the game and is the arbiter in disputes. It also runs and administers several major events, of which the Open Championship is the most important. It derives considerable revenue from what has now become a large-scale commercial enterprise, and ploughs the money back into the development of the game, benefiting all aspects from junior golf to the training of greenkeepers.

But the Royal & Ancient is also a private golf club and is used by its members as such. There are two major meetings of the members each year, in the spring and the autumn, when the club's competitions are played – for the Silver Cross of St Andrews in the spring and the Gold Medal in the autumn. The George Glennie Medal is awarded annually for the lowest aggregate score over the two meetings. These are also enjoyable social occasions, when members from all over the world gather to swap tales of golfing triumph and disaster.

Medal Day 1894 (left)
This painting, hanging in the clubhouse of the R & A, depicts future British Prime Minister Arthur James Balfour playing himself in as the club's captain during the Autumn Meeting of 1894. The names of all 191 figures are known. Apparently, Balfour hit a fine drive.

Ticket to St Andrews (right)
This coveted tag shows the bearer was a guest of the Royal & Ancient Club at the 1990 Open. The annual event is run by the R & A.

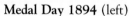

Leaping the burn

In their enthusiasm to follow the action during the final round of the 1927 Open, members of the gallery hurdle the Swilcan Burn. The Open was won by the legendary Bobby Jones with a score of 285.

ULTIMATE SAND TRAPS

There are 112 bunkers, and in preparation for the 2000 Open all were rebuilt with revetted faces, a form of construction that involves building up the face of the bunker using squares of turf. The result is extremely steep faces, almost vertical in some cases, and makes them very serious hazards. Many are hidden from view, a result perhaps of the fact that, in days past, the course was played in a clockwise

Pre-war guide

A spectators' guide to the 1939 Open, the last held for seven years. It was won by Dick Burton, breaking the run of American wins at St Andrews. The first post-war Open was also at St Andrews in 1946.

homeward stretch. The exception is the last hole, where tradition demands that the flag is white. The course has changed little in its layout over the years but has been lengthened somewhat to accommodate improvements in performance and equipment among the top players. For the 2000 Open

Training for golf

This 1920s poster was distributed by the London and North Eastern Railway, which served St Andrews at that time. The growth in the popularity of golf was closely tied to the spread of railways, giving easy access to these remote locations.

direction and not in the current anti-clockwise route. Tiger Woods was quick to realize in 2000 that avoiding the bunkers was vital to victory. Not once in four rounds did Woods find sand off the tee on his way to victory.

Many of these treacherous obstacles have fascinating names. The most famous is known as Hell, a huge pit of sand that

Championship five holes were increased by a total of just over 180 yards to take the course length to 7,115 yards. But apart from the new tees built to add this extra length, the course was much the same for Tiger Woods when he won the Championship in 2000 as it was for Tom Kidd when he won the first Open over the Old Course in 1873. The key to success over the Old Course is to avoid the fearsome and often deep bunkers.

Faldo's triumph

Confirming his position as one of the greats, Britain's Nick Faldo won the Open Championship at St Andrews in 1990. Here he holes out at the 18th in front of the huge crowds that St Andrews now attracts during the final round.

9 **Birdie chance** (left)
The 9th is a short par 4 at 356 yards and should leave a short chip to the flat green for big hitters. During championships, golfers look to this hole for a birdie. The bunkers can still catch the unwary, however.

ST ANDREWS
OLD
COURSE

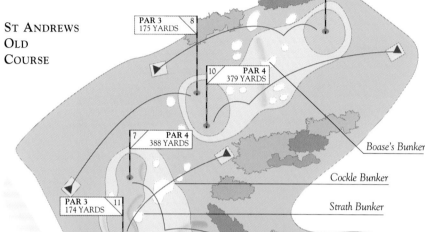

PAR 4 352 YARDS — 9

PAR 3 175 YARDS — 8

10 — **PAR 4** 379 YARDS

7 — **PAR 4** 388 YARDS

PAR 3 174 YARDS — 11

Boase's Bunker

Cockle Bunker

Strath Bunker

12 — **PAR 4** 314 YARDS

6 — **PAR 4** 412 YARDS

PAR 4 430 YARDS — 13

5 — **PAR 5** 568 YARDS

PAR 4 464 YARDS — 4

PAR 5 581 YARDS — 14

River Eden Estuary

Cottage Bunker

Formed by nature
The Old Course is on a strip of land jutting into the Eden Estuary. The land is mostly level, but has many bumps and depressions. Sea and wind have sculpted the layout, endowing it with a very different character from today's man-made courses.

Nick's Bunker

Coffin Bunkers

The Beardies   Elysian Fields   Hell Bunker   Ginger Beer Bunkers

THE NAMES OF THE OLD COURSE AT ST ANDREWS

1ST BURN	10TH BOBBY JONES
2ND DYKE	11TH HIGH (IN)
3RD CARTGATE (OUT)	12TH HEATHERY (IN)
4TH GINGER BEER	13TH HOLE O'CROSS (IN)
5TH HOLE O'CROSS (OUT)	14TH LONG
6TH HEATHERY (OUT)	15TH CARTGATE (IN)
7TH HIGH (OUT)	16TH CORNER OF DYKE
8TH SHORT	17TH ROAD
9TH END	18TH TOM MORRIS

The 4th hole takes its name from a ginger beer stall run there by David Anderson, known as Old Da', during the last century.

14 **Infernal hazard**
The key factor in playing the notorious 14th hole is to avoid the Beardies group of bunkers down the left side. The vast, deep Hell bunker defends the Long Hole from the second shot 100 yards from the green, at the end of the flat stretch of fairway that is known as the Elysian Fields. Many golfers who have not played safely, either to the left or the right side, have found themselves coming to terrible grief in this frightening cavern.

guards the 14th, the Long Hole. In front of the 7th green, the High Hole (out), is the huge Cockle bunker, and a few yards to its left Strath bunker eats into the front of the 11th. At the 16th, the Corner of the Dyke, a group of three bunkers are known as the Principal's Nose. Only one of them is visible from the tee and it lies in the centre of the fairway. Many are those who have felt confident that they have driven sufficiently well to pass the Principal's Nose, only to find their ball nestling deeply in Deacon Sime, a nasty little pot bunker some 30 yards further on. The notorious Road bunker, which eats into the front of the 17th, the Road Hole, has also claimed many a top player.

One golfer who fell foul of the Road bunker was poor Tommy Nakajima. The Japanese player was well placed in the 1978 Open Championship until he found this bunker. He will be long remembered for the four strokes it took him to escape, as will David Duval for his embarrassing visit to the same bunker in the 2000 Open. He also needed four strokes to escape.

15 Nervous ending
Not such a hard hole, the 18th still holds a few surprises, especially the Valley of Sin, a series of depressions in front of the green. Match pressure causes many a crisis at this relatively simple last hole.

CHAMPIONSHIP LENGTHS		
OUT	3,545 YARDS	PAR 36
IN	3,570 YARDS	PAR 36
TOTAL	7,115 YARDS	PAR 72

COURSE RECORD

62 CURTIS STRANGE, DUNHILL CUP 1987 (OLD YARDAGE)

OPEN CHAMPIONS AT ST ANDREWS

1873 TOM KIDD; 1876 BOB MARTIN; 1879 JAMIE ANDERSON; 1882 BOB FERGUSON; 1885 BOB MARTIN; 1888 JACK BURNS; 1891 HUGH KIRKALDY; 1895, 1900 J.H. TAYLOR; 1905, 1910 JAMES BRAID; 1921 JOCK HUTCHISON; 1927 BOBBY JONES †; 1933 DENSMORE SHUTE; 1939 DICK BURTON; 1946 SAM SNEAD; 1955 PETER THOMSON; 1957 BOBBY LOCKE; 1960 KEL NAGLE; 1964 TONY LEMA; 1970, 1978 JACK NICKLAUS; 1984 SEVE BALLESTEROS; 1990 NICK FALDO; 1995 JOHN DALY; 2000 TIGER WOODS

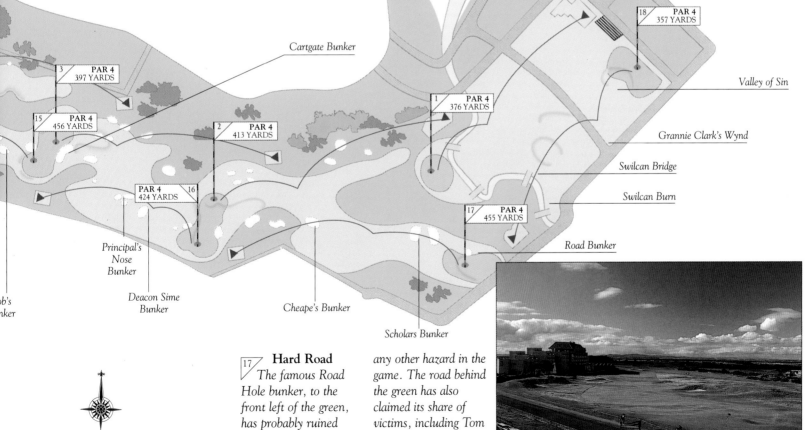

Cartgate Bunker

Royal & Ancient Clubhouse

Putting green

18 PAR 4 357 YARDS

Valley of Sin

3 PAR 4 397 YARDS

1 PAR 4 376 YARDS

Grannie Clark's Wynd

15 PAR 4 456 YARDS

2 PAR 4 413 YARDS

Swilcan Bridge

Swilcan Burn

PAR 4 424 YARDS 16

17 PAR 4 455 YARDS

Road Bunker

Principal's Nose Bunker

Deacon Sime Bunker

Cheape's Bunker

Scholars Bunker

b's nker

17 Hard Road
The famous Road Hole bunker, to the front left of the green, has probably ruined more scorecards than any other hazard in the game. The road behind the green has also claimed its share of victims, including Tom Watson in 1984.

EL SALER

EL SALER GOLF CLUB, EL SALER, VALENCIA, SPAIN

T HE COURSE DESIGNED *by Javier Arana at El Saler, near Valencia on the east coast of Spain, is one of Europe's best. Indeed, El Saler was, at one stage in its relatively short existence, rated by some players as the top course in continental Europe. The reliable climate, combined with intelligent use of the links-like terrain, make this course a true joy to play, as well as a tough challenge to match the more wind-blown courses of northern Europe.*

There are strong grounds for rating El Saler highly. At almost 6,500m in its championship guise, it is a stern test of golfing ability. Golf writer Peter Dobereiner once commented that "if it were transplanted to the west coast of Ireland, or to Scotland, exposed to the Atlantic gales, it would be a monster." This is indeed high praise.

The creator of this fine course, Javier Arana, is perhaps more widely remembered as a player than as a course architect, but his reputation as a designer is high. He has, however, confined his work to his native Spain, and it was not until the spread of European championship golf to that country in the early 1970s that the richness of his creations gained more

EL SALER CHAMPIONSHIP COURSE

Gulf of Valencia

Putting green

| 8 | PAR 4 |
| | 340 METRES |

| 7 | PAR 4 |
| | 340 METRES |

| 5 | PAR 5 |
| | 485 METRES |

| 9 | PAR 3 |
| | 145 METRES |

| 18 | PAR 4 |
| | 430 METRES |

| | PAR 5 | 15 |
| | 520 METRES | |

| 6 | PAR 4 |
| | 415 METRES |

| 4 | PAR 3 |
| | 175 METRES |

| 1 | PAR 4 |
| | 400 METRES |

| 3 | PAR 5 |
| | 485 METRES |

Clubhouse

1 **Pine green**
Umbrella pines grace the gentle inland landscape at the 1st. A drive right opens up the dogleg making the approach less difficult, but two greenside bunkers threaten, particularly one in the front right.

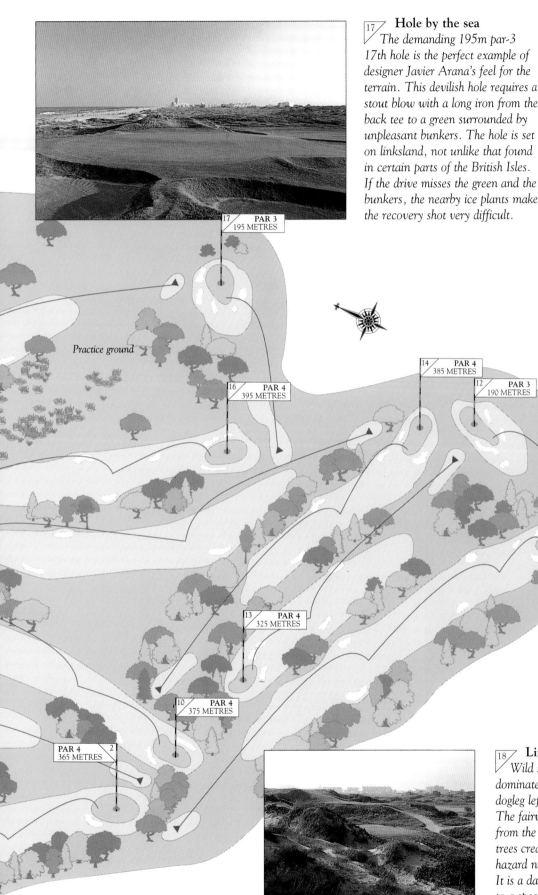

17 Hole by the sea
The demanding 195m par-3 17th hole is the perfect example of designer Javier Arana's feel for the terrain. This devilish hole requires a stout blow with a long iron from the back tee to a green surrounded by unpleasant bunkers. The hole is set on linksland, not unlike that found in certain parts of the British Isles. If the drive misses the green and the bunkers, the nearby ice plants make the recovery shot very difficult.

Practice ground

| 17 | PAR 3 |
| | 195 METRES |

| 14 | PAR 4 |
| | 385 METRES |

| 12 | PAR 3 |
| | 190 METRES |

| 16 | PAR 4 |
| | 395 METRES |

| 11 | PAR 5 |
| | 520 METRES |

| 13 | PAR 4 |
| | 325 METRES |

| 10 | PAR 4 |
| | 375 METRES |

| PAR 4 | 2 |
| 365 METRES | |

general acclaim. His Club de Campo course in Madrid and El Prat in Barcelona are highly thought of, but El Saler clearly rates as his masterpiece.

It covers an unusual combination of terrain, ranging from the umbrella pines of the farthest inland part of the course to the spectacular holes built among the sand dunes beside the Mediterranean. This is a combination that makes for a fascinating and varied challenge. Arana has made excellent use of the links environment in the seaside sections.

LANGER'S HOT ROUND
El Saler hosted a memorable Spanish Open in 1984. Bernhard Langer had to overcome the disruption of a robbery in his hotel bedroom, which relieved him of £3,000, and then a fine for slow play in the third round. On the final day he came back from seven strokes behind to win with a round of 62. The round included an amazing nine birdies in 11 holes from the 5th, and Langer, who went on to win the US Masters the following year, judged it to be the best he had ever played in his life. At the time, he also rated El Saler as one of the best courses in Europe.

The weather can be hot at El Saler in summer. However, with the variation in temperature between the sea and the land during the day, sea breezes can keep the air moving and cool things down. The clubhouse is close by one of Spain's magnificent paradors, the Parador Luis Vives, with its excellent hotel facilities.

18 Linksland
Wild sand dunes dominate the tee at the dogleg left par-4 18th. The fairway emerges from the links, with trees creating an added hazard near the green. It is a daunting finish to a spectacular course.

CHAMPIONSHIP LENGTHS		
OUT	3,150 METRES	PAR 36
IN	3,335 METRES	PAR 36
TOTAL	6,485 METRES	PAR 72

COURSE RECORD
62 BERNHARD LANGER, SPANISH OPEN 1984

SHINNECOCK HILLS

SHINNECOCK HILLS GOLF CLUB, SOUTHAMPTON, NEW YORK, USA

A S AMERICA'S FIRST 18-hole course, Shinnecock Hills has an important place in the history of golf in the New World. An early site of the importation of the game into the United States, it was heavily influenced by the traditional home of golf, Scotland, both in the choice of site and in the personalities associated with founding the course.

Shinnecock badge
Built on an Indian burial site, the course commemorates its native American link on its official badge.

After a short spell as professional at Westward Ho!, England, and then as professional and course designer at Biarritz in France, Scotsman Willie Dunn Jnr was persuaded, as were many before and after him, to move to the United States.

He was tempted there by a wealthy American, William K. Vanderbilt – the son of the founder of the Vanderbilt empire. He had seen Dunn stage an exhibition of his prowess as a player in southern France during the winter of 1890. On his return to the United States, Vanderbilt immediately started discussing

Rolling sandhills
Dunn and Vanderbilt chose the low-lying sandhills near the small resort of Southampton as a site for the course. Most of the work of cleaning off fairways and forming bunkers was done by hand.

with his friends the possibility of building a golf course at the fashionable summer resort of Southampton on Long Island, New York. Within a few months Willie Dunn, the former professional from Musselburgh, had quit France and was looking for a site where he could build a course for Vanderbilt. He chose a spot a couple of miles from the sea among sandhills reminiscent, in some ways, of his

native east coast of Scotland. Using the labour of Native Americans from a nearby reservation, and very little equipment other than a few roadscrapers drawn by horses, he laid out the first 12 holes at Shinnecock Hills, destined to be one of the world's most exclusive golf clubs.

These first holes were ready for play by late summer 1891. The members brought in Stanford White, one of the top architects of the day, to design and build a suitable clubhouse in the style of the surrounding area. By the summer of the following year it was ready for occupation, with locker rooms, shower baths and even a grill room. Shinnecock Hills was by far the best-appointed golf club in the United States.

The course was extended to 18 holes the following year and the game rapidly developed an influential following among the wealthy elite who spent their summers in fashionable Southampton. They even imported the custom of playing in red coats which had prevailed in the early days of the game in Britain.

INDIAN RELICS

It was not unusual for players to find some strange objects emerging when they played bunker shots on the original 12-hole layout. Old whiskey flasks and even human bones were excavated by overzealous use of the niblick. The explanation for these bizarre discoveries lies in the fact that scattered across the sandy land were some ancient Native Americans burial mounds, a few of which Willie Dunn shaped into bunkers.

Today the clubhouse built by Stanford White is still at the heart of the rambling Shinnecock Hills Club and, although the course that Dunn laid out may have

Red coats (below)
For a while after their founding, the members of Shinnecock wore red jackets when playing, after the early British tradition that evolved to warn others on the links that golfers were coming.

Hill house (right)
Nick Price drives towards the clubhouse in the 1995 US Open. The original building was opened in 1892, and forms the core of the club complex today.

Junior Scot (above)
Willie Dunn Jnr was brought from Europe to design Shinnecock.

SHINNECOCK HILLS CHAMPIONSHIP COURSE

4 **Protected dogleg**
Two huge bunkers guard the corner of the 382-yard 4th, a sharp dogleg right which, though not overly long, does demand care. A drive safely to the left will leave a short iron approach to a green fearsomely defended by a group of six bunkers.

changed a great deal in the interim, the values and traditions for which it has always stood remain very much the same. The club was one of the five founder members of the USGA in 1894.

The present course mostly dates back to 1931 when Dick Wilson was called in to make changes. It had soon become clear that because of its shortness – it was under 5,000 yards for the second-ever US Open which was played there in 1896 – the original course was not suitable for championship golf. Today it is still under 7,000 yards, not long by present-day championship standards, but it has been reprieved as a Major championship venue. It was chosen to stage the 1986 US Open, which was won by Ray Floyd. Three players, Chip Beck, Lanny Wadkins and Mark Calcavecchia, broke the course

CHAMPIONSHIP LENGTHS		
OUT	3,374 YARDS	PAR 35
IN	3,366 YARDS	PAR 35
TOTAL	6,740 YARDS	PAR 70

COURSE RECORD

65 C. BECK, M. CALCAVECCHIA,
L. WADKINS, US OPEN 1986

US OPEN CHAMPIONS AT SHINNECOCK HILLS

1896 JAMES FOULIS; 1986 RAY FLOYD;
1995 COREY PAVIN

6 PAR 4 456 YARDS

3 PAR 4 456 YARDS

7 PAR 3 184 YARDS

4 PAR 4 382 YARDS

PAR 3 169 YARDS 17

PAR 3 221 YARDS 2

8 PAR 4 361 YARDS

PAR 4 391 YARDS 1

9 **Good drive**
Shinnecock Hills puts a premium on good driving. Typical is the par-4 411-yard 9th hole, where an enormous mound has to be carried by the drive. Only a well-struck shot over the mound can take some of the difficulty out of the approach shot, which is played uphill to the partially hidden green.

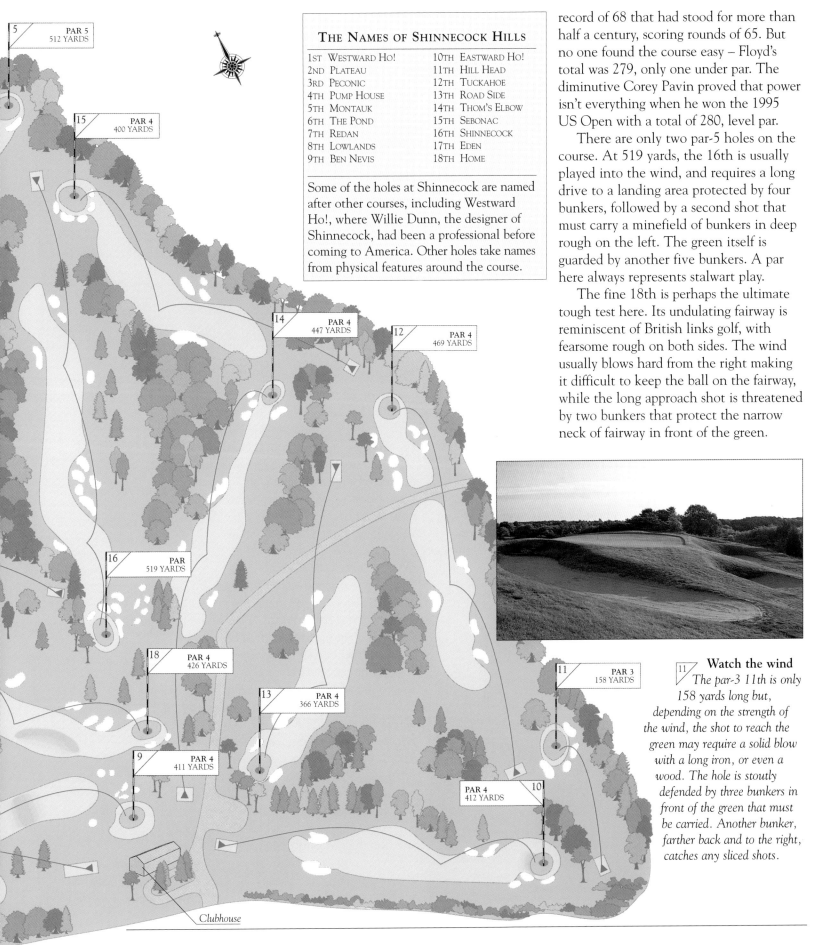

THE NAMES OF SHINNECOCK HILLS

1ST	WESTWARD HO!	10TH	EASTWARD HO!
2ND	PLATEAU	11TH	HILL HEAD
3RD	PECONIC	12TH	TUCKAHOE
4TH	PUMP HOUSE	13TH	ROAD SIDE
5TH	MONTAUK	14TH	THOM'S ELBOW
6TH	THE POND	15TH	SEBONAC
7TH	REDAN	16TH	SHINNECOCK
8TH	LOWLANDS	17TH	EDEN
9TH	BEN NEVIS	18TH	HOME

Some of the holes at Shinnecock are named after other courses, including Westward Ho!, where Willie Dunn, the designer of Shinnecock, had been a professional before coming to America. Other holes take names from physical features around the course.

record of 68 that had stood for more than half a century, scoring rounds of 65. But no one found the course easy – Floyd's total was 279, only one under par. The diminutive Corey Pavin proved that power isn't everything when he won the 1995 US Open with a total of 280, level par.

There are only two par-5 holes on the course. At 519 yards, the 16th is usually played into the wind, and requires a long drive to a landing area protected by four bunkers, followed by a second shot that must carry a minefield of bunkers in deep rough on the left. The green itself is guarded by another five bunkers. A par here always represents stalwart play.

The fine 18th is perhaps the ultimate tough test here. Its undulating fairway is reminiscent of British links golf, with fearsome rough on both sides. The wind usually blows hard from the right making it difficult to keep the ball on the fairway, while the long approach shot is threatened by two bunkers that protect the narrow neck of fairway in front of the green.

Watch the wind
The par-3 11th is only 158 yards long but, depending on the strength of the wind, the shot to reach the green may require a solid blow with a long iron, or even a wood. The hole is stoutly defended by three bunkers in front of the green that must be carried. Another bunker, farther back and to the right, catches any sliced shots.

Clubhouse

SUNNINGDALE

SUNNINGDALE GOLF CLUB, SUNNINGDALE, ASCOT, BERKSHIRE, ENGLAND

M ANY PUNDITS BELIEVE *that the perfect round of golf was played over the Sunningdale Old course by the great Bobby Jones in 1926 during a qualifying round for the Open Championship, held later that year at Royal Lytham. He scored 33 on the front nine and 33 on the back for a round of 66, composed of 33 strokes and 33 putts, with not a 5 on the card. The stage upon which this magical performance was played out could not have been more appropriate – the Old course at Sunningdale is a fine, traditional example of heathland golf only a few miles from the centre of London.*

Course symbol
A beautiful spreading oak tree makes up the crest of Sunningdale. It is a representation of the tree by the 18th green, next to the course's clubhouse.

To play at Sunningdale is to enjoy one of golf's great experiences. Jones certainly felt that to be the case because, after scoring 68 in the second qualifying round in which his only blemish was a single 5, he declared to the world that he would "like to take the course home".

When golf moved inland away from its original linksland environment, it soon became obvious that rough heathland with its heather, firm turf and well-drained soil was perfect for the game. Indeed, golf played on heathland shared many of the characteristics of seaside golf.

The man who had the vision to create a course on the heathland at Sunningdale, west of London, was T.A. Roberts. In 1898 he built a house on the land and negotiated a lease with the owners, St John's College, Cambridge. The lease permitted Roberts to have a course, and some housing, built. It may therefore have been the first property development in England linked to a golf course.

WOODED HEATHLAND
The course builder was Willie Park Jnr, son of the first Open Champion and twice winner of the title himself. The land on which he laid out the original course had a markedly different appearance from that which one sees in the present day. When the course was opened for play in 1901 there were no trees to obscure the views across the heath. Since then, thousands of trees have been encouraged to grow. Today, virtually every hole runs through great stands of pine and birch, creating a wonderful atmosphere of tranquillity that is hard to equal on any other course.

Golf-course architect Harry Colt, who was secretary at Sunningdale for 17 years, made some improvements to the course to compensate for the increased distances players were able to accomplish with the

Attractive features
The natural beauty of the countryside at Sunningdale made a perfect venue for the 1997 Women's British Open. Nancy Lopez plays out of a bunker (right) but it was Karrie Webb who was to win by an eight-shot victory. The spreading oak by the clubhouse (above) has provided shade for the caddies for many years.

Trees on the heath
Once, Sunningdale was a comparatively bleak and treeless heath. But in the last 80 years the land has seen the growth of pine and birch trees.

Willie Park Jnr
Park built the Old course in 1900.

arrival of the Haskell ball. In 1922 Colt also built the New course at Sunningdale, which is rather different in character. In many ways the New course is more demanding, although it is less intricate than its older companion. But it, too, is an excellent example of heathland golf, with its rolling fairways and crisp turf. An iron shot can clip the ball off this type of turf with a satisfactory feeling rarely experienced on modern courses, which owe more to man than nature.

To putt on those splendid Sunningdale greens, so fast of pace and of such delicate texture, is heaven indeed for those who are able to understand and appreciate the difference from less subtle surfaces. Sunningdale is one of that rare breed of course where the playing conditions vary little with the changing seasons. The greens retain their speed and firmness even during the winter months, making it a truly year-round course.

In common with all great courses, Sunningdale has a marvellous finishing hole, but one of the hazards at the 18th is relatively new. In 1940 a German bomb

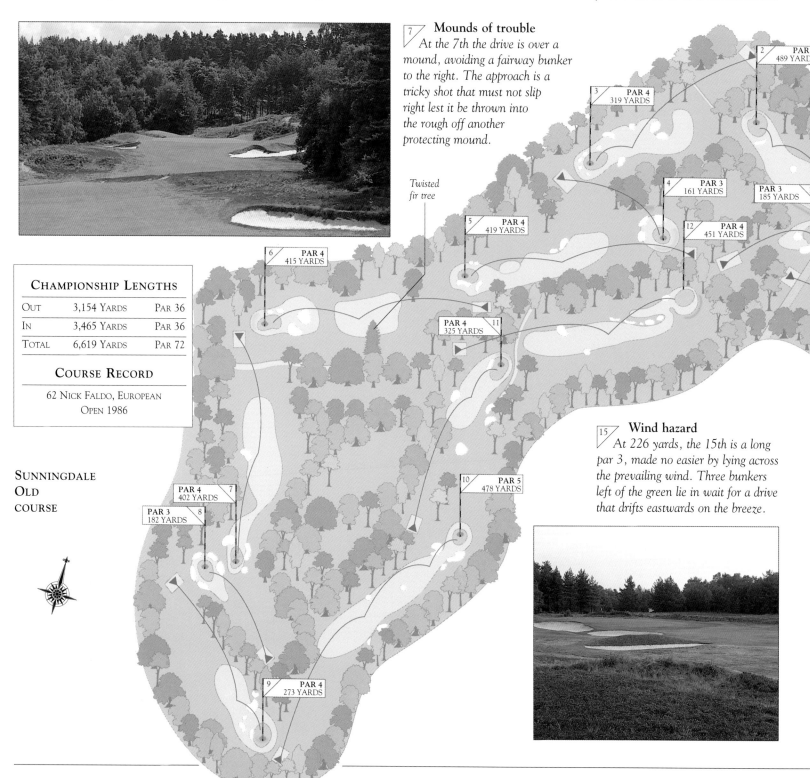

7 Mounds of trouble
At the 7th the drive is over a mound, avoiding a fairway bunker to the right. The approach is a tricky shot that must not slip right lest it be thrown into the rough off another protecting mound.

Twisted fir tree

2	PAR 5 489 YARDS
3	PAR 4 319 YARDS
4	PAR 3 161 YARDS
PAR 3 185 YARDS	13
5	PAR 4 419 YARDS
12	PAR 4 451 YARDS
6	PAR 4 415 YARDS
PAR 4 325 YARDS	11
10	PAR 5 478 YARDS
PAR 4 402 YARDS	7
PAR 3 182 YARDS	8
9	PAR 4 273 YARDS

CHAMPIONSHIP LENGTHS

Out	3,154 Yards	Par 36
In	3,465 Yards	Par 36
Total	6,619 Yards	Par 72

COURSE RECORD

62 Nick Faldo, European Open 1986

SUNNINGDALE
OLD
COURSE

15 Wind hazard
At 226 yards, the 15th is a long par 3, made no easier by lying across the prevailing wind. Three bunkers left of the green lie in wait for a drive that drifts eastwards on the breeze.

Clubhouse

18 PAR 4
432 YARDS

Oak tree

17 PAR 4
421 YARDS

1 PAR 5
494 YARDS

16 PAR 4
438 YARDS

14 PAR 5
509 YARDS

PAR 3
226 YARDS 15

18 **Home** (right)
A long drive uphill is required at the 18th. It must avoid a deep bunker to the left and heavy rough on the right to leave any chance of getting home at this 432-yard par 4. The second shot is aimed at the big oak tree, which stands sentinel between the clubhouse and green. The shot has to carry a string of four bunkers across the fairway.

17 **Green slopes** (above)
The green at the 17th has subtle slopes and is protected with four bunkers. The approach shot is fairly simple, so long as the drive has found the fairway. Missing the fairway, however, is easy to do. The drive at this hole, typical of many on the Old course, is played from an elevated tee down into a fairway that slopes gently and invitingly away. A copse of trees around the driving distance menaces a shot aimed too far left, but devilish bunkers protect the right side in the corner of the slight dogleg and must be avoided at all costs.

left a huge crater, providing the chance to put in the extra bunker protection the hole now enjoys. A feature of the Old course is that the ball rolls well. In fact, despite being almost 500 yards long, the par-5 1st can often be comfortably reached in two shots when the course is fast in the summer months.

POWER PLAY
While Sunningdale generates splendid enjoyment, and is a sufficient challenge for the amateur player, it is vulnerable to the power and strength of the modern tournament professional, particularly if the ground has been a little softened by rain. It says a lot that the professional course record, held by Nick Faldo, is as low as 62. Another example of the course's vulnerability was given by Ian Woosnam in 1988, when the Welshman won the Panasonic European Open at Sunningdale with a remarkable score of 260, 20 strokes under the card (for the European Open two tees are moved forward, reducing the par to 70).

Even if the Sunningdale course is less menacing to the great players than some of the other courses they have to master on their Tour, it does have its own strengths. Above all, at the Old course the players enjoy a form of golf more virtuous and loyal to the game's traditional origins than is to be found at most other venues on the circuit.

TRYALL

TRYALL GOLF, TENNIS AND BEACH CLUB, HANOVER, MONTEGO BAY, JAMAICA, WEST INDIES

T HE BRITISH PLANTERS, *many of them Scots, who ran the sugar plantations in Jamaica in the nineteenth century introduced golf to this beautiful Caribbean island. Tryall, the most western of the island's courses and only half an hour from the international airport at Montego Bay, is its most famous, although it was built as recently as 1957. Like other Caribbean islands it is susceptible to any winds going and Patty Sheehan, winner of the 1990 Jamaica Classic, called the event "The War of the Winds".*

Built by a group of Texas businessmen, the course is in an undulating lush landscape rising hundreds of feet around the historic Tryall Great House, the centrepiece of the resort and a legacy of the days of the sugar plantations. Views from the course, which is part of the Tryall Golf, Tennis and Beach Club, are breathtaking.

UPHILL STRUGGLE

The severe slopes overlooking Sandy Bay on the western tip of Jamaica were not promising material for a quality golf course, but architect Ralph Plummer managed to create sufficient flat fairway areas, even though the majority of tee-shots are either uphill or downhill. This makes it possible to hit positive shots to difficult green positions.

At only 6,772 yards, Tryall is not long by comparison with many courses, but what the course lacks in length it more than compensates for in the speed of its sloping greens and its challenging tees. For championship events the course starts at the hole that is normally the 8th for members and visitors, an alteration introduced to meet the needs of television. Tryall boasts many spectacular holes, none more so than the par-3 15th on the championship layout. The tee-shot must carry water all the way to the green. Thick vegetation catches anything cut, often throwing the ball into the water.

CHAMPIONSHIP LENGTHS		
OUT	3,459 YARDS	PAR 36
IN	3,313 YARDS	PAR 35
TOTAL	6,772 YARDS	PAR 71

COURSE RECORD
62 BIAH MARAGH AND PAUL AZINGER
1995

5 Sharp green
At 213 yards the championship 5th is not excessively long, but it is one of the toughest par-3 holes to be found anywhere in the world. The green slopes sharply from left to right, and only a perfect tee-shot placed below the hole will do. Four putts are not uncommon on this wickedly fast green. The ocean backdrop is a spectacular distraction.

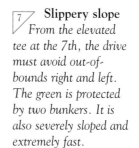

7 Slippery slope
From the elevated tee at the 7th, the drive must avoid out-of-bounds right and left. The green is protected by two bunkers. It is also severely sloped and extremely fast.

PAR 4
429 YARDS
9

PAR 4
482 YARDS
1

PAR 4
450 YARDS
7

PAR 3
170 YARDS
3

6 PAR 4
373 YARDS

5 PAR 3
213 YARDS

4 PA
500 YAR

14 **Caribbean blue**
The dazzling Caribbean laps in behind the 14th green on one of the toughest holes on the championship course. A lake guards the corner of the dogleg left and the second shot into the prevailing wind demands a long carry. The approach to the green is difficult to judge but the ocean view is breathtaking.

**TRYALL
CHAMPIONSHIP
COURSE**

Sandy Bay

Clubhouse

| 10 | PAR 4 |
| 391 YARDS |

4 YARDS   8

| 2 | PAR 4 |
| 404 YARDS |

| 11 | PAR 4 |
| 342 YARDS |

| 18 | PAR 4 |
| 434 YARDS |

| 13 | PAR 3 |
| 193 YARDS |

| PAR 4 | 12 |
| 373 YARDS |

| 17 | PAR 5 |
| 510 YARDS |

| 14 | PAR 5 |
| 521 YARDS |

| 15 | PAR 3 |
| 175 YARDS |

| 16 | PAR 4 |
| 367 YARDS |

Panorama in paradise
This is the view from the Tryall Great House east along the course towards the famous Round Hill Hotel in the distance. For championship events the course ends below the House.

Three major course changes were made for the inaugural Johnny Walker World Championship in 1991. A new par-3 15th hole with a more than eye-catching carry over the water was introduced and immediately became the course's feature hole. The 16th became a severe dogleg and the opening par 3 was dropped from the layout. Fred Couples won it that year and again here in 1995. In between, Nick Faldo (1992), Larry Mize (1993) and Ernie Els (1994) were also Johnny Walker World Champions at Tryall.

TURNBERRY

TURNBERRY HOTEL AND GOLF COURSES, TURNBERRY, AYRSHIRE, SCOTLAND

F RANK HOLE'S NAME *is not widely known in the world of international golf, but the game owes him a great debt. It was he who, in a persistent post-war campaign, managed to extract from the British government enough compensation money to attempt to recreate the Turnberry golf courses, after they had been dug up to build an airfield during the Second World War.*

Beacon of light
Part of the Turnberry crest is the lighthouse, which stands on the headland between the Firth of Clyde and Turnberry Bay.

Hole succeeded brilliantly and, with the help of architect Mackenzie Ross, rebuilt and redesigned the courses, rescuing them from under the runways. In the process he resurrected one of the great golf resorts.

Turnberry lies at the southernmost end of a huge stretch of classic linksland along the Ayrshire coast in the west of Scotland. Its Ailsa course is by common consent one of the most beautiful and challenging golf courses in the world, set among scenery on the grand scale.

SPECTACULAR LANDSCAPE
High on the hill overlooking the links is the famous Turnberry Hotel, whose white facade and russet red roof make an attractive landmark on the skyline. Behind stretches the rich agricultural land of Ayrshire, while at sea, across the Firth of Clyde, lies the stark beauty of the Isle of Arran with the Mull of Kintyre beyond.

To the left is the intriguing silhouette of Ailsa Craig, a great, round island of granite,

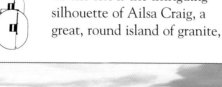

Flying course
During the Second World War, Turnberry (right) became an airfield, parts of which are still visible today. It was built for pilots being trained to fly Liberator bombers (above), which were used for sorties against German submarines.

which the locals call Paddy's Milestone. It towers out of the waters of the Firth close to where the great ships from the yards of Clydebank once used to run the measured mile as part of their sea trials. Today only a few still recall when the stones for another of Scotland's great sporting traditions, curling, were hewn from the granite of Ailsa Craig.

Turnberry's is not a long history by the standards of the courses that currently occupy the Open rota. All of it is contained within this century, and twice during that period the courses have been torn up to make way for military aircraft. In the First World War it was the Royal Flying Corps that built a training airfield.

Shared glory (above)
In the 1977 Open at Turnberry, Tom Watson (right) beat Jack Nicklaus in the legendary "Duel in the Sun".

Shortly afterwards the rebuilding work of Major C.K. Hutchinson, in collaboration with James Braid, restored the courses and they were available for play for a short while until the outbreak of the Second World War. This time it was the Royal Air Force that tore up the courses to build a three-runway airfield, the crumbling remains of which can still be seen today.

Many thought the courses would never be revived after the war, but Hole took on the challenge. With the help of the hotel company's superintendent of grounds and golf courses, and of a firm of English contractors, Hole and Ross created, in the design of the Ailsa course, one of Britain's greatest championship links. The second course at Turnberry, formerly known as

Landmark (above)
The lonely rock of Ailsa Craig has stood sentinel to the world's great golfers as they have striven to dominate the compelling Ailsa course.

Spectacle (right)
Nick Price approaches a huge gallery of spectators in front of the imposing Turnberry Hotel at the 18th, on his way to a dramatic win at the 1994 Open Championship.

the Arran, has had a complete redesign and been renamed the Kintyre. Course designer Donald Steel has considerably strengthened what is a superb complement to its more famous sister and a worthy venue for any championship. A new Colin Montgomery Links Golf Academy has been added to the resort's facilities.

The courses are very much part of the hotel operation at Turnberry. The two have always been linked. The 3rd Marquis of Ailsa, who was captain at Prestwick in 1899, and after whom the championship course is named, leased the land to the Glasgow and South Western Railway Company. Willie Fernie, professional at Troon farther up the coast, had designed two 13-hole courses on the site by 1905. When, shortly afterwards, the Turnberry Hotel was completed, the railway company took over the courses.

9 **Over the sea**
The 9th has a precipitous championship tee perching on a rocky promontory above the waters of the Firth of Clyde. A shot of more than 200 yards across the sea is required to make the carry to the safety of the fairway on the other side of a small bay. The 8th green lies to the right of the 9th tee, protected by its three bunkers.

THE NAMES OF TURNBERRY

1ST AILSA CRAIG	10TH DINNA FOUTER
2ND MAK SICCAR	11TH MAIDENS
3RD BLAE WEARIE	12TH MONUMENT
4TH WOE-BE-TIDE	13TH TICKLY TAP
5TH FIN' ME OOT	14TH RISK-AN-HOPE
6TH TAPPIE TOORIE	15TH CA CANNY
7TH ROON THE BEN	16TH WEE BURN
8TH GOAT FELL	17TH LANG WHANG
9TH BRUCE'S CASTLE	18TH AILSA HAME

Most Ailsa course names describe hole features, disguised in local Scottish dialect, but the 9th is named after the nearby remains of a castle said to have been used by the Scottish king, Robert the Bruce.

It took over 40 years for Turnberry to rise to championship standard, after its reconstruction by Hole and Ross. Since hosting the Amateur Championship in 1961, the Ailsa course has been the venue for many important events. It has staged the Open Championship three times. The first time, in 1977, saw the great battle between Jack Nicklaus and Tom Watson which became known as "The Duel in the Sun".

TURNBERRY AILSA COURSE

Turnberry Sands

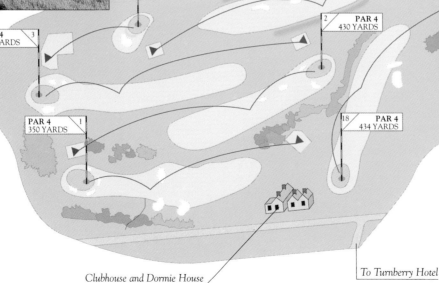

5 **In the valley**
The 5th is a tough par 4 of 442 yards that lies in a sweeping valley between the dunes. Players need a good drive down the right to miss two large bunkers lying in the corner of the dogleg. The fairway then turns left, following the shore, to a green screened by a bunker short and left, and other bunkers eating into the surface.

6 PAR 3 231 YARDS
5 PAR 4 442 YARDS
17 PAR 5 497 YARDS
4 PAR 3 165 YARDS
2 PAR 4 430 YARDS
3 PAR 4 462 YARDS
1 PAR 4 350 YARDS
18 PAR 4 434 YARDS

Practice area

Clubhouse and Dormie House

To Turnberry Hotel

CHAMPIONSHIP LENGTHS

OUT	3,494 YARDS	PAR 35
IN	3,482 YARDS	PAR 35
TOTAL	6,976 YARDS	PAR 70

COURSE RECORD

63 GREG NORMAN, THE OPEN 1986

OPEN CHAMPIONS AT TURNBERRY

1977 TOM WATSON; 1986 GREG NORMAN; 1994 NICK PRICE

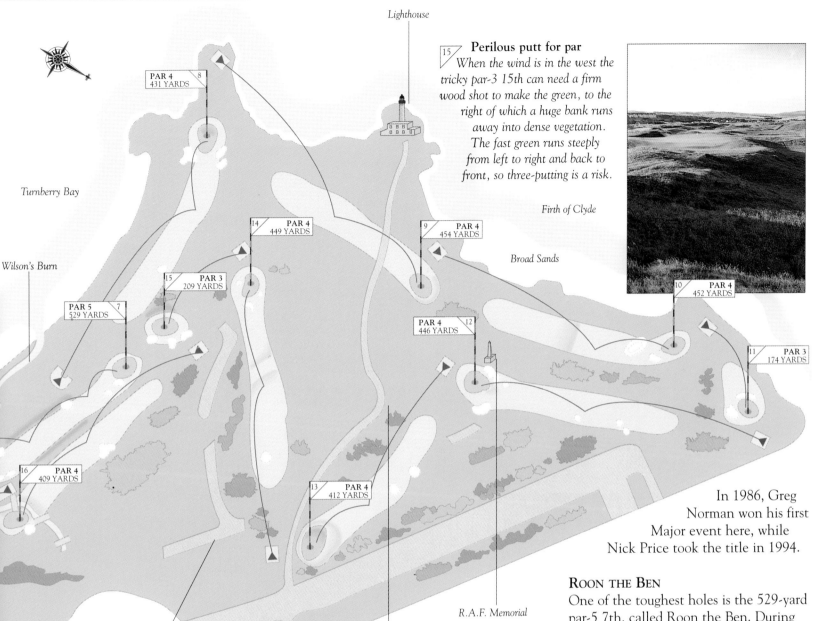

Lighthouse

PAR 4
431 YARDS | 8

Turnberry Bay

Wilson's Burn

PAR 5
529 YARDS | 7

14 | PAR 4
449 YARDS

15 | PAR 3
209 YARDS

9 | PAR 4
454 YARDS

Firth of Clyde

Broad Sands

10 | PAR 4
452 YARDS

PAR 4
446 YARDS | 12

11 | PAR 3
174 YARDS

16 | PAR 4
409 YARDS

13 | PAR 4
412 YARDS

R.A.F. Memorial

Airfield runways

Lighthouse Road

Perilous putt for par
15 *When the wind is in the west the tricky par-3 15th can need a firm wood shot to make the green, to the right of which a huge bank runs away into dense vegetation. The fast green runs steeply from left to right and back to front, so three-putting is a risk.*

In 1986, Greg Norman won his first Major event here, while Nick Price took the title in 1994.

ROON THE BEN
One of the toughest holes is the 529-yard par-5 7th, called Roon the Ben. During the 1973 John Player Classic, Tom Weiskopf, one of the longest hitters in the game, produced two strokes of masterly power and precision to conquer this long hole. With the wind blowing strongly into his face and from the left, Weiskopf found the fairway right of the bunker with a majestic drive. He then struck a spoon of such purity that it did not waver by a yard from the line on which it was struck and flew like a bullet to the front of the green.

Another notable challenge is the 497-yard par-5 17th, named Lang Whang. This means "a long hit" and sums up exactly what is required. The drive is from a high tee down to the fairway, from where the hole rises to a green protected by three bunkers.

Big drive
7 *The par-5 7th dog-legs left and runs along a shelf between the dunes with the sea hard on the left. To get to the green in two demands a huge first drive, especially to clear the lone deep bunker at the corner of the dogleg. A vast and cavernous bunker guards the left approach to the green and two deep ones guard the front right.*

VALDERRAMA

VALDERRAMA GOLF CLUB, SOTOGRANDE, CADIZ, SPAIN

A MERICAN GOLF-COURSE architect Robert Trent Jones long maintained that the course at Valderrama in the south of Spain is one of his finest achievements and that it truly belongs among the world's great courses. As a challenging European Tour and Ryder Cup venue its reputation is well secured.

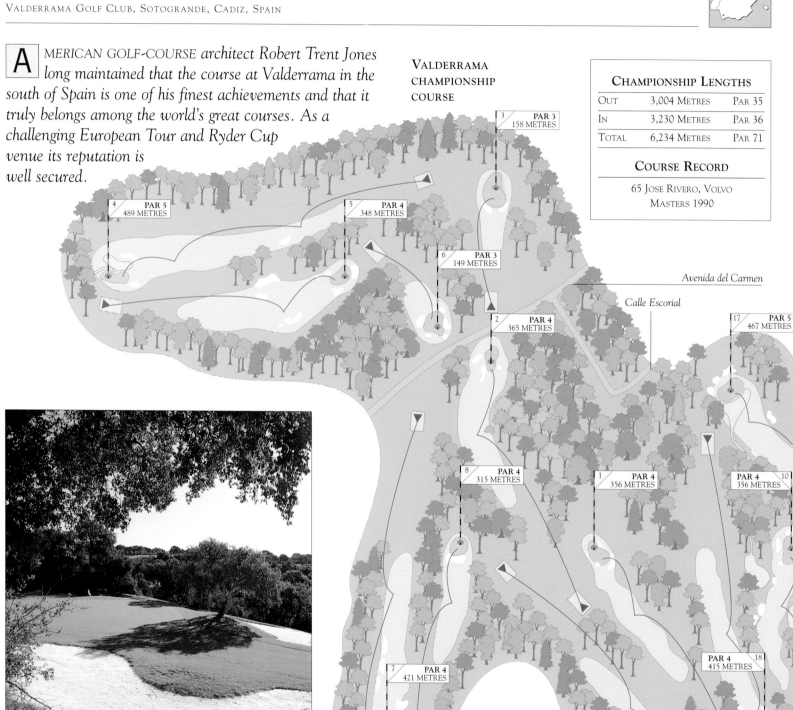

VALDERRAMA CHAMPIONSHIP COURSE

CHAMPIONSHIP LENGTHS		
OUT	3,004 METRES	PAR 35
IN	3,230 METRES	PAR 36
TOTAL	6,234 METRES	PAR 71

COURSE RECORD
65 JOSE RIVERO, VOLVO MASTERS 1990

Avenida del Carmen

Calle Escorial

3 PAR 3 158 METRES

4 PAR 5 489 METRES

5 PAR 4 348 METRES

6 PAR 3 149 METRES

2 PAR 4 365 METRES

17 PAR 5 467 METRES

8 PAR 4 315 METRES

1 PAR 4 356 METRES

10 PAR 4 356 METRES

7 PAR 4 421 METRES

18 PAR 4 415 METRES

9 PAR 4 403 METRES

5 **Tree trouble**
Bunkers threaten the tee-shot on both sides of the 5th fairway, which swings gently left. Uniquely, the approach shot is threatened by a cork tree, the foliage of which blocks the direct line. The safe line is to the left, away from front and back bunkers.

Trent Jones designed and built the course, originally known as Los Aves, in a fine location on a hill above the old village of Sotogrande. Sitting on the verandah at Augusta National in 1983, Severiano Ballesteros, who had just won the US Masters, mentioned to Trent Jones that he attributed much of his success to two weeks' practice at Los Aves.

In 1985 industrialist Jaime Ortiz-Patino and seven of his golfing friends acquired the course and formed the Valderrama Golf Club with the aim of making it an attractive private club. Trent Jones was brought in again to remodel the course and made some subtle but very significant changes, without altering the intrinsic character of the layout. He described it at the time as

"polishing the diamond to improve the shot values in some areas of the course". The object was to make it a magnificent, challenging championship layout and there is no doubt at all that he has succeeded.

EUROPE'S AUGUSTA?

Valderrama has been widely acclaimed as one of golf's outstanding tests when tackled from the championship tees. It has hosted nine Volvo Masters, the 1997 Ryder Cup, and the World Golf Championship in 1999 and 2000.

Ronan Rafferty, winner of the Volvo Masters and the Volvo Order of Merit in 1989, has described Valderrama's back nine as "probably more difficult than any other course in Europe . . . You are always looking for pars; birdies are a bonus."

The final four holes are generally accepted by players as the most punishing on the European Tour. However, playing from tees farther forward, those who pursue the royal and ancient game in a less rarefied atmosphere than the touring professional still experience immense enjoyment on Robert Trent Jones's creation.

The course is situated near the Mediterranean, and sea breezes play an important part when deciding how to tackle each hole. The trees, too, are a hazard, and the spectacular panoramic views may be distracting. The club itself exudes an air of quiet elegance and charm usually encountered only in clubs of much greater antiquity. Some devotees believe that Valderrama has become the Augusta of Europe.

Test of accuracy (left)
The par-4 2nd is more a test of precision than strength. The fairway is lined by trees on both sides and the drive must find the left of the fairway to leave a clear view of the green. The approach, played to an elevated green guarded by two bunkers, demands care. The green is no safe haven as the borrows are subtle and putts can be tricky, especially when the pin is in the centre of the green.

Tee up for three
All the single-shot holes on the championship course at Valderrama are spectacular, but the 12th is by far the hardest. The tee-shot is played from an elevated tee to a green set amidst cork trees. When the wind blows it is a very difficult green to hit, and anything off-target is almost sure to find one of the surrounding bunkers. The green itself is not easy, as it undulates and slopes from front to back.

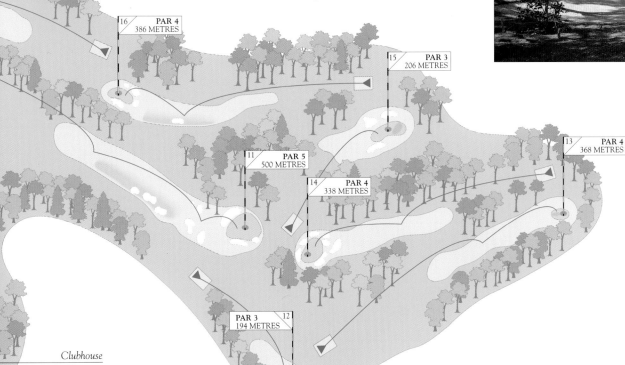

16 / PAR 4 386 METRES

15 / PAR 3 206 METRES

11 / PAR 5 500 METRES

14 / PAR 4 338 METRES

13 / PAR 4 368 METRES

PAR 3 194 METRES / 12

Clubhouse

WENTWORTH

WENTWORTH CLUB, VIRGINIA WATER, SURREY, ENGLAND

T HE WEST COURSE *at Wentworth, home of the World Match Play and PGA Championships, is one of the most famous of England's inland courses. Since 1964, when the World Match Play was first played, there have been some remarkably low scores, prompting Wentworth-watchers to wonder whether modern golf equipment and softer greens might have pulled the teeth of this great course. But Wentworth West, nicknamed the Burma Road, remains one of Britain's longest, toughest layouts.*

Work began on Wentworth in 1923. It was one of the first developments in Britain to be based on the American country club idea, where a wide range of other leisure facilities is laid on as well as golf courses.

The Wentworth project was to include within its 1,750 acres (708ha) provision for large houses, each set in at least an acre (0.4ha) of ground, close to the fairways. Respected golf architect Harry S. Colt directed the planning and building of two 18-hole and a short nine-hole course.

PAR 4
481 YARDS

14 PAR 3
179 YARDS

PAR 4
442 YARDS 13

PAR 5
509 YARDS 12

11 PAR 4
403 YARDS

PAR 5
497 YARDS 4

6 PAR 4
354 YARDS

PAR 3
191 YARDS 5

PAR 3
184 YARDS 10

PAR 4
396 YARDS 7

PAR 4
452 YARDS 9

8 PAR 4
400 YARDS

West Drive

3 **Three-tiered green**
The long par-4 3rd is uphill all the way. The drive must not only be long but must also avoid a dangerous bunker on the right. There is another bunker farther down the fairway and two bunkers guard the green itself. Recent alterations to the fearsome two-tiered green, where three and often four putts were once common, have been widely welcomed as being for the better.

Railway

WENTWORTH WEST COURSE

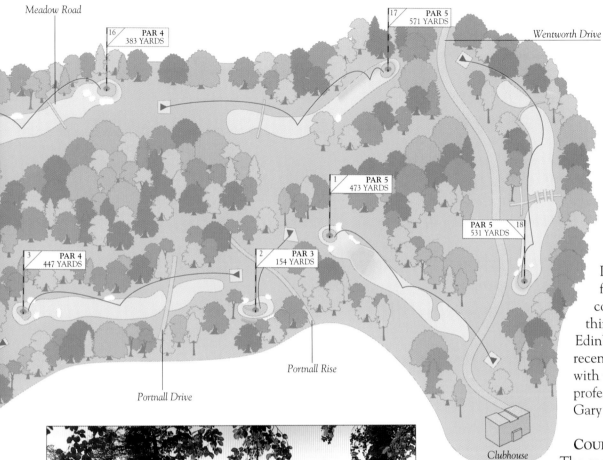

Meadow Road

16 **PAR 4**
383 YARDS

17 **PAR 5**
571 YARDS

Wentworth Drive

1 **PAR 5**
473 YARDS

PAR 5
531 YARDS 18

3 **PAR 4**
447 YARDS

2 **PAR 3**
154 YARDS

Portnall Rise

Portnall Drive

Clubhouse

CHAMPIONSHIP LENGTHS		
OUT	3,364 YARDS	PAR 36
IN	3,683 YARDS	PAR 37
TOTAL	7,047 YARDS	PAR 73

COURSE RECORD
63 WAYNE RILEY, PGA CHAMPIONSHIP 1991

What Colt created has stood the test of time. Lying in a marvellous stretch of sandy heathland to the south-west of London, the East course was finished before the longer West course, which opened in 1927. A third 18-hole course, called the Edinburgh, has been built more recently to a design by John Jacobs, with former Wentworth club professional Bernard Gallacher and Gary Player as design consultants.

COURSES FOR THE WEALTHY

The courses were built in a fine setting amid woodland of fir and silver birch, and today masses of rhododendrons add to the aesthetic appeal of the estate. Henry Cotton once described the clubhouse as "one of the most beautiful in England".

There may be some truth in the suggestion that Wentworth provides "millionaires' golf", but this does not detract from the quality of the golf the courses offer. There have been many great and memorable events held there over the years. In 1926 an informal match was played between the professionals of Great Britain and America, which the British won comfortably. It was not the first match between the countries but was, in effect, the forerunner of the Ryder Cup (which was also played here in 1953). In the World Match Play, Gary Player scored five victories in nine appearances, Arnold Palmer had two wins, and Seve Ballesteros won four times between 1981–85. Ernie Els had three consecutive victories in the 1990s, and Colin Montgomerie had a similar record in the PGA Championship.

18 **Drama hole**
A long, well-placed drive will open up the par-5 18th. The green can be reached in two shots, but bunkers right and left make the green difficult to hold with a long second shot. The 18th hole has been the site of much World Match Play drama.

2 **Over the road** (right)
At 154 yards, the 2nd on the Wentworth West course is the first and the shortest of the one-shot holes. The shot is played from an elevated tee, across a road that is in a dip, up to an elevated green protected by two bunkers in front and a third at the back left. The green slopes from back to front, and care is required on the putting surface if no more than the allotted two strokes are to be taken.

WINGED FOOT

WINGED FOOT GOLF CLUB, MAMARONECK, NEW YORK, USA

W HEN THE MEMBERS *of the New York Athletic Club decided they wanted a suburban golf club of their own, they asked the somewhat eccentric American course architect A.W. Tillinghast to build it for them. The architect received a less than comprehensive brief, being simply instructed by the good gentlemen of New York to "give us a man-sized course". Part of Tillinghast's response was the West course at Winged Foot, which not only met the members' requirements but may even have exceeded the brief, as it proved to be one of the toughest courses in the length and breadth of the United States.*

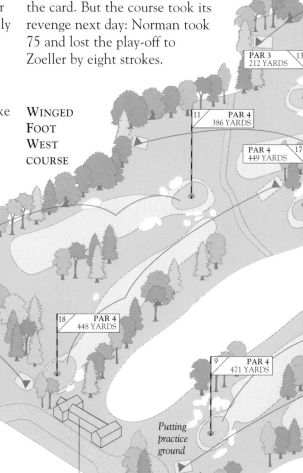

18 **Great putt**
At the dramatic 18th, the fairway is narrow, and the green has fearsome undulations. These did not bother Greg Norman in the 1984 US Open. It was here that he holed a massive putt from off the left edge for a birdie to force a play-off against Fuzzy Zoeller.

Tillinghast built many fine courses, including Baltusrol and Quaker Ridge, but Winged Foot was probably his most ambitious undertaking. During its construction he cut down nearly 8,000 trees and removed over 7,000 tons of rock. The West course was built in 1923, along with another 18-hole layout, the East course, which some still argue is just as difficult. But the West at Winged Foot is the accepted championship course and has been host to the US Open four times.

Eight of the par 4s on the West course are more than 400 yards long and extremely demanding. Only the best amateurs can hope to reach the majority of these greens in two shots and many top professionals find it difficult. These long two-shot holes are the principal reason

why Winged Foot is so difficult. There have, in fact, been many "big score" victories in the US Open at Winged Foot. In 1929 Bobby Jones and Al Espinosa were both 14 over par when they tied for the championship, and 30 years later Billy Casper had to single-putt no fewer than 31 greens to win with a score of 282.

WINNING OVER PAR
In its wisdom the USGA decided to make the course even tougher before the 1974 US Open. Hale Irwin's winning score of 287 – seven over the par for that championship – was a reflection of just how difficult it had become. Fuzzy Zoeller and Greg Norman reduced the course

to more manageable proportions in the 1984 US Open, when Norman staged a remarkable last-round challenge to tie Zoeller on 276 – four under the card. But the course took its revenge next day: Norman took 75 and lost the play-off to Zoeller by eight strokes.

WINGED FOOT WEST COURSE

PAR 3
212 YARDS
13

PAR 4
386 YARDS
11

PAR 4
449 YARDS
17

10
PAR 3
190 YARDS

18
PAR 4
448 YARDS

9
PAR 4
471 YARDS

Putting practice ground

10 **Tough 10th**
The green at this par 3 is protected by two deep, kidney-shaped bunkers. Behind, a house has its garden within 30ft (9m) of the green, and on the left trees catch hooked or pulled shots.

Clubhouse

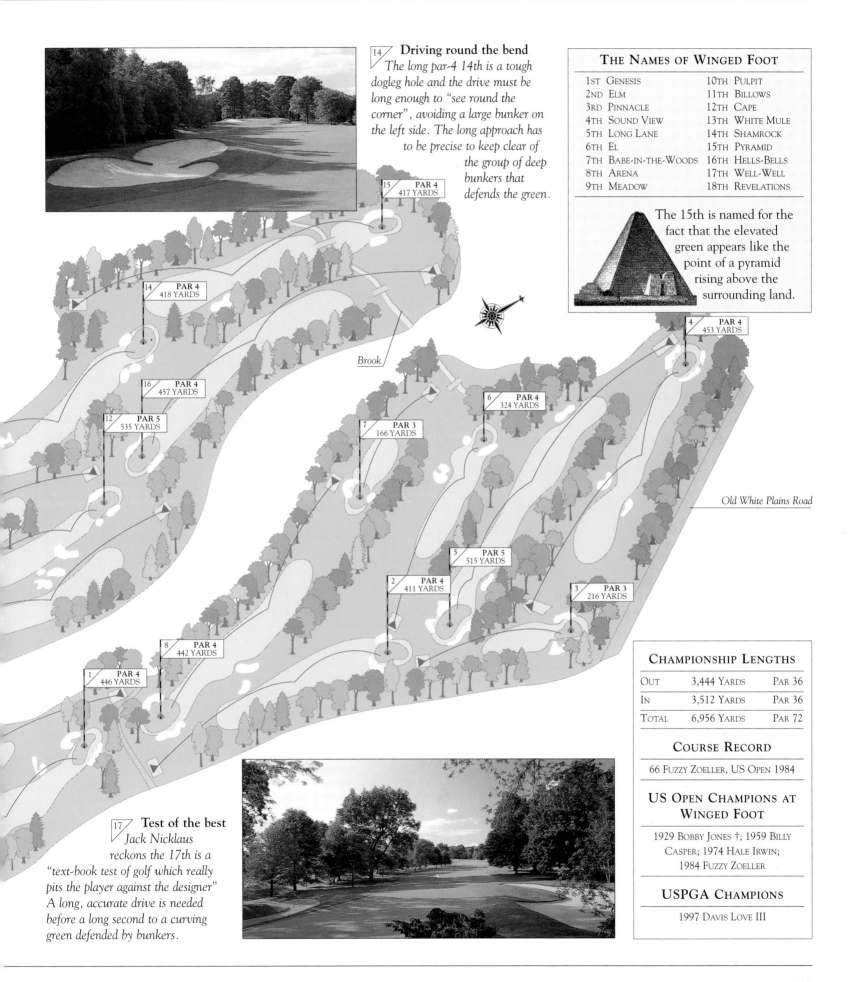

14 **Driving round the bend**
The long par-4 14th is a tough dogleg hole and the drive must be long enough to "see round the corner", avoiding a large bunker on the left side. The long approach has to be precise to keep clear of the group of deep bunkers that defends the green.

THE NAMES OF WINGED FOOT

1ST	GENESIS	10TH	PULPIT
2ND	ELM	11TH	BILLOWS
3RD	PINNACLE	12TH	CAPE
4TH	SOUND VIEW	13TH	WHITE MULE
5TH	LONG LANE	14TH	SHAMROCK
6TH	EL	15TH	PYRAMID
7TH	BABE-IN-THE-WOODS	16TH	HELLS-BELLS
8TH	ARENA	17TH	WELL-WELL
9TH	MEADOW	18TH	REVELATIONS

The 15th is named for the fact that the elevated green appears like the point of a pyramid rising above the surrounding land.

15 PAR 4 417 YARDS

14 PAR 4 418 YARDS

Brook

4 PAR 4 453 YARDS

16 PAR 4 457 YARDS

6 PAR 4 324 YARDS

12 PAR 5 535 YARDS

7 PAR 3 166 YARDS

Old White Plains Road

5 PAR 5 515 YARDS

2 PAR 4 411 YARDS

3 PAR 3 216 YARDS

8 PAR 4 442 YARDS

1 PAR 4 446 YARDS

17 **Test of the best**
Jack Nicklaus reckons the 17th is a "text-book test of golf which really pits the player against the designer" A long, accurate drive is needed before a long second to a curving green defended by bunkers.

CHAMPIONSHIP LENGTHS

OUT	3,444 YARDS	PAR 36
IN	3,512 YARDS	PAR 36
TOTAL	6,956 YARDS	PAR 72

COURSE RECORD

66 FUZZY ZOELLER, US OPEN 1984

US OPEN CHAMPIONS AT WINGED FOOT

1929 BOBBY JONES †; 1959 BILLY CASPER; 1974 HALE IRWIN; 1984 FUZZY ZOELLER

USPGA CHAMPIONS

1997 DAVIS LOVE III

THE WORLD OF GOLF

S INCE THE NINETEENTH *century, golf has spread from its traditional home on the east coast of Scotland to virtually all corners of the planet, from New Zealand's South Island to the north-west of the American continent. Although the majority of the world's courses are located in either North America or the British Isles, the rest are scattered across the continents of the world. Indeed, such is the hold of golf on the sporting imagination that Antarctica is the only continent on which golf is not played. These maps show the location of over a hundred courses featured in this Championship Courses chapter.*

UNITED KINGDOM AND IRELAND

Royal Dornoch (below) *Undulating fairways, dunes, and hummocks make for pure Scottish links.*

Augusta (left) *The most manicured woodland course in the world? Azaleas and magnolias produce a blaze of colour in this secluded, world-famous home to the Masters.*

NORTHERN IRELAND

REPUBLIC OF IRELAND

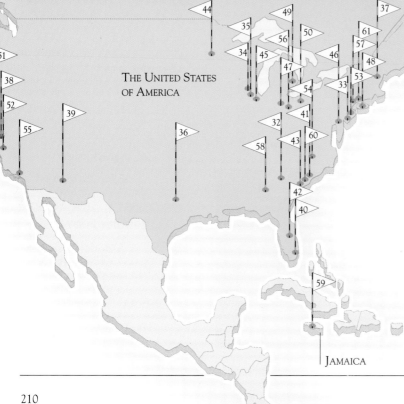

THE UNITED STATES OF AMERICA

UNITED STATES AND WEST INDIES

CANADA AND SOUTH AMERICA

JAMAICA

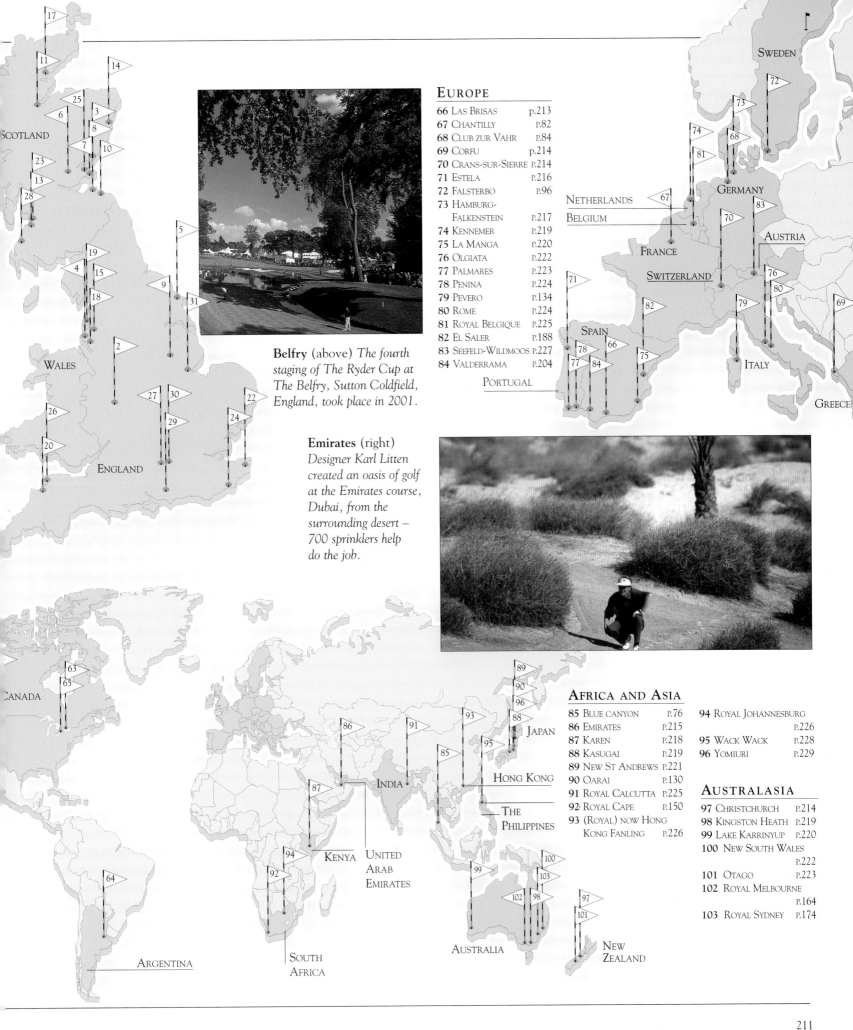

EUROPE

Belfry (above) *The fourth staging of The Ryder Cup at The Belfry, Sutton Coldfield, England, took place in 2001.*

Emirates (right) *Designer Karl Litten created an oasis of golf at the Emirates course, Dubai, from the surrounding desert – 700 sprinklers help do the job.*

AFRICA AND ASIA

AUSTRALASIA

WORLD DIRECTORY OF COURSES

I N THE SECOND *section of this chapter are a further
50 of the world's outstanding championship courses.
The layouts featured here – ancient and historic links as
well as lesser-known gems tucked away in unlikely
settings – present a wide array of golfing challenges.*

*The awesome antiquity of Prestwick, birthplace of the
Open Championship and its home for its first 12 years
(and 12 more times after that), contrasts with the New St
Andrews Club in Japan, for example, where an electronic
trolley system transports players' clubs around the course.*

*There is the miracle of the green oasis in the desert that is
the Emirates course in Dubai, and the sheer charm of
Corfu. These spectacular courses complete a collection of
over one hundred of the world's greatest courses, which
represents outstanding golf on an international scale.
Across their fairways is written the history – and
continuing development – of a royal and ancient game
whose beginnings were uncertain, but whose appeal is
international and whose future is assured.*

BANFF

BANFF, ALBERTA, CANADA

The Canadian Pacific Railway
Company built the original nine
holes amidst the spectacle of the
Canadian Rockies in 1911 for
guests at its splendid Banff
Springs Hotel. German prisoners-
of-war built an additional nine
during the First World War before
Canadian architect Stanley
Thompson was commissioned to
redesign the course in 1927. The
8th hole, known as the Devil's
Cauldron, is recognized as one
of the great holes in world golf.

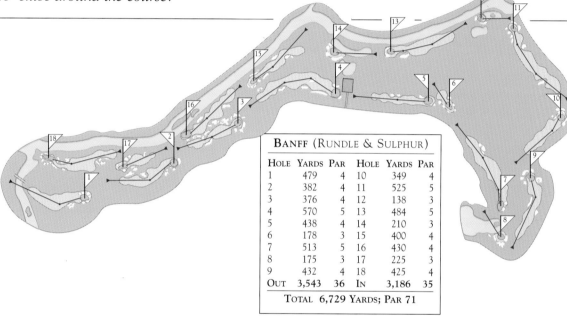

BANFF (RUNDLE & SULPHUR)					
HOLE	YARDS	PAR	HOLE	YARDS	PAR
1	479	4	10	349	4
2	382	4	11	525	5
3	376	4	12	138	3
4	570	5	13	484	5
5	438	4	14	210	3
6	178	3	15	400	4
7	513	5	16	430	4
8	175	3	17	225	3
9	432	4	18	425	4
OUT	3,543	36	IN	3,186	35
TOTAL 6,729 YARDS; PAR 71					

THE BELFRY (BRABAZON)					
HOLE	YARDS	PAR	HOLE	YARDS	PAR
1	418	4	10	275	4
2	349	4	11	420	4
3	465	4	12	235	3
4	579	5	13	394	4
5	399	4	14	194	3
6	396	4	15	550	5
7	183	3	16	410	4
8	460	5	17	575	5
9	400	4	18	474	4
OUT	3,649	37	IN	3,527	36
TOTAL 7,176 YARDS; PAR 73					

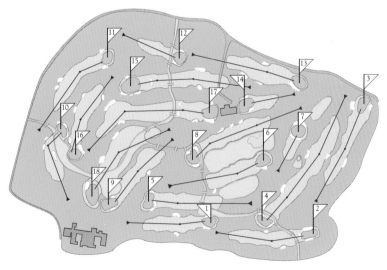

THE BELFRY

WISHAW, WARWICKSHIRE, ENGLAND

Two dramatic Ryder Cup encounters
between the professionals of Europe
and the US, disputes over its
selection as a venue, and hosting
the 2001 Ryder Cup, have made
The Belfry one of the best-known
courses in Britain. Transformed by
Peter Alliss and Dave Thomas from
farmland into an American-style
course, its showpieces are the 10th,
reachable with the drive across its
guarding lake by big hitters, and the
18th, which carries water twice, first
off the tee, and again with the
second shot to the three-tier green.

LAS BRISAS

MARBELLA, MALAGA, SPAIN

Water dominates this Robert Trent Jones layout, built in a valley beneath the Sierra Blanca. Opened in 1968, it is a sterner test than Jones's earlier work at Sotogrande. He has combined the aquatic threat on this course with some fearsome contouring in the greens. The par-3 16th rates as probably the most difficult hole, with the green sloping wickedly towards the water in front of it. Las Brisas has been the venue for the Spanish Open and for the World Cup.

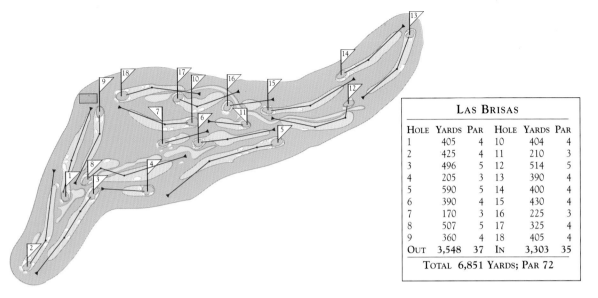

LAS BRISAS					
HOLE	YARDS	PAR	HOLE	YARDS	PAR
1	405	4	10	404	4
2	425	4	11	210	3
3	496	5	12	514	5
4	205	3	13	390	4
5	590	5	14	400	4
6	390	4	15	430	4
7	170	3	16	225	3
8	507	5	17	325	4
9	360	4	18	405	4
OUT	3,548	37	IN	3,303	35
TOTAL 6,851 YARDS; PAR 72					

BUTLER NATIONAL

OAK BROOK, CHICAGO, ILLINOIS, USA

George Fazio designed this course in Chicago's suburbs. Eleven of its 18 holes are threatened by water hazards. The lake at the par-4 14th has to be carried twice and it poses a major threat to the left of the green on the previous hole, the tough par-3 13th. The par-3 5th has a carry over water of 201 yards from the championship tee. Butler is renowned for the difficulty of its greens, which have subtle contours requiring particular care in judgement of the line.

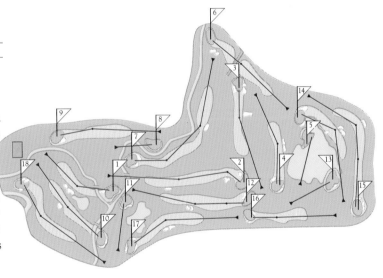

BUTLER NATIONAL					
HOLE	YARDS	PAR	HOLE	YARDS	PAR
1	372	4	10	446	4
2	563	5	11	193	3
3	433	4	12	482	5
4	406	4	13	197	3
5	201	3	14	430	4
6	443	4	15	583	5
7	623	5	16	385	4
8	195	3	17	459	4
9	431	4	18	464	4
OUT	3,667	36	IN	3,639	36
TOTAL 7,306 YARDS; PAR 72					

CHICAGO

WHEATON, ILLINOIS, USA

The Chicago Golf Club is the oldest 18-hole course in the United States. It was formed at Belmont, Illinois, in 1892 with a nine-hole course laid out by Charles Blair Macdonald, which was extended to 18 holes in 1893. In 1894, the club moved to its Wheaton site with an 18-hole layout again designed by Macdonald. That same year it was one of the five clubs that formed the United States Golf Association. Chicago has hosted the US Open three times and the US Amateur four times.

CHICAGO					
HOLE	YARDS	PAR	HOLE	YARDS	PAR
1	450	4	10	139	3
2	440	4	11	410	4
3	219	3	12	414	4
4	536	5	13	149	3
5	320	4	14	351	4
6	395	4	15	393	4
7	207	3	16	525	5
8	413	4	17	382	4
9	406	4	18	425	4
OUT	3,386	35	IN	3,188	35
TOTAL 6,574 YARDS; PAR 70					

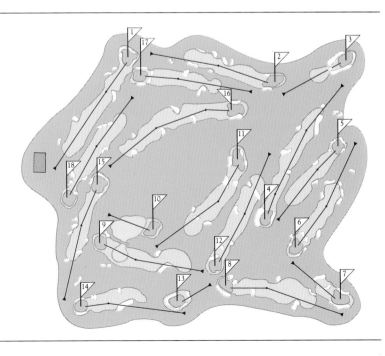

CHRISTCHURCH

SHIRLEY, CHRISTCHURCH, NEW ZEALAND

This course was established in 1873 by expatriate Scots. It moved from its original site at Hagley Park partly because of the interference of horned cattle, and it features the early Scottish practice of nine holes out and nine holes back. The 5th is a daunting par 5 of 539m that doglegs to the left in the landing area for the drive. A solitary bunker guards the green on the front left. The club has hosted the New Zealand Open Championship 13 times.

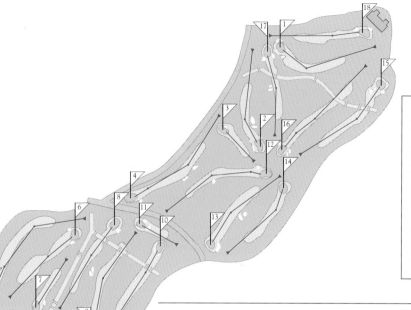

CHRISTCHURCH					
HOLE	METRES	PAR	HOLE	METRES	PAR
1	330	4	10	398	4
2	302	4	11	130	3
3	133	3	12	415	5
4	489	5	13	393	4
5	539	5	14	334	4
6	366	4	15	407	4
7	183	3	16	480	5
8	389	4	17	343	4
9	439	4	18	320	4
OUT	3,170	36	IN	3,220	37
TOTAL 6,390 METRES; PAR 73					

CORFU

CORFU, GREECE

Designed by Donald Harradine, the Corfu Golf and Country Club is one of the hidden golfing gems of Europe. It lies in the peaceful and verdant Ropa Valley on this romantic Greek island in the Ionian Sea. Although not long by the standards of some courses, Corfu nonetheless presents an exciting challenge, with several water hazards and great stands of mature cypress, pine and eucalyptus.

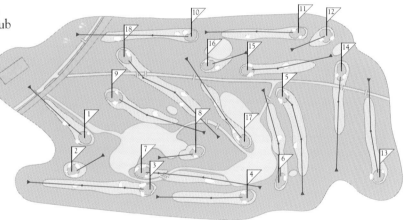

CORFU					
HOLE	METRES	PAR	HOLE	METRES	PAR
1	303	4	10	404	4
2	144	3	11	381	4
3	469	5	12	157	3
4	374	4	13	368	4
5	435	5	14	300	4
6	326	4	15	339	4
7	500	5	16	201	3
8	197	3	17	406	4
9	398	4	18	481	5
OUT	3,146	37	IN	3,037	35
TOTAL 6,183 METRES; PAR 72					

CRANS-SUR-SIERRE

MONTANA, SWITZERLAND

Founded in 1924, this golf club is set on a mountain plateau at a height of 5,000ft (1,600m) in the Berner Alps. The 6,165m course is shortened by the greater distance the ball travels in the rarefied air. Despite being under snow for the winter months, the course always returns to fine condition in time for the Swiss Open, which has been staged there since 1939. Crans-sur-Sierre is the largest club in Switzerland with some 1,500 members and enjoys a link with the Hong Kong Club, Fanling.

CRANS-SUR-SIERRE					
HOLE	METRES	PAR	HOLE	METRES	PAR
1	490	5	10	370	4
2	395	4	11	190	3
3	165	3	12	355	4
4	460	4	13	185	3
5	315	4	14	520	5
6	295	4	15	475	5
7	275	4	16	290	4
8	160	3	17	315	4
9	565	5	18	345	4
OUT	3,120	36	IN	3,045	36
TOTAL 6,165 METRES; PAR 72					

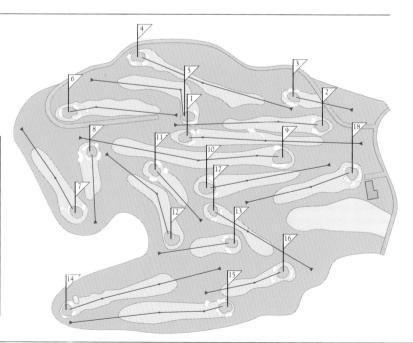

DORAL

MIAMI, FLORIDA, USA

Of the four courses at this Florida resort complex, the Blue course enjoys a worldwide reputation. Known as the "Blue Monster", the course is truly of championship standard and home of the Doral Open, a major early-season fixture on the US Tour. Dick Wilson was responsible for designing the course and its memorable finishing hole running alongside a lake. Close by, the 9th is similarly exacting, requiring a 163-yard carry over water all the way to the green.

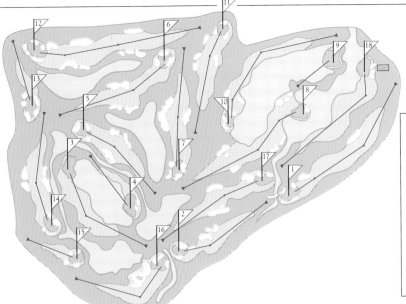

DORAL (BLUE)					
HOLE	YARDS	PAR	HOLE	YARDS	PAR
1	514	5	10	563	5
2	355	4	11	348	4
3	398	4	12	591	5
4	237	3	13	246	3
5	371	4	14	418	4
6	427	4	15	174	3
7	415	4	16	360	4
8	528	5	17	406	4
9	163	3	18	425	4
OUT	3,408	36	IN	3,531	36
TOTAL 6,939 YARDS; PAR 72					

THE DUNES

MYRTLE BEACH, SOUTH CAROLINA, USA

Designed in 1948 and one of Robert Trent Jones's earliest courses, The Dunes is now the centre of one of the world's busiest golf resorts. Bearing all the Jones hallmarks (large teeing areas, fairway bunkers and massive greens), the course also has water, trees and swampland. The 576-yard 13th is the most famous hole, tracing a semi-circle around a lake to a well-bunkered green. It may tempt unwary golfers to try too short a line over the water.

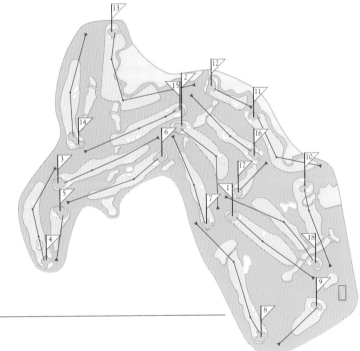

THE DUNES					
HOLE	YARDS	PAR	HOLE	YARDS	PAR
1	424	4	10	381	4
2	422	4	11	358	4
3	431	4	12	191	3
4	508	5	13	576	5
5	203	3	14	455	4
6	436	4	15	531	5
7	397	4	16	360	4
8	535	5	17	178	3
9	188	3	18	441	4
OUT	3,544	36	IN	3,471	36
TOTAL 7,015 YARDS; PAR 72					

EMIRATES

DUBAI, UNITED ARAB EMIRATES

In less than two years a barren stretch of desert scrubland was miraculously transformed into a lush, green, manicured golf course by designer Karl Litten. Daytime temperatures in Dubai range between 30–45°C (86–112°F), requiring that almost a million gallons (4.5 million litres) of water be pumped on to the course through 500 sprinkler heads every 24 hours. So successful is the course that the Desert Classic is now recognized as a regular part of the European Tour.

EMIRATES					
HOLE	YARDS	PAR	HOLE	YARDS	PAR
1	433	4	10	549	5
2	351	4	11	169	3
3	530	5	12	467	4
4	184	3	13	550	5
5	435	4	14	434	4
6	450	4	15	177	3
7	184	3	16	392	4
8	434	4	17	351	4
9	463	4	18	547	5
OUT	3,464	35	IN	3,636	37
TOTAL 7,100 YARDS; PAR 72					

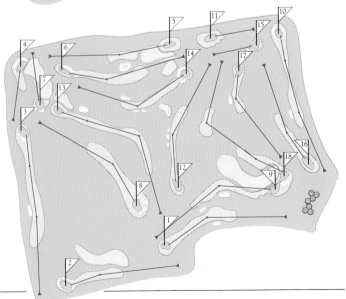

ESTELA

ESTELA, POVOA DE VARZIM, PORTUGAL

Always within sight or sound of the sea, this is a true Scottish-style links course on the north coast of Portugal. Constantly swept by breezes off the Atlantic, the often narrow fairways consist of fine, crisp turf while the rough is a mixture of sand and ground-hugging scrub. Two lakes on both front and back nines give a special beauty to the course. Most holes run out and back along the shore, so the wind is often across the line of the shot.

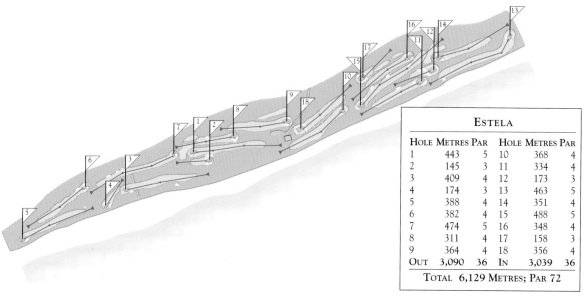

ESTELA					
HOLE	METRES	PAR	HOLE	METRES	PAR
1	443	5	10	368	4
2	145	3	11	334	4
3	409	4	12	173	3
4	174	3	13	463	5
5	388	4	14	351	4
6	382	4	15	488	5
7	474	5	16	348	4
8	311	4	17	158	3
9	364	4	18	356	4
OUT	3,090	36	IN	3,039	36
TOTAL 6,129 METRES; PAR 72					

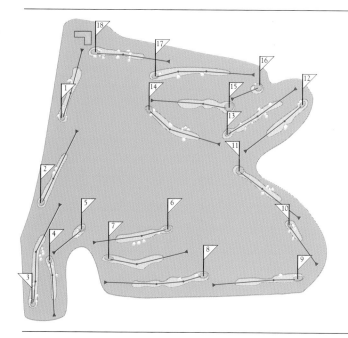

FORMBY

FORMBY, MERSEYSIDE, ENGLAND

The original nine holes of the completely natural golf course at Formby, which first came into being in 1884, were subsequently made up to the accepted 18 holes in the 1890s. The only changes to this links course since then have been necessitated by rapid erosion in the 1970s. Three new holes had to be brought into play to replace the original 8th, 9th and 10th, but the course has nonetheless stayed true to its nature, characterized by heather and stands of pine.

FORMBY					
HOLE	YARDS	PAR	HOLE	YARDS	PAR
1	415	4	10	188	3
2	381	4	11	384	4
3	518	5	12	405	4
4	312	4	13	380	4
5	162	3	14	420	4
6	402	4	15	403	4
7	377	4	16	127	3
8	493	5	17	494	5
9	450	4	18	390	4
OUT	3,510	37	IN	3,191	35
TOTAL 6,701 YARDS; PAR 72					

GLENEAGLES

AUCHTERARDER, PERTHSHIRE, SCOTLAND

James Braid laid out the many excellent holes of the King's and Queen's courses in their spectacular Perthshire hills setting as the first phase of the Gleneagles development. Both of the courses were actually in play ten years before the opening of the hotel, which was delayed until 1924 by the First World War. A third championship standard course, designed by Jack Nicklaus, was renamed the PGA Centenary Course in 2001.

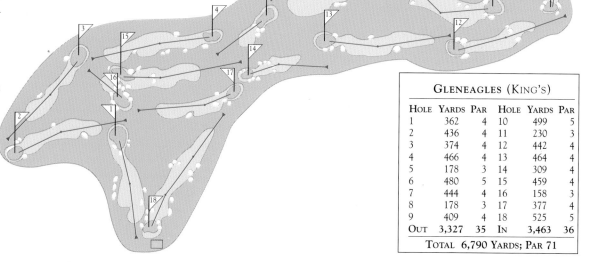

GLENEAGLES (KING'S)					
HOLE	YARDS	PAR	HOLE	YARDS	PAR
1	362	4	10	499	5
2	436	4	11	230	3
3	374	4	12	442	4
4	466	4	13	464	4
5	178	3	14	309	4
6	480	5	15	459	4
7	444	4	16	158	3
8	178	3	17	377	4
9	409	4	18	525	5
OUT	3,327	35	IN	3,463	36
TOTAL 6,790 YARDS; PAR 71					

GRAND CYPRESS
ORLANDO, FLORIDA, USA

The influence of the Old Course at St Andrews is obvious in the design of the New course at the Grand Cypress Resort in Florida. Course designer Jack Nicklaus features double greens, pot bunkers, wild rough and even a version of the famous Swilcan Bridge over a burn at the 1st. The large greens allow a pitch-and-run shot to come into play. The 140 bunkers include one at the 15th that is reminiscent of Hell bunker at St Andrews.

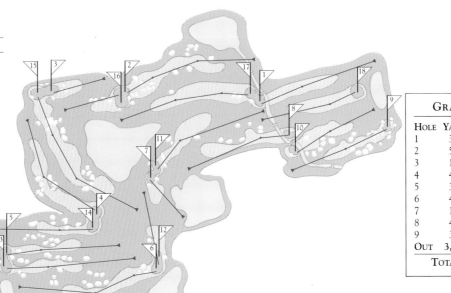

GRAND CYPRESS (NEW)					
HOLE	YARDS	PAR	HOLE	YARDS	PAR
1	362	4	10	330	4
2	514	5	11	430	4
3	179	3	12	207	3
4	440	4	13	431	4
5	393	4	14	371	4
6	496	5	15	570	5
7	182	3	16	190	3
8	440	4	17	485	5
9	382	4	18	371	4
OUT	3,388	36	IN	3,385	36
TOTAL 6,773 YARDS; PAR 72					

GULLANE
GULLANE, EAST LOTHIAN, SCOTLAND

There are three courses located in this small East Lothian village. The Number 1 probably just has the edge on the other two. From its lofty position, the course holds a commanding position over its more distinguished neighbour, Muirfield, and enjoys glorious views across the Firth of Forth. The greens are renowned for their quality, and share the same fine texture as the adjacent Open Championship course. The inward nine is the longer and more testing.

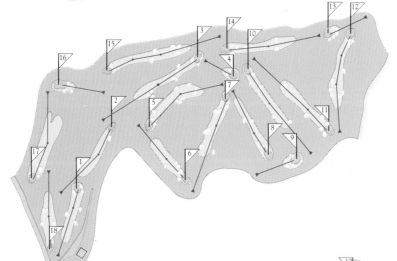

GULLANE (NUMBER 1)					
HOLE	YARDS	PAR	HOLE	YARDS	PAR
1	302	4	10	466	4
2	379	4	11	471	4
3	496	5	12	480	5
4	144	3	13	170	3
5	450	4	14	435	4
6	324	4	15	537	5
7	398	4	16	186	3
8	332	4	17	390	4
9	151	3	18	355	4
OUT	2,976	35	IN	3,490	36
TOTAL 6,466 YARDS; PAR 71					

HAMBURG-FALKENSTEIN
HAMBURG, GERMANY

The Falkenstein course was laid out by English architects Harry S. Colt, Charles Alison and John Morrison between 1928 and 1930, and later modernized by Dr Bernhard von Limburger. The course, built amid sandy terrain of heather and pine, is characterized by its narrow, tree-lined fairways and fast greens. Many of the holes are doglegs, and bunkers are used only where they will achieve maximum effect. Bernhard Langer won his first German Open here in 1981, scoring a course-record round of 64.

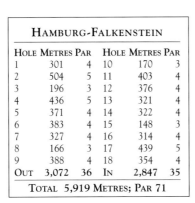

HAMBURG-FALKENSTEIN					
HOLE	METRES	PAR	HOLE	METRES	PAR
1	301	4	10	170	3
2	504	5	11	403	4
3	196	3	12	376	4
4	436	5	13	321	4
5	371	4	14	322	4
6	383	4	15	148	3
7	327	4	16	314	4
8	166	3	17	439	5
9	388	4	18	354	4
OUT	3,072	36	IN	2,847	35
TOTAL 5,919 METRES; PAR 71					

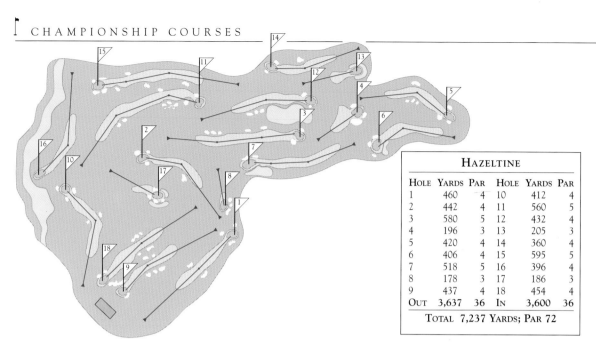

HAZELTINE

CHASKA, MINNESOTA, USA

The Hazeltine National Golf Club was the scene of Tony Jacklin's famous victory in the 1970 US Open, when he became the first home-based Briton to win the US title for 50 years. The club had been founded by former USGA president Totten Heffelfinger only a decade earlier, but the Robert Trent Jones layout has undergone extensive modifications since Jacklin's victory. Hazeltine hosted the US Open Championship for the second time in 1991.

HAZELTINE					
HOLE	YARDS	PAR	HOLE	YARDS	PAR
1	460	4	10	412	4
2	442	4	11	560	5
3	580	5	12	432	4
4	196	3	13	205	3
5	420	4	14	360	4
6	406	4	15	595	5
7	518	5	16	396	4
8	178	3	17	186	3
9	437	4	18	454	4
OUT	3,637	36	IN	3,600	36
TOTAL 7,237 YARDS; PAR 72					

THE JOCKEY CLUB

SAN ISIDRO, BUENOS AIRES, ARGENTINA

Dr Alister MacKenzie, famous for several of the world's greatest courses, took an extremely flat piece of ground at The Jockey Club and built two outstanding courses on it. Of the two, the Red course is the more famous; it features clever mounding and contouring and subtle Mackenzie bunkering. The Red course is short but testing and hosted the 1970 World Cup. However, golf here is regarded merely as a subsidiary adjunct to horse-racing and polo.

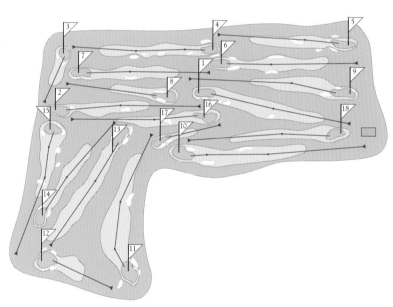

THE JOCKEY CLUB (RED)					
HOLE	YARDS	PAR	HOLE	YARDS	PAR
1	425	4	10	465	5
2	354	4	11	523	5
3	145	3	12	168	3
4	483	5	13	436	4
5	340	4	14	392	4
6	367	4	15	505	5
7	418	4	16	429	4
8	208	3	17	180	3
9	442	4	18	348	4
OUT	3,182	35	IN	3,446	37
TOTAL 6,628 YARDS; PAR 72					

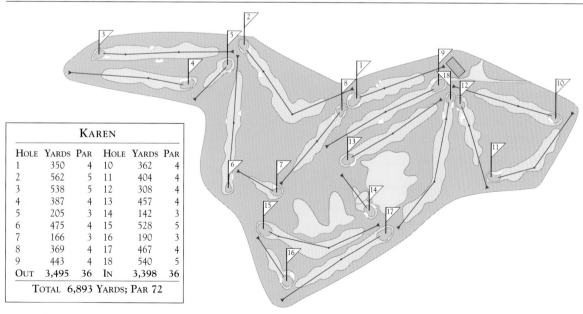

KAREN					
HOLE	YARDS	PAR	HOLE	YARDS	PAR
1	350	4	10	362	4
2	562	5	11	404	4
3	538	5	12	308	4
4	387	4	13	457	4
5	205	3	14	142	3
6	475	4	15	528	5
7	166	3	16	190	3
8	369	4	17	467	4
9	443	4	18	540	5
OUT	3,495	36	IN	3,398	36
TOTAL 6,893 YARDS; PAR 72					

KAREN

NAIROBI, KENYA

Baroness Karen von Blixen, author of *Out of Africa*, once owned the property on which is now laid out the beautiful Karen course. Twelve miles (19km) to the west of Nairobi, the setting is full of birdsong, botanical beauty and challenge for the golfer. Back-to-back par 5s at the 2nd and 3rd, one a 90-degree dogleg, the other straight, give a rather unbalanced feel to the first nine. Length is not the problem at the 142-yard par-3 14th, but there is an abundance of water to add difficulty.

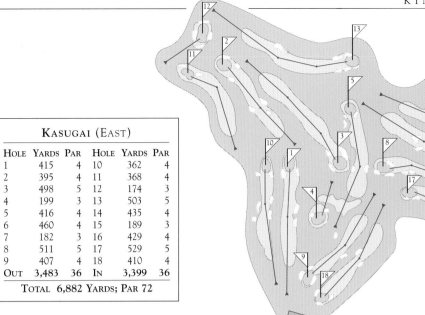

KASUGAI

NAGOYA, AICHIKEN, JAPAN

The "cut and fill" construction method, in which heavy equipment removes the tops of hills and deposits the earth in the valley below to build up the fairways, was used at Kasugai. Seichi Inoue designed the layouts. There are two courses, the East and West, with the East having been the venue for the Japan Open in 1975. Severe slopes present an arduous test and a conifer-planting operation has given definition to the fairways on both courses.

KASUGAI (EAST)					
HOLE	YARDS	PAR	HOLE	YARDS	PAR
1	415	4	10	362	4
2	395	4	11	368	4
3	498	5	12	174	3
4	199	3	13	503	5
5	416	4	14	435	4
6	460	4	15	189	3
7	182	3	16	429	4
8	511	5	17	529	5
9	407	4	18	410	4
OUT	3,483	36	IN	3,399	36
TOTAL 6,882 YARDS; PAR 72					

KENNEMER

KENNEMER, ZANDVOORT, NETHERLANDS

Perhaps the supreme links course on the European continent, Kennemer was designed by H.S. Colt in the late 1920s in an area of massive dunes and stands of pine trees. Kennemer has returning nines, reminiscent of Muirfield, rather than the more common out-and-back format. The imposing thatched clubhouse enjoys a perfect position on one of the highest sandhills. The design takes full advantage of elevated tees and greens, and of valley fairways.

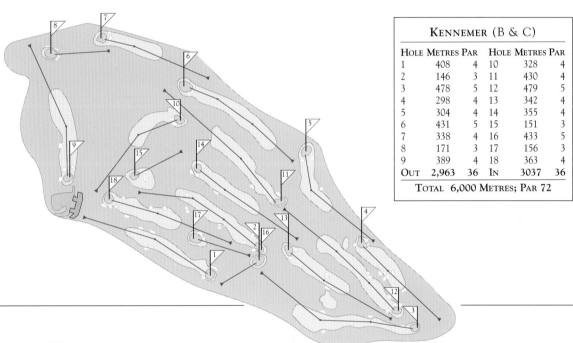

KENNEMER (B & C)					
HOLE	METRES	PAR	HOLE	METRES	PAR
1	408	4	10	328	4
2	146	3	11	430	4
3	478	5	12	479	5
4	298	4	13	342	4
5	304	4	14	355	4
6	431	5	15	151	3
7	338	4	16	433	5
8	171	3	17	156	3
9	389	4	18	363	4
OUT	2,963	36	IN	3037	36
TOTAL 6,000 METRES; PAR 72					

KINGSTON HEATH

CHELTENHAM, VICTORIA, AUSTRALIA

The original course was swallowed up in the expansion of Melbourne, but the new design, constructed in 1925, is on a fine area of sandy sub-soil close to Royal Melbourne Golf Club. Dr Alister MacKenzie, of Augusta fame, introduced a new bunkering plan in 1928 when the old timber clubhouse was demolished to make way for a new brick construction. In 1944 a huge bush fire engulfed most of the course, almost reaching the clubhouse and necessitating an impressive replanting operation.

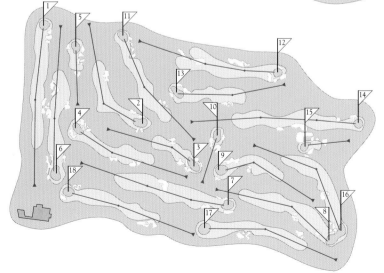

KINGSTON HEATH					
HOLE	METRES	PAR	HOLE	METRES	PAR
1	419	4	10	131	3
2	334	4	11	368	4
3	271	4	12	442	5
4	356	4	13	324	4
5	173	3	14	502	5
6	397	4	15	142	3
7	459	5	16	386	4
8	394	4	17	418	4
9	324	4	18	391	4
OUT	3,127	36	IN	3,104	36
TOTAL 6,231 METRES, PAR 72					

LAKE KARRINYUP

KARRINYUP, PERTH, WEST AUSTRALIA

The main feature is the massive lake, which comes into play on the 3rd, and particularly on the 8th, where the tee-shot must be solidly struck. The fairways are wide, bunkers a prominent design feature and the greens large and subtly shaped. Wind is a constant factor on this fine course and when it is against at the long 16th, two powerful hits are needed to reach the green in regulation.

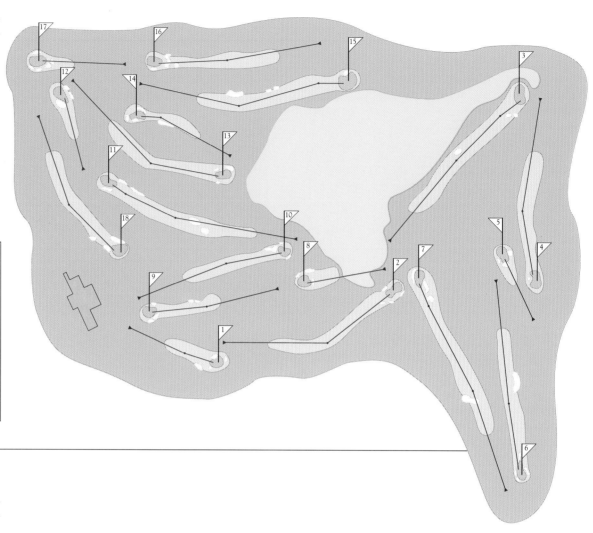

LAKE KARRINYUP					
HOLE	METRES	PAR	HOLE	METRES	PAR
1	272	4	10	340	4
2	430	4	11	460	5
3	475	5	12	150	3
4	390	4	13	385	4
5	150	3	14	260	4
6	390	4	15	485	5
7	537	5	16	400	4
8	178	3	17	180	3
9	335	4	18	370	4
OUT	3,157	36	IN	3,030	36
TOTAL 6,187 METRES; PAR 72					

LA MANGA

CARTAGENA, MURCIA, SPAIN

Both the North and South courses at La Manga are typified by wide fairways, large, flat, white sand bunkers and generously sized greens. There are scores of palm trees, lakes in profusion and numerous "barrancas" – deep ravines filled with rough and rocks that can ruin a score. The South course is the longer of the two and water comes into play on more than half of the holes. The 8th and 9th holes are a stiff examination of golfing ability, especially when the wind blows.

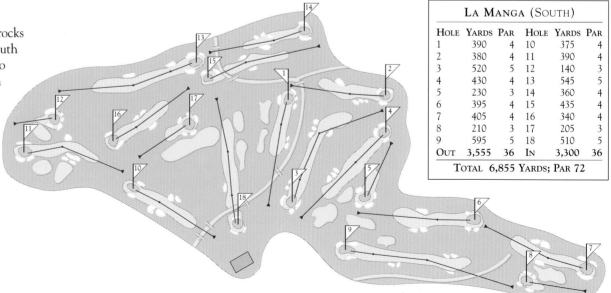

LA MANGA (SOUTH)					
HOLE	YARDS	PAR	HOLE	YARDS	PAR
1	390	4	10	375	4
2	380	4	11	390	4
3	520	5	12	140	3
4	430	4	13	545	5
5	230	3	14	360	4
6	395	4	15	435	4
7	405	4	16	340	4
8	210	3	17	205	3
9	595	5	18	510	5
OUT	3,555	36	IN	3,300	36
TOTAL 6,855 YARDS; PAR 72					

NAIRN

HOLE	YARDS	PAR	HOLE	YARDS	PAR
1	395	4	10	536	5
2	486	5	11	160	3
3	396	4	12	444	4
4	144	3	13	431	4
5	385	4	14	219	3
6	183	3	15	306	4
7	550	5	16	425	4
8	355	4	17	377	4
9	359	4	18	554	5
OUT	3,253	36	IN	3,452	36
TOTAL 6,705 YARDS; PAR 72					

NAIRN

NAIRN, NAIRNSHIRE, SCOTLAND

The links at Nairn on the Moray Firth is one of the most underrated courses in world golf. Archie Simpson designed the first layout of this course in 1887 but changes were made by James Braid and Old Tom Morris. Three holes (the 13th, 14th and 15th) loop from the shore; the remainder follow the out-and-back pattern of early courses.

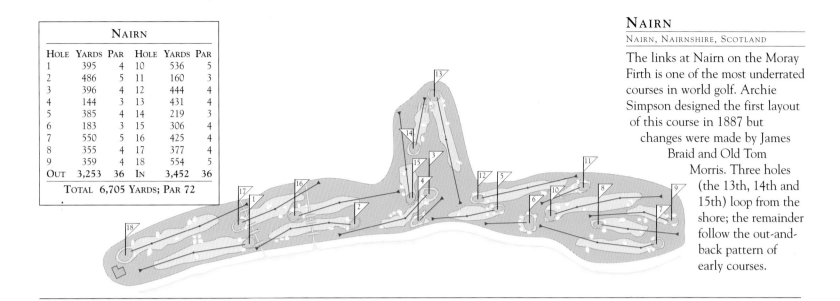

NATIONAL GOLF LINKS OF AMERICA

SOUTHAMPTON, NEW YORK, USA

Charles Blair Macdonald invested in five years' study of British links courses before building his course on the shores of Peconic Bay on eastern Long Island. A telescope at the clubhouse recalls the days when wealthy members arrived by private yacht. Opened in 1909, the balanced layout concentrates on strategy. Despite a well-deserved reputation, the National has hosted only one major event, the Walker Cup in 1922.

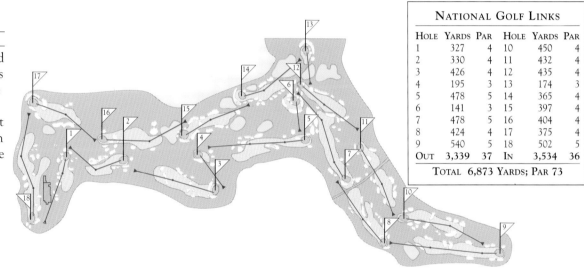

NATIONAL GOLF LINKS					
HOLE	YARDS	PAR	HOLE	YARDS	PAR
1	327	4	10	450	4
2	330	4	11	432	4
3	426	4	12	435	4
4	195	3	13	174	3
5	478	5	14	365	4
6	141	3	15	397	4
7	478	5	16	404	4
8	424	4	17	375	4
9	540	5	18	502	5
OUT	3,339	37	IN	3,534	36
TOTAL 6,873 YARDS; PAR 73					

NEW ST ANDREWS

TOCHIGI, JAPAN

Situated outside Tokyo, this course is a monument to new technology. The 18-hole New course, designed by Jack Nicklaus and Desmond Muirhead, is a great challenge. Golf bags are carried on an electronic trolley system controlled by the caddies. Nine holes on the New course are floodlit for evening play. The nine-hole Old course, with its replica of the Swilcan Bridge, is modelled on the club's Scottish namesake. A monorail transports players to the course from the clubhouse.

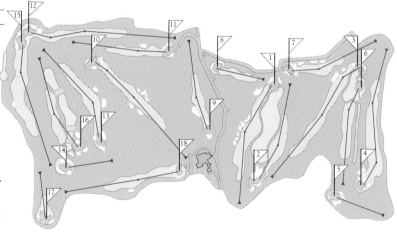

NEW ST ANDREWS (NEW)					
HOLE	METRES	PAR	HOLE	METRES	PAR
1	410	4	10	447	5
2	349	4	11	334	4
3	494	5	12	498	5
4	487	5	13	379	4
5	194	3	14	144	3
6	339	4	15	429	4
7	318	4	16	341	4
8	169	3	17	181	3
9	320	4	18	394	4
OUT	3,080	36	IN	3,147	36
TOTAL 6,227 METRES; PAR 72					

NEW SOUTH WALES

MATRAVILLE, NSW, AUSTRALIA

Built by Dr Alister MacKenzie on a headland separating the Pacific Ocean from Botany Bay, this superb course – tight fairways, difficult rough and strategic bunkering – is open to every bit of wind from any direction. The 181m 6th hole played over an inlet is a design feature that has since been copied all over the world. Taken over by the army in 1942, this great links required a massive restoration project to restore it to its former glory.

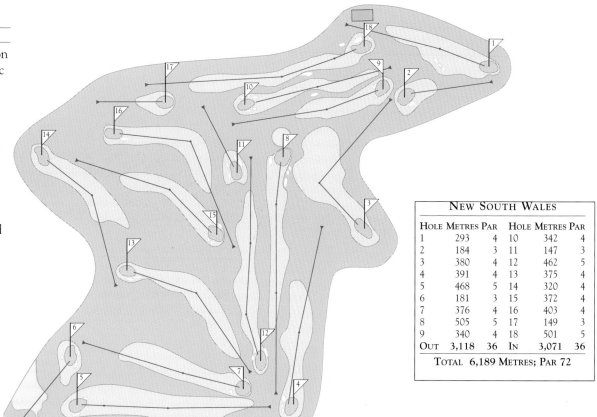

NEW SOUTH WALES					
HOLE	METRES	PAR	HOLE	METRES	PAR
1	293	4	10	342	4
2	184	3	11	147	3
3	380	4	12	462	5
4	391	4	13	375	4
5	468	5	14	320	4
6	181	3	15	372	4
7	376	4	16	403	4
8	505	5	17	149	3
9	340	4	18	501	5
OUT	3,118	36	IN	3,071	36
TOTAL 6,189 METRES; PAR 72					

OLGIATA

LARGO OLGIATA, ROME, ITALY

There was sufficient land available when Ken Cotton, a graduate of Cambridge University, England, designed this course in 1961 to allow him to create each hole in an individual setting. He took full advantage of the sweeping undulations of the site and its many mature trees to create a well-balanced layout that demands every shot in the book. When the course staged the World Cup seven years after its inauguration, Al Balding holed a bunker shot for an eagle-3 at the 17th to secure victory for the Canadian team.

OLGIATA					
HOLE	YARDS	PAR	HOLE	YARDS	PAR
1	377	4	10	396	4
2	212	3	11	431	4
3	465	4	12	427	4
4	399	4	13	430	4
5	487	5	14	170	3
6	427	4	15	503	5
7	195	3	16	202	3
8	377	4	17	520	5
9	552	5	18	427	4
OUT	3,491	36	IN	3,506	36
TOTAL 6,997 YARDS; PAR 72					

OLYMPIC

SAN FRANCISCO, CALIFORNIA, USA

This lakeside course was already in existence on the western edge of San Francisco, close to the Pacific, when the Olympic Club decided to get into golf and acquire it for their own members to use. They immediately planted the whole area with cypress, eucalyptus and pine. Since that date in 1922, the trees have come to dominate the course, providing extremely tight driving lines and small target areas. The course has been used three times for the US Open.

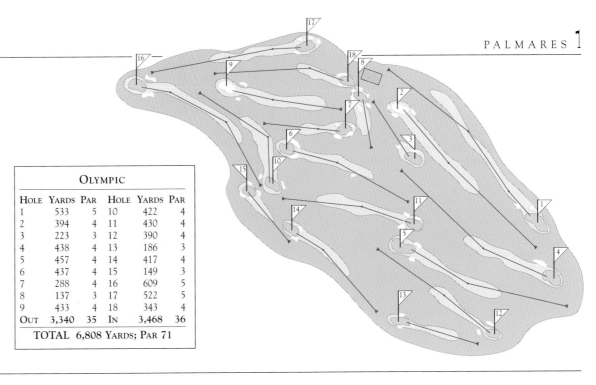

OLYMPIC					
HOLE	YARDS	PAR	HOLE	YARDS	PAR
1	533	5	10	422	4
2	394	4	11	430	4
3	223	3	12	390	4
4	438	4	13	186	3
5	457	4	14	417	4
6	437	4	15	149	3
7	288	4	16	609	5
8	137	3	17	522	5
9	433	4	18	343	4
OUT	3,340	35	IN	3,468	36
TOTAL 6,808 YARDS; PAR 71					

OTAGO

MAORI HILL, DUNEDIN, NEW ZEALAND

Many times the setting for the New Zealand Amateur and Professional Open Championships, the Balmacewen course at Otago is made particularly difficult by its hilly terrain, surrounded by native bush. The 361m par-4 11th is a classic driving hole, with a steep gradient on the right, mirrored by a creek on the opposite side. When he was once playing Bob Charles in an exhibition match, Arnold Palmer solved the problem this hole poses by driving the green.

OTAGO (BALMACEWEN)					
HOLE	METRES	PAR	HOLE	METRES	PAR
1	533	5	10	360	4
2	297	4	11	361	4
3	284	4	12	164	3
4	367	4	13	537	5
5	374	4	14	408	4
6	346	4	15	190	3
7	165	3	16	266	4
8	280	4	17	272	4
9	374	4	18	370	4
OUT	3,020	36	IN	2,928	35
TOTAL 5,948 METRES; PAR 71					

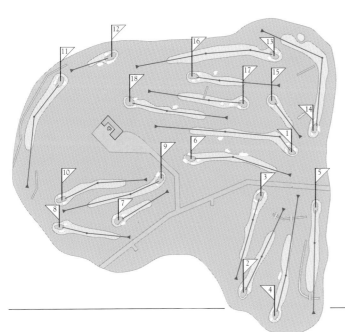

PALMARES

LAGOS, ALGARVE, PORTUGAL

One of the longest established golf courses located on Portugal's Algarve coast, Palmares manages to combine the best of all possible worlds. The clubhouse is set on a hillside and commands superb views over the course and the coast. The 1st hole drops downhill out of the trees to a stretch of five pure links holes situated between the railway and the shore. The course then climbs back up the slope for the remaining holes, which are played over gently undulating parkland.

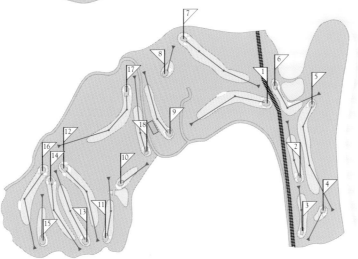

PALMARES					
HOLE	METRES	PAR	HOLE	METRES	PAR
1	418	4	10	165	3
2	321	4	11	271	4
3	287	4	12	400	4
4	142	3	13	386	4
5	550	5	14	347	4
6	344	4	15	212	3
7	462	5	16	418	4
8	142	3	17	458	5
9	317	4	18	321	4
OUT	2,983	36	IN	2,978	35
TOTAL 5,961 METRES; PAR 71					

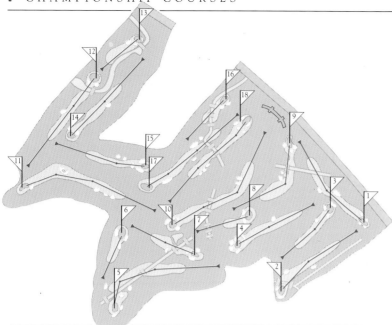

PENINA
PORTIMÃO, ALGARVE, PORTUGAL

Built on bare, flat ricefields, the course that Henry Cotton designed, and which he made his home for a great part of his later life, has been transformed, since it was first laid out in 1964, by more than 350,000 trees and shrubs.

Cotton visualized the effect of this planting and his vision has become a reality. The course is monstrously long from the championship tees, and every shot has to be carefully planned – just as the maestro intended.

PENINA					
HOLE	METRES	PAR	HOLE	METRES	PAR
1	407	4	10	498	5
2	388	4	11	494	5
3	306	4	12	385	4
4	353	4	13	185	3
5	451	5	14	358	4
6	176	3	15	301	4
7	310	4	16	192	3
8	171	3	17	476	5
9	386	4	18	436	5
OUT	2,948	35	IN	3,325	38
TOTAL 6,273 METRES; PAR 73					

PRESTWICK
PRESTWICK, AYRSHIRE, SCOTLAND

Prestwick is the home of the Open Championship, which was played here for the first 12 years of its existence, beginning in 1860. The Open returned 12 more times, but by 1924 the event had outgrown the restricted area in which the course is set. Prestwick remains a monument to the early days of golf, with fast-running, bumpy fairways, deep bunkers and many blind shots in unpredictable winds. Many of the holes remain unchanged from the early days.

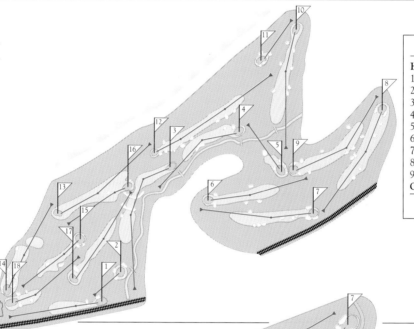

PRESTWICK					
HOLE	YARDS	PAR	HOLE	YARDS	PAR
1	346	4	10	454	4
2	167	3	11	195	3
3	500	5	12	513	5
4	382	4	13	460	4
5	206	3	14	362	4
6	400	4	15	347	4
7	430	4	16	298	4
8	431	4	17	391	4
9	458	4	18	284	4
OUT	3,320	35	IN	3,304	36
TOTAL 6,624 YARDS; PAR 71					

ROME
ACQUASANTA, ROME, ITALY

This golf course is set among the glorious relics of Ancient Rome, with impressive views of aqueducts and of the Appian Way. It is situated in low, rolling hills with well-positioned trees that provide an extra hazard on the fairways. The ground is maintained in good condition and is consistently well watered. The greens and their approaches are mainly flat, with few features to help the golfer judge distances. Although the course is not long, players find it a sufficiently tough challenge.

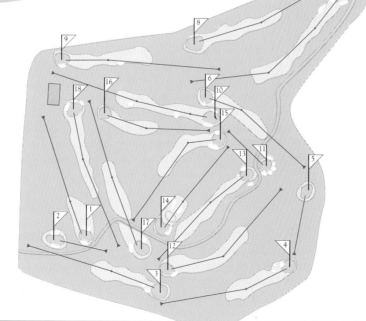

ROME					
HOLE	METRES	PAR	HOLE	METRES	PAR
1	305	4	10	444	5
2	141	3	11	120	3
3	317	4	12	408	4
4	359	4	13	348	4
5	197	3	14	331	4
6	351	4	15	329	4
7	504	5	16	319	4
8	368	4	17	391	4
9	398	4	18	370	4
OUT	2,940	35	IN	3,060	36
TOTAL 6,000 METRES; PAR 71					

ROYAL ABERDEEN
BRIDGE OF DON, ABERDEEN, SCOTLAND

While the club is more than 200 years old, this fine course over which members now play was built in 1888, after two earlier moves. The first hole plays down towards the sea and then the course veers northwards along the shore in true links fashion. There is great variation in the direction of play, with holes angled away from, or back towards, the shore. Subtle doglegs are created by setting tees in the dunes at an angle to the shallow valley of the fairways.

ROYAL ABERDEEN					
HOLE	YARDS	PAR	HOLE	YARDS	PAR
1	409	4	10	342	4
2	530	5	11	175	3
3	223	3	12	404	4
4	436	4	13	375	4
5	326	4	14	390	4
6	486	5	15	341	4
7	375	4	16	389	4
8	147	3	17	180	3
9	453	4	18	434	4
OUT	3,385	36	IN	3,030	34
TOTAL 6,415 YARDS; PAR 70					

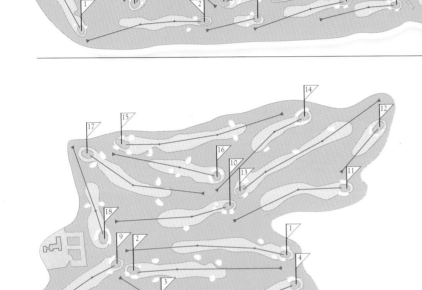

ROYAL BELGIQUE
TERVUREN, BELGIUM

This course was established by royal decree in 1904 and laid out to a design by Tom Simpson. In an area of parkland, he created a short but interesting test of golf, with eight par-4s under 380m, but still demanding thought and accuracy for the second shot through the careful use of bunkers and through tightening up the line of the tee-shot. The Belgian king is honorary president, and the clubhouse, once the Château of Ravenstein, is a national monument.

ROYAL BELGIQUE					
HOLE	METRES	PAR	HOLE	METRES	PAR
1	449	5	10	319	4
2	384	4	11	381	4
3	143	3	12	177	3
4	379	4	13	477	5
5	476	5	14	302	4
6	191	3	15	408	4
7	341	4	16	307	4
8	330	4	17	383	4
9	307	4	18	279	4
OUT	3,000	36	IN	3,033	36
TOTAL 6,033 METRES; PAR 72					

ROYAL CALCUTTA
TOLLYGUNGE, CALCUTTA, INDIA

Founded in 1829, Royal Calcutta was the first golf club established outside of the British Isles. To compensate for its low-lying, flat terrain, small lakes or tanks were dug to supply the earth needed to raise tees and greens. Even so, the highest point on the course is only 6ft (1.8m) above the level of the River Ganges. No hole is free from watery problems and with trees in abundance, few bunkers are required to make this long course difficult and demanding.

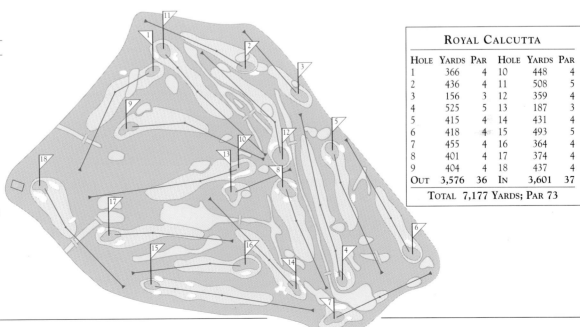

ROYAL CALCUTTA					
HOLE	YARDS	PAR	HOLE	YARDS	PAR
1	366	4	10	448	4
2	436	4	11	508	5
3	156	3	12	359	4
4	525	5	13	187	3
5	415	4	14	431	4
6	418	4	15	493	5
7	455	4	16	364	4
8	401	4	17	374	4
9	404	4	18	437	4
OUT	3,576	36	IN	3,601	37
TOTAL 7,177 YARDS; PAR 73					

HONG KONG, FANLING
NEW TERRITORIES, HONG KONG

Formerly the Royal Hong Kong, the club has come a long way since its inception at Happy Valley in 1889. Then, it was not possible to have bunkers or holes because the ground was shared with polo players and cricketers. It now has three 18-hole courses on the mainland at Fanling. The Old course, built in the 1900s, includes a picturesque loop (starting at the 10th hole) that is crucial to success on the back nine, yet all holes call for accurate driving and confident chipping.

HONG KONG, FANLING (OLD)					
HOLE	YARDS	PAR	HOLE	YARDS	PAR
1	325	4	10	396	4
2	292	4	11	467	4
3	157	3	12	162	3
4	395	4	13	397	4
5	190	3	14	498	5
6	496	5	15	377	4
7	179	3	16	205	3
8	339	4	17	474	5
9	514	5	18	376	4
OUT	2,887	35	IN	3,352	36
TOTAL 6,239 YARDS; PAR 71					

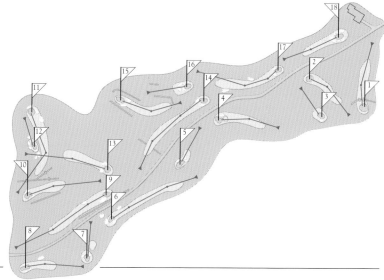

ROYAL JOHANNESBURG
TRANSVAAL, SOUTH AFRICA

At 6,825m, the East course may seem daunting, but it is set in the high veldt country of the Rand, 6,000ft (1,830m) above sea level, where the thin air allows golfers to hit the ball undreamed-of distances. A prime location for the South African Open, the East course favours long, accurate hitters, as its driving areas are squeezed by trees or well-placed bunkers. There is a good variety of holes as the course layout dips and climbs through a wooded valley.

ROYAL JOHANNESBURG (EAST)					
HOLE	METRES	PAR	HOLE	METRES	PAR
1	473	5	10	469	4
2	228	3	11	467	4
3	418	4	12	186	3
4	444	4	13	359	4
5	145	3	14	398	4
6	530	5	15	199	3
7	384	4	16	448	4
8	489	5	17	354	4
9	366	4	18	468	5
OUT	3,477	37	IN	3,348	35
TOTAL 6,825 METRES; PAR 72					

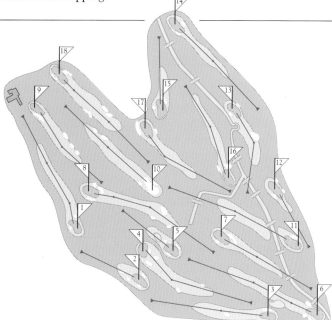

SAUNTON
BRAUNTON, DEVON, ENGLAND

Superbly situated on Devon's north coast, just the other side of the Taw Estuary from Westward Ho!, this old-established course has the river, the Atlantic and golden sands as its backdrop. Used during the Second World War as a battle school, Saunton did not re-open until Herbert Fowler's original East course had been revamped and restored by Ken Cotton in 1951. At that time, three new holes were brought into play, the 1st and the last two, and the course provides a good test of shot-making ability.

SAUNTON (EAST)					
HOLE	YARDS	PAR	HOLE	YARDS	PAR
1	470	4	10	337	4
2	476	5	11	362	4
3	402	4	12	418	4
4	444	4	13	136	3
5	112	3	14	461	4
6	370	4	15	485	5
7	428	4	16	430	4
8	380	4	17	202	3
9	382	4	18	408	4
OUT	3,464	36	IN	3,239	35
TOTAL 6,703 YARDS; PAR 71					

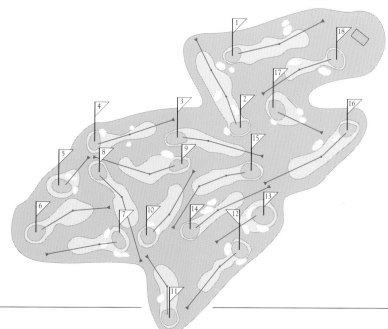

SCIOTO

COLUMBUS, OHIO, USA

Built on land once the home of Wyandotte Indians, the Scioto Country Club was laid out to a design by Donald Ross in 1916. A classic course, it is one of the best created by this architect. It is a strategic course, demanding careful assessment and shot-making, the very qualities that have made Jack Nicklaus, who learned his golf at Scioto, possibly the world's greatest player. The long 505-yard par-5 8th stands out as one of the toughest holes.

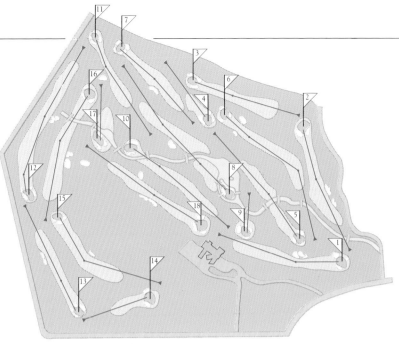

			SCIOTO			
HOLE	YARDS	PAR		HOLE	YARDS	PAR
1	418	4		10	424	4
2	459	4		11	365	4
3	377	4		12	545	5
4	194	3		13	436	4
5	438	4		14	238	3
6	527	5		15	408	4
7	372	4		16	425	4
8	505	5		17	209	3
9	162	3		18	445	4
OUT	3,452	36		IN	3,495	35
		TOTAL 6,947 YARDS; PAR 71				

SEEFELD-WILDMOOS

SEEFELD, TIROL, AUSTRIA

Located at 4,300ft (1,310m), this course was designed by Donald Harradine. When it emerges from its snow cover for a six-month golf season, the layout reveals itself to be extremely tight, requiring great accuracy. The mountain terrain is in places exploited to dramatic effect, as at the par-3 9th, where the tee towers 195ft (60m) above the green. Harradine has made sparing use of bunkers, relying instead on the abundant pine and birch trees to provide hazards.

			SEEFELD-WILDMOOS			
HOLE	METRES	PAR		HOLE	METRES	PAR
1	436	5		10	360	4
2	363	4		11	282	4
3	294	4		12	518	5
4	349	4		13	156	3
5	218	3		14	534	5
6	351	4		15	379	4
7	519	5		16	293	4
8	243	4		17	165	3
9	163	3		18	337	4
OUT	2,936	36		IN	3,024	36
		TOTAL 5,960 METRES; PAR 72				

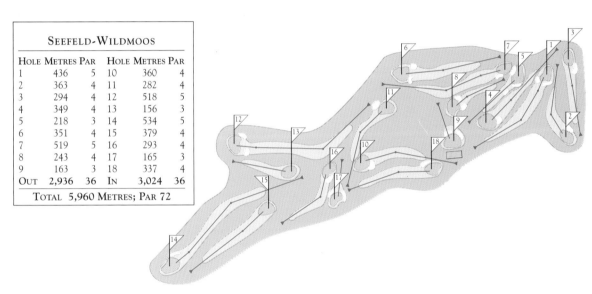

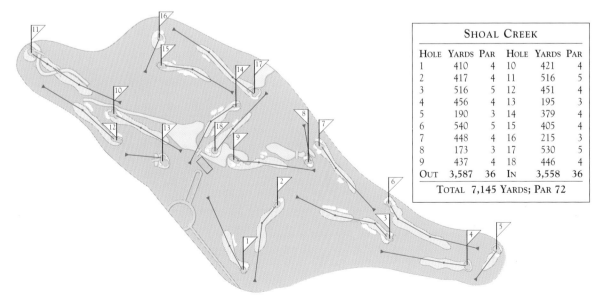

			SHOAL CREEK			
HOLE	YARDS	PAR		HOLE	YARDS	PAR
1	410	4		10	421	4
2	417	4		11	516	5
3	516	5		12	451	4
4	456	4		13	195	3
5	190	3		14	379	4
6	540	5		15	405	4
7	448	4		16	215	3
8	173	3		17	530	5
9	437	4		18	446	4
OUT	3,587	36		IN	3,558	36
		TOTAL 7,145 YARDS; PAR 72				

SHOAL CREEK

BIRMINGHAM, ALABAMA, USA

Originally designed by Jack Nicklaus as a members' course, Shoal Creek was torn apart by the professionals during the 1984 USPGA Championship. Before it hosted the event again in 1990, Nicklaus was called back to bring more trouble into play and to lengthen many of the holes. With its fierce rough, the course was almost too difficult second time around. Trees, lakes and creeks combine with creative bunkering and large, well-contoured greens to achieve a fine test of golfing skill.

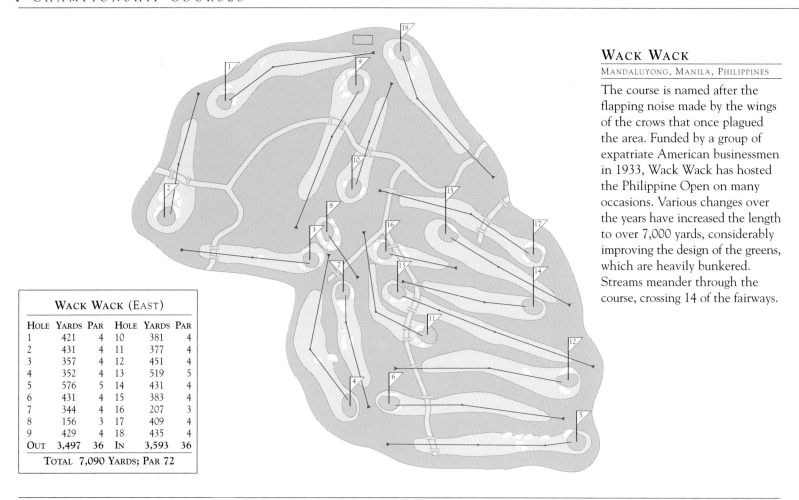

WACK WACK

MANDALUYONG, MANILA, PHILIPPINES

The course is named after the flapping noise made by the wings of the crows that once plagued the area. Funded by a group of expatriate American businessmen in 1933, Wack Wack has hosted the Philippine Open on many occasions. Various changes over the years have increased the length to over 7,000 yards, considerably improving the design of the greens, which are heavily bunkered. Streams meander through the course, crossing 14 of the fairways.

WACK WACK (EAST)					
HOLE	YARDS	PAR	HOLE	YARDS	PAR
1	421	4	10	381	4
2	431	4	11	377	4
3	357	4	12	451	4
4	352	4	13	519	5
5	576	5	14	431	4
6	431	4	15	383	4
7	344	4	16	207	3
8	156	3	17	409	4
9	429	4	18	435	4
OUT	3,497	36	IN	3,593	36
TOTAL 7,090 YARDS; PAR 72					

WALTON HEATH

TADWORTH, SURREY, ENGLAND

Although Walton Heath is not far from London, there is a distinct seaside quality about its short heathland turf, deep bunkers and large, rolling greens. The Old course was for many years the home of the original Matchplay Championship. "Exposed to all the breezes that blow", according to Bernard Darwin, the course has a demanding nature, typified by the 517-yard par-5 14th with its long carry from the tee and bunker-strewn journey to the green.

WALTON HEATH (OLD)					
HOLE	YARDS	PAR	HOLE	YARDS	PAR
1	442	4	10	138	3
2	289	4	11	384	4
3	441	4	12	371	4
4	391	4	13	513	5
5	427	4	14	517	5
6	174	3	15	408	4
7	494	5	16	510	5
8	400	4	17	181	3
9	399	4	18	404	4
OUT	3,457	36	IN	3,426	37
TOTAL 6,883 YARDS; PAR 73					

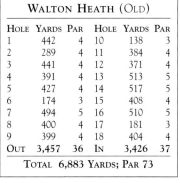

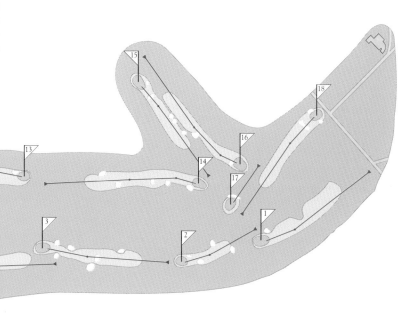

WILD DUNES

CHARLESTON, SOUTH CAROLINA, USA

Architect Tom Fazio felt he had the perfect material to work with when he designed this course on the Isle of Palms in South Carolina. A prehistoric hurricane is believed to have created the huge ridge of dunes 50ft (15m) high that dominate the back nine of this layout. The front nine has holes carved from the maritime forest of palmetto, loblolly pine and magnolia. The course threads its way through marsh and sand, with two classic links holes to finish.

WILD DUNES (LINKS)					
HOLE	YARDS	PAR	HOLE	YARDS	PAR
1	501	5	10	331	4
2	370	4	11	376	4
3	420	4	12	192	3
4	170	4	13	427	4
5	505	5	14	489	5
6	421	4	15	426	4
7	359	4	16	175	3
8	203	3	17	405	4
9	451	4	18	501	5
OUT	3,400	36	IN	3,322	36
TOTAL 6,722 YARDS; PAR 72					

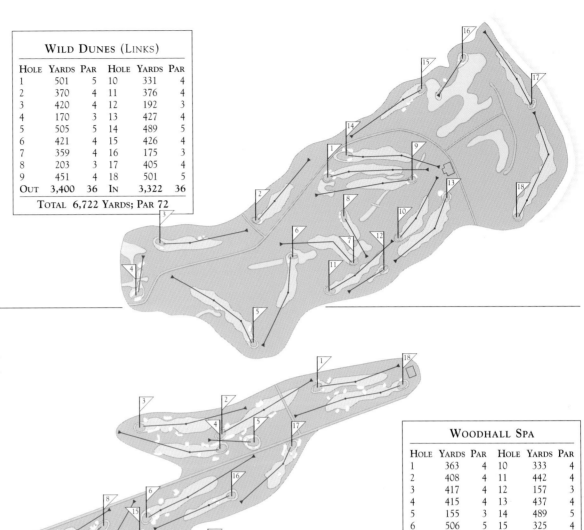

WOODHALL SPA

LINCOLNSHIRE, ENGLAND

Harry Vardon laid out the first course at Woodhall Spa in 1905, but it was subsequently redesigned by Harry S. Colt in 1912. The outstanding present layout is that of Colonel S.V. Hotchkin. The bunkers that guard the three short holes are deep and intimidating; the 560-yard 9th has its fairway completely blocked by bunkers, which come into play against a headwind.

WOODHALL SPA					
HOLE	YARDS	PAR	HOLE	YARDS	PAR
1	363	4	10	333	4
2	408	4	11	442	4
3	417	4	12	157	3
4	415	4	13	437	4
5	155	3	14	489	5
6	506	5	15	325	4
7	438	4	16	398	4
8	193	3	17	322	4
9	560	5	18	544	5
OUT	3,455	36	IN	3,447	37
TOTAL 6,902 YARDS; PAR 73					

YOMIURI

TOKYO, JAPAN

In common with many other Japanese courses, there are two greens at every hole, one for use in summer, the other for winter.

There are times when this arrangement interferes with the best tactical bunkering for each green, but in general it works well.

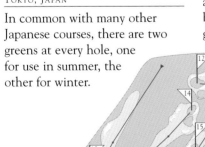

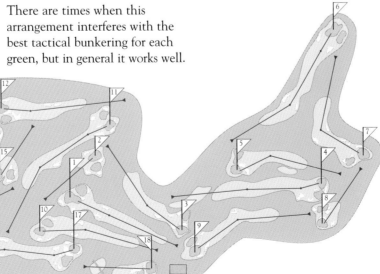

YOMIURI					
HOLE	YARDS	PAR	HOLE	YARDS	PAR
1	396	4	10	425	4
2	180	3	11	507	5
3	403	4	12	432	4
4	508	5	13	450	4
5	384	4	14	364	4
6	541	5	15	194	3
7	389	4	16	410	4
8	197	3	17	510	5
9	448	4	18	224	3
OUT	3,446	36	IN	3,516	36
TOTAL 6,962 YARDS; PAR 72					

THE HALL
OF FAME

Golf has thrown up an extraordinary number of outstanding characters, sportsmen and women of the most striking personality and individuality. Professional golfers are now among the highest paid of the world's athletes, but they are also among the most respected, because of their rigorous adherence to the rules of their game and respect for its traditions.

Tobacco-tin greats: Abe Mitchell, George Duncan, Harry Vardon, James Braid

This chapter lists more than 100 outstanding men and women who have made a special individual contribution to golf. It is a list that comprises not only the great champions but also architects and administrators who have played a significant role in the history of golf.

A statistics box, within each player's entry, records selective career highlights, with major championship victories, tour records and international team events.

Bobby Jones, Grand Slam winner in 1930

Different strokes for different champions (left)
British Open Champion (1996) Tom Lehman does not have a classic swing – his lateral movement into impact is more pronounced than most top-class players – but it works for him.

PETER ALLISS

BORN BERLIN, GERMANY, 28 FEBRUARY 1931

S ON OF THE *well-known professional Percy Alliss, Peter was born in Berlin, where his father was serving as a professional, but was brought up in England, at Ferndown in Dorset. As a boy he was seldom far from the famous courses in that area. It was obvious from the start that he was a naturally gifted player of the game.*

Ryder Cup stalwart
Between 1959 and 1969 Peter Alliss was chosen for every Ryder Cup team except one. In 1965 he won his singles match against Billy Casper by one hole (below). However the Americans dominated the event.

Peter Alliss was selected to represent England as a Boy International in 1946, and was hailed as a future champion by such an experienced observer as Leonard Crawley. He turned professional a few weeks later, while still only 15.

NIGHTMARE SHOT

In 1953 Alliss was thrown into the deep end when he was invited to play for Great Britain in the Ryder Cup at Wentworth, at the tender age of 22. It turned out to be a harrowing experience that might have seriously damaged his career. The key event occurred at the last hole in his singles match against Jim Turnesa. Confronting a pitch shot to the green in the tightest possible situation, Alliss hit a nightmare fluff, which was to haunt him for years. It allowed Turnesa to win by one hole, and the United States to win the Cup by that one match. British team captain Henry Cotton was furious. Alliss himself forgot that other players, including Bernard Hunt, had also failed at this last hole. He took his narrow defeat, and the overstated and absurd newspaper headlines that followed it, very badly.

It was several years before Alliss recovered from this experience, but

Voice of golf
Today Peter Alliss is recognized as golf's outstanding commentator, commanding huge respect on both sides of the Atlantic.

Putting trouble
Throughout his career, Alliss was plagued by erratic putting. It never quite matched the quality of the rest of his game.

Television. While Tony Jacklin, Sandy Lyle and Nick Faldo have won the Major titles at golf, the voice of golf in the United Kingdom for many years has been that of Peter Alliss.

There has never been any doubt of Alliss's popularity. In 1987, he was made captain of the British PGA, based at The Belfry, a course that he had been in part responsible for designing.

PETER ALLISS

WON SPANISH OPEN 1956, 1958; BRITISH PGA 1957, 1962, 1965; ITALIAN OPEN 1958; PORTUGUESE OPEN 1958; BRAZILIAN OPEN 1961. RYDER CUP 1953, 1957–69. WORLD CUP 1954–55, 1957–59, 1961–62, 1964, 1966–67. VARDON TROPHY 1964, 1966. BRITISH PGA CAPTAIN 1962, 1987.

ultimately it may have provoked him into greater efforts. In 1956 he won his first important championship, the Spanish Open, and in 1958, his best year, he took the Italian and Portuguese Open titles, as well as the Spanish Open for a second time. He went on to win 23 other significant tournaments up to 1969.

Peter Alliss played in eight Ryder Cup matches, as well as ten World Cup clashes for England. Yet he never won the Open Championship, though many supporters felt he should have done so.

When his putting – never the strongest point of his game – finally went into decline, Alliss was embraced by BBC

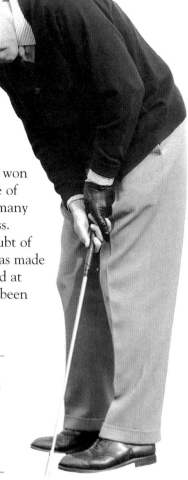

ISAO AOKI

BORN ABIKO, JAPAN, 31 AUGUST 1942

WHEN HE WAS *a boy, Isao Aoki caddied at his local club at Abiko, and used to play in the early mornings and the evenings, or whenever else the course was clear. Turning professional in 1964, it was not until 1971 that he won his first tournament. After that success, he rapidly became Japan's first international star.*

Aoki's victories include two Japan Opens and five Japan PGA Matchplay titles. In 1978 he won the World Matchplay at Wentworth and the following year lost by only one hole to Bill Rogers.

In 1978, at St Andrews, he led the field in the Open Championship at the end of the first round and shared the lead after two rounds, only to finish seventh, as he did in 1979. His first US Tour win was the Hawaiian Open in 1983, which he achieved with a spectacular eagle at the last hole, sinking his third shot from thick rough to win by one stroke. Earlier in that year he also won the European Open in Britain. Aoki established himself as one of the heroes of Japanese golf.

Gentleman golfer
Tall and good-looking, Aoki was always well known for his excellent manners on the course.

Aoki joined the Senior PGA Tour in 1992 and immediately became a prolific winner, including victories in the Japan Senior Open from 1994 to 1997.

Getting on line (right)
Aoki lines up a putt – his short game helped make him one of the world's outstanding players.

ISAO AOKI

WON JAPAN PGA 1973, 1981, 1986;
WORLD MATCHPLAY 1978;
EUROPEAN OPEN 1983; JAPAN OPEN
1983, 1987; HAWAIIAN OPEN 1983.
DUNHILL CUP 1985, 1999, 2000. FOUR
TOURS CHAMPIONSHIP 1985, 1987–88.

PAUL AZINGER

BORN HOLYOKE, MASSACHUSETTS, USA, 6 JANUARY 1960

IN THE *1993 USPGA Championship at the Inverness Club in Toledo, Ohio, Paul Azinger trailed Greg Norman by one stroke going into the final round. A closing three under par round of 68 put him in a tie with the Australian and into a thrilling play-off which Azinger won with a second extra hole par.*

It was the highlight of a remarkable season for the "Zinger", as he is widely known, and confirmed him as one of the game's new breed of superstars. He had come a long way from the days when he couldn't break 40 for nine holes as a senior in high school. Azinger learned quickly, and after Florida State University turned professional in 1981. The next year he was out on the Tour; by 1987 he was second on the money list and a dollar millionaire.

"Zinger" swinger
Not noted for his swinging style, Azinger nonetheless gets results, here helping the US team retain the Ryder Cup at The Belfry in 1993.

Azinger is not considered one of the classic swingers but he has one of the most effective methods on the Tour. In 1993 he kept the longest active winning streak going on the US Tour with three victories including wins in the Memorial Tournament and the New England Classic. Azinger has performed outstandingly on three US Ryder Cup teams and represented the United States in the World Cup, and the 2000 Presidents Cup when he was co-captain.

AGAINST ADVERSITY
The discovery of cancer in his right shoulder blade in 1993 was a major setback but the condition was diagnosed early enough to give him every confidence that he would make a complete recovery, and he fought the condition with great fortitude. He made a full recovery and was soon back in the winner's circle again.

PAUL WILLIAM AZINGER

WON US TOUR
CHAMPIONSHIP 1992;
USPGA 1993.
WINNER OF 12 US TOUR
EVENTS 1987–2000.
RYDER CUP 1989–93.
WORLD CUP 1989.
USPGA PLAYER OF THE
YEAR 1987. BEN HOGAN
AWARD 1995.

JOHN BALL, see page 236

SEVE BALLESTEROS

BORN PEDREÑA, SPAIN, 9 APRIL 1957

L ONG BEFORE SEVERIANO *Ballesteros beat Jack Nicklaus and Ben Crenshaw by three strokes to win the 1979 Open Championship at Royal Lytham and St Annes, it was obvious that golf had a refreshingly new and precocious talent. The young man from the north coast of Spain turned professional at 17 and took the game by storm. In five years he developed from a raw youngster into one of the world's leading players.*

There can be little argument that Seve Ballesteros is one of the greatest players of all time. Where precisely he is placed in the final order of merit will depend upon which criteria are applied. If the yardstick is the number of Majors won, then the Spaniard will be well down the league compared with Jack Nicklaus. But it can be safely argued that in Seve's generation Majors have been much harder to win.

Ballesteros has won just five Majors compared to Nicklaus's 20 – the Open Championship three times and the Masters twice. Some feel his remarkable talent should have delivered more.

Gracias amigos (below)
Seve acknowledges the tumultuous applause of the gallery after his popular victory in the Open Championship at St Andrews in 1984.

Mastering Augusta (above)
On his way to winning the US Masters for the second time, Ballesteros was watched by a tense crowd at Augusta in 1983.

Ballesteros is the youngest of four brothers who all became professional golfers. He taught himself to play by sneaking on to the Santander Golf Course, which was out of bounds to him, to learn under cover of dusk. The eight-year-old Seve practised every conceivable shot with just one club – an old 3-iron – which may just possibly account for his amazing ability in later life to invent brilliant recovery shots from seemingly impossible situations.

"PARKING LOT CHAMPION"

When he emerged on to the professional stage, Ballesteros brought with him a swashbuckling, go-for-everything attitude that the game had not seen since the legendary Arnold Palmer. Seve would hit it, find it and hit it again, aiming at the pin with every shot. The crowds loved him. When he won his first British Open title in 1979 he was christened the

Playing for Europe (left)
Seve took particular delight in the defeat of the Americans by the European team in the Ryder Cup in 1985 and 1987 and particularly when he was Captain of the winning European side at Valderrama in 1997.

After his second Open victory, achieved amid memorable scenes at St Andrews in 1984, Seve seemed to lose his winning touch and showed a distressing tendency to "choke" at crucial moments. But then came his triumph at the rain-interrupted Open at Royal Lytham in 1988, and Ballesteros was back on top of the world.

SEVERIANO BALLESTEROS

WON OPEN CHAMPIONSHIP 1979, 1984, 1988; US MASTERS 1980, 1983; WORLD MATCHPLAY 1981–82, 1984–85, 1991. BRITISH PGA 1983, 1991. WINNER OF 48 EUROPEAN TOUR EVENTS 1976–95. WORLD CUP 1975–77, 1991. RYDER CUP 1979, 1983–95 (NON-PLAYING CAPTAIN 1997). DUNHILL CUP 1985–86, 1988. SEVE BALLESTEROS TROPHY 2000 (PLAYING CAPTAIN). HARRY VARDON TROPHY 1976–78, 1986, 1988, 1991. EUROPEAN TOUR GOLFER OF THE YEAR 1986, 1988, 1991. WORLD GOLF HALL OF FAME 1997

Captain's winnings (below)
Ballesteros boosted his colleagues' confidence as non-playing Captain in the 1997 Ryder Cup.

Long but wide (above)
One of the longest hitters on the Tour, Seve tends to miss by a lot whenever he plays a shot off line.

"parking-lot champion" by the American press, after he had played his second at the 16th hole from among the cars. As Ballesteros revealed later, the drive had been deliberately hit down that side of the hole because the prevailing wind made it difficult to attack the green from the left. Far from being a wild shot, it had been a calculated tactic that brought him a birdie – typical of Seve's genius for the unexpected.

The following year he won the Masters and led the European challenge into the decade that was to see the American supremacy in world golf overturned. He won a second green jacket in 1983.

Europe's inspiration (above)
Ballesteros spurred Europe's triumph with his singles match win against Curtis Strange in the 1987 Ryder Cup at Muirfield Village, Ohio.

JOHN BALL

BORN HOYLAKE, ENGLAND, 24 DECEMBER 1862; DIED 1940

A NY ATTEMPT TO *assess John Ball's status among golfers of all time is futile – he is too remote from the modern game. But he was unquestionably the outstanding amateur of his own era, at a period when there were many top-class amateurs who were as good as most professionals. Quiet and modest, Ball shunned the limelight. Yet in his prime he drew an enormous following, particularly in his home area, where he was considered unbeatable.*

John Ball was born at Hoylake, Cheshire, where his father, a first-class golfer, owned the Royal Hotel next to land that was soon to become the links of the Royal Liverpool Golf Club. Ball was able to use the course in his youth and soon became a formidable young player.

He first played in the Open Championship in 1878 at the precocious age of 15; he lost the play-off for fourth place, taking a small cash prize. When some years later the question of amateur status was raised, the age limit for winning money was fixed at 16, so that Ball could avoid being classed as a professional. In 1885 he reached the semi-final of the first Amateur Championship, going on to win

Well out (right)
John Ball played his way out of bunkers with a mashie, never resorting to a niblick.

Palm grip
As was usual in his day, Ball gripped the club in his palms.

the title at Prestwick in 1888 and again at Hoylake in 1890. In the latter year he also became the Open Champion at Prestwick.

He was the first golfer from outside Scotland to win the title, and also the first player to win the Open and Amateur titles in the same year. Ball never won the Open again, but he won the Amateur eight times, the last time in 1912. He entered for the final time in 1921 when, aged 58, he still reached the fifth round.

MANUFACTURING SHOTS

Ball had a complete mastery over every club he used. He was adept at playing half and quarter shots with any club; no one was more versatile. He refused to recognize the necessity for a niblick and played from even the worst lies in bunkers with his mashie. In his young days Ball was always an immensely long hitter; as he grew older he lost some of his length, but he always retained uncanny accuracy with his irons.

JOHN BALL JNR

WON OPEN CHAMPIONSHIP 1890; BRITISH AMATEUR CHAMPIONSHIP 1888, 1890, 1892, 1894, 1899, 1907, 1910, 1912.

Amateur caricature
In 1892, the year of his third Amateur Championship victory, Ball was caricatured by "Lib" – Italian artist Liberio Prosperi – in Vanity Fair. In 1977 Ball's contribution to golf was recognized with his induction into the World Golf Hall of Fame.

MILLER BARBER

BORN SHREVEPORT, LOUISIANA, USA, 31 MARCH 1931

Golfing half-century
Miller Barber had more success as a 50-year-old on the Senior Tour than he had ever enjoyed previously.

K NOWN FOR MANY *years as "X" because of his dislike of the limelight, Miller Barber is, nonetheless, a genial and friendly individual. He is also a fine player and always a delight to watch. It is a great source of regret to Barber that he never won a Major title in his 20 years on the US Tour, but he has moved on to become an exceptionally proficient performer among the Seniors, accumulating prize money in excess of $2 million.*

After a successful career on the amateur circuit, Miller Barber turned professional in 1958. He joined the USPGA Tour the following year.

His swing was unorthodox, with a pronounced "flying" right elbow on the backswing, but it proved effective, and he became a very competitive player. After completing his apprentice years, he scored his first win on the Tour in 1964.

Seniors silver
Barber and his wife enjoy holding the USPGA Seniors trophy in 1981.

CONSISTENT VICTORIES

Barber won a US Tour victory every year between 1967 and 1974, an eight-year sequence equalled by very few players. His most significant triumph came in the World Open in 1973, a marathon event played over eight rounds that carried the first $100,000 prize in golf history.

Surprisingly, in the Majors Barber was rarely in the running, though in the 1969 US Open only a disastrous last round robbed him of the chance of glory. When Barber reached the age to qualify for the USPGA Senior Tour in March 1981, it was a different story. He won both the major events on the Senior Tour in his first two years – the USPGA Seniors in 1981 and the USGA Senior Open in 1982.

Barber has played in more US Senior Tour events than any other player in golf history. He became the first Senior Tour Player to earn $2 million in combined career earnings and the first Senior Tour player to win $2 million in Senior Tour career money. "X", now into his 70s, continues to grace the Senior Tour and regularly beats his age in tournament play.

MILLER WESTFORD BARBER JNR

WON WORLD OPEN 1973; USPGA
SENIORS 1981; USGA SENIOR OPEN 1982,
1984, 1985; US SENIOR PLAYERS 1983.
WINNER OF 11 US TOUR EVENTS 1964–78,
24 US SENIOR TOUR EVENTS 1981–89.
RYDER CUP 1969–71. ARNOLD PALMER
AWARD 1981–82.

PATTY BERG

BORN MINNEAPOLIS, MINNESOTA, USA, 13 FEBRUARY 1918

PATTY BERG IS not only one of the outstanding players of the modern women's game, but has also been among its great ambassadors. Her marvellous personality, exceptional golfing talents and striking good looks were evident from her early days as an amateur. In 1935, aged only 17, she was narrowly defeated in the final of the US Women's Amateur Championship by Glenna Collett Vare. Berg went on to win the Women's Amateur three years later and she was twice selected to represent the United States in the Curtis Cup competition.

Fine start
At the Sunningdale Ladies' Golf Course, Berg drives from the first tee.

Berg's greatest contribution to the game, came after she joined the professional ranks in 1940. The Second World War intervened before her professional career got into its stride, but after the war her game blossomed. In her lifetime she won more than 80 tournaments, 41 of them after the US LPGA was founded in 1948. She was a founder member of that association and also became its first president.

BERG IN THE MONEY
Berg won the first US Women's Open Championship, and the $5,600 first prize, in 1946 at the Spokane Country Club in Washington State. The $19,700 purse was then the largest in the history of women's golf. This was the only time the Women's Open was a matchplay event. Berg's total of 145 in the medal-qualifying round was seven strokes better than her nearest rival, Babe Zaharias. Berg went on to beat Betty Jameson in the final.

Patty won the World Championship four times, and she was three times the leading money winner on the LPGA

Early success
Two years before turning professional, Berg won this trophy at Westmoreland as the 1938 USGA Women's Amateur Champion.

Tour, in 1954, 1955 and 1957. In 1953 she recorded six victories on the Tour and she repeated this feat two years later. She also received the Vare Trophy three times for achieving the lowest scoring average of the year.

Berg frequently proved capable of performing outstanding feats of scoring. One round of 64 stood as a record at the Richmond Club in California for well over a decade.

By the time she played in her last Women's Tour event in 1962, Patty Berg had won 57 professional tournaments. She did not retire from the game altogether, but set herself to pass on her experience to others. In the summer of 1991, Patty Berg recorded a hole-in-one at the age of 73.

PATRICIA JANE BERG

WON US WOMEN'S AMATEUR 1938; WESTERN OPEN 1941, 1943, 1948, 1951, 1955, 1957, 1958; US WOMEN'S OPEN 1946; TITLEHOLDERS CHAMPIONSHIP 1937, 1938, 1939, 1948, 1953, 1955, 1957. WINNER OF 29 AMATEUR EVENTS 1934–40; 57 PROFESSIONAL EVENTS 1941–62. CURTIS CUP 1936, 1938. LPGA HALL OF FAME 1951. VARE TROPHY 1953, 1955, 1956. BOB JONES AWARD 1963. WORLD GOLF HALL OF FAME 1974. BEN HOGAN AWARD 1975. OLD TOM MORRIS AWARD 1986. PATTY BERG AWARD 1989.

TOMMY BOLT

BORN HAWORTH, OKLAHOMA, USA, 31 MARCH 1918

WITH A VOLCANIC *temperament and a smooth artistic style, Tommy "Thunderbolt" Bolt was one of the United States' longest-lasting tournament stars. He won the US Open in 1958 and came close to winning the USPGA tournament at Palm Beach in 1971, when in his 50s, finishing third behind Jack Nicklaus and Billy Casper.*

Thunderbolt (right)
Tommy Bolt had an excellent swing that partly compensated for his shaky putting.

Lake throw (left)
Bolt reacts to a bad shot by throwing his club into a lake during the 1960 US Open.

Most of the stories about Tommy Bolt are of his tantrums. He threw so many clubs, it is said, that once when he abused his caddie for handing him a 2-iron for a 7-iron shot, the lad explained: "It's the only iron we have left." After being beaten four and three by Eric Brown in the 1957 Ryder Cup at Lindrick, he remarked: "This isn't golf; it's war."

It was probably because of Bolt's fiery personality that he became a great shotmaker, engineering shots from strange places that few people would have considered possible. He was a truly fine swinger and, had he been blessed with a more equable temperament, he would surely have won many more tournaments.

THOMAS BOLT

WON US OPEN 1958; WORLD SENIORS 1969. WINNER OF 15 US TOUR EVENTS 1951–61. RYDER CUP 1955–57.

SIR MICHAEL BONALLACK

BORN CHIGWELL, ENGLAND, 31 DECEMBER 1934

SIR MICHAEL BONALLACK *has the finest record of all modern British amateurs. Strangely, he was not a great driver of the golf ball, but he did not need to be. It was his short game that won him so many important tournaments, including the British Amateur Championship five times between 1961 and 1970.*

Another honour
As Captain of the Royal & Ancient Golf Club, Sir Michael added another honour to his distinguished career.

down, and his eyes almost touching what appeared to be a short-shafted putter. This style was unusually effective.

Sir Michael Bonallack was appointed Secretary of the Royal & Ancient Golf Club in 1983. When he retired from the post in 2000, he was nominated as Captain of the R & A, the only individual ever to have held both positions.

When he won the 1963 English Amateur Championship in a 36-hole final match against Alan Thirwell, Sir Michael got up-and-down in two from off the greens no fewer than 22 times. In the 1970 British Amateur, he stood one down at lunch against Bill Hyndman, yet won by eight and seven.

Sir Michael's putting stance was highly individual and most unusual. He stood with his legs wide apart, his head

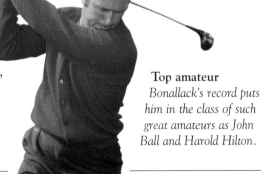

Top amateur
Bonallack's record puts him in the class of such great amateurs as John Ball and Harold Hilton.

SIR MICHAEL FRANCIS BONALLACK, OBE

WON BRITISH AMATEUR 1961, 1965, 1968, 1969, 1970. WALKER CUP 1957–73 (CAPTAIN 1969–71). EISENHOWER TROPHY 1960–72 (CAPTAIN 1968–72). BOB JONES AWARD 1972. SECRETARY R & A GOLF CLUB 1983–99, R & A CAPTAIN 1999–2000.

JAMES BRAID

BORN EARLSFERRY, SCOTLAND, 6 FEBRUARY 1870; DIED 1950

J AMES BRAID WAS *the first golfer to win five Open Championship titles, and he did it in the short space of ten years – between 1901 and 1910. One of the greatest golfers of all time, he also won the first Matchplay professional tournament in 1903, a victory he repeated on three more occasions. He enjoyed a long career, coming second in the 1927 Matchplay event at the age of 57.*

Braid was born in Earlsferry and showed great promise as a youngster on the links at Elie. He was a joiner and worked in St Andrews; it was there that he had an accident with some lime, which affected his eyes, causing some difficulty with his

Commanding skill
Braid dominated professional golf in the early twentieth century. The skill he shows in this photograph of 1900 – one year before his first Open win – brought him great success.

sight. Despite this early setback, he continued to show great aptitude for golf. He was a long hitter and a master of all clubs – except the putting cleek, which often let him down on the "short ones". He was so keen that he often practised in the evening, even though he had to walk many miles from work to the links.

Golf was in his family – he had cousins who were top-class golfers – so eventually he was persuaded to take a job in golf, against his parents' advice. Using his skill as a joiner to become a clubmaker, he went south, starting work in the Army and Navy Stores, London, in 1893.

EARLY SUCCESSES

Braid began to play golf in London at the weekends, and soon word spread around that the young Scot was something of a player. A match was arranged between Braid and the reigning Open Champion, J.H. Taylor. Braid succeeded in halving the match after being two down with two to play, a result that secured him a job as a professional at Romford.

More successes soon followed. He had entered, from Elie, for the 1894 Open at St George's and finished tenth. In 1896 at

Popular player
Known affectionately as "Jimmy", as in this 1907 cartoon (above) by "Spy" (Sir Leslie Ward), Braid was a tall, unassuming man. Despite his run of early successes, he changed little from the courteous young professional of 1900 (right).

Muirfield he was entered from Romford, and finished sixth. A year later he was runner-up to Harold Hilton at Hoylake: his putting – still his weakness – let him down in a final round of 79 to the winner's 75. He finally achieved his first Major success in 1901, at Muirfield, when he became the Open Champion.

CHAMPIONSHIP GOLF

His next Open victory was recorded at St Andrews in 1905. He won by five strokes, in spite of trouble in the final round. He was twice on the railway, at the 15th and 16th holes; on the second occasion, he found his ball right up against the rail, but

Elder statesman (above)
As one of the founders of the British PGA, Braid did much to promote the stature of the professional golfer and to advance the reputation of the game.

he still managed to get out in two shots, and recorded a six, which was far from disastrous. Characteristically, he remained quite calm and deliberate, even in such highly pressured situations.

Braid defended his title successfully the following year at Muirfield, won again at Prestwick in 1908, and yet again at St Andrews in 1910. By then, he had moved to Walton Heath, the club with which he

Putting to victory
Putting was originally a weak point in Braid's game. His breakthrough came when he changed his cleek for a putter; success soon followed in the Open Championship of 1901.

would be connected for the rest of his life. It was typical of his unassuming nature that, although he was an honorary member at Walton Heath for 25 years, he always entered the clubhouse by the back door.

Braid played for Britain against the United States in 1921, and appeared eight times in the professional Scotland versus England internationals during the period up to the First World War. A true ambassador for professional golf, he was a founding member of the PGA and later became its president, a position in which he was renowned for his wisdom and patient advocacy of moderation.

BRAID'S LEGACY

Braid was consulted for many years about the design and layout of golf courses and he made a notable contribution – many are the courses that bear his mark. At a time when professional course design was in its infancy, he brought to the task his immense experience and much thought. Perhaps his best-known creation is the King's Course at Gleneagles, where he imaginatively used a lovely setting.

To the end of his life he remained an enthusiast for the game and there were few days on which he did not play. Respected as one of the greatest of golfers and the finest of men, he died in 1950.

JAMES BRAID

WON OPEN CHAMPIONSHIP 1901, 1905, 1906, 1908, 1910; PGA MATCHPLAY 1903, 1905, 1907, 1911. GREAT BRITAIN V USA 1921. SCOTLAND V ENGLAND EIGHT TIMES 1903–12. WORLD GOLF HALL OF FAME 1976.

Eternal enthusiast
In his later years Braid could still be guaranteed to return a score less than his age. He approached each game with the same keenness he had shown as a young man, never playing carelessly.

JACK BURKE

J ACK BURKE HAD *every encouragement to become a fine professional player. His father was a golf professional, who only just failed to win the US Open in 1920, finishing one stroke behind Ted Ray. Young Jack became a professional in 1940 when he was 17, but he did not start to win tournaments until 1950. Between then and 1963, he had 17 wins on the US circuit.*

JACK BURKE JNR

WON US MASTERS 1956;
USPGA 1956. RYDER CUP
1951–59 (CAPTAIN 1957, NON-
PLAYING CAPTAIN 1973). VARDON
TROPHY 1952. USPGA PLAYER
OF THE YEAR 1956. USPGA
HALL OF FAME 1975.

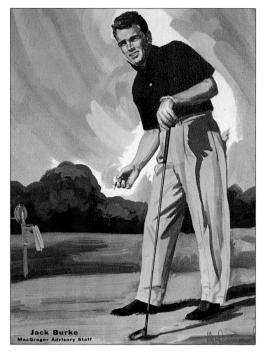

Burke was runner-up in the US Masters of 1952, but he had to wait until 1956 to win a Major – and then he won two, in what was by far his most successful year.

In the US Masters, Burke played extremely steadily in difficult conditions and came from the pack to win by one stroke from Ken Venturi, who had had an eight-stroke lead over him before the final round. Later in the year, Burke captured the USPGA Championship at Boston, in its penultimate year as a matchplay tournament. He came from behind in both the semi-final round and the final, eventually defeating Ted Kroll through a display of superior putting.

In the eight games he played in the Ryder Cup between 1951 and 1957, Burke lost only once. He is now professional at a course that he owns in Texas.

Golf promotion
Burke was one of several prominent players paid by the MacGregor company to advertise their range of clubs and balls.

SIR GUY CAMPBELL

B OTH A PROFICIENT *amateur golfer and a respected journalist, Major Sir Guy Campbell is also remembered for his provocative golf-course designs. With J.S.F. Morrison, he restored the Prince's course at Sandwich after the Second World War.*

Sir Guy's playing career was at its peak in the Edwardian era. In 1907 he reached the semi-finals of the British Amateur Championship, where he lost to the eventual winner, John Ball. He played three times for Scotland v England between 1909 and 1911.

In 1920 he joined the staff of *The Times* and for many years was a prolific contributor, often assisting Bernard Darwin. Sir Guy Campbell was never

afraid to say what he thought, and his dry humour often tempered straightforward and sharp comment. He was a noted authority on the history of golf – his great-grandfather being Robert Chambers, an early writer about the game, from whom Sir Guy must have inherited something in the style and the quality of his writing.

His favourite course always remained the Old Course at St Andrews, where he holed in one at the 8th in 1918, during a game against the 1904 Open Champion Jack White.

St Andrews favourite
Sir Guy was a familiar figure at St Andrews, where his name is kept alive by an annual foursomes trophy that he presented in 1910.

MAJOR SIR GUY COLIN CAMPBELL, 4TH BARONET

SCOTLAND V ENGLAND 1909–11.

JoAnne Carner

Born Kirkland, Washington, USA, 4 April 1939

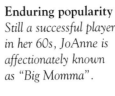

Enduring popularity
Still a successful player in her 60s, JoAnne is affectionately known as "Big Momma".

J OANNE CARNER HAD a glittering 14-year career as an amateur and, since 1970, has had an equally fine career as a professional. She was only 15 years old when, as JoAnne Gunderson, she took the US Junior title, and 18 when she first won the US Women's Amateur Championship. She won this title four more times before finally turning professional.

As a professional, Carner amassed a total of 42 tournament wins between 1970 and 1990. She has twice been US Women's Open Champion and five times holder of the Vare Trophy, awarded for the lowest scoring average in the year's LPGA Tour.

Sam Snead, in 1984, assessed Carner as the best woman player he had ever seen, although it has been her power and her scoring ability, rather than her swing, that have impressed Snead most. An athlete with a special interest in physical training,

Hard graft (above)
Power play has always been Carner's natural game – putting is relatively hard work.

JoAnne is a hitter rather than a swinger, a sturdy lady now known affectionately throughout the Tour as "Big Momma". Never very keen on practising, she believes in keeping it simple. "Turn round to the right on the backswing," she says, "then let the legs swing the club through powerfully along the right line up to a full finish. It's as simple as that."

Elusive Third Open
In 1987, at the age of 48, Carner came within a play-off of winning her third US Women's Open. She was eventually beaten by Britain's Laura Davies.

JoAnne Carner's record is a quite remarkable one. Her career earnings are close to $3 million and she continued to be a force on the LPGA Tour into her 60s.

JoAnne Gunderson Carner

Won US Women's Amateur 1957, 1960, 1962, 1966, 1968; US Women's Open 1971, 1976. Winner of 43 LPGA Tour events 1970–85. Curtis Cup 1958–64. Solheim Cup (Captain 1994). US LPGA Tour Leading Money Winner 1974, 1982–83. Vare Trophy 1974, 1975, 1981, 1982, 1983. Bob Jones Award 1981. LPGA Hall of Fame 1982. World Golf Hall of Fame 1985.

JoAnne and Nancy (above)
Two of the greatest American women golfers of modern times, Nancy Lopez (left) and JoAnne Carner, are joined in friendly rivalry.

JOE CARR

BORN DUBLIN, IRELAND, 18 FEBRUARY 1922

S WASHBUCKLING JOE CARR *was how the popular newspapers described the Dublin amateur in the 1950s when he was, without doubt, a world-class force in golf. The exciting manner in which he won every Irish title again and again captured the public's heart and imagination.*

Carr's victories in the East and West of Ireland Amateur Open Championships spanned the years from 1941 to 1969. He represented his country in every possible golf event, including the World Cup, usually reserved for professionals. At one time he held the course record at 12 clubs.

Despite his obvious qualities, Carr's record in Walker Cup matches was not impressive. Out of 20 matches played,

Walker fixture
Joe Carr on his way to winning the 1959 Berkshire Trophy, one of the official Walker Cup trials. He played in the Walker Cup ten times, but sadly, most of his performances were unimpressive.

Carr won just five. So it gave him great pleasure when his son Roddy won three out of four matches in the 1971 Walker Cup, with one match halved, and thus helped defeat the United States.

Carr was awarded the Hagen Trophy in 1967 for his contribution to Anglo-American goodwill. Six years earlier he had won the USGA Bob Jones Award for sportsmanship. So popular was he during his playing career that, two decades later, he was still an honorary member of most golf clubs in Ireland, as well as several elsewhere in the world. He was Captain of the Royal & Ancient in 1991–92.

JOSEPH BENEDICT CARR

WON IRISH OPEN AMATEUR 1946, 1950, 1954, 1956; BRITISH AMATEUR 1953, 1958, 1960; IRISH AMATEUR 1954, 1957, 1963, 1964, 1965, 1967. WALKER CUP 1947–63, 1967 (NON-PLAYING CAPTAIN 1965, CAPTAIN 1967). EISENHOWER TROPHY 1958–60 (NON-PLAYING CAPTAIN 1964–66). BOB JONES AWARD 1961. CAPTAIN R & A CLUB 1991–92.

BILLY CASPER

BORN SAN DIEGO, CALIFORNIA, USA, 24 JUNE 1931

D URING THE FINAL *round of the 1966 US Open at the Olympic Club in San Francisco, Billy Casper stood seven strokes behind the great Arnold Palmer with nine holes to play. Then, in one of the most remarkable fightbacks in the history of golf, Casper made up the difference to tie. He went on to beat Palmer in the play-off the following day by four strokes, 69 to 73. It was the highest point of a most distinguished golfing career.*

Billy Casper won two other Majors: he had become US Open Champion for the first time at Winged Foot in 1959, and in 1970 he won the Masters at Augusta after a play-off with Gene Littler.

Casper is a giant of American golf in physique as well as in performance. His golfing record is outstanding, but he has also been plagued by weight problems, particularly in the latter part of his career.

WILLIAM EARL CASPER JNR

WON US OPEN 1959, 1966; US MASTERS 1970; US SENIOR OPEN 1983. US SENIOR PLAYERS 1988. WINNER OF 51 US TOUR EVENTS 1956–75. RYDER CUP 1961–75 (NON-PLAYING CAPTAIN 1979). VARDON TROPHY 1960, 1963, 1965–66, 1968. USPGA PLAYER OF THE YEAR 1966, 1970. WORLD GOLF HALL OF FAME 1978. USPGA HALL OF FAME 1982.

Olympic victory (above)
The 1966 US Open Champion savours his memorable triumph over Arnold Palmer at the Olympic Club in San Francisco.

Eye-catching outfits (right)
An extremely powerful player, Billy Casper graced the US Senior Tour with his marvellous game and outrageous plus-fours.

BOB CHARLES

BORN CARTERTON, NEW ZEALAND, 14 MARCH 1936

B OB CHARLES *is the only left-handed golfer and the only New Zealander ever to have won the Open Championship – or indeed any one of the four Majors – and he is recognized as the finest left-hander ever to have played the game. He is also possibly the finest putter the world has ever seen. As well as winning the British Open at Royal Lytham and St Annes in 1963, Charles was twice runner-up in the Championship.*

Spectators talked about the last-green carry-on in the final round of the 1963 British Open for weeks. Was it shocking behaviour, or show-business fun? Little-known Phil Rodgers, from San Diego, California, was level with Bob Charles at the head of the field. The American knocked in his putt, pulled off his cap and covered the hole and ball in a comical music-hall mime of relief. Waiting, with a short putt to tie, was an unamused Bob Charles. Would this elaborate charade upset him? It did not, and his own putt went in to force a play-off.

The way in which Bob Charles putted on that occasion meant that there was never much doubt that he would win – and he did. The tall New Zealander from the North Island went on to a magnificent tournament-winning career.

BEST LEFT-HANDER
Although he won the New Zealand Open as an amateur in 1954, Charles did not turn professional until 1960. He then won the New Zealand Open three more times as a professional, as well as many other New Zealand tournaments. His other successes included the 1962 and 1974 Swiss Opens, the 1968 Canadian Open, the World Matchplay in 1969, the 1972 Dunlop Masters and four US tournaments.

Playing on (below)
Bob Charles contests the Seniors British Open in 1988.

Master of the art (above)
Possibly the finest putter the world has ever seen, left-hander Bob Charles demonstrates his great skill to spellbound spectators on the 5th green at Royal Lytham and St Annes during the 1963 Open Championship, which he won.

At the age of 40, Charles was already thinking of retiring to his farm in New Zealand. But he has found he can win too much money on the US Senior Tour to retire.

With the help of modern equipment, in his 50s Charles hits the ball farther than he managed when younger and just as straight. There was a short spell when his magnificent touch with the putter deserted him, but wearing spectacles has put him back on form. In 1986, his first year on the Senior Tour, Charles won $570,000. By 2000 he had surpassed earnings of $8 million on the Senior Tour.

ROBERT JAMES CHARLES CBE, OM (NZ)

WON NEW ZEALAND OPEN 1954, 1966, 1970, 1973;
OPEN CHAMPIONSHIP 1963; CANADIAN OPEN 1968;
WORLD MATCHPLAY 1969; SOUTH AFRICAN OPEN
1973; SENIORS BRITISH OPEN 1989, 1993.
EISENHOWER TROPHY 1960, WORLD CUP 1962–68,
1971–72, DUNHILL CUP 1985–86. SENIOR BRITISH OPEN
1983, 1993. WINNER OF 23 US SENIOR TOUR EVENTS
1987–96. ARNOLD PALMER AWARD 1988–89.
BRYON NELSON AWARD 1988–89, 1993.

SIR HENRY COTTON

BORN HOLMES CHAPEL, ENGLAND, 26 JANUARY 1907; DIED 1987

W HEN HENRY COTTON *was only 11 years old he autographed a photo of himself; he was a schoolboy playing at being a champion. It was only a youthful daydream, of course, but Henry Cotton went on to become that champion of his dreams, one of the greatest players of any era. His record of three British Open victories remains the best of any British player since the Great Triumvirate at the turn of the century.*

Delicate touch (right)
Henry Cotton believed that the hands were the key to the correct execution of golf shots.

Early talent (above)
As a 20-year-old, Cotton competed in the 1927 Open Championship at St Andrews, finishing ninth.

Thomas Henry Cotton was born in 1907, the son of a prosperous iron founder. His father sent him to Alleyn's public school, giving him a far more privileged start in life than that enjoyed by most other professional golfers of his day, who came from lowly backgrounds.

At school Henry was a better cricketer than golfer, but his headmaster banned him from cricket after he refused a caning. Asked what he would do when the rest of the boys were playing cricket, Cotton

replied: "I'll play golf, sir." And that is what he did. Precociously talented, Cotton turned professional at the age of 16. In 1927, when he was still only 20, he finished ninth in the Open at St Andrews, won that year by Bobby Jones.

HEADING WESTWARD

Cotton was so impressed by the young American that he decided to cross the Atlantic "to find out what made them tick". He finished third in his first event on American soil and was well on his way

to stardom. He had an obsessive drive for perfection and practised for long and aching hours. It paid off in the Open at Sandwich in 1934. Cotton led the field by ten strokes after three rounds, including a 65 that was to remain a Championship record for the next 43 years. Despite a last round of 79, he finally ended the American supremacy in the event with a five-stroke victory.

Three years later, in the Open Championship at Carnoustie, he was opposed by the full strength of the visiting

Cotton as innovator (below)
These 1939 "anti-shank" irons were designed by Cotton. A crank in the shaft leaves the face of each iron free of the bulbous joint between shaft and head that caused "shanking".

American Ryder Cup team. It was during this Open that Cotton played what is still held to be one of the greatest rounds ever in the competition, a 71 in torrential rain on a waterlogged course, to take the title.

The war years undoubtedly robbed Cotton of more honours, but he won the Open Championship for a third time in 1948, setting a record for the Muirfield course of 66. He was a member of four Ryder Cup teams, twice as captain. He wrote a weekly newspaper column on golf for more than 30 years and was the author

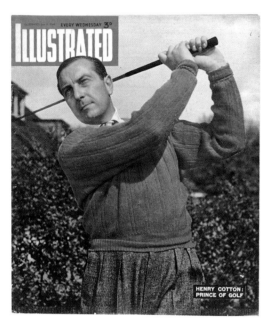

of many excellent books on the game he did so much to popularize. Indeed, he became so popular that he even topped the bill in a variety show with a golf act.

KNIGHTED BUT NOT CONFERRED
At the end of his career he became involved in golf-course architecture; his designs included the famous Penina course in Portugal. He was knighted, very belatedly, in 1987, but died before the honour could be officially conferred. Outstanding as his playing record was, Cotton will be remembered equally for his contribution to improving the standing of the golf professional. He took the pro out of the caddie shed and made him respectable. Cotton handed on to others his own vision of golf as a "noble occupation".

Strong hands (right)
The Henry Cotton method placed the emphasis on strong, educated hands to "whip" the clubhead square through the ball at impact. Other significant elements were a braced left leg and a high finish to the swing.

Cover shot (left)
In 1946, when Cotton was featured by Illustrated magazine, he was nearing the end of his career at the top.

The Dunlop 65
In 1934 Henry Cotton played a record round of 65 during his Open Championship victory at Sandwich. To mark this outstanding feat, Dunlop named their rubber-core ball the 65.

SIR THOMAS HENRY COTTON

WON MAR DEL PLATA OPEN 1930; BELGIAN OPEN 1930, 1934, 1938; PGA MATCHPLAY 1932, 1940, 1946; OPEN CHAMPIONSHIP 1934, 1937, 1948; ITALIAN OPEN 1936; GERMAN OPEN 1937, 1938, 1939; FRENCH OPEN 1946, 1947. RYDER CUP 1929, 1937, 1947 (CAPTAIN 1947, NON-PLAYING CAPTAIN 1953). CAPTAIN PGA 1934, 1948. HARRY VARDON TROPHY 1938. WORLD GOLF HALL OF FAME 1980.

Golfer and author
Cotton was the author of several important golf books and wrote a regular newspaper column.

FRED COUPLES

BORN SEATTLE, WASHINGTON, USA, 3 OCTOBER 1959

W HEN FRED COUPLES *won the US Masters at Augusta in 1992 he joined that elite band of professional golfers who have won one of the game's four Major championships. But it meant more than that to the young player who was almost as good at soccer in his youth as he was at golf.*

Hard hitting
Couples is renowned for the great length of his shots and, as a result, has earned himself the nickname "Boom Boom".

Couples' Augusta victory firmly established him as one of the modern golf superstars and one of the most popular winners of the coveted green jacket. Fred was introduced to golf by his father who worked in the Seattle Parks and Recreation Department. At the University of Houston he played on the same golf team as fellow professional-to-be Wayne McAllister and CBS broadcaster, Jim Nantz.

Couples turned professional in 1980 and qualified for the Tour the same year. In his rookie year Couples won close to $80,000 – 53rd on the money list.

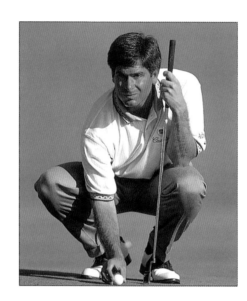

UP, DOWN, AND UP AGAIN
It was in 1983 that he first gave a clear indication of his potential when he won the Kemper Open in a five-way play-off. The following year he added the Players Championship in spectacular style by breaking the course record at Sawgrass with a dazzling eight under par round of 64, a record he would break by a stroke in 1992. After that victory Couples went into something of a slump as did his prize money for the next two years. But in 1987 he found the elusive winning touch again, took his career earnings to more than $1 million and has never looked back.

He took the 1992 season by storm, winning not only the US Masters but also the Nissan Los Angeles Open and the Nestlé Invitational, finishing the season as the Tour's leading money winner with more than $1.3 million.

Couples was voted PGA Tour Player of the Year in 1991 and again in 1992. He

Smooth and unruffled
Couples is one of the most relaxed and unflustered players in the game. His lazy, looping swing is deceptively powerful and if his sometimes vulnerable holing out of short putts were ever to match his spectacular ability through the green, he would undoubtedly have already accrued more than one Major championship.

has played in five US Ryder Cup teams and, partnered with Davis Love III, won four consecutive World Cup of Golf titles. Couples also represented the United States in the Dunhill Cup from 1991 to 1994.

Back problems have haunted Couples for many years but he continues to earn huge sums of money on Tour and remains one of the game's most popular characters. Off the course Fred Couples has a passion for antiques and vintage cars, as well as taking a keen interest in other sports.

FREDERICK STEPHEN COUPLES

WON US PLAYERS CHAMPIONSHIP 1984, 1996. WORLD CHAMPIONSHIP 1991, 1995; US MASTERS 1992. WINNER OF 14 US TOUR EVENTS 1983–98. RYDER CUP 1989–1997. FOUR TOURS CHAMPIONSHIP 1990–91. WORLD CUP 1992–95 (INDIVIDUAL WINNER 1994). PRESIDENTS CUP 1994–98. ARNOLD PALMER AWARD 1992. USPGA PLAYER OF THE YEAR 1992. VARDON TROPHY 1991, 1992.

BEN CRENSHAW

BORN AUSTIN, TEXAS, USA, 11 JANUARY 1952

T HERE IS PROBABLY *no player in the modern professional game who is more loved and admired by his fans and fellow players than Ben Crenshaw. Certainly, there is no other American golfer with a comparable respect for the great legends and traditions of the game. At his home in Austin, Texas, Crenshaw has a fine collection of antique clubs, golf books and memorabilia that he has lovingly acquired over the course of an impressive career.*

Even before turning professional in 1973, Ben Crenshaw had proved himself an exceptionally talented golfer. He was leading amateur in the US Open at the age of 18 and winner of the Fred Haskins Trophy three years in a row as the outstanding college player.

He made his mark on the professional game with startling rapidity. His first entry brought him victory in the 1973 San Antonio Texas Open, and this win was immediately followed by a second place in the eight-round World Open. Inevitably, he was soon being tagged as the natural successor to Jack Nicklaus.

THE NEARLY MAN

In 1975 Crenshaw came third in the US Open, hitting an iron shot into the water when he seemed set to qualify for the play-off, and the following year he was second on the US money list. But he did not go on to realize the full extent of his undoubted potential. He was acclaimed as among the best putters in the history of golf, but his tee-shots could be wayward. Over the years he gained an unwelcome reputation as the "nearly man".

Crenshaw finished runner-up twice in the British Open, in 1978 and 1979, twice in the US Masters, in 1976 and 1983, and once in the USPGA Championship, at Oakland Hills in 1979, when he lost a sudden-death play-off to David Graham.

A great golfer and golf historian
Ben Crenshaw's sure putting touch has helped him secure two US masters, but his knowledge of the history of the game is also highly accomplished.

He finally got his name on a Major title in 1984, winning the US Masters in a dramatic finish at Augusta. Going into the last round, he trailed fellow Texan Tom Kite by two strokes. Kite faded, however, while Crenshaw played a final round of 68, which included some marvellous long putts, and gave him a two-stroke victory over Tom Watson. The euphoria of 1984 was followed by a slump. It was discovered that "Gentle Ben", as he is known on the Tour, had an overactive thyroid. Fortunately, he was soon returned to full health.

In 1995 Crenshaw won an emotional second Masters victory. Earlier in the week he had been a pallbearer at the funeral of his long-time friend and mentor, the golf teacher and author Harvey Penick, and was in tears when he holed the winning putt.

In 1999 he captained the US Ryder Cup team to victory in the infamous matches at Brookline as his tournament career began to slowly wind down.

Crenshaw once said: "I do not think I could go on living unless I felt that one day I might win the Open Championship at St Andrews." This obsession shows Crenshaw's sense of the history of the game (and he is acknowledged as one of golf's great historians and collectors). He once recalled playing the last round of the 1978 Open at the "home of golf" in mystical terms: "Suddenly I felt I was walking not on the fairway at all but slightly above it," Crenshaw said, "and I was walking with the ghosts of the great players of the past who had trodden these famous links. I wondered how Old Tom Morris would have played the stroke I faced. It was the most eerie sensation."

In that year and again in 1979, Crenshaw narrowly failed to win the Open Championship. If his highest ambition was ever fulfilled, and he won the Open at St Andrews, there would never have been a more popular victory.

BEN DANIEL CRENSHAW

WON IRISH OPEN 1976; MEXICAN OPEN 1981; US MASTERS 1984, 1995. US TOUR CHAMPIONSHIP 1986. WINNER OF 19 US TOUR EVENTS 1973–95. EISENHOWER TROPHY 1972. WORLD CUP 1987–88 (INDIVIDUAL WINNER 1988). RYDER CUP 1981–83, 1987, 1995 (NON-PLAYING CAPTAIN). FOUR TOURS CHAMPIONSHIP 1988. DUNHILL CUP 1995. BOB JONES AWARD 1991.

LAURA DAVIES

BORN COVENTRY, ENGLAND, 5 OCTOBER 1963

EARLY IN 1987, *Laura Davies was invited to play in one of the early season tournaments on the US Women's Tour. The American authorities refused to allow her to play, saying that European women golfers had not yet made sufficient impact in the United States. Later that year, Laura made them eat their words – in a three-way play-off, she won the US Women's Open.*

Double champion
(below)
Davies shows off a brace of trophies: the candlesticks from the British Open, the cup from the US Open.

LAURA J. DAVIES CBE

WON WOMEN'S BRITISH OPEN 1986; US WOMEN'S OPEN 1987. USLPGA CHAMPIONSHIP 1994, 1996. EVIAN MASTERS 1995–96. DU MAURIER CLASSIC 1996; USLPGA TOUR CHAMPION 1988. WINNER OF 31 LADIES EUROPEAN TOUR EVENTS 1985–99 (ORDER OF MERIT WINNER 1985–86, 1992, 1992, 1996). PLAYER OF THE YEAR 1996, 1999, VIVIEN SAUNDERS TROPHY 1986, 1992–93, 1998–99). WINNER OF 19 US LPGA TOUR EVENTS 1987–2000 (LEADING MONEY WINNER 1994, PLAYER OF THE YEAR 1996). CURTIS CUP 1984. SOLHEIM CUP 1990–2000. LET HONORARY MEMBER 1993.

In 1984, at the age of 20, Laura Davies was selected for the British Curtis Cup team. The following year she turned professional, borrowing £1,000 from her mother to help her do so. After a few months she was able to pay all the money back. Later in her rookie year she won the Hennessy Cognac Ladies' Cup in France, and at the end of the year found herself at the top of the WPGA Order of Merit.

In 1986 Davies headed the money list again, winning the Women's British Open. As British Open Champion, she

Not a winner this time
Laura Davies agonizes over a missed putt during her failed bid for the 1989 US Women's Open.

ventured to the United States, finishing eleventh in the US Women's Open. The following year, she came back to win.

In 1988 Davies won twice in the United States and three times in Europe. She was in the Solheim Cup team which won a famous victory over the Americans at Dalmahoy, Scotland in 1992 (avenging a defeat in the first match between Europe and the US in 1990), and in the winning European team again in 2000 at Loch Lomond.

Driving to the top (right) *At 5ft 10in (1.78m) and strongly built, Laura Davies hits the ball farther than most male golfers.*

ROBERT DE VICENZO, see page 346

By that year, Laura Davies had also accumulated 31 Ladies European Tour events (winning the Order of Merit five times), and 19 US LPGA Tour events which also earned her Player of the Year in 1996.

JOHN DALY

BORN CARMICHAEL, CALIFORNIA, USA, 28 APRIL 1966

Massive drives
Daly wields 300-yard drives as an average.

N O GOLFER IN *recent history has ridden the emotional roller coaster more hair-raisingly than John Daly. A Cinderella appearance on the world's golfing stage in 1991 saw him step up from ninth alternate to a fairy-tale victory in the USPGA Championship at Crooked Stick, Indianapolis. He'd driven 500 miles from Memphis and teed up the following day without a practice round.*

That three-stroke victory was followed, in turn, by his first public admission of a deep-seated alcohol problem, an astounding win in the Open Championship at the Home of Golf in 1995, and further battles with the bottle which prompted more than one visit to the Betty Ford Clinic for alcohol dependency.

But what first drew the American public's attention to the podgy young player was the staggering distance he could achieve with every club in the bag. Wielding his clubs unlike any other player on tour – his endless backswing heaving the club well past the gurus' accepted norm – he dominated one obvious statistic throughout the 1990s and into the new millennium, with average drives of 300 yards.

His win at St Andrews in 1995 (67-71-73-71) came out of the blue. It was his only top ten finish that season, but he had to survive a 70-foot putt on the 72nd hole by Italian Costantino Rocca, which meant a four-hole play-off. Daly won by four strokes, aided considerably by Rocca's triple-bogey seven at the 17th.

JOHN PATRICK DALY

WON USPGA 1991; OPEN CHAMPIONSHIP 1995.
WINNER OF 4 US TOUR EVENTS 1991–95 DUNHILL
CUP 1993, 1998. WORLD CUP 1998.

JIMMY DEMARET

BORN HOUSTON, TEXAS, 24 MAY 1910; DIED 28 DECEMBER 1983.

T HE FIRST PLAYER *to win the US Masters three times (only Nicklaus and Palmer won more), Jimmy Demaret was one of the most popular professionals throughout the 1940s and 1950s. He made a name for himself as one of the game's most flamboyant characters, wearing much more colourful clothing than his competitors.*

Three-time winner
Demaret made a dramatic comeback at the 1950 US Masters, overcoming Jim Ferrier with a seven-shot swing in the last six holes.

Demaret could also claim to have compiled a Ryder Cup record second to none. In the three contests immediately after the Second World War he won all six ties – three foursomes and three singles – never being taken past the 16th green.

His first win at Augusta National, in 1940, was his sixth successive tournament victory that year – at a time when he was also entertaining audiences as a singer in a Houston night-club. In his first-round 67, he completed the inward half in 30 (a record until Mark Calcavecchia's 29 in 1992), beating Lloyd Mangrum by four strokes with a 280 aggregate.

JAMES NEWTON DEMARET

WON US MASTERS 1940, 1947, 1950. WINNER OF 31
US TOUR EVENTS 1939–51 (LEADING MONEY WINNER
1947). VARDON TROPHY 1947. RYDER CUP 1947–51.
WORLD CUP 1960. USPGA HALL OF FAME 1960.
WORLD GOLF HALL OF FAME 1983.

GEORGE DUNCAN

BORN METHLICK, SCOTLAND, 16 SEPTEMBER 1883; DIED 1964

G EORGE DUNCAN HAD *a lovely natural swing and was always good to watch. He was a very fast player with all his strokes, including putts, and walked quickly as well. He would have found the dawdling pace of the modern game very tiresome. As a golfer he commanded great respect from his fellow professionals, and whenever he played he was followed by an admiring crowd.*

Duncan was born in 1883, son of the village policeman at Methlick, Aberdeen. In 1906 he first played in the Open Championship at Muirfield, finishing in eighth place, and he was in the top ten six times before the First World War. The war interrupted his career, but in 1920, at Deal, he at last became Open Champion. He started with two disastrous rounds of 80, and was well behind the leader. But a 71 in the morning and a 72 in the afternoon ensured him the title.

It was a source of amazement to his fellows that this was his only Open Championship victory, though he was runner-up in 1922 at St George's, very nearly tying with the winner, Walter Hagen. After a magnificent final round of 69, Duncan needed to sink a putt on

Hasty player
George Duncan's style matched the title of his book: Golf at a Gallop.

the last hole, but it just failed to drop. Duncan also won the PGA Matchplay Championship in 1913, and twice lost in the final of that tournament.

INTERNATIONAL SUCCESSES
Duncan played against the United States in 1921 and 1926, and in the first three Ryder Cup matches, captaining the side in 1929. He won all his singles matches in these international encounters, beating Walter Hagen twice – the second time, in 1929, by a resounding ten and eight. Although he was quick, Duncan was never

careless. He was noted for his accurate wood shots played, of course, at great speed. He was always a mercurial player, but when he was in the mood, anything was possible. Duncan was also good at diagnosing faults, and helped many of the top players to correct errors in their game.

GEORGE DUNCAN

WON BELGIAN OPEN 1912; PGA MATCHPLAY 1913; FRENCH OPEN 1913, 1927; OPEN CHAMPIONSHIP 1920; IRISH OPEN 1927. REPRESENTED GB v US 1921, 1926. RYDER CUP 1927–31 (CAPTAIN 1929).

Open action (left)
George Duncan playing on the 8th green at Troon during the Open Championship of 1923.

High temper (right)
Duncan's impatient personality was caricatured in the "Men of the Moment in Sport" cigarette-card series of 1928.

WILLIE DUNN JNR

BORN MUSSELBURGH, SCOTLAND, 1865; DIED 1952

*W*ILLIE DUNN JNR *came from a famous Musselburgh golfing family. His father and uncle had played in the famous match against Allan Robertson and Tom Morris in 1849. "Young Willie" had pronounced views on how to play and many of his ideas, rejected in Britain at the time, have since gained approval. He was undoubtedly well ahead of his time – as early as the turn of the twentieth century, for instance, he experimented with steel shafts and a sort of wooden tee-peg, instead of the pinch of sand that was then standard practice. He was also an innovative course designer towards the end of the nineteenth century.*

Born at Musselburgh in 1865, Willie Dunn trained as a golf professional and greenkeeper. His brother Tom, 16 years his senior, was already an established pro and course designer. Willie gained much experience from him.

Willie Dunn played in the Open Championship from 1882 to 1886 without any great success, his best placing being ninth at Musselburgh in 1883. He later moved to Biarritz in the south-west of France as professional and helped his brother to lay out the new course there.

After completing his work in France, Dunn was persuaded to go to the United States. He crossed the Atlantic in March 1891. Within three months of arriving in the New World, with very limited equipment and using Native Americans from a nearby reservation for labour, he had built a 12-hole course at Shinnecock Hills on New York's Long Island.

INNOVATIVE DESIGN

Later extended to 18 holes, Shinnecock was the first seaside course to be created in North America. It also set a trend as the first incorporated club in the United States, and it had the first American clubhouse. "Young Willie" – as he was known to distinguish him from his father – was soon much in demand for advice and practical help. He is rightly

considered the first golf-course designer of the new school and had a significant effect on the future of golf.

In 1894 Dunn won the first US Open (at that time an unofficial matchplay event) at the St Andrew's Club in Yonkers, New York, defeating his fellow Scot, Willie Campbell, by two holes in the final.

The following year, when the US Open had the official blessing of the USGA and adopted the strokeplay formula, Dunn finished as runner-up to Horace Rawlins, failing to win the championship by just two strokes.

Golf in the family
Willie Dunn Jnr was born into a famous golfing family. This golfing tableau from around 1854 shows his father Willie Dunn Snr teeing off, while also in the foreground stand (left to right) Allan Robertson and Old Tom Morris.

Dunn stayed on the East Coast of the United States until 1910 as professional and greenkeeper at several clubs, before moving west to Ohio and then by stages across the continent until he at last reached California.

Dunn's fortunes varied and there were times when he was far from well-off, but the rise in the popularity of golf in the United States over this period ensured he would be a well-known and respected figure in the country for many years.

His two nephews, Seymour Dunn and John Duncan Dunn, both became golf-course designers and teachers. Willie Dunn returned to Britain in 1940 and lived there until his death in 1952.

Studio portrait
Dunn's bold spirit and keen mind are clearly visible in this studio photograph.

WILLIAM DUNN JNR

WON UNOFFICIAL US OPEN 1894. NOTED GOLF-COURSE
DESIGNER AND INSTRUCTOR.

DAVID DUVAL

BORN JACKSONVILLE, FLORIDA, USA, 9 NOVEMBER 1971

T HREE SECOND PLACES *in his US Tour rookie year, 1995, were a harbinger of future greatness for David Duval, yet after some wonderful golf – and the attendant multi-million dollar prize money – a major still eluded him five years later.*

Possessing a deceptively languid swing yet one of the Tour's longest hitters, Duval won the last three tournaments of 1997 to finish runner-up in the Money List. He climbed to top money winner in 1998 ($2,591,000), adding more than a million to that the following year, partly thanks to the "Tiger factor" that came in to play in negotiations to renew network TV contracts in the USA.

Such was the consummate ease with which Duval was playing early in 1999 (he had won four times before the US Masters, a feat not achieved since Johnny Miller in 1974), he dislodged Woods from the official World Number One spot, a position Woods had held for 41 consecutive weeks. Woods had to wait until the USPGA Championship in mid-August to regain top place.

Duval has also shown himself to be a man for the big occasion. In three successive years from 1998 at the Masters he tied second, sixth and third; at the US Open he shared seventh twice, and eighth; at the British Open he tied tenth in 1998. Two years later at St Andrews had Duval only offered any vestige of a challenge to Tiger Woods as the two were paired on the final day the elusive Major title might have been his.

Teeing off six strokes behind Woods, Duval outscored the champion-elect by three strokes on the front nine, but a two-shot swing on the tenth (Woods a birdie, Duval a bogey) sealed Wood's victory.

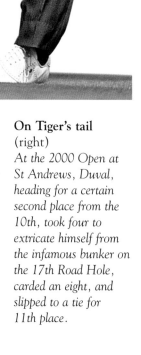

Low scoring record (left) *Low scoring and David Duval go together. His 59 to win the 1999 Bob Hope Chrysler Classic at Palm Springs tied the USPGA Tour's low round, and it was also the lowest final round in the tour's history.*

Like father, like son (above) *There was plenty to celebrate in the Duval household on 28 March 1999. While David was winning the Players Championship at*

Sawgrass his father Bob did likewise at the Emerald Coast Classic, thus becoming the first father-son duo to win PGA and Seniors tournaments on the same weekend.

On Tiger's tail (right) *At the 2000 Open at St Andrews, Duval, heading for a certain second place from the 10th, took four to extricate himself from the infamous bunker on the 17th Road Hole, carded an eight, and slipped to a tie for 11th place.*

DAVID ROBERT DUVAL

WON US TOUR CHAMPIONSHIP 1997; WORLD SERIES OF GOLF 1998; US PLAYERS CHAMPIONSHIP 1999. WINNER OF 12 US TOUR EVENTS 1997–2000. ARNOLD PALMER AWARD 1998. VARDON TROPHY 1998. WALKER CUP 1991. PRESIDENTS CUP 1996–2000. RYDER CUP 1999. WORLD CUP 2000.

ERNIE ELS

BORN JOHANNESBURG, SOUTH AFRICA, 17 OCTOBER 1969

B LESSED WITH ONE *of the most fluid, rhythmical actions ever seen in the game, Ernie Els slipped comfortably into the sobriquet adopted in the late 1990s by the media and fellow players, "The Big Easy".*

Having acquired a scratch handicap by the age of 14 in his native Johannesburg and shown equal promise as a tennis player, Ernie Els focused his sporting attention on the smaller ball, turned professional six years later, and began annexing various South African titles in 1992.

TRIUMPHS IN THE USA

But his influence on the world stage emerged in 1994 at Oakmont when, having survived a final-round 73 in the US Open, he joined Colin Montgomerie and Loren Roberts in an 18-hole play-off. When the Scot dropped out with a 78, the two others, tying on 74, played two extra holes, Els triumphing at the 20th for his first major championship.

Three years later, at Congressional CC, Maryland, Els picked up his second US title and became the first non-American since Scots immigrant Alex Smith (1906 and 1910) to win more than one US Open Championship. Els's final-round 69, and especially a decisive birdie at the tough 17th hole, secured victory by a stroke over Colin Montgomerie.

Els also made a significant impact in head-to-head encounters. He became the first player in the history of the World Matchplay Championship at Wentworth to win three in a row (1994–96), and reached the 1997 final, only to lose to his beaten finalist the previous year, Vijay Singh.

Flawless putting (right)
For a highly powerful player, Els has a great delicacy of touch around the green.

Top talent (above)
Despite being overshadowed by the feats of Tiger Woods, Els's record in the 1990s is impressive.

Though only one US Tour victory came his way in 2000, the modified Stableford tournament at Castle Rock, Colorado, Els won the game's biggest cheque, $2 million, when he beat Lee Westwood in a play-off for the Sun City Challenge. A year previously his winning cheque at the same event was $1 million. But of more significance the same year was Els' runner-up position in no fewer than three of the four majors – the Masters, the US Open and the British Open.

Gentle swing (right)
Els's almost leisurely swing, an exemplar to teaching professionals the world over, allied to a flawless putting stroke, had won him two US Open titles by the age of 27.

THEODORE ERNEST ELS

WON SOUTH AFRICAN OPEN 1992, 1996, 1998; US OPEN 1994, 1997; WORLD MATCHPLAY 1994–96; WORLD CHAMPIONSHIP 1994; MILLION DOLLAR CHALLENGE 1999–2000. WORLD CUP 1992–93, 1996–97 (INDIVIDUAL WINNER 1996). PRESIDENTS CUP 1996–2000. EUROPEAN TOUR HONORARY MEMBER 1999.

NICK FALDO

BORN WELWYN GARDEN CITY, ENGLAND, 18 JULY 1957

O N A DULL, *misty Sunday afternoon at Muirfield in 1987, Nick Faldo produced 18 consecutive pars in the final round of the Open Championship to beat American Paul Azinger in a nail-biting finish and prove himself among the great players of the modern game. That Muirfield victory came at the end of a long road for Faldo who, after a spectacular start to his career, had lost his way and long failed to break through into the big time as so many had expected.*

Watchful guru (above)
Coach David Leadbetter looks on as Faldo, his pupil, practises for the 1989 Open at Royal Troon.

Faldo took up golf in 1972, when he was 14, inspired by seeing Jack Nicklaus playing in the Masters on a new colour television his parents had just bought. He was transfixed by the marvellous backdrop of the Augusta course and by watching the man he now considers to be "the greatest golfer in the history of the game". A mere three years later, after learning the game

from professional Ian Connelly at Welwyn Garden City Golf Club, Nick Faldo became the youngest player ever to win the English Amateur Championship. He turned professional in 1976, already possessing one of the most fluent and elegant golf swings in the game.

RYDER SUCCESSES

Faldo won his first professional event in 1977 and became the youngest player, up to then, ever to play in the Ryder Cup. Partnered by Peter Oosterhuis, he won his foursomes and fourball matches, including among his victims Ray Floyd and the man he had watched on television five years earlier, Jack Nicklaus.

Faldo continued to dominate in Europe – in 1983 he won five tournaments and headed the money list. In 1984 he won in the United States for the first time at the Heritage

Precocious talent (above)
As soon as he took up golf at the age of 14, Faldo showed exceptional talent. He won the English Amateur shortly after his 18th birthday.

Delicate touch (left)
Faldo shows great assurance in his short putts. His ability on the greens made a vital contribution to his 1989 US Masters win.

Ryder Cup record
Faldo was a major factor in European Ryder Cup successes, appearing in 11 consecutive events from 1977–1997 – a record for the old millennium.

Classic. But his level of success was not as great as expected and he began to feel that his swing was not consistent enough to take him to the very top.

HARD TIMES
After meeting David Leadbetter, an English-born coach working in the United States, Faldo decided to remodel his swing. It took two hard years to make the change and there were times when, as Faldo admits, he was very low. In the 1985 Ryder Cup at The Belfry he dropped himself from Tony Jacklin's team when he felt the pressure had become too much.

In 1987 Faldo won the Spanish Open on a very tough Las Brisas course and then headed to Muirfield to play in the Open Championship, which he won with that marvellous final round of 18 consecutive pars, proof of the consistency of his new swing. In 1988 he could have been US Open Champion, had his putt gone down on the final green at Brookline; he went on to lose the play-off to Curtis Strange. The following year he went to Augusta and became only the second British player to win the Masters, beating Scott Hoch in virtual darkness at the second extra hole of a cliff-hanger play-off.

Faldo had established himself as almost certainly the best player in the world. Talk turned towards a possible "Grand

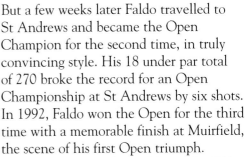

Slam" victory in all the four Majors in 1990. In April Faldo won the Masters again, defeating veteran Ray Floyd in another play-off, again at the second extra hole.

In the US Open at Medinah, however, his putt went astray by a fraction of an inch on the final green, he missed the play-off, and the dream was gone.

But a few weeks later Faldo travelled to St Andrews and became the Open Champion for the second time, in truly convincing style. His 18 under par total of 270 broke the record for an Open Championship at St Andrews by six shots. In 1992, Faldo won the Open for the third time with a memorable finish at Muirfield, the scene of his first Open triumph.

After the glory days of the early 1990s Faldo's game went into something of a decline. Often his private life made bigger headlines than his golf and he also parted company with his long-time guru, David Leadbetter. He moved to the United States and into golf course design.

NICHOLAS ALEXANDER FALDO, MBE

WON BRITISH PGA 1978, 1980–81, 1989; OPEN CHAMPIONSHIP 1987, 1990, 1992; VOLVO MASTERS 1988; US MASTERS 1989–90, 1996; WORLD MATCHPLAY 1989, 1992. WORLD CHAMPIONSHIP 1992. WINNER OF 27 EUROPEAN TOUR EVENTS 1977–94. HARRY VARDON TROPHY 1983, 1992. EUROPEAN TOUR GOLFER OF THE YEAR 1989–90, 1992. RYDER CUP 1977–97. WORLD CUP 1977, 1991, 1998. DUNHILL CUP 1985–88, 1991, 1993. FOUR TOURS CHAMPIONSHIP 1986–87, 1990. USPGA PLAYER OF THE YEAR 1990. WORLD GOLF HALL OF FAME 1997.

Surrendering to joy (left)
Nick Faldo celebrates after holing the putt that brought him his first Masters victory in 1989. His dramatic play-off with Scott Hoch took place in near darkness.

Working back to form (right)
Towards the end of the 1990s there were signs of an improvement in Faldo's form, after something of a slump in the mid-1990s. His desire and potential for further success remains undaunted.

MAX FAULKNER

BORN BEXHILL, ENGLAND, 29 JULY 1916

A FTER HE WON *the 1951 Open Championship with a last-hole trick shot at Royal Portrush, Northern Ireland, there was no stopping Max Faulkner. He could have made a fortune – on the stage. Instead he told and retold how he "swerved" his second shot to the green at the last hole, forced to do so following a wild tee-shot.*

Serious practice
Warming up at Wentworth for the Ryder Cup match of 1953, Faulkner draws a curious gallery, while Sam Snead looks on unconcerned.

Max the entertainer
Faulkner gives a characteristic grimace as he drives off the tee. He never missed a chance to make spectators laugh.

There was no stroke Max could not play, and no gag he was afraid to pull, turning up for big tournaments with weird putters, including one that was made of driftwood, or in garish outfits, such as purple plus-fours. But he could be a serious man too, and on tense days during an Open Championship he would sometimes slip away for a few hours of quiet fishing.

Max Faulkner won many professional tournaments, including the Spanish Open three times. In 1957, when he played in the winning Ryder Cup team at Lindrick, he was dropped from the singles because the British captain, Dai Rees, thought that he looked too highly strung.

MAX FAULKNER

WON OPEN CHAMPIONSHIP 1951; PGA MATCHPLAY 1953; PGA SENIORS 1968, 1970; SPANISH OPEN 1952, 1953, 1957. RYDER CUP 1947–53, 1957.

RAY FLOYD

BORN FORT BRAGG, NORTH CAROLINA, USA, 4 SEPTEMBER 1942

A PPROACHING THE AGE of 50, *Ray Floyd needed only to win one Open Championship to join the immortals – Sarazen, Hogan, Nicklaus and Player – who had won all four Majors. And who was to say he would not do it? In 1990, aged 47, he finished the Masters tied for first place with Nick Faldo, only to lose in the play-off.*

Floyd won the St Petersburg Open when he was only 20, but he was better known at the time as the party-going manager of an all-girl rock band called "The Ladybirds". He did have another win two years later, in 1965, but it was not until 1969 that he really came to the fore as a golfer, winning three big tournaments, including the USPGA Championship. His name was made.

Then, suddenly, that name disappeared from the leader boards. For a full six years Floyd could not win again. At last, towards the end of 1975, he did take a tournament. To prove he was back on top, he then won the 1976 US Masters in the most majestic style.

MASTERS TRIUMPH

In the first round he finished with a 65. In the second it was a 66. This 131 for two rounds was a record, as was his three-round total of 201. In the final round, he missed just one makable putt, which would have given him a new record for the tournament. As it was, he equalled Jack Nicklaus's existing Masters record by finishing on 271.

Also in 1976 Floyd was second in the USPGA and fourth in the Open Championship. In 1978 he came second to Jack Nicklaus in the Open at St Andrews. Then, in 1979, the wheels seemed to come off again. He failed to qualify for the US Open, was 36th in the British Open, 17th in the US Masters

Ageing gracefully
Something of a playboy in his younger years, Ray Floyd matured into one of the most successful players ever.

and only 62nd in the USPGA Championship. It was 1982 before the flamboyant Floyd won a significant competition again, the USPGA at Southern Hills. He was now 40 years old, but his opening round of 63 was, by his own reckoning, the best golf he had ever played in his life. In 1986, he won the US Open at Shinnecock Hills with a final round of 66. Then came the 1990 US Masters. After the third round Floyd was in front with a score of 206. But victory was not to be. He shot a last round of 72 and tied with Nick Faldo. On the second hole of the play-off he dumped his ball in the water that fronts the 11th green.

Floyd captained the 1989 US Ryder Cup team which tied with Europe at The Belfry. He moved on to the lucrative US Seniors' Tour in 1993, and by 1998 had won more than $6 million.

Putting power
Floyd's putting was one of the most effective parts of his game in his Masters and USPGA wins.

RAYMOND LORAN FLOYD

WON USPGA 1969, 1982; US MASTERS 1976;
US PLAYERS CHAMPIONSHIP 1981; US OPEN 1986.
US SENIOR TOUR CHAMPIONSHIP 1992, 1994. WINNER OF
22 US TOUR EVENTS 1963–92, 14 US SENIOR TOUR EVENTS
1992–2000. RYDER CUP 1969, 1975–77, 1981–85, 1991–93
(NON-PLAYING CAPTAIN 1989). DUNHILL CUP 1985–86.
FOUR TOURS CHAMPIONSHIP 1985. VARDON TROPHY 1983.
WORLD GOLF HALL OF FAME 1989.

Popular winner
Floyd (right) receives the USPGA Trophy in 1982, his second victory in the event.

ED FURGOL

BORN NEW YORK, USA, 22 MARCH 1917

AFTER ED FURGOL'S *left arm had been badly smashed in a childhood accident, every medical effort was made to repair the damage, but he was never able to straighten the arm again beyond 45 degrees. When the darkly good-looking Furgol decided to take up golf, most people thought he was simply wasting his time.*

Yet Furgol created his own very effective swing, disproving the theory that good golf must be played with a straight left arm. He began playing sizzling shots and, in 1945, quit a dull job to turn professional.

Nine years later, in the US Open of 1954, Furgol found himself needing a last-hole par at Baltusrol, New Jersey, to hold off Gene Littler and win the title. He stood on the tee, a tall figure with a "different" stance to suit his buckled left arm, and let fly. The ball was never going to hit the fairway and ended in trouble. Yet Furgol threaded his second shot out of trouble, scored his par, and collected the trophy.

That year the USPGA made him Player of the Year and, to prove it was no fluke, Furgol helped win the 1955 World Cup, taking the individual title as well.

Taking a challenge
Furgol's left arm was permanently bent, a serious disability for a golfer, but he overcame this handicap to win the US Open in 1954.

Bent-arm swing (left)
Ordinary golfers loved Ed Furgol because he showed that it was not absolutely necessary to possess a perfect swing in order to become a professional golf champion.

EDWARD FURGOL

WON US OPEN 1954. WINNER OF FOUR
US TOUR EVENTS 1954–57. WORLD CUP
1955 (INDIVIDUAL WINNER). RYDER CUP
1957. USPGA PLAYER OF THE YEAR
1954. BEN HOGAN AWARD 1955.

SERGIO GARCIA

BORN CASTELLON, SPAIN, 9 JANUARY 1980

A FTER A GLITTERING *career as an amateur, Spaniard Sergio Garcia, then 19, burst upon the professional scene in 1999, nowhere more spectacularly than at the USPGA Championship at Medinah, where he became the youngest player to lead the event since it changed from matchplay in 1958.*

Garcia's opening 66 at the 1999 USPGA was eclipsed by his final-round pursuit of Tiger Woods, made memorable by his incredible 6-iron recovery shot from behind a tree on the 452-yard 16th hole.

As his ball was heading for the green Garcia raced after it, leaping all the while to get a better view – and that one stroke and its immediate aftermath became synonymous with the character of Garcia, redolent of the dashing exploits of his mentor, Severiano Ballesteros.

Having been at one stage five strokes behind Woods, Garcia eventually lost by one, a feat which catapulted him into the 1999 Ryder Cup match at Brookline, where he had the joint best record of the match – 3¹/₂ points from a possible five.

Spanish succession
(right) *Fittingly for a player who looked to Ballesteros as a mentor, Garcia won the Seve Ballesteros Trophy at Sunningdale in 2000.*

Cracking start
(below) *In only his sixth start as a professional on the European Tour, Garcia won the 1999 Murphy's Irish Open at Druids Glen, and three months later the Linde German Masters.*

His three wins and a half came in partnership with Jesper Parnevik, but he lost his singles tie to Jim Furyk.

PRECOCIOUS SUCCESS
Record-breaking and Garcia are never far apart. At the age of 15 years and one month he became, as an amateur, the youngest player to make the cut in a European Tour event (The Turespana Open Mediterrania at Valencia); was the first British Amateur Champion to win the low-amateur award, at the Masters in 1999; won the PGA Catalonian Open as a 17-year-old; and in his first USPGA tournament as a professional, the Byron Nelson Classic, he fired an opening 62 before finishing in a tie for third place.

More infamously, he finished last in the 1999 British Open at Carnoustie after rounds of 89 and 83. Just two weeks later came his daunting display at Medinah against Woods.

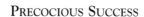

SERGIO GARCIA
FERNANDEZ

WON BRITISH AMATEUR
CHAMPIONSHIP 1998;
IRISH OPEN 1999;
GERMAN MASTERS 1999.
EISENHOWER TROPHY
1996–98. RYDER CUP 1999.
DUNHILL CUP 1999. SEVE
BALLESTEROS TROPHY 2000.
EUROPEAN TOUR ROOKIE
OF THE YEAR 1999.

Youthful emotions
(right) *Occasionally Garcia has allowed his emotions to get the better of him, notably when he kicked one of his shoes into an advertising hoarding after a tee shot, and in an altercation with an amateur partner during a pro-am.*

DAVID GRAHAM

BORN WINDSOR, NSW, AUSTRALIA, 23 MAY 1946

D AVID GRAHAM STARTED *playing with left-handed clubs as a 14-year-old, and only changed to right-handed after three years. After a spell as a club pro in Tasmania, he joined the Tour at home, late in the 1960s, and soon won the Victoria and Tasmania Opens. These victories encouraged him to go further afield, and he has since achieved success the world over, including wins in the 1979 USPGA and the 1981 US Open.*

In 1970 David Graham won the World Cup for Australia with Bruce Devlin, and he was twice a member of the winning team in the Dunhill Cup at St Andrews. Also in Britain, he took the World Matchplay title in 1976, defeating Hale Irwin in the final at the 38th hole.

Graham moved to Dallas, Texas to become a regular of the US Tour and in 1996 he joined the Senior Tour where he won more than $1 million in his first year.

Deliberate style
A player of great determination and courage, Graham's game is very accurate; he drops few strokes through lack of care.

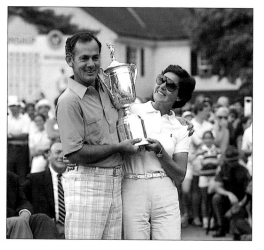

Shared euphoria (above)
Graham celebrates with his wife, Maureen, after victory in the 1981 US Open at Merion, with a last round of 67, three strokes clear.

ANTHONY DAVID GRAHAM

WON FRENCH OPEN 1970; WORLD MATCHPLAY 1976; AUSTRALIAN OPEN 1977; USPGA CHAMPIONSHIP 1979; US OPEN 1981; LANCÔME TROPHY 1981, 1982. WORLD CUP 1970. DUNHILL CUP 1985–86, 1988. PRESIDENTS CUP (NON-PLAYING CAPTAIN 1994).

HUBERT GREEN

BORN BIRMINGHAM, ALABAMA, USA, 28 DECEMBER 1946

A LTHOUGH ALL GOOD *golfers swing differently, it has often been said that they are all the same in the impact area. If this were not so, they would not hit the ball where they intend to and in the way they intend. Hubert Green's style is one of the few that makes people doubt the full truth of this law.*

Players' champion
Hubert Green (right), the 1985 USPGA Champion, receives his trophy at Cherry Hills.

Green crouches over the ball, his knees very bent. His hands at the address are well ahead of the ball. His backswing is short, his downswing fast. He seems to flick the ball away, but with great power. On the putting green this stance is further exaggerated and he uses a two-handed grip that, to purists, does not look correct. Youngest of four in a family of golfers,

Green joined the US Tour in 1970. He won the US Open and the Irish Open in 1977, and the USPGA Championship in 1985. He also tied for second in the 1978 US Masters, when Gary Player shot a final 64 to snatch the title and Hubert contrived to miss a 3ft (1m) putt to tie. In 1996 Green joined the US Senior Tour.

HUBERT MYATT GREEN

WON US OPEN 1977; USPGA 1985. WINNER OF 19 US TOUR EVENTS 1971–85. RYDER CUP 1977–79, 1985. WORLD CUP 1977.

RALPH GULDAHL

BORN DALLAS, TEXAS, USA, 22 NOVEMBER 1912; DIED 1987

T EXAN RALPH GULDAHL *was not perhaps the most popular player in the professional game, but he commanded the highest respect. Born in the same year as Sam Snead, Ben Hogan and Byron Nelson, Guldahl had won the US Open twice in succession before Nelson or Hogan had their names on the trophy – Snead never did.*

Ralph Guldahl was not a charismatic figure. He was a very careful player, always ready to take his time. He seemed almost to go into a trance over his putts and would not play until absolutely ready. The result was outstandingly steady and successful golf. Other players of the period made more impact, but Guldahl earned his place in the golfing record books.

Unorthodox style
Guldahl was a big man with an awkward swing; his backswing was fast. He rocked back on his heels after impact, but he developed great power and managed to control the cut shot that his swing created.

RALPH GULDAHL

WON WESTERN OPEN 1936, 1937, 1938; US OPEN 1937, 1938; US MASTERS 1939. RYDER CUP 1937. USPGA HALL OF FAME 1963. WORLD GOLF HALL OF FAME 1981.

❮ WALTER HAGEN, see page 266

SANDY HERD

BORN ST ANDREWS, SCOTLAND, 24 APRIL 1868; DIED 1944

S ANDY HERD WAS *a real St Andrews man, born and raised within the sound of well-struck golf balls on the Old Course. He stuck to the old-fashioned palm grip of the nineteenth-century Scottish golfer and to the old gutta ball until well into his 30s. Herd was a formidable matchplayer, like Walter Hagen later, but without Hagen's relaxed temperament. Herd went for everything. He was always in a hurry to win – often too much of a hurry.*

Sandy Herd's name would be better known now had he not been a contemporary of the Great Triumvirate of Vardon, Braid and Taylor. Although he had several victories over Vardon to his credit, in strokeplay he could rarely beat him or the other two great golfers of the time. Vardon won the Open Championship six times, Taylor and Braid

Lining up
Herd focused on the clubface and its intended line and angle at impact.

five times each, but Herd only once. That victory came at Royal Liverpool in 1902 when he beat Vardon and Braid by one stroke, 307 to their 308.

DASH AND COURAGE
In his youth Herd was known as a "fine fighter", a man of dash, courage and staying power, but lacking in self-restraint. His impatience seemed to be reflected in his ferocious waggle. But Bernard Darwin wrote: "The number of his waggles is only exceeded by that of his friends. I cannot conceive that Sandy ever had an enemy. If he lives to be a hundred he will still be the same fine, sturdy, independent, ever-youthful creature." In fact, he was still playing an occasional tournament approaching 70.

ALEXANDER HERD

WON OPEN CHAMPIONSHIP 1902; PGA MATCHPLAY 1906, 1926.

WALTER HAGEN

BORN ROCHESTER, NEW YORK, USA, 21 DECEMBER 1892; DIED 1969

I N LIFE, SAID *Walter Hagen, one should always take time "to smell the flowers along the way" – and he did. He said he never wanted to be a millionaire, he just wanted to live like one – and he did. He was a showman, a great golfer and a tremendous matchplayer. He won 11 Major tournaments, including four consecutive USPGA titles from 1924 to 1927, and he completely altered the status of the golf professional in society.*

When Francis Ouimet won the US Open from Vardon and Ray in 1913, Walter Hagen, almost unnoticed, was in fourth place. The next year he made his mark, winning the Open at the Midlothian, Chicago, starting with a record round of 68. He won again in 1919, immediately after the First World War.

KEEPING UP APPEARANCES
Hagen was ambitious to succeed on the other side of the Atlantic, however, although British snobbery did not appeal to him. When he arrived at Deal for the 1920 Open Championship, he was not allowed into the clubhouse. No professional was.

So Hagen hired a Daimler, a chauffeur and a footman, parked the Daimler outside the clubhouse front door, and had his footman collect him and his gear each day as he arrived at the 18th. He finished 53rd, but that did not worry him. He had made his point.

It was this assertive spirit that his friend Gene Sarazen was remembering

Looking good
The stylishness of Hagen's golfing outfits, unusual at that period, contributed greatly to his popularity.

when he wrote: "All the professionals who have a chance to go after the big money today should say a silent thanks to Walter each time they stretch a cheque between their fingers. It was Walter who made professional golf what it is."

Although he won the French Open that year, Hagen returned from Europe flat broke. He borrowed the taxi fare from the docks to the Delmonico Hotel, rented the best suite, ordered a case of Scotch and $500 to be sent up and relaxed. "A couple of tournaments and he was back in the black," Sarazen reported. Hagen simply refused to allow any worries to disturb his relaxation. In 1921 he returned to challenge for the British Open at St Andrews, coming sixth. In 1922 he won at Sandwich. In 1923 he lost by one stroke at Troon to Arthur Havers. In 1924 he won again at Hoylake. He did not cross the Atlantic in 1925, but in 1926 he was third behind Bobby Jones and Al Watrous at Lytham. After another year away, he was Open Champion again both at Sandwich in 1928 and at Muirfield in 1929. It was a truly remarkable record of success.

SERIOUS SHOWMANSHIP
Hagen was a showman, but he meant business. At Troon in 1923 he had whittled away at Havers's lead and arrived at the 72nd hole needing a birdie to tie. He hit his approach shot into a bunker, looked over the situation, and just failed to sink his bunker shot.

In 1926 at Lytham, needing an eagle to tie with Bobby Jones, he walked up to the green before playing his second, surveyed the green, and then asked the referee if he would kindly have the pin removed. He played a beautiful second that finished only a couple of feet from the hole. Despite his successes in the

Humble roots
The poor boy from Rochester grew up to grace cigarette cards – looking every bit the debonair millionaire that he had become.

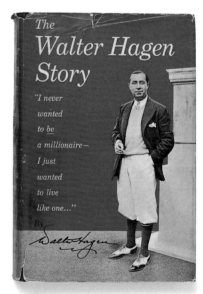

Putting it into words
Walter Hagen gave a suitably lively account of his successes – and his failures – in a popular autobiography.

Crowd pleaser (left)
Hagen was one of the most popular sportsmen of the 1920s. In 1924, at Hoylake, the fans look on as the Open Champion receives his wife's congratulations.

Practice style (right)
Hagen is kitted out for a practice round before the 1924 Open at Hoylake – he won the Championship.

player instead of a champion golfer, and this may have accounted for his wide stance and swaying backswing when he drove. He wanted distance, wherever the ball went. If it went into the woods, he would play out of them. When the ball was on the green, he would probably sink the putt. (It was Walter Hagen who showed the legendary Bobby Locke how to putt.) He used an extremely light grip, making a full, free swing with his arms, and he kept his head very still indeed.

Bobby Jones once said that he loved to play golf with Hagen: "He goes along chin-up, smiling away, never grousing about his luck, playing the ball as he finds it." In the 1924 British Open, Hagen started with a 77. "That would have crushed a less gallant spirit," commented Sarazen. It did not crush Hagen. He won.

WALTER CHARLES HAGEN

WON US OPEN 1914, 1919; USPGA 1921, 1924, 1925, 1926, 1927; OPEN CHAMPIONSHIP 1922, 1924, 1928, 1929. RYDER CUP 1927–35 (CAPTAIN 1927–35, NON-PLAYING CAPTAIN 1937). USPGA HALL OF FAME 1940. WORLD GOLF HALL OF FAME 1974.

❨ HAROLD HILTON, see page 270

British and US Opens, however, Hagen's main strength was at matchplay. When the USPGA Championship was a matchplay event, Walter won in 1921, beating Jim Barnes three and two. In the 1923 final at Pelham, he lost to Gene Sarazen at the 38th hole. Then he beat Jim Barnes again in 1924, Bill Mehlhorn in 1925, Leo Diegel in 1926 and Joe Turnesa in 1927.

Always the gentleman (below)
As 1929 Open Champion, Hagen (left) receives the congratulations of a young Henry Cotton.

RELAXED SPORTSMAN
Hagen may have been flamboyant, but he was a true gentleman. In 1928 he was beaten 18-and-17 by Archie Compston in a 72-hole match at Moor Park. His own story of that match shows only admiration for Compston. "His every shot was masterful," he wrote later in his autobiography, *The Walter Hagen Story*. "He gave me the worst beating of my career and I had only one statement to make to the British press: 'When you are laid out good and flat, you must not squawk!'"

Hagen's golf swing reflected his attitude to life: it was totally tension-free. He might have been a first-class baseball

BEN HOGAN

Born Dublin, Texas, USA, 13 August 1912; Died 1997

T HE CAREER OF *Ben Hogan was slow to take off. After turning professional in 1931, he took seven years to record his first win. From 1940 onwards he dominated the US money list, but he still had to wait until after the Second World War to win a Major – the USPGA Championship of 1946 at Portland. By the age of 36, however, Hogan was almost indisputably the best golfer in the world. It was at this high peak of his career that fate struck him a cruel blow.*

In 1948, a wonderful year for golf in the United States, Hogan won a great trio of titles: the US Open, the USPGA Championship and the Western Open. His galleries always attracted fellow professionals – they all hoped that some of the Hogan magic might rub off on them.

But on Wednesday, 2 February 1949, as Hogan and his wife Valerie were driving east of Pecos, Texas, they collided with a Greyhound bus in light fog. Hogan was critically injured. News of the accident flashed across America and there

Smile of success (below)
Hogan poses in untypically relaxed style after his 1953 US Open win.

Champion of Carnoustie (above)
Ben Hogan drives off during his assault on the Open Championship in 1953.

were chilling reports from the hospital that the great golfer might not survive his horrific injuries.

But Hogan survived. Very slowly and painfully he learned to walk again. Then he ventured on to a golf course on a motor scooter and built up his shattered body with exercises. By January 1950, he was on the practice ground at Riviera in Los Angeles, ready to take on such players as Lloyd Mangrum and Jimmy Demaret.

A huge crowd gathered to see whether their sporting idol could make a comeback after such physical damage. When the starter introduced him on the first tee, the gallery roared. Hogan fired a 73; despite the painful walk, he was back.

American hero
One of the greatest golfers of all time, Ben Hogan dominated the American game after the Second World War.

TRIUMPH OVER INJURY

Three weeks later Hogan went to the Greenbrier and won the White Sulphur Springs tournament, scoring a staggering total of 259. By the time he turned up at Merion to contest the US Open that June, the interest of the media and the public had been raised to fever pitch.

Although still clearly feeling the effects of his serious injury, a bandaged Hogan fought his way through two rounds on the final day to force a three-way tie with George Fazio and Lloyd Mangrum.

Comeback award
The Ben Hogan Award, a bronze sculpture of the golfer, is given every year to a golfer who has made a comeback from injury or physical disability.

Ben Hogan on canvas (right)
This dignified portrait of the great golfer was painted by J. Anthony Wills in 1967.

there was a fast-running stream of water, squirming like a serpent across the finishing holes. US journalists likened playing at Carnoustie to golf on the moon. But Hogan charted the course for a week and practised hitting drives to different parts of the fairways to find the smart way in. The quality of his performance, once the Championship began, brought tears to the eyes.

CONQUERING THE HEIGHTS
Every round Hogan played was lower than the one before – from 73 down to a last-round 68. Despite bumpy fairways and stampeding galleries, he won the title, and returned home to a ticker-tape parade and a chat with President Dwight D. Eisenhower.

WILLIAM BENJAMIN HOGAN

WON USPGA 1946, 1948; US OPEN 1948, 1950, 1951, 1953; US MASTERS 1951, 1953; OPEN CHAMPIONSHIP 1953. WINNER OF 63 US TOUR EVENTS 1938–59. RYDER CUP 1947, 1951 (CAPTAIN 1947, NON-PLAYING CAPTAIN 1949, 1967). WORLD CUP 1956, 1958 (INDIVIDUAL WINNER 1956). VARDON TROPHY 1940, 1941, 1948. USPGA PLAYER OF THE YEAR 1948, 1950, 1951, 1953. USPGA HALL OF FAME 1953. WORLD GOLF HALL OF FAME 1974. BOB JONES AWARD 1976.

Hollywood connection (right)
Hogan with his wife Valerie and actor Glenn Ford (right) who played Hogan in the film Follow the Sun.

Somehow he found the reserves of strength he needed to score a 69 in the play-off, defeating Mangrum by a clear margin of four strokes.

Hogan's comeback went on from success to success. In 1951 he won the Masters with a final round of 68, and kept his Open title at Oakland Hills with a last-round 67. Two years later he surpassed every previous performance by winning all three Majors in which he competed – the US Open at Oakmont, the Masters, and the Open Championship at Carnoustie in Scotland.

Hogan hated overseas travel and had never played in the British Open. To a visiting American in 1953, Carnoustie was quite a contrast to anything in Texas. The food was different, so Hogan ate lunch in his car. The winds swept in and

Hogan was never to reach such heights again, but he refused to retire. He was still capable of taking tenth place in the US Masters in 1967, at the age of 54.

Hogan's drive for perfection did not make him popular with everyone. But it is no surprise that his life was made into a Hollywood movie. In the whole history of golf, his was the greatest story ever told.

Treasured memories
Hogan is still revered by golfers worldwide, as this celebratory USGA exhibition showed.

GOLF: THE LIFEWORK OF BEN HOGAN
JULY 9 TO NOVEMBER 2, 1990
USGA MUSEUM AND LIBRARY

HAROLD HILTON

BORN WEST KIRBY, ENGLAND, 12 JANUARY 1869; DIED 1942

T HE GREAT AMATEUR *player Harold Hilton was not the most elegant swinger of a golf club, but he was one of the outstanding players of his or of any other generation. He was the only amateur player to win the Open Championship in Britain, apart from his contemporary John Ball and the immortal Bobby Jones.*

Hilton learned to play golf at the Royal Liverpool Club, where John Ball was also a member, and at one time his handicap was plus ten. He was short, only 5ft 7in (1.7m) tall, but he was extremely strong for his size and powerfully built.

He won the Open Championship at Muirfield in 1892, the first year it was held over 72 holes, and at Hoylake in 1897. He was four times British Amateur Champion. When he won the US Amateur Championship in 1911, he

Popular portrait
As Harold Hilton was the best amateur golfer of his era, his image was featured on cards of all kinds.

Facing front (left)
A firm believer in the follow-through, Hilton would throw his weight forward on to his left leg after every shot.

became the first player to hold the amateur titles on both sides of the Atlantic in the same year. Only Lawson Little, Bobby Jones and Bob Dickson have emulated that feat.

In *Golfing By-paths* (1946), Bernard Darwin described Hilton's unusual style as "a little man jumping on his toes and throwing himself and his club after the ball with almost frantic abandon." But it was a style that worked. Only John Ball and Freddie Tait posed any threat to Hilton's preeminence in the amateur game. A methodical player, he was also a great golf student and wrote sagely on the subject. In 1911 he became the first editor of *Golf Monthly*, the oldest monthly golf magazine.

HAROLD HORSFALL HILTON

WON OPEN CHAMPIONSHIP 1892, 1897; IRISH AMATEUR 1897, 1900, 1901, 1902; BRITISH AMATEUR 1900, 1901, 1911, 1913; US AMATEUR 1911.
WORLD GOLF HALL OF FAME 1978

HORACE HUTCHINSON

BORN LONDON, ENGLAND, 16 MAY 1859; DIED 1932

A S WELL AS *being a top-ranked golf player, Horace Hutchinson was one of the first people to write seriously about the game. Although himself a flamboyant player, and a master of the unorthodox, in his writing he always preached orthodoxy. He was also much admired by his contemporaries as a golf administrator.*

Horace's uncle was one of the founder members of the Royal North Devon Club at Westward Ho!, and by the age of 13 young Horace was playing there.

He quickly showed himself to be a fine player. When he was 16 he won the club's tournament, which carried with it the club captaincy. He was soon amongst the finest amateurs of the day. He played in the first Oxford v Cambridge match in

Unerring ability
Horace Hutchinson was renowned for his skill at driving and for being able to play recovery shots from every kind of bad lie.

1878 and took part in the first Amateur Championship in 1885, when he lost in the final to A.F. MacFie. In 1886 he won the final easily to become Amateur Champion and successfully defended his title the following year in a scintillating contest against John Ball.

Horace Hutchinson's great strength was his short game and there have been few better putters in any period. He mastered, too, the important art of hitting the ball low into the wind.

He had great influence in the game, especially through his books and prolific magazine writing, and in 1908 he became the first English commoner to be captain of the Royal & Ancient Golf Club.

HORATIO GORDON HUTCHINSON

WON BRITISH AMATEUR 1886, 1887. LEADING AMATEUR IN OPEN CHAMPIONSHIP 1885. CAPTAIN ROYAL & ANCIENT GOLF CLUB 1908.

HALE IRWIN

BORN JOPLIN, MISSOURI, USA, 3 JUNE 1945

TALL, STYLISH AND *powerful, Hale Irwin was one of the most consistent American golfers of the 1970s and 1980s. More athletic than he appeared – he was a first-class American college football player – he built his game around control. Irwin's game is about rhythm, swinging on-plane and staying out of trouble.*

Not a slugger
With enough natural strength not to need to hit the ball really hard, Hale Irwin plays a neat and tidy game that shows great control.

Recipe for success (above)
Competitive spirit, consistency and all-round competence have characterized Hale Irwin's game over the 20 years that he has remained at the top of the golfing profession.

Odd meal
Irwin gnaws at his club in frustration during the 1987 US Open at Olympic.

When Hale Irwin came to the final green at Medinah in the 1990 US Open, he hit his second shot to the edge of the sloping green 45ft (13.5m) from the cup. He knew he needed to get down in two more to stand any chance of winning.

Irwin struck the putt firmly and it raced in a wide curve across the green, up the slope and round into the hole. He ran round the green doing a version of an Indian war dance. In his heart he agreed with Greg Norman, his playing partner: "You could just have seen the putt that wins the tournament." It was not quite that easy. Irwin went into an 18-hole play-off with Mike Donald that ended in a tie. But then Irwin won the 19th hole and, at 45, became the oldest man ever to win the US Open.

GOLDEN YEARS

Until his 1990 Open victory, Irwin's best years appeared to be behind him. A professional since 1968, he had first won the US Open at Winged Foot in 1974, when the course was set up so sternly that only one of the first four finishers broke 70 in any round. He won the title again at Inverness, Ohio, in 1979, despite a last round of 75.

Between 1973 and 1981, Irwin was only twice out of the top seven on the US money list. He might have taken the British Open title at Royal Birkdale in 1983, but for the 2in (5cm) putt that he missed at the 14th hole of the third round.

Since joining the US Senior Tour in 1995, Irwin has won 29 of its events. In 1998 he was voted the Senior Tour Player of the Year for the second straight season after seven victories, including two Major championships, and a new single-season earnings record of $2,861,945.

HALE S. IRWIN

WON US OPEN 1974, 1979, 1990; WORLD MATCHPLAY 1974, 1975. WINNER OF 20 US TOUR EVENTS 1971–90. WORLD CUP 1974, (INDIVIDUAL WINNER 1979). RYDER CUP 1975–81, 1991. WORLD GOLF HALL OF FAME 1992. ARNOLD PALMER AWARD 1997–98

TONY JACKLIN

BORN SCUNTHORPE, ENGLAND, 7 JULY 1944

WHEN TONY JACKLIN won the US Open at Hazeltine in 1970, he became the first British player for 70 years to hold both the British and US Open titles at the same time. Hailed as a national hero, he was awarded an OBE and went on to become the chief inspiration for the developing European Tour. In the 1980s, Jacklin achieved fresh prominence as an inspirational captain of the European Ryder Cup team and in the 1990s, back in the United States, he prepared himself for a comeback to full-time tournament golf on the US Seniors Tour.

Big shot
With great natural ability, Jacklin was one of the best strikers in the history of the game.

Being the son of a lorry driver in the English steel town of Scunthorpe, Lincolnshire, seems an unlikely background from which to launch a bid for golf fame and fortune. But from the age of nine, Jacklin developed a burning ambition to be the best and his talent was precocious enough to help him achieve it. At the age of 13 he won the Lincolnshire Boys' Championship, and held the title for the next two years. At 16 he beat the leading professional by nine strokes to add the Lincolnshire Open to his successes.

TRANSATLANTIC SUCCESS

Jacklin turned professional in 1962 and in 1963 he was named Rookie of the Year. By 1968 Jacklin had joined the US Tour and won the Jacksonville Open with a record score, proving that he could take on and beat the top Americans. This was emphatically confirmed by his victory in the Open Championship at Royal Lytham and St Annes in 1969, which made him the first Briton to hold the title for 18 years. The following year he took on the Americans on their home ground, winning the US Open at Chaska, Minnesota, by seven strokes with a score of 281, the biggest winning margin since Jim Barnes' nine-stroke win in 1921.

Tony Jacklin was the new hope of Europe. When he went to St Andrews shortly afterwards, the galleries flocked to see him defend his Open Championship crown and keep the Americans at bay. But his defence was dogged by the most cruel luck.

Jacklin began by producing golf of such masterful quality he went to the turn in 29 strokes, but his momentum was broken by a cloudburst. The following day, the magic was missing and Jacklin could only manage to finish fifth.

SHATTERING BLOW

Two years later, at Muirfield, Jacklin looked set to win the Open Championship again when Lee Trevino, level with Jacklin at the 17th, played through the back of the green in four strokes. Safely on in three, Jacklin seemed almost home and dry. But Trevino then flukily holed his chip shot from off the green, and Jacklin was so shaken by this shot that he three-putted.

Trevino went on to win a championship he admitted later he had mentally conceded. It was a shattering blow.

Home win
Tony Jacklin kisses the trophy after his Open Championship triumph in 1969. Jacklin's victory interrupted an overseas domination of the Championship that had begun with Bobby Locke's win at Royal Lytham in 1952.

UPS AND DOWNS

Jacklin bounced back as Ryder Cup captain and inspired a new crop of outstanding young European players to a near victory at the first attempt in Florida in 1983. Two years later, the Europeans had an emotional victory at The Belfry. Then, in 1987, Jacklin led his team to even greater glory, winning for the first time in America. After a draw at The Belfry in 1989, he bowed out as captain, having presided over the start of a new era in European golf.

When he appeared to have found salvation for the putting problems that dogged the final years of his regular tour career with the new long-handled putter, he moved to America to try to qualify for the US Senior Tour. With invitations he played in several events, winning twice, but his efforts to become a regular Senior Tour player sadly petered out.

ANTHONY JACKLIN, CBE

WON DUNLOP MASTERS 1967, 1973; OPEN CHAMPIONSHIP 1969; US OPEN 1970; LANCÔME TROPHY 1970; BRITISH PGA 1972, 1982; ITALIAN OPEN 1973; GERMAN OPEN 1979. WINNER OF 14 PGA EUROPEAN TOUR EVENTS 1965–82. WORLD CUP 1966, 1970–72. RYDER CUP 1967–79 (NON-PLAYING CAPTAIN 1983–89). HONORARY LIFE PRESIDENT BRITISH PGA.

Clutching the cup
The sheer joy of victory over the United States, in the United States, was plainly evident in Captain Tony Jacklin's face at Muirfield Village in 1987. Jacklin's Europeans beat Nicklaus's US team 15 to 13, spurred on by Jacklin's unceasing encouragement as non-playing captain. American dominance of the Ryder Cup had been shattered.

LEE JANZEN

BORN AUSTIN, MINNESOTA, USA, 28 AUGUST 1964

LEE JANZEN WAS *15 years old when he won his first tournament as a member of the Greater Tampa Golf Association. While at Florida Southern University a string of golf victories indicated that he was heading for the top.*

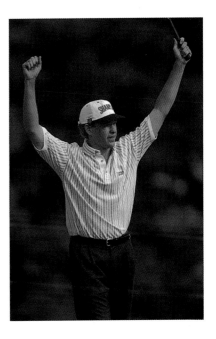

Janzen turned professional immediately he left college but it was three years before he qualified for the US Tour, in the autumn of 1989. Three years after that he was a dollar millionaire and had a reputation as one of the most consistent players around.
Janzen's rise through the professional ranks has been meteoric: by 1992 he had moved up to ninth place in the money list. That was the year of his first US Tour victory in the Northern Telecom Open when he played the final three rounds in 17 under par.

HEADLINE HITTER

But it was in 1993 that Janzen really hit the headlines. At the US Open at Baltusrol, Lee returned four rounds in the 60s to win by two strokes over a luckless Payne Stewart. His 272 total tied with Jack Nicklaus for the lowest cumulative score in the history of the US Open. Earlier in the year he won the Phoenix Open for his second US Tour victory. Further laurels came as a member of the victorious US Ryder Cup team in 1993. Janzen then repeated another US Open victory in 1998, and again it was a close call against Payne Stewart – 280 against 281. Janzen remains an unspectacular player, far from being the longest hitter on Tour, but he has the ability to produce spectacular scores from a golf game that has no apparent weaknesses.

Two-time US Open Champion
Janzen's first win in a major championship, the 1993 US Open, earned him a hefty $290,000 and a ten-year automatic entry to US Tour tournaments. In 1998 he secured his second US Open victory.

LEE MACLEOD JANZEN

WON US OPEN 1993, 1998. US PLAYERS CHAMPIONSHIP 1995. WINNER OF 8 US TOUR EVENTS 1992–98. RYDER CUP 1993, 1997. DUNHILL CUP 1995. PRESIDENTS CUP 1998.

BOBBY JONES

BORN ATLANTA, GEORGIA, USA, 17 MARCH 1902; DIED 1971

D URING 1936, SIX years after he had retired from championship golf with no worlds left to conquer, Bobby Jones made a sentimental return trip to St Andrews as an ordinary holidaymaker, to have a round over the famous Old course with some friends. It was not long before the word was out that Bobby Jones was back in the "home of golf"; when he arrived on the 1st tee, he found that some 2,000 of the Auld Grey Toon's inhabitants had turned out to watch him play, and that the number grew as the round progressed.

Jones recalled that day some 22 years later, when, confined to a wheelchair and in declining health, he returned to St Andrews to be made a freeman of the city. "That spontaneous welcome was bound to be touching and it did something to me," he said. "I played golf as I had not done for more

Enthralled spectators (above)
Delighting the crowd, Jones uses his mashie during the British Open at St Andrews in 1927, in which he made a record score of 285.

than four years or ever since." And he further added: "I could take out of my life everything except my experiences at St Andrews and I'd still have had a rich, full life."

The son of an Atlanta attorney, Bobby Jones was a sickly child, and there was grave concern that he would not survive infancy. When he was five years old, he was introduced to golf while on holiday, and he and a friend built their own two-hole course. A member at the nearby East Lake Country Club found an old cleek and cut it down for him.

Boy hero (left)
Bobby Jones was a precociously talented golfer. In 1916, at Merion, in his very first appearance in a US Amateur Championship at the tender age of 14, he played well enough to reach the quarter-finals of the tournament.

Flowing swing (right)
Jones's style was greatly influenced by Stewart Maiden, who was the professional at East Lake, Georgia. The young Bobby had followed the quiet Scotsman every time he played and would mimic his flowing, rhythmical swing.

PERSEVERANCE
It was not the ideal club for a youngster to learn to play with, but he persevered. It gives a clue as to why one of the strongest parts of Jones's game at the height of his powers was his long-iron play.
When the Jones family moved permanently to East Lake and Bobby's interest developed in what was still a relatively new game in the United States, he was greatly influenced by the East Lake Club professional, an expatriate Scot, Stewart Maiden.

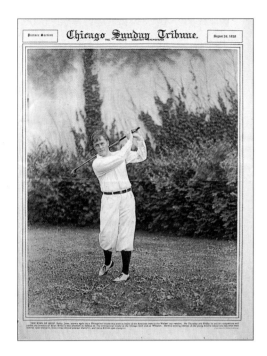

Chicago Sunday Tribune

Homage to greatness (left)
A Chicago Sunday Tribune *of 1928 pays tribute to Bobby Jones's position as the greatest golfer of his era.*

Crowd puller (right)
Jones won his first Open Championship at Royal Lytham in 1926. His swift method of play ensured him many admirers.

By the time he was 14 years old, Bobby Jones was not only good enough to play in the US Amateur Championship but to get to the quarter-final. There was a lean period as he grew out of his frail early years and developed into a strong young

man, but by 1923 he was the US Open Champion and well on the way to becoming the greatest player of his era. In the eight-year period from that first US Open victory, Jones won a total of 13 national championships, including his Grand Slam of 1930 – the Open and Amateur Championships of both Britain and the United States. He became a national hero, the most popular sportsman in American history. Thousands flocked to see him play; few realized that he did not like crowds and felt irritated, threatened and shut in by them.

In 1930, with three legs of his Grand Slam already secure and only the US Amateur at Merion standing between him and a unique sporting triumph, Bobby Jones – bothered by the crowds – suddenly lost his form. However, after a quiet final practice elsewhere, at Pine Valley, he returned to Merion for the Championship in much better heart and back to his usual form. He won comfortably in the end and, at the age of only 28, walked off the stage

of competitive golf for ever. Jones's retirement dream was to build his own golf course, where he and his friends could play privately, away from the attentions of well-meaning but intrusive golf fans. The result was the Augusta National Golf Club, since 1934 the permanent home of the US Masters (see page 68).

TRUE AMATEUR

Bobby Jones's record as a truly amateur player will live for ever in the history of the game of golf. Despite many lucrative offers, he never turned professional, earning his living from his legal practice throughout his playing career.

It was not just his record that made Bobby Jones unique. His contribution to the special ethic and the great traditions of golf was equally remarkable.

Today, in the USGA museum in Far Hills, New Jersey, there is a room dedicated to the memory of Bobby Jones, where the artifacts of his incredible career are on display. Across the Atlantic, the 10th hole on the Old Course at St Andrews now bears his name, and his portrait hangs proudly in the Big Room of the Royal & Ancient Golf Club as a permanent memorial to the greatest amateur player in the game's history.

ROBERT TYRE JONES JNR

WON US OPEN 1923, 1926, 1929, 1930; US AMATEUR 1924, 1925, 1927, 1928, 1930; OPEN CHAMPIONSHIP 1926, 1927, 1930; BRITISH AMATEUR 1930. USA v GB 1921. WALKER CUP 1922–30 (CAPTAIN 1928, 1930). NON-PLAYING CAPTAIN EISENHOWER TROPHY 1958. USPGA HALL OF FAME 1940. WORLD GOLF HALL OF FAME 1974.

Ticker-tape welcome
New York mayor James J. Walker congratulates Bobby Jones on his Grand Slam wins in 1930.

Room to reflect
The Robert T. Jones Jnr room at Far Hills is filled with memorabilia, including Jones's 32 competition medals.

ANDREW KIRKALDY

BORN DENHEAD, SCOTLAND, 18 MARCH 1860; DIED 1934

A NDREW KIRKALDY SHOWED *great talent for golf at an early age, figuring as runner-up in the Open Championship of 1879 at the age of 19. He was a beautiful player to watch. Large, squarely built and strong, he was noted for his long, low drives, particularly into a wind. A golfer of the top class, he was unlucky never to achieve the highest peak, a victory in the Open.*

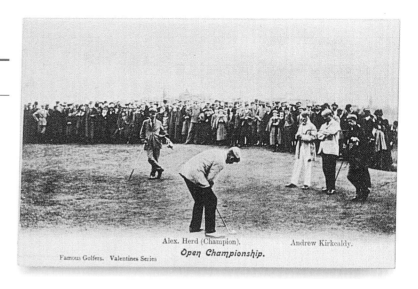

Alex. Herd (Champion).   Andrew Kirkcaldy.
Open Championship.
Famous Golfers. Valentines Series

Kirkaldy was born in Denhead, outside St Andrews, in 1860. He was the son of a miner who had been a soldier in the Crimean War. The family was very poor. After his successful appearance in the 1879 Open, he joined the Army and was in the Black Watch when they went to war in Egypt in 1882. He fought at Tel-el-Kebir, showing great dash and gallantry, always ready to be among the leaders in an attack, regardless of danger. This devil-may-care attitude was characteristic of the man and of the game of golf he played.

BACK FROM THE WARS

Kirkaldy lost many potential golfing years to soldiering, but he soon picked up the game again on his return. After a brief spell as a professional in England, at Winchester, he went back home to St Andrews and remained at the "home of golf" for the rest of his days.

Returning to the Open in 1888, he finished sixth. The following year he tied for the Championship with Willie Park Jnr at Musselburgh, but lost the play-off. In 1891 he was again second; this time the winner was his brother, Hugh. This was the first instance of brothers occupying the top two places in the British Open.

Clubhouse portrait
This somewhat dour portrait of Andrew Kirkaldy by W.O. Hutchison hangs in the clubhouse of the Royal & Ancient Golf Club at St Andrews.

Local rivals
This early postcard in the Valentine series features Andrew Kirkaldy and Sandy Herd.

Although three times runner-up, three times third and twice fourth, Andrew Kirkaldy was never to win the Open. But he was involved in many big matches, usually on the winning side. In 1895, for instance, a year when the Open was held at St Andrews, the reigning Open Champion, J.H. Taylor, issued a challenge to any golfer to play a 36-hole match over the New Course. Andrew Kirkaldy picked up the gauntlet and, in a tense game, scraped out a win on the last green.

SCOTTISH HUMOUR

Kirkaldy was a person of great character, kind-hearted but prepared to express himself fluently and vividly in broad Scots. Stories abound of Kirkaldy's humour. He was a source of enormous amusement to those able to understand him, but was quickly impatient of anyone who sought to patronize him. Few tried it twice.

After the death of Tom Morris, Kirkaldy was appointed honorary professional to the Royal & Ancient Club, a post he held from 1910 to 1933. He died in 1934 at the age of 74.

ANDREW KIRKALDY

RUNNER-UP IN THE OPEN CHAMPIONSHIP 1879, 1889, 1891. HONORARY PROFESSIONAL ROYAL & ANCIENT GOLF CLUB 1910–33.

TOM KITE

BORN AUSTIN, TEXAS, USA, 9 DECEMBER 1949

Top money winner
Kite has accumulated more money (in 1989 alone he topped the US money list with $1,395,278) than anyone else in the history of the game, largely through the strength of his putting. If Kite drove as well as he pitches and putts, he would have won twice as many tournaments.

W INNING HAS ALWAYS *been Tom Kite's problem. He was the first man to reach $5 million in earnings on the US Tour. By the end of 1989 he had earned Tour prize money totalling $5,600,691, ahead even of Jack Nicklaus, who had won $5,102,420 in all his years as top man. Yet Nicklaus had 71 Tour wins to his credit, while Kite had only 13. Even allowing for the effects of inflation on prize money, the contrast is significant.*

Kite had ten top-ten finishes on the US Tour in each of the three years from 1987 to 1989; in 1981 he had 21. By 1990 he had secured 19 top-ten finishes in the four Majors. Yet he had never actually won a Major and had only twice won more than one Tour event in a season.

Kite's propensity to near-misses started early: he came second in the US Amateur in 1970. He turned professional in 1972 and was named Rookie of the Year in 1973, his first full season on the Tour.

HIGH FLYER
In 1978 he was joint second to Nicklaus at St Andrews in the Open Championship, along with Ben Crenshaw, Ray Floyd and Simon Owen. He has been joint second twice in the Masters. In 1983 he joined Ben Crenshaw in second place when Seve Ballesteros won after a last-round 69. In the 1986 Masters he joined Greg Norman in second place, one shot behind Nicklaus. On the 72nd hole he needed to sink a 12ft (4m) putt to tie, but missed.

Kite had come close to winning Majors but had not quite succeeded until he arrived at Pebble Beach, California, in 1992. In an historic US Open, Kite was rewarded for his perseverance and took his first Major title with a score of 285.

In 1997 Kite was non-playing Captain of the losing US Ryder Cup team at Valderrama, and by 2000 he was playing on both the regular and senior tours. In that year he won more than $1 million on the Senior Tour alone.

A MAJOR ACHIEVEMENT

After two decades as the best player never to have won any of the game's Majors, Tom Kite finally had his reward. In 1992, at the US Open at Pebble Beach, Kite battled his way through the wind on the final day to overtake Jeff Sluman and Colin Montgomerie to claim victory. Kite's run of near-misses was over.

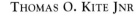

THOMAS O. KITE JNR

WON EUROPEAN OPEN 1980; US PLAYERS CHAMPIONSHIP 1989; US TOUR CHAMPIONSHIP 1989; US OPEN 1992. WINNER 19 US TOUR EVENTS 1976–93. EISENHOWER TROPHY 1970. WALKER CUP 1971. RYDER CUP 1979–89, 1993. WORLD CUP 1984–85. FOUR TOURS CHAMPIONSHIP 1987, 1989. DUNHILL CUP 1989–90, 1992, 1994. BOB JONES AWARD 1979. VARDON TROPHY 1981, 1982. ARNOLD PALMER AWARD 1981, 1989. USPGA PLAYER OF THE YEAR 1989.

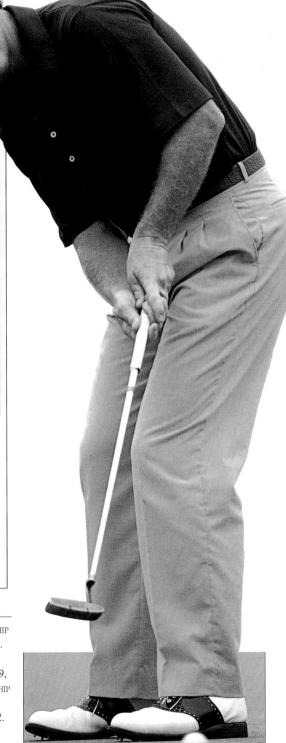

JOHNNY LAIDLAY

BORN HADDINGTONSHIRE, SCOTLAND, 5 NOVEMBER 1860; DIED 1940

W HEN JOHN LAIDLAY *was 12 years old, he went to Loretto School, Musselburgh, which lies just by the famous old links. Here he soon showed his great golfing skill, and by the time he was 16 he had achieved a round with a four at each hole. This was with the guttie ball, and no mean feat. Laidlay joined Luffness when he was 18 and soon won his first medal. In the 1880s and early 1890s he was the leading Scottish amateur player.*

Golfing innovator
Johnny Laidlay was first to use what has become known as the Vardon Grip. He was also responsible for introducing the game to Egypt.

In the British Amateur Championship in the years from 1888 to 1894, Laidlay always reached at least the semi-final; he was in five finals, including four in a row, and won the title twice, in 1889 and 1891. He was leading amateur in the Open Championship on four occasions, and was runner-up in 1893. He played in the Open for the last time in 1906, but continued to enter the Amateur until 1920, when he was close to 60.

Laidlay had an individual and unusual style of play. Nearly every shot was played off a firm left side; although he broke almost every rule of style, he had great control over all his shots. His swing was often described as "peculiar" and he used a light grip, but he still developed power even off a half-swing.

Immaculate short game
Using a cleek gave Laidlay a feel for the low run-up.

JOHN ERNEST LAIDLAY

WON BRITISH AMATEUR
CHAMPIONSHIP 1889, 1891.
SCOTLAND V ENGLAND
1902–11.

BERNHARD LANGER

BORN ANHAUSEN, GERMANY, 27 AUGUST 1957

T HERE ARE FEW *of the great players who have not suffered from that terrible affliction known as the "yips", which manifests itself as an involuntary lunge on short putts, reducing grown men to the consistency of jelly, with accompanying suicidal tendencies, on the green. The "yips" mostly affects top players late in their careers: Ben Hogan, Sam Snead and Harry Vardon are classic examples of players so afflicted. In the case of the German player Bernhard Langer, however, it is not something that has crept up on him; he has suffered from this terrible burden through most of his golfing career.*

It is a tribute not only to the quality of the rest of Langer's game, but also to his quite remarkable tenacity and determination, that he has at least three times been able sufficiently to overcome the problem to become one of the great players in the modern game. Indeed, he has, paradoxically, become an outstanding putter.

Rewards of victory
Bernhard Langer's international status was finally confirmed when he won the US Masters in 1985. He was only the second European to wear the coveted Green Jacket.

Coming from a nation that had not even produced a good touring professional, let alone an international super-star, Langer's achievements since he turned professional in 1972 have been quite remarkable. He joined the European Tour in 1976, but made little impression until 1980. That year he found some relief from his putting problems when he came across a second-hand ladies' putter at Sunningdale during the Hennessy Cup matches. It was an Acushnet Bull's Eye, which he acquired for £5. After thickening the grip a little, Langer immediately pressed this cheap purchase into service.

The new putter worked well in the Hennessy, and Langer then reeled off a stream of rounds in the low and middle 60s, before crowning the season by

Steady and sure
Bernhard Langer won 37 European Tour Events from 1980 to 1997 and was the second leading money earner on that Tour.

Elusive title
The Open Championship still eludes the German gentleman of golf, though he has won the US Masters twice.

"Broomhandle" putter
Langer displays his unorthodox putter and putting grip which has helped him conquer the "yips".

winning the Dunlop Masters at St Pierre. The following year, with the "yips" at bay, he played in 17 events, finished in the top ten in 14 of them, and was runner-up six times. He won his own country's Open Championship, as well as the Bob Hope British Classic. He headed the European money list that year and played in the European Ryder Cup team for the first time. He established himself as a regular member of the team, making a major contribution to its success in the 1980s.

RETURN OF THE JINX

The following year the old problem with the short putts returned, although Langer remained an excellent putter from the longer distances. Again he sought refuge in a different putter, but he found that a change of grip had as much effect. Alternating between a conventional grip for the longer putts and a left-hand-below-the-right grip on the short ones, he was back in business again.

In 1984 Langer headed the European money list again, along with four European Tour event wins. From then on he concentrated on the US Tour and shocked the Americans in 1985 by brilliantly winning the US Masters. For good measure, the following week he won the Sea Pines Heritage Classic. He played much less often in Europe, but returned to carry off the British PGA Championship and the Irish Open in

1987. Despite a very limited schedule, he finished in fifth place in the European Order of Merit that year.

In 1988 the "yips" were back but Langer cured them yet again with a strange combination grip in which the right hand clamped the grip to the left forearm. It was good enough to take the German to his second victory in the Masters at Augusta in 1993 with a score of 277.

Finally Langer decided that the long-handled putter was the ultimate solution to his putting woes and he continues to be a major challenger on the European Tour with his "broomhandle" after more than two decades at the top.

In 1999 he was bidding for the tenth successive Ryder Cup appearance but finished just outside the automatic selection group.

BERNHARD LANGER

WON GERMAN OPEN 1981, 1982, 1985, 1986, 1993; US MASTERS 1985, 1993; EUROPEAN OPEN 1985, 1995; HERITAGE CLASSIC 1985. AUSTRALIAN MASTERS 1985; BRITISH PGA 1987, 1993, 1995. VOLVO MASTERS 1994. WINNER OF 37 PGA EUROPEAN TOUR EVENTS 1980–97. EUROPEAN TOUR GOLFER OF THE YEAR 1985, 1993. RYDER CUP 1981–97. WORLD CUP 1976–80, 1990–94, 1996 (INDIVIDUAL WINNER 1993). FOUR TOURS CHAMPIONSHIP 1985–87, 1989–90. DUNHILL CUP 1992 1994, 2000. SEVE BALLESTEROS TROPHY 2000. HARRY VARDON TROPHY 1981, 1984.

TOM LEHMAN

BORN AUSTIN, MINNESOTA, USA, 7 MARCH 1959

T HE TERM "OVERNIGHT success" would find no room in any appraisal of Tom Lehman's professional career. Rather "late developer" seems a more apt description. Having turned professional in 1982 he spent the next three years languishing in the lower reaches of the USPGA Tour, tried his hand in Asia, Europe and South Africa before returning to the Nike/Hogan Tour in 1990.

At the age of 33 he faced up to the USPGA Tour for a second time and this time the transformation in his fortunes was spectacular. A second and two third-place finishes marked his 1992 and 1993 seasons (and a total of $1 million), the most notable a tie for third place in the Masters in 1993. He went one better at Augusta the next year, behind José-Maria Olazábal, and in 1996 Lehman became holder of the British Open title.

US WINNER AT BRITISH OPEN

Lehman's victory at Royal Lytham and St Annes, apart from giving him tour exemptions in Britain and the USA until 2006, was also the first at that venue by an American professional (amateur Bobby Jones had won the first

Not a classic swing (right)
Lehman does not possesses a classic swing, along the lines of a Snead or an Elkington, but it is reassuringly repetitive.

USPGA Player of the Year 1996 (above)
Lehman was also briefly top of the world rankings.

time the Open was played there, in 1926), and Lehman also had the satisfaction of setting a course-record 64, in the third round, which gave him a six-stroke cushion over Nick Faldo. The Minnesotan ultimately scooped the coveted Claret Jug by three shots, from Ernie Els and Mark McCumber.

Two weeks earlier Lehman had high hopes of victory in the US Open at Oakland Hills, but was pipped over the closing holes by Steve Jones, and shared second place with Davis Love III. Such was Lehman's consistency in the US Open that for the four years from 1995 he was never worse than fifth. Lehman romped the Tour Championship later in 1996 by six strokes, and was leading money winner with a then record $1,780,159.

THOMAS EDWARD LEHMAN

WON OPEN CHAMPIONSHIP 1996; US TOUR CHAMPIONSHIP 1996. WINNER OF 5 US TOUR EVENTS 1994–2000. ARNOLD PALMER AWARD 1996. USPGA PLAYER OF THE YEAR 1996. VARDON TROPHY 1996. PRESIDENTS CUP 1996–96, 2000. RYDER CUP 1995–99. WORLD CUP 1996. DUNHILL CUP 1999–2000.

TONY LEMA

BORN OAKLAND, CALIFORNIA, USA, 25 FEBRUARY 1934; DIED 1966

I N A FATEFULLY *short career, Tony Lema showed the world that he was an extraordinary golfer. He burst into the limelight by winning three tournaments in 1962 and then, in his very first appearance in the Masters at Augusta in 1963, came within one stroke of taking Jack Nicklaus into a play-off. The following year, in his first venture overseas, he won the Open Championship.*

Easy and gifted (right)
Displaying a relaxed swing, the young Lema captivated crowds with his fluid style and easy charm.

Defending champion
Tony Lema defends his title in the Open Championship at Birkdale in 1965. He was beaten by Australian Peter Thomson.

Tony Lema had been a caddie, a Marine in the Korean War and an assistant in the pro shop at the San Francisco Golf Club before he joined the US Tour in 1959.

Starting unpromisingly, he struggled for three years before attaining his first success.

A tall, handsome man with a good-looking, long-legged swing, Tony Lema naturally caught the eye. After his first tournament victory, at Orange County in 1962, he was nicknamed "Champagne Tony", because he had promised the press he would break open a bottle when he won. The nickname suited his style of living, which was easy and expensive.

NATURAL TALENTS

In 1963, as well as almost tying Nicklaus in the Masters, he came fourth in the US money list. But it was his triumph in the Open Championship at St Andrews in 1964 that made his name a legend.

Lema arrived late for the Championship, leaving himself only one day to look over the course. He had never played golf on a links before in his life, yet he won easily, by five strokes from Jack Nicklaus.

Lema's opening round was a 73, but after that his scores were 68, 68 and 70. Lema gave much of the credit for his Open success to his caddie, Tip Anderson. He said he just did as Tip told him. But in fact he found, as did the St Andrews crowds, that he was a natural links golfer. He played the chip-and-run as to the manner born. Indeed, for his second shot on the 72nd hole he played a true Scots run-up through the Valley of Sin, instead of a pitch. And naturally he got his birdie.

It looked on the cards that Lema would retain his Open title at Royal Birkdale in 1965 when he led after two rounds, but he eventually lost out to Peter Thomson. Nevertheless, Lema had an immensely successful season in the United States in that year, coming second to Nicklaus on the money list.

Tragically, Tony Lema never lived to complete another Tour. He was killed in a plane crash, with his wife Betty alongside him, in 1966. It was one of life's bitter ironies that the aircraft crashed on a golf course, at Lansing, Illinois.

ANTHONY DAVID LEMA

WON OPEN CHAMPIONSHIP 1964. RYDER CUP 1963–65. WORLD CUP 1965.

JUSTIN LEONARD

BORN DALLAS, TEXAS, USA, 15 JUNE 1972

T HE YOUTHFUL-LOOKING *American Justin Leonard wrote his name into the record books when he won the 1997 British Open at Royal Troon. At 25, he had become the youngest Open champion since Seve Ballesteros achieved that feat at the age of 22 in 1979. However, subsequently, the Texan has struggled to come to terms with a game that, increasingly, is dominated by the bigger hitters.*

Open in his grasp
Much was expected of Leonard when he went on to win the Open at Troon in 1997 but, to date at least, he has not become the dominant force some commentators believed he would. It remains to be seen how often he can win over the 7,000-yard-plus courses that have become the norm on the Tour.

There is no doubt that his victory in the Open Championship at Troon was the highlight of Justin Leonard's career to date. It came when he mastered the bright but blustery conditions to finish three strokes ahead of Sweden's Jesper Parnevik and Northern Ireland's Darren Clarke to win the oldest, and arguably most prestigious, title in the professional world of golf.

Prior to that victory, Leonard had already earned a reputation as a golfer to watch. In 1992, at the age of 20, he had

won the US Amateur and then in 1996, during just his second full season on the USPGA Tour, he won his first Tour title at the Buick Open, a victory he replicated early in the following year when he added the Kemper Open title to his record.

In 1998, he won one of the year's richest prizes when he came from five shots behind to overtake Lee Janzen and

Testing his mettle
Although he has earned the big bucks, Leonard's mettle to win further majors remains to be tested.

win the Players Championship at Sawgrass, Florida, but in 1999 he did not add to his haul of trophies, albeit that he earned more than $2 million dollars as consolation.

NOT A POWER PLAYER
Some people were beginning to wonder if the diminutive Leonard was starting to struggle against the group of power hitters who dominate the game in the new millennium but he silenced at least some of the doubters when he bounced back to win the Westin Texas Open in the autumn of 2000, a victory that helped him to accumulate more than $2 million for the second successive season.

However, the jury is still out on Leonard, but there is no doubting the Texan's ability, nor his battling qualities.

JUSTIN CHARLES GARRET LEONARD

WON US AMATEUR 1992; OPEN CHAMPIONSHIP 1997; US PLAYERS CHAMPIONSHIP 1998. WINNER OF 5 US TOUR EVENTS 1996–2000. EISENHOWER TROPHY 1992. WALKER CUP 1993. PRESIDENTS CUP 1996–98. RYDER CUP 1997–1999. DUNHILL CUP 1997. WORLD CUP 1997

GENE LITTLER

BORN SAN DIEGO, CALIFORNIA, USA, 21 JULY 1930

A NY DISCUSSION ON *the great swings in the history of tournament golf must mention the skill of Gene Littler. Sportswriters christened him "Gene the Machine" because of the silky smoothness of his action. Some think he may have had the best swing of them all. Certainly, the great Gene Sarazen thought highly enough of it to comment early in Littler's career: "Here's a kid with a perfect swing like Sam Snead's – only better."*

Gene the Machine
Described by sportswriters as mechanical, Gene Littler's swing was the result of hours of practice.

Littler burst on the scene by winning the US Amateur in 1953, and shocked the professional game the following year by winning the San Diego Open while still an amateur. Although Littler took the glory at San Diego, runner-up Dutch Harrison took the money, which, not surprisingly, prompted Littler to turn professional the following week.

Victory meant he avoided the need to qualify as a tournament professional or for any USPGA event that year. In fact,

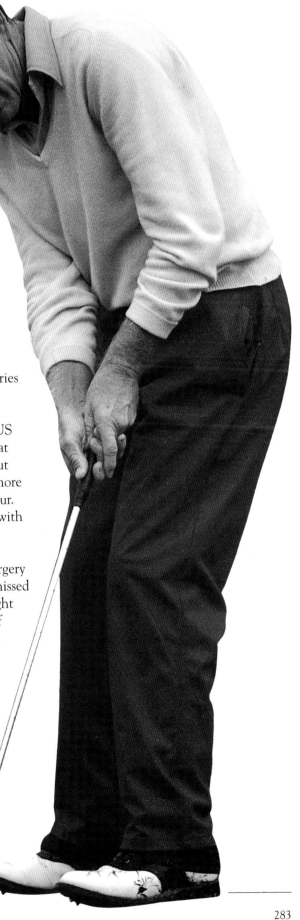

for the rest of his career he never had to qualify for a Tour event. The following year he won four times, including the Tournament of Champions, which he successfully defended over the next two years.

EARLY PROMISE UNFULFILLED

That remarkable series of three victories in a row in such a prestigious event confirmed Littler as a major figure in world golf. When he won the 1961 US Open at Oakland Hills, it seemed that many more victories would be his. But Littler lacked the fierce drive to do more than make a good living from the Tour. He preferred to spend time at home with his family and his hobby – he had a passion for classic cars.

In 1972 Littler had to undergo surgery for cancer of the lymph glands and missed almost the entire season. But he fought back and continued to earn plenty of money on the Tour well into his 50s.

EUGENE ALEX LITTLER

WON US AMATEUR 1953; US OPEN 1961.
WINNER OF 29 US TOUR EVENTS 1954–77.
WALKER CUP 1953. RYDER CUP 1961–71,
1975. BOB JONES AWARD 1973. BEN HOGAN
AWARD 1973. USPGA HALL OF FAME 1982.
WORLD GOLF HALL OF FAME 1990.

Man of courage (right)
Littler won the Ben Hogan Award in 1973 for his fightback after illness.

BOBBY LOCKE

BORN GERMISTON, SOUTH AFRICA, 20 NOVEMBER 1917; DIED 1987

B OBBY LOCKE PLAYED *golf from his earliest years: by the time he was eight, he had a handicap of 14; at nine, he played in his first competition. His handicap was already down to scratch by the age of 16. He continued to make astonishing progress, winning the Transvaal Open in 1934 and soon becoming known throughout his home country, South Africa, as "the golfing robot".*

Early days (right)
At the Transvaal Open in 1934, Locke was already cultivating the image that was to be his trademark, wearing full plus-fours and a white cap.

Locke soon dominated the golf scene in South Africa. In 1935 he won the South African Amateur, recovering from a dire situation in the semi-final to win at the 38th hole, and doing the same in the final, again winning at the 38th. The South African Open followed immediately, and Locke won the tournament by three strokes.

CAREER MOVES

At this time Locke was working for the Rand Mining House, and in 1936 they sent him to work at their London office. In Britain he played often with Leonard Crawley, one of the best amateurs of the time, who helped him a great deal. He met Harry Vardon, competed for the Harry Vardon Cup, and won easily. He lost early on in the Amateur Championship, but achieved a respectable eighth place in the Open Championship.

Returning home in 1937, he again won both the South African Amateur and Open, and in 1938, aged only 20, he turned professional. Beginning his professional career in spectacular fashion, he won the South African Open and the Irish Open in 1938, and followed up with a tenth place in the British Open.

The Second World War interrupted Locke's career, although he still managed to play some golf, despite flying many hundreds of hours in the South African Air Force. Resuming his career after the war, Locke went to the United

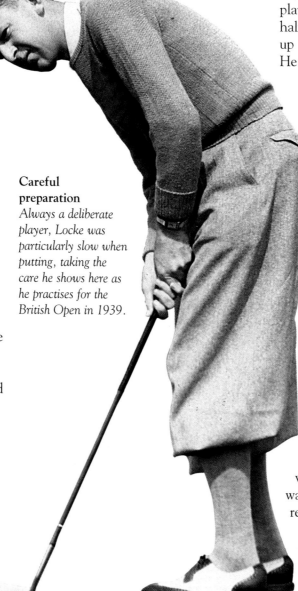

Careful preparation
Always a deliberate player, Locke was particularly slow when putting, taking the care he shows here as he practises for the British Open in 1939.

States, where his excellent results and style of play drew him a large following. He played in 59 tournaments in two and a half seasons, winning 13, finishing runner-up in ten and coming third seven times. He came third in the US Open of 1947, and also won the Canadian Open. To these achievements he added the British Open title, winning at Sandwich in 1949 after a tie with Harry Bradshaw from Ireland.

As Open Champion Locke decided to stay in Britain, so starting a row in the United States, where it was said that he had committed himself to playing in various tournaments. His sponsors were not pleased, well aware of his crowd-drawing power. The USPGA said he had violated contracts, and Locke was barred from the US Tour.

PROFESSIONAL JEALOUSY

There was more than a suspicion that his success and the jealousy of some of the Tour professionals had not helped his cause. In 1951 Locke was reinstated after opinion veered to his side and a compromise was reached, but he never played regularly in the United States again. Despite controversies off the course, Locke meanwhile retained the Open in 1950 at Troon, and he won it again in 1952. When he scored his fourth Open triumph at

St Andrews in 1957, he became the eighth player to have won the Championship four times or more. His career came to an abrupt end in 1959, when he was involved in a serious car accident.

CONTROLLED SKILL

Not always a popular player, Locke was sometimes thought to be distant on a golf course. He certainly concentrated hard, and had no time for unnecessary conversation. Some of his outwardly unemotional behaviour stemmed from the early firmness of his father, who had threatened to remove the young Bobby's golf clubs for good if he persisted in his childish tantrums.

Locke also had an unusual style that led to his hooking nearly all his shots, even his putts. It infuriated some of his biggest critics, who failed to understand that his hook was completely under control and that the ball nearly always landed on the spot he had selected for it.

Aiming right
So pronounced was the Bobby Locke hook that he aimed to the right of his target by almost 45 degrees to counteract it.

British Open win
Runner-up Harry Bradshaw (left) congratulates Locke after the South African's victory in the 1949 Open.

ARTHUR D'ARCY LOCKE

WON SOUTH AFRICAN OPEN 1935, 1937, 1938, 1939, 1940, 1946, 1950, 1951, 1955; IRISH OPEN 1938; NEW ZEALAND OPEN 1938; DUTCH OPEN 1939; CANADIAN OPEN 1947; OPEN CHAMPIONSHIP 1949, 1950, 1952, 1957; FRENCH OPEN 1952, 1953. GERMAN OPEN 1954. WORLD CUP 1953–56, 1960. HARRY VARDON TROPHY 1946, 1950, 1954. WORLD GOLF HALL OF FAME 1977.

HENRY LONGHURST

BORN BROMHAM, ENGLAND, 18 MARCH 1909; DIED 1978

W RITER AND TALENTED *amateur golfer Henry Longhurst decided in 1937 that there was room on the market for a book to be called simply* Golf. *However, it caused a furore because it told readers how to play the game and Longhurst, a university graduate and an amateur, was not supposed to gain financially from anything to do with a sport played solely for enjoyment.*

Despite the whisperings, Longhurst continued to turn out delightful golf writing – and his amateur status was not taken away by the R & A. After the Second World War he became golf writer for the *Sunday Times* and then teamed up with the BBC in its radio and television coverage of the game. His voice became equally familiar to American TV viewers.

His straightforward commentating style proved extremely popular and his delivery was much imitated. He may have been the first commentator to say: "What a dreadful shot – an awful fluff", instead of "Bad luck!"

Public office
Political ambitions took Longhurst to Parliament (1943–45).

HENRY CARPENTER LONGHURST, CBE

WON GERMAN AMATEUR 1936. RUNNER-UP SWISS AMATEUR 1928; FRENCH AMATEUR 1937. HONORARY MEMBER R & A GOLF CLUB.

Jovial figure
Longhurst was a relaxed commentator, often especially witty near the 19th hole.

NANCY LOPEZ

BORN TORRANCE, CALIFORNIA, USA, 6 JANUARY 1957

N ANCY LOPEZ *is not only an outstanding golfer, but also a personality with the sort of star appeal that draws new spectators to the game. During her first full year as a professional in 1978, when she won five consecutive tournaments, attendances for the US LPGA Tour tripled.*

Introduced to golf by her father at the age of eight, Nancy very quickly became an exceptionally good player, winning the New Mexico Women's Amateur when she was only 12. By the time she was 15 she had won the USGA Junior Girls' title, which she successfully defended for the next two years.

AMATEUR TO PROFESSIONAL

In 1975 Lopez finished runner-up in the US Women's Open while still an amateur and only 18 years old. The following year she played in the winning US team in the Espirito Santo and the Curtis Cup.

Clearly destined for the professional ranks, she joined the LPGA Tour in 1977 and soon hit a winning streak. Her first full season, in 1978, was outstandingly

Great concentration (above)
A consistent technique and a highly developed power of concentration have been the two elements at the heart of Lopez's success.

Big swing
Nancy Lopez's unconventional swing action has always been the most controversial part of her game, but it gives her great length.

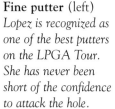

Fine putter (left)
Lopez is recognized as one of the best putters on the LPGA Tour. She has never been short of the confidence to attack the hole.

successful. She won nine tournaments, including a record five in a row, and among her victories was the LPGA title.

The whole sporting world was forced to take notice of the young lady with the rather loopy swing. Little wonder that she was named Rolex Player of the Year and Rookie of the Year. She also collected the Vare Trophy for the best tournament average and, to add to these distinctions, she was named *Golf Magazine* Player of the Year.

BREAKING RECORDS

Lopez's swing may have been strange to look at, but it was remarkably consistent. Eight wins in the following year led to another Rolex Player of the Year award. Her stroke average of 71.20 for 1979 set an all-time LPGA record, until she lowered it again in 1985 to 70.73. These successes put her at the top of the 1979 LPGA money list, with total winnings of nearly $200,000.

In 1982 Lopez married the baseball star Ray Knight, and in the following year the couple had cause for a double celebration – their first child was born and Nancy's total prize money rose past $1 million, after only five years playing golf on the professional circuit. Lopez treated herself to generous time off during this period, but despite playing only a limited schedule she won the Uniden LPGA Invitational and the Chevrolet World Championship of Women's Golf in 1984.

This was a foretaste of further triumphs that lay ahead. In 1985 she took the LPGA Tour by storm, finishing in the top ten in 21 of the 25 events in which she played. She won five times, including a second LPGA Championship and the Portland Ping Championship, which was

finally decided only by a tense sudden-death play-off against Lori Garbacz. Nancy's winnings for the year totalled more than $416,000, the first time that the $400,000 mark had been passed on the LPGA Tour. She set a further record in 1985 by winning the Henredon Classic with a score of 268 – an extraordinary 20 under par. Her total of 25 birdies over the four rounds of the event was also a record.

In 1987 the birth of Nancy's second child restricted her competitive appearances, but she soon returned and was part of the victorious US team in the inaugural Solheim Cup against the Europeans. In 1997 she won her

48th career title and also finished second in the US Women's Open. She was the first woman in US Women's Open history to shoot four rounds in the 60s but still lost by one stroke to Alison Nicholas. Though she has won three LPGA titles and career earnings over $5 million, the US Women's Open still eludes her.

SWINGING ACROSS THE LINE

Nancy Lopez is one of the outstanding stars of women's golf and one of the most popular players in the game, but her technique has always been a subject of considerable controversy. She has an unusual swing that some purists contend has several faults. Her action takes the club very much to the outside, with a pronounced bowing of the left wrist, but she attacks the ball strongly from the inside on the downswing and hits the ball extremely far. This length, combined with a delicate touch, a marvellous putting stroke and an aggressive approach to the game, made her a formidable player.

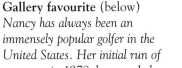

Gallery favourite (below)
Nancy has always been an immensely popular golfer in the United States. Her initial run of successes in 1978 drew a whole new public to women's golf and she has kept her appeal down the years.

NANCY MARIE LOPEZ

WON LPGA CHAMPIONSHIP 1978, 1985, 1989. WINNER OF 48 LPGA TOUR EVENTS 1978–97. CURTIS CUP 1976. ESPIRITO SANTO TROPHY 1976. VARE TROPHY 1978, 1979, 1985. SOLHEIM CUP 1990. LPGA PLAYER OF THE YEAR 1978, 1979, 1985, 1988. LPGA HALL OF FAME 1987. WORLD GOLF HALL OF FAME 1989. BOB JONES AWARD 1998

Rising standards
Lopez won 17 of her first 50 professional tournaments, and her example has since inspired other women golfers to raise their game, making victory ever more difficult to achieve. She has never lost the will to win, however.

DAVIS LOVE III

BORN CHARLOTTE, NORTH CAROLINA, USA, 13 APRIL 1964

W HEN FIRING ON *on all cylinders – as he was when he won the 1997 USPGA Championship at Winged Foot – there are few better golfers to watch than Davis Love III. He has the same sort of powerful but graceful swing that Tom Weiskopf used to have but, like the 1973 British Open champion, a question remains as to whether he has won as many major titles as he should have done.*

The records show that Davis Love III has won a string of USPGA Tour titles since he emerged on Tour in 1986. He has also done well enough to represent America in five World Cups, four Ryder Cups and four Presidents Cups, but there is still debate over whether he has achieved quite as much as his talent suggests he should have.

Anyone who watched Love demolish the field while finishing five strokes ahead of Justin Leonard at the 1997 USPGA Championship at Winged Foot would have wagered significant sums of money that it would be the first of many majors Love would win but, to date, he has still to repeat that success in the four championships that matter most.

Love titles (right)
Love won his first US Tour title at the 1987 MCI Heritage Classic, an event he has won twice more since, and by 2001 had added 14 more victories to his name, including individual honours at the 1995 World Cup.

World Cup (below)
From 1992–95 Love teamed up with friend and compatriot Fred Couples to win four successive World Cups.

USPGA champion
(right and opposite)
Love claims what is still his only major title – the USPGA trophy in 1997.

Until his victory in the AT&T Pebble Beach Pro-Am in January 2001 he won just once in America, (1998, MCI Classic) and once in Japan (1998, Chunichi Crowns), a rather meagre haul for such a naturally gifted golfer.

Love III was taught golf by his father, Davis Love II, who was tragically killed in a plane crash in 1988. Young Davis learned well, winning the North and South Amateur and representing the US in the 1985 Walker Cup before turning professional later that year. During that Walker Cup at Pine Valley Peter McEvoy, the GB & I player at the wrong end of a five and three drubbing in the singles from Love, said that he thought the American would make a major impact on the game.

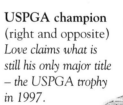

DAVIS MILTON LOVE III

WON HERITAGE CLASSIC 1987, 1991–92, 1998; US PLAYERS CHAMPIONSHIP 1992; USPGA 1997. WINNER OF 13 US TOUR EVENTS 1987–98. WALKER CUP 1985. DUNHILL CUP 1992. WORLD CUP 1992–95, 1997 (INDIVIDUAL WINNER 1995). RYDER CUP 1993–99. PRESIDENTS CUP 1994–2000.

SANDY LYLE

BORN SHREWSBURY, ENGLAND, 9 FEBRUARY 1958

A LTHOUGH BORN IN *England, Sandy Lyle adopted his father's Scottish nationality after he turned professional in 1977. When he won the Open at Sandwich in 1985, he was the first Scot to win it for more than 60 years and the first Briton for 16 years. When he won the US Masters in 1988, he was the first Briton ever to win the event. And he won both Majors in his own way – calmly, casually and cheerfully, with the odd wayward shot only underlining the sheer brilliance of the rest of his game.*

Kilted master (right)
As US Masters champion, Lyle returned to Augusta to defend his title in 1989 proudly wearing his kilt with the Green Jacket.

Swing changes
Sandy Lyle has worked hard to find a method that would regain his form.

Lyle was a junior champion at 14 and English Amateur Strokeplay Champion at 17. He won this title again at the age of 19, played in the Walker Cup and then turned professional. Two years later he was in the Ryder Cup team.

It was towards the end of 1977 that he joined the professional ranks, and early in 1978 he won his first tournament, the Nigerian Open, achieving a record-breaking round of 61 in the process. He went on to win

Mild elation (below)
Lyle had an agonizing wait, while his rivals slowly finished their rounds, before he could lift the familiar claret jug trophy at the 1985 British Open at Royal St George's, Sandwich.

all around the world, in Europe, Japan, Hawaii and the mainland United States. Lyle won the Open Championship at Royal St George's, Sandwich, in 1985 with rounds of 68, 71, 73 and 70, beating Payne Stewart of the United States by just a single stroke. In difficult situations, Lyle's calmness ensured success, again also most notably with his bunker shot on the 18th at the 1988 US Masters. In the three years after his victory in the Open Championship in 1985, he won five times on the US Tour, including his success in the US Masters at Augusta in 1988. In the autumn of that year he beat his constant rival, Nick Faldo, in the final of the World Matchplay.

Lyle's game went into a slump in the 1990s and although there were signs of improvement in 1993, he was not selected to play in the European Ryder Cup team that year.

IRONING OUT HIS SWING
Powerfully built and 6ft 1in (1.85m) tall, Sandy Lyle has always been a great iron player – but with a slightly suspect swing. As Seve Ballesteros said of him: "When he is good he is the best and there is no one to touch him, but when he is bad he is almost the worst." Lyle remains a gallery favourite around the world and, for a while, was easily spotted thanks to a major swing change which involved taking the club to the top of the swing and then stopping completely before the downswing. It gave him the best form for some years.

ALEXANDER WALTER BARR LYLE, MBE

WON EUROPEAN OPEN 1979; OPEN CHAMPIONSHIP 1985; US PLAYERS CHAMPIONSHIP 1987; US MASTERS 1988; WORLD MATCHPLAY 1988. VOLVO MASTERS 1992. WINNER OF 17 PGA EUROPEAN TOUR EVENTS 1979–92. WALKER CUP 1977. RYDER CUP 1979–87. WORLD CUP 1979–80, 1987 (INDIVIDUAL WINNER 1980). DUNHILL CUP 1985–90, 1992. FOUR TOURS CHAMPIONSHIP 1985–87. HARRY VARDON TROPHY 1979, 1980, 1985.

ALISTER MACKENZIE

BORN WAKEFIELD, ENGLAND, 30 AUGUST 1870; DIED 1934

D R ALISTER MACKENZIE *was one of the true giants of golf-course architecture, making his reputation in the United States after the First World War. Surprisingly, he was never a professional golf player – indeed, he was unique among the great course designers in not being a very good player at all. Yet his contribution to the game was outstanding, consisting of a number of the world's greatest courses, including Cypress Point in California and Augusta National, the home of the US Masters.*

In the second half of the nineteenth century many more people were attracted to the game of golf, partly because of the arrival of the gutta percha ball, which had replaced the feathery and made the game easier and less expensive.

As golf spread rapidly from Scotland, where it had its natural roots, to England and then to every corner of the world, more golf courses had to be built, and built quickly. Thus the profession of golf-course architect was born. Of the many who have been involved in this relatively young profession, few have had more influence than Dr Alister MacKenzie.

ART OF CAMOUFLAGE
Although he was born in England, Alister MacKenzie was definitely a Scot by nationality, with an enthusiasm for the game of golf. Training initially as a doctor, he served as a surgeon with the Somerset Regiment in the Boer War in South Africa, but his interests were already elsewhere. He was fascinated by the art of camouflage at which the Boers were particularly adept. It was his eye for

Course doctor
Alister MacKenzie trained in medicine, but later changed his profession to become one of the world's top course designers.

A new ball game
The introduction of the gutta percha ball encouraged more people to take up golf and so increased the need for courses.

detail and skill at disguising pitfalls that he was to put to good use on his return to Scotland, when he became increasingly involved in golf-course design.

MacKenzie's career in course design blossomed after he met Harry S. Colt, then a prominent designer, in 1907. Together they designed the course at Alwoodley, near Leeds, where MacKenzie was secretary. With the outbreak of war in 1914, he served not as a medical man, but as an expert in camouflage.

BUILDING A REPUTATION
After the First World War MacKenzie concentrated his energies on course design, a subject on which he had clear views. He wanted all artificial features to look natural, every hole to have its own character, and sufficient variety to require the use of every type of club. With an increasing number of courses built to his designs – especially in the north of

England – his name soon spread across the world. His greatest courses include the West course at Royal Melbourne in Australia and Tiritangi in New Zealand.

His reputation was assured after he built the famous Cypress Point course on the Monterey Peninsula in California in 1928. It was after playing this marvellous MacKenzie layout that Bobby Jones invited the Doctor to help him build Augusta National. Unfortunately MacKenzie did not live to see the course completed – he was able to see the finished construction work but not the course fully covered in grass. He did not know that Augusta National, as home to the US Masters, was to become one of the most famous courses in the world.

DR ALISTER MACKENZIE

DESIGNER OF AUGUSTA NATIONAL, CYPRESS POINT, ROYAL MELBOURNE, AND MANY OTHER COURSES WORLDWIDE.

GRAHAM MARSH

BORN KALGOORLIE, WESTERN AUSTRALIA, 14 JANUARY 1944

MANY PEOPLE ARE *surprised when they learn that Australian Graham Marsh, brother of the famous Test cricketer Rodney Marsh, has won over 60 tour events worldwide, from Scotland to Thailand, from Denmark to Japan, and from Australia to India. A success too on the US Seniors' Tour, Marsh won the 1997 US Senior Open.*

GRAHAM VIVIAN MARSH MBE

WON HERITAGE CLASSIC 1977; WORLD MATCHPLAY 1977; BRITISH MASTERS 1979; EUROPEAN OPEN 1981; AUSTRALIAN MASTERS 1982; US SENIOR OPEN 1997; THE TRADITION 1999. DUNHILL CUP 1985. FOUR TOURS CHAMPIONSHIP 1985–88, 1991.

It was after seeing Marsh play in the Australian Amateur in 1967 that Peter Thomson urged him to turn professional. In 1970 Marsh travelled to Europe, where he won the Swiss Open. Soon after, he began his extraordinary career in Japan, winning 20 tournaments there by 1990.

In 1977 Marsh won the World Matchplay title at Wentworth, beating Ray Floyd five and three, after defeating Hale Irwin seven and six in the semi-final. Never a player to produce high drama, this modest, cheerful man has shown the world the value of a simple method, consistency and a persistent nature which he has now taken to the US Seniors Tour.

Lasting success
In a career that has already spanned more than two decades, Marsh now looks to the Seniors' golf for new successes.

PHIL MICKELSON

BORN SAN DIEGO, CALIFORNIA, USA, 16 JUNE 1970

AMATEURS TRIUMPH IN USPGA *tournaments at much the same rate as blue moons appear in the sky. Scott Verplank's 1985 win in the Western Open was the first in 31 years, but six years later Phil Mickelson, then a student at Arizona State University and the reigning US amateur champion, did it again.*

Amateur success (below) *As a young left-hander, Phil Mickelson was an acclaimed US Amateur Champion.*

To much local acclaim Phil Mickelson won the Tucson Northern Telecom Open – and a year later he began what was to become one of US golf's most glittering careers.

FAMILY TIES

Mickelson had attracted much media attention at the championship by claiming he would leave the course if his wife went into labour so that he could attend the birth of their first child. As it happened, their daughter Amanda was born the day after the final round.

He is right-handed in everything he does except golf and attributes this seeming anomaly to the fact that he mirror-imaged his father when he was child. Phil's father was a keen player and when he practised he made his son stand in front of him so that he could keep an eye on him. Phil had a golf club in his hands from the age of 18 months and although his father tried to turn him round to play the more conventional way he kept going back to the mirror image of his father's swing.

SUPERB SHORT GAME

Mickelson's short game is the envy of almost every player on the USPGA Tour. When he was six or seven years old the family had a chipping green set up in the back yard and Phil would practise for hours on days when his parents couldn't take him to the golf course. He credits his creativity around the greens to those hours of practice when he moved all over the back yard to hit chip shots because he became bored hitting the same shot all the time.

PHILIP ALFRED MICKELSON

WON US AMATEUR 1990; WORLD SERIES OF GOLF 1996; US TOUR CHAMPIONSHIP 2000. WINNER OF 17 US TOUR TITLES 1991–2000. WALKER CUP 1989–91. PRESIDENTS CUP 1994–2000. RYDER CUP 1995–99. DUNHILL CUP 1996.

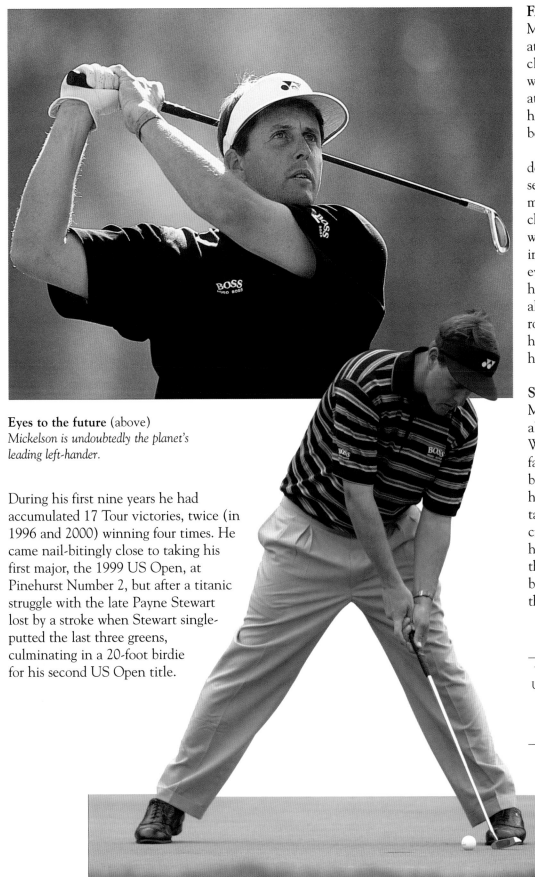

Eyes to the future (above)
Mickelson is undoubtedly the planet's leading left-hander.

During his first nine years he had accumulated 17 Tour victories, twice (in 1996 and 2000) winning four times. He came nail-bitingly close to taking his first major, the 1999 US Open, at Pinehurst Number 2, but after a titanic struggle with the late Payne Stewart lost by a stroke when Stewart single-putted the last three greens, culminating in a 20-foot birdie for his second US Open title.

Serious challenger (left) *Mickelson seemed to be one of the few players in the world who could offer Tiger Woods (four years his junior) any sort of credible challenge as the new century unfolded.*

CARY MIDDLECOFF

BORN HALLS, TENNESSEE, USA, 6 JANUARY 1921; DIED 1998

D URING THE 1955 US Masters, Dr Cary Middlecoff rolled in an 80ft (24m) putt on the 13th green of the final round for an eagle; he went on to win the coveted Green Jacket by a record seven strokes from Ben Hogan. It was perhaps the crowning moment of a very successful professional career for the tall dentist from Tennessee.

Middlecoff won his state Amateur four times in a row from 1940 before joining the professional ranks in 1947. Two years later he was the US Open Champion. From 1949 to 1956, "The Doc" was never out of the top-ten money winners on the US Tour. His best year was 1955 when he won the Masters and five other Tour events.

SLOW BUT SURE
Middlecoff was noted for the slowness of his play, cautiously setting himself up for each shot. It was a style that often paid dividends. He won the US Open again in 1956, and the next year narrowly lost it in an 18-hole play-off with Dick Mayer.

This was not the only notable play-off in Middlecoff's career. In 1949, in the Motor City Open, he tied with Lloyd Mangrum on 273 and the match went to sudden-death. It turned out to be the longest sudden-death play-off in USPGA history, lasting for 11 holes before play was halted because night was falling. Middlecoff and Mangrum shared the title and the $5,000 first prize.

DR CARY MIDDLECOFF

WON US OPEN 1949, 1956;
US MASTERS 1955. WINNER OF 40 US
TOUR EVENTS 1945–61. WORLD CUP 1959.
RYDER CUP 1953–55, 1959. VARDON
TROPHY 1956. USPGA HALL OF FAME
1974. WORLD GOLF HALL OF FAME 1986.

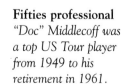

Fifties professional
"Doc" Middlecoff was a top US Tour player from 1949 to his retirement in 1961.

JOHNNY MILLER

BORN SAN FRANCISCO, CALIFORNIA, USA, 29 APRIL 1947

T ALL, BLOND AND handsome, Johnny Miller showed early that he had the makings of a golfing superstar. In 1966 he went to San Francisco intending to be a caddie in the US Open, but played instead and finished eighth. Turning professional in 1969, he was soon challenging Nicklaus for the unofficial title of world's leading golfer, winning eight US tournaments in 1974. Yet he failed to sustain his form. By 1978 he had dropped to 111th in the US money list.

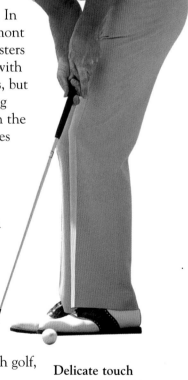

At his peak Johnny Miller was a formidable performer in the Majors. In 1973 he won the US Open at Oakmont with a final round of 63. At the Masters in 1975 he nearly caught Nicklaus with a 65 and a 66 in the last two rounds, but lost out by one stroke. The following year he travelled to Britain and won the Open at Royal Birkdale by six strokes from Nicklaus and Ballesteros.

SHORT OF THE BEST
Then, quite suddenly, the magic seemed to vanish. Miller was to win again, but never to dominate. Between 1980 and 1988 he won six tournaments in the United States – not a bad record, but not magnificent either. What had happened? Quite early on in his career, Miller said that he became bored with too much golf, even when he was winning.

A Mormon with deeply held beliefs, he became much more interested in his family – he has six children – than in his golf. When he lost his winning swing, he did not feel he had either the time or

Delicate touch
At the height of his powers in the 1970s, Johnny Miller had a magical touch with the putter that brought him the highest prizes.

Rivals at the top
Johnny Miller (left) and Jack Nicklaus were victorious partners in the 1983 Chrysler Team International. In the mid-1970s Miller was hailed as the "new Nicklaus", but his career did not sustain the same heights as his great rival.

In control (below)
Miller combined elegance with power and control.

the desire to recapture it. In his view, there were greater things in life than triumphs on the golf course. He still accumulated prize money – in 1984 his career earnings passed the $2 million mark. But money was not everything for him either.

Miller would prefer to be remembered for his 63 in the US Open at Oakmont, with four straight birdies to begin with and five more later, or for his final 66 at Royal Birkdale in 1976, with its par-birdie-eagle mid-round. Today he is best known as an outspoken US TV golf commentator.

JOHN LAURENCE MILLER

WON US OPEN 1973; OPEN CHAMPIONSHIP 1976. WINNER OF 24 US TOUR EVENTS 1971–94. LEADING MONEY WINNER 1974. WORLD CUP 1973, 1975, 1980 (INDIVIDUAL WINNER 1973, 1975). RYDER CUP 1975, 1981. USPGA PLAYER OF THE YEAR 1974. WORLD GOLF HALL OF FAME 1996.

ABE MITCHELL

BORN EAST GRINSTEAD, ENGLAND, 19 JANUARY 1887; DIED 1947

A BE MITCHELL HAS *always been rated the best golfer never to have won the Open Championship. He had particularly large hands and struck the ball with great power, together with a certain elegance. Almost every amateur who saw him wanted to copy his style – including Samuel Ryder, the founder of the Ryder Cup.*

Ryder hired Abe Mitchell as his private tutor and, in 1926, watched him lead a British team to victory – 13$\frac{1}{2}$ matches to 1$\frac{1}{2}$ – against a team of American professionals. Sam Ryder instantly decided to put up a solid gold trophy for future international matches.

Mitchell should have captained the first Ryder Cup team to sail for the United States in 1927, but he fell ill with appendicitis. He played in 1929, 1931 and 1933, however, winning four of his six matches in the tournaments.

Golf writer Bernard Darwin attributed Mitchell's relative lack of success to his peaceful nature, commenting: "He would rather be in his back garden."

HENRY ABRAHAM MITCHELL

WON PGA MATCHPLAY 1919, 1920, 1929. RYDER CUP 1929–33.

Quiet genius
Abe was a gentle soul, but a powerful hitter.

In the English rain (below)
Mitchell plays himself out of a damp lie during the Amateur Championship of 1912.

COLIN MONTGOMERIE

BORN GLASGOW, SCOTLAND, 23 JUNE 1963

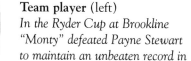

A S A YOUNGSTER *Colin Montgomerie took to golf easily: after all he was Scottish, his father was to become secretary of the Royal Troon Golf Club, and as a boy he displayed a rare talent. Even a brief stint working in a biscuit factory and studying Business and Law in the United States could not dissuade him from a life in golf.*

In 1987 he won the Scottish Amateur Championship, and the next year was Rookie of the Year, finishing 92nd in the Order of Merit with more than £60,000 in prize money. The following year he doubled his earnings and began a steady advance up the Order of Merit table. In 1990 he was 14th and by the time he had won his second Volvo Tour event, the Scandinavian Masters, he was fourth. Although he did not win an event in 1992, Montgomerie finished third in the Order of Merit, runner-up in no fewer than seven events and established himself as one of the new European superstars.

But 1993 was to prove the big year for him. On the last day of the Heineken Open in Holland, "Monty" shot a brave 69 into the teeth of a gale. There was a lightning strike as he walked onto the final green, but the Scot holed out for a brilliant victory. An equally important victory was at the Volvo Masters at Valderrama where he sealed the number one spot in the 1993 Volvo Order of Merit.

ORDERS OF MERIT

From that point on Monty dominated the European Order of Merit through the remainder of the decade. In 1999 he won an unprecedented seventh successive Volvo Order of Merit, a record unlikely to be equalled, let alone beaten.

"Monty" was voted the Asprey and Garrard Golfer of the Year for the fourth time in five years and won five European titles as well as the World Matchplay at Wentworth. It was a remarkable year in which he also won the Standard Life Loch Lomond in his native Scotland and successfully defended the Volvo PGA Championship. His European earnings were a record £1,302,057. He was finally pipped as Europe's number one at the end of the 2000 season by Lee Westwood.

Team player (left)
In the Ryder Cup at Brookline "Monty" defeated Payne Stewart to maintain an unbeaten record in five Ryder Cup singles, 1991–99.

Elusive US Open (right)
Montgomerie finished second twice to Ernie Els in the 1994 and 1997 US Open Championships.

COLIN STUART MONTGOMERIE
MBE

WON VOLVO MASTERS 1993. ANDERSON CONSULTING WORLD CHAMPIONSHIP 1997; VOLVO PGA 1998–2000; WORLD MATCHPLAY 1999. WINNER OF 24 EUROPEAN TOUR EVENTS 1989–2000. HARRY VARDON TROPHY 1993–99. EUROPEAN TOUR GOLFER OF THE YEAR 1995–97, 1999. EISENHOWER TROPHY 1984–86. WALKER CUP 1985–87. DUNHILL CUP 1988, 1991–98, 2000. WORLD CUP 1988, 1991–93, 1997–99 (INDIVIDUAL WINNER 1997). RYDER CUP 1991–99. FOUR TOURS CHAMPIONSHIP 1991.

Honoured UK player (left)
Montgomerie was honoured for his services to golf with an MBE, which he received from Her Majesty the Queen at an investiture in Buckingham Palace in 1998.

US problems (right)
Unsavoury gallery behaviour in the US has marred his attempts to secure a major US title.

OLD TOM MORRIS

BORN ST ANDREWS, SCOTLAND, 16 JUNE 1821; DIED 1908

O LD TOM MORRIS *was, by the last two decades of the nineteenth century, the most famous golfer alive. Four times winner of the Open Championship, he became an institution in his home town of St Andrews. His advice was much sought after, both as a player and as a designer of new courses. Even after he finally gave up competing in the Open when he was 75, he never lost his enthusiasm for the ancient game.*

Tom Morris played golf at St Andrews from his early childhood. At the age of 18, he was apprenticed to Allan Robertson to make feathery balls. The two were also partners on the golf course. Their most famous victory was a dramatic win against the Dunn twins over three greens in 1849.

Morris and Robertson eventually quarrelled over the introduction of the guttie ball, and in 1851 Tom moved to Prestwick as greenkeeper. There he played a part in arranging the first Open Championship in 1860 and participated in the tournament, starting as favourite but finishing runner-up to Willie Park Snr. Tom Morris went on to win the Championship four times, the last in 1867 when he was 46 years old.

COMING HOME

In 1865 Old Tom was brought back to St Andrews by the Royal & Ancient Club as greenkeeper. He subsequently became professional to the R & A, a post he held until his death. He was also busy as a golf-course designer.

Old Tom died in 1908 at the age of 87, never recovering after falling down stairs at the New Golf Club in St Andrews. At his funeral great crowds gathered to mourn a man loved by all, generous by nature and gentle in character.

Sporting family (right)
As his youngest son, also called Tom, began to show exceptional golfing talent, father Tom became known as Old Tom. This postcard is just one of the hundreds of printed memorabilia that pay tribute to the outstanding family talent.

Old faithful (left)
The iron-headed putting cleek with a hickory shaft that belonged to Tom Morris.

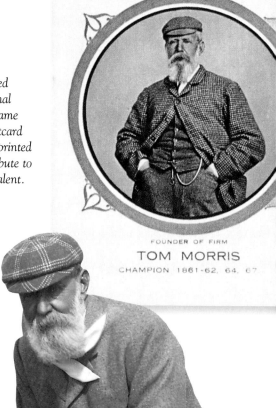

FOUNDER OF FIRM
TOM MORRIS
CHAMPION 1861-62, 64, 67.

TOM MORRIS SNR

WON OPEN CHAMPIONSHIP 1861, 1862, 1864, 1867.
HONORARY PROFESSIONAL ROYAL & ANCIENT GOLF CLUB.
WORLD GOLF HALL OF FAME 1976.

Striking oils (below)
Old Tom Morris, 81, as painted by Sir George Reid. Morris is said to have commented, when shown the finished painting, "Well, the cap's like mine".

Grand old man (above)
Old Tom Morris continued to play golf even into his 80s.

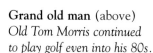

YOUNG TOM MORRIS

BORN ST ANDREWS, SCOTLAND, 20 APRIL 1851; DIED 1875

W HEN YOUNG TOM Morris was 13 years old he went with his famous father to a tournament on the North Inch at Perth in Scotland. Because of his background he was not allowed to enter as an amateur, but was matched against a local youngster who was rather older and considered to be a coming champion. The local boy lost and Young Tom Morris was on the road to immortality.

SON OF FOUNDER
TOM MORRIS, JUNR.
(YOUNG TOMMY)
CHAMPION 1868-69, 70, 72.
WINNER OF CHAMPIONSHIP BELT AND 1st
CHAMPIONSHIP MEDAL
RECORD ST ANDREWS COURSE 1869 77 STROKES

Championship Belt (below)
In 1860 Prestwick Golf Club paid £25 for a red leather belt, decorated in silver, as a trophy for the Open. After winning the Open three times consecutively, Young Tom Morris retained the Belt in 1870.

Young talent (above)
Young Tom was broad-shouldered, had strong hands and played quickly and powerfully. But there was a sensitivity that gave his short game great accuracy – he was one of the best putters ever.

Handing on (below)
In a career lasting less than ten years, Young Tom Morris eclipsed his father as a golfer. Here the two men are photographed together not long before Young Tom's tragically early death in 1875.

Shortly after the match in Perth, Young Tom won a tournament at Montrose and then, at 16, tied with Willie Park Snr, already three times Open Champion, and Bob Andrew, another established player, at Carnoustie. Morris won the play-off.

In the same year of 1867, Young Tom made his second appearance in the Open Championship, finishing fourth. He won the tournament the following year, recording the first hole-in-one in the history of the Open. When he repeated the victory in 1869 and again in 1870, he won the Open Championship Belt outright under the rules of the competition. With no trophy to be played for, the tournament lapsed in 1871.

UNMATCHED SUCCESS
When the Championship was reintroduced the following year, the present trophy, the claret jug, was put up for competition. Young Tom won again to make it four victories in a row, a feat that has never been matched since.

Young Tom was runner-up in 1874 at Musselburgh, but this was to be his last Open Championship. When his wife died in childbirth

in 1875 Tom was inconsolable. He died a few months later, many believed of a broken heart, aged only 24. Young Tom Morris was by far the outstanding golfer of his era and one of the greatest ever seen.

TOM MORRIS JNR

WON OPEN CHAMPIONSHIP 1868, 1869, 1870, 1872.
WORLD GOLF HALL OF FAME 1975.

Death of a young hopeful
A memorial to Tom was erected by his parents in the grounds of at St Andrews Cathedral.

KEL NAGLE

BORN SYDNEY, NEW SOUTH WALES, AUSTRALIA, 21 DECEMBER 1920

S TARTING AS A *professional's assistant at the age of 15, Kel Nagle had to wait until well after the Second World War to become a touring professional. This delay may have been the making of him. When young he had been a long, wild hitter, but in maturity learned patience and calmness.*

In his 30s Nagle built up a fine winning record in New Zealand and Australia. Then he came to Britain and became internationally known by winning the Centenary Open at St Andrews in 1960. He started with a 69 and a 67. A third-round 71 put him in the lead. Arnold Palmer was four strokes behind but fought back to two behind and

Centenary winner
Nagle brandishes the Open jug and a replica presented specially for his Centenary victory.

then, as Nagle prepared to putt on the tricky 17th, Palmer birdied the 18th. A tremendous cheer went up, but Nagle calmly sank a putt of 10ft (3m) for a par 4. A safe four on the last gave him victory.

In 1965 Nagle's steadiness nearly won him the US Open. He tied with Gary Player but lost the play-off. Passing 50, he won the 1971 World Seniors, a victory repeated in 1975.

Kel Nagle's record proves that good golf requires accuracy more than length, and that accuracy, once acquired, tends to last.

KELVIN DAVID GEORGE NAGLE

WON NEW ZEALAND OPEN 1957, 1958, 1962, 1964, 1967, 1968, 1969; AUSTRALIAN OPEN 1959; OPEN CHAMPIONSHIP 1960; FRENCH OPEN 1961; CANADIAN OPEN 1964. WORLD SENIORS 1971, 1975. PGA SENIORS 1971, 1973, 1975. WORLD CUP 1954–55, 1958–62, 1965–66. HONORARY MEMBER R & A GOLF CLUB.

TOMMY NAKAJIMA

BORN KIRYU CITY, JAPAN, 20 OCTOBER 1954

I T IS A HAPPY *circumstance that Tsuneyuki "Tommy" Nakajima is an oriental philosopher of some experience, as well as a truly fine golfer. A successful star in his own country both as amateur and professional, but he has never won a top tournament abroad. He has come close but never managed to make a breakthrough.*

Golf philosopher
Tommy Nakajima plays beautifully – in Japan. He was leading money winner four times and once won nine tournaments in a year.

In 1978, at the Open Championship at St Andrews, he was doing well until he putted his third shot on the 17th into the notorious Road Bunker. It took him four shots to get the ball out and he finished the hole bravely with a nine. Many now know the bunker as "The Sands of Nakajima". At Turnberry in 1986, he was only a stroke behind Greg Norman at the start of the final round but three-putted the 1st green, then bogeyed the 3rd while Norman birdied. Then in the World

Matchplay he played superbly, only to lose to Sandy Lyle at the 38th hole. In the 1987 US Open at Olympic, his ball stuck in a tree and it took him several shots to get it out. Japan remains his happier hunting ground.

TSUNEYUKI NAKAJIMA

WON JAPAN AMATEUR 1973; JAPAN PGA 1977, 1983–84, 1986, 1992; JAPAN OPEN 1985–86, 1990–91. FOUR TOURS CHAMPIONSHIP 1986–88. DUNHILL CUP 1986. LEADER JAPAN ORDER OF MERIT 1982–83, 1985–86. WORLD CUP 1996.

BYRON NELSON

BORN FORT WORTH, TEXAS, USA, 4 FEBRUARY 1912

BYRON NELSON *was born in the same year and district as Ben Hogan, and for several years they were caddie colleagues. But Nelson found his "secret" before Hogan and had retired by the time Ben reached his peak. At his best, in 1945, Nelson scored 11 consecutive US Tour wins.*

Nelson's first few years on the circuit were unsuccessful. In 1935 he finished the US Open at Oakmont with an appalling total of 317. It was almost literally too much, but after many hours of practice and experimentation, Nelson discovered his own personal best swing. He won the Masters for the first time in 1937, the US Open in 1939, and the USPGA in 1940.

Wartime golf
Nelson putts at Inverness, Ohio, in a War Bond Invitation event in 1944. His record would have been even better had war not disrupted his career.

He won the Masters again in 1942, just before it was halted because of the Second World War. A Tour of sorts continued, and in 1944 he won 13 out of 23 events.

After the war ended in 1945, Nelson had his greatest year. He won 18 of the 30 tournaments he entered, finishing second in seven others. His scoring average was 68.3 per round. In strokeplay tournaments, his average lead over those who came second was 6.3 strokes – a still unbeaten

In retirement
At the age of 74 Byron Nelson was still enjoying his golf, far from the pressures of top competition.

record. In 1946 he won the first two tournaments and was runner-up in the US Open after a play-off, but he realized he was no longer in peak condition. In 1955 he won the French Open on a vacation trip to Europe, but that was the end. He returned to his Texas ranch and attended tournaments only as a TV commentator.

What was his "secret"? He stood close to the ball, bending to allow his arms to hang freely. He restricted his hip turn and started back with a slight lateral sway. He restricted the "roll of the wrists" coming into impact and kept the back of his left hand square to the arc from 30in (75cm) before impact to 30in after. And he kept his left arm straight. It certainly worked for him.

JOHN BYRON NELSON JNR

WON US MASTERS 1937, 1942; US OPEN 1939; USPGA 1940, 1945. WINNER OF 52 US TOUR EVENTS 1935–51. RYDER CUP 1937, 1947 (NON-PLAYING CAPTAIN 1965). VARDON TROPHY 1939. USPGA HALL OF FAME 1953. WORLD GOLF HALL OF FAME 1974. BOB JONES AWARD 1974.

Touring for MacGregor (below)
The MacGregor Golf Company, a leading manufacturer of clubs and balls in the United States, employed Nelson as a touring pro.

Byron Nelson
MacGregor Advisory Staff

LARRY NELSON

BORN FORT PAYNE, ALABAMA, USA, 10 SEPTEMBER 1947

S TEADY, CONSISTENT, UNDRAMATIC, *Larry Nelson is unique among top golfers in one respect: he learned his golf from a book and did not even hit a golf ball until he was 21. It was a mere five years later, in 1974, that he won his way on to the American Tour, qualifying through his performance in a tournament that was only the second four-round event in which he had ever played.*

A naturally self-effacing character, Nelson made only a modest impact at the top level until 1979. In that year he won two tournaments on the US Tour and finished second in the US Order of Merit, accumulating $281,000 in prize money.

Nelson never achieved such a high position in the Order of Merit again, but he scored some outstanding successes. He won the USPGA Championship in 1981, beating Fuzzy Zoeller by four strokes at the Atlanta Athletic Club, and two years later he achieved victory in the US Open at Oakmont. Seven strokes adrift after two rounds, a third-round 65 left him only one behind the leaders, Tom Watson and

Severiano Ballesteros. The last round developed into a straight fight between Nelson and Watson. The two men were tied when Nelson sank a 60ft (18m) putt that settled the issue at the 16th.

He won the USPGA Championship again in 1987 and registered his tenth US Tour victory the following year. But it is in the Ryder Cup that Nelson's record of success has been most dramatic.

FIVE STRAIGHT WINS

In 1979, at the Greenbrier Club, Nelson won all five Ryder Cup matches in which he played, beating young Seve Ballesteros by three and two in the singles. At Walton Heath in 1981 he again came through, winning all four of his games. He finally lost a Ryder Cup match for the first time at Muirfield Village in 1987. He was then 40 years old.

Larry Nelson grips the club as Ben Hogan advised, stands like Hogan, concentrates on swinging on-plane and has his left wrist bowed out through impact. With 11 US Senior Tour wins (1998–2000) and the Arnold Palmer and Jack Nicklaus awards in 2000, it works just as efficiently at it always did.

Ryder pals (above) *Larry Nelson (left), an outstanding Ryder Cup performer, with team-mate Lanny Wadkins.*

Oakmont winner *Nelson hugs the US Open trophy after his 1983 win at Oakmont Country Club.*

LARRY GENE NELSON

WON USPGA 1981, 1987; US OPEN 1983.
WINNER OF 10 US TOUR EVENTS 1979–88.
RYDER CUP 1979–81, 1987.

Bunker sandstorm
Nelson blasts his way out of trouble – not a common experience for such a careful golfer.

JACK NEWTON

BORN SYDNEY, NEW SOUTH WALES, AUSTRALIA, 30 JANUARY 1950

T *HE WORLD LOST a fine competitive golfer when Jack Newton walked into the propeller of a Cessna aeroplane at Sydney's Mascot airport in 1983. He lost his right arm and right eye, bringing his tournament career to an end. Newton has not abandoned the game, however, and remains an inspiration to all disabled golfers.*

Crowd pleaser
Newton was a great favourite among the galleries until his tragic accident in 1983.

A fine all-round sportsman, Newton became a golf professional in 1971. Venturing to Europe, he won two tournaments in 1972. In 1975 he came close to winning the Open at Carnoustie. He tied Tom Watson and then lost the play-off by one stroke. The deciding strokes were a chip-in from off the green by Watson on the 13th and an approach into the sand by Newton on the 18th.

Then came his tragic accident. Some 18 months later he was back on the course, determined to become the best despite his disabilities.

JACK NEWTON

WON DUTCH OPEN 1972; BENSON & HEDGES INTERNATIONAL 1972; PGA MATCHPLAY 1974; BUICK OPEN 1978; AUSTRALIAN OPEN 1979.

❮ JACK NICKLAUS, see page 304

Disabled inspiration
Jack Newton in 1990.

NORMAN VON NIDA

BORN STRATHFIELD, QUEENSLAND, AUSTRALIA, 14 FEBRUARY 1914

N *ORMAN VON NIDA is respected not only as a great Australian tournament player, but also as one of the game's most eminent teachers. He won the Australian Open three times and his country's PGA title four times.*

The early progress of von Nida's career was cruelly interrupted by the outbreak of the Second World War, just after he had begun his first assault on the US Tour. After the war, in 1946, he travelled to Britain with only £17 in his pocket and a month to go before the first tournament.

But von Nida, affectionately known as "The Von", was nothing if not resourceful. He was soon among the top money winners and finished his first season in Britain in second place in the

"The Von" in action
Norman von Nida tees off at Royal Lytham and St Annes in 1947. The Australian made a major impact on golf in Britain during the post-war period.

Order of Merit. The following year he created a record by winning three tournaments in a sequence of four. He also won or tied four other events to set a new money record of £3,263 for the year.

Von Nida was a colourful figure, never slow to express his views. After an incident with US Ryder Cup player Henry Ransom during the Lower Rio Grande Valley Open in 1948, a fist-fight developed. The press blamed von Nida, but in fact he had been attacked first. After the local sheriff pulled them apart, Ransom was disqualified from the event.

The Von's reputation as a teacher is highly respected and he has worked with distinguished Australian players such as Greg Norman and David Graham.

NORMAN GEORGE VON NIDA

WON AUSTRALIAN PGA 1946, 1948, 1950, 1951; DUNLOP MASTERS 1948; AUSTRALIAN OPEN 1950, 1952, 1953. WORLD CUP 1956. HARRY VARDON TROPHY 1947.

JACK NICKLAUS

BORN COLUMBUS, OHIO, USA, 21 JANUARY 1940

T HERE HAS NEVER *been a player quite like Jack William Nicklaus in the history of golf. His record is by any standards truly remarkable. Since the age of 14 he has been winning tournaments and setting records with prodigious regularity. At the same time Nicklaus has followed a parallel career as a golf-course designer, a role in which he has almost equalled his influence as a player.*

Nicklaus took up golf at the age of ten. By the time he was 19 he had won his first US Amateur Championship and was in the Walker Cup team. Two years later, he won the Amateur again, after setting a record 282 for an amateur in the 1960 US Open, finishing second to Arnold Palmer.

It was a meteoric start to a career that dominated golf for a quarter of a century. By 1986, when Nicklaus won the Masters for the sixth time at the age of 46, he had won 18 Major championships – seven

more than any other player – and he had earned more money than anyone in the history of the game. That victory at Augusta was the highlight of the 25th season of his professional career. He had played in 100 Major championships, finishing in the top three 45 times – an achievement that even the remarkable Tiger Woods will find very hard to emulate.

TO BE THE BEST
Nicklaus has won every honour that it is possible to win in golf, many of them several times; only the record for the highest number of USPGA tournament wins is missing from his collection. In the

Cup team (above)
Jack Nicklaus (left) and Arnold Palmer (right) won the World Cup for the United States four times in the 1960s.

process he has become one of the most popular men active in any field of sporting endeavour and highly respected as an ambassador for the game he loves.

As Nicklaus's domination of the game increased over the years, so did his popularity with the galleries. As a stern, slightly overweight and crew-cut youngster, Nicklaus was not popular, particularly when he first emerged to challenge the superiority of the great Arnold Palmer. But by the beginning of the 1970s he had lost weight, grown his hair and assumed a relaxed appearance. This did wonders for his image, although it did not affect the intense concentration behind the steely blue eyes, which could be as cold as ice one moment and then melt into a disarming smile the next. The secret of Nicklaus's success has much to do with his capacity for intense concentration, but he was also blessed from the start with immense physical strength,

Smiling bear (left)
In the 1980s, Jack Nicklaus approached his golf as a pleasure rather than a job, but the will to win was still there.

First-time winner (left)
In April 1990 Nicklaus won the first Senior event he contested, the Tradition at Desert Mountain.

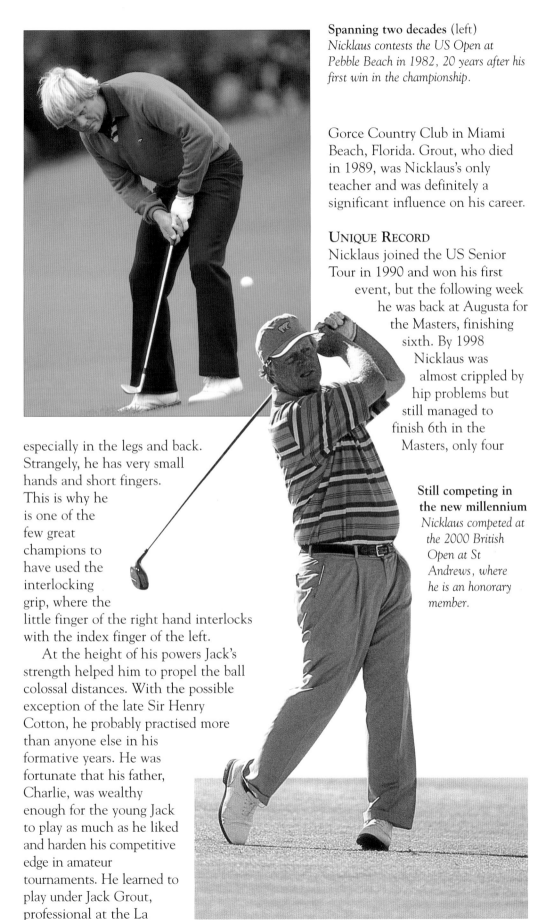

Spanning two decades (left) *Nicklaus contests the US Open at Pebble Beach in 1982, 20 years after his first win in the championship.*

Gorce Country Club in Miami Beach, Florida. Grout, who died in 1989, was Nicklaus's only teacher and was definitely a significant influence on his career.

UNIQUE RECORD

Nicklaus joined the US Senior Tour in 1990 and won his first event, but the following week he was back at Augusta for the Masters, finishing sixth. By 1998 Nicklaus was almost crippled by hip problems but still managed to finish 6th in the Masters, only four

Still competing in the new millennium *Nicklaus competed at the 2000 British Open at St Andrews, where he is an honorary member.*

The bear and the tiger *Two of golf's greatest legends together at the 2000 USPGA Championship at Valhalla, Georgia, USA.*

strokes behind the winner, Mark O'Meara. He ended his remarkable run of 154 straight appearances in major championships when he decided not to play in the PGA Championship at Sahalee CC that year.

Successful surgery to his hip allowed Nicklaus to return to competitive golf and now into his 60s he continues to drive the ball almost as far as he did as a youngster, albeit aided to some extent by advances in equipment.

Jack Nicklaus's record at the top level of golf is unique. He has been the greatest player of his or any other era so far. Tiger Woods has set out to challenge that record, but despite his phenomenal start he still has a long hard road ahead of him.

JACK WILLIAM NICKLAUS

WON US AMATEUR 1959, 1961; US OPEN 1962, 1967, 1972, 1980; US MASTERS 1963, 1965–66, 1972, 1975, 1986; USPGA 1963, 1971, 1973, 1975, 1980; OPEN CHAMPIONSHIP 1966, 1970, 1978. THE TRADITION 1990–91, 1995–96; US SENIOR PLAYERS 1990; US PGA SENIORS' 1991; US SENIOR OPEN 1991, 1993. WINNER OF 70 US TOUR EVENTS 1962–86 (LEADING MONEY WINNER 1964–65, 1967, 1971–73, 1975–76). USPGA PLAYER OF THE YEAR 1967, 1972–73, 1975–76. WALKER CUP 1959–61. EISENHOWER TROPHY 1960. WORLD CUP 1963–64, 1966–67, 1971, 1973 (INDIVIDUAL WINNER 1963–64, 1971). RYDER CUP 1969–77, 1981 (NON-PLAYING CAPTAIN 1983, 1987). PRESIDENTS CUP (NON-PLAYING CAPTAIN 1998). WORLD GOLF HALL OF FAME 1974. BOB JONES AWARD 1975. PLAYER OF THE CENTURY 1988. HONORARY MEMBER ROYAL & ANCIENT GOLF CLUB.

especially in the legs and back. Strangely, he has very small hands and short fingers. This is why he is one of the few great champions to have used the interlocking grip, where the little finger of the right hand interlocks with the index finger of the left.

At the height of his powers Jack's strength helped him to propel the ball colossal distances. With the possible exception of the late Sir Henry Cotton, he probably practised more than anyone else in his formative years. He was fortunate that his father, Charlie, was wealthy enough for the young Jack to play as much as he liked and harden his competitive edge in amateur tournaments. He learned to play under Jack Grout, professional at the La

GREG NORMAN

BORN MOUNT ISA, QUEENSLAND, AUSTRALIA, 10 FEBRUARY 1955

G REG NORMAN *was a latecomer to golf, taking up the game at the age of 17. Yet within two years he was down to scratch and had embarked on a meteoric career that took him to the position of the world's number one player. He turned professional in 1976 and in only his fourth tournament, the West Lakes Classic in Australia, he led by ten strokes going into the last round – victory was a formality. By the end of the season he had been selected to play for Australia in the World Cup. He had played in just six professional events.*

Long and straight (right)
Australian superstar Greg Norman has always been noted for the impressive power and perfect straightness of his long hitting.

THE ROUGH WITH THE SMOOTH

In the 1986 Open Championship at Turnberry, Norman dominated the tournament with a great display of long, straight hitting on a course with wasp-waisted fairways and with severe rough waiting for those who missed them. Norman's strength, and the improvement in his short game, helped him to a second-round 63 and a 69 on the final day, to secure a comfortable victory by five strokes. Here he plays a delicate pitch from wet rough and celebrates his triumph on the last green.

At the heart of Norman's extraordinary talent is an ability to propel a golf ball vast distances. But, unlike many others who have had similar reputations, he is also a straight hitter. Norman's long game was remarkable from the very beginning, but he had to work hard on his short game. Here he was helped in no small measure by the great Australian player and teacher, Norman von Nida. The work Greg Norman devoted to improving his putting stroke paid off handsomely, for today the Great White Shark is considered one of the most reliable putters in the game of golf.

WORLDWIDE VICTORIES
Since Norman's first tournament win, victories have flowed in a steady stream all over the world. He joined the European Tour the year after he turned professional and won the Martini International on his way to finishing 20th in the Order of Merit. By 1980 he had beaten Sandy Lyle in the final to win the first of three World Matchplay titles he would take in a seven-year period; also in 1980, he finished second on the European money list, topped the Australian Order of Merit, and won the Australian Open.

Two years later, in 1982, despite a restricted schedule, Norman emerged as the top money winner in Europe in a remarkable season that saw him, among other triumphs, become the first player to defend successfully the Dunlop Masters title.

Norman saw the European campaign as an apprenticeship, once reaching the top there, for taking on the lucrative US Tour. By 1986 he was top of the US money list with more than $650,000.

The hat

Norman's own-branded sportswear, including his trademark hat is known throughout the golf world.

SUPERSTAR STATUS

In 1986 he won twice on the US Tour, was runner-up four times, and finished in the top ten in more than half of the 19 events he played. Norman had arrived in the golfing superstar bracket.

In that year Norman had also been well placed to win both the US Masters at Augusta and the US Open at Shinnecock Hills. At Augusta he lost the Masters by blocking a 4-iron wildly into the crowd at the last, when a four would have given him a tie with Jack Nicklaus. At Shinnecock Hills, he was in the lead going into the final round, but then shot a disastrous 75.

It was a different story in the Open Championship at Turnberry. Here, Greg Norman's ability as a long, straight hitter was a definite advantage on the narrow fairways. His second round of 63, with

three putts on the last green, equalled the Championship record. After coping well with the wet and windy conditions of the third round, he led by one stroke going into the final 18 holes. When he holed a 40-yard bunker shot at the 3rd for a birdie, Norman suddenly had a five-stroke lead to win his first major comfortably.

TOUGH AT THE TOP

In the big events he seems to have suffered more at the hands of fate than most golfers. Bob Tway holed a bunker shot at the last hole to beat him in the 1986 USPGA; he was beaten in a play-off

Back on form
(above)
In 2000 Norman was back in the Top 50 Official World Golf Ranking at 43rd, and climbing up steadily.

Great White Shark
On home territory in 2000 (right). Norman also swung his club at the spectacular closing ceremony for the 2000 Sydney Olympics.

for the US Masters when Larry Mize chipped into the hole in 1987; and after shooting 64 in the final round of the 1989 Open at Troon, he lost in a three-way play-off to Mark Calcavecchia. However, in 1993 Norman won his second Open at Royal St George's, restoring his position at the top of the Sony World Rankings.

A persistent shoulder injury took its toll on Norman in the late 1990s and he took some time to recover from surgery.

In 1998, still recovering, he played a very much reduced schedule but still became the first player to pass the $12 million mark in career earnings at the Dotal-Ryder Open. He threatened at the Masters in a titanic struggle before having to give way to José-Maria Olazábal and finished 6th in the British Open at Carnoustie. On September 12th, 1999 he fell out of the Top 50 in the Official World Golf Ranking for the first time.

GREGORY JOHN NORMAN

WON WORLD MATCHPLAY 1980, 1983, 1986; AUSTRALIAN OPEN 1980, 1985, 1987, 1995–97; WORLD MATCHPLAY 1980, 1983, 1986; AUSTRALIAN MASTERS 1981, 1983–84, 1987, 1989–90; OPEN CHAMPIONSHIP 1986, 1993. WINNER OF 14 EUROPEAN TOUR EVENTS 1977–94. WINNER OF 18 US TOUR EVENTS 1984–97. US PLAYERS CHAMPIONSHIP 1994. USPGA PLAYER OF THE YEAR 1995. WORLD CUP 1976, 1978. DUNHILL CUP 1985–90, 1992, 1994–96. VARDON TROPHY 1989–90, 1994. AUSTRALASIAN TOUR LEADING MONEY WINNER 1980, 1983–84, 1986, 1988. FOUR TOURS CHAMPIONSHIP 1985–87, 1989. HARRY VARDON TROPHY 1982. ARNOLD PALMER AWARD 1986, 1990, 1995. PRESIDENTS CUP 1996–2000.

JOSÉ-MARIA OLAZÁBAL

BORN FUENTERRABIA, SPAIN, 5 FEBRUARY 1966

AFTER A GLITTERING amateur career there was little doubt that Spain's José-Maria Olazábal would become one of the game's outstanding professional players. An impressive tally of PGA European Tour wins, Ryder Cup performances, and two US Masters victories confirmed him as the successor to his fellow Spaniard, Severiano Ballesteros.

José-Maria learned to play at the Real Golf Club de San Sebastian in northern Spain where his father was a greenkeeper and his mother worked as a cleaner. His passion for the game and determination to win brought him a string of amateur successes, including the Italian and the British Amateur Championships, when he was still only 18.

He won the European Tour Qualifying School in 1985, and finished second in the Order of Merit in 1986, winning more than £155,000. Although Olazábal failed to produce a victory in 1987 and slipped back to 17th in the Order of Merit, he emerged as a key figure in the European Ryder Cup team which scored an historic

Keeping his cool
(right) *Erratic driving had plagued Olazábal's form in 1993 and prevented him extending his winning streak of at least one PGA European Tour event each season 1988–92. No such problem marred his determined victory at the 1994 US Masters.*

A Very Good Year
(right) *Olazábal tied for fourth place in the 2000 USPGA Championship, and won the B & H International, thus ending a two-year drought after winning the Dubai Desert Classic in 1998.*

Supreme short game
Blessed with a brilliant short game, Olazábal remains one of the game's finest putters.

"away" victory over the USA. He struck up a remarkable team partnership with Seve Ballesteros which proved so valuable to the Europeans in five Ryder Cup encounters.

In 1990 he took America by storm, winning the World Series of Golf by a record 12 strokes. Up until 1992 he was only once out of the top seven in the official Order of Merit. After suffering something of a slump in 1993, Olazábal made a gritty comeback, winning his first Major title, the 1994 US Masters.

Soon after his first major victory, Olazábal was struck down by a rare foot ailment, which severely curtailed his tournament schedule, and at one point threatened to end his career completely. He was forced to watch the 1995 Masters from his bed due to illness and could not compete for the Ryder Cup team. The foot problem was eventually diagnosed as rheumatoid polyarthritis in three joints in his right foot and two in his left. It confined him to bed for almost 18 months

before German doctor Hans-Wilhelm Muller-Wohlfahrt successfully treated him.

By 1999 "Ollie" was back and he could not have made a more sensational return. At the Masters at Augusta he produced sensational golf and a wonderful putting touch to win his second green jacket.

In 2000 he ended a two-year spell without a European Tour victory when he won the Benson & Hedges International title at The Belfry, scene of so much of his Ryder Cup success. A remarkable second-round 62 at the USPGA Championship at Valhalla gave him a tie for 4th place.

JOSÉ-MARIA OLAZÁBAL MANTEROLA

WON BRITISH AMATEUR 1984. WORLD SERIES OF GOLF 1990, 1994; US MASTERS 1994, 1999; VOLVO PGA 1994. WINNER OF 18 PGA EUROPEAN TOUR EVENTS 1986–2000; 5 US TOUR EVENTS 1990–99; EISENHOWER TROPHY 1982–84; WORLD SERIES OF GOLF 1990. RYDER CUP 1987–93, 1997–99. WORLD CUP 1989, 2000. FOUR TOURS CHAMPIONSHIP 1987, 1989. DUNHILL CUP 1986–89, 1992–93, 1998–2000. SEVE BALLESTEROS TROPHY 2000. BEN HOGAN AWARD 1999.

CHRISTY O'CONNOR

BORN GALWAY, IRELAND, 21 DECEMBER 1924

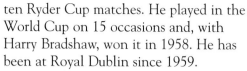

O NE OF THE *best professionals ever to have come from Ireland, Christy O'Connor was a prominent member of the group of players who developed professional golf in the British Isles in the days before the start of the European Tour, at a time when world golf was dominated by the United States.*

Although he never achieved his ambition of winning the Open Championship, O'Connor came near to it three times. He was joint runner-up in 1965 at Birkdale and twice took third place – in 1958 at Royal Lytham and in 1961 at Birkdale.

He was, however, a prolific winner of other tournaments, and won the Irish Professional Championship ten times. He was a regular selection for the Ryder Cup team; no other player has taken part in ten Ryder Cup matches. He played in the World Cup on 15 occasions and, with Harry Bradshaw, won it in 1958. He has been at Royal Dublin since 1959.

An Irishman with great charm, Christy O'Connor had a big following from his earliest days. The crowds flocked to see him and to enjoy his company. One of his characteristics was to improve his scores throughout a tournament and to reserve his best for the last. On many occasions, he "stole" a win after all had seemed lost. In his later years, O'Connor has remained an intuitive striker of the ball.

Last GB & I win
At Lindrick in 1957, O'Connor helped Great Britain and Ireland win the Ryder Cup for the first time for 34 years and for the last time ever. He remained a formidable competitor, playing golf in the spirit intended.

CHRISTY O'CONNOR

WON DUNLOP MASTERS 1956, 1959; PGA MATCHPLAY 1957; IRISH OPEN 1964, 1966–67, 1972. WINNER OF 24 EUROPEAN TOUR EVENT 1955–72.WORLD SENIORS 1976–77; PGA SENIORS 1976–77, 1979, 1981–82, 1983. RYDER CUP 1955–73. WORLD CUP 1956–64, 1966–69, 1971, 1975. HARRY VARDON TROPHY 1961–62.

CHRISTY O'CONNOR JNR

BORN GALWAY, IRELAND, 19 AUGUST 1948

A PERFECTLY STRUCK *2-iron to within tap-in distance at the last hole in the 1989 Ryder Cup remains, for all who saw it, a vivid memory of a titanic struggle that resulted in the famous trophy remaining on the European side of the Atlantic. The stroke was played by Christy O'Connor Jnr, nephew of the legendary O'Connor Snr.*

Christy O'Connor is one of the most popular players ever to grace the European golf scene. His shot at The Belfry gave him a one-hole victory over long-hitting Fred Couples of the United States. It also gained a vital point for the Europeans. O'Connor's reaction when he arrived on the green to take the cheers of the crowd forms another indelible picture of that marvellous match. Moving on to the senior tour, he made a sensational start on both sides of the Atlantic. He won an emotional victory in the 1999 Senior British Open, dedicating his victory to his son Darren who tragically died in a car accident.

CHRISTY PATRICK O'CONNOR

WON SIX PGA EUROPEAN TOUR EVENTS 1975–92. IRISH OPEN 1975; BRITISH MASTERS 1992. WORLD CUP 1974–75, 1978, 1985, 1989, 1992. RYDER CUP 1975, 1989. DUNHILL CUP 1985, 1989, 1992.

Steady record (right)
O'Connor has been a consistent performer on the European Tour.

Captain's thanks (left)
Captain Tony Jacklin congratulates Christy O'Connor after his historic putt that beat Fred Couples in the 1989 Ryder Cup.

MARK O'MEARA

BORN GOLDSBORO, NORTH CAROLINA, USA, 13 JANUARY 1957

T HROUGHOUT THE 1980S and 1990s Mark O'Meara was one of America's most successful golfers. During those two decades he amassed no fewer than 20 professional victories around the world, but it was not until he won both the Masters and the British Open in the same year –1998 – that he began to receive the accolades his talent clearly deserved. Mark O'Meara must have been beginning to wonder if he would ever win a major title. He had already competed in 15 US Opens, 15 USPGAs, 14 Masters and 13 British Open Championships when he arrived at Augusta for the 1998 Masters.

Even then, all he had to show for his efforts was a haul of five second-place finishes. O'Meara seemed destined to be forever regarded as one of golf's "nearly men" but that was before he transformed his career with two major victories in the space of four short months.

FINALLY THE BRIDEGROOM

The first of the victories that elevated O'Meara into the upper echelons of the game came when he finished with a birdie-birdie burst to edge out Fred Couples and David Duval to win the 1998 Masters.

Then he confirmed his new status later on that summer when he defeated Brian Watts in a four-hole play-off for the British Open at Royal Birkdale. All of a sudden the 41-year-old

Sweet success
Barely four months after winning the 1998 US Masters, O'Meara was kissing the Claret Jug as British Open victor as well.

Team player (above) *From 1998 O'Meara played key roles in US victories in the Ryder Cup, Presidents Cup, and World Cup.*

player had become the oldest man ever to win two major titles in one calendar year. O'Meara was no longer the bridesmaid but a *bona fide* superstar.

O'Meara first hit the headlines by defeating John Cook in the 1979 US Amateur final. He went on to win 20 tour titles around the world from 1984 to the end of 1987, before achieving the double that made him the unanimous choice as the Jack Nicklaus USPGA Player of the Year for 1998. O'Meara now lives on the same Florida estate as his friend and rival, Tiger Woods.

MARK O'MEARA

WON US AMATEUR 1979; PEBBLE BEACH NATIONAL PRO-AM 1985, 1989–90, 1992, 1997. US MASTERS 1998; OPEN CHAMPIONSHIP 1998; WORLD MATCHPLAY 1998. WINNER OF 16 US TOUR EVENTS 1984–98. USPGA PLAYER OF THE YEAR 1998. RYDER CUP 1985, 1989–91, 1997–99. DUNHILL CUP 1985–87, 1996–99. FOUR TOURS CHAMPIONSHIP 1985. PRESIDENTS CUP 1996–98. WORLD CUP 1999

FRANCIS OUIMET

BORN BROOKLINE, MASSACHUSETTS, USA, 8 MAY 1893; DIED 1967

*T*HE TRIUMPH OF *20-year-old amateur Francis Ouimet in the 1913 US Open Championship was a turning point in the history of American golf. Until that moment, the game had been perceived as the preserve of the rich, but this marvellous victory by a young man from an ordinary American family fired the imagination of the whole country. It set in motion the steady rise of the game's popularity in the United States.*

Francis Ouimet (pronounced "Wimmet") did not come from a wealthy background, but fortunately when he was a youngster his family, who lived in Brookline, moved to a house near the Country Club, and he was allowed to play on the course.

He was a caddie from the age of 11, although he had to give up this job at 16 to avoid losing his amateur status. By the time he was 19, he was a more than useful player and won the Massachusetts State Championship. He took time off work to play in the US Amateur in 1913, but thought he would not get leave to play in the US Open later in the same year, even though it was being held at Brookline, his local course.

Ouimet's boss, however, saw to it that he played. By the time Ouimet stood on the 13th tee in the final round, Harry

People's champion
A stamp was issued in the United States in 1988 to celebrate the 75th anniversary of Ouimet's famous win in the 1913 US Open.

Vardon and Ted Ray, the two leading British professionals, seemed to have the Open sewn up. They had already finished and had tied, well ahead of the American field. Yet Ouimet completed the last six holes in two under par to tie with the British pair, and then, contrary to all expectations, went on to win the play-off.

HIGH REGARD

The rest of Ouimet's career was something of an anti-climax. The following year he won the US Amateur and the French Amateur, and was fifth in the US Open. He won the US Amateur again in 1931. He played in the first Anglo-American match in 1921 and participated in every Walker Cup from 1922 to 1949.

He was a modest, sincere individual with a delightful character, and was held in the highest regarded by his fellow golfers. In 1951 he became the first American to be elected captain of the Royal & Ancient Golf Club.

Amateur rivals
As the non-playing captain of the US Walker Cup team in 1947, Ouimet (left) ties an armband on the opposing captain, John Beck.

R & A captain
Ouimet is resplendent in his red coat as the first American captain of the Royal & Ancient Golf Club in 1951.

FRANCIS DE SALES OUIMET

WON US OPEN 1913; FRENCH AMATEUR 1914; US AMATEUR 1914, 1931. WALKER CUP 1922–34 (CAPTAIN 1932–34, NON-PLAYING CAPTAIN 1936–49). PGA HALL OF FAME 1940. CAPTAIN R & A GOLF CLUB 1951. BOB JONES AWARD 1955. WORLD GOLF HALL OF FAME 1974.

"JUMBO" OZAKI

BORN KAIMAN TOWN, TOKUSHIMA, JAPAN, 24 JANUARY 1947

I F THE ADULATION *and hoopla that surrounds Tiger Woods's every move on a golf course smacks of pop idolatry, then visitors to Japan will know that the same level of adoration was accorded "Jumbo" Ozaki long before "Tigermania". At the same time, it has been fashionable to disparage Ozaki's home-based achievements since his only "away" win was the 1972 New Zealand PGA title.*

Moreover, "Jumbo" did tie for sixth place in the 1989 US Open, eighth in the Masters in 1973, and 14th in the 1978 British Open Championship.

His third successive win in the 1996 Dunlop Phoenix International, Japan's richest tournament, was also his 100th victory, and though eligible to join the lucrative US Seniors Tour he chose to continue his career in his homeland.

FROM BASEBALL TO GOLF

The eldest of three golfing brothers, Masashi Ozaki first drew attention in the mid-60s as a baseball pitcher – his high school team won the national championship. He then signed for a Japanese professional team, the Nishitetsu Lions but switched to golf and became a professional in 1970. Ozaki then began what was the most illustrious career of any Asian golfer, and over the next 30 years had chalked up more than 110 wins in Japan.

Record breaker (below) *In 2000, Ozaki became the oldest winner, aged 53, on the Japanese tour by taking the Sun-Chlorella Classic.*

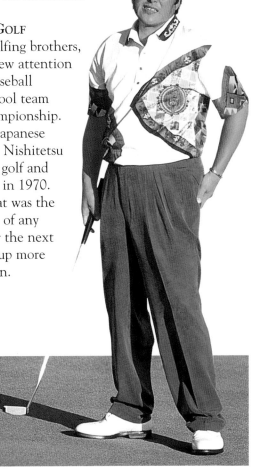

MASASHI "JUMBO" OZAKI

WON JAPAN PGA 1971, 1974, 1989, 1991, 1993; NEW ZEALAND PGA 1972; JAPAN OPEN 1974, 1988–89, 1992, 1994. JAPAN MATCHPLAY 1989. WORLD CUP 1974, 1988. PRESIDENTS CUP 1996.

ALF PADGHAM

BORN CATERHAM, ENGLAND, 2 JULY 1906; DIED 1966

A LF PADGHAM WAS *a tall, slim man who had a lovely natural swing reminiscent of the great Harry Vardon. His long game was always immaculate, but his putting variable. Padgham was one of the group of British players who upheld the professional flag during the 1930s. His great year was 1936 when he carried all before him, crowning his season by becoming Open Champion.*

Padgham had been threatening to win the Open Championship for some time before his 1936 victory at Hoylake. He came third in 1934, was runner-up in 1935, and was never out of the top seven from 1932 through to 1938.

A member of the British team that played in South Africa in 1936–37, he started with a victory, but then seemed to lose his touch and was never quite able to regain it. He was one of several fine players who missed productive years because of the Second World War.

Alf Padgham was not a charismatic figure. He dressed sombrely, often in a waterproof jacket, and although he had a great sense of humour it usually revealed itself only to his friends. In public he was shy and could appear somewhat taciturn.

Card player (above) *A 1930s cigarette card bears witness to Alf Padgham's fame.*

ALFRED HARRY PADGHAM

WON PGA MATCHPLAY 1931, 1935; IRISH OPEN 1932; GERMAN OPEN 1934; OPEN CHAMPIONSHIP 1936; DUTCH OPEN 1938. RYDER CUP 1933–37. CAPTAIN BRITISH PGA 1936.

❮ ARNOLD PALMER, see page 316

Practical skills (left) *Though an effective player, Padgham's style was not eye-catching.*

JESPER PARNEVIK

BORN DANDERYD, STOCKHOLM, SWEDEN, 7 MARCH 1965

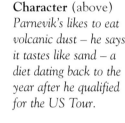

*A*T A TIME *when tournament golf had many great players but a diminishing number of personalities, the arrival of Jesper Parnevik on the scene brought some badly needed colour. The son of Sweden's most famous comedian, Jesper is known the world over as the man who eats volcanic dust, has a retro dress sense and wears his golf cap with the peak turned up. He also happens to be a highly talented professional who has earned superstar status.*

Parnevik turned professional in 1986 after learning to play by hitting floating balls into a lake behind his family home. His first European Tour victory was in the Bells Scottish Open in 1993 and he became the first Swede to win a European Tour event in his home country with his victory in the 1995 Scandinavian Masters, an event he was to win again in 1998.

In 1995 he went to the US Tour Qualifying School and finished fourth, prompting his decision to play most of his golf in the United States. He took up residence in Florida and in 1998 won his first US Tour event, the Phoenix Open.

The following year he won again, at the Greater Greensboro Chrysler Classic, where he led from start to finish and then lit a victory cigar on the final green before holing the winning putt.

In 2000 he became a multiple tournament winner with victories in the Bob Hope Chrysler Classic and the GTE Byron Nelson Classic, finishing eighth in the money list with close to $2.5 million. He might well have finished even higher but for increasing hip pain, which eventually required corrective surgery.

Character (above)
Parnevik's likes to eat volcanic dust – he says it tastes like sand – a diet dating back to the year after he qualified for the US Tour.

Consistent (below)
Parnevik has so far won an equal number of Tour events on both sides of the Atlantic – four apiece to date.

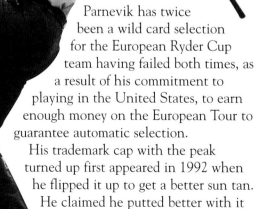

JESPER BO PARNEVIK

WON SCOTTISH OPEN 1993; SCANDINAVIAN MASTERS 1995, 1998. WINNER OF 4 EUROPEAN TOUR EVENTS 1993–98, 4 US TOUR EVENTS 1998–2000. EISENHOWER TROPHY 1984–86. DUNHILL CUP 1993–95, 1997. WORLD CUP 1994–95. RYDER CUP 1997–99.

Amusing antics (right)
A tough and talented pro lurks underneath.

Parnevik has twice been a wild card selection for the European Ryder Cup team having failed both times, as a result of his commitment to playing in the United States, to earn enough money on the European Tour to guarantee automatic selection.

His trademark cap with the peak turned up first appeared in 1992 when he flipped it up to get a better sun tan. He claimed he putted better with it up and has kept it that way since.

SE RI PAK

BORN DAEJEON, KOREA, 28 SEPTEMBER 1977

F EW PLAYERS, MEN or women, can boast a victory in their first major championship, but South Korea's Se Ri Pak, in her rookie year on the LPGA Tour, did just that, winning the McDonalds LPGA Championship at Wilmington, Delaware, in 1998, leading from start to finish. She trumped that a couple of months later, becoming, at the age of 20, the youngest-ever winner of the US Women's Open title.

But that championship, played over the tough Blackwolf Run course in Kohler, Wisconsin, turned into a marathon against 20-year-old amateur, Jenny Chuasiriporn, from Duke University, North Carolina.

Title chaser
Pak won 8 LPGA events 1998–99, but titles in 2000 were more elusive.

The 92-hole tournament was the longest in US women's golfing history. Pak, who stands unusually upright at the address position, wasn't finished.

Six days later she won the Jamie Farr Kroger Classic by nine strokes (biggest winning margin of the season), and thus became only the third player in LPGA history to win the US Open and the tournament immediately after it. She added four more LPGA wins in 1999, including a successful defence of the Jamie Farr Classic.

SE RI PAK
OM (KOR)

WON LPGA CHAMPIONSHIP 1998; US WOMEN'S OPEN 1998; LPGA TOUR CHAMPIONSHIP 1999.

Merited awards
In 1998 Pak received LPGA Rookie of the Year and the Korean Order of Merit.

WILLIE PARK JNR

BORN MUSSELBURGH, SCOTLAND, 4 FEBRUARY 1864; DIED 1925

W ILLIE PARK'S FATHER was the first Open Champion, and won the Championship four times. From him Willie learned to love the game, and it was natural that he should inherit much of his father's skill. An exceptional golfer, he was also a successful businessman, expanding his father's club- and ball-making business, designing approximately 170 courses, authoring several golf instruction books, and inventing several new golf clubs.

Famous putter
Park regarded putting as the most important aspect of his game. He used a special putting cleek, with a goose-neck, offset head.

Park Royal
This 56-sided ball, the Royal, was invented by Willie Park Jnr in 1896. Park claimed the hexagonal panels slowed the ball on the green.

Park was tall and had an easy and unhurried swing that developed great power. He seemed to strike the ball quite effortlessly. His putting was magnificent and at times almost uncannily accurate. With his famous putter "Old Pawky", he was hard to beat.

Park won the Open Championship twice, at Prestwick in 1887 and at Musselburgh in 1889, after a tie with Andrew Kirkaldy. At Prestwick in 1898 he decided to play safe at the last hole for the four he thought he needed to tie with Vardon, only to find that Vardon had made a three and that he was thus only the runner-up. At that time there were no scoreboards around the course and a player had to rely on reports from spectators to keep track of the developing scores.

Willie Park was a great player of challenge matches. His most famous encounter was a two-green contest with Harry Vardon in 1899 at North Berwick and Ganton. Special trains were run and the crowd at North Berwick was estimated at 10,000. Vardon won easily. Park was active in golf all his life. His 1896 book, *The Game of Golf*, was the first complete book on golf by a professional.

WILLIAM PARK JNR

WON OPEN CHAMPIONSHIP 1887, 1889.

ARNOLD PALMER

BORN LATROBE, PENNSYLVANIA, USA, 10 SEPTEMBER 1929

THE POPULARITY OF *golf today – both as a spectator and a participant sport – probably owes more to the influence of Arnold Palmer than to anyone else who has ever played the game. The arrival of Palmer on the golf scene, coinciding as it did with the explosion of television as the medium for the masses, brought the game to the attention of millions. And when the business acumen of American lawyer Mark McCormack was added to this potent combination, professional golf hit the big time.*

Change of champions (left)
Kel Nagle congratulates Palmer on his 1961 British Open win at Birkdale.

Legendary strength (below)
Palmer has always been a marvellous athlete, immensely strong with huge shoulders and hands.

A shot at success (above)
A good approach shot to the 18th green at Wentworth helps Palmer to victory in the Piccadilly World Matchplay in 1964.

Arnold Palmer brought something new and different to the game: excitement and naked aggression. When Palmer hit a golf ball, the crowds came out in their thousands to cheer and join what became known as "Arnie's Army".

Palmer, the son of a professional, took to the game at a very young age. He had plenty of natural ability, but an early incident helped turn a young man with considerable talent into one of the greatest names in the history of sport. Playing in a junior match while still at school, the young Arnold Palmer, furious at duffing a shot, threw his club over some trees in a fit of temper. On the way home his father, Deacon, turned on him. "Pap told me", Palmer recalled, "that this is a gentleman's game and he was ashamed of me. If I ever did such a thing again he was through with me as a golfer."

EARLY TRAGEDY

A little later in Palmer's youth, another incident occurred that deeply affected his life. A new-found friend, Buddy Worsham, was killed in a road accident; Palmer was so shaken by this tragedy that he dropped out of the education system and enlisted in the US Coast Guard for three years.

However, he won the Ohio State Amateur while on leave and, in 1954, after his discharge from the Coast Guard, also won the US Amateur Championship. He then turned professional and met Mark McCormack. The professional game was never the same again. With McCormack handling the business side, Palmer was able to concentrate on what he did best – playing golf. He had a superb putting touch, immense physical strength, fierce determination to go for everything, and an uncanny ability to power his way out of trouble when things went wrong. Palmer's motto was: "If you can see it, you can hole it." It was a philosophy that made him the most exciting player in the game's history, until, perhaps, the arrival of Tiger Woods. Palmer was always pure theatre and his swashbuckling style helped to make him the people's hero.

Palmer's all-or-nothing attitude dazzled the British golfing public when he first crossed the Atlantic in the early 1960s to breathe new life into the by then slightly flagging Open Championship. He single-handedly revived its fortunes.

Famous figure (right)
Arnold Palmer was an unmistakable figure at numerous US Masters tournaments. He achieved nine top-five finishes at Augusta, including four victories.

Palmer power (left)
Palmer fights his way out of trouble in the 1982 US Open.

Precision putter (right)
A marvellous putting touch was responsible for many of Palmer's spectacular successes.

ARNOLD DANIEL PALMER

WON US AMATEUR 1954; US MASTERS 1958, 1960, 1962, 1964; US OPEN 1960; OPEN CHAMPIONSHIP 1961–62; WORLD MATCHPLAY 1964, 1967; USPGA SENIORS 1980, 1984; US SENIOR OPEN 1981. WINNER OF 60 US TOUR EVENTS 1955–73. RYDER CUP 1961–67, 1971–73 (CAPTAIN 1963, NON-PLAYING CAPTAIN 1975). WORLD CUP 1960, 1962–64, 1966–67 (INDIVIDUAL WINNER 1967). USPGA PLAYER OF THE YEAR 1960, 1962. VARDON TROPHY 1961–62, 1964, 1967. BOB JONES AWARD 1971. WORLD GOLF HALL OF FAME 1974. USPGA HALL OF FAME 1980.

When he kept coming back to the event, the other top American players followed him, thus restoring the tournament to its premier position in world golf.

Apart from his two British Open victories, he won the Masters four times and finished second twice. He won only one US Open, though he was runner-up four times, and, as a tribute to his contribution to the US Open Palmer was extended a special invitation to play in the 1994 Championship.

Palmer was never better than second in the USPGA and was the leading US money winner in 1958, 1960, and 1962–63. He later helped to establish the immense popularity of the US Senior Tour winning ten events from 1980–88 as well as the US Senior Players in 1984–85.

A fond farewell
In 1995 Palmer bade a sentimental farewell to the British Open with a final wave from the Swilcan Bridge.

GARY PLAYER

BORN JOHANNESBURG, SOUTH AFRICA, 1 NOVEMBER 1935

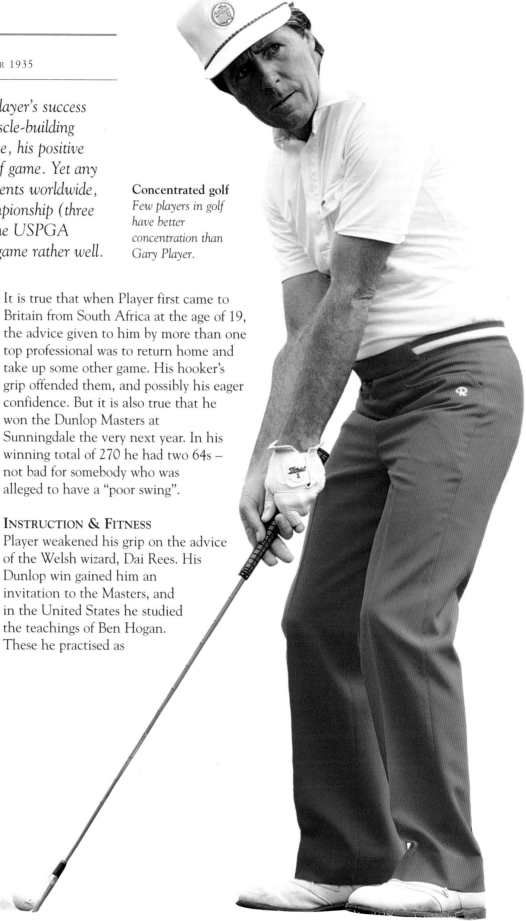

MOST COMMENTATORS PUT *Gary Player's success down to his determination, his muscle-building exercises, his diet, his unrelenting practice, his positive thinking – anything, it seems, but his golf game. Yet any golfer who wins more than 100 tournaments worldwide, including the US Open, the Open Championship (three times), the Masters (three times), and the USPGA (twice), must surely be able to play the game rather well.*

Concentrated golf
Few players in golf have better concentration than Gary Player.

It is true that when Player first came to Britain from South Africa at the age of 19, the advice given to him by more than one top professional was to return home and take up some other game. His hooker's grip offended them, and possibly his eager confidence. But it is also true that he won the Dunlop Masters at Sunningdale the very next year. In his winning total of 270 he had two 64s – not bad for somebody who was alleged to have a "poor swing".

INSTRUCTION & FITNESS

Player weakened his grip on the advice of the Welsh wizard, Dai Rees. His Dunlop win gained him an invitation to the Masters, and in the United States he studied the teachings of Ben Hogan. These he practised as

Man in black (above) *In his early days Player always wore black – it became his trademark.*

GARY JIM PLAYER

WON OPEN CHAMPIONSHIP 1959, 1968, 1974; US MASTERS 1961, 1974, 1978; USPGA 1962, 1972; US OPEN 1965; WORLD MATCHPLAY 1965–66, 1968, 1971, 1973. US PGA SENIORS 1986, 1988, 1990; US SENIOR OPEN 1987–88. US SENIOR PLAYERS 1987; SENIOR BRITISH OPEN 1988, 1990, 1997. WINNER OF 21 US TOUR EVENTS 1958–78, 19 US SENIOR TOUR EVENTS 1985–98. WORLD CUP 1956–60, 1962–68, 1971–73, 1977 (INDIVIDUAL WINNER 1965, 1977). DUNHILL CUP 1991. BOB JONES AWARD 1966. WORLD GOLF HALL OF FAME 1974.

diligently as Hogan himself. Player was also one of the first golfers to believe in being physically fit and he worked hard to build up his strength.

In 1956 he won the first of his 13 South African Open titles, and in 1958 recorded the first of seven wins in the Australian Open. In 1959 he opened his account in the Majors, winning the Open Championship at Muirfield. In 1965, when he took the US Open title at St Louis after a tie with Kel Nagle, he became one of only four golfers to win all four Majors.

Player's second Open Championship win in 1968 – a tense struggle with Jack Nicklaus in foul weather at Carnoustie – and his second USPGA Championship at Oakland Hills in 1972 held out the prospect of winning all four Majors twice.

ROUND UNDER 60

In 1974 Player not only won the Masters and the Open Championship at Royal Lytham – four shots ahead of Peter Oosterhuis – but shot one round of 59 in the Brazilian Open. His final victory in the Masters, in 1978 at the age of 42, was his ninth Major win. But he never won a second US Open.

Player was also the king of matchplay. In 1965 he had his first and most dramatic win in the World Matchplay. Seven down to Tony Lema after 19 holes, he clawed back to win at the 37th; in the final he beat Peter Thomson. He beat Nicklaus in the same competition by six and four in 1966 and again by five and four in 1971.

First win (above) *In 1956, the 20-year-old Player received a £500 cheque for his first key event, the Dunlop Masters at Sunningdale.*

Player – the designer (below) *Player has been a hugely successful golf-course architect. He has been involved in over 100 golf courses.*

When Gary Player joined the Senior PGA Tour in 1985 he won his first tournament at the start of a senior career which has been just as successful and more lucrative than his regular tour years. He has won consistently and received countless awards for his contribution to the game of golf.

In 1998 just two months short of his 63rd birthday he became the second oldest winner on the Senior Tour with a one-stroke victory at the Northville Long Island Classic and the day before had captured his fourth consecutive MasterCard Champions title.

Black-and-white (below) *Player advertised his presence well at the 2000 British Open at St Andrews, where he is an honourary member.*

NICK PRICE

BORN DURBAN, SOUTH AFRICA, JANUARY 28 1957

I N 1994 *NICK PRICE confirmed his superstar status with one of the most prolific years ever on Tour. He won six events including the British Open and the USPGA Championship, becoming one of only three players to win two major titles in the same season – and only one of six players since 1945 to capture successive major titles.*

Club class (right)
Price exchanges clubs with his caddie at the Cisco World Matchplay at Wentworth. He is also a great team player and has been a member of eight Dunhill Cup teams for Zimbabwe.

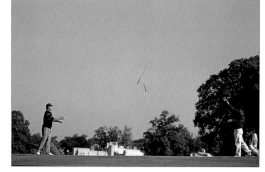

The Zimbabwean's British Open victory at Turnberry was achieved in grand style with an eagle-birdie-par finish over the last three holes to make up a two-stroke deficit on Sweden's Jesper Parnevik. It was a sweet moment for Price. A few weeks later he leapt to a five-stroke lead in the USPGA Championship at Southern Hills and then cruised to a comfortable six-stroke victory over Corey Pavin.

It all seemed a far cry from the boy who served for two years in the Rhodesian Air Force. But at the age of 17 he had won the Junior World Championship, and by 1975 he was playing the South African and European Tours as an amateur. He turned professional in 1977 and his runner-up place in both the 1982, and notably against Seve Ballesteros in the 1986 British Open Championship gave an indication of his potential.

Price had joined the US Tour in 1983 to become an immediate success. However, by his own standards he suffered something of a slump in the mid 1990s and did not record a victory, although he had five top-ten finishes each year and finished 30th and 50th,

respectively, on the money list. In 1997 he returned to his winning ways with victory in the 1997 MCI Classic and climbed back into the top 20 on the money list. Through the 1990s Nick Price won 15 times, a record equalled only by Tiger Woods.

Price is right (right)
Price resides in the United States but has represented Zimbabwe with great pride.

NICHOLAS RAYMOND LEIGE PRICE

WON USPGA 1992, 1994; US PLAYERS CHAMPIONSHIP 1993; OPEN CHAMPIONSHIP 1994. WINNER OF 16 US TOUR EVENTS 1983–98. ARNOLD PALMER AWARD 1993–94. USPGA PLAYER OF THE YEAR 1993–94. VARDON TROPHY 1993, 1997. EISENHOWER TROPHY 1976. DUNHILL CUP 1993–2000. WORLD CUP 1993. PRESIDENTS CUP 1994–2000.

A winning spree
Having clinched two major titles in 1994, Price then won three events in a row, the Canon Greater Hartford Open, Sprint Western Open and Federal Express St Jude Classic.

A year to savour (right)
In 1993 Price finished top of the money list and was voted PGA Player of the Year.

TED RAY

BORN JERSEY, CHANNEL ISLANDS, 28 MARCH 1877; DIED 1943

L IKE THE GREAT *Harry Vardon, Ted Ray was born in Jersey. As a young player, Ray had high hopes of following in the footsteps of his famous Channel Island contemporary. It was cruel fortune that he arrived on the professional golf scene just when the Great Triumvirate of Harry Vardon, James Braid and J.H. Taylor was at its peak, leaving little but the pickings for other golfers. There was inspiration nonetheless to be found from their lead and Ray learned much from playing with and against them.*

In 1899 Ted Ray played his first Open Championship, making the top ten in 1902. From 1906 onwards he was always in the leading group and he came third in 1908. But it was not until 1912 that he finally won his first Open title.

Ray reached the first Matchplay final in 1903, losing to James Braid. Although he never won this tournament, he reached the final in both 1911 and 1912.

Second best
Ted Ray had a fine swing and was a great player, but lived in the shadow of the legendary Vardon.

In 1913, Ray accompanied Harry Vardon on a record-breaking trip to the United States, playing a series of matches and exhibitions. The high point of the tour was the US Open at Brookline, when both of them tied with the unknown American youngster Francis Ouimet; it was Ouimet who won the play-off.

Ray returned with Vardon to the United States in 1920 for another very successful tour. At Inverness he won the US Open, becoming one of only three British players to win both the British and US Opens. He twice played for Great Britain against the United States, and was in the first Ryder Cup match.

RICH CAREER
Ted Ray had a long and successful career. He continued to play in the Open Championship until 1932, coming close to winning the event at Prestwick in 1925, when he finished runner-up to Jim Barnes by a single stroke.

A professional at Ganton for some years (following Harry Vardon) Ted Ray moved to the Oxhey Club in Hertfordshire where he served from 1912 until his retirement in 1941.

EDWARD RAY

WON OPEN CHAMPIONSHIP 1912;
US OPEN 1920. GB v USA 1921, 1926.
RYDER CUP 1927 (CAPTAIN).

Ambassadors of golf
Ray (left) visited New York with Vardon in 1913. Their tour attracted huge public interest.

Vintage player
Ted Ray continued to play in championship golf well into his 50s. The familiar plus-foured figure was seldom to be seen on the course without his pipe.

DAI REES

BORN BARRY, WALES, 31 MARCH 1913; DIED 1983

W ELSHMAN DAI REES *was an incredible dynamo of a man. He won his first British PGA Matchplay Championship at the age of 23, defeating Ernest Whitcombe in 1936. A year later, he beat the legendary Byron Nelson in a Ryder Cup clash. And, at the end of his career, at the age of 60, he finished second in the Martini Tournament after younger men had suggested he really ought to quit.*

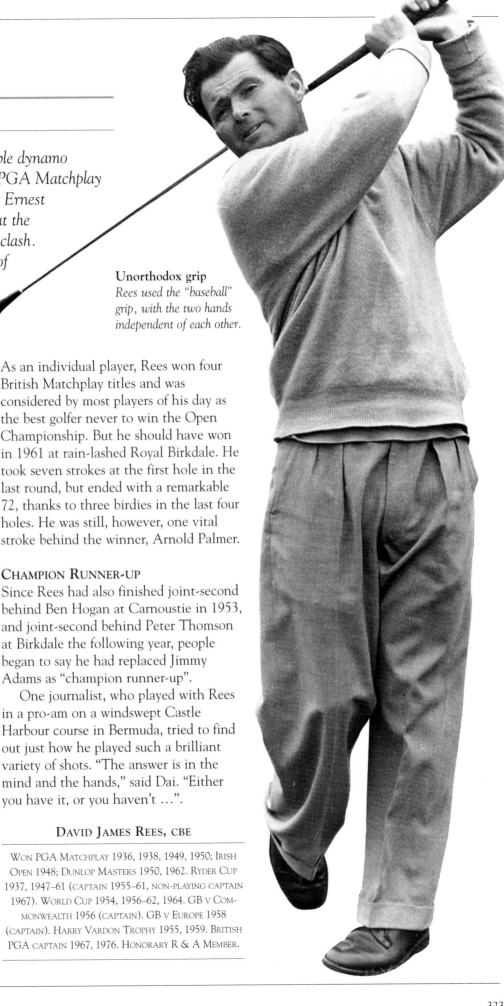

Unorthodox grip
Rees used the "baseball" grip, with the two hands independent of each other.

Winning the Ryder Cup
Rees captained the 1957 team that won the Ryder Cup for Britain for the first time in 24 years.

Rees's energetic life included military service in Africa in the Second World War, when he kept his two-handed swing together by hitting boot-polish tins with an old club he had found. One of the many highlights of his post-war career was a game with King George VI, whom he helped reach the turn in 38 in foursomes, much to the delight of both players.

Dai Rees had an extremely successful international career. He played in nine Ryder Cup matches between 1937 and 1961, and he was captain of the 1957 British team that defeated the United States at Lindrick, Yorkshire – the last time that Great Britain and Ireland won before the event was broadened to bring in European players in 1979.

As an individual player, Rees won four British Matchplay titles and was considered by most players of his day as the best golfer never to win the Open Championship. But he should have won in 1961 at rain-lashed Royal Birkdale. He took seven strokes at the first hole in the last round, but ended with a remarkable 72, thanks to three birdies in the last four holes. He was still, however, one vital stroke behind the winner, Arnold Palmer.

CHAMPION RUNNER-UP

Since Rees had also finished joint-second behind Ben Hogan at Carnoustie in 1953, and joint-second behind Peter Thomson at Birkdale the following year, people began to say he had replaced Jimmy Adams as "champion runner-up".

One journalist, who played with Rees in a pro-am on a windswept Castle Harbour course in Bermuda, tried to find out just how he played such a brilliant variety of shots. "The answer is in the mind and the hands," said Dai. "Either you have it, or you haven't …".

DAVID JAMES REES, CBE

WON PGA MATCHPLAY 1936, 1938, 1949, 1950; IRISH OPEN 1948; DUNLOP MASTERS 1950, 1962. RYDER CUP 1937, 1947–61 (CAPTAIN 1955–61, NON-PLAYING CAPTAIN 1967). WORLD CUP 1954, 1956–62, 1964. GB V COMMONWEALTH 1956 (CAPTAIN). GB V EUROPE 1958 (CAPTAIN). HARRY VARDON TROPHY 1955, 1959. BRITISH PGA CAPTAIN 1967, 1976. HONORARY R & A MEMBER.

ALLAN ROBERTSON

BORN ST ANDREWS, SCOTLAND, 11 SEPTEMBER 1815; DIED 1859

A LLAN ROBERTSON WAS *the first professional golfer to gain real public recognition and the outstanding player of his day. He was a great ambassador for the game, a highly respected individual who could associate comfortably with everyone, lord or labourer. When he died at the age of 44 in 1859, the year before the Open Championship was first contested, a member of the Royal & Ancient Club intoned: "They may shut up their shops and toll their bells, for the greatest among them is gone."*

Robertson in oils
The artist who painted this contemporary portrait of Robertson is unknown. The ball he holds may be presumed to be a feathery of his own manufacture.

Allan Robertson's family had lived in St Andrews for generations. His grandfather, Peter Robertson, had been a ball-maker and professional golfer, and his father, David, was also a ball-maker and an accomplished golfer. It was not surprising that Allan followed the family tradition.

His earliest playthings were small clubs and he was seldom off the links. When he became a working man, he would go down to play at first light before anyone else was

Winning partnership
Allan Robertson (right) and Old Tom Morris are said to have never lost a match playing together.

around and while the dew was still on the ground. He was out on the course again after work if it was still light enough. As a young man he swept the board among all other players and was recognized as the undisputed champion golfer of his age.

During his lifetime the town of St Andrews was resurrected by Sir Hugh Lyon Playfair. Allan Robertson did for golf at St Andrews what Provost Playfair did for the town. His own keenness and dedication, both to the game and to St Andrews Links, helped popularize golf and drew people to the town to play.

Robertson was not only a brilliant player, but also a man of great honour on and off the course. He wore a habitually droll expression; nothing ever disturbed him when he was playing.

Tom Morris – "Old" Tom Morris as he would later be known – was apprenticed to Robertson as a ball-maker. At that time only two or three featheries could be

turned out by one man in a day's work. Consequently they were expensive. In addition to supplying local demand, balls were exported all over Britain and even to the Colonies. In Robertson's best year some 2,500 balls were produced.

RIFT OVER RUBBER

When the use of gutta percha made much cheaper balls possible, Robertson was dismayed because he thought his business would be ruined. Although later, in 1852, he would relent, at first he refused to have anything to do with the new rubber substance. This caused a rift with Tom Morris, who left to set up on his own.

Although Robertson quarrelled with Morris in business, he continued to play with him as a partner at golf. It was said of Robertson that he never lost a match, but this does not seem to have been strictly the case. However, he did lose very few, though in his later years he seems to have avoided head-on singles confrontations with some of the better players. It is almost certainly true that he was never defeated when he was playing with Old Tom Morris as a partner.

There were many famous matches. One of the earliest was in 1840 when Robertson defeated Tom Alexander, a ball-maker from Musselburgh, and one of the best players of the day. There was also a series of singles against Willie Dunn from Musselburgh. But perhaps the most famous match of all was when Robertson and Morris took on Willie and his twin brother, Jamie Dunn, in 1849 in a contest over three greens. The stake was £400, an enormous sum of money at the time.

BATTLE OF GIANTS

In the first match, at Musselburgh, the Dunns won easily over the 36 holes. At St Andrews the home pair won, everything then resting on the final match at North Berwick. Rival crowds turned up to support each pair, and the referee had considerable difficulty in keeping order as the excitement mounted.

With eight holes of the 36 left to play, the Dunns were four up. Odds of 20 to one were being offered against the Dunn brothers losing, but a storming finish by Robertson and Morris saw them all square

with two to go, and the St Andrews pair went on to win both final holes to record a truly remarkable victory.

Allan Robertson was a short man, but he was of robust stature, with a thick neck and a stoop. He was noted for his long cool swing. If his driving was attractive to watch, his short game was quite exquisite. He was at his best with his half and quarter shots to the flag.

Robertson was the first to hole the Old Course at St Andrews in under 80 strokes, a remarkable feat that he accomplished playing with Mr Bethune of Blebo in 1858, the year before his death. His score was an outward nine of 40 and a homeward nine of 39, a total achieved on a course that was much rougher than it is today.

Dressed in his red jacket and with his customary cap, he was almost part of the scenery at St Andrews. He enjoyed the best of health until the very year he died. He never recovered from an attack of jaundice in the spring of 1859, and he died early in the following September.

The Royal & Ancient Club passed a resolution: "This meeting has heard with deep regret of the death of Allan Robertson, and they desire to record on their minutes the opinion, universally

entertained, of the almost unrivalled skill with which he played the game of golf, combining a ready and correct judgement with most accurate execution. They desire also to express the sense of propriety of his whole conduct, and unvarying civility …".

Robertson's club and ball
With this playclub and gutta percha ball, preserved in the Royal & Ancient Golf Club collection, Allan Robertson recorded a round of 79 on the Old Course at St Andrews in 1858, becoming the first player to complete the course in under 80. He died the following year.

ALLAN ROBERTSON

A RENOWNED GOLFER AND MAKER OF CLUBS AND BALLS.

Links with the past
Allan Robertson stands third from the right in this photograph taken around 1850. Teeing-up is R & A captain Frank Wemyss; second from the left is Old Tom Morris.

DOUG SANDERS

BORN CEDARTOWN, GEORGIA, USA, 24 JULY 1933

ALTHOUGH A FINE *player, Doug Sanders failed to achieve success and acclaim commensurate with his undoubted skill. Never winning a Major title, Sanders nevertheless built up an impressive record. Between 1955 and 1972 he won a total of 20 US Tour events and was regularly amongst the top 60 money winners.*

Avoiding trouble
Sanders plays out of the rough at Hoylake in 1968.

Sanders was runner-up in the USPGA Championship in 1959, runner-up in the US Open in 1961, and fourth in the US Masters in 1966. He was also twice runner-up in the British Open, in 1966 and in 1970. On the second occasion, in 1970, Sanders had a short putt on the last green at St Andrews to win, but after agonizing over the shot for some time, he missed. The following day he lost the play-off to Jack Nicklaus.

Sanders's technique is unusual: he uses a short backswing that, it was once said, could be completed in a phone box. However, his great strength ensures that he plays all the shots well. An entertaining golfer on the course, Doug Sanders has a serious side too, preferring to put much of his earnings from golf back into the game to encourage youngsters.

DOUGLAS GEORGE SANDERS

WON CANADIAN OPEN 1956. WINNER OF 20 US TOUR EVENTS 1956–72. RYDER CUP 1967.

Colourful character
Sanders has always cut a flamboyant figure on the course and has an extensive collection of garish clothes.

GENE SARAZEN

BORN HARRISON, NEW YORK, USA, 27 FEBRUARY 1902; DIED 1999

LIKE MANY PLAYERS *of his era, Gene Sarazen (born Eugene Saraceni) began his golf career as a caddie. He had left school early to help his father as a carpenter, but for health reasons he was advised to find an outdoor job. As a caddie he played regularly and made spectacular progress. By the age of 21 he had won three Major events.*

When the young Sarazen was appointed to an assistant pro's job in Fort Wayne, club members there helped him to enter the 1920 US Open. He finished well down the order, but he could clearly live in the big time and his confidence grew.

In 1921 he again fared poorly in the Open, but he knocked reigning champion Jock Hutchison out of the USPGA Championship (then a matchplay event). In 1922 he won the US Open at Skokie and the USPGA at Oakmont, becoming the first player to win both events in the same year. This was an extraordinary feat for a player who was only 20 years old.

At this time Sarazen became firm friends with Walter Hagen, a golfer ten years his senior. Hagen had missed the USPGA that year, so a 72-hole match was arranged between the two – the "World Championship" – and Sarazen

Gum king
Sarazen was featured as a sporting hero on this gum card in 1933, the year of his third USPGA victory.

Custom built
In the early 1930s, Sarazen designed the first sand iron. With its heavy sole, it transformed bunker shots.

Natural talent
Sarazen had a lovely, natural swing and, although only 5ft 4in (1.62m) tall, he was a powerful player.

all four of the current Majors. As late as 1940 Sarazen lost a play-off for the US Open title.

Twice winner of the USPGA Seniors Championship, in 1954 and 1958, Sarazen never lost his love of the game. In 1973, at the age of 71, he went to the Open Championship at Troon on a sentimental journey – 50 years after he had failed to qualify there, despite being the reigning USPGA and US Open Champion. Sarazen celebrated his return to Troon by holing in one with a 5-iron at the famous 8th hole. The following day, at the same

hole, he found a greenside bunker with his tee-shot, and then holed the shot from the sand with his sand iron for an almost unbelievable two – he had not needed to use his putter on the 8th hole at all.

Eugene Sarazen

Won US Open 1922, 1932; USPGA 1922, 1923, 1933; Open Championship 1932; US Masters 1935; USPGA Seniors 1954, 1958. Winner of 38 US Tour events 1922–41. Ryder Cup 1927–37. USPGA Hall of Fame 1940. World Golf Hall of Fame 1974. Old Tom Morris Award 1988. Bob Jones Award 1992.

won. He went on to defend his USPGA title successfully at Pelham in 1923, taking his list of victories in the Majors to three by the time he was 21.

Gene Sarazen played a good deal of exhibition golf in the following years and experimented with changes to his swing. But it was not a success and he failed to make much impact at the top level for some years. It was not until 1930 that he again did well in a Major, finishing as runner-up in the USPGA Championship.

Major Successes
After several attempts, Sarazen finally won the British Open at Prince's in 1932, and later that year he became the US Open Champion at Fresh Meadow. In 1933 he came close to successfully defending his Open Championship title at St Andrews and won the USPGA Championship for the third time in Milwaukee.

Sarazen missed the first US Masters in 1934 because he was playing exhibition golf in Australia, but he won the next year, when he produced one of the most famous strokes in the history of the game. At the par-5 15th hole, in the last round, he holed a full 4-wood shot over the water for an albatross-two (also known as a double eagle) to enable him to tie with Craig Wood after 72 holes. He then won the play-off. This victory gave Sarazen the distinction of being the first player to win

Life at the top (above)
A relaxed and confident Sarazen sailed to England with his wife in 1924. Only 22, he had already won three Major championships.

In retirement (right)
Known affectionately as "The Squire", because of his interest in farming, Sarazen continued to enjoy a game of golf and the life outdoors well past normal retirement age.

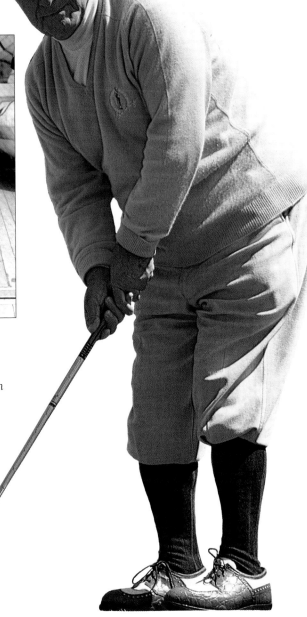

VIJAY SINGH

BORN LAUTOKA, FIJI, 22 FEBRUARY 1963

F IJIAN VIJAY SINGH *is living proof that hard work does pay off: he came from humble beginnings and was once reduced to earning a meagre living as a club pro in Borneo. But he cast aside these disadvantages to become one of the finest golfers in the world.*

On new shoulders
(left) *Singh receives the coveted Green Jacket from 1999 Masters Champion José-Maria Olazábal.*

Sure shot (left) *At the end of the 1980s Singh made his mark on the European Tour winning six times in five years before switching to the USPGA Tour.*

Select group (right) *On winning the 2000 Masters, Singh joined the select group of Woods, Daly, Stewart, Janzen, O'Meara, Els, Price and Faldo to win two or more Majors during the 1990s.*

Fiji's only world-class golfer has become something of a legend among his contemporaries, and is widely regarded as the hardest worker the game has seen since Ben Hogan in his prime. All Singh's endless hours of practice have paid off now that he has won two Majors and almost 30 other tournaments worldwide.

Singh learned the game from his father, an aeroplane technician who also happened to teach golf, and Vijay showed sufficient aptitude for the game to turn professional in 1982.

EARLY STRUGGLES

Vijay translates as "victory" in Hindi and his name is entirely appropriate given the manner in which he has garnered trophies during the past decade and a half. But, to begin with, he struggled to earn a living competing in regional events in Asia, Australia and wherever else he could play in an event. At one point, penniless and

String of successes
(right) *Since joining the US tour Singh has gone on to even greater things, winning nine times in America, once more in Europe and becoming the proud possessor of two Major titles.*

❲ SAM SNEAD, see page 332

disillusioned, Vijay turned his back on competitive golf to become a club pro in Borneo, but soon changed his mind and decided to give Tour golf another try. Singh's first win was the 1984 Malaysian PGA Open but it was not until 1988, when he won the Nigerian Open and then joined the European Tour, that he started to make his mark.

Switching his allegiance to the USPGA Tour, the Fijian's first major success came when he defeated Steve Stricker by two strokes to win the 1998 USPGA Championship at Sahalee and then, in 2000, he added a second, finishing three strokes ahead of Ernie Els at the Masters. That victory denied Tiger Woods the chance to win the modern Grand Slam of golf, all four major titles in the same year.

VIJAY SINGH

WON WORLD MATCHPLAY 1997; USPGA 1998; US MASTERS 2000. WINNER OF 7 EUROPEAN TOUR EVENTS 1989–97, 9 US TOUR EVENTS 1993–2000. US TOUR ROOKIE OF THE YEAR 1993. EISENHOWER TROPHY 1980. PRESIDENTS CUP 1994–2000.

LEADERS

HOLE	1	2	3	4	5	6	7	8	9	10	11	12	13	14	15	16	17	18
PAR	4	5	4	3	4	3	4	3	4	4	4	3	5	4	5	3	4	4

		1	2	3	4	5	6	7	8	9	10	11	12	13	14	15	16	17	18
7	SINGH	7	7	6	6	6	7	8	7	9	7	7	7	6	7	7	7	7	
4	DUVAL	4	5	5	5	5	6	6	7	8	5	4	5	5	6	6	6	6	6
3	ROBERTS	4	4	4	4	4	4	5	6		4	5	5	6	7	7	7	7	
3	ELS	3	3	3	3	3	3	3	4	4	4	4	4	4	5	4	4	4	4
1	WOODS	1	2	2	3	3	2	2	3	4	1	1	2	2	2	2	2	2	2
1	LOVE III	0	0	0	0	0	0	0	0	0	0	0	1	2	1	1	2	2	3
0	LEHMAN	1	0	0	0														
1	MICKELSON	1	2	2	2	2					1	1	2	3	2	1	2	2	2
1	FRANCO	0	0	0	0	0					1	1	2	1	2	2	2	2	2
2	SUTTON	2	1	1	1	1	1				2	1	1	0	0	1	0	0	1

17

ANNIKA SORENSTAM

BORN STOCKHOLM, SWEDEN, 9 OCTOBER 1970

T HE FINEST GOLFER of either sex ever to have emerged from Sweden is undoubtedly Annika Sorenstam. Indeed, but for the presence of her great rival, Australia's Karrie Webb, Sorenstam would be the dominant golfer of the current era. Most significant of all she passed a landmark in women's golf in 2001 by scoring the first ever sub-60 score in a tournament, having already become the first to record an annual stroke average of under 70 (69.9).

There is little doubt that women's golf still does not attract as much attention as it should from male golfers, but the attractive and effervescent 30-year-old has done much to transcend this divide. Like Karrie Webb, England's Laura Davies and very, very few others, Sorenstam's name is well known in even the most chauvinistic male circles and her reputation is undoubtedly deserved, given the enormous impact she has had on the worldwide women's game since turning professional in 1993.

Sorenstam, who hails from Stockholm but now spends most of her time in the United States, picked up a club for the first time when she was 12 years old and in no time at all had developed into one of the world's leading amateur golfers. Between 1987 and 1992, she was an ever-

No.2
During 2000, Sorenstam, whose sister, Charlotta, is also a leading professional, won five events in all, including women's golf's richest prize at the Evian Masters, solidifying her place behind Karrie Webb as a strong No.2 on the official World Rankings.

Back to back (left) *Sorenstam won the US Women's Open in 1995 and 1996.*

Sorenstam and the Solheim Cup (above) *Sorenstam has competed in four successive Solheim Cups from 1994.*

International (right) *Sorenstam has won both the Australian Ladies Open and Ladies Masters, and also won once in Japan.*

present force in the Swedish national side. She won several national titles in her home country, emerged triumphant in seven collegiate tournaments while on a golf scholarship at the University of Texas and then, to cap it all, also won the 1992 World Amateur Championship and, later the same year, finished runner-up in the American Women's Amateur.

Given such success on the amateur stage, much was expected of Sorenstam when she turned professional at the end of 1992 and she certainly did not disappoint, winning the 1993 WPGET Rookie of the Year Award in Europe and then doing the same thing on the US Tour 12 months later. Since then, Sorenstam has gone on to win three Majors (consecutive US Opens, and the Nabisco Championship – her third consecutive 2001 US LPGA Tour success).

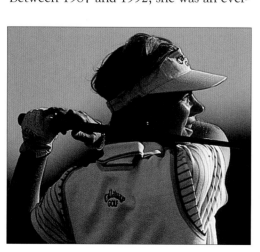

ANNIKA SORENSTAM

WON US WOMEN'S OPEN 1995–96; LPGA TOUR CHAMPIONSHIP 1997; EVIAN MASTERS 2000. WINNER OF 6 LET EVENTS 1995–2000 (ROOKIE OF THE YEAR 1993). ORDER OF MERIT WINNER 1995, 2000. WINNER OF 23 LPGA TOUR EVENTS 1995–2000 (ROOKIE OF THE YEAR 1994). LEADING MONEY WINNER 1995, 1997–98. PLAYER OF THE YEAR 1995, 1997–98.

SAM SNEAD

BORN ASHWOOD, VIRGINIA, USA, 27 MAY 1912

S AM SNEAD FINISHED *in third place in the USPGA* *Championship in August 1974, behind Lee Trevino and Jack Nicklaus and ahead of Gary Player; a few months before, he had been runner-up in the Los Angeles Open. He was 62 years old. It was hard to detect much difference between the quality of his play then and nearly 40 years earlier, when he had made his first appearance as a rookie touring professional in the US Ryder Cup team. Snead, it seemed, could go on for ever.*

Slammin' Sam (above)
*Part of the Ryder Cup team in 1953,
Snead is pictured in action at Wentworth.*

Serious business
Sam Snead walks from the clubhouse at St Andrews on his way to winning the Open Championship in 1946, the first Open to be played after the Second World War.

Natural ability
(right)
If a poll were ever taken to determine the player from any generation who had the best swing, Sam Snead would have to figure prominently among the leaders.

The secret of Snead's golfing longevity, apart from an unbounded enthusiasm for the game, has much to do with his swing. Although he was self-taught, he developed one of the most elegant swings in the history of the game.

Legend has it that Snead climbed down from the trees and, on his way down, broke off a limb that he fashioned into a golf club. He then went on to win golf tournaments barefooted. The truth is not as harsh.

TALENTED FAMILY

Sam Snead, the youngest son of five, did grow up in the backwoods and did carve out clubs from the limbs of swamp maple. The family was not well-off, although there was enough for them to foster their talents in sport and music.

The young Sam started hitting a ball around with pieces of stick cut to shape, but as the distinguished American golf writer, Dick Aultman, pointed out "there were far more amateur whiskey distillers than professional golf instructors around Ashwood, Virginia, during the 1920s." Sam, in fact, learned to play by watching his oldest brother, Homer, hit massive drives across the fields on their cow-and-chicken farm. Young Sam soon graduated to old, cast-off clubs and became a

caddie at The Homestead, a club near his home. Caddying at Hot Springs and later Cascade led eventually to an assistant's post at the Greenbrier at White Sulphur Springs, West Virginia. It was there one day that he made up a four with Lawson Little, for two consecutive years the British and US Amateur Champion, and with past US Open Champions, John Goodman and Billy Burke. Sam's round of 61 startled and impressed the others and led to his receiving some support from his club members to try his hand at playing on the professional circuit.

He went to California for the start of the 1937 season, and in his third outing won the Oakland Open with four sub-par rounds and a total of 270. During the season he won five times and was also runner-up in the US Open, a position he was destined to hold four times.

Snead was a charismatic figure – the hillbilly mountain boy from Virginia. The American public had not had a golfing

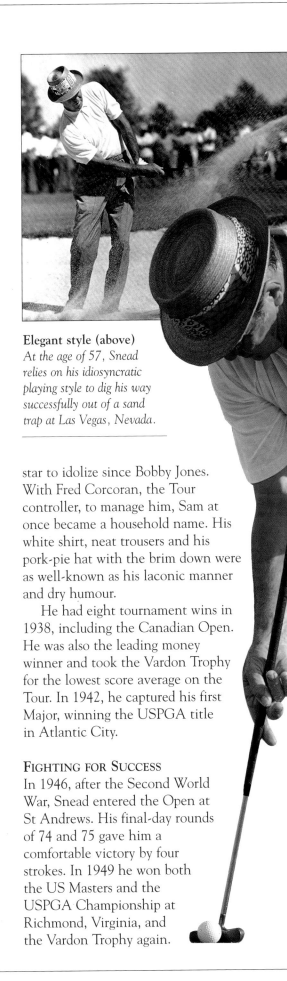

Elegant style (above)
At the age of 57, Snead relies on his idiosyncratic playing style to dig his way successfully out of a sand trap at Las Vegas, Nevada.

star to idolize since Bobby Jones. With Fred Corcoran, the Tour controller, to manage him, Sam at once became a household name. His white shirt, neat trousers and his pork-pie hat with the brim down were as well-known as his laconic manner and dry humour.

He had eight tournament wins in 1938, including the Canadian Open. He was also the leading money winner and took the Vardon Trophy for the lowest score average on the Tour. In 1942, he captured his first Major, winning the USPGA title in Atlantic City.

FIGHTING FOR SUCCESS
In 1946, after the Second World War, Snead entered the Open at St Andrews. His final-day rounds of 74 and 75 gave him a comfortable victory by four strokes. In 1949 he won both the US Masters and the USPGA Championship at Richmond, Virginia, and the Vardon Trophy again.

The sidewinder (below)
Plagued by putting problems in later life, Sam Snead uses his famous "sidewinder" technique, which is a variation of the banned "croquet" style. He faces the hole, standing to one side of the ball, and swings the putter with his right hand low down the shaft.

He was also the leading money winner for the second time and Player of the Year. In all, Snead won the Vardon Trophy four times and was leading money winner three times in the course of his career.

"Slammin' Sam", as he became known, was a founder of the US Senior Tour. He won the USPGA Seniors title six times, the World Seniors five times, and altogether has more Senior tournament wins to his credit than anyone else.

Although Sam Snead cultivated a hillbilly image, he has been astute in managing his affairs and is an amusing speaker when persuaded to talk. He has passed on his golfing knowledge in many books and articles.

SAMUEL JACKSON SNEAD

WON USPGA 1942, 1949, 1951; OPEN CHAMPIONSHIP 1946; US MASTERS 1949, 1952, 1954; USPGA SENIORS 1964, 1965, 1967, 1970, 1972, 1973. WORLD SENIORS 1964, 1965, 1970, 1972, 1973. WINNER OF 81 US TOUR EVENTS 1936–65. RYDER CUP 1937, 1947–55, 1959 (CAPTAIN 1951, 1959, NON-PLAYING CAPTAIN 1969). WORLD CUP 1954, 1956–62 (INDIVIDUAL WINNER 1961). VARDON TROPHY 1938, 1949–50, 1955. USPGA PLAYER OF THE YEAR 1949. USPGA HALL OF FAME 1953. WORLD GOLF HALL OF FAME 1974.

Prize catch
Having teed off first – as is traditional – at the US Masters, the three times Masters Champion Snead, still a country boy at heart, stops off along the course for a quiet spot of fishing.

CRAIG STADLER

BORN SAN DIEGO, CALIFORNIA, USA, 2 JUNE 1953

CRAIG STADLER IS *a formidable golfer, although his form has been variable over the years. Not a man to dissemble, when his game is going badly he often finds difficulty in hiding his annoyance with himself. But he is a good-hearted and genuine person, instantly recognizable from his bushy moustache and known, inevitably, as "The Walrus".*

Stadler had a distinguished career as an amateur before turning professional in 1975 at the age of 22. He won the World Junior in 1971, the US Amateur in 1973, and was an All-America university player in 1974 and 1975. He represented the United States in the Walker Cup of 1975.

In his first few years as a professional Stadler made only a moderate living. His breakthrough came with his first two wins

Gentle approach
For such a bulky man, Stadler has a great delicacy of touch around the green.

on the Tour in 1980, a year in which he finished eighth in the US money order. His big year, however, was 1982, when he won the Masters and three other tournaments – the Tucson Open, the Kemper Open and the World Series. He ended the season by taking the Arnold Palmer Award as the leading money winner on the Tour.

Stadler has twice played in the Ryder Cup and has also won the 1985 European Masters and the 1990 Scandinavian Enterprise Open. He is a big man and he has had to fight a weight problem. But the power of his hitting more than makes up for the jibes he has to suffer from the press and from his fellow professionals.

CRAIG ROBERT STADLER

WON US AMATEUR 1973; US MASTERS 1982. US TOUR CHAMPIONSHIP 1991. WINNER OF 12 US TOUR EVENTS 1980–96. WALKER CUP 1975. RYDER CUP 1983–85. ARNOLD PALMER AWARD 1982.

JAN STEPHENSON

BORN SYDNEY, NEW SOUTH WALES, AUSTRALIA, 22 DECEMBER 1951

FROM HER EARLIEST *days as an Australian schoolgirl champion, Jan Stephenson made her mark as a supremely talented golfer. Her talent, good looks and engaging personality made her one of the most outstanding players in women's golf in the 1970s and 1980s.*

Distractions (right)
Often admired for her blonde good looks and fashion on the course as much as her play, Jan once commented after winning the US Women's Open in 1983 that "perhaps people would now watch her as a golfer".

Consistently in the top 15 money winners on the US LPGA list from 1976 and well into the 1980s, Jan Stephenson won her first New South Wales Girls' title when just 13 years old and went on to win it five times. Four times she won the State Junior title and twice the State Amateur.

She turned professional in 1973 and joined the US LPGA the following year. In that year Jan was named Rookie of the Year and went on to win 16 LPGA events from 1976 to 1987.

Off the tournament trail she was the first woman player to take an interest in golf-course design.

JAN STEPHENSON

WON AUSTRALIAN LADIES OPEN 1973, 1977; PETER JACKSON CLASSIC 1981; LPGA CHAMPIONSHIP 1982; US WOMEN'S OPEN 1983; LADIES' FRENCH OPEN 1985. WINNER OF 16 LPGA EVENTS 1976–87.

⟨ PAYNE STEWART, see page 336

CURTIS STRANGE

BORN NORFOLK, VIRGINIA, USA, 20 JANUARY 1955

C ONSISTENCY HAS BEEN *the hallmark of Curtis Strange's success. His secret lies in hitting greens with uncanny regularity and holing a significant number of putts. In 1988, Strange became the first player to earn more than $1 million in one season on the US Tour, but his finest triumph was winning consecutive US Open Championships in 1988 and 1989.*

By the time he was eight years old Curtis Strange was playing golf every day. He was the son of a golf professional in Norfolk, Virginia, and the game has always been part of his life. As an amateur he developed into a long hitter. When he was 19, Strange was selected for the Eisenhower Trophy team, and the following year he played in the US Walker Cup victory over Great Britain and Ireland.

Strange turned professional in 1976 and qualified for the US Tour in 1977, but finished well down the money list in 1977 and 1978.

Alone with his thoughts (right)
Strange is an introspective individual, occasionally abrupt in his dealings with other people, notably the press.

Down the creek (below)
Strange's hopes of winning the 1985 Masters sank when he found the water of Rae's Creek at the 13th hole.

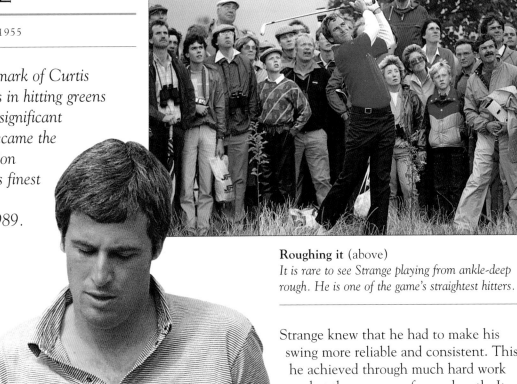

Roughing it (above)
It is rare to see Strange playing from ankle-deep rough. He is one of the game's straightest hitters.

Strange knew that he had to make his swing more reliable and consistent. This he achieved through much hard work and at the expense of some length. It was hard work well rewarded, for Strange soon emerged as a major force in world golf, winning his first US Tour event in 1979, and the next year finishing third in the US money list. He was runner-up in the Masters in 1985 and runner-up in the USPGA Championship at Kemper Lakes in 1989.

Strange's first US Open win, at Brookline in 1988, came after a play-off with Nick Faldo: Strange won by 71 to 75. His successful defence of the title the next year, at Oak Hill, made him the first winner of consecutive Opens since Hogan. Known as "The Grinder", he has been a master of the art of winning at golf.

CURTIS NORTHRUP STRANGE

WON CANADIAN OPEN 1985, 1987; US OPEN 1988, 1989. US TOUR CHAMPIONSHIP 1988. WINNER OF 17 US TOUR EVENTS 1979–89. EISENHOWER TROPHY 1974. WALKER CUP 1975. RYDER CUP 1983–89, 1995 (NON-PLAYING CAPTAIN 2001). FOUR TOURS CHAMPIONSHIP 1985, 1987–89. DUNHILL CUP 1987–91, 1994. ARNOLD PALMER AWARD 1985, 1987, 1988. USPGA PLAYER OF THE YEAR 1988.

PAYNE STEWART

BORN SPRINGFIELD, MISSOURI, USA, 30 JANUARY 1957; DIED 1999.

T HE TRAGIC DEATH of Payne Stewart in a freak aeroplane accident in 1999 robbed golf not only of a great champion but one of the most colourful characters of the modern game.

Stewart died only weeks after winning his second US Open title in dramatic fashion at Pinehurst and the world of golf was stunned by his loss. He had boarded a chartered, twin-engine Lear 35 and was on his way to Texas to discuss a proposed new course near Dallas, and then on to play in the Tour Championship in Houston for the top 30 on the USPGA Tour's money list.

1999 US Open Champion (below) A wonderful highlight in an all too short career.

Victory at Pinehurst Number 2 (right) Stewart dramatically holed a curling right to left 15ft (4.5m) putt on the final green to hold off Phil Mickelson by one stroke and clinch the 1999 US Open title.

his first major title, the USPGA. Two years later he defeated Scott Simpson in a memorable US Open at Hazeltine for his second major. Both had finished six under par after 72 holes before Stewart went on to win the title by two strokes in the 18-hole play-off.

In 1998 Stewart lost a US Open title to Lee Janzen that he should really have won, but the following year he found redemption at Pinehurst's famous Number 2 course.

WILLIAM PAYNE STEWART

WON USPGA 1989; US OPEN 1991, 1999; DUTCH OPEN 1991. WINNER OF 11 US TOUR EVENTS 1982–99. FOUR TOURS CHAMPIONSHIP 1986–87, 1989–90. RYDER CUP 1987–93, 1999. WORLD CUP 1987, 1990 (INDIVIDUAL WINNER 1990). DUNHILL CUP 1993, 1999.

Flair (right) In Britain they call them "plus fours" and in the United States they call them "knickers"; Stewart made them his instantly recognizable trademark.

TRAGIC LOSS

The aircraft suffered a loss of cabin pressure and flew a ghostly journey halfway across the United States with its windows iced over and its six occupants incapacitated before nose-diving into a grassy field. Everyone aboard was killed. It was a tragic end to a colourful career and for a man who was instantly recognized by his flamboyant golf dress.

However, his sometime outrageous dress did nothing to disguise the fact that Payne Stewart was one of the best all-rounders in the game. In 1989 he topped the $1 million earnings mark, was an established US Ryder Cup player and won

Colourful clothes (right) Stewart often wore golf shirts in the colours of US football teams, gold-tipped shoes, and brightly coloured flat caps.

FREDDIE TAIT

BORN EDINBURGH, SCOTLAND, 11 JANUARY 1870; DIED 1900

WHEN FREDDIE TAIT *was killed leading his men into battle in the Boer War at Koodoosberg Drift, a great player was lost to the game of golf. He was much loved and admired as a kind and courteous man, and his death cast a great shadow across Scotland. Although he shunned the limelight and tried various subterfuges to avoid publicity, he collected a following wherever he went.*

Mark of respect
Lieutenant Tait of the Black Watch was greatly admired by his fellow soldiers.

A man and his dog
A posthumous portrait of Tait, with his terrier Nails, was painted by J.H. Lorimer.

Young Freddie took to the links from the age of five. He soon displayed remarkable ability and, by the age of 12, had played St Andrews' Old Course in less than a 100 strokes, a marked achievement at that time for one so young. Tait hit the ball as hard as he could, but he soon developed an unhurried and comfortable swing, displaying a sizeable reserve of power and great control.

Tait joined the Royal & Ancient Club in 1890 and, that same year, lowered the Old Course record to 77 in a match against the former Amateur Champion A.F. MacFie. Four years later he reduced it again to 72.

Freddie Tait first played in the Open Championship in 1891 and was three times leading amateur in the event. He won the Amateur Championship in 1896 at Sandwich, trouncing Harold Hilton eight and seven in the final. After winning the Amateur again in 1898, at Hoylake, he lost to John Ball at the 37th hole in an epic final at Prestwick in 1899.

Today he is remembered through the Freddie Tait Medal, which is played for annually in St Andrews.

FREDERICK GUTHRIE TAIT

WON BRITISH AMATEUR CHAMPIONSHIP 1896, 1898; ST GEORGE'S CHALLENGE TROPHY 1896, 1898, 1899.

J.H.TAYLOR

BORN NORTHAM, ENGLAND, 19 MARCH 1871; DIED 1963

JOHN HENRY TAYLOR, *known throughout his career as "J.H.", was the first to come to prominence of the immortal Triumvirate – Vardon, Braid and Taylor – who dominated golf in the latter part of the nineteenth and early part of the twentieth centuries. Between them, they won no fewer than 16 Open Championships, Taylor winning five and being runner-up in six others.*

J.H. Taylor was born close to the famous links of Westward Ho! where he worked as a youngster. His father had died when J.H. was an infant and he left school at the age of 11. By the age of 20, he had matured into a fine player and went to Burnham and Berrow as greenkeeper and professional, first making his mark by beating Andrew Kirkaldy. Shortly afterwards, he took over from Andrew Kirkaldy as professional at Winchester and later moved to Royal Mid-Surrey, where he was the resident professional for 47 years until he retired in 1946.

Side line
An official picture of J.H. Taylor taken as he prepared to leave for Egypt, where he was to design a new golf links in partnership with Fred Hawtree.

THE ROAD TO FAME

Taylor's first Open Championship was in 1893 and he led at one stage, but it was the following year that was to put J.H. Taylor on the road to becoming the greatest name in the land. The 1894 Open was played at Sandwich, the first time it had been played outside of Scotland, and after 36 holes J.H. was in the lead. He went on to win by five strokes and broke the domination the Scots had exercised over the Open from its beginnings in 1860.

In 1895 he took on the Scots again in their own heartland at St Andrews, and despite an opening round of 86 he won by a clear four strokes. This established him as the dominant player in the game. The following year he suffered something of a setback when he was beaten in a challenge match by the up-and-coming Harry Vardon. Nor did he win at the Open one month later. Taylor, with a three-stroke lead going into the final round, could only tie with Vardon and then lost the 36-hole play-off.

He had his revenge in 1900 at St Andrews, when he won with a score of 309, becoming only the fifth man in the history of the event to break 80 in each round, and beating Vardon by eight strokes. James Braid finished third.

In a brilliant career, Taylor also won the French Open in 1908 and 1909, the German Open in 1912, and

was runner-up to Vardon in the 1900 US Open at Wheaton, Illinois. He was regarded as the pioneer of professional golf and was instrumental in the formation of the Professional Golfers' Association in Britain, doing much to elevate the status of the game. Referring to his contribution to the status of golfers, Bernard Darwin wrote that J.H. Taylor had "turned a feckless company into a self-respecting and respected body of men".

Despite his lack of early formal education, J.H. was a public speaker of rare charm. He realized early in

Postcard fame (below)
J.H. enjoyed the great prestige he earned as a successful golfer and its accompanying spin-offs, such as opportunities for advertising.

J. H. TAYLOR.

Opening shot (above)
J.H. drives during the opening of St George's Golf Club, Weybridge.

Stylish play (right)
Taylor's distinctive style is captured on this cigarette card.

his career that this was necessary if he was to speak for his word-shy fellow professionals. He was honoured many times in his career, including honorary membership of the Royal & Ancient Golf Club in 1949. The Royal North Devon Golf Club bestowed on him their highest honour by electing him President in 1957.

J.H. Taylor was the last survivor of the Triumvirate. He was a month short of his 92nd birthday when he died in 1963.

Useful tips (right)
Taylor often gave displays of golfing technique on private and public courses, as well as in famous stores such as Harrods.

JOHN HENRY TAYLOR

WON OPEN CHAMPIONSHIP 1894, 1895, 1900, 1909, 1913; PGA MATCHPLAY 1904, 1908; FRENCH OPEN 1908, 1909; GERMAN OPEN 1912. RYDER CUP (NON-PLAYING CAPTAIN 1933). HONORARY MEMBER R & A GOLF CLUB. WORLD GOLF HALL OF FAME 1975.

PETER THOMSON

BORN MELBOURNE, AUSTRALIA, 23 AUGUST 1929

P ETER THOMSON, WINNER of five Open Championships in Britain, is the greatest golfer to emerge from Australia. His last Open victory, at Royal Birkdale in 1965, proved to be the finest of his career. He beat a field including Tony Lema, Jack Nicklaus and Arnold Palmer, finally quashing the suggestion that he owed his spectacular record of success in Europe and Australia to weak opposition.

Talking with Thomson, one gets the strong impression that he would have been a success at anything to which he turned his hand. Intelligent and well-read, he claims that you can tell a top player simply by meeting him and seeing him under pressure. "The super player has one vital quality – calmness," he says.

Nowhere is that quality needed more than on the inward nine holes of an Open Championship on the last day, and that was often when Thomson showed his class as a player. A man blessed with outstanding confidence, he burst into British golf in the 1950s and took it apart, beating such fine players as Christy O'Connor, Dai Rees and Max Faulkner. Only Bobby Locke, from South Africa, proved a match for Thomson. The two

First touch (right)
Thomson receives the claret jug in 1954 after the first of his five British Open victories.

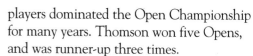

players dominated the Open Championship for many years. Thomson won five Opens, and was runner-up three times.

He would often start a tournament quietly with a couple of ordinary rounds, but finish strongly. His famous victory in the 1965 Open was a classic example. In the last round, playing with the defending champion Tony Lema in a wind that swirled across the Royal Birkdale links, Thomson put on a superb show. A perfect drive at the last hole set him up. He then swept a 3-iron on to the green, and his four gave him the title by two strokes.

St Andrews revisited
Thomson plays a quiet round at St Andrews, the scene of his second Open Championship in 1955.

Strong nerves under pressure (left and opposite) *Thomson had the quality he himself identified as the mark of a top player – calmness under stress.*

PETER WILLIAM THOMSON, CBE

WON NEW ZEALAND OPEN 1950–51, 1953, 1955, 1959–61, 1965, 1971; AUSTRALIAN OPEN 1951, 1967, 1972; OPEN CHAMPIONSHIP 1954–56, 1958, 1965; PGA MATCHPLAY 1954, 1961, 1966–67; BRITISH MASTERS 1961, 1968; USPGA SENIORS 1984; BRITISH PGASENIORS 1988. WINNER OF 11 US SENIOR TOUR EVENTS 198–85. DUNLOP MASTERS 1961, 1968. WORLD CUP 1953–57, 1959–62, 1965, 1969. HONORARY MEMBER R & A GOLF CLUB.

LEE TREVINO

BORN DALLAS, TEXAS, USA, 1 DECEMBER 1939

L OOKING BACK ON *the career of Lee Buck Trevino, Mexican-American school drop-out, ex-Marine sergeant and all-round golfing hustler, golf history will probably have to rank him among the greatest ten players the world has ever seen. In the summer of 1971, the "Merry Mex" won three Open Championships – of the United States, Britain and Canada – within the space of one month. He is unquestionably one of the most entertaining golfers in the professional game.*

The illegitimate son of an immigrant Mexican grave-digger, Lee Trevino came from the humblest of backgrounds. "Rich people like to talk about their backgrounds," Trevino recalls today. "We were too poor to care. We just managed to exist." Their four-room plank house had neither electricity nor running water.

The only reason young Lee began playing golf was that his home stood in a hay field next to the Glen Lakes Country Club. "In those days I used to practise golf shots off the mud. Today I put a new ball on pegs with my own name on them. Sure, I've come a long way."

EARLY DAYS
Trevino left school early and became a local greenkeeper. He caddied when he could, played a few holes at dusk, but only took a serious interest in golf after he joined the Marines at 17. Asked if he played any sport, he casually mentioned golf; the Marines gave him a try and he shot a round of 66. When his unit transferred to the Far East, he played in Japan, Taiwan and the Philippines.

Returning home to Texas after his discharge in 1961, Trevino found plenty of filled wallets waiting to be tapped by a golfing hustler in local money matches. At this stage in his game, he would often play with just one club, a rusty but trusty 3-iron, and he would give his opponent handicap shots just to increase the wager.

Supermex
Trevino's attitudes stem from a tough childhood in Texas as a Mexican immigrant. On his cap he sports the Mexican sombrero that has become his emblem.

Down the line (above)
Trevino's swing keeps the club travelling down the line longer than that of any other player.

While working in the evenings, Trevino would attract a crowd by playing with a Dr Pepper bottle at Hardy's Pitch-n-Putt. The bottle, wrapped in adhesive tape, could hit the ball a good, solid blow and Trevino, hustling against wealthy opponents using conventional clubs, would make around $200 a week. He also developed a patter that would get laughs and, maybe, distract. Trevino later described this experience as a good grounding for success on the glamorous international scene: "Pressure is when you've got $3 in your pocket and you're playing for $10."

PROFESSIONAL SUCCESS
Although he turned professional in 1960, it was a long time before Trevino made any impact on the US Tour. In 1967 he earned a respectable fifth place in the US Open and was named Rookie of the Year – enough to persuade Trevino to join the Tour full-time. But he was still a complete outsider when he came to the 1968 Open at Oak Hill, Rochester, and won in a spectacular manner, defeating the

legendary Jack Nicklaus by four strokes and becoming the first player to break 70 in all four rounds of the Championship. The golfing world greeted this unorthodox character, with his inimitable style of play, as a major new superstar.

ON TOP OF THE WORLD
Trevino reached his peak in the early 1970s. He was leading money winner on the US Tour at the start of the decade, and then came his extraordinary winning streak in 1971 when he won three Opens. Trevino went on to retain the British Open title at Muirfield the following year, holing four pitch shots during the week to snatch the Championship from Tony Jacklin – "God is a Mexican" was Trevino's comment.

After this purple patch he was never quite as successful again, although his further victories included two USPGA Championships and the British Masters title. He has never won the US Masters, apparently finding difficulty with the course – and sometimes also with the attitudes he perceives at Augusta.

Trevino's drive has a very individual style. He lines his body up to the left of the target and swings back outside the line, returning the clubhead straight down

Master putter
Trevino is known for his control and his swing, but it is often overlooked how good a putter he is.

the line into the ball. His accuracy is such that it has been said the only time he leaves the fairway is to make a telephone call. He is also one of the most brilliant golf-course strategists.

ON-COURSE ANTICS
Almost as striking as his golf, however, is his behaviour on the course. When he took his clubs to the British Isles, it was as though a circus act had arrived. At Muirfield, Neil Coles, a serious English professional, asked the R & A if they minded that he play with someone other than Trevino, as the Trevino "chat" distracted him so much. At Wentworth, Tony Jacklin asked if their match could possibly be played with a certain degree of silence, so he could concentrate. "Sure", said Trevino, "you don't have to say a word – you just have to listen!" Other antics included producing a rubber snake on the first tee before the 1971 US Open play-off against Jack Nicklaus, which Trevino won.

Despite all his wins and the wealth they have brought, Lee Trevino has never lost sight of his poor beginnings. "A lot of guys on the Tour gripe about the travel and the food, and losing their laundry," says Trevino. "But no matter how bad the

food is, I've eaten worse. And I couldn't care less about the dry cleaning because I remember when I only had one shirt."

Success has not been smooth: after winning a million, he lost it in a failed business venture. But Lee picked himself up and won several millions more, ending up as a celebrity on the US Senior Tour, where he took more money in 1990 than the winner of the regular US Tour.

LEE BUCK TREVINO

WON US OPEN 1968, 1971; OPEN CHAMPIONSHIP 1971–72; CANADIAN OPEN 1971, 1977, 1979; USPGA 1974, 1984; LANCÔME TROPHY 1978, 1980; US PLAYERS CHAMPIONSHIP 1980; BRITISH MASTERS 1985. US SENIOR OPEN 1990; USPGA SENIORS' 1992, 1994. WINNER OF 27 US TOUR EVENTS 1968–84. LEADING MONEY WINNER 1970. WINNER OF 29 US SENIOR TOUR EVENTS 1990–2000. WORLD CUP 1968–71, 1974 (INDIVIDUAL WINNER 1969). RYDER CUP 1969–75, 1979–81 (NON-PLAYING CAPTAIN 1985). VARDON TROPHY 1970–72, 1974, 1980. USPGA PLAYER OF THE YEAR 1971. BEN HOGAN AWARD 1980. ARNOLD PALMER AWARD 1990, 1992; JACK NICKLAUS AWARD 1990, 1992, 1994; BRYON NELSON AWARD 1990–92. WORLD GOLF HALL OF FAME 1981.

Low scorer (below)
Trevino won the Vardon Trophy five times. The Trophy is awarded to the player with the lowest scoring average on the USPGA Tour.

Wit and wisdom
In the 1980s, Trevino applied his gift for witty commentary, which had often annoyed his fellow players on the course, to television coverage.

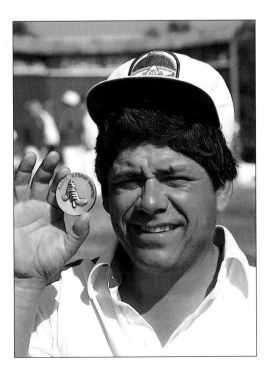

HARRY VARDON

BORN JERSEY, CHANNEL ISLANDS, 9 MAY 1870; DIED 1937

H ARRY VARDON WAS one of the greatest players ever to grace the game of golf. He may well have been the purest striker of a golf ball there has ever been. As the leading member of the Great Triumvirate, with his colleagues James Braid and J.H. Taylor, Vardon dominated golf around the beginning of the twentieth century, winning a record total of six Open Championships.

Postcard hero
One of Vardon's strengths was his ability with the driver, shown in a postcard of the time.

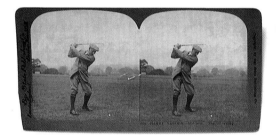

Double image (above)
Vardon's style of play was presented as a model for aspiring golfers in this 1910 stereoscopic photo.

Escape (left)
Stymied by his opponent, Vardon chips a shot over the obstructing ball.

Ace of clubs (right)
Harry Vardon was a supremely successful competitive golfer and did much to increase the popularity of the game. At his best, around the start of the twentieth century, he was virtually invincible.

Harry Vardon was born at Grouville on Jersey, where there was little opportunity for him to play, but his interest in golf awoke early. He was acting as a caddie by the age of seven. When his brother Tom went to England and found that he could make money as a professional, Harry soon decided to follow in his footsteps.

He took a job at a nine-hole course at Ripon in Yorkshire, despite having only played a few dozen games in his life. He soon moved on to Bury St Edmunds and then to Ganton, back in Yorkshire. It was from there that he established his fame as not only the greatest player of his time, but also a leading popularizer of the game.

SIX OPEN TRIUMPHS

Between them the Great Triumvirate won 16 British Opens. Vardon won six of them, a record that still stands today. In 1893 he made his first appearance in the Open Championship, at Prestwick, but he made little impression. The following year he finished fifth at Sandwich, the first time the Open was played in England and the first time J.H. Taylor won it.

In 1895 Vardon came to prominence when he led the Open after the first round at St Andrews, only to finish in ninth place; Taylor won again to establish himself as the leading player of the day.

But the members at Ganton were so confident of the ability of their own professional that they raised the money for a

Man of bronze
As a golfing hero, Vardon was depicted in many different ways. This bronze figurine by Hal Ludlow captures the essence of Vardon's effortless swing.

twice in all the matches he played. He also won the US Open at Wheaton, Illinois.

Harry Vardon was at his greatest over a seven-year period between 1896 and 1903. Then he was struck down with tuberculosis, a serious illness from which he never completely recovered. Although he could not again attain the dominance that he had once enjoyed, he still won the Open Championship on two more occasions, in 1911 and 1914.

Vardon's illness was blamed in some quarters for a later and sad decline in his ability with the putter, particularly with the short putts. In his book *This Game of Golf*, Henry Cotton recalled being startled by the putting of the great man, by then well past his best.

about the stiff left arm, the great man replied simply: "I like playing against people with stiff left arms." Vardon was rare among the great players in not taking a divot with any of his shots. So accurate was he with all his clubs that he could always sweep the ball off the turf cleanly, hardly disturbing the surface at all.

THE VARDON GRIP

Harry Vardon popularized the overlapping grip, in which the little finger of the right hand overlaps the index finger of the left in the right-handed grip. It became known as the Vardon Grip, although he did not in fact invent it. The great amateur player Johnny Laidlay is thought to have been the first to use this style of grip, which is still the most popular among today's top professionals.

HARRY VARDON

WON OPEN CHAMPIONSHIP 1896, 1898, 1899, 1903, 1911, 1914; US OPEN 1900; PGA MATCHPLAY 1912. LEADING MEMBER OF THE GREAT TRIUMVIRATE OF VARDON, BRAID AND TAYLOR. WORLD GOLF HALL OF FAME 1974.

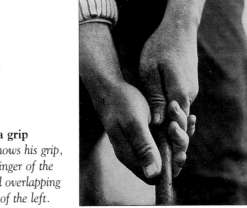

Getting a grip
Vardon shows his grip, the little finger of the right hand overlapping the index of the left.

Vardon versus Ray (below)
Ted Ray watches the flight of the ball as Vardon tees off at the 6th during the Open Championship at Muirfield in 1912. Ray beat Vardon into second place that year.

challenge match between Vardon and Taylor. Vardon won by eight and six decisively. A month later the Open was played at Muirfield, and Harry Vardon found himself in another battle with Taylor. With one round still to play, Vardon was three behind, but he fought his way back and finished in a tie. In the play-off, which in those days was over 36 holes, Vardon won by four strokes. With Braid and Taylor, he was to dominate the Championship for the next two decades.

At a time when there were very few tournaments in Britain or America, other than the Open Championships, competition play for professionals was largely confined to money matches, challenges and exhibitions. When he was at the height of his powers around the turn of the century, Vardon spent almost a year touring the United States and playing exhibitions. He was beaten only

Cotton described "the unbelievable jerking of the clubhead, in an effort to make contact with the ball from two feet or less from the hole". This was an affliction that had affected Vardon to some degree throughout his career, but was more than compensated for by his uncanny accuracy, elegance and purity of stroke.

His swing was much more upright than was the vogue of the time, and he played with a slightly bent left arm and a flying right elbow, when the fashion was for a rigid left arm. Asked once what he thought

JESSIE VALENTINE

BORN PERTH, SCOTLAND, 18 MARCH 1915

BORN DURING THE *First World War, Janet (Jessie) Valentine was the daughter of a noted golf and cricket professional. She was only 5ft 1in (1.55m) tall, but from the beginning of her career she had a neat and compact swing that gave her great control for such a slight person. Always ready to accept a challenge, she was an attacking player with a strong competitive streak.*

Valentine came to prominence in 1936. Selected for the Curtis Cup, she sank a famous long putt on the last green to win her final singles and square the match. In the same year, she beat Pam Barton at the 37th hole of the French Ladies' final.

Jessie Valentine went on to win a hatful of other championships, and was an almost automatic choice for British international teams until the late 1950s.

Leading Scot
Jessie Valentine was a formidable competitor, winning three British Ladies' and six Scottish Ladies' Championships over two decades.

JANET VALENTINE (NÉE ANDERSON), MBE

WON FRENCH LADIES' AMATEUR 1936; BRITISH LADIES' AMATEUR 1937, 1955, 1958; SCOTTISH LADIES' AMATEUR 1938, 1939, 1951, 1953, 1955, 1956; WORPLESDON MIXED FOURSOMES 1963–65. CURTIS CUP 1936–38, 1950–58. GB v COMMONWEALTH 1953, 1955 (NON-PLAYING CAPTAIN 1959).

❮ HARRY VARDON, SEE PAGE 344

ROBERTO DE VICENZO

BORN BUENOS AIRES, ARGENTINA, 14 APRIL 1923

ARGENTINIAN GOLFER *Roberto de Vicenzo will always be remembered for his victory in the British Open at Hoylake in 1967 at the age of 44 – the oldest winner since Old Tom Morris. A frank, wholehearted person, he always enjoyed great popularity.*

Son of a poor family in Buenos Aires, Roberto de Vicenzo turned professional in 1938. Six years later he first won the Argentinian Open and established himself as the leading South American player for the next three decades.

He won six tournaments on the US circuit and national Opens in Belgium, the Netherlands, Spain, Germany and France, but he struggled to reach his main goal of winning the British Open. He was

Late riser
De Vicenzo rose to his greatest heights after reaching the age of 40.

runner-up in 1950 and third no fewer than six times, before he was finally successful at Hoylake at his nineteenth attempt. A last round of 70 kept him two strokes ahead of runner-up Jack Nicklaus. It was an emotional occasion and de Vicenzo's victory was one of the most popular in the history of the event.

The Argentinian might have won another Major in 1968, but for an error in marking his card. He would have forced a play-off with Bob Goalby for the Masters title, had he not signed for a four at the 17th, instead of the birdie-three he had played. The score had to stand.

ROBERTO DE VICENZO

WON OPEN CHAMPIONSHIP 1967; USPGA SENIORS 1974; USGA SENIOR OPEN 1980. WINNER OF OVER 40 EVENTS WORLDWIDE 1944–74. WORLD CUP (REPRESENTING ARGENTINA) 1953–55, 1962–66, 1968–74, (REPRESENTING MEXICO) 1956, 1959, 1960–61 (INDIVIDUAL WINNER 1962, 1970). BOB JONES AWARD 1970. USPGA HALL OF FAME 1979. WORLD GOLF HALL OF FAME 1989.

GLENNA COLLETT VARE

BORN NEW HAVEN, CONNECTICUT, USA, 20 JUNE 1903; DIED 1989

G| LENNA COLLETT VARE *dominated ladies' golf in the United States for many years during the 1920s and 1930s. One of the first women to hit the ball freely, she could drive great distances. She played with extreme concentration, but at the same time with a bubbling, infectious enthusiasm.*

The American did not take up golf until she was 14, but by the age of 19 she had defeated Cecil Leitch, the British Ladies' Champion, three times. She won her first US Ladies' title in 1922 and her last in 1935. Her total of six wins was a record for USGA events. From 1928 to 1931 she won 19 consecutive matches, also a record.

Collett never won the British Ladies', although she twice reached the final, in 1929 and 1930. The 1929 final against Joyce Wethered at St Andrews was one of the best ever seen. After playing the first nine holes in 34 strokes to go five up, the American player could not withstand Wethered's comeback and lost at the 35th.

Glenna Collett was certainly the finest American woman golfer of her time. She married businessman Edwin Vare in 1931.

GLENNA COLLETT VARE

WON US LADIES' AMATEUR 1922, 1925, 1928, 1929, 1930, 1935; CANADIAN LADIES' 1923, 1924. CURTIS CUP 1932–38, 1948 (CAPTAIN 1936, 1948, NON-PLAYING CAPTAIN 1934, 1950). BOB JONES AWARD 1965. WORLD GOLF HALL OF FAME 1975.

Title shot (above)
Glenna playing in the 1925 Ladies' Amateur Championship at Troon.

Off duty (below)
Glenna Collett Vare relaxes during her first appearance in the Curtis Cup in 1932.

KARRIE WEBB

BORN AYR, QUEENSLAND, AUSTRALIA, 21 DECEMBER 1974

F| IRST WINNER OF *the US Women's Open in the new millennium, Karrie Webb has had a golfing career whose statistics since 1996 are mind-boggling. There was a spell as 1999 ended and the new century began when she was either first or second in eight consecutive tournaments, going back to October 1999.*

Runaway
(below)
Webb won by five strokes at the 35th US Women's Open in Illinois.

Among her five firsts was the opening major in 2000, the Nabisco Championship at Rancho Mirage, California. From day one the cry had been "who's gonna be second?" as the Australian turned in a 14 under par total of 274, ten clear of Dottie Pepper and the largest winning margin in the tournament's history.

The LPGA knew they had a budding talent as early as the tour's final qualifying school of 1995, when Webb, nursing a broken wrist bone, came second. Her rookie year was stunning – four victories (beaten in history only by Nancy Lopez's nine). Webb became the first rookie – on either the LPGA or the USPGA Tour – to win $1 million (in a mere ten months and ten days).

Prolific winner (right)
Webb won seven times in the LPGA's 50th anniversary year.

KARRIE WEBB

WON WOMEN'S BRITISH OPEN 1995, 1997; LPGA TOUR CHAMPIONSHIP 1996; AUSTRALIAN LADIES MASTERS 1998–2000; US WOMEN'S OPEN 2000. WINNER OF 23 LPGA EVENTS 1995–2000

❮ TOM WATSON, SEE PAGE **348**

TOM WATSON

BORN KANSAS CITY, MISSOURI, USA, 4 SEPTEMBER 1949

T OM WATSON IS *rare among his generation of American professionals in being a devotee of traditional British links golf. Most of his compatriots would have the element of chance, so much a part of hard, seaside links golf, taken out of the equation. But at his best Watson thrived on the unpredictable British courses.*

Watson's first British Open victory was a memorable occasion. Coming to the final hole in the play-off against Jack Newton at Carnoustie in 1975, he faced a tough 2-iron shot over the burn in front of the green. Newton was in a greenside bunker, and a four would be good enough for Watson to win. The young man from Kansas City, who had only been a professional for four years, struck a majestic shot to the heart of the green for a memorable victory that catapulted him into golf's major league.

GOLFING PSYCHOLOGIST

Watson had been the top player on the Stanford University golf team, but he was not one of the golf-scholarship students that American universities were turning out tailor-made for the professional Tour. He went to Stanford to study and graduated in psychology.

The following year he joined the USPGA Tour but success was slow in coming. Although there was no doubting his rare talent, Watson was reputed to be frightened of winning. American sports journalists were keen to write off a player they christened "Huckleberry Finn".

But Watson was not frightened to win – he had simply not learned how. In 1974 he found out, winning the Western Open. The same year he led the US Open by a stroke going into the last

Road victim (above)
Close to retaining the Open Championship at St Andrews in 1984, Watson hit his second shot against the wall at the notorious 17th hole and never recovered.

Watson's guru
Byron Nelson (above) was Tom Watson's mentor, helping perfect his game in the 1970s.

Happy Tom (below)
Watson rejoices at winning the 1982 US Open at Pebble Beach.

round, only to finish joint fifth. Then came that dramatic play-off against the luckless Australian, Jack Newton, the last time the Open was played at Carnoustie before it was removed from the rota for 24 years.

This first British Open victory initiated a golden age for Watson. As well as four more Open Championships, he won the Masters twice, in 1977 and 1981, and topped the US money list four years in a row from 1977 to 1980.

DUEL IN THE SUN
His greatest single triumph was the Open Championship of 1977 at Turnberry. In a week of high sunshine and even higher drama, Watson and Jack Nicklaus fought out one of the most dramatic matches in the history of golf.

Bent jug (left)
Watson holds a damaged trophy after winning at Royal Birkdale in 1983 – it had been dropped and was bent as a result.

The two players were so far ahead of the field that it became a head-to-head battle – a battle that will be forever remembered as "The Duel in the Sun". For 70 holes Watson had never held the lead, but going to the last he was one ahead. After finding the gorse with his drive, Nicklaus manufactured a birdie with a monster putt, forcing Watson to birdie for victory. Tom's 7-iron approach finished close to the hole and he tapped in to win. In 1982 Watson won both the Open Championship and the US Open, which had eluded him for so long, and in 1984 he topped the US money list for the fifth time.

UNFULFILLED POTENTIAL

Yet it still seems that Watson failed to realize his full potential. At St Andrews in 1984 he might easily have equalled the legendary Harry Vardon's total of six Open victories, had he not fallen victim to the notorious 17th Road Hole in the

Senior hitter (above) *Watson's first victory on the Senior Tour made him the third youngest player ever to win such an event, at 50 years and 15 days.*

final round. This failure was a turning point in his career. At the height of his powers as one of golf's best putters, Watson began to suffer problems with the "short ones" and knew his halcyon days were over. After winning 34 titles on the USPGA Tour Tom Watson joined the Senior Tour in 1999 and won his first title in his second event.

THOMAS STURGES WATSON

WON OPEN CHAMPIONSHIP 1975, 1977, 1980, 1982–83; US MASTERS 1977, 1981; US OPEN 1982; US TOUR CHAMPIONSHIP 1987; US SENIOR TOUR CHAMPIONSHIP 2000. WINNER OF 34 US TOUR EVENTS 1974 –98. LEADING MONEY WINNER 1977–80, 1984. USPGA PLAYER OF THE YEAR 1977–80, 1982, 1984. VARDON TROPHY 1977–79. RYDER CUP 1977, 1981–83, 1989 (NON-PLAYING CAPTAIN 1993). BOB JONES AWARD 1987. WORLD GOLF HALL OF FAME 1988.

Two of the greats (left) *Watson and Faldo check their line during a practice round at the 2000 Open Championship.*

Battling on (above) *Watson tied for 6th place with Clark Dennis and Greg Norman at the 1994 US Open at Oakmont.*

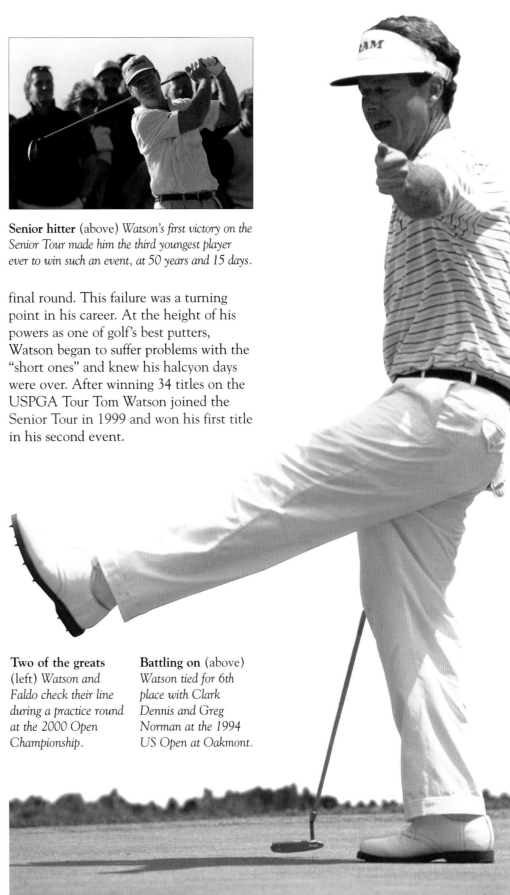

TOM WEISKOPF

BORN MASSILLON, OHIO, USA, 9 NOVEMBER 1942

L OOKING AT THE record of Tom Weiskopf, there are many who will conclude that he has done less than justice to an exceptional talent. He has one of the great golf swings of the modern game – "majestic" is the word most frequently used to describe it. Yet, despite one of the best careers ever on the US Tour, he has won only one Major. In truth, he should have won many more.

Weiskopf took up golf at the age of 15 and within a few months was a low-handicap player. After he joined the US Tour in 1964, it quickly became apparent that golf had found a new and remarkable talent. "Long Tom"

Triumph at Troon
Weiskopf sinks a putt during the 1973 Open Championship. His Open victory was the summit of his career and earned him the durable respect of the British golfing public.

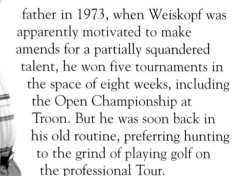

Elegance and power
Weiskopf's long smooth swing had an elegance unusual in a tall man.

Matchplay (above)
Weiskopf defending his World Matchplay title at Wentworth in 1973.

Weiskopf was one of the longest hitters the game had ever seen. Added to a delicate touch with the putter, this made him a formidable force.

Throughout his career, however, Weiskopf has also had a reputation for unpredictable temperament and motivation. He once turned down a place in the American Ryder Cup team because he preferred to go on a hunting trip. If he applied himself he could be almost unbeatable. Following the death of his

father in 1973, when Weiskopf was apparently motivated to make amends for a partially squandered talent, he won five tournaments in the space of eight weeks, including the Open Championship at Troon. But he was soon back in his old routine, preferring hunting to the grind of playing golf on the professional Tour.

Although Tom Weiskopf won only one Major championship, he came close on many other occasions. He was runner-up in the US Open once, at Atlanta in 1976, and finished third in that championship twice. He was also four times runner-up in the US Masters.

THOMAS DANIEL WEISKOPF

WON WORLD MATCHPLAY CHAMPIONSHIP 1972; OPEN CHAMPIONSHIP 1973; CANADIAN OPEN 1973, 1975. US SENIOR OPEN 1995. WINNER OF 15 US TOUR EVENTS 1968–82, 4 US SENIOR TOUR EVENTS 1994–96. WORLD CUP 1972. RYDER CUP 1973–75.

JOYCE WETHERED

BORN LONDON, ENGLAND, 17 NOVEMBER 1901; DIED 1997

T HE GREAT AMATEUR *Bobby Jones once stated that, in his opinion, Joyce Wethered (Lady Heathcoat-Amory) had "the best swing of either man or woman" that he had ever seen. She was undoubtedly one of the supreme lady golfers of all time.*

As a child Joyce Wethered lived in the south of England, but her parents had a holiday home next to the links at Dornoch in Sutherland, Scotland. She and her elder brother, Roger, used to play golf every day when they were there.

Roger became a first-class player and his sister was able to play against him and his friends. This helped her game immensely. She developed into an exceptional player, noted for her magnificent swing and her accuracy.

Joyce's record in competitive golf was outstanding. She played five times in the English Ladies' Amateur Championship and won each time. In all she played 33 matches in the event, winning every one. It was a similar story in the British Ladies' Amateur Championship. She won the title four times and lost only two matches.

English winner (right)
In five consecutive English Ladies' Championships, Joyce Wethered played 33 matches without losing.

Lady rivals (left)
Joyce Wethered (left) and Cecil Leitch line up to contest the British Ladies' Championship at Troon in 1925.

Enjoying the game
Joyce Wethered played most of her golf purely for pleasure. She first retired from serious competition at the remarkably early age of 24.

In her first English Ladies' final, played at Sheringham in 1920, Wethered met the holder, Cecil Leitch. A cult figure with a large following, Leitch was expected to win easily, but Wethered achieved a victory by two and one, recording one of the biggest upsets in the history of the event.

FAMOUS VICTORY

Joyce Wethered returned from four years' retirement to score a memorable victory over the US Ladies' Champion, Glenna Collett, in the final of the British Ladies' at St Andrews in 1929. Wethered was five down after nine holes as Collett went to the turn in 34. But Wethered played the next 18 holes superbly for 73, and won on the penultimate green by three and one.

Wethered played in the first Curtis Cup match in 1932, but thereafter appeared only in the Worplesdon Mixed Foursomes, which she won eight times.

JOYCE WETHERED
(LADY HEATHCOAT-AMORY)

WON BRITISH LADIES' 1922, 1924, 1925, 1929; ENGLISH LADIES' 1920, 1921, 1922, 1923, 1924; WORPLESDON MIXED FOURSOMES 1922, 1923, 1927, 1928, 1931, 1932, 1933, 1936. CURTIS CUP 1932 (CAPTAIN). WORLD GOLF HALL OF FAME 1975.

LEE WESTWOOD

BORN WORKSOP, ENGLAND, 24 APRIL 1973

WHENEVER THE TOPIC *of talented players who've failed to win a Major is raised, the names of Duval, Mickelson, Montgomerie and Lee Westwood are foremost in any discussion. Lee, as well as being the youngest, could also be the first to unburden himself of that tag.*

Giving the impression of consummate unflappability, the young Englishman has steadily carved a niche for himself in world golf since his first European Tour win in 1996, and can boast success in every golf-playing continent.

What first drew overseas attention to his scoring ability was his USPGA Tour win in the 1998 McDermott-Freeport Classic in New Orleans, his 15-under total of 273 providing a three-stroke victory. Despite this boost, he only just made the cut the following week at the Masters, eventually finishing 44th. But in November of that year he underlined his

Best by date
In his best season ever Lee made a Tour record of £1,858,000 and beat Monty in a play-off for the World Matchplay.

ability to travel well with his third successive win in the Taiheiyo Masters, and a triumph at the Dunlop Phoenix.

While Montgomerie was tucking away seven successive European Tour Order of Merit wins (1993–99), Westwood latterly seemed his heir apparent, and in 2000 he finally usurped the Scot – and in some style. Having suffered a crisis of confidence when tying 54th at the Benson & Hedges in mid-May and lying a distant 33rd on the Money List, he had an amazing run in his next six events – first, tied second, tied fourth, tied fifth, first and first. And with six European Tour victories in a season he became only the fourth player (after Faldo, Ballesteros and Montgomerie) to do so.

LEE JOHN WESTWOOD

WON JAPANESE MASTERS 1996–98; VOLVO MASTERS 1997; AUSTRALIAN OPEN 1997; EUROPEAN OPEN 1999–2000; WORLD MATCHPLAY 2000. WINNER OF 14 EUROPEAN TOUR EVENTS 1996–2000. HARRY VARDON TROPHY 2000. EUROPEAN TOUR GOLFER OF THE YEAR 1998, 2000. DUNHILL CUP 1996–99. RYDER CUP 1997–99. SEVE BALLESTEROS TROPHY 2000.

MICKEY WRIGHT

BORN SAN DIEGO, CALIFORNIA, USA, 14 FEBRUARY 1935

MICKEY WRIGHT MUST *rank as one of the all-time great women golfers. Her 82 victories on the US LPGA Tour included four US Women's Opens and four LPGA Championships, and for six years she recorded the most victories in a season. Her extraordinary 13 wins out of 32 starts in 1963 is a record that is unlikely to be overtaken.*

Wright was encouraged to play golf by her father, himself a keen golfer. At 19 she was leading amateur in the US Women's Open and decided to turn professional. Her first tournament win followed in 1956. After a great career at the top, an injury to her wrist and a painful foot forced her to leave the circuit in 1969.

Glittering career
Wright's success at both junior and then professional level owed much to her powerful game, hard work and faultless swing.

MARY KATHRYN WRIGHT

WON US WOMEN'S OPEN 1958–59, 1961, 1964; LPGA CHAMPIONSHIP 1958, 1960–61, 1963; WESTERN OPEN 1962–63, 1966. WINNER OF 82 LPGA EVENTS 1956–73. LEADING MONEY WINNER 1961–64. VARE TROPHY 1960–64. LPGA HALL OF FAME 1964. WORLD GOLF HALL OF FAME 1976.

KATHY WHITWORTH

BORN MONAHANS, TEXAS, USA, 27 SEPTEMBER 1939

K ATHY WHITWORTH IS *not only the most successful player ever in women's golf, she is also the most prolific winner – male or female – in the history of the professional game. In a remarkable career that has spanned more than 30 years, Whitworth has won 88 US LPGA Tour events. Of all the major women's championships, only the US Women's Open eludes her.*

Kathy Whitworth took up golf at the age of 15 but made little impression as an amateur, winning only a couple of State titles, before she joined the professional ranks in December 1958. She was into her fourth season on the LPGA Tour before she won a tournament – the 1962 Kelly Girl Open – but once she had made the breakthrough she just kept on winning. For a 17-year spell she won at least one event each year and at her peak in 1968 she won no fewer than ten in the season.

SOLHEIM CUP CAPTAIN
Whitworth was honoured as one of the great ambassadors for women's professional golf by being appointed the non-playing captain of the US team in the inaugural Solheim Cup – the women's equivalent of the Ryder Cup – in 1990. In the first of these biennial matches, Whitworth led the US LPGA to victory against the Women Professional Golfers' European Tour.

KATHRYNNE ANN WHITWORTH

WON TITLEHOLDERS CHAMPIONSHIP 1965–66. WINNER OF 88 LPGA EVENTS 1962–85. LPGA CHAMPIONSHIP 1967, 1971, 1975. LEADING MONEY WINNER 1965–68, 1970–73. LPGA PLAYER OF THE YEAR 1966–69, 1971–73. SOLHEIM CUP 1990–92 (NON-PLAYING CAPTAIN). VARE TROPHY 1965–67, 1969–72. LPGA HALL OF FAME 1975. WORLD GOLF HALL OF FAME 1982. PATTY BERG AWARD 1987.

High accuracy (right)
Never a classic swinger, Whitworth's strength was her ability to keep the ball in play.

Hard-earned riches
A career that was a model of consistency brought high financial rewards: Kathy Whitworth was the first player to win $1 million on the LPGA Tour and remains one of the world's top money winners.

TIGER WOODS

BORN CYPRESS, CALIFORNIA, USA, 30 DECEMBER 1975

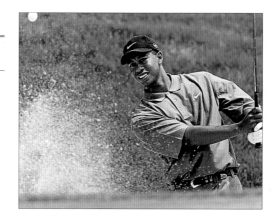

Records tumbling down (left and right) *In 1999 Woods won the US Open at Pebble Beach by 15 strokes, the World Golf Championships-NEC Invitational by 11 strokes and the British Open by eight strokes.*

PROBABLY NO ONE *in the history of golf has taken the game by such storm as Tiger Woods. Even before his first win in a major championship he seemed to have transcended the game itself, and some were even saying he had reinvented it. "Tigermania" arrived after Woods won his third successive US Amateur title in August 1995.*

In the family (above) *Tiger with his father, Earl, and his Thai-born mother. The son was already in the golfing limelight at the age of two thanks to his proud parents*

Another day, another trophy (below) *Tiger takes the 1999 USPGA Championship.*

The legendary Bobby Jones had won five US Amateur titles but never more than two in succession as Tiger had done. Eldrick "Tiger" Woods set out on his professional career with the equivalent of $60 million in endorsements from Nike and Titleist and golf, the world was already beginning to learn, would never be the same again.

THROUGH THE PORTALS OF HISTORY

There was a time when Tiger Woods would not have been allowed through the gates of Augusta National Golf Club in Georgia but in April 1997, after four of the most incredible days in the history of the Masters, the young man from Orlando, Florida, virtually owned the place.

His four-round total of 270 broke almost every record for low scoring, including the lowest winning score, the widest winning margin (he won by nine strokes) and he became the youngest winner of the famous green jacket at 21 years, three months and 15 days, a record previously held by Seve Ballesteros at the age of 23 years and three days in 1980.

In 1999 Tiger won his second Major, the USPGA Championship as a prelude to the 2000 season, which firmly established him as one of the all-time greats of the game.

GOLFING PRODIGY

He was named "Tiger" after a Vietnamese soldier who was a friend of his father, Earl Woods, in Vietnam, and as early as the age of two Tiger Woods was in the golfing limelight, putting against Bob Hope in a television show.

A year later he had shot 48 for nine holes and was featured in the American golf magazine *Golf Digest* at the age of five.

Three in a row (below) *Tiger at the Memorial, Muirfield Village in 2000. The year before he added the USPGA Championship to his British Open and US Open to make it three Majors in a row – a feat no one had accomplished since Ben Hogan in 1953 – and became only the fifth player in history to win all four of golf's modern major championships.*

ELDRICK "TIGER" WOODS

WON US AMATEUR 1994–96; US MASTERS 1997, 2001; USPGA 1999, 2000; WGC INVITATIONAL 1999, 2000; US TOUR CHAMPIONSHIP 1999; WGC STROKEPLAY 1999; US OPEN 2000, OPEN CHAMPIONSHIP 2000; WGC TEAM 2000. 2001 US PLAYERS. WINNER OF 24 US TOUR EVENTS 1996–2000. ARNOLD PALMER AWARD 1997, 1999, 2000. USPGA PLAYER OF THE YEAR 1997, 1999, 2000. VARDON TROPHY 1999, 2000. RYDER CUP 1997–99.

IAN WOOSNAM

BORN OSWESTRY, ENGLAND, 2 MARCH 1958

ALTHOUGH BORN ON *the English side of the border, Ian Woosnam considers himself a Welshman. He is only 5ft 4in (1.62m) tall, but one of the longest hitters in the modern game. He is also one of the most successful and in 1991 he hit the top spot in the world rankings. The only prize to elude him was a win in one of the Majors. But that was before the 1991 US Masters.*

Fight back (right)
Renowned for his tenacity and his determination to win, Ian Woosnam fought his way to fourth place in the 1990 Open at St Andrews.

Woosnam turned professional in 1976, but it was sometime before his quality showed. In 1982 he finished eighth in the European Order of Merit, and in 1985 he played in the triumphant European Ryder Cup team. But 1987 was his first big year.

It began with a victory at the Hong Kong Open, followed by five wins on the European Tour, which made him leading money winner. He became the first British player to win the World Matchplay title, beating Sandy Lyle in the final.

Winning millions
In 1987, repeated successes worldwide brought Woosnam over £1 million in prize money. He headed the European Order of Merit.

INTERNATIONAL SUCCESS

The Ryder Cup was next: Woosnam played in the team that recorded the first European win on American soil. He added a victory for Wales in the World Cup, taking the individual title.

Woosnam came third in the 1986 Open Championship. The next year he was European Tour Golfer of the Year, and second to Curtis Strange in the 1989 US

Open at Oak Hill. He topped the Volvo Order of Merit in 1990, and a string of early wins made him number one in the Sony World Rankings in 1991.

Then came the US Masters at Augusta. He arrived on the last tee tied with Tom Watson and José-Maria Olazábal on 11 under par. His rivals found trouble and Woosnam needed a par 4 to win. He hit the ball hard with his driver but hooked it on to the members' practice ground leaving an 8-iron to the green. He came up short, but putted to within 6ft of the pin. "Woosie" kept his nerve to win.

Top form (left)
As part of the winning European side in the Ryder Cup of 1985, Ian Woosnam enjoyed the taste of success – if somewhat dangerously – with his young team-mate Paul Way.

BABE ZAHARIAS,
see page 358

IAN HAROLD WOOSNAM, MBE

WON SCOTTISH OPEN 1987, 1990, 1996; WORLD MATCHPLAY 1987, 1990; VOLVO PGA 1988, 1997; BRITISH PGA 1988; EUROPEAN OPEN 1988; US MASTERS 1991. WINNER OF 28 EUROPEAN TOUR EVENTS 1982–97. WORLD CUP 1980, 1982–85, 1987, 1990–94 (INDIVIDUAL WINNER 1987, 1991). RYDER CUP 1983–97. DUNHILL CUP 1985–86, 1988–91, 1993, 1995, 2000. FOUR TOURS CHAMPIONSHIP 1985–87, 1989–90. HARRY VARDON TROPHY 1987, 1990.

FUZZY ZOELLER

BORN NEW ALBANY, INDIANA, USA, 11 NOVEMBER 1951

F UZZY ZOELLER NOT only brings a lighter side to the game of golf but also a standard of play that at times can challenge the very best. Indeed, if Zoeller had not been troubled by back problems throughout his career he might well have won more than the two Major championships he already has to his credit.

Zoeller joined the US Tour in 1975 after a modest career as an amateur. He was soon among the money winners and by 1978 he had topped the $100,000 mark in earnings for the season.

He arrived for the US Masters in 1979 lying third in the US money list for the year. After a three-way play-off with Ed Sneed and Tom Watson, he won with a birdie 3 at the second extra hole.

In the 1984 US Open, he was in a play-off again. This time against Greg Norman, who had holed a massive 40ft (12m) putt on the 18th to save par. Fuzzy waved a white towel in mock surrender, but parred the hole to finish in a tie. Winning the play-off brought him his second Major title.

FRANK URBAN ZOELLER

WON US MASTERS 1979; US OPEN 1984. WINNER OF 10 US TOUR EVENTS 1979–86. RYDER CUP 1979, 1983–85. BOB JONES AWARD 1985. BEN HOGAN AWARD 1986

Winning in style
During the play-off with Greg Norman at the 1984 US Open, powerful driving allied to precision putting won Zoeller the title.

Major touch (above)
Zoeller's 1984 victory in the US Open was his second win in a Major event despite the pressure of injury.

Funny man (left)
Zoeller always combines skill with entertainment and attracts a large, enthusiastic following on the course.

BABE ZAHARIAS

BORN PORT ARTHUR, TEXAS, USA, 26 JUNE 1914; DIED 1956

O NE OF THE *most gifted all-round athletes in sporting history, Babe Zaharias astonished the world with her ability in every sport she chose to play. She originally made her living as a baseball and basketball player, and went on to win gold medals in the 1932 Olympic Games in field and track events. As a woman golfer she was supreme in the period after the Second World War, heading the US money list every year from 1948 to 1951.*

The professional way (right)
Babe Zaharias drives during an open tournament at Wentworth between professional American golfers and English amateurs in 1951.

ALL-ROUND ATHLETE

Babe Zaharias was not only an outstanding golfer, but also an enormously successful all-round athlete, whether winning a javelin event or relaxing with a game of billiards. She also excelled at baseball, basketball, tennis, hurdling, the high jump, diving, roller-skating and bowling. No other woman has matched her range of skills.

Born Mildred Didriksen (later changed to Didrikson), it was through her prowess at baseball that she earned her nickname "The Babe" – after the legendary baseball player Babe Ruth – when she hit five home runs in one game. In 1932 she entered eight events in the National Track and Field Championships and won six of them, setting four world records in the process. At the Los Angeles Olympic Games that year, she won the javelin, the 80m hurdles and the high jump; her victories in all three made her world-famous. However, the celebrations were slightly marred when – after setting a new world record – she was disqualified from the high jump for using the revolutionary Western Roll technique of jumping, which was judged "unladylike".

TURNING POINT

It was during those Olympic Games that the famous American sportswriter Grantland Rice persuaded 18-year-old Babe to turn her athletic prowess to the royal and ancient game of golf. She was a natural and delighted everyone with the distance she could hit the ball – hardly surprising for a woman who could generate sufficient speed and power with her right arm to win an Olympic gold medal in the javelin. Although her amazing power was her principal golfing asset, she was sufficiently adroit in the other disciplines of the game eventually to become one of the great players.

AMATEUR DISQUALIFICATION

Just as some of the gilt had been rubbed off her incredible success in the Los Angeles Olympics, so she had to face disappointment in the early stages of her golf career. She won the 1935 Texas Amateur Women's Invitational – the second event she ever contested – but two weeks later the USGA ruled that she was a professional, because of her baseball and basketball earnings, and she was barred from amateur competition.

In 1938 Babe married a wrestler, George Zaharias, giving her financial security, and five years later she regained

Victorious fling
Semi-finalists Babe Zaharias (left) and Jean Donald celebrate Babe's progression to the final of the 1947 British Ladies' Amateur at Gullane.

her amateur status in golf. She went on to win 17 tournaments in a row in 1946–47, including the 1946 US Women's Amateur and the 1947 British Ladies' Amateur, becoming the first American ever to win this British title since its instigation in 1893. In the six rounds of the competition, she lost only four holes.

In August 1947, Zaharias joined the professional ranks through choice and became a key figure in the evolution of women's professional golf in the United States. "The Babe" became a founder and charter member of the LPGA. She was the leading money winner on the professional Tour for four consecutive

American breakthrough
In 1947 Zaharias became the first American to win the British Ladies' Amateur, a title that had eluded her great predecessor Glenna Collett Vare.

Stamp of history
An official first-day cover of 1981, issued from the World Golf Hall of Fame, commemorates Babe Zaharias's remarkable contribution to golf.

years from 1948 and won a total of 31 US professional events in an illustrious career, including the Titleholders Championship three times and the Western Open Championship four times.

Zaharias was the most graceful of athletes and yet she could strike a golf ball as powerfully as any man. Stories of her striking power are legion, including the claim that, at the Gullane course on the east coast of Scotland, she was once through the back of the green at the 540-yard 15th with a drive and a 4-iron.

She once shocked officials at the same course by appearing in red-and-white chequered shorts and was asked to change. Her influence on women's golf was immense; she brought the crowds flocking in their thousands to see her play.

Zaharias took a team of American women players to Britain in 1951. In a match against a team of scratch London

amateurs, including the former English Champion Leonard Crawley, Babe's team won all their singles, playing the men even. In her match against Crawley, Zaharias not only won, but added insult to injury by having earlier rejected the chivalrous offer of "the ladies' tees".

Tragically, Babe Zaharias contracted cancer and underwent major surgery in 1953. Such was her determination that she fought back, and the following year won an astonishing five events – including her third US Women's Open by 12 strokes – and another two tournaments in 1955.

MILDRED ELLA DIDRIKSON ZAHARIAS

WON WESTERN OPEN 1940, 1944, 1945, 1950; US WOMEN'S AMATEUR 1946; BRITISH LADIES' AMATEUR 1947; TITLEHOLDERS CHAMPIONSHIP 1947, 1950, 1952; US WOMEN'S OPEN 1948, 1950, 1954.
WINNER OF 41 LPGA EVENTS 1940–55. LEADING MONEY WINNER 1950–51. VARE TROPHY 1954. LPGA HALL OF FAME 1951. BOB JONES AWARD 1957. WORLD GOLF HALL OF FAME 1974. USPGA HALL OF FAME 1976.

RECORDS AND REFERENCE

The first Open Championship was played in 1860 over the 12-hole course at Prestwick. Only eight players took part over three rounds on a wild October day. It was an inauspicious start to the most vulnerable of the great golfing events, but the roll of winners, in the world's oldest championship, now provides a perfect mirror to reflect the development of the game and the fluctuation in fortunes from one country to another. Although the Open Championship led the way, other great events soon followed. There are now hundreds around the world, but only four are recognized as golf's Majors: the Open Championships of Britain and the United States, the Masters Tournament at Augusta, and the USPGA Championship.

Programme for the 1965 US Open at Bellerive

This chapter lists the winners of the major men's, women's and team's professional and amateur championships, and top money earners up to the end of 2000 (unless otherwise stated).

US Ryder Cup team 1999 (left) *Captain Ben Crenshaw, surrounded by his US players, holds the trophy donated by Samuel Ryder in 1927.*

A commemorative plate for the 1989 Ryder Cup, tied between Europe and the United States.

THE OPEN CHAMPIONSHIP

ROYAL & ANCIENT GOLF CLUB

Golf's oldest and most prestigious championship was first proposed at the October meeting of the Prestwick Golf Club in 1856, but it was 1860 before it was played. The eight entrants played three rounds of the 12 holes of the Prestwick links. Willie Park Snr from Musselburgh won the original trophy, the Championship Belt, with a score of 174.

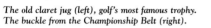

The old claret jug (left), golf's most famous trophy.
The buckle from the Championship Belt (right).

Winners and runners-up GB, except where stated

Year	Venue	Winner	Runner-up	Margin	Score
1860	Prestwick	Willie Park Snr	Tom Morris Snr	2	174
1861	Prestwick	Tom Morris Snr	Willie Park Snr	4	163
1862	Prestwick	Tom Morris Snr	Willie Park Snr	13	163
1863	Prestwick	Willie Park Snr	Tom Morris Snr	2	168
1864	Prestwick	Tom Morris Snr	Andrew Strath	2	167
1865	Prestwick	Andrew Strath	Willie Park Snr	2	162
1866	Prestwick	Willie Park Snr	David Park	2	169
1867	Prestwick	Tom Morris Snr	Willie Park Snr	2	170
1868	Prestwick	Tom Morris Jnr	Robert Andrew	2	157
1969	Prestwick	Tom Morris Jnr	Tom Morris Snr	3	154
1870	Prestwick	Tom Morris Jnr	David Strath, Bob Kirk	12	149

Young Tom Morris won the original trophy, the Championship Belt, outright after three consecutive wins, and the Open lapsed for one year. It resumed in 1872 with a new trophy, the famous claret jug, subscribed for by the R & A, the Prestwick Club and the Honourable Company of Edinburgh Golfers.

Year	Venue	Winner	Runner-up	Margin	Score
1872	Prestwick	Tom Morris Jnr	David Strath	3	166
1873	St Andrews	Tom Kidd	Jamie Anderson	1	179
1874	Musselburgh	Mungo Park	Tom Morris Jnr	2	159
1875	Prestwick	Willie Park Snr	Bob Martin	2	166
1876	St Andrews	Bob Martin	David Strath •	*	176
1877	Musselburgh	Jamie Anderson	Bob Pringle	2	160
1878	Prestwick	Jamie Anderson	Bob Kirk	2	157
1879	St Andrews	Jamie Anderson	Andrew Kirkaldy, James Allan	3	169
1880	Musselburgh	Bob Ferguson	Peter Paxton	5	162
1881	Prestwick	Bob Ferguson	Jamie Anderson	3	170
1882	St Andrews	Bob Ferguson	Willie Fernie	3	171
1883	Musselburgh	Willie Fernie	Bob Ferguson	*	159
1884	Prestwick	Jack Simpson	Douglas Rolland, Willie Fernie	4	160
1885	St Andrews	Bob Martin	Archie Simpson	1	171
1886	Musselburgh	David Brown	Willie Campbell	2	157
1887	Prestwick	Willie Park Jnr	Bob Martin	1	161
1888	St Andrews	Jack Burns	Ben Sayers, David Anderson Jnr	1	171
1889	Musselburgh	Willie Park Jnr	Andrew Kirkaldy	*	155
1890	Prestwick	John Ball Jnr †	Willie Fernie, Archie Simpson	3	164
1891	St Andrews	Hugh Kirkaldy	Andrew Kirkaldy, Willie Fernie	2	166

Competition thereafter extended from 36 to 72 holes

Year	Venue	Winner	Runner-up	Margin	Score
1892	Muirfield	Harold Hilton †	John Ball, Jnr, † Sandy Herd, Hugh Kirkaldy	3	305
1893	Prestwick	Willie Auchterlonie	Johnny Laidlay †	2	322

Year	Venue	Winner	Runner-up	Margin	Score
1894	St George's (Sandwich)	John H. Taylor	Douglas Rolland	5	326
1895	St Andrews	John H. Taylor	Sandy Herd	4	322
1896	Muirfield	Harry Vardon	John H. Taylor	*	316
1897	Royal Liverpool (Hoylake)	Harold Hilton †	James Braid	1	314
1898	Prestwick	Harry Vardon	Willie Park Jnr	1	307
1899	St George's (Sandwich)	Harry Vardon	Jack White	5	310
1900	St Andrews	John H. Taylor	Harry Vardon	8	309
1901	Muirfield	James Braid	Harry Vardon	3	309
1902	Royal Liverpool (Hoylake)	Sandy Herd	Harry Vardon, James Braid	1	307
1903	Prestwick	Harry Vardon	Tom Vardon	6	300
1904	Royal St George's (Sandwich)	Jack White	John H. Taylor, James Braid	1	296
1905	St Andrews	James Braid	John H. Taylor, Rowland Jones	5	318
1906	Muirfield	James Braid	John H. Taylor	4	300
1907	Royal Liverpool (Hoylake)	Arnaud Massy (Fr)	John H. Taylor	2	312
1908	Prestwick	James Braid	Tom Ball	8	291
1909	Cinque Ports (Deal)	John H. Taylor	James Braid, Tom Ball	6	295
1910	St Andrews	James Braid	Sandy Herd	4	299
1911	Royal St George's (Sandwich)	Harry Vardon	Arnaud Massy (Fr)	*	303
1912	Muirfield	Ted Ray	Harry Vardon	4	295
1913	Royal Liverpool (Hoylake)	John H. Taylor	Ted Ray	8	304
1914	Prestwick	Harry Vardon	John H. Taylor	3	306
1920	Cinque Ports (Deal)	George Duncan	Sandy Herd	2	303
1921	St Andrews	Jock Hutchison (US)	Roger Wethered †	*	296
1922	Royal St George's (Sandwich)	Walter Hagen (US)	George Duncan, Jim Barnes (US)	1	300
1923	Troon	Arthur Havers	Walter Hagen (US)	1	295
1924	Royal Liverpool (Hoylake)	Walter Hagen (US)	Ernest Whitcombe	1	301
1925	Prestwick	Jim Barnes (US)	Archie Compston, Ted Ray	1	300
1926	Royal Lytham & St Annes	Bobby Jones (US) †	Al Watrous (US)	2	291
1927	St Andrews	Bobby Jones (US) †	Aubrey Boomer, Fred Robson	6	285
1928	Royal St George's (Sandwich)	Walter Hagen (US)	Gene Sarazen (US)	2	292
1929	Muirfield	Walter Hagen (US)	Johnny Farrell (US)	6	292
1930	Royal Liverpool (Hoylake)	Bobby Jones (US) †	Macdonald Smith (US), Leo Diegel (US)	2	291
1931	Carnoustie	Tommy Armour (US)	Jose Jurado (Arg) †	1	296
1932	Prince's (Sandwich)	Gene Sarazen (US)	Macdonald Smith (US)	5	283
1933	St Andrews	Densmore Shute (US)	Craig Wood (US)	*	292
1934	Royal St George's (Sandwich)	Henry Cotton	Sid Brews (SA)	5	283
1935	Muirfield	Alf Perry	Alf Padgham	4	283
1936	Royal Liverpool (Hoylake)	Alf Padgham	Jimmy Adams	1	287

Year	Venue	Winner	Runner-up	Margin	Score
1937	Carnoustie	Henry Cotton	Reg Whitcombe	2	290
1938	Royal St George's (Sandwich)	Reg Whitcombe	Jimmy Adams	2	295
1939	St Andrews	Dick Burton	Johnny Bulla (US)	2	290
1946	St Andrews	Sam Snead (US)	Bobby Locke (SA), Johnny Bulla (US)	4	290
1947	Royal Liverpool (Hoylake)	Fred Daly (NI)	Reg Horne, Frank Stranahan (US) †	1	293
1948	Muirfield	Henry Cotton	Fred Daly (NI)	5	284
1949	Royal St George's (Sandwich)	Bobby Locke (SA)	Harry Bradshaw (Ire)	*	283
1950	Troon	Bobby Locke (SA)	Roberto de Vicenzo (Arg)	2	279
1951	Royal Portrush	Max Faulkner	Antonio Cerda (Arg)	2	285
1952	Royal Lytham & St Annes	Bobby Locke (SA)	Peter Thomson (Aus)	1	287
1953	Carnoustie	Ben Hogan (US)	Frank Stranahan (US) †, Dai Rees, Peter Thomson (Aus), Antonio Cerda (Arg)	4	282
1954	Royal Birkdale	Peter Thomson (Aus)	Syd Scott, Dai Rees, Bobby Locke (SA)	1	283
1955	St Andrews	Peter Thomson (Aus)	Johnny Fallon	2	281
1956	Royal Liverpool (Hoylake)	Peter Thomson (Aus)	Flory van Donck (Bel)	3	286
1957	St Andrews	Bobby Locke (SA)	Peter Thomson (Aus)	3	279
1958	Royal Lytham & St Annes	Peter Thomson (Aus)	Dave Thomas	*	278
1959	Muirfield	Gary Player (SA)	Fred Bullock, Flory van Donck (Bel)	2	284
1960	St Andrews	Kel Nagle (Aus)	Arnold Palmer (US)	1	278
1961	Royal Birkdale	Arnold Palmer (US)	Dai Rees	1	284
1962	Troon	Arnold Palmer (US)	Kel Nagle (Aus)	6	276
1963	Royal Lytham & St Annes	Bob Charles (NZ)	Phil Rodgers (US)	*	277
1964	St Andrews	Tony Lema (US)	Jack Nicklaus (US)	5	279
1965	Royal Birkdale	Peter Thomson (Aus)	Brian Huggett, Christy O'Connor Snr (Ire)	2	285
1966	Muirfield	Jack Nicklaus (US)	Doug Sanders (US), Dave Thomas	1	282
1967	Royal Liverpool (Hoylake)	Roberto de Vicenzo (Arg)	Jack Nicklaus (US)	2	278
1968	Carnoustie	Gary Player (SA)	Jack Nicklaus (US), Bob Charles (NZ)	2	289
1969	Royal Lytham & St Annes	Tony Jacklin	Bob Charles (NZ)	2	280
1970	St Andrews	Jack Nicklaus (US)	Doug Sanders (US)	*	283
1971	Royal Birkdale	Lee Trevino (US)	Lu Liang Huan (Tai)	1	278
1972	Muirfield	Lee Trevino (US)	Jack Nicklaus (US)	1	278
1973	Troon	Tom Weiskopf (US)	Johnny Miller (US), Neil Coles	3	276
1974	Royal Lytham & St Annes	Gary Player (SA)	Peter Oosterhuis	4	282
1975	Carnoustie	Tom Watson (US)	Jack Newton (Aus)	*	279
1976	Royal Birkdale	Johnny Miller (US)	Jack Nicklaus (US), Seve Ballesteros (Sp)	6	279
1977	Turnberry	Tom Watson (US)	Jack Nicklaus (US)	1	268

Year	Venue	Winner	Runner-up	Margin	Score
1978	St Andrews	Jack Nicklaus (US)	Ben Crenshaw (US), Tom Kite (US), Ray Floyd (US), Simon Owen (NZ)	2	281
1979	Royal Lytham & St Annes	Seve Ballesteros (Sp)	Ben Crenshaw (US), Jack Nicklaus (US)	3	283
1980	Muirfield	Tom Watson (US)	Lee Trevino (US)	4	271
1981	Royal St George's (Sandwich)	Bill Rogers (US)	Bernhard Langer (WG)	4	276
1982	Royal Troon	Tom Watson (US)	Nick Price (Zim), Peter Oosterhuis	1	284
1983	Royal Birkdale	Tom Watson (US)	Andy Bean (US), Hale Irwin (US)	1	275
1984	St Andrews	Seve Ballesteros (Sp)	Tom Watson (US), Bernhard Langer (WG)	2	276
1985	Royal St George's (Sandwich)	Sandy Lyle	Payne Stewart (US)	1	282
1986	Turnberry	Greg Norman (Aus)	Gordon J. Brand	5	280
1987	Muirfield	Nick Faldo	Paul Azinger (US), Rodger Davis (Aus)	1	279
1988	Royal Lytham & St Annes	Seve Ballesteros (Sp)	Nick Price (Zim)	2	273
1989	Royal Troon	Mark Calcavecchia (US)	Wayne Grady (Aus), Greg Norman (Aus)	*	275
1990	St Andrews	Nick Faldo	Payne Stewart (US), Mark McNulty (Zim)	5	270
1991	Royal Birkdale	Ian Baker-Finch (Aus)	Mike Harwood (Aus)	2	272
1992	Muirfield	Nick Faldo	John Cook (US)	1	272
1993	Royal St George's (Sandwich)	Greg Norman (Aus)	Nick Faldo	2	267
1994	Turnberry	Nick Price (Zim)	Jesper Parnevik (Swe)	1	268
1995	St Andrews	John Daly (US)	Costantino Rocca (It)	*	282
1996	Royal Lytham & St Annes	Tom Lehman (US)	Mark McCumber (US), Ernie Els (SA)	2	271
1997	Royal Troon	Justin Leonard (US)	Darren Clarke (NI), Jesper Parnevik (Swe)	3	272
1998	Royal Birkdale	Mark O'Meara (US)	Brian Watts (US)	*	280
1999	Carnoustie	Paul Lawrie	Jean van de Velde (Fr), Justin Leonard (US)	*	290
2000	St Andrews	Tiger Woods (US)	Thomas Björn (Den), Ernie Els (SA)	8	269

1915–19 not played (First World War)
1940–45 not played (Second World War)
† amateur
* play-off
• Tied but refused to play off

2001 David Duval (US)
2002 Ernie Els (RSA) T. Levet (FRA
2003 Ben Curtis (US) T. Björn (PEN)
2004 Todd Hamilton (US) V. Singh (FIJ)
E. Els (RSA)

OPEN FACT FILE
Most wins: 6, Harry Vardon (GB) 1896, 1898, 1899, 1903, 1911, 1914
Biggest victory margin: 13 strokes, Tom Morris Snr (GB) 1862
Lowest winning aggregate: 267, Greg Norman (Aus) 1993
Lowest round: 63, Mark Hayes (US) 1977, Isao Aoki (Jap) 1980, Greg Norman (Aus) 1986, Paul Broadhurst (GB) 1990, Jodie Mudd (US) 1991, Nick Faldo (GB) 1993, Payne Stewart (US) 1993
Youngest winner: 17 years, 5 months, 8 days, Tom Morris Jnr (GB) 1868
Oldest winner: 46 years, 99 days Tom Morris Snr (GB) 1867
Biggest winning span: 19 years, John H. Taylor (GB) 1894–1913
Most consecutive wins: 4, Tom Morris Jnr (GB) 1868–70, 1872
Lowest final round by a champion: 64, Greg Norman (Aus) 1993
Most used course: 26, St Andrews

THE US OPEN CHAMPIONSHIP

UNITED STATES GOLF ASSOCIATION

A young English-born player, Horace Rawlins, was the first winner of the US Open over a nine-hole course at Newport, Rhode Island, in 1895, the year after the formation of the USGA. His winning score of 173 for 36 holes – two better than Willie Dunn – won him a cheque for $150 out of the grand total of $335 that was played for. The championship was extended to 72 holes in 1898 when eight rounds of the nine-hole course at Myopia Hunt Club, Hamilton, Massachusetts, were played. Needless to say, the prize money has risen over the years: by 2000 it was $4.5 million with the winner receiving $800,000.

The present-day US Open trophy (left) is an exact replica of the original which was unfortunately destroyed in a fire in 1946.

Winners and runners-ups US, except where stated

Year	Venue	Winner	Runner(s)-up	Margin	Score
1895	Newport	Horace Rawlins	Willie Dunn	2	173
1896	Shinnecock Hills	James Foulis	Horace Rawlins	3	152
1897	Chicago	Joe Lloyd	Willie Anderson	1	162

Competition thereafter extended from 36 to 72 holes

Year	Venue	Winner	Runner(s)-up	Margin	Score
1898	Myopia Hunt Club	Fred Herd	Alex Smith	7	328
1899..	Baltimore	Willie Smith	George Low, Val Fitzjohn, W. H. Way	11	315
1900	Chicago	Harry Vardon (GB)	John H. Taylor (GB)	2	313
1901	Myopia Hunt Club	Willie Anderson	Alex Smith	*	331
1902	Garden City	Laurie Auchterlonie	Stewart Gardner, Walter Travis †	6	307
1903	Baltusrol	Willie Anderson	David Brown	*	307
1904	Glen View	Willie Anderson	Gil Nicholls	5	303
1905	Myopia Hunt Club	Willie Anderson	Alex Smith	2	314
1906	Onwentsia	Alex Smith	Willie Smith	7	295
1907	Philadelphia Cricket Club	Alex Ross	Gil Nicholls	2	302
1908	Myopia Hunt club	Fred McLeod	Willie Smith	*	322
1909	Englewood	George Sargent	Tom McNamara	4	290
1910	Philadelphia Cricket Club	Alex Smith	John McDermott, Macdonald Smith	*	298
1911	Chicago	John McDermott	Mike Brady, George Simpson	*	307
1912	CC of Buffalo	John McDermott	Tom McNamara	2	294
1913	The Country Club (Brookline)	Francis Ouimet †	Harry Vardon (GB), Ted Ray (GB),	*	304
1914	Midlothian	Walter Hagen	Chick Evans †	1	290
1915	Baltusrol	Jerome Travers †	Tom McNamara	1	297
1916	Minikahda	Chick Evans †	Jock Hutchison	2	286
1919	Brae Burn	Walter Hagen	Mike Brady	*	301
1920	Inverness	Ted Ray (GB)	Jack Burke, Leo Diegel, Jock Hutchison, Harry Vardon (GB)	1	295
1921	Columbia	Jim Barnes	Walter Hagen, Fred McLeod	9	289
1922	Skokie	Gene Sarazen	John Black, Bobby Jones †	1	288
1923	Inwood	Bobby Jones †	Bobby Cruickshank	*	296
1924	Oakland Hills	Cyril Walker	Bobby Jones †	3	297
1925	Worcester	Willie MacFarlane	Bobby Jones †	*	291
1926	Scioto	Bobby Jones †	Joe Turnesa	1	293
1927	Oakmont	Tommy Armour	Harry Cooper	*	301

Year	Venue	Winner	Runner(s)-up	Margin	Score
1928	Olympia Fields	Johnny Farrell	Bobby Jones †	*	294
1929	Winged Foot	Bobby Jones †	Al Espinosa	*	294
1930	Interlachen	Bobby Jones †	Macdonald Smith	2	287
1931	Inverness	Billy Burke	George Von Elm	*	292
1932	Fresh Meadow	Gene Sarazen	Phil Perkins (GB), Bobby Cruickshank	3	286
1933	North Shore	Johnny Goodman †	Ralph Guldahl	1	287
1934	Merion Cricket Club	Olin Dutra	Gene Sarazen	1	293
1935	Oakmont	Sam Parks, Jnr	Jimmy Thomson	2	299
1936	Baltusrol	Tony Manero	Harry Cooper	2	282
1937	Oakland Hills	Ralph Guldahl	Sam Snead	2	281
1938	Cherry Hills	Ralph Guldahl	Dick Metz	6	284
1939	Philadelphia	Byron Nelson	Craig Wood, Densmore Shute	*	284
1940	Canterbury	Lawson Little	Gene Sarazen	*	287
1941	Colonial	Craig Wood	Densmore Shute	3	284
1946	Canterbury	Lloyd Mangrum	Vic Ghezzi, Byron Nelson	*	284
1947	St Louis	Lew Worsham	Sam Snead	*	282
1948	Riviera	Ben Hogan	Jimmy Demaret	2	276
1949	Medinah	Cary Middlecoff	Sam Snead, Clayton Heafner	1	286
1950	Merion	Ben Hogan	Lloyd Mangrum, George Fazio	*	287
1951	Oakland Hills	Ben Hogan	Clayton Heafner	2	287
1952	Northwood	Julius Boros	Ed Oliver	4	281
1953	Oakmont	Ben Hogan	Sam Snead	6	283
1954	Baltusrol	Ed Furgol	Gene Littler	1	284
1955	Olympic	Jack Fleck	Ben Hogan	*	287
1956	Oak Hill	Cary Middlecoff	Ben Hogan, Julius Boros	1	281
1957	Inverness	Dick Mayer	Cary Middlecoff	*	282
1958	Southern Hills	Tommy Bolt	Gary Player (SA)	4	283
1959	Winged Foot	Billy Casper	Bob Rosburg	1	282
1960	Cherry Hills	Arnold Palmer	Jack Nicklaus †	2	280
1961	Oakland Hills	Gene Littler	Bob Goalby, Doug Sanders	1	281
1962	Oakmont	Jack Nicklaus	Arnold Palmer	*	283
1963	The Country Club (Brookline)	Julius Boros	Jacky Cupit, Arnold Palmer	*	293
1964	Congressional	Ken Venturi	Tommy Jacobs	4	278
1965	Bellerive	Gary Player (SA)	Kel Nagle (Aus)	*	282
1966	Olympic	Billy Casper	Arnold Palmer	*	278
1967	Baltusrol	Jack Nicklaus	Arnold Palmer	4	275
1968	Oak Hill	Lee Trevino	Jack Nicklaus	4	275
1969	Champions	Orville Moody	Deane Beman, Al Geiberger, Bob Rosburg	1	281
1970	Hazeltine National	Tony Jacklin (GB)	Dave Hill	7	281
1971	Merion	Lee Trevino	Jack Nicklaus	*	280
1972	Pebble Beach	Jack Nicklaus	Bruce Crampton (Aus)	3	290
1973	Oakmont	Johnny Miller	John Schlee	1	279
1974	Winged Foot	Hale Irwin	Forrest Fezler	2	287
1975	Medinah	Lou Graham	John Mahaffey	*	287
1976	Atlanta Athletic Club	Jerry Pate	Tom Weiskopf, Al Geiberger	2	277
1977	Southern Hills	Hubert Green	Lou Graham	1	278

Year	Venue	Winner	Runner(s)-up	Margin	Score
1978	Cherry Hills	Andy North	Dave Stockton, J. C. Snead	1	285
1979	Inverness	Hale Irwin	Gary Player (SA), Jerry Pate	2	284
1980	Baltusrol	Jack Nicklaus	Isao Aoki (Jap)	2	272
1981	Merion	David Graham (Aus)	George Burns, Bill Rogers	3	273
1982	Pebble Beach	Tom Watson	Jack Nicklaus	2	282
1983	Oakmont	Larry Nelson	Tom Watson	1	280
1984	Winged Foot	Fuzzy Zoeller	Greg Norman (Aus)	*	276
1985	Oakland Hills	Andy North	Dave Barr (Can) T. C. Chen (Tai) Denis Watson (SA)	1	279
1986	Shinnecock Hills	Ray Floyd	Lanny Wadkins, Chip Beck	2	279
1987	Olympic	Scott Simpson	Tom Watson	1	277
1988	The Country Club (Brookline)	Curtis Strange	Nick Faldo (GB)	*	278
1989	Oak Hill	Curtis Strange	Chip Beck, Mark McCumber, Ian Woosnam (GB)	1	278
1990	Medinah	Hale Irwin	Mike Donald	*	280
1991	Hazeltine National	Payne Stewart	Scott Simpson	*	282
1992	Pebble Beach	Tom Kite	Jeff Sluman	2	285
1993	Baltusrol	Lee Janzen	Payne Stewart	2	272
1994	Oakmont	Ernie Els (SA)	Loren Roberts, Colin Montgomerie (GB)		279
1995	Shinnecock Hills	Corey Pavin	Greg Norman (Aus)	2	280
1996	Oakland Hills	Steve Jones	Tom Lehman, Davis Love III	1	278
1997	Congressional	Ernie Els (SA)	Colin Montgomerie (GB)	1	276
1998	Olympic	Lee Janzen	Payne Stewart	1	280
1999	Pinehurst (Number 2)	Payne Stewart	Phil Mickelson	1	279
2000	Pebble Beach	Tiger Woods	Miguel Angel Jiménez (Sp), Ernie Els (SA)	15	272

1917–18 not played (First World War)
1942–45 not played (Second World War)
† *amateur*

* *play-off*

US OPEN FACT FILE
Most wins: 4, Willie Anderson (US) 1901, 1903, 1904, 1905
Bobby Jones (US) 1923, 1926, 1929, 1930
Ben Hogan (US) 1948, 1950, 1951, 1953
Jack Nicklaus (US) 1962, 1967, 1972, 1980
Biggest victory margin: 15 shots, Tiger Woods (US) 2000
Lowest winning aggregate: 272, Jack Nicklaus (US) 1980, Lee Janzen (US) 1993,
Tiger Woods (US) 2000
Lowest round: 63, Johnny Miller (US) 1973, Tom Weiskopf (US) 1980,
Jack Nicklaus (US) 1980
Youngest winner: 19 years, 10 months, 12 days, John McDermott (US) 1911
Oldest winner: 45 years, 15 days, Hale Irwin (US) 1990
Biggest winning span: 18 years, Jack Nicklaus (US) 1962–80
Most consecutive wins: 3, Willie Anderson (US) 1903–05
Lowest final round by a champion: 63, Johnny Miller (US) 1973
Most used courses: 7, Baltusrol, Oakmont

THE USPGA CHAMPIONSHIP
UNITED STATES PROFESSIONAL GOLFERS' ASSOCIATION

The USPGA Championship was first played in 1916 at Siwanoy, New York. It was a matchplay event until it moved to a 72-hole strokeplay format in 1958. The founding of the event was one of the first actions of the newly formed Professional Golfers' Association of America in 1916. It is recognized as one of golf's four Major championships and performance in the USPGA Tour determines which players can enter. Walter Hagen and Jack Nicklaus share the record for the most wins with five.

The USPGA Championship trophy (left) was presented to the Association by Rodman Wanamaker, the Philadelphia millionaire who first conceived of the event.

Winners and runners-up US, except where stated

Year	Venue	Winner	Runner(s)-up	Margin
1916	Siwanoy	Jim Barnes	Jock Hutchison	1 up
1919	Engineers	Jim Barnes	Fred McLeod	6 & 5
1920	Flossmoor	Jock Hutchison	J. Douglas Edgar	1 up
1921	Inwood	Walter Hagen	Jim Barnes	3 & 2
1922	Oakmont	Gene Sarazen	Emmet French	4 & 3
1923	Pelham	Gene Sarazen	Walter Hagen	at 38th
1924	French Lick	Walter Hagen	Jim Barnes	2 up
1925	Olympia Fields	Walter Hagen	Bill Mehlhorn	6 & 5
1926	Salisbury	Walter Hagen	Leo Diegel	5 & 3
1927	Cedar Crest	Walter Hagen	Joe Turnesa	1 up
1928	Five Farms	Leo Diegel	Al Espinosa	6 & 5
1929	Hillcrest	Leo Diegel	Johnny Farrell	6 & 4
1930	Fresh Meadow	Tommy Armour	Gene Sarazen	1 up
1931	Wannamoisett	Tom Creavy	Densmore Shute	2 & 1
1932	Keller	Olin Dutra	Frank Walsh	4 & 3
1933	Blue Mound	Gene Sarazen	Willie Goggin	5 & 4
1934	Park	Paul Runyan	Craig Wood	at 38th
1935	Twin Hills	Johnny Revolta	Tommy Armour	5 & 4
1936	Pinehurst	Densmore Shute	Jimmy Thomson	3 & 2
1937	Pittsburgh	Densmore Shute	Harold McSpaden	at 37th
1938	Shawnee	Paul Runyan	Sam Snead	8 & 7
1939	Pomonok	Henry Picard	Byron Nelson	at 37th
1940	Hershey	Byron Nelson	Sam Snead	1 up
1941	Cherry Hills	Vic Ghezzi	Byron Nelson	at 38th
1942	Seaview	Sam Snead	Jim Turnesa	2 & 1
1944	Manito	Bob Hamilton	Byron Nelson	1 up
1945	Morraine	Byron Nelson	Sam Byrd	4 & 3
1946	Portland	Ben Hogan	Ed Oliver	6 & 4
1947	Plum Hollow	Jim Ferrier (Aus)	Chick Harbert	2 & 1
1948	Norwood Hills	Ben Hogan	Mike Turnesa	7 & 6
1949	Hermitage	Sam Snead	Johnny Palmer	3 & 2
1950	Scioto	Chandler Harper	Henry Williams Jnr	4 & 3
1951	Oakmont	Sam Snead	Walter Burkemo	7 & 6
1952	Big Spring	Jim Turnesa	Chick Harbert	1 up
1953	Birmingham	Walter Burkemo	Felice Torza (It)	2 & 1
1954	Keller	Chick Harbert	Walter Burkemo	4 & 3
1955	Meadowbrook	Doug Ford	Cary Middlecoff	4 & 3
1956	Blue Hill	Jack Burke Jnr	Ted Kroll	3 & 2
1957	Miami Valley	Lionel Hebert	Dow Finsterwald	2 & 1

Competition changed from matchplay to strokeplay.

Year	Venue	Winner	Runner(s)-up	Margin	Score
1958	Llanerch	Dow Finsterwald	Billy Casper	2	276
1959	Minneapolis	Bob Rosburg	Jerry Barber, Doug Sanders	1	277
1960	Firestone	Jay Hebert	Jim Ferrier (Aus)	1	281
1961	Olympia Fields	Jerry Barber	Don January	*	277
1962	Aronimink	Gary Player (SA)	Bob Goalby	1	278
1963	Dallas	Jack Nicklaus	Dave Ragan	2	279
1964	Columbus	Bobby Nichols	Jack Nicklaus, Arnold Palmer	3	271
1965	Laurel Valley	Dave Marr	Billy Casper, Jack Nicklaus	2	280
1966	Firestone	Al Geiberger	Dudley Wysong	4	280
1967	Columbine	Don January	Don Massengale	*	281
1968	Pecan Valley	Julius Boros	Bob Charles (NZ), Arnold Palmer	1	281
1969	NCR (Dayton)	Ray Floyd	Gary Player (SA)	1	276
1970	Southern Hills	Dave Stockton	Arnold Palmer, Bob Murphy	2	279
1971	PGA National (Palm Beach)	Jack Nicklaus	Billy Casper	2	281
1972	Oakland Hills	Gary Player (SA)	Tommy Aaron, Jim Jamieson	2	281
1973	Canterbury	Jack Nicklaus	Bruce Crampton (Aus)	4	277
1974	Tanglewood	Lee Trevino	Jack Nicklaus	1	276
1975	Firestone	Jack Nicklaus	Bruce Crampton (Aus)	2	276
1976	Congressional	Dave Stockton	Ray Floyd, Don January	1	281
1977	Pebble Beach	Lanny Wadkins	Gene Littler	*	282
1978	Oakmont	John Mahaffey	Jerry Pate, Tom Watson	*	276
1979	Oakland Hills	David Graham (Aus)	Ben Crenshaw	*	272
1980	Oak Hill	Jack Nicklaus	Andy Bean	7	274
1981	Atlanta Athletic Club	Larry Nelson	Fuzzy Zoeller	4	273
1982	Southern Hills	Ray Floyd	Lanny Wadkins	3	272
1983	Riviera	Hal Sutton	Jack Nicklaus	1	274
1984	Shoal Creek	Lee Trevino	Gary Player (SA), Lanny Wadkins	4	273
1985	Cherry Hills	Hubert Green	Lee Trevino	2	278
1986	Inverness	Bob Tway	Greg Norman (Aus)	2	276
1987	PGA National (Palm Beach)	Larry Nelson	Lanny Wadkins	*	287
1988	Oak Tree	Jeff Sluman	Paul Azinger	3	272
1989	Kemper Lakes	Payne Stewart	Andy Bean, Mike Reid, Curtis Strange	1	276
1990	Shoal Creek	Wayne Grady (Aus)	Fred Couples	3	282
1991	Crooked Stick	John Daly	Bruce Lietzke	3	276
1992	Bellerive	Nick Price (Zim)	John Cook, Jim Gallagher Jnr, Gene Sauers, Nick Faldo (GB)	3	278
1993	Inverness	Paul Azinger	Greg Norman (Aus)	*	272
1994	Southern Hills	Nick Price (Zim)	Corey Pavin	6	269
1995	Riviera	Steve Elkington (Aus)	Colin Montgomerie (GB)	*	267
1996	Valhalla	Mark Brooks	Kenny Perry	*	277
1997	Winged Foot	Davis Love III	Justin Leonard	5	269
1998	Sahalee	Vijay Singh (Fij)	Steve Stricker	2	271
1999	Medinah	Tiger Woods	Sergio Garcia (Sp)	1	277
2000	Valhalla	Tiger Woods	Bob May	*	270

1917–18 not played (First World War)
1942–45 not played (Second World War)
*† amateur   * play-off*

USPGA FACT FILE
Most wins: 5, Walter Hagen (US) 1921, 1924, 1925, 1926, 1927
Jack Nicklaus (US) 1963, 1971, 1973, 1975, 1980
Biggest victory margin: matchplay, 8 & 7, Paul Runyan (US) 1938
Strokeplay, 7 strokes, Jack Nicklaus (US) 1980
Lowest aggregate: 267, Steve Elkington (Aus) & Colin Montgomerie (GB) 1995
Lowest round: 63, Bruce Crampton (Aus) 1975, Ray Floyd (US) 1982, Gary Player (SA) 1984,
Vijay Singh (Fij) 1993, Michael Bradley (US) 1995, Brad Faxon (US) 1995,
José-Maria Olazábal (Sp) 2000
Youngest winner: 20 years, 5 months, 20 days, Gene Sarazen (US) 1922
Oldest winner: 48 years, 4 months, 18 days, Julius Boros (US) 1968
Biggest winning span: 17 years, Jack Nicklaus (US) 1963–80
Most consecutive wins: 4, Walter Hagen (US) 1924–27
Lowest final round by a champion: 64, Steve Elkington (Aus) 1995
Most used courses: 3, Firestone, Oakmont, Southern Hills

THE MASTERS TOURNAMENT

AUGUSTA NATIONAL GOLF CLUB

The Masters Tournament, held annually at the Augusta National Golf Club, is an invitation event with strict qualifying conditions. It was first played in 1934 as the Augusta National Invitation Tournament after Bobby Jones decreed that the suggested name, The Masters Tournament, was "too presumptuous". He eventually relented and the Masters name was officially adopted in 1938.

This silver plaque (left) used to be presented to the Masters Champion each year. Now a smaller version of the permanent trophy kept at Augusta is given (see page 68).

Winners and runners-up US, except where stated

Year	Winner	Margin	Runner(s)-up	Score
1934	Horton Smith	1	Craig Wood	284
1935	Gene Sarazen	*	Craig Wood	282
1936	Horton Smith	1	Harry Cooper	285
1937	Byron Nelson	2	Ralph Guldahl	283
1938	Henry Picard	2	Ralph Guldahl, Harry Cooper	285
1939	Ralph Guldahl	1	Sam Snead	279
1940	Jimmy Demaret	4	Lloyd Mangrum	280
1941	Craig Wood	3	Byron Nelson	280
1942	Byron Nelson	*	Ben Hogan	280
1946	Herman Keiser	1	Ben Hogan	282
1947	Jimmy Demaret	2	Byron Nelson, Frank Stranahan †	281
1948	Claude Harmon	5	Cary Middlecoff	279
1949	Sam Snead	3	Johnny Bulla, Lloyd Mangrum	282
1950	Jimmy Demaret	2	Jim Ferrier (Aus)	283
1951	Ben Hogan	2	Skee Riegel	280
1952	Sam Snead	4	Jack Burke, Jnr	286
1953	Ben Hogan	5	Ed Oliver	274
1954	Sam Snead	*	Ben Hogan	289
1955	Cary Middlecoff	7	Ben Hogan	279
1956	Jack Burke, Jnr	1	Ken Venturi †	289
1957	Doug Ford	3	Sam Snead	283
1958	Arnold Palmer	1	Doug Ford, Fred Hawkins	284
1959	Art Wall, Jnr	1	Cary Middlecoff	284
1960	Arnold Palmer	1	Ken Venturi	282
1961	Gary Player (SA)	1	Charlie Coe †, Arnold Palmer	280
1962	Arnold Palmer	*	Gary Player (SA), Dow Finsterwald	280
1963	Jack Nicklaus	1	Tony Lema	286

Year	Winner	Margin	Runner(s) up	Score
1964	Arnold Palmer	6	Dave Marr, Jack Nicklaus	276
1965	Jack Nicklaus	9	Arnold Palmer, Gary Player (SA)	271
1966	Jack Nicklaus	*	Tommy Jacobs, Gay Brewer	288
1967	Gay Brewer	1	Bobby Nichols	280
1968	Bob Goalby	1	Roberto de Vicenzo (Arg)	277
1969	George Archer	1	Billy Casper, George Knudson (Can), Tom Weiskopf	281
1970	Billy Casper	*	Gene Littler	279
1971	Charles Coody	2	Johnny Miller, Jack Nicklaus	279
1972	Jack Nicklaus	3	Bruce Crampton (Aus), Bobby Mitchell, Tom Weiskopf	286
1973	Tommy Aaron	1	J. C. Snead	283
1974	Gary Player (SA)	2	Tom Weiskopf, Dave Stockton	278
1975	Jack Nicklaus	1	Johnny Miller, Tom Weiskopf	276
1976	Ray Floyd	8	Ben Crenshaw	271
1977	Tom Watson	2	Jack Nicklaus	276
1978	Gary Player (SA)	1	Hubert Green, Rod Funseth, Tom Watson	277
1979	Fuzzy Zoeller	*	Ed Sneed, Tom Watson	280
1980	Seve Ballesteros (SP)	4	Gibby Gilbert, Jack Newton (Aus)	275
1981	Tom Watson	2	Johnny Miller, Jack Nicklaus	280
1982	Craig Stadler	*	Dan Pohl	284
1983	Seve Ballesteros (SP)	4	Ben Crenshaw, Tom Kite	280
1984	Ben Crenshaw	2	Tom Watson	277
1985	Bernhard Langer (WG)	2	Curtis Strange, Seve Ballesteros (SP), Ray Floyd	282
1986	Jack Nicklaus	1	Greg Norman (Aus), Tom Kite	279
1987	Larry Mize	*	Seve Ballesteros (SP), Greg Norman (Aus)	285
1988	Sandy Lyle (GB)	1	Mark Calcavecchia	281
1989	Nick Faldo (GB)	*	Scott Hoch	283
1990	Nick Faldo (GB)	*	Ray Floyd	278
1991	Ian Woosnam (GB)	1	José-Maria Olazábal (SP)	277
1992	Fred Couples	2	Ray Floyd	275
1993	Bernhard Langer (Ger)	4	Chip Beck	277
1994	José-Maria Olazábal (SP)	2	Tom Lehman	279
1995	Ben Crenshaw	1	Davis Love III	274
1996	Nick Faldo (GB)	5	Greg Norman (Aus)	276
1997	Tiger Woods	12	Tom Kite	270
1998	Mark O'Meara	1	David Duval, Fred Couples	279
1999	José-Maria Olazábal (SP)	2	Davis Love III	280
2000	Vijay Singh (Fiji)	3	Ernie Els (SA)	278
2001	Tiger Woods	2	David Duval	272

1943–45 not played (First World War)
* play-off   † amateur

MASTERS FACT FILE
Most wins: 6, Jack Nicklaus (US) 1963, 1965, 1966, 1972, 1975, 1986
Biggest victory margin: 12 shots, Tiger Woods (US) 1997
Lowest winning aggregate: 270, Tiger Woods (US) 1997
Lowest round: 63, Nick Price (Zim) 1986, Greg Norman (Aus) 1996
Youngest winner: 21 years, 3 months, 15 days, Tiger Woods (US) 1997
Oldest winner: 46 years, 2 months, 23 days, Jack Nicklaus (US) 1986
Biggest winning span: 23 years, Jack Nicklaus (US) 1963–86
Most consecutive wins: 2, Jack Nicklaus (US) 1965–66, Nick Faldo (GB) 1989–90
Lowest final round by a champion: 64, Gary Player (SA) 1978

US MULTIPLE MAJOR WINNERS

TOP 40 PLAYERS

Jack Nicklaus, one of only five men (along with Gene Sarazen, Ben Hogan, Gary Player and Tiger Woods) to win all four titles, has won an amazing 18 majors – nine ahead of his nearest challenger, Walter Hagen. The record for the most wins (six) in any one major is shared by Nicklaus (Masters Tournament) and Harry Vardon (Open Championship).

Winners US, except where stated

Rank	Player	Masters Tournament	US Open	Open Championship	USPGA	Total
1	Jack Nicklaus	6	4	3	5	18
2	Walter Hagen		2	4	5	11
3	Ben Hogan	2	4	1	2	9
	Gary Player (SA)	3	1	3	2	9
5	Tom Watson	2	1	5		8
6	Harry Vardon (GB)		1	6		7
	Bobby Jones		4	3		7
	Gene Sarazen	1	2	1	3	7
	Sam Snead	3		1	3	7
11	Arnold Palmer	4	1	2		7
	Lee Trevino		2	2	2	6
	Nick Faldo (GB)	3		3		6
13	James Braid (GB)			5		5
	John H. Taylor (GB)			5		5
	Byron Nelson	2	1		2	5
	Peter Thomson (Aus)			5		5
	Seve Ballesteros (SP)	2		3		5
	Tiger Woods	1	1	1	2	5
19	Tom Morris Snr (GB)			4		4
	Tom Morris Jnr (GB)			4		4
	Willie Park Snr (GB)			4		4
	Willie Anderson		4			4
	Jim Barnes		1	1	2	4
	Bobby Locke (SA)			4		4
	Ray Floyd	1	1		2	4
26	Jamie Anderson (GB)			3		3
	Bob Ferguson (GB)			3		3
	Tommy Armour		1	1	1	3
	Densmore Shute		1		2	3
	Ralph Guldahl	1	2			3
	Henry Cotton (GB)			3		3
	Jimmy Demaret	3				3
	Cary Middlecoff	1	2			3
	Julius Boros		2		1	3
	Billy Casper	1	2			3
	Larry Nelson		1		2	3
	Hale Irwin		3			3
	Nick Price (Zim)			1	2	3
	Payne Stewart		2		1	3

MEN'S TOURS

USPGA TOUR LEADING MONEY WINNERS

Since 1981, the Arnold Palmer Award has been awarded annually to the USPGA Tour's leading money winner.

Year	Player *(US except where stated)*	Total money winnings
1934	Paul Runyan	$6,767
1935	Johnny Revolta	$9,543
1936	Horton Smith	$7,682
1937	Harry Cooper	$14,138
1938	Sam Snead	$19,534
1939	Henry Picard	$10,303
1940	Ben Hogan	$10,655
1941	Ben Hogan	$18,358
1942	Ben Hogan	$13,143
1943	*No Statistics Compiled*	
1944	Byron Nelson (War Bonds)	$37,967
1945	Byron Nelson (War Bonds)	$63,335
1946	Ben Hogan	$42,556
1947	Jimmy Demaret	$27,936
1948	Ben Hogan	$32,112
1949	Sam Snead	$31,593
1950	Sam Snead	$35,758
1951	Lloyd Mangrum	$26,088
1952	Julius Boros	$37,032
1953	Lew Worsham	$34,002
1954	Bob Toski	$65,819
1955	Julius Boros	$63,121
1956	Ted Kroll	$72,835
1957	Dick Mayer	$65,835
1958	Arnold Palmer	$42,607
1959	Art Wall	$53,167
1960	Arnold Palmer	$75,262
1961	Gary Player (SA)	$64,540
1962	Arnold Palmer	$81,448
1963	Arnold Palmer	$128,230
1964	Jack Nicklaus	$113,284
1965	Jack Nicklaus	$140,752
1966	Billy Casper	$121,944
1967	Jack Nicklaus	$188,998
1968	Billy Casper	$205,168
1969	Frank Beard	$164,707
1970	Lee Trevino	$157,037
1971	Jack Nicklaus	$244,490
1972	Jack Nicklaus	$320,542
1973	Jack Nicklaus	$308,362
1974	Johnny Miller	$353,021
1975	Jack Nicklaus	$298,149
1976	Jack Nicklaus	$266,438
1977	Tom Watson	$310,653
1978	Tom Watson	$362,428
1979	Tom Watson	$462,636
1980	Tom Watson	$530,808

Year	Player	Total money winnings
1981	Tom Kite	$375,698
1982	Craig Stadler	$446,462
1983	Hal Sutton	$426,668
1984	Tom Watson	$476,260
1985	Curtis Strange	$542,321
1986	Greg Norman (Aus)	$653,296
1987	Curtis Strange	$925,941
1988	Curtis Strange	$1,147,644
1989	Tom Kite	$1,395,278
1990	Greg Norman (Aus)	$1,165,477
1991	Corey Pavin	$979,430
1992	Fred Couples	$1,344,188
1993	Nick Price (Zim)	$1,478,557
1994	Nick Price (Zim)	$1,499,927
1995	Greg Norman (Aus)	$1,654,959
1996	Tom Lehman	$1,780,159
1997	Tiger Woods	£2,066,833
1998	David Duval	$2,591,031
1999	Tiger Woods	$6,616,585
2000	Tiger Woods	$9,188,321

USPGA TOUR RECORDS
Most times leading money winner: 8, Jack Nicklaus (1964–76)
Most tournament wins: 81, Sam Snead (1936–65)
Most wins in a year: 18, Byron Nelson (1945)
Biggest winning margin: 16 strokes – J. Douglas Edgar (GB) (1919 Canadian Open), Joe Kirkwood, Snr (Aus) (1924 Corpus Christi Open), Bobby Locke (SA) (1948 Chicago Victory National Championship)
Lowest Aggregate (72 holes): 256, Mark Calcavecchia (2001 Phoenix Open)
Lowest round: 59, Al Geiberger (1977 Memphis Classic), Chip Beck (1991 Las Vegas Invitational), David Duval (1999 Bob Hope Chrysler Classic)

PGA EUROPEAN TOUR

ORDER OF MERIT WINNERS

The Harry Vardon Trophy is awarded annually to the leading player in the European Tour Order of Merit.

Year	Player	Country
1937	Charles Whitcombe	England
1938	Henry Cotton	England
1939	Reg Whitcombe	England
1946	Bobby Locke	South Africa
1947	Norman von Nida	Australia
1948	Charlie Ward	England
1949	Charlie Ward	England
1950	Bobby Locke	South Africa
1951	John Panton	Scotland
1952	Harry Weetman	England
1953	Flory van Donck	Belgium
1954	Bobby Locke	South Africa
1955	Dai Rees	Wales
1956	Harry Weetman	England
1957	Eric Brown	Scotland

Year	Player	Country	Winnings in US $
1958	Bernard Hunt	England	
1959	Dai Rees	Wales	
1960	Bernard Hunt	England	
1961	Christy O'Connor	Ireland	
1962	Christy O'Connor	Ireland	
1963	Neil Coles	England	
1964	Peter Alliss	England	
1965	Bernard Hunt	England	
1966	Peter Alliss	England	
1967	Malcolm Gregson	England	
1968	Brian Huggett	Wales	
1969	Bernard Gallacher	Scotland	
1970	Neil Coles	England	
1971	Peter Oosterhuis	England	
1972	Peter Oosterhuis	England	
1973	Peter Oosterhuis	England	
1974	Peter Oosterhuis	England	
1975	Dale Hayes	South Africa	
1976	Severiano Ballesteros	Spain	21,495
1977	Severiano Ballesteros	Spain	28,699
1978	Severiano Ballesteros	Spain	47,178
1979	Sandy Lyle	Scotland	39,808
1980	Sandy Lyle	Scotland	43,346
1981	Bernard Langer	W. Germany	81,036
1982	Greg Norman	Australia	66,406
1983	Nick Faldo	England	119,416
1984	Bernard Langer	W. Germany	139,344
1985	Sandy Lyle	Scotland	162,553
1986	Severiano Ballesteros	Spain	242,209
1987	Ian Woosnam	Wales	253,717
1988	Severiano Ballesteros	Spain	451,560
1989	Ronan Rafferty	Northern Ireland	400,311
1990	Ian Woosnam	Wales	574,167
1991	Severiano Ballesteros	Spain	545,354
1992	Nick Faldo	England	708,522
1993	Colin Montgomerie	Scotland	613,683
1994	Colin Montgomerie	Scotland	762,719
1995	Colin Montgomerie	Scotland	835,052
1996	Colin Montgomerie	Scotland	875,146
1997	Colin Montgomerie	Scotland	798,948
1998	Colin Montgomerie	Scotland	993,077
1999	Colin Montgomerie	Scotland	1,302,056
2000	Lee Westwood	England	1,858,602

PGA EUROPEAN TOUR RECORDS (*Official events only since formation of European tour in 1971*)
Most Order of Merit Victories: 7, Colin Montgomerie (1993–99)
Most tournament wins: 48, Seve Ballesteros (Sp) 1976–95)
Most wins in a year: 6, Seve Ballesteros (Sp) (1986)
Biggest winning margin: 15 strokes – Tiger Woods (US) 2000 US Open
Lowest aggregate (72 holes): 258, David Llewellyn (1988 AGF Biarritz Open), Ian Woosnam (1990 Torras Monte Carlo Open)
Lowest round: 60, Baldovino Dassau (It), David Llewellyn, Ian Woosnam, Darren Clarke (twice) (NI), Johan Ryström (Swe), Paul Curry, Jamie Spence, Bernhard Langer (Ger)

THE US WOMEN'S OPEN CHAMPIONSHIP
UNITED STATES GOLF ASSOCIATION

The US Women's Open dates back to 1946 when Patty Berg, then a professional for six years, defeated Betty Jameson by five and four in Spokane after a 36-hole qualifying event. The following year the championship was altered to a 72-hole strokeplay format. The event is primarily for women professionals, but amateurs can compete. Unsurprisingly, it has been dominated by American players, but Europe (six wins), Australia (two), Uruguay, and South Korea have also been successful in the premier major of the women's game.

Winners US, except where stated

Year	Winner	Venue	Margin
1946	Patty Berg	Spokane	5 & 4
Competition thereafter changed from matchplay to strokeplay			**Score**
1947	Betty Jameson	Greensboro	295
1948	Babe Zaharias	Atlantic City	300
1949	Louise Suggs	Landover	291
1950	Babe Zaharias	Wichita	291
1951	Betsy Rawls	Atlanta	293
1952	Louise Suggs	Bala	284
1953	Betsy Rawls	Rochester	302 *
1954	Babe Zaharias	Salem	291
1955	Fay Crocker (Ur)	Wichita	299
1956	Kathy Cornelius	Duluth	302 *
1957	Betsy Rawls	Winged Foot	299
1958	Mickey Wright	Bloomfield Hills	290
1959	Mickey Wright	Pittsburgh	287
1960	Betsy Rawls	Worcester	292
1961	Mickey Wright	Baltusrol	293
1962	Murle Lindstrom	Myrtle Beach	301
1963	Mary Mills	Kenwood	289
1964	Mickey Wright	San Diego	290†
1965	Carol Mann	Atlantic City	290
1966	Sandra Spuzich	Hazeltine National	297
1967	Catherine Lacoste † (Fr)	Hot Springs	294
1968	Susie Berning	Moselem Springs	289
1969	Donna Caponi	Scenic Hills	294
1970	Donna Caponi	Muskogee	287
1971	JoAnne Gunderson Carner	Erie	288
1972	Susie Berning	Winged Foot	299
1973	Susie Berning	Rochester	290
1974	Sandra Haynie	La Grange	295
1975	Sandra Palmer	Atlantic City	295
1976	JoAnne Gunderson Carner	Springfield	292 *
1977	Hollis Stacy	Hazeltine National	292
1978	Hollis Stacy	Indianapolis	289
1979	Jerilyn Britz	Brooklawn	284
1980	Amy Alcott	Richland	280
1981	Pat Bradley	La Grange	279
1982	Janet Alex	Del Paso	283
1983	Jan Stephenson (Aus)	Cedar Ridge	290
1984	Hollis Stacy	Salem	290
1985	Kathy Baker	Baltusrol	280
1986	Jane Geddes	NCR (Dayton)	287 *

Year	Winner	Venue	Margin
1987	Laura Davis (GB)	Plainfield	285 *
1988	Liselotte Neumann (Swe)	Baltimore	277
1989	Betsy King	Indianwood	278
1990	Betsy King	Duluth	284
1991	Meg Mallon	Colonial	283
1992	Patty Sheehan	Oakmont	280
1993	Lauri Merten	Crooked Stick	280
1994	Patty Sheehan	Indianwood	277
1995	Annika Sorenstam (Swe)	The Broadmoor	278
1996	Annika Sorenstam (Swe)	Pine Needles	272
1997	Alison Nicholas (GB)	Pumpkin Ridge	274
1998	Se Ri Pak (S Kor)	Blackwolf Run	290 *
1999	Juli Inkster	Old Waverly	272
2000	Karrie Webb (Aus)	Merit Club	282

* play-off   † amateur   Most wins – 4, Betsy Rawls, Mickey Wright

THE US LPGA CHAMPIONSHIP

UNITED STATES LADIES PROFESSIONAL GOLF ASSOCIATION

The Inaugural LPGA Championship in 1955 was contested over 54 holes followed by matchplay to determine money distribution. Thereafter, the second-longest running women's major has been held over 72 holes strokeplay.

Winners US, except where stated

Year	Winner	Venue	Margin
1955	Beverly Hanson	Orchard Ridge	(4 & 3) 220
1956	Marlene Hagge	Forest Lake	291*
1957	Louise Suggs	Churchill Valley	285
1958	Mickey Wright	Churchill Valley	288
1959	Betsy Rawls	Sheraton Hotel	288
1960	Mickey Wright	Sheraton Hotel	292
1961	Mickey Wright	Stardust	287
1962	Judy Kimball	Stardust	282
1963	Mickey Wright	Stardust	294
1964	Mary Mills	Stardust	278
1965	Sandra Haynie	Stardust	279
1966	Gloria Ehret	Stardust	282
1967	Kathy Whitworth	Pleasant Valley	284
1968	Sandra Post (Can)	Pleasant Valley	294*
1969	Betsy Rawls	Concord	293
1970	Shirley Englehorn	Pleasant Valley	285*
1971	Kathy Whitworth	Pleasant Valley	288
1972	Kathy Ahern	Pleasant Valley	293
1973	Mary Mills	Pleasant Valley	288
1974	Sandra Haynie	Pleasant Valley	288
1975	Kathy Whitworth	Pine Ridge	288
1976	Betty Burfeindt	Pine Ridge	287
1977	Chako Higuchi (Jap)	Bay Tree Golf Plantation	279
1978	Nancy Lopez	Jack Nicklaus Golf Center	275
1979	Donna Caponi	Jack Nicklaus Golf Center	279
1980	Sally Little (SA)	Jack Nicklaus Golf Center	285
1981	Donna Caponi	Jack Nicklaus Golf Center	280
1982	Jan Stephenson (Aus)	Jack Nicklaus Golf Center	279
1983	Patty Sheehan	Jack Nicklaus Golf Center	279

Year	Winner	Venue	Score
1984	Patty Sheehan	Jack Nicklaus Golf Center	272
1985	Nancy Lopez	Jack Nicklaus Golf Center	273
1986	Pat Bradley	Jack Nicklaus Golf Center	277
1987	Jane Geddes	Jack Nicklaus Golf Center	275
1988	Sherri Turner	Jack Nicklaus Golf Center	281
1989	Nancy Lopez	Jack Nicklaus Golf Center	274
1990	Beth Daniel	Bethesda	280
1991	Meg Mallon	Bethesda	274
1992	Betsy King	Bethesda	267
1993	Patty Sheehan	Bethesda	275
1994	Laura Davies (GB)	Du Pont	279
1995	Kelly Robbins	Du Pont	274
1996	Laura Davies (GB)	Du Pont	213 ✤
1997	Chris Johnson	Du Pont	281*
1998	Se Ri Pak (S Kor)	Du Pont	273
1999	Juli Inkster	Du Pont	268
2000	Juli Inkster	Du Pont	281*

* play-off   ✤ reduced to 54 holes because of rain.
Most wins – 4, Mickey Wright   **Sponsors** – Mazda (1987–93), McDonald's (1994–)

THE WOMEN'S BRITISH OPEN CHAMPIONSHIP

LADIES GOLF UNION

Launched in 1976, this event overcame early difficulties to become European women's golf's most cherished prize. Thriving under Weetabix cereal sponsorship, it became sanctioned with the US LPGA Tour in 1994 and achieved major status in 2001.

Winners GB, except where stated   Not played 1983

Year	Winner	Venue	Score
1976	Jennifer Lee Smith†	Fulford	299
1977	Vivien Saunders	Lindrick	306*
1978	Janet Melville†	Foxhills	310
1979	Alison Sheard (SA)	Southport & Ainsdale	301
1980	Debbie Massey (US)	Wentworth	294
1981	Debbie Massey (US)	Northumberland	295
1982	Marta Figueras-Dotti (Sp)†	Royal Birkdale	296
1984	Ayako Okamoto (Jap)	Woburn	289
1985	Betsy King (US)	Moor Park	300
1986	Laura Davies	Royal Birkdale	283
1987	Alison Nicholas	St. Mellion	296
1988	Corinne Dibnah (Aus)	Lindrick	295*
1989	Jane Geddes (US)	Ferndown	274
1990	Helen Alfredsson (Swe)	Woburn	288*
1991	Penny Grice-Whittaker	Woburn	284
1992	Patty Sheehan (US)	Woburn	207✤
1993	Karen Lunn (Aus)	Woburn	275
1994	Lisolette Neumann (Swe)	Woburn	280
1995	Karrie Webb (Aus)	Woburn	278
1996	Emilee Klein (US)	Woburn	277
1997	Karrie Webb (Aus)	Sunningdale	269
1998	Sherri Steinhauer (US)	Royal Lytham & St. Annes	292
1999	Sherri Steinhauer (US)	Woburn	283
2000	Sophie Gustafson (Swe)	Royal Birkdale	282

* play-off   ✤ reduced to 54 holes because of rain. **Most wins** – 2, Debbie Massey, Karrie Webb, Sherri Steinhauer.   **Sponsors** – Hitachi (1984), Burberry's (1985), Weetabix (1987–)

THE NABISCO CHAMPIONSHIP

MISSION HILLS COUNTRY CLUB

The opening LPGA major of the season, this glittering event is staged each spring in Rancho Mirage, California. Jane Blalock won the inaugural Colgate Dinah Shore Winners Circle (as it was then known) in 1972, but major championship status was not conferred until 1983. The winner receives the Nabisco Dinah Shore Trophy, named after the late tournament host, and traditionally celebrates by jumping into the lake at the 18th hole!

Winners US, except where stated

Year	Winner	Score	Year	Winner	Score
1983	Amy Alcott	282	1992	Dottie Mochrie (Pepper)	279*
1984	Juli Inkster	280*	1993	Helen Alfredsson (Swe)	284
1985	Alice Miller	275	1994	Donna Andrews	276
1986	Pat Bradley	280	1995	Nanci Bowen	285
1987	Betsy King	283*	1996	Patty Sheehan	281
1988	Amy Alcott	274	1997	Betsy King	276
1989	Juli Inkster	279	1998	Pat Hurst	281
1990	Betsy King	283	1999	Dottie Pepper	269
1991	Amy Alcott	273	2000	Karrie Webb (Aus)	274
			2001	Annika Sorenstam (Swe)	281

* *Denotes play-off*
Most wins – 3, Amy Alcott, Betsy King   **Sponsors** – Colgate (1972–81), Nabisco (1982–)

WOMEN MULTIPLE MAJOR WINNERS

Patty Berg holds the record for most women's major wins (15) and most wins (7) in an individual Major (Western Open, Titleholders). The women's Majors have seen changes over the years, the latest being the Women's British Open replacing the Du Maurier Classic in 2001. Four women: Louise Suggs, Mickey Wright, Pat Bradley and Juli Inkster have won all four designated Majors available to them at the time.

Winners US, except where stated

		Western Open (1935–63)	Titleholders Championship (1937–66, 1972)	DuMaurier Classic (1979–2000)	US Women's Open (1946–)	LPGA Championship (1955–)	Nabisco Championship (1983–)	Total
1	Patty Berg	7	7		1			15
2	Mickey Wright	3	2		4	4		13
3	Louise Suggs	4	4		2	1		11
4	Babe Zaharias	4	3		3			10
5	Betsy Rawls	2			4	2		8
6	Kathy Whitworth	1	2		3			6
	Pat Bradley			3	1	1	1	6
	Patty Sheehan				2	3	1	6
	Betsy King				2	1	3	6
	Juli Inkster			1	1	2	2	6
11	Amy Alcott			1	1		3	5
12	Susie Berning	1			3			4
	Donna Caponi				2	2		4
	Sandra Haynie			1	1	2		4
	Hollis Stacy			1	3			4
	Laura Davies (GB)			1	1	2		4
17	Betty Jameson	2			1			3
	Beverly Hanson	1	1			1		3
	Annika Sorenstam (Swe)			2		1		3
	Mary Mills			1	2			3
	Jan Stephenson (Aus)			1	1	1		3
	Nancy Lopez				3			3
	Karrie Webb (Aus)			1	1		1	3
	Meg Mallon			1	1	1		3

WOMEN'S TOURS

UNITED STATES LADIES PROFESSIONAL GOLF ASSOCIATION TOUR
LEADING MONEY WINNERS

Year	Winners US, except where stated		Winnings in US$	
1950	Babe Zaharias	14,800	1977	Judy Rankin	122,890
1951	Babe Zaharias	15,087	1978	Nancy Lopez	189,814
1952	Betsy Rawls	14,505	1979	Nancy Lopez	197,489
1953	Louise Suggs	19,816	1980	Beth Daniel	231,000
1954	Patty Berg	16,011	1981	Beth Daniel	206,998
1955	Patty Berg	16,492	1982	JoAnne Carner	310,400
1956	Marlene Hagge	20,235	1983	JoAnne Carner	291,404
1957	Patty Berg	16,272	1984	Betsy King	266,771
1958	Beverly Hanson	12,639	1985	Nancy Lopez	416,472
1959	Betsy Rawls	26,774	1986	Pat Bradley	492,021
1960	Louise Suggs	16,892	1987	Ayako Okamoto (Jap)	466,034
1961	Mickey Wright	22,236	1988	Sherri Turner	350,851
1962	Mickey Wright	21,641	1989	Betsy King	654,132
1963	Mickey Wright	31,269	1990	Beth Daniel	863,578
1964	Mickey Wright	29,800	1991	Pat Bradley	763,118
1965	Kathy Whitworth	28,658	1992	Dottie Pepper	693,335
1966	Kathy Whitworth	33,517	1993	Betsy King	595,992
1967	Kathy Whitworth	32,937	1994	Laura Davies (GB)	687,201
1968	Kathy Whitworth	48,379	1995	Annika Sorenstam (Swe)	666,533
1969	Carol Mann	49,152			
1970	Kathy Whitworth	30,235	1996	Karrie Webb (Aus)	1,002,000
1971	Kathy Whitworth	41,181	1997	Annika Sorenstam (Swe)	1,236,789
1972	Kathy Whitworth	65,063			
1973	Kathy Whitworth	82,864	1998	Annika Sorenstam (Swe)	1,092,748
1974	JoAnne Carner	87,094			
1975	Sandra Palmer	76,374	1999	Karrie Webb (Aus)	1,591,959
1976	Judy Rankin	150,734	2000	Karrie Webb (Aus)	1,876,853

WOMEN'S TOURS RECORDS

Most times leading money winner – 8, Kathy Whitworth (1965–73)
Most Tournament wins – 88, Kathy Whitworth (1962–85)
Most wins in a year – 13, Mickey Wright (1963)
Biggest winning margin – 14 strokes – Louise Suggs (1949 US Women's Open), Cindy Mackey (1986 Mastercard International Pro-Am)
Lowest Aggregate (72 Holes) – 261, Se Ri Pak (S Kor) (1998 Jamie Farr Kroger Classic), Annika Sorenstam (Swe) (2001 Standard Register Ping)
Lowest round – 59, Annika Sorenstam (Swe) (2001 Standard Register Ping)

TOUR CHAMPIONSHIP

UNITED STATES LADIES PROFESSIONAL GOLF ASSOCIATION

First staged in 1996, this season-ending event on the US LPGA Tour features the top 30 players on the yearly money list. There have been no multiple winners so far.

Winners US, except where stated

Year	Venue	Winner	Score
1996	Desert Inn	Karrie Webb (Aus)	272
1997	Desert Inn	Annika Sorenstam (Swe)	277*
1998	Desert Inn	Laura Davies (GB)	277
1999	Desert Inn	Se Ri Pak (S Kor)	276*
2000	LPGA International	Dottie Pepper	279

* *play-off*   **Sponsors:** ITT (1996–97), PageNet (1998–99), Arch Wireless (2000)

LADIES EUROPEAN TOUR

ORDER OF MERIT / LEADING MONEY WINNERS

GB, unless stated

1979	Alison Sheard (SA) *	£4,965
1980	Muriel Thomson	£8,008
1981	Jenny Lee Smith	£13,519
1982	Jenny Lee Smith	£12,551
1983	Muriel Thomson	£9,226
1984	Dale Reid	£28,239
1985	Laura Davies	£21,736
1986	Laura Davies	£37,500
1987	Dale Reid	£53,815
1988	Marie-Laure Taya (de Lorenzi) (Fr)	£99,360
1989	Marie-Laure de Lorenzi (Fr)	£77,534
1990	Trish Johnson	£83,043
1991	Corinne Dibnah (Aus)	£89,058
1992	Laura Davies	£66,333
1993	Karen Lunn (Aus)	£81,266
1994	Liselotte Neumann (Swe)	£102,750
1995	Annika Sorenstam (Swe)	£130,324
1996	Laura Davies	£110,880
1997	Alison Nicholas	£94,589
1998	Helen Alfredsson (Swe)	£125,975
1999	Laura Davies	£204,522
2000	Annika Sorenstam (Swe)	£208,283

* Catherine Panton-Lewis won Order of Merit
Alison Sheard was Leading Money Winner

WOMEN'S EUROPEAN TOUR RECORDS

Most times leading money winner – 5, Laura Davies (1985–99)
Most tournament wins – 31, Laura Davies
Most wins in a year – 7, Marie-Laure Taya (de Lorenzi) (Fr) (1988)
Biggest winning margin – 16 strokes, Laura Davies (1995 Guardian Irish Holidays Open)
Lowest Aggregate (72 holes) 267, Laura Davies (1988 Biarritz Ladies Open and 1995 Guardian Irish Holidays Open
Lowest round – 62, Trish Johnson (1996 Ladies French Open)

EVIAN MASTERS

ROYAL GOLF CLUB EVIAN

This exclusive, stylish and prestigious tournament on the French shores of Lake Geneva was launched in 1994. It became cosanctioned with the US LPGA Tour in 2000, when its £1 million ($1.5 million) prize money made it the second richest event in women's golf.

1994	Helen Alfredsson (Swe)	287
1995	Laura Davies (GB)	271
1996	Laura Davies (GB)	274
1997	Hiromi Kobayashi (Jap)	274*
1998	Helen Alfredsson (Swe)	277
1999	Catrin Nilsmark (Swe)	279
2000	Annika Sorenstam (Swe)	276*

* *play-off*
Most wins – 2, Laura Davies, Helen Alfredsson

THE RYDER CUP

PROFESSIONAL GOLF ASSOCIATION/ PGA EUROPEAN TOUR/ UNITED STATES PROFESSIONAL GOLF ASSOCIATION

A match between the professional golfers of Britain and the United States at Wentworth in 1926 was the forerunner of the Ryder Cup. The first official match was played the next year after Samuel Ryder, a seed merchant from St Albans, England, offered a gold cup for a biennial match between teams representing Great Britain and Ireland and the United States. In 22 matches between 1927 and 1977, Great Britain and Ireland won only three times. The match had become so one-sided that, in 1977, it was decided to include European players in the team from the rapidly developing European Tour. This change led to the end of the Americans' long dominance of the event.

The famous trophy (left), given by Samuel Ryder, cost £750 ($3,600) in 1927.

Year	Venue	Winners/Captain		Opponents/Captain		Margin
1927	Worcester (Mass)	US	Walter Hagen	GB	Ted Ray	9½–2½
1929	Moortown	GB	George Duncan	US	Walter Hagen	7–5
1931	Scioto	US	Walter Hagen	GB	Charles Whitcombe	9–3
1933	Southport & Ainsdale	GB	J. H. Taylor*	US	Walter Hagen	6½–5½
1935	Ridgewood	US	Walter Hagen	GB	Charles Whitcombe	9–3
1937	Southport & Ainsdale	US	Walter Hagen*	GB	Charles Whitcombe	8–4
1947	Portland	US	Ben Hogan	GB	Henry Cotton	11–1
1949	Ganton	US	Ben Hogan*	GB	Charles Whitcombe *	7–5
1951	Pinehurst	US	Sam Snead	GB	Arthur Lacey*	9½–2½
1953	Wentworth	US	Lloyd Mangrum	GB	Henry Cotton*	6½–5½
1955	Thunderbird (Palm Springs)	US	Chick Harbert	GB	Dai Rees	8–4
1957	Lindrick	GB	Dai Rees	US	Jack Burke	7½–4½
1959	Eldorado (Palm Desert)	US	Sam Snead	GB	Dai Rees	8½–3½
1961	Royal Lytham & St Annes	US	Jerry Barber	GB	Dai Rees	14½–9½
1963	East Lake (Atlanta)	US	Arnold Palmer	GB	Johnny Fallon*	23–9
1965	Royal Birkdale	US	Byron Nelson*	GB	Harry Weetman*	19½–12½
1967	Champions (Houston)	US	Ben Hogan*	GB	Dai Rees*	23½–8½
1969	Royal Birkdale *tied*	US	Sam Snead* *and*	GB	Eric Brown*	16–16
1971	Old Warson (St Louis)	US	Jay Hebert*	GB	Eric Brown*	18½–13½
1973	Muirfield (Scotland)	US	Jack Burke*	GB & Ire	Bernard Hunt*	19–13
1975	Laurel Valley	US	Arnold Palmer*	GB & Ire	Bernard Hunt*	21–11
1977	Royal Lytham & St Annes	US	Dow Finsterwald*	GB & Ire	Brian Huggett*	12½–7½
1979	Greenbrier	US	Billy Casper*	Eur	John Jacobs*	17–11
1981	Walton Heath	US	Dave Marr*	Eur	John Jacobs*	18½–9½
1983	PGA National (Palm Beach)	US	Jack Nicklaus*	Eur	Tony Jacklin*	14½–13½
1985	The Belfry	Eur	Tony Jacklin*	US	Lee Trevino*	16½–11½
1987	Muirfield Village	Eur	Tony Jacklin*	US	Jack Nicklaus*	15–13
1989	The Belfry *tied*	Eur	Tony Jacklin* *and*	US	Ray Floyd*	14–14
1991	Kiawah Island	US	Dave Stockton*	Eur	Bernard Gallacher*	14½–13½
1993	The Belfry	US	Tom Watson*	Eur	Bernard Gallacher*	15–13

Year	Venue	Winners/Captain	Opponents/Captain	Margin
1995	Oak Hill	Eur Bernard Gallacher*	US Larry Wadkins*	14¹/₂–13¹/₂
1997	Valderrama	Eur Seve Ballesteros*	US Tom Kite*	14¹/₂–13¹/₂
1999	Brookline	US Ben Crenshaw*	Eur Mark James*	14¹/₂–13¹/₂

* nonplaying captain

RYDER CUP FACTFILE
Overall record - US 24 wins, GB/GB & Ire/Eur 7 wins, 2 ties
US home record – won 15, lost 2
GB/GB & Ire/Eur home record – won 5, lost 9, tied 2
Most Appearances – 11 matches, Nick Faldo (GB & Ire/Eur), 1977–97
Most points – 25, Nick Faldo (GB & Ire/Eur), 1977–97

SOLHEIM CUP

LET & LPGA

The Solheim Cup, the women's equivalent to the Ryder Cup, is a biennial match between the Ladies European Tour and America's Ladies Professional Golf Association Tour. It is sponsored by the Karsten Manufacturing Corporation, makers of the world famous Ping golf clubs and named after the company's late founder, Karsten Solheim. The cup itself is fashioned from Ireland's renowned Waterford Crystal.

Year	Venue	Winners/Captain	Opponents/Captain	Margin
1990	Lake Nona (Florida)	US Kathy Whitworth*	Eur Mickey Walker*	11¹/₂–4¹/₂
1992	Dalmahoy (Scotland)	Eur Mickey Walker*	US Kathy Whitworth* †	11¹/₂–6¹/₂
1994	The Greenbrier (W Virginia)	US JoAnne Carner*	Eur Mickey Walker*	13–7
1996	St Pierre (Wales)	US Judy Rankin*	Eur Mickey Walker*	17–11
1998	Muirfield Village (Ohio)	US Judy Rankin*	Eur Pia Nilsson*	16–12
2000	Loch Lomond (Scotland)	Eur Dale Reid*	US Pat Bradley*	14¹/₂–11¹/₂

* nonplaying captain † returned home due to bereavement; Alice Miller took over the captaincy

SOLHEIM CUP FACTFILE
Overall record – US 4 wins, Eur 2 wins   **US home record** – won 3, lost 0   **Eur home record** – won 2, lost 1   **Most appearances** – 6 matches, Helen Alfredsson (Eur), Laura Davies (Eur), Trish Johnson (Eur), Liselotte Neumann (Eur), Alison Nicholas (Eur), Dottie Pepper (US), 1990–2000   **Most points** – 14, Laura Davies (Eur), Dottie Pepper (US), 1990–2000

THE PRESIDENTS CUP

US PGA/ INTERNATIONAL PGA TOURS

A biennial team matchplay event, played in non-Ryder Cup years, between the US PGA Tour and an International team comprising players from the rest of the world except Europe. Teams are 12-a-side and a past or present president or prime minister of the host country acts as Honorary Chairman. The first four matches have all been won by the home team.

Year	Venue	Winners/Captain	Opponents/Captain	Margin
1994	Robert Trent Jones GC (Virginia)	US Hale Irwin	International David Graham	20–12
1996	Robert Trent Jones GC (Virginia)	US Arnold Palmer	International Peter Thomson	16¹/₂–15¹/₂
1998	Royal Melbourne (Australia)	International Peter Thomson	US Jack Nicklaus	20¹/₂–11¹/₂
2000	Robert Trent Jones GC (Virginia)	US Ken Venturi	International Peter Thomson	21¹/₂–10¹/₂

Most wins – 3, US

THE WALKER CUP

ROYAL & ANCIENT GOLF CLUB/ UNITED STATES GOLF ASSOCIATION

Like the Ryder Cup, the Walker Cup began as an unofficial match between players from Britain and the United States, this time amateurs rather than professionals. It was played as an annual event for three years before becoming a biennial match from 1926 onward. Although the US has dominated proceedings, GB & Ireland have performed admirably in recent years, claiming three victories in the last six matches

The impressive Walker Cup trophy (left) was named after the man who donated it, George H. Walker, the president of the USGA.

Year	Venue	Winners/Captain	Opponents/Captain	Margin
1922	National Golf Links	US William Fownes	GB Robert Harris	8–4
1923	St. Andrews	US Robert A. Gardner	GB Robert Harris	6¹/₂–5¹/₂
1924	Garden City	US Robert A. Gardner	GB Cyril Tolley	9–3
1926	St. Andrews	US Robert A. Gardner	GB Robert Harris	6¹/₂–5¹/₂
1928	Chicago	US Bobby Jones	GB William Tweddell	11–1
1930	Royal St. George's (Sandwich)	US Bobby Jones	GB Roger Wethered	10–2
1932	Brookline	US Francis Ouimet	GB Tony Torrance	9¹/₂–2¹/₂
1934	St. Andrews	US Francis Ouimet	GB Hon. Michael Scott	9¹/₂–2¹/₂
1936	Pine Valley	US Francis Ouimet*	GB William Tweddell	10¹/₂–1¹/₂
1938	St. Andrews	GB John Beck*	US Francis Ouimet*	7¹/₂–4¹/₂
1947	St. Andrews	US Francis Ouimet*	GB John Beck*	8–4
1949	Winged Foot	US Francis Ouimet*	GB Laddie Lucas*	10–2
1951	Royal Birkdale	US William Turnesa	GB Raymond Oppenheimer*	7¹/₂–4¹/₂
1953	Kittansett	US Charlie Yates*	GB Tony Duncan*	9–3
1955	St. Andrews	US William C. Campbell*	GB Alec Hill*	10–2
1957	Minikahda	US Charles Coe*	GB Gerald Micklem*	8¹/₂–3¹/₂
1959	Muirfield (Scotland)	US Charles Coe	GB Gerald Micklem*	9–3
1961	Seattle	US Jack Westland*	GB Charles Lawrie*	11–1
1963	Turnberry	US Richard Tufts*	GB Charles Lawrie*	14–10
1965	Baltimore *tied*	US John Fischer* *and*	GB Joe Carr*	12–12
1967	Royal St. George's (Sandwich)	US Jess Sweetser*	GB Joe Carr	15–9
1969	Milwaukee	US Billy Joe Patton*	GB Michael Bonallack	13–11
1971	St. Andrews	GB Michael Bonallack	US John Winters*	13–11
1973	Brookline	US Jess Sweetser*	GB David Marsh*	14–10
1975	St. Andrews	US Ed Updegraff*	GB David Marsh*	15¹/₂–8¹/₂
1977	Shinnecock Hills	US Lou Oehmig*	GB Sandy Saddler*	16–8
1979	Muirfield (Scotland)	US Dick Siderowf*	GB Rodney Foster*	15¹/₂–8¹/₂
1981	Cypress Point	US Jim Gabrielsen*	GB & Ire Rodney Foster*	15–9
1983	Royal Liverpool (Hoylake)	US Jay Sigel	GB & Ire Charlie Green*	13¹/₂–10¹/₂
1985	Pine Valley	US Jay Sigel	GB & Ire Charlie Green*	13–11
1987	Sunningdale	US Fred Ridley*	GB & Ire Geoffrey Marks*	16¹/₂–7¹/₂
1989	Peachtree	GB & Ire Geoffrey Marks*	US Fred Ridley*	12¹/₂–11¹/₂
1991	Portmarnock	US James Gabrielsen*	GB & Ire George Macgregor*	14–10

Year	Venue	Winners/Captain	Opponents/Captain	Margin
1993	Interlachen	US Vinny Giles*	GB & Ire George Macgregor*	19–5
1995	Royal Porthcawl	GB & Ire Clive Brown*	US Downing Gray *	14–10
1997	Quaker Ridge	US Downing Gray*	GB & Ire Clive Brown	18–6
1999	Nairn	GB & Ire Peter McEvoy*	US Danny Yates*	15–9

nonplaying captain

WALKER CUP FACTFILE
Overall record – US 31 wins, GB/GB & Ire 5 wins, 1 tie
US home record – won 16, lost 1, tied 1
GB/GB & Ire home record – won 4, lost 15
Most appearances – 10 matches, Joe Carr (GB), 1947– 67
Most points – 20½, Jay Sigel (US) 1977–93

THE CURTIS CUP
LADIES' GOLF UNION/ UNITED STATES GOLF ASSOCIATION

The first Curtis Cup match between the amateur women of Britain and the US took place in 1932, but unofficial matches between the two countries had been played from 1905. The cup was donated by the Curtis sisters, both winners of the US Women's Amateur Championship. GB & Ireland's 1986 win was the first American home defeat in any of the four main transatlantic team events.

Harriot and Margaret Curtis gave the trophy (left) for a biennial match between amateur women of the United States and the British Isles.

Year	Venue	Winners/Captain	Opponents/Captain	Margin
1932	Wentworth	US Marion Hollins*	British Isles Joyce Wethered	5½–3½
1934	Chevy Chase	US Glenna Collett Vare	British Isles Doris Chambers*	6½–2½
1936	Gleneagles *tied*	US Glenna Collett Vare* *and*	British Isles Doris Chambers*	4½–4½
1938	Essex (Mass)	US Frances Stebbins*	British Isles Kathleen Wallace-Williamson*	5½–3½
1948	Birkdale	US Glenna Collett Vare	British Isles Doris Chambers*	6½–2½
1950	Buffalo	US Glenna Collett Vare*	British Isles Diana Critchley*	7½–1½
1952	Muirfield (Scotland)	British Isles Lady Katherine Cairns*	US Aniela Goldthwaite*	5–4
1954	Merion	US Edith Flippin*	British Isles Baba Beck*	6–3
1956	Prince's (Sandwich)	British Isles Zara Bolton*	US Edith Flippin*	5–4
1958	Brae Burn *tied*	British Isles Daisy Ferguson* *and*	US Virginia Dennehy *	4½–4½
1960	Lindrick	US Mildred Prunaret*	British Isles Maureen Garrett*	6½–2½
1962	Broadmoor	US Polly Riley*	British Isles Frances Smith*	8–1
1964	Royal Porthcawl	US Helen Hawes*	British Isles Elsie Corlett*	10½–7½
1966	Hot Springs	US Dorothy Porter*	British Isles Zara Bolton*	13–5
1968	Royal County Down (Newcastle)	US Evelyn Monsted*	GB & Ire Zara Bolton*	10½–7½
1970	Brae Burn	US Carol Cudone*	GB & Ire Jeanne Bisgood*	11½–6½

Year	Venue	Winners/Captain	Opponents/Captain	Margin
1972	Western Gailes	US Jean Crawford*	GB & Ire Frances Smith*	10–8
1974	San Francisco	US Allison Choate*	GB & Ire Belle Robertson*	13–5
1976	Royal Lytham & St Annes	US Barbara McIntire*	GB & Ire Belle Robertson*	11½–6½
1978	Apawamis	US Helen Sigel Wilson*	GB & Ire Carol Comboy*	12–6
1980	St Pierre	US Nancy Syms*	GB & Ire Carol Comboy*	13–5
1982	Denver	US Betty Probasco*	GB & Ire Maire O'Donnell*	14½–3½
1984	Muirfield (Scotland)	US Phyllis Preuss* Diane Bailey*	GB & Ire	9½–8½
1986	Prairie Dunes	GB & Ire Diane Bailey*	US Judy Bell*	13–5
1988	Royal St George's (Sandwich)	GB & Ire Diane Bailey*	US Judy Bell*	11–7
1990	Somerset Hills	US Lesley Shannon*	GB & Ire Jill Thornhill*	14–4
1992	Royal Liverpool (Hoylake)	GB & Ire Liz Boatman*	US Judy Oliver*	10–8
1994	The Honors Course (Chattanooga) *tied*	GB & Ire Liz Boatman* *and*	US Lancy Smith*	9–9
1996	Killarney	GB & Ire Ita Butler*	US Martha Lang*	11½–6½
1998	Minikahda	US Barbara McIntire*	GB & Ire Ita Butler*	10–8
2000	Ganton	US Jane Booth*	GB & Ire Claire Dowling*	10–8

nonplaying captain

CURTIS CUP FACTFILE
Overall record – US 22 wins, British Isles/GB & Ire 6 wins, 3 ties
US home record – won 12, lost 1, tied 2
British Isles/GB & Ire home record – won 5, lost 10, tied 1
Most appearances – 11 matches, Carol Semple Thompson (US) 1974–2000
Most points – 19, Carol Semple Thompson (US), 1974–2000

WORLD CUP GOLF
INTERNATIONAL FEDERATION OF PGA TOURS

Founded in 1953, as the Canada Cup by Canadian businessman John Jay Hopkins, the World Cup, as it was renamed in 1967, is an international team competition for professionals, with each country represented by two players. In 2000 the World Cup became the team event of the World Golf Championships and a new format (36 holes fourballs and 36 holes foursomes) was introduced. Previously run by the International Golf Association, it had been contested over 72 holes strokeplay, with the winners being the team with the lowest combined aggregate. In addition, an individual award (International Trophy) was presented to the player with the lowest aggregate. The event was not staged in 1981 and 1986.

(until 1966, Canada Cup)

Year	Venue	Winners	Score	Leading Individual(s)	Score
1953	Montreal	Argentina (Roberto de Vicenzo, Antonio Cerda)	287	Antonio Cerda (Arg)	140•
1954	Laval-sur-Lac	Australia (Peter Thomson, Kel Nagle)	556	Stan Leonard (Can)	275
1955	Washington	US (Ed Furgol, Chick Harbert)	560	Ed Furgol (US)	279*
1956	Wentworth	US (Ben Hogan, Sam Snead)	567	Ben Hogan (US)	277

Year	Venue	Winners	Score	Leading Individual(s)	Score
1957	Tokyo	Japan (Torakichi Nakamura, Koichi Ono)	557	Torakichi Nakamura (Jap)	274
1958	Mexico City	Ireland (Harry Bradshaw, Christy O'Connor Snr)	579	Angel Miguel (Sp)	286*
1959	Royal Melbourne	Australia (Kel Nagle, Peter Thomson)	563	Stan Leonard (Can)	275*
1960	Portmarnock	US (Arnold Palmer, Sam Snead)	565	Flory van Donck (Bel)	279
1961	Puerto Rico	US (Jimmy Demaret, Sam Snead)	560	Sam Snead (US)	272
1962	Buenos Aires	US (Arnold Palmer, Sam Snead)	557	Roberto de Vicenzo (Arg)	276
1963	St Nom-La-Breteche	US (Jack Nicklaus, Arnold Palmer)	482	Jack Nicklaus (US)	237•
1964	Maui (Hawaii)	US (Jack Nicklaus, Arnold Palmer)	554	Jack Nicklaus (US)	276
1965	Madrid	South Africa (Harold Henning, Gary Player)	571	Gary Player (SA)	281
1966	Tokyo	US (Jack Nicklaus, Arnold Palmer)	548	George Knudson (Can)	272*
1967	Mexico City	US (Jack Nicklaus, Arnold Palmer)	557	Arnold Palmer (US)	276
1968	Olgiata (Rome)	Canada (Al Balding, George Knudson)	569	Al Balding (Can)	274
1969	Singapore	US (Orville Moody, Lee Trevino)	552	Lee Trevino (US)	275
1970	Buenos Aires	Australia (Bruce Devlin, David Graham)	544	Roberto de Vicenzo (Arg)	269
1971	Palm Beach	US (Jack Nicklaus, Lee Trevino)	555	Jack Nicklaus (US)	271
1972	Royal Melbourne	Taiwan (Hsieh Min-Nan, Lu Liang-Huan)	438*	Hsieh Min-Nan (Tai)	217•
1973	Marbella	US (Johnny Miller, Jack Nicklaus)	558	Johnny Miller (US)	277
1974	Caracas (Venezuela)	South Africa (Bobby Cole, Dale Hayes)	554	Bobby Cole (SA)	271
1975	Bangkok	US (Lou Graham, Johnny Miller)	554	Johnny Miller (US)	275
1976	Palm Springs (California)	Spain (Seve Ballesteros, Manuel Pinero)	574	Ernesto Acosta (Mex)	282
1977	Manila	Spain (Seve Ballesteros, Antonio Garrido)	591	Gary Player (SA)	289
1978	Hawaii	US (John Mahaffey, Andy North)	564	John Mahaffey (US)	281
1979	Glyfada	US (John Mahaffey, Hale Irwin)	575	Hale Irwin (US)	285
1980	Bogota (Colombia)	Canada (Dan Halldorson, Jim Nelford)	572	Sandy Lyle (Scot)	282
1982	Acapulco (Mexico)	Spain (Jose-Maria Canizares, Manuel Pinero)	563	Manuel Pinero (Sp)	281
1983	Pondok Inah (Jakarta)	US (Rex Caldwell, John Cook)	565	Dave Barr (Can)	276
1984	Olgiata (Rome)	Spain (Jose-Maria Canizares, Jose Rivero)	414*	Jose-Maria Canizares (Sp)	205•
1985	La Quinta (California)	Canada (Dan Halldorson, Dave Barr)	559	Howard Clark (Eng)	272
1987	Kapalua (Hawaii)	Wales (Ian Woosnam, David Llewellyn)	574*	Ian Woosnam (Wal)	274
1988	Royal Melbourne	US (Ben Crenshaw, Mark McCumber)	560	Ben Crenshaw (US)	275
1989	Las Brisas (Spain)	Australia (Peter Fowler, Wayne Grady)	278	Peter Fowler (Aus)	137•
1990	Grand Cypress (Orlando)	Germany (Bernhard Langer, Torsten Giedeon)	556	Payne Stewart (US)	271
1991	La Querce (Italy)	Sweden (Anders Forsbrand, Per-Ulrik Johansson)	563	Ian Woosnam (Wal)	273
1992	La Moraleja (Spain)	US (Fred Couples, Davis Love III)	548	Brett Ogle (Aus)	270*
1993	Lake Nona (Florida)	US (Fred Couples, Davis Love III)	556	Bernhard Langer (Ger)	272

Year	Venue	Winners	Score	Leading Individual(s)	Score
1994	Dorado Beach (Puerto Rico)	US (Fred Couples, Davis Love III)	536	Fred Couples (US)	265
1995	Mission Hills (China)	US (Fred Couples, Davis Love III)	543	Davis Love III (US)	267
1996	Erinvale (Cape Town)	South Africa (Ernie Els, Wayne Westner)	547	Ernie Els (SA)	272
1997	Kiawah Island (S Carolina)	Ireland (Padraig Harrington, Paul McGinley)	545	Colin Montgomerie (Sco)	266
1998	Gulf Harbour (Auckland)	England (Nick Faldo, David Carter)	568	Scott Verplank (US)	279
1999	Mines Resort (Malaysia)	US (Tiger Woods, Mark O'Meara)	545	Tiger Woods (US)	263
2000	Buenos Aires (Argentina)	US (Tiger Woods, David Duval)	254		

* play-offs
• played over 36 holes in 1953 and 1989, 63 holes in 1963, 54 holes in 1972 and 1984
Most wins (Team – 23, US) (Individual – 3, Jack Nicklaus)

Sponsors: Philip Morris (1989, 1991–92), Kraft General Foods (1990), Heineken (1993–96), EMC (2000)

VOLVO PGA CHAMPIONSHIP

BRITISH PROFESSIONAL GOLFERS' ASSOCIATION

Now firmly established as the flagship event of the European Tour, this championship commenced at Pannal Golf Club, in Yorkshire, England in 1955, but from 1984 has found a permanent home at the Tour's Wentworth headquarters. Until 1966 it was restricted to UK and Irish professionals only. The following two years saw both closed and open events contested, but from 1969 it has been an open event, though it wasn't staged in 1970 and 1971. Colin Montgomerie became the first man to win three consecutive titles in 2000.

Winners GB, except where stated

Year	Winner	Venue	Score
1955	Ken Bousfield	Pannal	277
1956	Charlie Ward	Maesdu	282
1957	Peter Alliss	Maesdu	286
1958	Harry Bradshaw (Ire)	Llandudno	287
1959	Dai Rees	Ashburnham	283
1960	Arnold Stickley	Coventry	247 •
1961	Brian Bamford	Royal Mid-Surrey	266
1962	Peter Alliss	Little Aston	287
1963	Peter Butler	Royal Birkdale	306
1964	Tony Grubb	Western Gailes	287
1965	Peter Alliss	Prince's (Sandwich)	286
1966	Guy Wolstenholme	Saunton	278
1967✣	Brian Huggett	Thorndon Park	271 (c)
1967	Malcolm Gregson	Hunstanton	275
1968✣	Peter Townsend	Royal Mid-Surrey	275 (c)
1968	David Talbot	Dunbar	276
1969✣	Bernard Gallacher	Ashburnham	293
1972	Tony Jacklin	Wentworth	279
1973	Peter Oosterhuis	Wentworth	280
1974	Maurice Bembridge	Wentworth	278
1975	Arnold Palmer (US)	Royal St George's (Sandwich)	285
1976	Neil Coles	Royal St George's (Sandwich)	280*
1977	Manuel Pinero (Sp)	Royal St George's (Sandwich)	283
1978	Nick Faldo	Royal Birkdale	278

375

Year	Winner	Venue	Score
1979	Vicente Fernandez (Arg)	St Andrews	288
1980	Nick Faldo	Royal St George's (Sandwich)	283
1981	Nick Faldo	Ganton	274
1982	Tony Jacklin	Hillside	284*
1983	Seve Ballesteros (Sp)	Royal St George's (Sandwich)	278
1984	Howard Clark	Wentworth	204 ••
1985	Paul Way	Wentworth	282*
1986	Rodger Davis (Aus)	Wentworth	281*
1987	Bernhard Langer (W Ger)	Wentworth	270
1988	Ian Woosnam	Wentworth	274
1989	Nick Faldo	Wentworth	272
1990	Mike Harwood (Aus)	Wentworth	271
1991	Seve Ballesteros (Sp)	Wentworth	271*
1992	Tony Johnstone (Zim)	Wentworth	272
1993	Bernhard Langer (Ger)	Wentworth	274
1994	José-Maria Olazábal (Sp)	Wentworth	271
1995	Bernhard Langer (Ger)	Wentworth	279
1996	Costantino Rocca (It)	Wentworth	274
1997	Ian Woosnam	Wentworth	275
1998	Colin Montgomerie	Wentworth	274
1999	Colin Montgomerie	Wentworth	270
2000	Colin Montgomerie	Wentworth	271

* play-off •Due to bad weather, reduced to 63 holes, ••Due to bad weather, reduced to 54 holes, (c) closed ✢ Two events 1967 and 1968; none in 1970 and 1971
Most wins – 4, Nick Faldo
Sponsors: Schweppes (1967–69), Viyella (1972–74), Penfold 1975–77), Colgate (1978–79), Sun Alliance (1980–83), Whyte & Mackay (1984–87), Volvo (1988–)

THE PLAYERS CHAMPIONSHIP
US TOURNAMENT PLAYERS

Launched in 1974 as the Tournament Players Championship, but renamed as the Players Championship in 1988, this unoffical "fifth Major" has been contested each spring at the Tournament Players Club at Sawgrass in Florida since 1982.

Winners US, except where stated

Year	Winner	Score	Year	Winner	Score
1974	Jack Nicklaus	272	1988	Mark McCumber	273
1975	Al Geiberger	270	1989	Tom Kite	279
1976	Jack Nicklaus	269	1990	Jodie Mudd	278
1977	Mark Hayes	289	1991	Steve Elkington (Aus)	276
1978	Jack Nicklaus	289	1992	Davis Love III	273
1979	Lanny Wadkins	283	1993	Nick Price (Zim)	270
1980	Lee Trevino	278	1994	Greg Norman (Aus)	264
1981	Ray Floyd	285	1995	Lee Janzen	283
1982	Jerry Pate	280	1996	Fred Couples	270
1983	Hal Sutton	283	1997	Steve Elkington (Aus)	272
1984	Fred Couples	277	1998	Justin Leonard	278
1985	Calvin Peete	274	1999	David Duval	285
1986	John Mahaffey	275	2000	Hal Sutton	285
1987	Sandy Lyle (GB)	274	2001	Tiger Woods	274

Most wins – 3, Jack Nicklaus   **Venues**: Atlanta (1974), Colonial (1975), Inverrary (1976), Sawgrass (1977–81); TPC Sawgrass (1982–)

THE AMATEUR CHAMPIONSHIP
ROYAL & ANCIENT GOLF CLUB

The Amateur Championship was officially inaugurated in 1886, but it is accepted that the first was actually played the year before. The Royal Liverpool Club, Hoylake, issued invitations in 1885 for an Open Amateur Tournament to be played during the club's spring meeting. Allan F. MacFie, a Scots member of the host club, beat 43 others to win. Below are listed the winners from after World War II.

Winners and runners-up GB, except where stated

Year	Venue	Winner	Runner-up	Margin
1946	Birkdale	James Bruen (Ire)	Robert Sweeny (US)	4 & 3
1947	Carnoustie	William Turnesa (US)	Richard Chapman (US)	3 & 2
1948	Royal St George's (Sandwich)	Frank Stranahan (US)	Charles Stowe	5 & 4
1949	Portmarnock	Max McCready (Ire)	William Turnesa (US)	2 & 1
1950	St Andrews	Frank Stranahan (US)	Richard Chapman (US)	8 & 6
1951	Royal Porthcawl	Richard Chapman (US)	Charles Coe (US)	5 & 4
1952	Prestwick	Harvie Ward (US)	Frank Stranahan (US)	6 & 5
1953	Royal Liverpool (Hoylake)	Joe Carr (Ire)	Harvie Ward (US)	2 holes
1954	Muirfield	Douglas Bachli (Aus)	William C. Campbell (US)	2 & 1
1955	Royal Lytham & St Annes	Joseph Conrad (US)	Alan Slater	3 & 2
1956	Troon	John Beharrell	Leslie Taylor	5 & 4
1957	Formby	Reid Jack	Harold Ridgley (US)	2 & 1
1958	St Andrews	Joe Carr (Ire)	Alan Thirlwell	3 & 2
1959	Royal St George's (Sandwich)	Deane Beman (US)	Bill Hyndman (US)	3 & 2
1960	Royal Portrush	Joe Carr (Ire)	Bob Cochran (US)	8 & 7
1961	Turnberry	Michael Bonallack	James Walker	6 & 4
1962	Royal Liverpool (Hoylake)	Richard Davies (US)	John Povall	1 hole
1963	St Andrews	Michael Lunt	John Blackwell	2 & 1
1964	Ganton	Gordon Clark	Michael Lunt	at 39th
1965	Royal Porthcawl	Michael Bonallack	Clive Clark	2 & 1
1966	Carnoustie	Bobby Cole (SA)	Ronnie Shade	3 & 2•
1967	Formby	Robert Dickson (US)	Ron Cerrudo (US)	2 & 1
1968	Troon	Michael Bonallack	Joe Carr (Ire)	7 & 6
1969	Royal Liverpool (Hoylake)	Michael Bonallack	Bill Hyndman (US)	3 & 2
1970	Royal County Down (Newcastle)	Michael Bonallack	Bill Hyndman (US)	8 & 7
1971	Carnoustie	Steve Melnyk (US)	James Simons (US)	3 & 2
1972	Royal St George's (Sandwich)	Trevor Homer	Alan Thirlwell	4 & 3
1973	Royal Porthcawl	Dick Siderowf (US)	Peter Moody	5 & 3
1974	Muirfield	Trevor Homer	Jim Gabrielsen (US)	2 holes
1975	Royal Liverpool (Hoylake)	Vinny Giles (US)	Mark James	8 & 7
1976	St Andrews	Dick Siderowf (US)	John Davies	at 37th
1977	Ganton	Peter McEvoy	Hugh Campbell	5 & 4
1978	Troon	Peter McEvoy	Paul McKellar	4 & 3
1979	Hillside	Jay Sigel (US)	Scott Hoch (US)	3 & 2
1980	Royal Porthcawl	Duncan Evans	David Suddards (SA)	4 & 3

Year	Venue	Winner	Runner-up	Margin
1981	St Andrews	Philippe Ploujoux (Fr)	Joel Hirsch (US)	4 & 2
1982	Royal Cinque Ports (Deal)	Martin Thompson	Andrew Stubbs	4 & 3
1983	Turnberry	Philip Parkin	Jim Holtgrieve (US)	5 & 4
1984	Formby	José-Maria Olazábal (Sp)	Colin Montgomerie	5 & 4
1985	Royal Dornoch	Garth McGimpsey	Graham Homewood	8 & 7
1986	Royal Lytham & St Annes	David Curry	Geoff Birtwell	11 & 9
1987	Prestwick	Paul Mayo	Peter McEvoy	3 & 1
1988	Royal Porthcawl	Christian Hardin (Swe)	Ben Fouchee (SA)	1 hole
1989	Royal Birkdale	Stephen Dodd	Craig Cassells	5 & 3
1990	Muirfield	Rolf Muntz (Neth)	Michael Macara	7 & 6
1991	Ganton	Gary Wolstenhome	Bob May (US)	8 & 6
1992	Carnoustie	Stephen Dundas	Bradley Dredge	7 & 6
1993	Royal Portrush	Iain Pyman	Paul Page	at 37th
1994	Nairn	Lee James	Gordon Sherry	2 & 1
1995	Royal Liverpool	Gordon Sherry	Michael Reynard	7 & 6
1996	Turnberry	Warren Bladon	Roger Beames	1 hole
1997	Royal St George's	Craig Watson	Trevor Immelmann (SA)	3 & 2
1998	Muirfield	Sergio Garcia (Sp)	Craig Williams	7 & 6
1999	Royal County Down	Graeme Storm	Aran Wainwright	7 & 6
2000	Royal Liverpool	Mikko Ilonen (Fin)	Christian Reimbold (Ger)	2 & 1

• *Final played over 18 holes*
Most wins – 8, John Ball (all before First World War)

THE US AMATEUR CHAMPIONSHIP

UNITED STATES GOLF ASSOCIATION

The Newport Club, Rhode Island, was the venue for the first US Amateur Championship in 1895. It was won by Charles Blair Macdonald, a pioneer of golf in the US. There were only 32 entries, and matches were played over 18 holes with a 36-hole final. The championship continued under matchplay rules until 1965, when it became a 72-hole strokeplay event. The event was changed yet again in 1973, when it reverted to matchplay. The only player to have won the event five times was the legendary Bobby Jones, whose dominance of the amateur game during the 1920s was indisputable. He won in 1924, 1925, 1927, 1928, and 1930. In that last year he also won the British Open at Royal Liverpool, the US Open at Interlachen, and the British Amateur Championship at St Andrews, an astounding series of victories known as the Impregnable Quadrilateral. Eighteen-year-old Tiger Woods became the youngest champion in 1994, and two years later, the first to win threee consecutive titles. Below are listed the winners from after Second World War.

Winners and runners-up US, except where stated

Year	Venue	Winner	Runner-up	Margin
1946	Baltusrol	Stanley Bishop	Smiley Quick	at 37th
1947	Pebble Beach	Robert Riegel	John Dawson	2 & 1
1948	Memphis	William Turnesa	Ray Billows	2 & 1
1949	Oak Hill	Charles Coe	Rufus King	11 & 10
1950	Minneapolis	Sam Urzetta	Frank Stranahan	at 39th
1951	Saucon Valley	Billy Maxwell	Joseph Gagliardi	4 & 3
1952	Seattle	Jack Westland	Al Mengert	3 & 2
1953	Oklahoma City	Gene Littler	Dale Morey	1 up
1954	Detroit	Arnold Palmer	Robert Sweeny	1 up
1955	Virginia	Harvie Ward	Bill Hyndman	9 & 8
1956	Knollwood	Harvie Ward	Charles Kocsis	5 & 4

Year	Venue	Winner	Runner-up	Margin
1957	Brookline	Hillman Robbins	Frank Taylor	5 & 4
1958	Olympic	Charles Coe	Tommy Aaron	5 & 4
1959	Broadmoor	Jack Nicklaus	Charles Coe	1 up
1960	St Louis	Deane Beman	Robert W. Gardner	6 & 4
1961	Pebble Beach	Jack Nicklaus	Dudley Wysong	8 & 6
1962	Pinehurst	Labron Harris	Downing Gray	1 up
1963	Wakonda	Deane Beman	Richard Sikes	2 & 1
1964	Canterbury	William C. Campbell	Edward Tutwiler	1 up

Competition changed from matchplay to strokeplay				**Score**
1965	Southern Hills	Robert Murphy		291
1966	Merion	Gary Cowan (Can)		285*
1967	Broadmoor	Robert Dickson		285
1968	Scioto	Bruce Fleisher		284
1969	Oakmont	Steve Melnyk		286
1970	Waverley	Lanny Wadkins		279
1971	Wilmington	Gary Cowan (Can)		280
1972	Charlotte	Vinny Giles		285

Reverted to matchplay				**Margin**
1973	Inverness	Craig Stadler	David Strawn	6 & 5
1974	Ridgewood	Jerry Pate	John Grace	2 & 1
1975	Virginia (Richmond)	Fred Ridley	Keith Fergus	2 up
1976	Bel-Air	Bill Sander	Parker Moore	8 & 6
1977	Aronimink	John Fought	Doug Fischesser	9 & 8
1978	Plainfield	John Cook	Scott Hoch	5 & 4
1979	Canterbury	Mark O'Meara	John Cook	8 & 7
1980	Pinehurst	Hal Sutton	Bob Lewis	9 & 8
1981	Olympic	Nathaniel Crosby	Brian Lindley	at 37th
1982	Brookline	Jay Sigel	David Tolley	8 & 7
1983	North Shore	Jay Sigel	Chris Perry	8 & 7
1984	Oak Tree	Scott Verplank	Sam Randolph	4 & 3
1985	Montclair	Sam Randolph	Peter Persons	1 up
1986	Shoal Creek	Buddy Alexander	Chris Kite	5 & 3
1987	Jupiter Hills	Billy Mayfair	Eric Rebmann	4 & 3
1988	Hot Springs	Eric Meeks	Danny Yates	7 & 6
1989	Merion	Chris Patton	Danny Green	3 & 1
1990	Englewood	Phil Mickelson	Manny Zerman (SA)	5 & 4
1991	Honors Course (Chattanooga)	Mitch Voges	Manny Zerman (SA)	7 & 6
1992	Muirfield Village	Justin Leonard	Tom Sherrer	8 & 7
1993	Champions	John Harris	Danny Ellis	5 & 3
1994	TPC, Sawgrass	Tiger Woods	Trip Kuehne	2 up
1995	Newport	Tiger Woods	Buddy Marucci	2 up
1996	Pumpkin Ridge	Tiger Woods	Steve Scott	at 38th
1997	Cog Hill	Matt Kuchar	Joel Kribel	2 & 1
1998	Oak Hill	Hank Kuehne	Tom McKnight	2 & 1
1999	Pebble Beach	David Gossett	Sun Yoon Kim (Kor)	9 & 8
2000	Baltusrol	Jeff Quinney	James Driscoll	at 39th

* *play-off*
Most wins – 5, Bobby Jones (before Second World War)

GLOSSARY

Albatross   British term for a score of three under the **par** for a hole. In the US it is known as a **double eagle**.

Anti-shank   Club design that attempts to eliminate the possibility of striking the ball with the **hosel**.

Approach   Shot played to the green from the **fairway** or **rough**.

Back nine   Second set of nine holes on an 18-hole golf course.

Baffy   Sturdy wooden club, now obsolete, similar to the modern 3- or 4-wood. It replaced the earlier "baffing spoon" and had a lofted face for high shots from the **fairway**.

Balata   Natural or synthetic compound used to make the cover for top-standard golf balls. Its soft, elastic qualities produce a high spin rate and it is favoured by tournament players.

Bent grass   Type of fine-leafed grass that produces an ideal surface for putting greens. It is, however, difficult to maintain in hot climates.

Birdie   Term used for a score of one under the **par** for a hole.

Bogey   Term used for a score of one over the **par** for a hole.

Boron   A strong metal powder often added during the construction of **graphite** shafts to provide added strength at the **hosel** end.

Borrow   British term for the amount a putt will deviate from a straight line due to the slope of the **green**.

Brassie   A wooden fairway club with a protective brass sole-plate, the equivalent of the modern 2-wood.

Break   American term for the amount that a putt will deviate from a straight line due to the slope of the **green**. The term in Britain is **borrow**.

Bulger driver   Designed to reduce the chances of striking the ball on the heel or toe of the club, the bulger had a convex face. Popular in the late nineteenth century, now obsolete.

Carry   Distance between the point from which a ball is played to the point where it lands. When the ball is hit over water or a bunker, it is said to "carry" the hazard.

Chip   Low running shot normally played from near the edge of the **green** towards the **hole**.

Chipper   Club with a relatively straight face used for playing the low **chip** from just off the **green**.

Cleek   Term of Scottish origin to describe an iron club roughly the equivalent of a modern 2-iron, although there were variations including short cleeks, long cleeks, driving cleeks and putting cleeks.

Couch grass   Grass often regarded as a weed, with long, creeping roots.

Cross bunker   Bunker lying across the line of the **fairway**.

Cut   To miss the cut is to fail to score low enough, usually over the first 36 holes of a 72-hole tournament, to qualify for the final two rounds.

Cut shot   Shot that makes the ball spin in a clockwise direction resulting in a left to right bending flight. It can either be deliberate or a mistake.

Divot   Piece of turf removed by the clubhead when a shot is played.

Dogleg   Hole that sharply changes direction left or right, normally in the landing area for the tee-shot.

Dormie   Term used in **matchplay** for the situation when a player is leading by as many holes as are left to play and therefore cannot be beaten.

Double-eagle   US term for three under the par for a hole. In Britain this score is known as an **albatross**.

Double green   Single putting surface shared by two **holes**, usually coming from opposite directions. They are a relic of the early days of golf when courses were played out and back over the same ground.

Driver   Club with a long shaft and little loft used for driving the ball the maximum distance from the **tee**.

Eagle   Term that denotes a score of two under the **par** for a **hole**.

Fairway   Area of closely mown turf between **tee** and **green**, which has as its boundary either longer grass known as semi-rough or completely uncut grass called **rough**.

Feathery   An early golf ball made by filling a leather pouch with boiled feathers. It was highly susceptible to damage and began to go out of use in the mid-1880s after the introduction of the cheaper **guttie** ball.

Fescue   A fine-leafed, deep-rooting species of grass common on seaside links and heathland courses in the British Isles, tolerant to drought conditions and providing an ideal surface for putting greens.

Flat swing   Backswing in which the plane is more horizontal than vertical. This is often regarded as a fault, but many fine players have had flat swings, including Ben Hogan.

Fourball   A match involving four players in teams of two, in which each player plays his own ball.

Foursome   A match involving four players in teams of two, in which each team plays one ball by alternate strokes. At the start of play each team decides which player will play the first tee-shot, after which they alternate the tee-shot on each hole.

Free drop   Ball dropped without penalty away from an immovable obstruction, or in other circumstances in accordance with the Rules of Golf.

Front nine   First nine **holes** on an 18-hole golf course. The second nine holes are known as the **back nine**.

Graphite (carbon fibre)   Carbon-based substance that when bonded in layers produces an exceptionally strong but very light material ideal for golf-club shafts and increasingly also employed in the manufacture of clubheads.

Great Triumvirate   Name given collectively to three outstanding British professionals who were active before the First World War: James Braid, J.H. Taylor and Harry Vardon.

Green   Area of closely mown grass specially prepared for putting, into which is cut the **hole**. It is separated from the fairway by the "apron", a fringe of grass longer than the green but shorter than the fairway. Originally the term "green" was used for a whole course.

Guttie   Ball introduced in 1848, made of gutta percha, a rubber-like substance obtained from the latex of a species of Malaysian tree.

Handicap   System that subtracts strokes from the scores of weaker players to enable people of varying abilities to play against each other on theoretically equal terms. The handicap is usually based on the average scores of a player set against a standard for a course.

Haskell ball   Name of the first **rubber-core ball**, which was invented in 1898 by Coburn Haskell.

Hole   General term for the whole region between the **tee** and **green**, but also the specific target in the ground of a standard $4\frac{1}{4}$in (108mm) in diameter.

Hook Stroke that bends sharply to the left, caused by the application of counter-clockwise spin, either deliberately or unintentionally.

Hosel Socket on an iron-headed club that serves to connect the iron clubhead to the shaft.

Interlocking grip Method of gripping the handle of the club in which the little finger of the right hand intertwines with the forefinger of the left hand. It is usually favoured by players with small hands or short fingers to maintain a firm grip.

Kweek grass Fine species of grass indigenous to South Africa. It is less than ideal on golf courses because it is extremely difficult to play on.

Lie Situation in which a ball finishes after completion of a stroke. The lie can vary from good to bad, depending on how far the ball has settled down in the grass or, in the case of a bunker, in the sand.

Links Stretch of seaside land used for playing golf. Linksland is usually low-lying, with sand dunes supporting fine, salt-resistant grasses. The word probably derives from the fact that linksland links the foreshore and agricultural land farther from the sea.

Loft Angle of slope of a face of a club away from the vertical. The loft increases with the number of the iron, giving a higher flight trajectory and less distance.

Lofter Early club with a loft equivalent to a modern 5- or 6-iron and used to strike the ball on a high trajectory. Also called a lofting iron, it superseded the wooden **baffy** for **approach** shots to the **green**.

Long iron Club with minimum degree of **loft** designed to perform long and accurate shots from the **fairway**.

LPGA Acronym for Ladies' Professional Golf Association.

Mashie Iron club that made its appearance in the late 1880s. It had loft equivalent to the modern 5-iron. J.H. Taylor was the first acknowledged master of the mashie.

Matchplay Form of competition in which the number of **holes** won or lost rather than the number of strokes taken determines the winner. The alternative is **strokeplay**.

Medium iron Modern iron club used for **approach** shots to the **green**, combining a medium length of flight with considerable accuracy.

Mixed foursome Foursome in which each team is made up of one male and one female player.

Niblick Early lofted iron, now obsolete, that was roughly equivalent to the modern 9-iron. It had a heavy head and a wide face and was used for extricating the ball from difficult lies or for lofting over hazards.

Off the pace American expression to describe the number of strokes or the position of a player behind the leader of a tournament – for instance, "two strokes off the pace".

Overclubbing Error caused by selecting a club that sends the ball farther than the intended distance.

Par Estimated standard score for a hole, based on the length of the hole and on the number of strokes a first-class player would expect to take to complete it in normal conditions.

PGA Acronym for Professional Golfers' Association.

Pitch Lofted shot to a green with little run at the end of its flight.

Playclub Old term for a driving club in common use up to the latter part of the nineteenth century, roughly equivalent to driver or 2-wood.

Pot bunker Small, round and deep bunker commonly found on traditional British links courses.

Pro-Am Form of the game in which a professional player forms a team with amateur players.

R & A The Royal & Ancient Golf Club of St Andrews.

Rookie A newcomer to the professional golf Tour.

Rough Area of unmown grass alongside the fairway that punishes an off-line shot.

Rubber-core ball The golf ball that revolutionized the game at the turn of the twentieth century. Also known as the **Haskell ball**.

Sand wedge Extremely lofted club, also known as a "sand iron", with a wide flange designed for playing from bunkers. US player Gene Sarazen is credited with its invention.

Short game Play within 100 yards (90m) of the green, especially chipping, bunker shots and putting.

Short iron Lofted iron club used for short **approaches** to the **green** or for lofting over obstacles or hazards.

Slice Shot carrying considerable clockwise spin that consequently curves violently to the right.

Spoon The traditional name for a lofted **fairway** wood, the equivalent of the modern 3-wood.

Strokeplay Form of competition in which the number of strokes a player takes to complete a round is compared with the other players' scores for a round. Strokeplay has largely supplanted **matchplay** in professional tournament golf.

Stymie Situation in which one player's ball blocked another player's ball's route to the hole. The stymied player was required to play over the top of the offending ball. The stymie was outlawed in 1951 by the **USGA** and the **R & A**.

Surlyn® Trademark of a thermoplastic resin similar to natural balata, used in ball manufacture. It is an extremely resilient material and virtually indestructible by clubs.

Sweet spot Precise point on the face of a golf club, usually in the centre, that will deliver the maximum possible mass behind the ball. A ball struck at this point will travel farther than one struck on any other part of the face.

Tee Closely mown area from which the first stroke on a hole is played. The term is also used to refer to the tee peg.

USGA Acronym for the United States Golf Association.

US LPGA United States Ladies Professional Golfers' Association.

USPGA United States Professional Golfers' Association.

Vardon grip Method of holding the handle of the club in which the little finger of the right hand overlaps the forefinger of the left. Popularized, but not invented, by Harry Vardon.

Whipping Waxed thread used to bind the area where the shaft meets the clubhead. Modern techniques have made this practice redundant.

Yips Nervous disorder that can destroy the ability to putt, turning the stroke into a twitch or a jerk. Ben Hogan and Bernhard Langer are two famous examples of top players who suffered from the yips.

INDEX

ACKNOWLEDGMENTS

AUTHOR'S ACKNOWLEDGMENTS THIS EDITION

I feel greatly honoured that former United States President George Bush contributed such a generous Foreword to this new edition and I am very grateful to him for his contribution. I am also indebted to Mr Tom Frechette and the other members of President Bush's personal staff who helped with the arrangements and made it possible.

I am greatly indebted to Colin Callander, Ron Marshall, and Richard Dyson for their contributions to this 3rd revision. I would also like to thank my good friend Ko Shioya and Takashi Sudo for their invaluable assistance with input from Japan and Nario

Kodato of the Oarai Golf Club and Mark Parsinen of The Kingsbarns Links for their generous help.

It has been a particular pleasure to work with James Harrison and Ted Kinsey at *KINSEY* & Harrison for the production of this edition. They have been stoic in their support and patient to a fault.

My thanks also go to publisher of this edition, Mike Edwards and to Sharon Lucas and Derek Coombes at DK Adult for their backup and encouragement throughout this project, and to David Lamb of DK Adult who has been such a loyal supporter and a valued friend from the very beginning.

Finally, I owe special thanks to my wife Jane for her meticulous research work and for being such a tower of strength during the compilation of this revision.

KINSEY & Harrison would like to thank Simon Roulstone for additonal course artwork, Trish Gant who took additional golf club photography, Bill Pickup and Sam Stokes at Spires Design, Abingdon, for the text conversion, Patricia Hymans for the revised index, and Nevada Bob's for loan of clubs.

AUTHOR'S ACKNOWLEDGMENTS PREVIOUS EDITION

I am very grateful to editorial director David Lamb for his encouragement from the beginning and for his support and understanding during the sometimes difficult early stages of this project. To Roger Smoothy, who has been an outstanding and diligent editor and a good friend throughout, I extend my sincere thanks. Carolyn King and Nick Harris have provided marvellous and vital support, and to them I also extend my warmest thanks.

Brian Rust and Caroline Murray have done valiant work on the design and have had excellent backing from the editorial and design teams at Dorling Kindersley who have a seemingly endless capacity for hard work. My grateful thanks go to them all.

I am also extremely grateful to the R & A Historian, Bobby Burnet, for his invaluable help and research in the history of the game and to Alick A. Watt, Alan Elliott, John Allan May, John Ingham, and Keith Mackie for their contributions. I have had outstanding cooperation and help from photographer Brian D. Morgan and the staff at Golf Photography International, Glasgow.

Finally, I owe a special debt of gratitude to my family and close friends who have supported me so stoically throughout this project and kept me going when dark clouds crossed the horizon.

Publisher's acknowledgments previous edition

Dorling Kindersley would like to thank the club secretaries, general managers, golf professionals, tournament officers, administrative staff, and members at the featured clubs for all their cooperation and goodwill. For providing valuable reference and information and verifying accuracy, special thanks are due to Donald E. Aitken, David C. Allen, Robert Alonzi, James H. Armstrong Jr., Christian Barras, Dorothy Bell, Marshal Bereton, A. Beveridge, Stan Bishop, Gil Blechman, Cam Boatwright, Rod Bogg, Commander J.M. Bradley, Peter Burford, Gerry Bywater, Cary Corbitt, Nancy Van Cott, Major A.S. Craven, N.T. Crewe, E.J. Davies, Chris Davis, Danette Dearborn, David E. Donaldson, Richard Doyle-Davidson, Gilberto Duavit, Jean Duysters, H.R. Ebrecht, Bud Erickson, Wilma Erskine, Eric Filfinger, Michael C. Franck, Brian Franke, William John Dennis Garvey, W.E. Geddes, R.J. Harper, C.L. Hart, Donald T. Hayes, Dr T.M. Healy, A. Heron, Captain R.J. Hitchen, Danna Holck, W.M. Hopley, Rick Jacobson, Ben Kern, Pasquale J. LaRocca, Nelson Long Jnr, F.J. Longden, Michael Lovett, Jim Lucius, Cliffe Mann, E.P. van Marken, Jim McPhilomy, J.D. Montgomerie, Robert Nelson, Sandra Nicolson, Mark De Noble, Jeanne Poepl, D. Patrick, Stefano Pilato, Air Vice-Marshal R.G. Price, Group Captain J.A. Prideaux, Antonio Ribeiro, Dennis Roberson, C.J. Rouse, J. Rutherford, Fernando Sagnier, Werner Seelos, S.R. Sharp, Douglas La Rue Smith, E.J.C. Smith, Masuo Someya, Diane Stracuzzi, Timothy K. Surlas, Margaret Swindell, A.J.B. Taylor, A. Thirlwell, Leon M. Thompson, Rodolfo B. Valdez, Major J.G. Vanreenen, Alfredo Vercelli, Ian C.R. Walker, Sean Walsh, G.E. Watts, Barry Weickel, John Weir, Robin H. White, R. Widuhrt, Ingrid Willstrand, E. Wilson, Jim Wisler, Christina Witchell and Allan Wood.

Thanks to the following people and organizations for their help during the creation of this book:
Eunice Paterson for production; Josephine Buchanan, Joanna Chisholm, Corinne Hall, Stephanie Jackson, Andrew Mikolajski, Caroline Ollard, Deborah Rhodes and Susannah Tapper for editorial assistance; John W.L. Adams, Sharon Clapson, Richard Dyson, Rhonda Jenkins at the USGA, David H. Linton and John T. Milton for research and fact-checking; Indexing Specialists (Hove, East Sussex) for compiling the index; Joanna Figg-Latham, Bob Gordon, Neville Graham, Lee Griffiths, Vanessa Hamilton, Clair Lidzey, Gurinder Purewall and Alistair Wardle for design assistance; Boyd Annison, Mark Annison and Keith Errington at Icon Associates and Salvatore Tomaselli for computer artworks; Rowan Clifford, Andy Farmer and Janos Marffy for illustrations; Penelope Chaplin and Pamela Thomas at DK Inc.Sarah Baddiel, The Golf Gallery for golfing ephemera, Phillips Auctioneers for antique golf equipment, Birdie Golf Ltd., Neil Jordan's Pro Shop, Lillywhites Ltd., Nevada Bob's, Dorlings Signs Ltd., Golfplans International, Strokesport for clubs and course reference. A. Davis de Montluzin at Jack Nicklaus Golf Services, Tom Fazio at Fazio Golf Course Designers Inc., Michael Gedye, Joe Hackler, Stuart MacPherson, and J.P. Richardson of Ordnance Survey (Air Photo Sales) for assistance with artwork reference; Karen Bednarski at the USGA Museum (Far Hills, New Jersey), Bob Gowland at Phillips, Mark Kiemele at Public Image, Katherine McCudden at Christies, James T. Strachan and James Watt (Dirleton) for providing photographs; Tim Ridley and Barnabus Kindersley for studio photography; Sean Arnold at Golf and Polo Antiques (Grays Antique Market), James Horsfield at Auchterlonie's, Leonard Jowett at John White & Sons and Mike Mander at The Royal Botanic Gardens (Kew) for providing materials for photography; Deborah Pownall for picture research.